KITCHEN GARDEN

S.H.

CROQUET LAWN

PADDOCK

PADDOCK

STABLES

COTTAGE

C. H. SPURGEON AUTOBIOGRAPHY

THE BANNER OF TRUTH TRUST
3 Murrayfield Road, Edinburgh EH12 6EL, UK
P.O. Box 621, Carlisle, PA 17013, USA

*

Autobiography first published in four volumes 1897–1900
Revised edition published by the Banner of Truth Trust
in two volumes. This second part first published 1973
© The Banner of Truth Trust 1973
Reprinted 1976
Reprinted 1983
Reprinted 1987
Reprinted 1995
Reprinted 2006

ISBN-10: 0 85151 182 1
ISBN-13: 978 0 85151 182 5

*

Printed in the U.S.A. by
Versa Press, Inc.,
East Peoria, IL

C. H. SPURGEON AUTOBIOGRAPHY

Volume 2: The Full Harvest
1860–1892

A revised edition, originally compiled
by Susannah Spurgeon and Joseph Harrald

THE BANNER OF TRUTH TRUST

C. H. Spurgeon in 1878

As long as there is breath in our bodies, let us serve Christ; as long as we can think, as long as we can speak, as long as we can work, let us serve him, let us even serve him with our last gasp; and, if it be possible, let us try to set some work going that will glorify him when we are dead and gone. Let us scatter some seed that may spring up when we are sleeping beneath the hillock in the cemetery.

C.H.S.

As for myself, I am compelled to say with solemn truthfulness that I am not content with anything I have ever done. I have half wished to live my life over again, but now I regret that my proud heart allowed me so to wish, since the probabilities are that I should do worse the second time. Whatever grace has done for me I acknowledge with deep gratitude; but so far as I have done anything myself I beg pardon for it. I pray God to forgive my prayers, for they have been full of fault; I beseech him to forgive even this confession, for it is not as humble as it ought to be; I beseech him to wash my tears and purge my devotions, and to baptize me into a true burial with my Saviour, that I may be quite forgotten in myself, and only remembered in him.

C.H.S.

CONTENTS

Contents

ILLUSTRATIONS

Illustrations

PREFACE

AFTER looking at one of the biographies of which he was the subject, Spurgeon once commented that the matter would never be rightly done till he took it in hand himself. It was a light-hearted saying but how many have since regretted that when his life was over at the age of fifty-seven there was no Autobiography among the one hundred and fifty volumes bearing his name! In 1894, two years after his death, the most complete *Life* was issued by G. Holden Pike, in six slim volumes. There followed, however, between 1897 and 1900, *C. H. Spurgeon's Autobiography, Compiled from his Diary, Letters and Records* in four large volumes. These were brought together through the labours of Mrs. C. H. Spurgeon and Spurgeon's private secretary. The major part of the contents of volumes one and two were reprinted in 1962, with the revised title *C. H. Spurgeon: The Early Years*, and this present volume now gives most of volumes three and four, thus completing his whole life in two volumes.

The fact that a decade has passed between the reprint of the first part of his *Autobiography* and this volume may suggest that the publishers have not been without difficulties in preparing the present work for the press. Such indeed has been the case. As we explained in our Preface to *The Early Years*, the volumes entitled *C. H. Spurgeon's Autobiography* were not autobiography in the customary sense of the term; they could not be for, as indicated above, Spurgeon completed comparatively little along this line. Nonetheless, Susannah Spurgeon and Joseph Harrald, by sifting the very large amount of material which Spurgeon spoke or wrote for everything of a biographical nature, went a considerable way towards making the contents of the four volumes autobiographical. Far enough, in their view, to justify the title. In the judgment of the present publishers they possibly erred in one respect: their material was too diffuse. Spurgeon himself once said, when reviewing the bulky two-volume *Memoirs of James Begg*, 'This is another case of a man buried beneath a pyramid of documents.' The four large volumes did not altogether avoid this danger. The method of revision employed in this reprint has been to prune out some of the secondary material—almost exclusively this was matter which was not Spurgeon's own. Considerably more material of this nature belonged to volumes three and four of the *Autobiography*, than to volumes one and two. We consequently found that in attempting to make certain improvements upon the work of Susannah Spurgeon and Joseph Harrald in this second and final volume—as we sought to do to a minor extent in *The Early Years*—our problems were altogether more complex. More was needed than careful abridgement. In some areas the work needed recasting and reshaping. At some points in the story, e.g. his visits to Scotland, his Jubilee of 1884, and his recurring illness, there was new material to be added. This extra material, which we have blended in, has been drawn from Spurgeon's magazine, *the Sword and the Trowel, The Life and Work* by G. H. Pike, *James Archer Spurgeon* by G. H. Pike, and a few other sources. The reader will thus find some facts and details which were not in the original volumes. One chapter which the present publishers have purposely left unrevised is that recording aspects of the 'Down-Grade' controversy. A fuller treatment of that subject is no doubt required and it would need to include more of Spurgeon's own words from *The Sword and the Trowel*.

For the most part, this present volume remains the work of the two first compilers and to them we would pay our tribute. His wife was the instrument of Spurgeon's first book, writing out and helping to choose the extracts which went into *Smooth Stones Taken From Ancient Brooks*, 1857, and it was fitting that her final work should be to bring out this record of his life. Surviving her husband by twelve years she died on October 22, 1903. Joined with her in the work, and without doubt taking the major share, was the Rev. Joseph William Harrald. Harrald was born in 1849 and, like Spurgeon, in East Anglia. He entered the Pastors' College in 1870, later that year he began work at Shoreham and there he remained till the late 1870's when Spurgeon—seeing his gifts as a short-hand writer and as a general aid—called on his help as a personal secretary. With characteristic humility and devotion to what he believed was God's will Harrald thenceforth laboured in everything with Spurgeon; in the latter's phrase, he was a true 'armour-bearer'. After his master's death there was no one more trustworthy than Harrald to supervise the revision of the large number of Spurgeon's sermons still to be published. His end came on July 1, 1912 at Shoreham whence he had retired. After a morning walk on the beach, he took his lunch and settled down to the revision of a sermon of Spurgeon's which he was getting ready for the Press. 'Later,' says his biographer, A. Harwood Field, 'it was found that he had gone home then, swiftly, silently, and sweetly. Kissed to sleep by the Saviour who had died for him.'

Susannah Spurgeon and Harrald gave their best to the preparation of this Autobiography because they believed that Spurgeon would continue to serve the Church of Christ in ages yet to come and that Christians would want to know what kind of man he was. This was faith not in his person but in the message of which God had made him such a powerful spokesman. 'I beseech you,' Spurgeon once said, 'to live not only for this age, but for the next also.' And thus he sought to live himself.

Spurgeon was the first great preacher of the Christian era to live in a world in which newspapers and publishers were revolutionizing means of communication. Within days, or at the most weeks, of preaching in London, his words were reported and read across the world. At one time his Sunday morning sermons given in the Tabernacle even appeared in several of the next day's newspapers in the United States! This was, as it were, a first instalment of how modern media can, in God's hand, bring the gospel to the nations. It was also no coincidence that Spurgeon was as gifted a writer as he was a preacher.

Extraordinary as the revival of interest in Spurgeon's writings may appear to be today, there is nothing remarkable in it. The truths he preached are too great to decay and wherever those truths are used by God's Spirit to quicken the churches, Spurgeon's testimony will be welcomed by Christians. Such is the case at the present time. In recent years the publishers have re-issued Spurgeon's annual College Conference Addresses, *An All-Round Ministry*, the six volumes of *The New Park Street Pulpit* and, most important of all, the republication of *The Metropolitan Tabernacle Pulpit* has been commenced. While the preparation of this present volume was being completed news came of new editions of Spurgeon's sermons being published in Germany and Yugoslavia—a reminder that the same message is in all lands the power of God unto salvation.

Spurgeon once used a legend from Nottinghamshire to illustrate the truth that the Word preached outlives the mortal messenger. In an earthquake of long ago the village of Raleigh was, with its church and dwellings, swallowed up and buried beneath the ground. Nothing remained save that at Christmas, so the story went, from deep down beneath the earth the old church bells could still be heard ringing by those who put their ears to the ground. Unlike the strange tale, it was no legend, said Spurgeon, 'that those preachers whose voices were clear and mighty for truth during life, continue to preach in their graves! Being dead, they yet speak'. In the last sermon but one that Spurgeon ever revised, which was upon the text, 'I shall not die, but live, and declare the works of the Lord,' he gave this testimony:

'Often, the death of a man is a kind of new birth to him; when he himself is gone physically, he spiritually survives, and from his grave there shoots up a tree of life whose leaves heal nations. O worker for God, death cannot touch thy sacred mission! Be thou content to die if the truth shall live the better because thou diest. Be thou content to die, because death may be to thee the enlargement of thine influence. Good men die as dies the seed-corn which thereby abideth not alone. When saints are apparently laid in the earth, they quit the earth, and rise and mount to Heaven-gate, and enter into immortality. No, when the sepulchre receives this mortal frame, we shall not die, but live.'

The Publishers,
The Grey House,
Edinburgh

February 14, 1973

It has always been a subject of satisfaction to me that Newington Butts was the site selected for the erection of the Tabernacle. It appears that in the old days of persecution, some Baptists were burnt 'at the Butts at Newington'—probably on the very spot where thousands have been brought to the Lord, and have confessed their faith in the identical way which cost their predecessors their lives. If this is not actually an instance in which 'the blood of the martyrs' has proved to be 'the seed of the church', it is certainly a most interesting and pleasing coincidence. Our district seems to have furnished other martyrs, for in a record dated 1546, we read: 'Three men were condemned as Anabaptists, and burnt in the highway beyond Southwark towards Newington'. Though that description is not very explicit, the region referred to could not have been very far from the place where, these many years, there has been gathered a great congregation of those believers whom some people still erroneously persist in calling 'Anabaptists', though we strenuously hold to 'one Lord, one faith, one baptism'—C.H.S., *in notes prepared for his Autobiography.*

I

Building 'Our Holy and Beautiful House'

On September 7, 1857, a meeting was held at New Park Street Chapel, for the double purpose of giving thanks to God for the success that had attended the Pastor's labours in gathering funds for the new Tabernacle, and of encouraging the people to do their utmost for the same object. On this occasion, Spurgeon said that the many thousands of hearers, who regularly worshipped at the Music Hall, proved that, as soon as a building could be erected to seat 5,000 persons, that number of friends might be safely calculated upon to fill it, and they would then have the best and strongest church in London. Sir Morton Peto had promised to get his agent to look out for a suitable site, and he had also guaranteed substantial help to the Building Fund, which continued to grow, though not as rapidly as the young Pastor desired.

The following resolution, preserved in the church-book, shows that, in July, 1858, the time appeared to have arrived for making a further advance in connection with the much-needed new Tabernacle:

'Meeting of the male members of the church,
Monday, July 26th, 1858.

Our Pastor convened this meeting in order to acquaint the church with the position of the great design for erecting a new Tabernacle, and also to obtain the opinion of the church as to immediate progress.

The church unanimously resolved—That the Committee be desired to proceed with all prudent speed, and agree that our Pastor should leave us alternate months, if he saw it necessary to do so, in order to collect the needful funds.

The meeting afforded a most pleasing proof of the unity and zeal of the brethren.'

It was not long after this time that the public announcement was made concerning the purchase of the freehold site for the new sanctuary; and on December 13, 1858, New Park Street Chapel was once more crowded with an eager and expectant audience, which had assembled 'to hear a statement of the progress made, and to devise steps for recruiting the funds necessary for building the proposed Tabernacle.' The venerable deacon James Low, presided; and deacon Thomas Cook, the Honorary Secretary, presented a report which contained the following information with regard to the financial and other progress made by the Building Committee:

'Their first efforts were directed to adopt measures for raising funds, and obtaining a site for the building, in both of which they have met with abundant success. Since the opening of the account, in September, 1856, to the present date, a period of 27 months, the sum of £9,418 19s. 7d. has been received, or an average of £348 17s. per month. The object, however, of paramount importance to the Committee was obtaining an eligible site for the building. This was, indeed, surrounded with innumerable difficulties, which seemed at times to be beyond the power of the Committee to overcome. At length, however, their labours were crowned with complete success, and they were rewarded for their long and tedious negotiation by obtaining the promise of the Fishmongers' Company to sell a portion of their land at Newington.'[1]

After several other ministers had addressed the meeting, Spurgeon said:

'I do not feel in speaking order tonight, because I seem to have something in my heart so big that I am not able to get it out. I cannot, however, resist the temptation of saying a few words on a topic which you may think far remote from the object of the meeting. The times in which we live are most wonderful; and I wish that this church should be in the future what it has been in the past —the advance-guard of the times. I cannot help observing that during the last four or five years a remarkable change has come over the Christian mind. The Church of England has been awakened. How has this been accomplished, and what means have been used? I cannot help remembering that God honoured us by letting us stand in the front of this great movement. From our example, the blessed fire has run along the ground, and kindled a blaze which shall not soon be extinguished. When I first heard that clergymen

---

[1] The site was formerly occupied by the Fishmongers' Company Almshouses. They bore the name of St. Peter's Hospital, and were built in 1618–36. They were rebuilt, in 1850–1, at East Hill, Wandsworth; and, after their removal, the land presented such a forlorn appearance that the building of the Tabernacle upon it was regarded as a great public improvement.

were to preach in Exeter Hall, my soul leaped within me, and I was ready to exclaim, "Lord, now lettest thou thy servant depart in peace!" When I heard that Westminster Abbey was opened on Sunday evenings for the preaching of the gospel, and then St. Paul's Cathedral, I was overwhelmed with gratitude, and prayed that only the truth as it is in Jesus might be preached in those places; and that the ministers might travail in birth for souls, that Christ might be formed in them the hope of glory. I never felt such union to the Church of England as I now do. The fact is that, when a youth in the country, I was accustomed to associate with the name of clergyman, fox-hunting and such-like amusements; I abhorred them, for I thought they were all like that. Now I see them anxious to win souls to Christ, I cannot help loving them; and as long as they go on to feel the value of souls, I shall continue to pray for them. Now, seeing that the Lord has thus honoured us to be leaders of others, we must continue to lead; we must not take one step backwards, but must still be the very van of the army. What if God should spread the late revival, and let the New Park Street Church still go on as the advance-guard of the host?

Now, as to the Tabernacle, I am quite certain that it will be built, and that I shall preach in it; and I have no doubt that the money will be forthcoming—that matter is no burden to me. Some of you have done a great deal, but you ought to have done a great deal more. There are others who, if measured by oughts, ought not to have done so much. We have not done badly, after all; for, after paying £5,000 for the site, we have a balance in hand of £3,600. I hope that you will all agree that the spot is a most eligible one; though some recommended Kensington, others Holloway, and others Clapham. Having secured the ground, the next thing we did was to advertise for plans, and the following is the circular issued to architects:

"The Committee for building the new Tabernacle for the congregation of the Rev. C. H. Spurgeon give notice that they are prepared to receive designs or models from architects or others for the erection of a building on land situate near The Elephant and Castle, Newington, for which they offer the following premiums: £50 for the best design, £30 for the second, and £20 for the third. The following are the conditions: The building to contain on basement floor (which is to be five feet below the level of footway) school-rooms, twelve feet high, for boys and girls, and lecture-hall to seat 800 persons. The chapel above to seat 3,000 persons, with

standing-room for not less than 1,000, and with not more than two
tiers of galleries. Each sitting to be not less than two feet six inches
by one foot seven inches. Gothic designs will not be accepted by the
Committee. The plan of the Surrey Music Hall has proved to be
acoustically good, and will be decidedly preferred. The total cost,
including architect's commission, warming, ventilation, lighting,
boundary walls, fences, paths, fittings, and every expense, to be
about £16,000. The architects competing will be requested to act as
judges, and to award the first and third premiums. The second
premium to be awarded by the Committee."

More than 250 architects have applied for this circular, all of
whom appear desirous to build the place; so that I anticipate we
shall have a very pretty Tabernacle picture-gallery by-and-by. There
are many friends with us tonight who attend the Music Hall; they
cannot get in here on a Sabbath evening, so they are obliged to be
content with half a loaf. For their sake, I want to see the new chapel
built, for I cannot bear the thought that so many should come here
Sabbath after Sabbath, unable to get inside the doors.

Now, as to money; we say that the building is to cost about
£16,000; but depend upon it, it will be £20,000. Someone asks,
perhaps, "How are we to get it?" Pray for it. When I thought of the
large sum, I said to myself, "It may as well be twenty thousand as
ten; for we shall get one amount as readily as the other." Brethren,
we must pray that God will be pleased to give us the money, and we
shall surely have it. If we had possessed more faith, we should have
had it before now; and when this Tabernacle is built, we shall find
money enough to build a dozen. Look at what Mr. Müller, of
Bristol, has done by faith and prayer. When this land was threatened
with famine, people said, "What will you do now, Mr. Müller?"
"Pray to God," was the good man's answer. He did pray, and the
result was, that he had an overwhelming increase. Do you ask,
"What is required of me tonight?" Let me remind you that all you
possess is not your own; it is your Master's; you are only stewards,
and must hereafter give an account of your stewardship.'

Evidently many who were present were touched by the Pastor's
words, for the sums collected and promised during the evening
amounted to nearly £1,000.

In February, 1859, the competing architects' drawings (sixty-two
sets and one model) were exhibited in the Newington Horse and

Carriage Repository, and proved exceedingly attractive both to the New Park Street congregation and the general public. By a vote taken among themselves, about forty of the competitors assigned the first premium (£50) to the design submitted by E. Cookworthy Robins. The following letter from Spurgeon to Mr. Robins shows that the Pastor himself placed the prize design among the first three, but that the drawings submitted by W. W. Pocock had been selected by himself and the Committee:

'Dear Sir,

I am requested by the Committee to forward the enclosed cheque for £50 as the first premium. In so doing, allow me to congratulate you upon the architectural taste which is so manifest in your drawings. In my own personal selection, your design was one of three which I considered to be pre-eminent among the many. We have inspected the designs with great care, and long deliberation; and, although we are compelled to prefer Mr. Pocock's design as the best basis for our future building, we could not but regret that we were thus compelled to lose your services in the erection. You may not be aware that we have received from private friends of yours, and persons for whom you have erected buildings, the most flattering testimonials of your ability. Since these were unsolicited on your part, and probably unknown to you, we thought them worthy of the highest consideration, and should have felt great pleasure in entrusting our great undertaking to your hands. Wishing you every prosperity,

I am,

Yours heartily,

C. H. SPURGEON.'

The Committee awarded the second premium (£30) to W. W. Pocock, and the Tabernacle was erected after his design, though with considerable modifications, including the abandonment of the towers at the four corners of the building. When Spurgeon found that they would probably cost about £1,000 each, he thought that amount of money could be more profitably expended, and therefore had them omitted, and the style of the structure was altered to the form which has since become familiar to hundreds of thousands of earnest worshippers from all quarters of the globe. The motto on the envelope accompanying Mr. Pocock's drawings was the word 'Metropolitan'—a singularly appropriate one, for the building erected under his superintendence was to contain that word in its official designation, The Metropolitan Tabernacle.[1]

When the plans were finally settled, and the tenders were received and opened, it was found that the highest amounted to £26,370, and the lowest to £21,500, with a saving of £1,500 if Bath instead of Portland stone should be used. This was the tender of William Higgs; and at the net estimate of £20,000, the very figures the Pastor had stated some months before, the contract was signed. Spurgeon often said that it was one of his chief mercies that Mr. Higgs was the builder of the Tabernacle, and it was a special cause of joy to many that the contract was secured by one of the Pastor's own spiritual children, who afterwards became an honoured deacon of the church, and one of the dearest personal friends and most generous helpers his minister ever had.

All needful preparations for the great building having been made, the foundation stone was laid by Sir Samuel Morton Peto, Bart., M.P., on Tuesday afternoon, August 16, 1859. About 3,000 persons were present at the ceremony, which was commenced with the singing of the hundredth Psalm, and prayer by Spurgeon; after which B. W. Carr read the statement, which he had drawn up on behalf of the deacons, rehearsing the history of the church. The closing paragraphs, narrating the unparalleled advance made during the five years from 1854 to 1859 at New Park Street, Exeter Hall, and the Surrey Gardens, reveal the need there was for a larger place of worship:

'From the day the Rev. Charles Haddon Spurgeon commenced his labours in our midst, it pleased the Lord our God to grant us a revival which has steadily progressed ever since. Among the earliest additions to our number, there were not a few disciples of Christ, who, after making a profession under faithful ministers long ago departed to their rest, had wandered about, and found no settled home. Many such were gathered into the fold of our fellowship. Here their souls have been restored, while they have found the presence of the good Shepherd, who maketh us to lie down in green pastures, and leadeth us beside the still waters. But the greater work was that of conversion. So did the Holy Ghost accompany the preaching of the gospel with Divine power, that almost every sermon proved the means of awakening and regeneration to some

---

[1] Each competitor had been required to attach a motto to his design.

[8]

who were hitherto "dead in trespasses and sins." Thus our church became an asylum for the aged, as well as a nursery for the babes of our Saviour's family. . . .

The prejudice against entering a Nonconformist sanctuary has, in many instances, been laid aside by those who have worshipped within the walls of an edifice (the Surrey Gardens Music Hall) that is justly accounted neutral ground, it being sacred or profane according to the temporary use it is made to serve. Every week has borne testimony to the saving influence of the gospel, as it has been proclaimed in the Music Hall to an assembly of 5,000 persons. Still, with so large a congregation, and so small a chapel, the inconvenience of a temporary meeting-place becomes more and more grievously felt. There is, and has been for the past two years, as fair an average of that large congregation, who are devout persons, and regular attendants, as in any sanctuary in London. Yet not one-third of them can find a place under the same ministry for more than one service during the week. The church members far exceed the extent of accommodation in our own chapel to provide all of them with sittings. It is only by having two distinct services that we can admit our communicants to the table of the Lord. The necessity therefore for the undertaking that we assemble to inaugurate, must be perceived by all. Every attempt to trace the popular demand for Evangelical teaching to spasmodic excitement has failed. The pastor of New Park Street Church has never consciously departed from the simple rule of faith recorded in the New Testament. The doctrines he has set forth are identical with those which have been received by godly men of every section of the Church since the days of the apostles. The services of religion have been conducted without any peculiarity or innovation. No musical or æsthetic accompaniments have ever been used. The weapons of our warfare are not carnal, but they are mighty. The history of our progress for five years is patent to the world. The example has been found capable of successfully stimulating other churches in their aggressive efforts to save perishing souls. With earnest individual and united prayer, each step has been taken; and to the exclusive honour and praise of our God, our stone of Ebenezer is this day laid.'

After the reading of the paper, Spurgeon explained: 'In the bottle which is to be placed under the stone, we have put no money—for one good reason, that we have none to spare. We have not put newspapers, because, albeit we admire and love the liberty of the press, yet that is not so immediately concerned in this edifice. The articles placed under the stone are simply these: the Bible, the Word of God, we put that as the foundation of our church. Upon this rock doth Christ build the ministration of His truth. We know of nothing else as our standard. Together with this, we have put *The Baptist Confession of Faith*, which was signed in the olden times by Benjamin Keach, one of my eminent predecessors. We put also *the declaration of the deacons*, which you have just heard read, printed on parchment. There is also an edition of Dr. Rippon's Hymn Book, published just before he died; and then, in the last place, there is a programme of this day's proceedings. I do not suppose that the New Zealander who, one day, is to sit on the broken arch of London Bridge, will make much out of it. If we had put gold and silver there, it is possible he might have taken it back to New Zealand with him; but I should not wonder, if ever England is destroyed, these relics will find their way into some museum in Australia or America, where people will spell over some of our old-fashioned names, and wonder whoever those good men could be who are inscribed here, as Samuel Gale, James Low, Thomas Olney, Thomas Cook, George Winsor, William P. Olney, George Moore, and C. H. Spurgeon. And I think they will say, "Oh! depend upon it, they were some good men, so they put them in stone there." These deacons *are* living stones, indeed; they have served this church well and long. Honour to whom honour is due. I am glad to put their names with mine here; and I hope we shall live together for ever in eternity.'

When Sir Morton Peto had duly laid the stone and offered his congratulations to the Pastor and to the Church, Spurgeon said:

'Before I speak about the building we are going to erect here, I want just to mention that I had a sweet letter from that eminent servant of God, John Angell James, of Birmingham, in reply to one I had written asking him to come to this meeting. He said, "I would have done so if I had been well enough, but I am unable to travel. My work is almost done, I cannot serve my Master much longer; but I can still do a little for Him. I preach perhaps once on the Sabbath, and I still continue to do what I can with my pen. What a mercy," he adds, "to have been permitted to serve my Master so long!" We frequently exchange notes, and in his last letter to me he said, "My dear brother, be on your watch-tower, and gird your sword on your thigh. The devil hates you more than most men, for you have done so much damage to his kingdom; and, if he can, he will trip you up." I am sure what good Mr. James says is true, but I know that he, and you, and many more of the Lord's people are praying that I may be upheld, and that we may successfully carry through this great undertaking. I never answer any slanders against myself, and very seldom answer any questions about what I mean to do. I am obliged to be a self-contained man, just going on my own way, and letting other people go in their own way. If I am wrong, I will be accountable to my own Master, but to no flesh living; and if I am right, the day will declare it. God knows how sincere are my intentions even when I may have acted unwisely.

I said, some time ago, when our brethren were half afraid, "The Tabernacle is to be built, and it will be built, and God will fill it with His presence and glory." There is no doubt whatever about the money being obtained. I scarcely know that I have asked an individual to give anything, because I have such a solid conviction that the money must come. I suppose that, out of all that is now in our hands, I have myself collected more than half through my preaching; and I daresay that is how the larger part of the remainder will come, through the kindness of the provincial and metropolitan churches, who have almost all treated me with the noblest generosity. I give this day my hearty thanks to all who have helped me; and I do not know but what I may as well add, to all who have not helped me. Many of them mean to do so, and therefore I will thank them beforehand.[1] There is one gentleman here today who is to address you. I think (albeit that he can speak admirably,) the best part of his speech will be made with his hand, for he has three thousand pounds with him to give as a noble donation from an aged servant of Christ, long sick and confined to his house, but who loves Christ's ministers, and desires to help Christ's cause. He would not like me to mention his name, and therefore I shall not do it.

And now, my dear friends, as to the place to be erected here. I have a word or two to say with regard to *its style*, with regard to *its purposes*, and with regard to *our faith and our prospects*.

It is to me a matter of congratulation that we shall succeed in building in this city a Grecian place of worship. My notions of architecture are not worth much, because I look at a building from a theological point of view, not from an architectural one. It seems to me that there are two sacred languages in the world. There was

---

[1] It should be remembered that Spurgeon did not attempt to exclude humour from speeches of this kind!

the Hebrew of old, and I doubt not that Solomon adopted Jewish architecture for the Temple—a Hebrew form and fashion of putting stones together in harmony with the Hebrew faith. There is but one other sacred language—not Rome's mongrel tongue—the Latin; glorious as that may be for a battle-cry, it is of no use for preaching the gospel. The other sacred language is the Greek, and that is dear to every Christian's heart. Our fullest revelation of God's will is in that tongue; and so are our noblest names for Jesus. The standard of our faith is Greek; and this place is to be Grecian. I care not that many an idol temple has been built after the same fashion. Greek is the sacred tongue, and Greek is the Baptist's tongue; we may be beaten in our own version, sometimes; but in the Greek, never. Every Baptist place should be Grecian—never Gothic. We owe nothing to the Goths as religionists. We have a great part of our Scriptures in the Grecian language, and this shall be a Grecian place of worship; and God give us the power and life of that master of the Grecian tongue, the apostle Paul, that here like wonders may be done by the preaching of the Word as were wrought by his ministry!

As for our faith, as a church, you have heard about that already. We believe in the five great points commonly known as Calvinistic; but we do not regard those five points as being barbed shafts which we are to thrust between the ribs of our fellow-Christians. We look upon them as being five great lamps which help to irradiate the cross; or, rather, five bright emanations springing from the glorious covenant of our Triune God, and illustrating the great doctrine of Jesus crucified. Against all comers, especially against all lovers of Arminianism, we defend and maintain pure gospel truth. At the same time, I can make this public declaration, that I am no Antinomian. I belong not to the sect of those who are afraid to invite the sinner to Christ. I warn him, I invite him, I exhort him. Hence, then, I have contumely on either hand. Inconsistency is charged against me by some people, as if anything that God commanded could be inconsistent; I will glory in such inconsistency even to the end. I bind myself precisely to no form of doctrine. I love those five points as being the angles of the gospel, but then I love the centre between the angles better still. Moreover, we are Baptists, and we cannot swerve from this matter of discipline, nor can we make our church half-and-half in that matter. The witness of our church must be one and indivisible. We must have one Lord, one faith, and one baptism. And yet dear to our hearts is that great article of the

Apostles' Creed, "I believe in the communion of saints." I believe not in the communion of Episcopalians alone; I do not believe in the communion of Baptists only, I dare not sit with them exclusively. I think I should be almost strict-communionist enough not to sit with them at all, because I should say, "This is not the communion of saints, it is the communion of Baptists." Whosoever loves the Lord Jesus Christ in verity and truth hath a hearty welcome, and is not only permitted, but invited to communion with the Church of Christ. However, we can say, with all our hearts, that difference has never lost us one good friend yet. I see around me our Independent brethren; they certainly have been to Ænon today, for there has been "much water" here; and I see round about me dear strict-communion brethren, and one of them is about to address you. He is not so strict a communionist but what he really in his own heart communes with all the people of God. I can number among my choicest friends many members of the Church of England, and some of every denomination; I glory in that fact. However sternly a man may hold the right of private judgment, he yet can give his right hand with as tight a grip to everyone who loves the Lord Jesus Christ.

Now with regard to *our prospects*. We are to build this place, and the prospect I anticipate is that it will be paid for before it is opened. I think it is likely to be so; because, if we carry out our intention, as a Committee, we have a notion that, if our friends do not give us liberal contributions, we will put up the carcass and roof it in, and allow them to come in and stand. Those who want seats can buy them. I am sure my people would soon get me a pulpit, and such is the zeal of our brethren that they would soon build me a baptistery. I leave it open for any generous friend here, who pleases to do so, to engage to provide some part of the Tabernacle, and to say, "I will give that." Churchmen give painted windows for their places of worship; and if some of you agree to give different parts of the chapel, it may be so erected. You must understand that our large expenditure is caused partly by the fact that we have immense school-rooms underground, and also a lecture-hall, holding between 800 and 900 persons, for church-meetings. This is necessary, because our church is of such an immense size, and our members come out to every service if possible; there is no church-edifice in London so well used as ours is; they hack it to pieces. We must build this Tabernacle strongly, I am sure, for our friends are always with us. They love to be at the prayer-meetings. There are no people who take out their quarter's seat-money so fully. They say, "We will hear all that we can;" and, depend upon it, they never give me a chance of seeing the seats empty. But our desire is, after we have fitted up our vestry, schools, and other rooms, that we shall be able to build other chapels. Sir Morton Peto is the man who builds one chapel with the hope that it will be the seedling for another; and we will pretty soon try *our* hands at it. Our people have taken to chapel-building, and they will go on with it. They built a chapel that held "near a thousand hearers, in Horse-lie-down," for Benjamin Keach; then they built one in Carter Lane for Dr. Gill; then one in Park Street for Dr. Rippon; and now we have set about building one here. God sparing my life, if I have my people at my back, I will not rest until the dark county of Surrey is covered with places of worship. I look on this Tabernacle as only the beginning; within the last six months, we have started two churches, one in Wandsworth and the other in Greenwich, and the Lord has prospered them, the pool of baptism has often been stirred with converts. And what we have done in two places, I am about to do in a third, and we will do it, not for the third or the fourth, but for the hundredth time, God being our helper. I am sure I may make my strongest appeal to my brethren, because we do not mean to build this Tabernacle as our nest, and then to be idle. We must go from strength to strength, and be a missionary church, and never rest until, not only this neighbourhood, but our country, of which it is said that some parts are as dark as India, shall have been enlightened with the gospel.'

The first donation to be laid on the foundation stone was one of £3,000 from a wealthy gentleman in Bristol who was at that time house-bound through sickness, but who also promised that if twenty others would give £100 each, he would add another £2,000 to match theirs. Many other donations were laid upon the stone before the proceedings ended. By the end of the day the contributions amounted to little short of £5,000.

In an evening meeting on the same day, the chair was taken by the Lord Mayor, Alderman Wire, who said that he looked on Spurgeon as one who was called to accomplish a great work for God. Among the speakers was the father of the young pastor. He confessed that he was there to acknowledge a fault. He had thought that his son had done wrong in not going to College, and again in coming to London; but he now saw that God had opened the way. 'Several told me', he said, 'that my son would not do in London; he had not sufficient education; but he had after all the best education, for God had been his teacher. If anything could have crowned my happiness, it would have been to see my son's grandfather present. He is always speaking about him'.

In January, 1860, the total receipts had grown to £16,868 6s. 2d., and on Monday evening, April 2, one more crowded meeting was held at New Park Street Chapel, under the presidency of the Pastor, 'to hear a statement as to the progress of the Building Fund, and to adopt measures for obtaining additional contributions.' Spurgeon mentioned that the number of members had nearly reached 1,500, and that there was a constant and regular stream of enquirers and candidates for church-fellowship; and he had no doubt that, soon after the new Tabernacle was opened, and all the organizations were in operation, they would have over 3,000 members in full communion with them. Mr. Cook reported that there had been received, up to that date, £18,904 15s. 2d., but it was estimated that a further sum of £12,000 would be required before the Tabernacle could be opened free of debt. Towards this amount, upwards of £500 was contributed that evening.

*

Soon after the building operations commenced[1] I went to the site with Mr. Cook, the Secretary of our Committee, and there, in the midst of the bricks, and mortar, and stone, and scaffold poles, and so on, we two knelt down, and prayed for the Lord's blessing on the whole enterprise, and also asked that no one of the many workmen employed might be killed or injured while they were helping to rear our new place of worship; and I was afterwards able to testify that our prayer-hearing God had graciously granted both of our requests.

I have one, among many reasons, for speaking with 'bated breath as to anything which God has wrought by me, because, in my heart of hearts, I am made to feel that the true honour belongs to unknown helpers, who serve the Lord, and yet have none of the credit of having done so. I cannot help being pushed to the front; but I envy those who have done good by stealth, and have refused to have their names so much as whispered. I do not think I ever told in public, until the night of my pastoral silver-wedding celebration (May 19, 1879), one fact which will ever live in my memory. The Tabernacle was to be built, and some £30,000 would be wanted.

[1] The remainder of this chapter is autobiographical material which Spurgeon had intended to use in narrating this portion of his life-story.

[15]

We did not know, when we started, that it would be so much; we thought about £12,000 or £15,000 would suffice, and we felt that we were rather bold to venture upon *that*. When we came to the undertaking of responsibilities, there was a natural shrinking on the part of the Committee with which we started. No one could be blamed; it was a great risk, and, personally, I did not wish anyone to undertake it. I was quite prepared for any risk; but then I had no money of my own, and so was a mere man of straw. There was, in some of our friends, a measure of fear and trembling, but I had none; I was as sure upon the matter as possible, and reckoned upon paying all the cost. This quiet assurance, however, had a foundation which reflects credit upon one who has for some years gone to his reward. When I was riding with a friend to preach in the country, a gentleman overtook us, and asked me if I would get out of the trap, and ride with him in his gig, as he wished to speak with me. I did so. He said, 'You have got to build that big place.' I said, 'Yes.' He said, 'You will find that many friends will feel nervous over it. Now, as a business man, I am sure you will succeed; and, beside that, God is with the work, and it cannot fail. I want you never to feel anxious or downcast about it.' I told him that it was a great work, and that I hoped the Lord would enable me to carry it through. 'What do you think,' he asked, 'would be required, at the outside, to finish it off altogether?' I replied, '£20,000 must do it in addition to what we have.' 'Then,' he said, 'I will let you have the £20,000, on the condition that you shall only keep what you need of it to finish the building. Mark,' he added, 'I do not expect to give more than £50; but you shall have bonds and leases to the full value of £20,000 to fall back upon.' This was truly royal. I told no one, but the ease of mind this act gave me was of the utmost value. I had quite as much need of faith, for I resolved that none of my friend's money should be touched: but I had no excuse for fear. God was very good to me; but, by this fact, I was disabled from all personal boasting. My friend gave his £50, and no more, and I felt deeply thankful to him for the help which he would have rendered had it been required. There were others who did like generous deeds anonymously, and among them was the giver of £5,000. If there be honours to be worn by anyone, let these dear brethren wear them.

While the Metropolitan Tabernacle was being completed Spurgeon took his first holiday since the commencement of his ministry in London. Few preachers have undertaken such a period of uninterrupted service as Spurgeon did from 1854 to 1860. It was reckoned that he preached an average of ten sermons a week, invitations which he found it difficult to refuse pouring in with great regularity from all quarters. Naturally most of his engagements were in the area of 'greater London', but the development of the railway enabled him to accept invitations from far afield. Some of his congregations numbered as many as 30,000 persons. The unrelieved strain at last began to produce symptoms which could not be ignored. Spurgeon himself, and his closest friends, alike realized that the only way to prevent a complete breakdown in health was to seek relaxation for a time in a district where he would be comparatively free from outside pressure. Accordingly a Continental tour was arranged.

This European tour, extending over eight weeks, was perhaps the most enjoyable holiday that Spurgeon ever had. Accompanied by his wife and two friends he left London shortly after a 'farewell meeting' on the evening of the 4th June 1860, and did not preach in London again until the 29th July. The account of his tour given in this chapter was delivered to an assembly in the half-finished Tabernacle in the middle of August.

2

In Calvin's Pulpit

I HAVE been requested by two well-known and deservedly eminent publishers to print some notes of my journey on the Continent; but I went there for rest and recreation, and I felt that this most sacred purpose could not be attained if I chained myself to the drudgery of book-writing. My congregation would have been disappointed if I had come home as tired as I went, and I could have had no solid excuse for ceasing my daily preaching if I had not really rested my weary brain. I believe, moreover, that the narrative of my journey will be far more valuable to me as a fountain of fresh illustrations and suggestions, than if I could pour it all out into a book. Will it not be better to retain my pearl, and let it glitter every now and then, than to melt it into one small draught, too shallow to satisfy the public thirst?

I went from St Katherine's Docks down the river, accompanied by my well-beloved deacons and several of my friends. At Gravesend they left me and my party, with the kindest wishes, and with many a prayer to God for our safety. The journey was rendered abundantly pleasant by the evening which we spent together in prayer and fellowship before our departure. I never heard such kind words and such loving prayers uttered concerning any human being as I heard that night concerning myself. There was nothing like fulsome flattery, all the glory was given to God; but every brother invoked such choice blessings upon my head that I went away with a rich cargo of joy, knowing that a full wind of prayer was following behind.

The captain of our vessel was from Essex, and as all Essex men have a high opinion of their countrymen, we soon found ourselves in full talk upon the excellences of our native county. Many were our anecdotes, and swiftly flew the time. Mine I have told so many times, I daresay you know them. Some of the captain's tales were new and original. I shall give you one, because it tends to illustrate the place in which we landed—Antwerp. That city is so full of images of the Virgin Mary that you cannot turn the corner of a street without seeing them, sometimes under a canopy of many colours, arrayed in all manner of imitation jewellery, and at other times in neat little niches which seem to have been picked out of the wall for their special accommodation. Sometimes Mary is represented by an ugly black doll, and at other times by a decent respectable statue. So many of these objects are there, that the sailors may be excused for imagining every image which they see to be a Virgin Mary. One of them, who landed there, went to buy some tobacco; and when he returned to the ship, his companions said, 'That is very good tobacco, Jack; where did you get it?' 'Oh!' he answered, 'you will know the shop, for there is a Virgin Mary sitting over the door, smoking a pipe.' I don't wonder at the man's blunder, for among so many idols one may easily mistake a Turk and his turban for the Virgin and her crown. I am sure they think vastly more of her than of our Lord Jesus Christ; for, though we saw many crucifixes, and many representations of the Saviour, yet even in their image-work it seemed to me that the Virgin Mary was *cent per cent* beyond the Lord Jesus Christ.

It happened the very day we landed at Antwerp that there was a grand procession just streaming in its full glory out of the cathedral, a fine and venerable building. There were priests in their robes, beadles resplendent in their livery, and a great number of men, whom I supposed to be penitents, carrying huge candles, certainly I should think two inches in diameter. These men walked two-and-two along the streets. Whether that burning of the candles typified the consumption of their sins, the melting of their church, or the illumination of soul which they so greatly needed, I do not know. There were also carried great lamps of silver, or electro-plate, very much like our own street lamps, only of course not quite so heavy; and these, too, when the sun was shining brightly, and there was no need of the slightest artificial light. In all solemnity, the men marched along, not in the dark cathedral, but in the open streets, with these candles and lanterns blazing and shaming the sunlight. Someone told me they were taking 'the most blessed and comfortable sacrament' to some sick people; but what the candles had to do with the sacrament, or the sacrament with the candles, or the people with the sacrament, I do not know. I noticed two little boys, very handsomely dressed, walking in the middle of the procession, and throwing flowers and oak leaves before the priests as they walked; so that, as they went along, their holy feet scarcely needed to touch the soil, or to be hurt with the stones. The presence of those children, full of infantile joy, relieved the soul for a moment, and bade us pray that our own little ones might take part in a nobler celebration when the Lord Himself should come in the glory of His Father. Almost every house had, just before the window, a little place for holding a candle; and as soon as the inmates heard the procession coming along, the candles were lighted. I noticed that, the moment it passed, the thrifty housewives blew out the lights, and so they saved their tallow if they did not save their souls. I enquired, and was informed—and I think on good authority— that even some of the Protestants in Antwerp burn these candles in front of their houses lest their trade should be hindered if they did not conform to the customs of the rest of the people; it is an unutterable disgrace to them if they do so. I would like to have seen Martin Luther with a candle before his door when the priests were passing, unless, indeed, he had burned the Pope's Bull before their eyes. He would sooner have died than have paid respect to a baptized heathenism, a mass of idolatries and superstitions. Never did I feel my Protestant feelings boiling over so tremendously as in this city of idols, for I am not an outrageous Protestant generally, and I rejoice to confess that I feel sure there are some of God's people even in the Romish Church, as I shall have to show you by-and-by; but I did feel indignant when I saw the glory and worship which belong to God alone, given to pictures, and images of wood and stone. When I saw the pulpits magnificently carved, the gems set in the shrines, the costly marbles, the rich and rare paintings upon which a man might gaze for a day, and see some new beauty in each face, I did not marvel that men were enchanted therewith; but when I saw the most flagrant violation of taste and of religion in their 'Calvarys' and cheap prints, my spirit was stirred within me, for I saw a people wholly given unto idolatry. They seem as if they could not live without Mary the Virgin, and without continually paying reverence and adoration to her.

We journeyed from Antwerp to Brussels. I cannot say that Brussels greatly interested me; I do not care much for places in which there is nothing but fine buildings and museums. I had much rather see an odd, old-fashioned city like Antwerp, with its sunny memories of Rubens, Quintin Matsys, and other princes in the realm of art. I think its singular houses, its quaint costumes, and its ancient streets, will never die out of my memory. In Brussels, I heard a good sermon in a Romish church. The place was crowded with people, many of them standing, though they might have had a seat for a halfpenny or a farthing; and I stood, too; and the good priest—for I believe he is a good man—preached the Lord Jesus with all his might. He spoke of the love of Christ, so that I, a very poor hand at the French language, could fully understand him, and my heart kept beating within me as he told of the beauties of Christ and the preciousness of His blood, and of His power to save the chief of sinners. He did not say, 'justification by faith,' but he did say, 'efficacy of the blood,' which comes to very much the same thing. He did not tell us we were saved by grace, and not by our works; but he did say that all the works of men were less than nothing when brought into competition with the blood of Christ, and that the blood of Jesus alone could save. True, there were objectionable sentences, as naturally there must be in a discourse delivered under such circumstances; but I could have gone to the preacher, and have said to him, 'Brother, you have spoken the truth;' and if I had been handling his text, I must have treated it in the same way that he did, if I could have done it as well. I was pleased to find my own opinion verified, in his case, that there are, even in the apostate church, some who cleave unto the Lord— some sparks of heavenly fire that flicker amidst the rubbish of old superstition, some lights that are not blown out, even by the strong wind of Popery, but still cast a feeble gleam across the waters sufficient to guide the soul to the rock Christ Jesus. I saw, in that church, a box for contributions for the Pope; he will never grow rich with what I put into it. I have seen money-boxes on the Continent for different saints—Santa Clara, St. Francis, St. Dominic; another box for the Virgin, and another for the poor; but I never could make out how the money got to the Virgin, and to Dominic, and to the rest of them; but I have a notion that, if you were to discover how the money gets to the poor, you would find how it reaches the saints.

After leaving Brussels, and getting a distant glimpse of the Lion Mound of Waterloo, we hurried down to Namur, and steamed along the Meuse—that beautiful river, which is said to be an introduction to the Rhine, but which to my mind is a fair rival to it; it quite spoiled me for the Rhine. Everywhere, on each side, there were new phases of beauty, and sweet little pictures which shone in the sunshine like small but exquisite gems. It was not one vast Koh-i-noor diamond; it was not sublimity mingling its awe with loveliness such as you would see in Switzerland with its majestic mountains, but a succession of beautiful pearls, threaded on the silver string of that swiftly-flowing river. It is so narrow and shallow that, as the steamboat glides along, it drives up a great wave upon the banks on either side. In some parts, along the river, there were signs of mineral wealth, and the people were washing the ironstone at the water's edge to separate the ore from the earth.

One thing which I saw here I must mention, as it is a type of a prevailing evil in Belgium. When there were barges of ironstone to be unloaded, *the women* bore the heavy baskets upon their backs. If there were coals or bricks to be carried, the women did it; they carried everything; and their lords and masters sat still, and seemed to enjoy seeing them at work, and hoped it might do them good, while they themselves were busily engaged in the important occupation of smoking their pipes. When we came to a landing-place, if the rope was to be thrown off so that the steam-boat might be secured, there was always a woman to run and seize it, and there stood a big, lazy fellow to give directions as to how she should do it. We joked with each other upon the possibility of getting our wives to do the like; but, indeed, it is scarcely a joking matter to see poor women compelled to work like slaves, as if they were only made to support their husbands in idleness. They were fagged and worn; but they looked more fully developed than the men, and seemed to be more masculine. If I had been one of those women, and I had got a little bit of a husband sitting there smoking his pipe, if there is a law in Belgium that gives a woman two months for beating her husband, I fear I should have earned the penalty. Anyhow, I would have said to him, 'I am very much obliged to you for doing me the honour of marrying me; but, at the same time, if I am to work and earn *your* living and my own, too, you will smoke your pipe somewhere else.' The fact is, my dear friends, to come to something that may be worth our thinking about, employment for women is greatly needed in our country, and the want of it is a very great evil; but it is not so much to be deplored as that barbarity which dooms women to sweep the streets, to till the fields, to carry heavy burdens, and to be the drudges of the family. We greatly need that watchmaking, printing, telegraphing, bookselling, and other indoor occupations should be more freely open to female industry, but may heaven save our poor women from the position of their Continental sisters! The gospel puts woman where she should be, gives her an honourable position in the house and in the Church; but where women become the votaries of superstition, they will soon be made the burden-bearers of society. Our best feelings revolt at the idea of putting fond, faithful, and affectionate women to oppressive labour. Our mothers, our sisters, our wives, our daughters are much too honourable in our esteem to be treated otherwise than as dear companions, for whom it shall be our delight to live and labour.

As everybody who goes on the Continent visits Cologne, so did we; but I must say of Cologne that I have a more vivid recollection of what I smelt than of what I saw. The Cologne odour is more impressive than the Eau de Cologne. I had heard Albert Smith say he believed there were eighty-three distinct bad smells in Cologne, and in my opinion he understated the number, for every yard presented something more terrible than we had ever smelt before. Better to pay our heavy taxes for drainage than live in such odours. Our filthy friend, the Thames, is as sweet as rose-water when compared with Cologne or Frankfort. Hear this, ye grumblers, and be thankful that you are not worse off than you are! We went down the Rhine; and it was just a repetition of what we saw down the Meuse, with the addition of castles and legends. My want of taste is no doubt the cause of my disappointment upon seeing this river. The lakes of Westmoreland and Cumberland, and the lochs of Scotland, fairly rival the Rhine, and are of much the same character.

We went across to Frankfort and Heidelberg, and then to Baden-Baden. Let me say a few words about Baden. I went to see the gaming-table there; it was, without exception, the most mournful sight I ever looked upon. The Conversation House at Baden is a gorgeous building. Wealth could not make it more splendid than it is. All the luxuries that can be gathered from the very ends of the earth are lavished there. It is a fairy palace, more like the fantastic creation of a dream than sober substantial fact. You are freely admitted; no charge is made, whilst the most beautiful music that can be found waits to charm your ear. Every place of amusement is free; even the public library is free. You ask me how all this is supported. To the left of the building there are two rooms for gaming. There is a long table, and a great crowd standing round it; the seats are all full, and there sit four men in the middle with long rakes, pulling money this way and that way, and shoving it here and there. I hardly ever saw such a mass of money, except upon a banker's counter. There are long piles of gold done up in marked quantities, and there are also heaps of silver money. You see a young man come in; he does not seem like a gambler. He puts down a half-napoleon as a mere joke: in a minute it is shovelled away; he has lost his money. He walks round again, and puts down another piece of gold; this time he wins, and he has two. By-and-by he will play more deeply, and the day will probably come when he will stake his all, and lose it. You may see women sitting there all night playing for high stakes. Some people win, but everybody must lose sooner or later, for the chances are dreadfully against any man who plays. The bank clears an enormous sum every year; I am afraid to mention the amount lest I should be thought to exaggerate. What staring eyes, what covetous looks, what fiery faces I saw there! And what multitudes go into that place happy, and return to curse the day of their birth! I had the sorrow of seeing some fools play. I saw young men, who lost so much that they had hardly enough to take them back to England. Such is the infatuation that I am not surprised when spectators are carried away by the torrent.

There are some who defend the system; I hold it to be fraught with more deadly evils than anything else that could be invented, even by Satan himself. I saw an old respectable-looking man put down ten pounds. He won, and he received twenty. He put down the twenty; he won again, and he had forty. He put down the forty, and received eighty. He put down the eighty, and took up one hundred and sixty pounds. Then he put it all in his pocket, and walked away as calmly as possible. The man would lose money by that transaction, because he would go back on the morrow, and probably play till he would sell the house that covers his children's heads, and pawn the very bed from under his wife. The worst thing that can happen to a man who gambles is to win. If you lose, it serves you right, and there is hope that you will repent of your folly; if you win, the devil will have you in his net so thoroughly that escape will be well-nigh impossible. I charge every young man here, above all things never have anything to do with games of chance. If you desire to make your damnation doubly sure, and ruin both body and soul, go to the gaming-table; but if not, avoid it, pass by it, look not at it, for it has a basilisk's eyes,[1] and may entice you; and it has the sting of an adder, and will certainly destroy you if you come beneath its deadly influence.

From Baden-Baden, we went to Freiburg, and afterwards to Schaffhausen. There, for the first time, we saw the Alps. It was a

---

[1] Basilisk: the King of Serpents, supposed to have the power to fascinate the creature on which it fixes its eye; in other words, to rob the creature of all power to escape or resist it.

wonderful sight, though in the dim distance we hardly knew whether we saw clouds or mountains. We had to hold a sort of controversy with ourselves—'Is that solid—that glittering whiteness, that sunny shimmering that we see there? Is it a bank of white mist? Is it cloud, or is it a mountain?' Soon you are assured that you are actually beholding the everlasting hills. If a man does not feel like praising God at such a moment, I do not think there is any grace in him; if there be anything like piety in a man's soul when he sees those glorious works of God, he will begin to praise the Lord, and magnify His holy Name. We went from Schaffhausen to Zurich. Everywhere there was something to delight us. The magnificent falls of the Rhine, the clear blue waters of the Zurich lake, the distant mountains, the ever-changing costumes of the people—all kept us wide awake, and gratified our largest love of novelties. All nature presented us with a vast entertainment, and every turn of the head introduced us to something new and beautiful.

At Zurich, I saw in the great fair what I also saw at Baden-Baden, a sight which gave me pleasure, namely, the little star of truth shining brightly amid the surrounding darkness. Opposite the house at Baden where Satan was ruining souls at the gaming-table, there was a stall at which an agent of the Bible Society was selling Bibles and Testaments. I went up and bought a Testament of him, and felt quite cheered to see the little battery erected right before the fortifications of Satan, for I felt in my soul it was mighty through God to the pulling down of the stronghold. Then, in the midst of the fair at Zurich, where the people were selling all manner of things, as at John Bunyan's Vanity Fair, there stood a humble-looking man with his stall, upon which there were Bibles, Testaments, and Mr. Ryle's tracts. It is always a great comfort to me to see my sermons, in French and other languages, sold at the same shops as the writings of that excellent man of God. There is the simple gospel in his tracts, and they are to my knowledge singularly owned of God. How sweet it is to see these dear brethren in other churches loving our Lord, and honoured by Him!

At Lucerne, we spent our third Sabbath day. Of all days in the year, Sabbath days on the Continent are the most wretched, so far as the public means of grace are concerned; this one, however, was spent in quiet worship in our own room. Our first Sabbath was a dead waste, for the service at church was lifeless, spiritless, graceless, powerless. Even the grand old prayers were so badly read that it was impossible to be devout while hearing them, and the sermon upon 'the justice of God in destroying the Canaanites' was as much adapted to convert a sinner, or to edify a saint, as Burke's Peerage, or Walker's Dictionary; there was nothing, however, Puseyistical or heretical. Far worse was our second Sunday, in Baden, which effectually prevented my attending Episcopal service again until I can be sure of hearing truthful doctrine. The preacher was manifestly a downright Puseyite because, during one part of the service, he must needs go up to the Roman Catholic altar, and there bow himself with his back to us. The images and idols were not concealed in any way; there they were in all their open harlotry, and I must say they were in full keeping with the sermon which was inflicted upon us. The preacher thought he would give us a smart hit, so he began with an attack upon all who did not subscribe to baptismal regeneration and sacramental efficacy. He did not care what we might say, he was certain that, when the holy drops fell from the fingers of God's ordained minister, regeneration there and then took place. I thought, 'Well, that is coming out, and the man is more honest than some of the wolves in sheep's clothing, who hold baptismal regeneration, but will not openly confess it.' The whole sermon through, he treated us to sacramental efficacy, and made some allusion to St. George's riots, saying that it was an awful thing that the servants of God were subjected to persecution, and then he told us we had not sufficient respect for our ministers, that the real ordained successors of the apostles were trodden down as mire in the streets.

I abstained from going to church after that; and if I were to continue for seven years without the public means of grace, unless I knew that a man of kindred spirit with Mr. Allen, Mr. Cadman, Mr. Ryle, and that holy brotherhood of Evangelicals, would occupy the pulpit, I never would enter an Anglican church again. These Puseyites make good Churchmen turn to the Dissenters, and we who already dissent, are driven further and further from the Establishment. In the name of our Protestant religion, I ask whether a minister of the Church of England is allowed to bow before the altar of a Popish church? Is there no rule or canon which restrains men from such an outrage upon our professed faith, such an insult to our Constitution? In the church at Lucerne, I think they had the head of John the Baptist, with some of the blood in a dish, and other relics innumerable; yet I was expected to go on Sunday, and worship there! I could not do it, for I should have kept on thinking of John the Baptist's head in the corner. Though I have a great respect for that Baptist, and all other Baptists, I do not think I could have controlled myself sufficiently to worship God under such circumstances.

We went up the Rigi, as everybody must do who visits the Alps, toiling up, up, up, ever so high, to see the sun go to bed; and then we were awakened in the morning, with a dreadful blowing of horns, to get up and see the sun rise. Out we went, but his gracious majesty, the sun, would not condescend to show himself; or, at least, he had been up half-an-hour before we knew it; so we all went down again, and that was the end of our glorious trip. Yet it was worth while to go up to see the great mountains all around us, it was a sight which might make an angel stand and gaze, and gaze again; the various sharp or rounded peaks and snowy summits are all worthy of the toil which brings them into view. The circular panorama seen from the Rigi-Kulm is perhaps unrivalled. There is the lake of Zug, there the long arms of Lucerne, yonder Mount Pilatus, and further yet the Black Forest range. Just at your feet is the buried town of Goldau, sad tomb in which a multitude were crushed by a falling mountain. The height is dizzy to unaccustomed brains, but the air is bracing, and the prospect such as one might picture from the top of Pisgah, where the prophet of Horeb breathed out his soul to God.

We went here, there, and everywhere, and saw everything that was to be seen; and, at last, after a long journey, we came to Geneva. I had received the kindest invitation from our esteemed and excellent brother, Dr. d'Aubigné. He came to meet me at the station, but he missed me. I met a gentleman in the street, and told him I was Mr. Spurgeon. He then said, 'Come to my house—the very house where Calvin used to live.' I went home with him; and after we found Dr. d'Aubigné and Pastor Bard, I was taken to the house of Mr. Lombard, an eminent banker of the city, and a godly and gracious man. I think I never enjoyed a time more than I did with those real true-hearted brethren. There are, you know, two churches there—the Established and the Free; and there has been some little bickering and some little jealousy, but I think it is all dying away; at any rate, I saw none of it, for brethren from both these churches came, and showed me every kindness and honour.

I am not superstitious, but the first time I saw the medal bearing the venerated likeness of John Calvin, I kissed it, imagining that no one saw the action. I was very greatly surprised when I received this magnificent present. On the one side is John Calvin with his visage worn by disease and deep thought, and on the other side is a verse fully applicable to him: 'He endured, as seeing Him who is invisible.' This sentence truly describes the character of that glorious man of God. Among all those who have been born of women, there has not risen a greater than John Calvin; no age before him ever produced his equal, and no age afterwards has seen his rival. In theology, he stands alone, shining like a bright fixed star, while other leaders and teachers can only circle round him, at a great distance—as comets go streaming through space—with nothing like his glory or his permanence. Calvin's fame is eternal because of the truth he proclaimed; and even in heaven, although we shall lose the name of the system of doctrine which he taught, it shall be that truth which shall make us strike our golden harps, and sing, 'Unto Him that loved us, and washed us from our sins in His own blood, and hath made us kings and priests unto God and His Father; to Him be glory and dominion for ever and ever;' for the essence of Calvinism is that we are born again, 'not of blood, nor of the will of the flesh, nor of the will of man, but of God.'

I preached in the cathedral at Geneva; and I thought it a great honour to be allowed to stand in the pulpit of John Calvin. I do not think half the people understood me; but they were very glad to see and join *in heart* with the worship in which they could not join with the understanding. I did not feel very happy when I came out in full canonicals, but the request was put to me in such a beautiful way that I could have worn the Pope's tiara, if by so doing I could have preached the gospel the more freely. They said, 'Our dear brother comes to us from another country. Now, when an ambassador comes from another land, he has the right to wear his own costume at Court; but, as a mark of great esteem, he sometimes condescends to the manners of the people he is visiting, and wears their Court dress.' 'Well,' I said, 'yes, that I will, certainly, if you do not require it, but merely ask it as a token of my Christian love. I shall feel like running in a sack, but it will be your fault.' It was John Calvin's gown, and that reconciled me to it very much. I do love that man of God; suffering all his life long, enduring not only persecutions from without but a complication of disorders from within, and yet serving his Master with all his heart.

I ask your prayers for the Church at Geneva. That little Republic stands now, like an island as it were, on each side shut in by France, and I can assure you there are no greater Anti-Gallicans in the whole world than the Genevese. Without knowing that I trod upon tender ground, I frequently said, 'Why, you are almost French people!' At last they hinted to me that they did not like me to say so, and I did not say it any more. They are afraid of being Frenchified: they cannot endure the thought of it; they know the sweets of liberty, and cannot bear that they should be absorbed into that huge monarchy. Dr. d'Aubigné charged me with this message, 'Stir up the Christians of England to make Geneva a matter of special prayer. We do not dread the arms of France, nor invasion; but something worse than that, namely, the introduction of French principles.' There is a French population constantly crossing the border; they bring in infidelity, and neglect of the Sabbath day, and Romanism is making very great advances. The brethren said, 'Ask the people to pray for us, that we may stand firm and true. As we have been the mother of many churches, desert us not in the hour of our need, but hold us up in your arms, and pray that the Lord may still make Geneva a praise throughout the earth.' After the service in the cathedral, it was arranged for me to meet the ministers; d'Aubigné was there, of course, and César Malan, and most of the noted preachers of Switzerland. We spent a very delightful evening together, talking about our common Lord, and of the progress of His work in England and on the Continent; and when they bade me 'Good-bye,' every one of those ministers—a hundred and fifty, or perhaps two hundred of them—kissed me on both cheeks! It was rather an ordeal for me, but it was meant to express their esteem and regard, and I accepted it in the spirit in which it was given. It was a peculiar pleasure to me to have the opportunity of visiting that great centre of earnest Protestantism, and of meeting so many of the godly and faithful men who had helped to keep the lamp of truth burning brightly. To my dying day, I shall remember those servants of Jesus Christ who greeted me in my Master's name, and loved me for my Master's sake. Hospitality unbounded, love unalloyed, and communion undisturbed, are precious pens with which the brethren in Geneva wrote their names upon my heart.

At last we got away from Geneva, and went off to Chamouni. What a glorious place that Chamouni is! My heart flies thither in recollection of her glories. The very journey from Geneva to Chamouni fires one's heart. The mind longs to climb the heavens as those mountains do. It seemed to sharpen my soul's desires and longings till, like the peaks of the Alps, I could pierce the skies. I cannot speak as I should if I had one of those mountains in view; if I could point out of the window, and say, 'There! see its frosted brow! see its ancient hoary head!' and then speak to you of the avalanches that come rattling down the side, then I think I could give you some poetry. We went up the Mer de Glace on mules. I had the great satisfaction of hearing three or four avalanches come rolling down like thunder. In descending, I was in advance, and alone; I sat down and mused, but I soon sprang up, for I thought the avalanche was coming right on me, there was such a tremendous noise. We crossed many places where the snow, in rushing down from the top, had swept away every tree and every stone, and left nothing but the stumps of the trees, and a kind of slide from the top of the mountain to the very valley. What extraordinary works of God are to be seen there! We have no idea of what God Himself is. As I went among those mountains and valleys, I felt like a little creeping insect. I sank lower and lower, and grew smaller and smaller, while my soul kept crying out

Great God, how infinite art Thou!
What worthless worms are we!

After leaving Chamouni, we came at last to what was to be the great treat of our journey, namely, the passage of the Simplon. The crossing of that mountain is an era in any man's life. That splendid road was carried over the Alps by Napoleon, not for the good of his species, but in order that he might transport his cannon to fight against Austria. Sir James Mackintosh described the Simplon road as 'the most wonderful of useful works.' There are other works which may contain more genius, and some which may seem to be more grand; but this, in the midst of the rugged stern simplicity of nature, seemed to say, 'Man is little, but over God's greatest works man can find a pathway, and no dangers can confine his ambition.' Where the rock was so steep that the road could not be made by any other means, workmen were hung down from the top in cradles, and they chipped a groove, and thus carried the road along the precipitous face of the rock; frequently, too, it was made to run through a huge tunnel cut in the solid rock. On and on we went up the enormous height until we came to the region of perpetual frost and snow. There one could make snowballs in the height of summer, and gather ice in abundance. On the top of the mountain stands the hospice; there were some four or five monks, who came out and asked us to enter; we did so, and would honour the religious feeling which dictates such constant hospitality. We were shown into a very nice room, where there was cake and wine ready, and if we had chosen to order it, meat, soup, and anything we liked to have, and nothing to pay. They entertain any traveller, and he is expected to pay nothing whatever for his refreshment; of course, no one who could afford it would go away without putting something into the poor-box. It pleased me to find that they were Augustinian monks because, next to Calvin, I love Augustine. I feel that Augustine's works were the great mine out of which Calvin dug his mental wealth; and the Augustinian monks, in their acts of charity, seemed to say, 'Our master was a teacher of grace, and we will practise it, and give to all comers whatsoever they shall need, without money and without price.' Those monks are worthy of great honour; there they are, spending the best and noblest period of their lives on the top of a bleak and barren mountain, that they may minister to the necessities of the poor. They go out in the cold nights, and bring in those that are frostbitten; they dig them out from under the snow, simply that they may serve God by helping their fellow-men. I pray God to bless the good works of these monks of the Augustinian Order, and may you and I carry out the spirit of Augustine, which is the true spirit of Christ, the spirit of love, the spirit of charity, the spirit which loves truth, and the spirit which loves man, and above all, loves the Man Christ Jesus! We never need fear, with our strong doctrines, and the spirit of our Master in us, that we shall be carried away by the heresies which continually arise, and which would deceive, if it were possible, even the very elect.

If any of you can save up money—after this Tabernacle is paid for—to go to Switzerland, you will never regret it, and it need not be expensive to you. If you do not find your head grow on both sides, and have to put your hands up, and say, 'I feel as if my brains are straining with their growth,' I do not think you have many brains to spare. As I have stood in the midst of those mountains and valleys, I have wished I could carry you all there. I cannot reproduce to you the thoughts that then passed through my mind; I cannot describe the storms we saw below us when we were on the top of the hill; I cannot tell you about the locusts that came in clouds, and devoured everything before them; time would utterly fail me to speak of all the wonders of God which we saw in nature and in providence. One more remark, and I have done. If you cannot

travel, remember that our Lord Jesus Christ is more glorious than
all else that you could ever see. Get a view of Christ, and you have
seen more than mountains, and cascades, and valleys, and seas can
ever show you. Thunders may bring their sublimest uproar, and
lightnings their awful glory; earth may give its beauty, and stars
their brightness; but all these put together can never rival *Him* of
whom Dr. Watts so well sang—

> *Now to the Lord a noble song!*
> *Awake, my soul, awake, my tongue;*
> *Hosannah to th' Eternal Name,*
> *And all His boundless love proclaim.*
>
> *See where it shines in Jesus' face,*
> *The brightest image of His grace;*
> *God, in the person of His Son,*
> *Has all His mightiest works outdone.*
>
> *The spacious earth and spreading flood*
> *Proclaim the wise and powerful God,*
> *And Thy rich glories from afar*
> *Sparkle in every rolling star.*
>
> *But in His looks a glory stands,*
> *The noblest labour of Thine hands;*
> *The pleasing lustre of His eyes*
> *Outshines the wonders of the skies.*
>
> *Grace! 'tis a sweet, a charming theme;*
> *My thoughts rejoice at Jesus' Name:*
> *Ye angels, dwell upon the sound,*
> *Ye heavens, reflect it to the ground!*

I would propose that the subject of the Ministry in this house, as long as this platform shall stand, and as long as this house shall be frequented by worshippers, shall be the person of Jesus Christ. I am never ashamed to avow myself a Calvinist; I do not hesitate to take the name of Baptist; but if I am asked what is my creed, I reply, 'It is Jesus Christ.' My venerated predecessor, Dr. Gill, has left a *Body of Divinity*, admirable and excellent in its way; but the Body of Divinity to which I would pin and bind myself for ever, God helping me, is not his system, or any other human treatise; but Christ Jesus, who is the sum and substance of the gospel, who is in himself all theology, the incarnation of every precious truth, the all-glorious personal embodiment of the way, the truth, and the life.—C. H. SPURGEON's First Words at the Tabernacle.

3

The Tabernacle Opened

On December 18, 1859, we commenced our third series of services at Exeter Hall, which ended on March 31, 1861. A few of my remarks upon leaving that place may fitly be quoted here:

'In the providence of God, we, as a church and people, have had to wander often. This is our third sojourn within these walls. It is now about to close. We have had at all times and seasons a compulsion for moving: sometimes, a compulsion of conscience; at other times, a compulsion of pleasure, as on this occasion. I am sure that, when we first went to the Surrey Music Hall, God went with us. Satan went, too, but he fled before us. That frightful calamity, the impression of which can never be erased from my mind, became, in the providence of God, one of the most wonderful means of turning public attention to special services; and I do not doubt that—fearful catastrophe though it was—it has been the mother of multitudes of blessings. The Christian world noted the example, and saw its after-success; they followed it, and to this day, in the theatre and the music-hall, the Word of Christ is preached where it was never preached before. Never could it be more manifestly seen than in that place, that the gospel, when proclaimed simply and earnestly, is the power of God unto salvation to every one that believeth.

In each of our movings we have had reason to see the hand of God, and here particularly; for many residents in the West End have in this place come to listen to the Word, who probably might not have taken a journey beyond the river. Here, God's grace has broken hard hearts; here have souls been renewed, and wanderers reclaimed. "Give unto the Lord, O ye mighty, give unto the Lord glory and strength. Give unto the Lord the glory due unto his name." And now we journey to the house which God has in so special a manner given to us, and this day would I pray as Moses did, "Rise up, Lord, and let thine enemies be scattered; and let them that hate thee flee before thee."

"But what enemies have we?" say you. We have multitudes. We

shall have to do battle in our new Tabernacle with that old enemy of the Church, the scarlet beast. Rome has built one of its batteries hard by our place, and there is one who styles himself "Archbishop of Southwark." Then we shall have another enemy, almost as our next-door neighbour—infidelity. *There*, has been one of its special places for display. Yet, comparatively speaking, infidelity is but a very puny adversary; it is not half so cunning as Popery, and hath nothing like its might. But worse than this, we shall have to deal with the indifference of the masses round about us, and with their carelessness concerning gospel truth, and with the prevailing sin and corruption; how shall we deal with all this? Shall we invent some socialistic system of reform? Shall we preach up some new method of political economy? No! the cross, the old cross is enough; this is the true Jerusalem blade, that divides like the razor of old with which Tarquin's augur cut the pebble. We will preach Christ as the sinner's Saviour, the Spirit of God as applying Christ's truth to the soul, and God the Father in His infinite sovereignty saving whom He wills, and in the bounty of His mercy willing to receive the vilest of the vile; and there is no indifference so callous, no ignorance so blind, no iniquity so base, no conscience so seared as not to be made to yield, when God wills it, before the might of His strength. So again I pray, "Rise up, Lord, and let these thine enemies be scattered; and let them that hate thee flee before thee." "Rise up, *Lord*!" O God the Father, rise up! Pluck thy right hand out of thy bosom, and let Thine eternal purposes be accomplished! O God the Son, rise up; show thy wounds, and plead before thy Father's face, and let thy blood-bought ones be saved! Rise up, O God the Holy Ghost; with solemn reverence, we do invoke thine aid! Let those who have hitherto resisted thee, now give way! Come thou, and melt the ice; dissolve the granite: break the adamantine heart; cut thou the iron sinew, and bow thou the stiff neck! Rise up, *Lord*—Father, Son, and Spirit—we can do nothing without thee; but if thou wilt arise, thine enemies shall be scattered, and they that hate thee shall flee before thee.'

*

The first meeting in the Tabernacle was held on Tuesday afternoon, August 21, 1860, while the building was still unfinished. The object of the gathering was twofold: first, to give thanks to God for the success which had thus far attended the enterprise; and, next, to raise as much as possible of the amount required to open the sanctuary free from debt. £22,196 19s. 8d. had been received up to that time, but more than £8,000 was still needed. Apsley Pellatt presided, and heartily congratulated the congregation upon being present in the largest place of worship in Great Britain for the use of Nonconformist Christians. Several representative speakers delivered interesting and sympathetic addresses, and Spurgeon gave the following detailed description of the main building in which the meeting was being held, and of the smaller rooms connected with it:

'You may perhaps guess the joy with which I stand before you to-day, but no man but myself can fathom its fulness, and I myself am quite unable to utter it. "Bless the Lord, O my soul: and all that is within me, bless his holy name." Much as I wish to express my gratitude, I must go at once to my business, and first say a few words about *the structure itself*. If the floor were to give way, our brethren, who are now upon the platform, would find themselves in the baptistery; and if, at any time, those of them who have never been baptized wish to be immersed in obedience to their Master's command, they will always find a willing servant in me. The baptistery will be usually uncovered, as we are not ashamed to confess our belief in believers' baptism.

On the occasion of the administration of the Lord's supper, the table will also stand here; and there are steps on each side at the back of the platform by which the deacons will descend to distribute the memorials of the Saviour's death. You see, above us, the pulpit, or platform, which might hold a large number of persons. I cannot stand like a statue when I preach; I prefer a wide range both of thought and action. The pulpit will also be convenient for public meetings, so that there will be no expense for erecting platforms. Concerning this vast chapel, I believe it is the most perfect triumph of acoustics that has ever been achieved. If it had been a failure at present, I should not have been at all disappointed, because the walls have yet to be covered with matched boarding, so that not a particle of brickwork is to be exposed—it being my theory that soft substances are very much the best for hearing, having proved in a great number of buildings that stone walls are the main creators of an echo, and having seen hangings put up to break the reverberation, and to give the speaker a hope of being heard.

It has been remarked by a great many friends, as they entered, that the building was not so large as they expected; and I was pleased to hear them say so, for it showed me that the structure did not appear huge and unsightly. To look very large, a building must be generally out of proportion, for when there is proportion, the idea of size is often lost. If you went down below, you would find the lecture-hall, about the same area as New Park Street Chapel, or rather larger; and the school-room, larger in its area than the venerable sanctuary in which my brother, Dr. Campbell, long preached the Word—I mean, the Tabernacle, Moorfields. I believe that four chapels like the one at Moorfields could be put into this building; two resting on the basement would only just fill up the same area, and then there would be room for two more on the top of them. Now, perhaps, you may get some idea of the size of the Tabernacle.

With regard to the appearance of the structure, I have this much to say; I think it is highly creditable to the architect. The omission of the towers has deprived him of much of the effect which he hoped to produce by his design, and is perhaps the reason why the roof seems to rise too much, but they will never be erected as long as I am here. I will have no ornament which has not a practical use, and I do not think those towers could have had any object except mere show. As for the front elevation, it is not surpassed by anything in London. The building has no extravagance about it, and yet, at the same time, it has no meanness. True, the roof rises to a very great height above the portico, and does not present a very architectural appearance from the Causeway, but we must recollect this—those who only look at the Tabernacle from the outside have not sub-scribed anything towards its erection, and therefore cannot judge of its true beauty.

The lecture-hall, beneath this platform, is for our church-meetings; it is rendered fully necessary, as we have now more than 1,500 members. The schoolroom will contain, I should think, 1,500 if not 2,000 children. There are large class-rooms, which will be used on the Sabbath day for classes, and on the week-days for my students. I have no doubt my friend, Mr. Rogers, who has so long been my excellent helper in that work—and to whom very much credit is due—will feel himself more comfortable when he has proper rooms in which all his young men can be taught in every branch necessary to give them a complete education for the ministry. There is a very fine room for the ladies' working meetings, which will also be available for a library—a place where the works of all our former Pastors will be collected and preserved, for you must know that, of old, our church has ever been prolific of good works, in both senses of that term. We have the almost innumerable works of Keach—they were so many that it was difficult to find them all. The chap-books, which used to be hawked about the country—printed from worn type on bad brown paper, and adorned with quaint illustrations, yet containing good, sound theology—I have no doubt interested the villagers, and greatly impressed the public mind at the time. Then we have the ponderous tomes of Gill, the tractates and hymns of Rippon, and the works of those who, since their day, have served us in the Lord. The pulpit of my glorious predecessor, Dr. Gill, will be brought here, and placed in the vestry below, that we may retain our ancient pedigree. It is said to have had a new bottom, and some of the four sides are new, yet I affirm it to be Dr. Gill's pulpit. I am as certain that it is so, as that I am the same man as I was seven years ago, though all the component parts of my body may have been changed in the meantime.

Behind the upper platform, there are three spacious rooms; in the centre, is the minister's vestry; to the right and left, are the rooms of the deacons and elders—the officers of the army on either side of the captain, so that they may be ready to go forward at the word of command. Then above them, on the third storey, there are three other excellent rooms, to be used for tract and Bible depositories, and for other schemes which we hope the church will undertake.

I have thus tried to explain the structure of the building to you; I do not think that anything else remains to be said about it, except I draw your attention to the staircases by which you ascend to the galleries, each gallery having a distinct entrance and staircase, so that there is no fear of any overcrowding. I will only say that a design was never carried out with more fidelity by any builder than this has been. There have been improvements made as we have gone on, but they always have been improvements, to which, if they did not seem absolutely necessary, the builder has objected, lest he should have any extras; and when we have compelled him to make them, he has done them as cheaply as possible. He is a man of whom I am proud that he is at once a member of the church, a member of the Building Committee, and the builder of this house of God. Mr. Higgs, besides being a most generous donor, gives us in solid brick and stone far more than he has done in cash. If I had ten thousand buildings to erect, I would never look to anybody else; I would stick to my first love, for he has been faithful and true.

I must pass on to another point, namely, *the present position of this project*. We have pushed beyond the era of objection to it. Now, those very wise friends (and they were very wise) who said the building ought not to be built, it would be too big, cannot undo it; the only thing they can do is to help us through with it, for so much money has been spent already that we cannot propose to pull it down, however absurd the structure may be. Some of our brethren have asked, "When Mr. Spurgeon dies, who will take his place?"— as if God could not raise up servants when He would, or as if we ought to neglect our present duty, because of something which may happen in fifty years' time. You say, perhaps, "You give yourself a long lease—fifty years." I don't know why I should not have it; it may come to pass, and will, if the Lord has so ordained. Dr. Gill was chosen Pastor of this church when he was twenty-two, and he was more than fifty years its minister; Dr. Rippon was chosen at the age of twenty, and he was Pastor for sixty-three years; I was nineteen when I was invited; and is it not possible that I also, by Divine grace, may serve my generation for a long period of time? At any rate, when I am proposing to commence a plan, I never think about whether I shall live to see it finished, for I am certain that, if it is God's plan, He will surely finish it, even if I should have to leave the work undone.

I said, just now, that this project has gone beyond the era of objections; it has even passed beyond the realm of difficulties. We have had many difficulties, but far more providences. The ground was as much given to us by God as if He had sent an angel to clear it for us. The money, too, has been given, even beyond our hopes, and we have had it from quarters where we should least have expected it. All the Christian Churches have contributed their portion, and almost all the ends of the earth have sent their offerings. From India, Australia, America, and everywhere, have we received something from God's people to help us in this work. We hope now we shall go on even to the end of it without feeling any diminution of our joy.'

It was most appropriate that the building which had been erected for a house of prayer should be opened with a meeting for prayer. Accordingly, at seven o'clock in the morning of Monday, March 18, 1861, more than a thousand people assembled in the Tabernacle. The Pastor presided, and among those who took part in the proceedings were representatives of the deacons and elders of the church, and students of the College. Fervency and intense earnestness marked the petitions. On the following Monday, at the same early hour, the Rev. George Rogers presided over the second prayer-meeting, and addressed the brethren in a sweet and savoury manner upon 'The House of God, the Gate of Heaven.' At three o'clock the same afternoon, the first sermon in the Tabernacle was preached by the Pastor from Acts 5. 42: 'And daily in the temple, and in every house, they ceased not to teach and preach Jesus Christ;'[1] and in the evening, Rev. W. Brock, of Bloomsbury Chapel, discoursed upon Philippians 1. 18: 'Christ is preached; and I therein do rejoice, yea, and will rejoice.' It was remarked at the time how well the two sermons were adapted to one another, although the ministers were quite unaware what text each had selected.

The following evening, more than three thousand of the contributors to the Building Fund assembled in the Tabernacle, under the presidency of Sir Henry Havelock. The Pastor had undertaken, in the month of January, to bring in £1,000, at the opening of the building, in addition to all that he had previously raised; and in the course of the meeting he announced that he had paid in £1,500, others had brought the total up to £3,700, so that the building was free from debt, although they still needed about £500 for various matters which could wait until the money was in hand.

On 'Good Friday,' March 29, the Pastor preached in the morning from Romans 3. 24, 25: 'Christ Jesus: whom God hath set forth to be a propitiation through faith in his blood,' and in the evening, from the Song of Solomon, 2. 16: 'My beloved is mine, and I am his.' It was a fitting finale to these services to be able to announce that the whole sum required had been given, and the building, free from debt, was ready for Divine worship on the following Lord's day. That Sabbath evening, March 31, the Pastor preached from 2 Chron. 5. 13, 14; and 7. 1–3; and speaking upon the glory of the Lord filling the house, uttered a prophecy which has been abundantly fulfilled in every particular: 'Let God send the fire of His Spirit here, and the minister will be more and more lost in his Master. You will come to think less of the speaker, and more of the truth spoken; the individual will be swamped, the words uttered will rise above everything. When you have the cloud, the man is forgotten; when you have the fire, the man is lost, and you only see his Master. Suppose the fire should come here, and the Master be seen more than the minister, what then? Why, this church will be-

---

[1] This sermon, along with the other special sermons and addresses which marked the opening of the Tabernacle, will be found in *The New Park Street* and *Metropolitan Tabernacle Pulpit*, vol. 7.

come two, or three, or four thousand strong! It is easy enough for God to double our numbers, vast though they are even now. We shall have the lecture-hall beneath this platform crowded at each prayer-meeting, and we shall see in this place young men devoting themselves to God; we shall find ministers raised up, and trained, and sent forth to carry the sacred fire to other parts of the globe. Japan, China, and Hindustan shall have heralds of the cross, who have here had their tongues touched with the Divine flame. Through us, the whole earth shall receive benedictions; if God shall bless us, He will make us a blessing to multitudes of others. Let God but send down the fire, and the biggest sinners in the neighbourhood will be converted; those who live in the dens of infamy will be changed; the drunkard will forsake his cups, the swearer will repent of his blasphemy, the debauched will leave their lusts—

> *Dry bones be raised, and clothed afresh,*
> *And hearts of stone be turned to flesh.'*

On Thursday evening, April 4, Dr. Octavius Winslow preached from the words, 'It is finished;' on Lord's day, April 7, the Pastor occupied the pulpit both morning and evening, and presided at the first communion service held in the Tabernacle; the next night, a family gathering of our own church was held under the presidency of the Pastor's father, Rev. John Spurgeon; and on the Tuesday evening, Rev. Hugh Stowell Brown, of Liverpool, preached on 'Christian Baptism,' and the Pastor conducted the first baptismal service, concerning which Dr. Campbell wrote, in *The British Standard*, April 12:

'The probable effects of the Metropolitan Tabernacle become the subject of interesting speculation. While these effects will be great and glorious, they will form no exception to the course of human affairs. Imperfection attaches to everything that appertains to man. The building will inevitably form a powerful magnet, especially to young people in all quarters of the city, who will hardly endure the old-fashioned churches and chapels of their fathers. The result will be to confer on it a leviathan monopoly. This monopoly will operate in two ways: it will bring multitudes from the world to Christ—an event in which we shall most sincerely rejoice. It will also draw multitudes from the churches to the water—an event in which we do not rejoice. This Metropolitan Tabernacle, we believe, will do more to make proselytes than all the other Baptist chapels in London united. It will lift the thing into respectability, and even dignity. It will become an object of ambition with sentimental young women and poetic young men to be plunged into a marble basin, so beautiful that it might adorn a palace, and so spacious that dolphins might play in it! Then, Mr. Spurgeon knows well how to go about this matter; his noble catholicity has not sufficed wholly to eliminate his baptismal bigotry. His manly eloquence will most powerfully minister to the triumph of the polished marble. He showed last Sabbath evening that, while prepared to die for the gospel, he is not less prepared to fight for the water. . . .

On the evening of Tuesday, the ordinance of baptism, by immersion, was administered to some twenty people. The interest of the thing was overpowering. There was the young orator, the idol of the assembly, in the water, with a countenance radiant as the light; and there, on the pathway was Mrs. Spurgeon, a most prepossessing young lady—the admiration of all who beheld her—with courtly dignity and inimitable modesty, kindly leading forward the trembling sisters in succession to her husband, who gently and gracefully took and immersed them, with varied remark and honied phrase, all kind, pertinent to the occasion, and greatly fitted to strengthen, encourage, and cheer. Emerging from the water, there were two portly deacons, in boxes at the side of the steps, with benignant smile, to seize their hands, and bring them up, throwing cloaks over them; two other deacons received them at the top of the steps, and other two politely led them backward to the vestry. It was quite an ovation, an era in the history of the neophytes. It had really not been wonderful if all the ladies in the place had been candidates for such distinction. We have ourselves seen several who were there, whose heads seem completely turned. Pædo-Baptist ministers, whatever their piety or ability, have no chance with Mr. Spurgeon in multiplying members. They operate only in one element, he in two: to him, the land and the water are alike productive. We shall not be surprised if, in seven more years, his church be doubled,[1] and the Metropolitan Tabernacle prove insufficient to accommodate even the members and their families. The largest chapel in the world, it will have the largest church. When then?'

[1] In much less than seven years after the opening service, the church-membership had been more than doubled, and 'the members and their families' could not have found sitting accommodation in the building if they had all tried to be present at any one time.

In the same article, Dr. Campbell thus referred to one of the many misleading paragraphs which continued to be inserted, from time to time, in various newspapers:

'The services of a Christian minister may, as a rule, be safely estimated by the light in which he is viewed by an ungodly world. If it exalt him, there is something wrong. It only "loves its own." But, if it pour out upon him the vials of its calumny, falsehood, and scorn, the presumption is, that he is faithful to his God, and the friend of his race. The most splendid illustration of the last century was Whitefield. . . . In our own times, the counterpart of Whitefield is Mr. Spurgeon. Regard being had to the changed and softened character of the times, he has been abused, slandered, libelled, and lied against quite as much. The London correspondent of a very able Scottish journal, professedly conducted on Christian principles, had the audacity, so late as last week, to write as follows: "Sympathetic Aberdonians need not trouble themselves to make up any more money-boxes for Mr. Spurgeon's Tabernacle. All the debts have been paid, and the chapel was opened on Sunday evening. As the Tabernacle is Mr. Spurgeon's own property, pew-rents and all, he will probably be able to enjoy his 'privilege' of riding in a carriage to the end of his days. This being the case, it is sincerely to be hoped that he will now finally dissociate the work of the gospel from the pursuit of mammon."

Now, the great fact alleged in the foregoing is an unmitigated falsehood; and, as to cupidity, it were quite as just and true to charge Mr. Spurgeon with the guilt of murder as with the worship of mammon! No man in this great metropolis preaches one-third so much for all Evangelical sects, on behalf of all sorts of charitable objects, and he *uniformly preaches for nothing*!

"But the carriage," says the correspondent. Well, the plain one-horse vehicle—what of that? Living where his health requires him to live, a few miles in the country, in a very plain and far from commodious habitation, some conveyance is absolutely necessary to his great and unceasing toils. Is that to be denied him? To economize a little horse-power, would you abridge his leviathan labours for the cause of God and the souls of men? It is a curious fact that the miserable malignants of a former day brought it as a charge against Wesley and Whitefield, and in our own times against Collyer and Hill, that they kept a carriage! This suggests the economist who wished the ointment to have been sold for the poor, "not that he cared for the poor; but because he was a thief, and had the bag." But enough: "Wisdom is justified of her children." All good and upright men "glorify God" in Charles Haddon Spurgeon. They desire for him life and length of days, with a continuance of all his gifts and all his graces, and an increase of favour with God and man. He is still in the morning of life; and we trust he may have before him at least half-a-century of usefulness and honour ere he be called to the Upper World to take his place—among prophets, apostles, martyrs, and evangelists, who have turned many to righteousness—to shine as a star for ever and ever.'

On Wednesday, April 10, a great communion service was held—probably the largest since the day of Pentecost—in order to set forth the essential oneness of the Church, and the real fellowship in the body of Christ which is the privilege of all her members. The following afternoon and evening, addresses were delivered upon the distinguishing doctrines of Calvinism—election, human depravity, particular redemption, effectual calling, and final perseverance. Spurgeon, in introducing the ministering brethren that day, began with certain remarks on the terms used:

'It may happen this afternoon that the term "Calvinism" may be frequently used. Let it not be misunderstood; we only use the term for shortness. That doctrine which is called "Calvinism" did not spring from Calvin; we believe that it sprang from the great founder of all truth. Perhaps Calvin himself derived it mainly from the writings of Augustine. Augustine obtained his views, without doubt, through the Spirit of God, from the diligent study of the writings of Paul, and Paul received them of the Holy Ghost, from Jesus Christ the great founder of the Christian dispensation. We use the term then, not because we impute an extraordinary importance to Calvin's having taught these doctrines. We would be just as willing to call them by any other name, if we could find one which would be better understood, and which on the whole would be as consistent with fact.'

Following that, Spurgeon observed that 'there is nothing upon which men need to be more instructed than upon the question of what Calvinism really is', and went on to controvert various 'infamous allegations' which have been brought against Calvinists. Refuting the charge that Calvinists dare not preach the gospel to the unregenerate, he said: 'Did not Bunyan plead with sinners, and whoever classed him with any but the Calvinists? Did not Charnock, Goodwin and Howe agonize for souls, and what were they but Calvinists? Did not Jonathan Edwards preach to sinners, and who more clear and explicit on these doctrinal matters? The works of our innumerable divines teem with passionate appeals to the unconverted. . . . Was George Whitefield any less seraphic? Did his eyes weep the fewer tears or his bowels move with the less compassion because he believed in God's electing love and preached the sovereignty of the most High?'

On the charge that those who hold Calvinistic views are the enemies of revivals, Spurgeon had this to say: 'Why, sirs, in the history of the church, with but few exceptions, you could not find a revival at all that was not produced by the orthodox faith. What was that great work which was done by Augustine, when the church suddenly woke up from the pestiferous and deadly sleep into which Pelagian doctrine had cast it? What was the Reformation itself but the waking up of men's minds to those old truths? . . . Need I mention to you better names than Huss, Jerome of Prague, Farel, John Knox, Wycliffe, Wishart and Bradford? Need I do more than say that these held the same views, and that in their day anything like an Arminian revival was utterly unheard of. . . . And then, let me say, if you turn to the continent of America, how gross the falsehood that Calvinistic doctrine is unfavourable to revivals! Look at that wondrous shaking under Jonathan Edwards and others which we might quote. Or turn to Scotland—what shall we say of M'Cheyne? What shall we say of those renowned Calvinists, Dr. Chalmers, Dr. Wardlaw, and before them, Livingstone, Haldane, Erskine, and the like? What shall we say of the men of their school but that, while they held and preached unflinchingly the great truths which we would propound today, yet God owned their word and multitudes were saved. And if it were not perhaps too much like boasting of one's own work under God, I might say, personally I have never found the preaching of these doctrines lull this church to sleep, but ever while they have loved to maintain these truths, they have agonized for the souls of men; and the sixteen-hundred or more whom I have myself baptized, upon profession of their faith, are living testimonies that these old truths in modern times have not lost their power to promote a revival of religion.'

At the first church-meeting held at the Tabernacle, on Monday evening, May 6, seventy-two persons were proposed for member-ship, and the Pastor wrote in the church-book as follows:

'I, Charles Haddon Spurgeon, the least of all saints, hereby set to my seal that God is true, since He has this day fulfilled my hopes, and given according to our faith. O Lord, be Thou praised world without end, and do Thou make me more faithful and more mighty than ever!

C. H. Spurgeon'.

The following inscription, also in the Pastor's handwriting, is signed by himself, the deacons, the elders, and a large number of the church-members, beginning with 'Susie Spurgeon':

'We, the undersigned members of the church lately worshipping in New Park Street Chapel, but now assembling in the Metropolitan Tabernacle, Newington, desire with overflowing hearts to make known and record the lovingkindness of our faithful God. We asked in faith, but our Lord has exceeded our desires, for not only was the whole sum given us, but far sooner than we had looked for it. Truly, the Lord is good, and worthy to be praised. We are ashamed of ourselves that we have ever doubted Him; and we pray that, as a church and as individuals, we may be enabled to trust in the Lord at all times with confidence, so that in quietness we may possess our souls. In the Name of our God we set up our banner. Oh, that Jehovah-Jireh may also be unto us Jehovah-shammah and Jehovah-shalom! To Father, Son and Holy Ghost we offer praise and thanksgiving, and we set to our seal that God is true'.

This entry closes the records in the church-book for the seven years from 1854 to 1861. It is worthy of note, as showing the un-paralleled growth of everything connected with the work, that the two previous church-books had respectively lasted from 1757 to 1808, and from 1808 to 1854; while the next one, commenced on May 7, 1861, ended on January 11, 1866, and the following volumes were generally filled in about five years. All are large thick quartos, uniform in size, and the complete series formed one of the most precious treasures saved from the disastrous fire on April 20, 1898.

During the month of May, 1861, four more church-meetings were held, at which seventy-seven additional members were pro-posed, and at the communion service on June 2, a hundred and twenty-one persons were received into full fellowship. This large increase was thus gratefully recorded at the church-meeting on

June 18: 'It was unanimously resolved that a record of our gratitude to God for His graciousness toward us should be made in the church-book. With our whole hearts, as a highly-favoured church and people, we magnify and extol the lovingkindness of our God in so singularly owning the Word proclaimed among us, by giving so many souls to be added to our number. To God be all the glory! Oh, that we may be more than ever devoted to His honour and service!'

The Tabernacle is so well proportioned that many persons fail to realize its vast size. The building is a rectangle, measuring outside the walls 174 feet in length, and 85 feet in width; inside, the extreme length, including the vestries, is 168 feet; the main auditorium being 146 feet long, 81 feet broad, and 62 feet high. Estimates as to the seating accommodation of the Tabernacle have varied considerably; but the actual number of sittings that could be let, previous to the fire,[1] was 3,600, and about 1,000 persons could occupy seats on the flaps in the aisles and other parts of the building. Many hundreds of additional hearers could find—and for thirty years did find—standing-room in the great house of prayer, so that the preacher had regularly before him, Sabbath by Sabbath, between five and six thousand immortal souls listening to his proclamation of the Word of life.

As an instance of the misleading notions that people have entertained concerning the capacity of large public buildings, it may be mentioned, on the authority of *The Builder*, May 4, 1861, that the Surrey Gardens Music Hall, which was supposed to hold 10,000 or 12,000 people, had a sitting area of 19,723 feet, while that of the Metropolitan Tabernacle was 25,225 feet!

At the annual church-meeting, on January 22, 1862, the Building Committee's audited balance-sheet was presented and adopted. It showed that the total expenditure up to that time had been £31,332 4s. 10d., all of which had been met. The two largest items in the account were—purchase of land, £5,000; and contract for the main building, £20,000. Among the receipts, the highest amounts were—collectors' accounts, £7,258 5s. 2d.; donations and subscriptions, £9,034 19s. 2d.; per Pastor C. H. Spurgeon, £11,253 15s. 6d.

After the Tabernacle was built, an earnest endeavour was made to retain New Park Street Chapel for the Baptist denomination, and

---

[1] A fire on April 20, 1898—six years after Spurgeon's death—destroyed most of the original building.

to make it, if possible, the abode of another church. For some years, preaching was carried on, a brother supported, and considerable expenses incurred; but it was clear that a self-sustaining interest was not to be gathered in the neighbourhood. John Collins worked very hard, and enjoyed much of the Divine blessing, but those who were converted under him had a pardonable tendency to gravitate towards the mother-church at the Tabernacle and it became evident beyond all question that it was useless for us to retain so large a building in such a situation, and so near our own. The property consisted of the chapel, schools, and almsrooms; and it was agreed, and arranged with the Charity Commissioners, that it should be sold, and the proceeds used for new schools and almsrooms.

In the *Memorials of William Higgs*, there is an interesting paragraph concerning this transaction: 'When the date of the auction was fixed, Mr. Higgs was requested to attend at the mart for the protection of the sale. He had before valued the property at a given sum, saying that he did not think it likely to fetch very much more. But, to the surprise of those friends who were also present, when this sum was reached, he himself put in a bid at a still higher figure, and ran up the amount until the property was knocked down to him at a price considerably greater than that which he had in the first instance named. He was, of course, joked a little about his bargain, but he quietly replied that no doubt it would prove a good one. And so it did; for, not very long afterwards, he went to Mr. Spurgeon with the news that he had sold the place at a profit of £500, adding that he had brought the money with him, as he could not, himself, think of keeping it.'

Sermons should have real teaching in them, and their doctrine should be solid, substantial and abundant. We do not enter the pulpit to talk for talk's sake; we have instructions to convey, important to the last degree, and we cannot afford to utter pretty nothings. Our range of subjects is all but boundless, and we cannot therefore be excused if our discourses are threadbare and devoid of substance. . . . The entire gospel must be presented from the pulpit; the whole faith once delivered to the saints must be proclaimed by us . . . so that the people may not merely hear, but *know* the joyful sound. . . .

Do not rehearse five or six doctrines with unvarying monotony of repetition. With abundant themes diligently illustrated by fresh metaphors and experiences, we shall not weary but, under God's hand, shall win our hearers' ears and hearts.—c.h.s. *in 'Lectures to my Students'*

4

Memorable Sermons and Services in the 1860's

AMONG the earliest of the memorable services at the Tabernacle was the one held on Lord's day morning, December 15, 1861. Late on the previous night, the Prince Consort had been 'called home;' and in commencing his sermon, Spurgeon read a few sentences which he had written with reference to that solemn event. He did not feel that he could at that time make further allusion to the Prince's departure, as he had prepared a discourse upon quite a different topic, but the following Sabbath morning he preached from Amos 3. 6, 'Shall there be evil in a city, and the Lord hath not done it?'—a sermon which was published under the title, 'The Royal Death-bed.'

Singularly enough, the next discourse claiming special notice also related to a great public calamity, namely, the Hartley Colliery explosion (near Tynemouth, Northumberland). On Thursday evening, January 30, 1862, Spurgeon preached from Job 14. 14, 'If a man die, shall he live again?'—a sermon which commenced thus: 'Once more the Lord has spoken; again the voice of Providence has proclaimed, "All flesh is grass, and all the goodliness thereof is as the flower of the field." O sword of the Lord, when wilt thou rest and be quiet? Wherefore these repeated warnings? Why doth the Lord so frequently and so terribly sound an alarm? Is it not because our drowsy spirits will not awaken to the realities of death? We fondly persuade ourselves that we are immortal; that, though a thousand may fall at our side, and ten thousand at our right hand, yet death shall not come nigh unto us. We flatter ourselves that, if we must die, yet the evil day is far hence. If we be sixty, we presumptuously reckon upon another twenty years of life; and a man of eighty, tottering upon his staff, remembering that some few have survived to the close of a century, sees no reason why he should not do the same. If man cannot kill death, he tries at least to bury him alive; and since death will intrude himself in our pathway, we endeavour to shut our eyes to the ghastly object. God in Providence is continually filling our path with tombs. With kings and princes, there is too much forgetfulness of the world to come; God has therefore spoken to *them*. They are but few in number; so one death might be sufficient in their case. That one death of a beloved and illustrious Prince will leave its mark on courts and palaces. As for the workers, they also are wishful to put far from them the thought of the coffin and the shroud: God has spoken to *them* also. They were many, so one death would not be sufficient; it was absolutely necessary that there should be many victims, or we should have disregarded the warning. Two hundred witnesses cry to us from the pit's mouth—a solemn fellowship of preachers all using the same text, "Prepare to meet thy God, O Israel!" If God had not thus spoken by the destruction of many, we should have said, "Ah! it is a common occurrence; there are frequently such accidents as these." The rod would have failed in its effect had it smitten less severely. The awful calamity at the Hartley Colliery has at least had this effect, that men are talking of death in all our streets. O Father of thy people, send forth thy Holy Spirit in richer abundance, that by this solemn chastisement higher ends may be answered than merely attracting our thoughts to our latter end! Oh, may hearts be broken, may eyes be made to weep for sin, may follies be renounced, may Christ be accepted, and may spiritual life be given to many survivors as the result of the physical death of those who now sleep in their untimely graves in Earsdon churchyard!'

In closing his discourse, the preacher pleaded for the widows and orphans who were suffering through the terrible calamity; and, though it was a wet week-night, and many who were present had already contributed to the Relief Fund, the congregation generously subscribed £120.

When Spurgeon was at Geneva, in 1860, he preached for Dr. Merle d'Aubigné as well as in the cathedral. It was therefore fitting that the Genevan divine should speak to the congregation at the Tabernacle when the opportunity occurred. On Lord's day morning, May 18, 1862, the Pastor purposely made his discourse somewhat shorter than usual; and, in closing it, said: 'My dear friend, Dr. d'Aubigné, is here this morning, having been called by the Bishop of London, according to the order of our beloved Queen, to preach in the Royal Chapel of St. James. In a kind note with which he favoured me last week he expressed a desire publicly to show his hearty fellowship with his brethren of the Free Churches of England, and I am delighted to welcome him in the Tabernacle, in the name of this church, and I may venture to add, in the name of all the Free Churches of England. May the historian of the Reformation continue to be honoured of the Lord his God!'

Dr. d'Aubigné, addressing the congregation, said: 'When I heard your dear Pastor reading to us the 16th chapter of Romans, I remembered those words which we find very often in the Epistles of Paul, "love to the saints" and "faith in the Lord". In that 16th chapter, we find a beautiful exhibition of love to the saints, the children of God. We see that it was written from the Church of Corinth, in Greece, to the Church in Rome. Observe how many Christians that Church of Corinth and the apostle Paul knew at Rome! We have a long catalogue of them—Priscilla, Aquila, Andronicus, and others. I must confess, my dear friends, to my regret, that in this great assembly I know only two or three people. I know your Pastor and my dear friend, Mr. Spurgeon; I know the name, but not the person, of Mr. North, upon my left; and I know the friend who has received me in your great city, Mr. Kinnaird— "Gaius, mine host," as the apostle says. But in this great assembly of six thousand men and women, and I hope brethren and sisters in Christ, I do not know anyone else. Well, my dear friends, I would ask you, do you know the names of many Christians in Geneva? Perhaps you do not know three; possibly, not two; perhaps, only one. Now, that is to me a demonstration that fraternity, or brotherly love, is not so intense in our time as it was in the days of the apostles. In the first century, for a man to give his name to the Lord was to expose himself to martyrdom; and Christians at that time formed only one household in the whole world, in Europe, Asia, and Africa. Let us remember that, and may we, by the Holy Ghost, say that we, who have been baptized with the blood and the Spirit of the Lord, have only one Father, one Saviour, one Spirit, one faith, and we are only one house, the house of the living God, the house of Christ, one house of the Holy Spirit in the whole world; not only in Europe, Asia, and Africa, but in America, in Australia, one house, one family. O my dear friends, let us grow in love to the brethren! . . .

Dear friends, we find in the Epistle to the Romans these words, "The whole church saluteth you." I have no official charge; but I may, in a Christian and fraternal spirit, say to you, the Genevese Church, the Church in Geneva saluteth you; and I would say, the whole Continental Church saluteth you, for we know you, and we love you, and the dear minister God has given you. Now we ask from you love towards us; we are doing what we can in that dark

Continent to spread abroad the light of Jesus Christ. In Geneva, we have an Evangelical Society which has that object before it, and we are also labouring in other places; we ask an interest in your prayers, for the work is hard among the Roman Catholics and the infidels of the Continent. The grace of our Lord Jesus Christ be with you all! Amen.'

During the terrible distress caused by the Lancashire cotton famine, Spurgeon preached, on Lord's day morning, November 9, 1862, a sermon on 'Christian Sympathy,' from Job 30. 25 : 'Did not I weep for him that was in trouble? Was not my soul grieved for the poor?' In appealing on behalf of the people in need, the Pastor urged these five reasons why they should be generously helped: (1) their poverty was not the result of their own fault; (2) the cause of their suffering was the national sin of slavery; (3) their heavy trials had been borne most patiently; (4) the distress was very widely spread; and (5) gratitude to God should move all who were able to give liberally to those who were in want. The appeal was most effective, for the congregation contributed £776 11s. 11d. towards the Famine Fund—probably the largest amount ever given from the Tabernacle to any outside object, and exceeding even the sum (£700) realized by the Fast day service at the Crystal Palace in aid of the Indian Relief Fund.

March 15, 1863, was a memorable morning at the Metropolitan Tabernacle, for Spurgeon then delivered the discourse which, when published, became No. 500. The text of it was, 1 Samuel 7. 12 : 'Then Samuel took a stone, and set it between Mizpeh and Shen, and called the name of it Ebenezer, saying, Hitherto hath the Lord helped us;' and the title was most appropriate, 'Ebenezer.' It was both autobiographical and historical, and contained many interesting allusions to the Lord's gracious help to both Pastor and people. In the introduction, the preacher said: 'Looking at God's hand in my own life, and acknowledging that hand with some record of thankfulness, I, your minister, brought by Divine grace to preach this morning the five hundredth of my printed sermons, consecutively published week by week, set up my stone of Ebenezer to God. I thank Him, thank Him humbly, but yet most joyfully, for all the help and assistance given in studying and preaching the Word to these mighty congregations by the voice, and afterwards to so many nations through the press. I set up my pillar in the form of this sermon. My motto this day shall be the same as Samuel's,

"Hitherto hath the Lord helped *me*"; and as the stone of my praise is much too heavy for me to set it upright alone, I ask you, my comrades in the day of battle, my fellow-labourers in the vineyard of Christ, to join with me in expressing gratitude to God, while together we set up the stone of memorial, and say, "Hitherto hath the Lord helped *us*." '

In many respects, the most memorable service ever held in the Tabernacle was the one on Lord's day morning, June 5, 1864, when Spurgeon preached his notable sermon on 'Baptismal Regeneration'. Concerning that discourse, the preacher wrote, more than ten years afterwards: 'It was delivered with the full expectation that the sale of the sermons would receive very serious injury; in fact, I mentioned to one of the publishers that I was about to destroy it at a single blow, but that the blow must be struck, cost what it might, for the burden of the Lord lay heavy upon me, and I must deliver my soul. I deliberately counted the cost, and reckoned upon the loss of many an ardent friend and helper, and I expected the assaults of clever and angry foes. I was not mistaken in other respects; but, in the matter of the sermons, I was altogether out of my reckoning, for they increased greatly in sale at once. That fact was not in any degree to me a test of my action being right or wrong; I should have felt as well content in heart as I am now as to the rightness of my course had the publication ceased in consequence; but, still, it was satisfactory to find that, though speaking out might lose a man some friends, it secured him many others; and if it overturned his influence in one direction, it was fully compensated elsewhere. No truth is more sure than this, that the path of duty is to be followed thoroughly if peace of mind is to be enjoyed. Results are not to be looked at; we are to keep our conscience clear, come what may; and all considerations of influence and public estimation are to be light as feathers in the scale. In minor matters, as well as in more important concerns, I have spoken my mind fearlessly, and brought down objurgations and anathemas innumerable; but I in nowise regret it, and shall not swerve from the use of outspoken speech in the future any more than in the past. I would scorn to retain a single adherent by such silence as would leave him under any misapprehension. After all, men love plain speech.'

A student who was in the Pastors' College in 1864—Samuel Blow —has preserved this interesting reminiscence of the day following the great deliverance: 'It was the custom of Mr. Spurgeon to revise his sermons on Monday mornings, and then, in the afternoon, to come to the class-room, and question us on history and other subjects in a homely and friendly way. Entering the room, and taking his seat, on this particular occasion, he told us that he had just been revising this special sermon, and he was certain it would cause a great stir and raise tremendous opposition when it appeared in print. He suggested that, instead of going through the usual course of instruction, we might devote the time to prayer, so the whole of that afternoon was spent in supplicating a blessing on the issue and circulation of that remarkable discourse showing the absurdity of the Baptismal Regeneration theory.'

Now that a whole generation has passed away since the sermon was delivered, it is difficult to realize the sensation which was caused when it appeared in print, and became generally known. A hundred thousand copies of it were speedily sold, and the circulation was still further increased by the many replies to it which were before long preached and published. Three weeks after its delivery, Spurgeon preached from Hebrews 13.13, 'Let us Go Forth'; and in quick succession followed two more special discourses in continuation of the controversy—'Children Brought to Christ, not to the Font'; and ' "Thus Saith the Lord" or, the Book of Common Prayer Weighed in the Balances of the Sanctuary.' All of them had an immense sale, and as each one was issued, it elicited answers from the Church of England side. Spurgeon collected a hundred and thirty-five sermons and pamphlets, and had them bound in three large octavo volumes; and, doubtless, others gathered together similar signs and tokens of the fray. One such set afterwards came into the Pastor's hands, and he found in it several contributions which were not contained in his own series. They were bound in two substantial volumes, and were evidently the result of the sympathetic labours of an ardent admirer, who recorded his opinions concerning the controversy in the following Preface: 'In 1864, the Rev. C. H. Spurgeon threw down the gauntlet of defiance to the Church of England upon the point of Infant Baptism and Regeneration; when, presto! such a theological battle ensued as was never before seen or heard of. The whole religious world of London flung itself into it; the press groaned under the infliction; the pamphlets which followed, *pro* and *con*, in prose and verse, serious and burlesque, being almost innumerable.'

It was a surprise and a disappointment to many friends of Spurgeon to find that his protest against the doctrine of Baptismal

Regeneration was, to some extent at least, weakened by a published letter from the Rev. Baptist Wriothesley Noel, who had himself left the Church of England, and become Pastor of the Baptist Church meeting in John Street Chapel, Bedford Row, and whose *Essay on the Union of Church and State* contained quite as vigorous a condemnation of the clergy as appeared in the sermon to which he objected. It is generally supposed, and was officially stated, on the authority of Mr. Arnold, the Secretary of the Evangelical Alliance, that Spurgeon's withdrawal from that body was the result of Baptist Noel's letter, but the following paragraph in *The Sword and the Trowel*, March, 1870, puts the matter in its true light:

'Our readers may have observed a letter written by us to an American paper explaining the reason why we cannot attend the meeting of the Evangelical Alliance at New York. We had to make the same explanation to the Dutch brethren when the Alliance met at Rotterdam, but, as we have no wish to disturb the peace of the Alliance, we have not agitated the question. It may, however, be as well to state that, about the time when Mr. Noel's letter appeared, objecting to certain expressions used by us in our notorious Baptismal Regeneration sermon, we received a letter from Mr. James Davis, the secretary of the Alliance, setting forth very strongly that our only alternative was either to retract our harsh language, or to withdraw from the Alliance. Knowing Mr. Noel's gentle spirit, we should not have taken much notice of his letter had we not been led to suppose, from the epistle of the secretary, that the Committee of the Alliance were of the same mind; and then, not being able to retract a syllable of our utterances, and being unwilling to embroil the Alliance in our conflict, we withdrew from it. We have since learned that the letter was unauthorized, and several members of the Alliance Committee have expressed regret that we acted upon it. We are in this state of the case absolutely passive; we do not wish to revive any personal question, or cause altercation; only it is clear to everyone that, under the circumstances, neither manliness nor Christian truthfulness will allow us to attend Alliance gatherings while we are practically under its ban.'

Happily, some few years afterwards, Spurgeon saw his way to rejoin the Alliance, and he remained a member of its Council until he was 'called home' in 1892. On many occasions, he spoke at meetings arranged in connection with the Alliance, the most memorable being the great gatherings at Exeter Hall and the Mildmay

Conference Hall, in 1888, for united testimony in regard to fundamental truth, just at the time when the 'Down-grade' Controversy was at its height, and thousands of lovers of Evangelical doctrine felt the need of a clear and emphatic 'declaration of those things which are most surely believed among us.' It is also noteworthy that, in the circular concerning the formation of the Pastors' College Evangelical Association, Spurgeon wrote: 'As a convenient summary of faith, we have adopted, with certain alterations and additions, the basis of the Evangelical Alliance, accepting it with the more readiness because so many believers of various churches have been content thus to set forth the main points of their agreement.'

The Baptismal Regeneration Controversy afforded Dr. Campbell the opportunity of publishing in *The British Standard* a series of articles, which extended over seventeen weeks, and were afterwards republished in a volume consisting of 330 small octavo pages. In the Introduction, he explained why he had not earlier taken part in the conflict: 'It was known to many that, between Mr. Spurgeon and myself, there had long been an intimate and cordial friendship, proofs and illustrations of which, on my part, had from time to time appeared in the columns of *The British Standard*, and other publications under my control. In his early days, I stood by him, when his advocates in the press were neither numerous nor, with one or two honourable exceptions, efficient, while his adversaries were both unscrupulous and powerful. Some surprise accordingly was felt, by our mutual friends, that I was not among the first to place myself at his side. They were at a loss to account for my seeming apathy, but, in this, they were guided by feeling rather than by judgment; they did not reflect that the state of things was entirely altered. Mr. Spurgeon was no longer a tender sapling that might receive benefit from the friendly shade of an elder tree, but an oak of the forest, whose roots had struck deep in the earth, and whose thick and spreading boughs bade defiance to the hurricane. They forgot that Mr. Spurgeon alone was more than a match for all his adversaries. Besides, a passing newspaper article, however strong or telling, although it might have gratified our mutual friends, would have been of small importance to the cause which I had so much at heart —the correction and purification of the Liturgy of the Established Church. . . . That subject is vital, not only to her real usefulness, but to her very existence as a Protestant Institution! The universality of the doctrine of Baptismal Regeneration will be the sure prelude to her overthrow, and the re-establishment of the Church of Rome, with all her darkness and bondage, misery and wickedness.'

The service at the Tabernacle on Lord's day evening, July 31, 1864, was a memorable one to Spurgeon and two of his hearers, and afterwards to many more when he related a singular circumstance which occurred in connection with his sermon that night. A man living in Newington had been converted through the Pastor's preaching and he became a regular worshipper at the Tabernacle. His wife, a very staunch member of the Church of England, strongly objected to his going, but he continued to attend notwithstanding all that she said.

One Sabbath night, after her husband had gone to the service, her curiosity overcame her prejudice, and she herself determined to go to hear what the preacher had to say. Not wishing to be known, she tried to disguise herself by putting on a thick veil and a heavy shawl, and sought still further to avoid observation by ascending to the upper gallery. She was very late in reaching the building, so, just as she entered, the preacher was announcing his text, and the first words that sounded in her ears were strikingly appropriate to her case, especially as she declared that Spurgeon pointed directly at her as he said, 'Come in, thou wife of Jeroboam; why feignest thou thyself to be another? for I am sent to thee with heavy tidings' (1 Kings 14. 6).

This singular coincidence further impressed her when, in the course of his sermon, the Pastor said:

'While thus speaking about the occasional hearer, an idea haunts my mind that I have been drawing somebody's portrait. I think there are some here who have had their character and conduct sketched out quite accurately enough for them to know who is meant. Do remember that, if the description fits you, it is meant for you; and if you yourself have been described, do not look about among your neighbours and say, "I think this is like somebody else". If it is like you, take it home to yourself, and God send it into the centre of your conscience, so that you cannot get rid of it! . . .

. . . I do not suppose there is anybody here disguised as to dress tonight, though such things may happen. The working man, who is afraid he shall be laughed at if he be known, may come here in disguise. Now and then a clergyman may come in, who would not be very comfortable in his conscience if it were known he did such a thing, and so he does not show himself exactly in his wonted garb. Notwithstanding, whoever you may be, disguised or not, it is of no use where God's gospel is preached. It is a quick discerner, and will find out the thoughts and intents of the heart. It will search you out, and unmask your true character, disguise yourself as you may.'

When the husband reached home, the woman revealed her secret, and said that he must, somehow, have let Spurgeon know that she was up in the gallery of the Tabernacle. The good man assured her that he was quite innocent, but she would not be convinced. The next day, when he saw the Pastor, he told him what a hard time he was having through his wife's singular experience the previous evening. The sermon was printed with the title 'A Hearer in Disguise'.

An almost exactly similar incident occurred several years before, when Spurgeon was preaching at New Park Street Chapel. On that occasion it was the wife of an eminent London doctor who wished to hear the young preacher without being recognized. She also had disguised herself, as she thought, effectually, but she was greatly surprised when she heard the announcement of the text which was so singularly suited to her: 'Come in, thou wife of Jeroboam; why feignest thou thyself to be another?'

At the Monday evening prayer-meeting at which Spurgeon related the incident linked with the sermon of July 31 he also mentioned the sermon at Exeter Hall in which he suddenly broke off from his subject, and pointing in a certain direction, said 'Young man, those gloves you are wearing have not been paid for: you have stolen them from your employer'. At the close of the service, a young man, looking very pale and greatly agitated, came to the room which was used as a vestry, and begged for a private interview with Spurgeon. On being admitted, he placed a pair of gloves upon the table, and tearfully said, 'It's the first time I have robbed my master, and I will never do it again. You won't expose me, sir, will you? It would kill my mother if she heard that I had become a thief'. The preacher had drawn the bow at a venture, but the arrow struck the target for which God intended it, and the startled hearer was, in that singular way, probably saved from committing a greater crime.

A service which became more memorable after several years had elapsed was that held on Lord's day morning, August 4, 1867, when the Pastor preached from Job 14.14: 'All the days of my appointed time will I wait, till my change come'. After the murder of President James A. Garfield (U.S.A.) in the summer of 1881, his widow wrote to Spurgeon: 'It is choice treasure from my storehouse of beautiful memories, that I sat beside General Garfield in the Metropolitan Tabernacle one bright summer Sunday morning (August 4, 1867), and listened to your voice. I have this morning re-read from his Journal his account of that day. A sentence from it may interest you. After describing his impressions of the great audience, of the preacher, and of the sermon, he adds: "God bless Mr. Spurgeon! He is helping to work out the problem of religious and civil freedom for England, in a way that he knows not of".'

One passage in the discourse was specially appropriate to the hundreds of Americans and other strangers from across the seas who were present: 'The Christian life should be one of waiting; that is, holding with a loose hand all earthly things. Many travellers are among us this morning; they are passing from one place to another, viewing divers countries; but as they are only travellers, and are soon to return to their homes, they do not speculate in the various businesses of Lombard Street or Cheapside. They do not attempt to buy large estates, and lay them out, and make gold and silver thereby; they know that they are only strangers and foreigners, and they act as such. They take such interest in the affairs of the country in which they are sojourning as may be becoming in those who are not citizens of it; they wish well to those among whom they tarry for a while; but that is all, for they are going home, therefore they do not intend to hamper themselves with anything that might make it difficult for them to depart from our shores'.

It was a notable occasion—Tuesday evening, March 2, 1869—when Spurgeon preached in the Tabernacle to several thousands of children. It was one of the very few occasions on which the young people of the congregation and of the Sunday-schools were assembled specially by themselves. The text was Psalm 71.17: 'O God, thou hast taught me from my youth;' and the sermon was one that boys and girls could easily understand and remember. It contained an unusually large number of anecdotes and illustrations, and in the course of it Spurgeon put several questions to his youthful auditors, which they answered promptly, and on the whole accurately. A brief extract will show the style of the sermon:

'Why should we go to God's school early? I think we ought to do so, first, because *it is such a happy school.* Schools used to be very miserable places, but, nowadays, I really wish I could go to school again. I went into the Borough Road School, the other day, into the Repository, where they sell slates, and pencils, and books, and all such things. The person who was there opened a box, and said to me, "Do you want to buy any of these things?" I said, "What are they? Why, they are toys, are they not?" He answered, "No, they are not toys: they are used for the lessons that are taught in the kindergarten school." I said, "Why, if I were to take them home, my boys would have a game with them, for they are only toys." "Just so," he replied, "but they are what are used in the kindergarten school to make learning the same as playing, so that little children should play while they are learning." Why, I thought, if that were so, I should like to go at once! Now, those who go to God's school are made much more happy than any toy can make children. He gives them real pleasure. There is a verse—I don't know how many of you can repeat it—I will say the first line; you say the second, if you can.

SPURGEON: *'Tis religion that can give*
CHILDREN: *Sweetest pleasures while we live;*
SPURGEON: *'Tis religion must supply*
CHILDREN: *Solid comfort when we die.*
SPURGEON: Yes, we made that out very well between us. Then, let us be off to God's school early, because it is such a happy school.'

Spurgeon delivered a similar discourse to a congregation of children on Lord's day afternoon, February 26, 1871, only on that occasion his subject consisted of Dr. Horatius Bonar's hymn, beginning 'I lay my sins on Jesus, The spotless Lamb of God.'

Towards the close of the sermon, Spurgeon related to the children this interesting reminiscence of his boyhood:

'Now the last wish is, "I long to be *with* Jesus." That is the best of all. But, dear boys and girls, you cannot sing that in your hearts unless you carry out the first part of the hymn, for we cannot be with Jesus till first He has taken upon Himself our sins, and made us like Himself. I do not think many of you go to a boarding-school, but I know what I used to do when I was at a school of that kind. I wanted to get home for the holidays; and six weeks before breaking-up time came, I made a little almanac. There was one square for every day, and, as the days passed, I used to mark them over with my pen, and make them black. Didn't I like to see them getting blotted! First I said, "There are only five weeks and six days before the holidays come," then it was, "five weeks and five days," and then, "five weeks and four days," and so on, till it was within a fortnight of the vacation, and then I began to feel that it was almost time to go home. You see, I was longing to go home; and that is how you and I will feel when we become like Jesus, we shall long to be with Jesus, where saints and angels sing His praises for ever. But, in order to be able to look at death in that light, we must first lay our sins on Jesus.'

*

How vividly this incident in my husband's boyhood recalls a similar one in much later days! He had been working at high pressure for a long time, and was greatly needing a rest. The time for the proposed holiday was fixed far in advance, and he looked forward to it with feverish impatience. It was referred to at all meal-times; and one day he said to me, 'Wifey, I wish I had a piece of string marked, and put in some prominent place, so that I could cut off each day as it passes.'

I immediately prepared a length of tape, with all the dates plainly written on it, and attached it to the chandelier which overhung the dining-table. It certainly was not an ornament to the room, but it gave him exceeding pleasure to clip off a piece of it day by day; so nobody cared how it looked, if he were gratified. It was very long when first put up, and he took as much delight as a little child would have done in watching it gradually grow shorter.

Friends would stare at it in wonder and curiosity, especially if they happened to be there at dividing time, when the scissors were produced, and with all due ceremony the symbol of the flight of another twenty-four hours was snipped off. Some laughed, some joked, some criticized; but he steadily persevered in his task until only an inch or two of the recording line was left hanging in its place, and we began to make preparations for the long-desired journey.

Alas, for those plans of ours which do not run parallel with God's will! My beloved became seriously ill when but a few days remained on the register, and that pathetic morsel of tape was cut down and removed, amidst tears of disappointment and sorrow for his sake. A sad period of suffering ensued, and one day he said, 'Wifey, we will never do that again; it will be better, in future, patiently to wait for the unfolding of God's purposes concerning us.'

*

Of all the memorable services away from the Tabernacle, the most notable were those held on the five Lord's day mornings March 24 to April 21, 1867, in the Agricultural Hall, Islington. It is difficult to tell the exact number of persons present—the estimates ranging from twelve to twenty-five thousand—but the congregations were the largest that Spurgeon ever addressed in any building with the exception of the Fast-day service at the Crystal Palace in 1857.

Not only were great crowds of hearers attracted, but the Word preached was blessed to very many of them, some of whom joined the neighbouring churches, while others found a spiritual home at the Tabernacle. The text on the first morning was Matthew 21.28–32, and in introducing his subject, the preacher said:

'The sight of this vast arena, and of this crowded assembly, reminds me of other spectacles which, in days happily long past, were seen in the amphitheatres of the old Roman Empire. Around, tier upon tier, were the assembled multitudes, with their cruel eyes and iron hearts; and in the centre stood a solitary, friendless man, waiting till the doors of the lions' den should be uplifted, that he might yield himself up a witness for Christ and a sacrifice to the popular fury. There would have been no difficulty then to have divided the precious from the vile in that audience. The most thoughtless wayfarer who should enter the amphitheatre would know at once who was the disciple of Christ and who were the enemies of the Crucified One. There stood the bravely-calm disciple, about to die, but all around, in those mighty tiers of the Colosseum, or of the amphitheatre of some provincial town, as the case might be, there sat matrons and nobles, princes and peasants, plebeians and patricians, senators and soldiers, all gazing downward with the same fierce, unpitying look, vociferous in the joy with which they beheld the agonies of a disciple of the hated Galilean, "butchered to make a Roman holiday."

Another sight is before us to-day, with much more happy associations; but, alas! it is a far more difficult task this day to separate the chaff from the wheat. Here, in this spacious arena, I hope there are hundreds, if not thousands, who would be prepared to die for our Lord Jesus, if such a sacrifice were required of them; and in yonder crowded seats, we may count by hundreds those who bear the Name and accept the gospel of Jesus of Nazareth; and yet, I fear me that, both in these living hills on either side, and upon this vast floor, there are many enemies of the Son of God, who are forgetful of His righteous claims, who have cast from them those "cords of a man" which should bind them to His throne, and have never submitted to the mighty love which showed itself in His cross and in His wounds. I cannot attempt the separation. You must grow together until the harvest. To divide you were a task which, at this hour, angels could not perform, but which, one day, they will easily accomplish, when, at their Master's bidding, the harvest being come, they shall gather together first the tares to bind them in bundles to burn them, and afterwards the wheat into Jehovah's barn. I shall not attempt the division, but I ask each man to attempt it for himself in his own case. I say unto you, young men and maidens, old men and fathers, this day examine yourselves whether you be in the faith.'

It is not a matter of surprise that the success of such a ministry as this should 'provoke to jealousy' various other branches of the Christian church, and not a few were inclined to believe that imitation was called for. The cry came at times from unexpected quarters; as for example from a High Churchman (writing in the second volume of *The Ingoldsby Letters*), who, despite his ecclesiastical principles, had braced himself to the ordeal of attendance at a service in the Tabernacle. Indeed, the repetition of the indiscretion testified to the deep impression made on the inquisitive mind by what it heard and saw. The narrative in 'The Letters' ran as follows:

'The hymn concluded, Mr. Spurgeon walked to the table, and taking his stand between it and the sofa, opened a large and handsome clasped Bible (the gift, I was told, of the congregation), and when he had found the place, which was on this occasion the latter part of the sixth chapter of Ephesians, he proceeded to read it with a slow and articulate voice, dwelling upon the more impressive passages, which he illustrated by a short extempore comment as he went along. This was a sermon in itself and was listened to with profound attention, and I will venture to say, corresponding edification, by all that multitude, who thus drank in the words of the Apostle, made plain and intelligible to the humblest comprehension, at the same time impressed upon all with a fervour and simplicity of illustration worthy both of the matter and object of the writer. . . .

All the learning and piety in the world will not supply the want of a good delivery, and the tact to suit your discourse to the character of your audience. Herein lies the first secret of Mr. Spurgeon's success. He has taken the measure of his congregation's taste and capacity, and adapts himself to it. Like the cunning doctor in Lucretius, he anoints the lips of his cup with honey, and so cheats his patients into swallowing the salutiferous draught. Religion was made agreeable to his hearers, but it is still religion. He makes it apparent both in his preaching and practice that her ways are ways of pleasantness and all her paths are peace.

The second great cause of Mr. Spurgeon's continued popularity is that he is mighty in the Scriptures. This is his deep well, and he is not sparing of its resources. He draws and draws again as he has occasion, and he does it without forcing. He has carefully studied John Bunyan, and copies him here with considerable skill.

Thirdly, he is evidently a man of prayer, and feels therein a hidden source of strength which will not fail him at his need. The same gift which empowers him to pour forth his two extempore prayers in the early part of the service, accompanies him throughout his sermon, and chastens and subdues even the more attractive portions of the discourse. In his lightest illustrations he does not forget the object and the occasion, and thus escapes splitting on a rock that has foundered many a preacher of oratorial power equal or even superior to his own.

He has, moreover, an accurate and quick ear and an expressive eye, developing in a remarkable degree the organ of language, aided by those of ideality, comparison, gaiety, wonder, veneration, and constructiveness. His manner is agreeable, and he is blest with a large fund of animal spirits and considerable strength. Such are Mr. Spurgeon's natural and acquired qualifications as a preacher, to which he has not disdained to add the great advantages of careful study and long cultivation. He understands, too, the art of concealing his art. He holds himself entirely under control. And if for a moment he appears to give way to the excitement of the topic and allows free rein to his tongue, he still has it under subjection, and returns to a quieter mood without effort and without constraint. His transitions are natural, and pleasantly relieve the outline of his bolder strokes. He is no windy orator, and knows when to pause, when to turn. He does not run either himself or his subject out of breath. His diction, though rapid, is sufficiently choice; his figures well selected and full of meaning. His energy is prodigious, and his earnestness bears all the appearance of sincerity and truth.'

It was very important that, during the short active lifetime of our Saviour—a little more than three years—He should confine His operation to a comparatively small district, so as to produce a permanent result there which would afterwards radiate over the whole world. He knew what was best for men, and therefore He restricted Himself to a very narrow area; and, my brethren and sisters, I am not sure that we are always wise when we want a great sphere. I have myself sometimes envied the man with about five hundred people to watch over, who could see them all, know them all, and enter into sympathy with them all, and so could do his work well. But, with so large a number as I have under my charge, what can one man do?—c.h.s. *in exposition of Matthew 15. 21*

5

The Pastor's Fellow-Workers

SINCE I came to London, I have seen the last of a former race of deacons—fine, gentlemanly men, rather stiff and unmanageable, not quite according to my mind, but respectable, prudent grandees of Dissent, in semi-clerical dress, with white cravats. The past generation of deacons is to be spoken of with reverence in all places where holy memories are cherished, but, out of them all, my friend, counsellor, and right hand, was Thomas Olney. Never did a minister have a better deacon, nor a church a better servant. He was for sixty years a member, for thirty-one years a deacon, and for fourteen years treasurer of the church. He was ever remarkable for his early and constant attendance at the prayer-meeting and other week-day services. He had a childlike faith and a manly constancy. To believe in Jesus, and to work for Him, were the very life of his new and better nature. He was eminently a Baptist, but he was also a lover of all good men. The poor, and especially the poor of the church, always found in him sincere sympathy and help. His name will be had in lasting remembrance.

Among my first London deacons was one very worthy man, who said to me, when I went to preach in Exeter Hall and the Surrey Gardens Music Hall, 'I am an old man, and I cannot possibly go at the rate you young people are going; but I don't want to hang on, and be a drag to you, so I will quietly withdraw, and go and see how I can get on with Mr. Brock.' I think that was the kindest thing that the good man could have done, and that it was probably the best course for himself as well as for us. I went over to see him, some time afterwards, and he asked me to take my two boys that he might give them his blessing. He said to me, 'Did I not do the very best thing I could have done by getting out of the way, and not remaining to hinder the work? I always read your sermons, and I send in my subscriptions regularly.' Dear good man, he died the next day.

My present staff of nine deacons consists of peculiarly lovable, active, energetic, warm-hearted, generous men, every one of whom seems specially adapted for his own particular department of service.

I am very thankful that I have never been the pastor of a dead church, controlled by dead deacons. I have seen such a thing as that with my own eyes, and the sight was truly awful. I recollect very well preaching in a chapel where the church had become exceedingly low, and, somehow, the very building looked like a sepulchre, though crowded that one night by those who came to hear the preacher. The singers drawled out a dirge, while the members sat like mutes. I found it hard preaching; there was no 'go' in the sermon, I seemed to be driving dead horses.

After the service, I saw two men, who I supposed were the deacons—the pillars of the church—leaning against the posts of the vestry door in a listless attitude, and I said, 'Are you the deacons of this church?' They informed me that they were the only deacons, and I remarked that I thought so. To myself I added that I understood, as I looked at *them*, several things which else would have been a riddle. Here was a dead church, comparable to the ship of the ancient mariner which was manned by the dead. Deacons, teachers, minister, people, all dead, and yet wearing the semblance of life.

> '*The helmsman steered, the ship moved on,*
>   *Yet never a breeze up-blew;*
> *The mariners all 'gan work the ropes,*
>   *Where they were wont to do;*
> *They raised their limbs like lifeless tools—*
>   *We were a ghastly crew.*'

All my church-officers are in a very real sense my brethren in Christ. In talking to or about one another, we have no stately modes of address. I am called 'the Governor'—I suppose, because I do not attempt to govern; and the deacons are known among us as 'Brother William,' 'Uncle Tom,' 'Dear Old Joe,' 'Prince Charlie,' 'Son of Ali,' and so on. These brethren are some of them esquires, who ought also to be M.P.'s, but we love them too well to dignify them. One day, I spoke rather sharply to one of them, and I think he deserved the rebuke I gave him, but he said to me, 'Well, that may be so, but I tell you what, sir, *I would die for you any day.*' 'Oh!' I replied, 'bless your heart, I am sorry I was so sharp, but, still, you did deserve it, did you not?' He smiled, and said he thought he did, and there the matter ended.

One of my deacons made a remark to me one night which would have mortally offended a more sensitive individual than I am. It was the first Sabbath in the month, the preaching service was over, and

we were just going down to the great communion in the Tabernacle. I enquired how many new members there were to be received,
and the answer was, 'Only seven.' In an instant, my good friend
said, 'This won't pay, Governor; running all this big place for seven
new members in a month!' He was quite right, although a Christian
church is not 'run' on exactly the same lines as a business undertaking; but I could not help thinking, at the time, that it would not
have done for some deacons to make such an observation to certain
ministers of my acquaintance; or if the remark had been made, it
would have been attended with very serious consequences. I know
one pastor who is very decidedly of opinion that the Lord never
made anyone equal in importance to a Baptist minister (that is,
himself), but it so happened that one of his church-officers had the
notion that a deacon is a being of a still higher order, so it was not
very surprising that the time came when they could no longer work
together harmoniously.

On going into the Tabernacle, one day, I gave directions about
some minor alterations that I wished to have made, not knowing at
the time that I was cancelling the orders given by the deacon who
had the main care of the building resting upon him. When he
arrived, in the evening, he saw what had been done, and at once
asked who had interfered with his instructions. The reply was, 'The
Governor, sir.' The spirit of unquestioning loyalty at once asserted
itself over any temporary annoyance he may have felt, and he said,
'Quite right; there must be only one captain in a ship;' and, for a
long while, that saying became one of our most familiar watch-
words. I have often been amazed at the devotion of our brethren; I
have told them many a time that, if they would follow a broomstick
as they have followed me, the work must succeed. To which William
Olney, as the spokesman for the rest, has answered, 'Yes, dear
Pastor; but it is because we have such absolute confidence in your
leadership that we are ready to follow you anywhere. You have
never misled us yet, and we do not believe you ever will do so.'

After one long illness, which kept me for many weeks out of the
pulpit, I said to the deacons, 'I am afraid you will get quite tired of
your poor crippled minister,' but one of the least demonstrative of
the brethren replied, 'Why, my dear sir, we would sooner have you
for one month in the year than anyone else in the world for the
whole twelve months!' I believe they all agreed with what he said,
for they have often urged me to go away for a long sea voyage, or to
rest for a year, or for several months at the least, but I have always

had one answer for them: 'It is not possible for me to leave my work for any lengthened period until the Lord calls me home; and, besides, there is a Scriptural reason why a minister should not be away from his people for more than six weeks at a time.' 'What is that?' they asked. 'Why, don't you remember that, when Moses was up in the mount with God for forty days, Aaron and the children of Israel turned aside to the worship of the golden calf?'

I had one most touching proof of a deacon's loving self-sacrifice and generosity. During a very serious illness, I had an unaccountable fit of anxiety about money matters. There was no real ground for apprehension, for my dear wife and I were scrupulously careful to 'owe no man anything,' and there was no pecuniary liability in connection with the Lord's work under my charge which need have caused me the slightest perplexity. I had fallen into one of those curious mental conditions that are often the result of extreme pain and weakness, in which the mind seems to lay hold of some impalpable object, and will not let it go. One of the brethren came to see me while I was in that sad state, and after trying in vain to comfort me, he said, 'Well, good-bye, sir, I'll see what I can do.' He went straight home, and before very long he came back to me bringing all the stocks and shares and deeds and available funds that he had. Putting them down on the bed where I was lying in great agony, he said, 'There, my dear Pastor, I owe everything I have in the world to you, and you are quite welcome to all I possess. Take whatever you need, and do not have another moment's anxiety.' Of course, as soon as I got better, I returned to my dear friend all that he had brought to me under such singular circumstances. Even if I had needed it, I could not have taken a penny of it, for it seemed to me very much as the water from the well of Bethlehem must have appeared to David. Happily, I did not require any part of the amount so freely placed at my disposal, but I could never forget the great kindness of the brother who was willing to give all that he had in order to allay the groundless fears of his sorely-afflicted minister.

Of late years we have heard a great deal against deacons, and have read discussions as to their office, evidently suggested by no idolatrous reverence for their persons. Many of our ministering brethren bitterly rate them, others tremble at the mention of their very name, and a few put on their armour and prepare to do battle with them wherever they go, as if they were the dragons of ministerial life. We ourselves are charged with having said that 'a deacon is worse than a devil, for if you resist the devil he will flee from you, but if you resist a deacon he will fly at you'. This is no saying of ours; we never had any cause to speak so severely, and although in some cases it is undoubtedly true, we have never had any experimental proof of it. Not one in a hundred of all the sayings fathered upon us are ours at all, and as to this one it was in vogue before we were born.

Our observation of deacons leads us to observe that, as a rule, they are quite as good men as the pastors, and the bad and good in the ministry and the diaconate are to be found in very much the same proportions. If there be lordly deacons, are there not lordly pastors? If there be ignorant, crotchety men among deacons, are there not their rivals in our pulpits? The church owes an immeasure-able debt of gratitude to those thousands of godly men who study her interests day and night, contribute largely of their substance, care for her poor, cheer her ministers, and in times of trouble as well as prosperity, remain faithfully at their posts. Whatever there may be here and there of mistake, infirmity, and even wrong, we are assured from wide and close observation, that the greater number of our deacons are an honour to our faith, and we may style them as the apostle did his brethren, the 'glory of Christ'.

Heaviest censure is occasionally deserved, but affectionate esteem is usually due. Deprive the church of her deacons, and she would be bereaved of her most valiant sons; their loss would be the shak-ing of the pillars of our spiritual house and would cause a desolation on every side. Thanks be to God, such a calamity is not likely to befall us, for the great Head of the church, in mercy to her, will always raise up a succession of faithful men, who will use the office well, and earn unto themselves a good degree and much boldness in the faith.

Much ought to be taken into consideration in estimating the character of men sustaining office in the church, for many difficulties may be incidental to the position, and this may mitigate the severity with which we ought to judge the men. Our brethren in the deacon's work are not so migratory as our ministers; they are frequently born to Christ in the churches in which they live and die; they cannot readily remove when evil days becloud the church, but remain chained to the oar to bear the odium of discontent and the sorrow of decay. No frequent removal secures for them a renewal of popu-larity elsewhere; their whole career for bad or good is remembered by one and the same constituency, and hence false steps are with great difficulty reprieved, and awkward disagreements are painfully remembered. With new ministers come new ways, and men in office, especially elderly men, cannot so easily learn and unlearn as young and fresh comers might desire. Perhaps cherished methods are crossed and hallowed ideas overthrown, and this is not the smallest trial of a good man's life. We almost think it needs a better man to make a good deacon than a good minister. *We* who preach the Word go first, and this pleases human nature; grace is needed to make older, wealthier, and often wiser men go second and keep their place without envyings and bickerings: thousands do this and are to be honoured for it.

When I came to New Park Street, the church had deacons, but no elders; and I thought, from my study of the New Testament, that there should be both orders of officers. They are very useful when we can get them—the deacons to attend to all secular matters, and the elders to devote themselves to the spiritual part of the work; this division of labour supplies an outlet for two different sorts of talent, and allows two kinds of men to be serviceable to the church; and I am sure it is good to have two sets of brethren as officers, instead of one set who have to do everything, and who often become masters of the church, instead of the servants, as both deacons and elders should be.

As there were no elders at New Park Street, when I read and expounded the passages in the New Testament referring to elders, I used to say, 'This is an order of Christian workers which appears to have dropped out of existence. In apostolic times, they had both deacons and elders, but, somehow, the church has departed from this early custom. We have one preaching elder—that is, the Pastor —and he is expected to perform all the duties of the eldership.' One and another of the members began to enquire of me, 'Ought not we, as a church, to have elders? Cannot we elect some of our brethren who are qualified to fill the office?' I answered that we had better not disturb the existing state of affairs, but some enthusiastic young men said that they would propose at the church-meeting that elders should be appointed, and ultimately we did appoint them with the unanimous consent of the members. I did not force the question upon them; I only showed them that it was Scriptural, and then of course they wanted to carry it into effect.

The church-book, in its records of the annual church-meeting held January 12, 1859, contains the following entry:

'Our Pastor, in accordance with a previous notice, then stated the necessity that had long been felt by the church for the appointment of certain brethren to the office of elders, to watch over the spiritual affairs of the church. Our Pastor pointed out the Scripture warrant for such an office, and quoted the several passages relating to the ordaining of elders: Titus 1. 5, and Acts 14. 23—the qualifications of elders; 1 Timothy 3. 1–7, and Titus 1. 5–9—the duties of elders; Acts 20. 28–35, 1 Timothy 5. 17, and James 5. 14; and other mention made of elders: Acts 11. 30, 15. 4, 6, 23, 16. 4, and 1 Timothy 4. 14.

Whereupon, it was resolved—That the church, having heard the statement made by its Pastor respecting the office of the eldership, desires to elect a certain number of brethren to serve the church in that office for one year, it being understood that they are to attend to the spiritual affairs of the church, and not to the temporal matters, which appertain to the deacons only.'

I have always made it a rule to consult the existing officers of the church before recommending the election of new deacons or elders, and I have also been on the look-out for those who have proved their fitness for office by the work they have accomplished in their private capacity. In our case, the election of deacons is a permanent one, but the elders are chosen year by year, though they usually continue in their office for life. This plan has worked admirably with us, but other churches have adopted different methods of appointing their officers. In my opinion, the very *worst* mode of selection is to print the names of all the male members, and then vote for a certain number by ballot. I know of one case in which a very old man was within two or three votes of being elected simply because his name began with A, and therefore was put at the top of the list of candidates.

My elders, usually about twenty-five in number, have been a great blessing to me; they are invaluable in looking after the spiritual interests of the church. The deacons have charge of the finance; but if the elders meet with cases of poverty needing relief, we tell them to give some small sum, and then bring the case before the deacons. I was once the unseen witness of a little incident that greatly pleased me. I heard one of our elders say to a deacon, 'I gave old Mrs. So-and-so ten shillings the other night.' 'That was very generous on your part,' said the deacon. 'Oh, but!' exclaimed the elder, 'I want the money from the deacons.' So the deacon asked,

'What office do you hold, brother?' 'Oh!' he replied, 'I see; I have gone beyond my duty as an elder, so I'll pay the ten shillings myself; I should not like "the Governor" to hear that I had overstepped the mark.' 'No, no, my brother,' said the deacon; 'I'll give you the money, but don't make such a mistake another time.'

Some of the elders have rendered great service to our own church by conducting Bible-classes and taking the oversight of several of our home-mission stations, while one or two have made it their special work to 'watch for souls' in our great congregation, and to seek to bring to immediate decision those who appeared to be impressed under the preaching of the Word. One brother has earned for himself the title of my hunting dog, for he is always ready to pick up the wounded birds. One Monday night, at the prayer-meeting, he was sitting near me on the platform; all at once I missed him, and presently I saw him right at the other end of the building. After the meeting, I asked him why he went off so suddenly, and he said that the gas just shone on the face of a woman in the congregation, and she looked so sad that he walked round, and sat near her, in readiness to speak to her about the Saviour after the service.

That same brother did a very unusual thing on another occasion. A poor fallen woman accosted him in the street, and in an instant he began to plead with her to leave her sinful ways, and come to Christ. Rain came on while he was talking to her, so he rapped at the door of the nearest house, and asked if he might stand in the passage while he spoke and prayed with a poor soul under conviction of sin. The good woman invited him into her front room, and when he thanked her for her kindness, he took the opportunity of asking her also if she knew the Lord. I believe he had the joy of leading both of them to the Saviour, and bringing them to join the church at the Tabernacle. Eternity alone will reveal how many have thus been arrested and blessed by a wise and winning word spoken in season, and accompanied by earnest prayer and clear Scriptural teaching concerning the way of salvation. Others of the elders have also exercised a most gracious ministry in various parts of the metropolis and in the home counties, through the agency of the Tabernacle Country Mission and Evangelists' Association. Many churches, that are now self-supporting and flourishing, were started in a very humble fashion by the brethren connected with one or other of these two useful Societies. The labours of the elders in visiting the sick, seeking to reclaim the wandering, pointing enquirers to the Saviour, and introducing candidates to the fellowship of the church, are recorded in the Lord's Book of Remembrance, and are gratefully recollected by their Pastor and fellow-members.

*

After the Tabernacle was opened, the church continued to grow so rapidly that it was found necessary, from time to time, to provide the Pastor with suitable helpers in his many-sided service. The following entry in the church-book shows the steps that were taken before a permanent appointment was made:

November 24, 1862. 'Our Pastor stated that he thought it desirable that we should revive the office of Teacher, which had formerly existed in this church, but had fallen into disuse. In looking over our church history, he found that, during the pastorate of William Rider, Benjamin Keach had laboured in the church under the name and title of Teacher, so that, upon the decease of William Rider, a Pastor was at once on the spot in the person of the mighty man of God who had for twenty years been recognized as a Teacher among us. Again, in the pastorate of Benjamin Keach, the church elected Benjamin Stinton to assist the Pastor as a Teacher, and it again happened that, on the removal of Benjamin Keach, Benjamin Stinton succeeded to the pastorate, and the church was spared the misery of long remaining without a Pastor, or seeking some unknown person from abroad. The Teacher, without dividing the unity of the pastorate, would, in the judgment of our Pastor, be a valuable aid for the edification of the saints in the matter of Word and doctrine. Our Pastor also remarked that, when the Holy Spirit manifestly made a man useful in the church, and bestowed on him the real qualifications for an office, it seemed but fitting and seemly that the church should humbly recognize the gift of the Lord, and accept the brother in the Lord's name.

In the outcome, two such teachers were appointed—John Collins followed by Thomas Ness—but after short periods of happy service both of them were called to hold pastorates elsewhere, and for the moment the experiment ended.

After the departure of Thomas Ness nearly two years were allowed to elapse before any further effort was made to relieve the Pastor from part at least of his ever-increasing burden of labour and responsibility. On October 16, 1867, a special church-meeting was held, of which the church-book contains the following record:

'For nearly fourteen years, we have, as a church, enjoyed a most

wonderful and uninterrupted prosperity, so that our present number of members is now more than 3,500—a number far too great
for the efficient oversight of one man.[1] Although our deacons and
elders labour abundantly, yet there is much work which no one can
do but the Pastor, and which one Pastor finds himself quite unable
to perform. The mere examination of candidates, and attending to
discipline, entail most laborious duties. Moreover, the Pastor's
labours in Exeter Hall, the Surrey Gardens Music Hall, our own
large Tabernacle, and the Agricultural Hall, have been most exhausting, and yet he has taken little rest, being perpetually occupied
in preaching the Word, having proclaimed the gospel throughout
England, Scotland, and Wales, and having journeyed for the same
purpose to Geneva, Paris, Holland, and Germany.

In addition to all this, numerous Institutions have grown up in
connection with our church, of which the chief are the College and
the Orphanage, both of which require much care and industry in
their right management. The Pastor conducts a magazine which
greatly aids him in raising funds, but which involves much writing.
He publishes a sermon every week. He has been one of the foremost
in founding the London Baptist Association, and serves on its
Committee, and accepts his share of work for other public Societies.
Last of all, he has been for some months laid prostrate by severe
illness, and will probably be attacked in the same manner again very
speedily unless some little respite can be afforded him. He is not
afraid of work, but he does not wish to commit suicide, and therefore asks for help.

The following resolution was then proposed by Deacon William
Olney, seconded by Elder Dransfield, supported by brethren Nisbet,
Miller, and Stringer, and carried unanimously: "That, in the opinion
of this church, the time has now arrived when some permanent help
should be obtained to assist our beloved Pastor in the very arduous
work connected with the pastorate of so large a church; also that
we consider the most likely person to discharge this duty to the
comfort of our Pastor, and the lasting benefit of the church, is our
Pastor's brother, the Rev. J. A. Spurgeon. It is therefore resolved
that an invitation be given to the Rev. James A. Spurgeon to give
as much of his time as he can spare from his present engagements to

[1] Many endeavours carried on by the church also came under this general oversight.
These included, in 1868: a Sunday-school containing 1,077 children, with 96 teachers,
and two other schools close by made up of 500 children and 45 teachers; a young
women's Bible-class, containing from 500 to 600 members; and two men's cate-
chism classes, averaging upwards of 100 each.

assist our Pastor in any way considered by him most advisable for the advantage of this church, for a period of three months, with a view to his being permanently engaged afterwards, if it is thought advisable at the expiration of that period; also that it be an instruction to our deacons to make any financial arrangement necessary to carry out this resolution." '

The three-months' probationary period having proved satisfactory to both Pastor and people, a special church-meeting was held in January, 1868, at which it was decided to invite James Archer Spurgeon, who was three years younger than his brother, to become Assistant or Co-Pastor of the Church. At the same time it was explained to him by letter that, should the Lord call his brother Charles home, it would not follow that he would automatically succeed him in the pastorate. Nor while he was Co-Pastor must he assume that the office gave him the right to occupy the pulpit at the Tabernacle in the absence or the illness of Charles. These delicate matters were stated with complete candour but in gracious words, and James Spurgeon found no difficulty in accepting the Church's stipulations. During the remainder of his brother's life 'he did a vast amount of daily routine work at the Tabernacle, of which the outside public heard little and knew less, but in the doing of which he proved the most effective assistant to the senior pastor that could possibly have been provided. . . . The two brothers appeared to be at one in everything; but the chief reason of their being able to work in unison as they did was that they were agreed in doctrine'.

If Charles was known to his elders and deacons as 'The Governor', James was known to them and to members of the Tabernacle as 'Mr. James'. To Church members at Croydon, where he also held a pastorate, the latter was known as Mr. Spurgeon; among outsiders he was recognized as Mr. James Spurgeon. 'Brother', remarked Charles to him one day, 'I am taking from you your very name—they call you Mr. James. If ever the Americans offer you a doctorship you must accept it, and then Dr. Spurgeon will be a sufficient distinction from Mr. Spurgeon'! The wish met with fulfilment, but not until after Charles's death, when the degree of LL.D was conferred on James by Colgate University, U.S.A.

Spurgeon used often to say that his best deacon was a woman— alluding to Mrs. Bartlett. In the summer of 1859, one of the teachers of New Park Street Sunday-school was going away for a month, and asked Mrs. Bartlett to take charge of her class during her absence; but, on presenting herself at the school, she was directed by the superintendent to the senior class. There were only three young women in attendance that afternoon, but in the course of the month the number had so increased that she was asked to continue as teacher. She did so, and before long the class had outgrown its accommodation, an experience which was again and again repeated until it was finally settled in the lecture-hall of the new Tabernacle, where there were some 600 or 700 regularly present. When Mrs. Bartlett was 'called home,' in 1875, it was estimated that between 900 and 1000 members of her class had joined the church at the Tabernacle, and Mr. Spurgeon thus wrote concerning his esteemed helper:

'Mrs. Bartlett was a choice gift from God to the church at the Tabernacle, and the influence of her life was far-reaching, stimulating many others besides those who by her means were actually led to the Saviour. We miss her sadly, but her spiritual children are with us still; they have stood the test of years, and the most searching test of all, namely, the loss of her motherly counsel and inspiring words. She did not build with wood, hay, and stubble, for the edifice remains, and for this let God be glorified.

She was a woman of intense force of character. She believed with all her heart, and therefore acted with decision and power. Hence, she did not constantly look to the Pastor for help in her appointed service; but, beginning in a small and quiet way, toiled on till everything grew around her to large proportions. She took small account of difficulty or discouragement, but trusted in God, and went on as calmly sure of success as if she saw it with her eyes. When anything flagged, she only seemed to throw out more energy, waited upon God with more fervency, and pushed forward with the resolve to conquer. Deborah herself could not have been more perfectly God-reliant than Mrs. Bartlett was. She did not beat the air, or run at an uncertainty, but such expressions as "I know God will help us. It must be done; it shall be done; sisters, you will do it!" were just the sort of speeches that we expected of her. She flamed in determined earnestness at times when only fire could clear a path, and then there was no withstanding her, as her class very well knew.

To her resolute will, God had added by His grace an untiring perseverance. On, and on, and on, year by year, she went at the same duty, and in the same way. New plans of usefulness for the class were opened up by her as she saw them possible and prudent, but the former things were never dropped for fresh ideas, and novel methods were not devised to the superseding of the well-tried plans. Her talk was always concerning "the old, old story," and never of new-fangled doctrines or imaginary attainments. She kept close to the cross, extolled her Saviour, pleaded with sinners to believe, and stirred up saints to holy living. Of her theme she never tired, nor would she allow others to tire. She looked as if it was treason to grow cold; her glance indicated that to be indifferent about the Redeemer's Kingdom was a shameful crime. From first to last of her long leadership of her class, she appeared to be almost equally energetic and intense.

It pleased God to make our sister an eminently practical woman. She was no dreamer of dreams, but a steady, plodding worker. She never wasted two minutes of her Pastor's time with marvellous methods, and miraculous plans; she instinctively saw what could be done, and what should be done, and she did it, looking to God for the blessing. Her class has raised large sums for the College, and has done actual service in more ways than we have space to tell, for she trained her disciples into a band of labourers, and kept them all at it to the utmost of their abilities. Her addresses were always practical; never speculative, or merely entertaining. She aimed at soul-winning every time she met the class, and that in the most direct and personal manner. In pursuing this object, she was very downright, and treated things in a matter-of-fact style. The follies, weaknesses, and temptations of her sex were dealt with very pointedly; and the griefs, trials, and sins of her class were on her heart, and she spoke of them as real burdens. Her talk never degenerated into story-telling, or quotations of poetry, or the exhibition of singularities of doctrine; but she went right at her hearers in the name of the Lord, and claimed their submission to Him.

Amid all her abounding labours, Mrs. Bartlett was the subject of frequent pain and constant weakness. She had the energy of vigorous health, and yet was almost always an invalid. It cost her great effort to appear on many occasions, but then she would often succeed best, as she pleaded with her hearers, "as a dying woman" to be reconciled to God. "Out of weakness . . . made strong," was her continual experience; in fact, much of her power lay in her weakness, for the observation of her pains and feebleness operated upon the sympathetic hearts of her young friends, and made them the more highly appreciate the counsels which cost her so much effort and self-denial. She has met many of her spiritual children above, and others are on the way to the sweet meeting-place. We are thankful for the loan we had of such a woman, thankful that she was not sooner removed as sometimes we feared she would have been, thankful that she has left a son to perpetuate her work, and thankful, most of all, that there is such a work to be perpetuated.'

On the monument over her grave in Nunhead Cemetery, is the following inscription, which was written by Mr. Spurgeon:

'In affectionate memory of
LAVINIA STRICKLAND BARTLETT,
Who departed to her blissful home, August 21, 1875, in her 69th year. The Pastors, Deacons, and Elders of the Church in the Metropolitan Tabernacle unite with her Class and the students of the College in erecting this memorial to her surpassing worth. She was indeed "a mother in Israel." Often did she say, "*Keep near the cross, my sister*".'

This chapter may be appropriately closed with Spurgeon's testimony to the piety and the unity of the Tabernacle church, together with a solemn warning as to what would happen if such a highly-favoured company of people should ever prove unfaithful: 'I thank God that we have a great many very warm-hearted, earnest Christians in connection with this church—I will make bold to say, such true and lovely saints as I never expected to live to see. I have beheld in this church apostolical piety revived; I will say it, to the glory of God, that I have seen as earnest and as true piety as Paul or Peter ever witnessed. I have marked, in some here present, such godly zeal, such holiness, such devotion to the Master's business, as Christ Himself must look upon with joy and satisfaction. God has been pleased to favour us with profound peace in the church. We have been disturbed by no word of false doctrine, by no uprising of heretics in our midst, or any separations or divisions. This is a blessed thing, but, still, Satan may make it a dangerous matter. We may begin to think that there is no need for us to watch, that we shall always be as we are; and deacons, and elders, and Pastor, and church-members, may all cease their vigilance, and then the "root of bitterness" may spring up in the neglected corner till it gets too deeply rooted for us to tear it up again. Though we are not free from ten thousand faults, yet I have often admired the goodness of God which has enabled us, with a hearty grip, to hold each other by the hand, and say, "We love each other for Christ's sake, and for the truth's sake, and we hope to live in each other's love till we die, wishing, if it were possible, to be buried side by side." I do thank God for this, because I know there is more than enough of evil among us to cause dissensions in our midst. We who bear office in the church have the same nature as others; and therefore, naturally, would seek to have the supremacy, and every man, if left to himself, would indulge an angry temper, and find many reasons for differing from his brother. We have all been offended often, and have as often offended others. We are as imperfect a band of men as might be found, but we are one in Christ. We have each had to put up with the other, and to bear and forbear; and it does appear to me a wonder that so many imperfect people should get on so well together for so long. By faith, I read over the door of our Tabernacle this text, "When He giveth quietness, who then can make trouble?"

Possibly, my brethren, many of you do not sufficiently prize the peace which reigns in our church. Ah! you would value it if you lost it. Oh, how highly you would esteem it if strife and schism should ever come into our midst! You would look back upon these happy days we have had together with intense regret, and pray, "Lord, knit us together in unity again; send us love to each other once more;" for, in a church, love is the essential element of happiness.

If we, as a church, prove unfaithful; if we leave our first love; if we do not plead in prayer, and seek the conversion of souls, God may take away His presence from us as He has done from churches that were once His, but which are not so now. The traveller tells you that, as he journeys through Asia Minor, he sees the ruins of those cities which once were the seven golden candlesticks, wherein the light of truth shone brightly. What will he now say of Thyatira? Where will he find Laodicea? These have passed away, and why may not this church? Look at Rome, once the glory of the Christian Church, her ministers many, and her power over the world enormous for good; and now she is the place where Satan's seat is, and her synagogue is a synagogue of hell. How is this? Because she departed from her integrity, she left her first love, and the Lord cast her away. Thus will He deal with us also if we sin against Him. You know that terrible passage: "Go ye now unto my place which was in Shiloh, where I set my name at the first, and see what I did to it for the wickedness of my people Israel." God first of all had the tabernacle pitched at Shiloh, but it was defiled by the sin of Eli's sons, so the tabernacle was taken away, and Shiloh became a wilderness. So may this flourishing church become. If justice should thus visit you, you may hold your prayer-meetings—probably those will soon cease—but of what avail will your formal prayers be? You may get whom you will to preach, but what of that? I know what you would do, if some of us were fallen asleep, and the faithful ones buried—if the Spirit of God were gone, you would say, "Well, we are still a large and influential congregation; we can afford to pay a talented minister, money will do anything;" and you would get the man of talents, and then you would want an organ and a choir, and many other pretty things which we now count it our joy to do without. Then, if such were the case, all these vain attempts at grandeur would be unsuccessful, and the church would ere long become a scorn and a hissing, or else a mere log upon the water. Then it would be said, "We must change the management," and there would be this alteration and that; but if the Lord were gone, what could you do? By what means could you ever make this church, or any other church, revive again? Alas! for the carnal, spasmodic efforts we have seen made in some churches! Prayer-meetings badly attended, no conversions, but still the people have said, "It is imperative upon us to keep up a respectable appearance; we must collect a congregation by our singing, by our organ, or some other outward attraction;" and angels might have wept as they saw the folly of men who sought almost anything except the Lord, who alone can make a house His temple, who alone can make a ministry to be a ministration of mercy, without whose presence the most solemn congregation is but as the herding of men in the market, and the most melodious songs but as the shoutings of those who make merry at a marriage. Without the Lord, our solemn days, our new moons, and our appointed feasts, are an abomination such as His soul hateth. May this church ever feel her utter, entire, absolute dependence upon the presence of her God, and may she never cease humbly to implore Him to forgive her many sins, but still to command His blessing to abide upon her! Amen.'

It can be argued, with small fear of refutation, that open-air preaching is as old as preaching itself. We are at full liberty to believe that Enoch, 'the seventh from Adam,' when he prophesied, asked for no better pulpit than the hillside, and that Noah, as a preacher of righteousness, was willing to reason with his contemporaries in the ship-yard wherein his marvellous ark was built. Certainly, Moses and Joshua found their most convenient place for addressing vast assemblies beneath the unpillared arch of heaven. Samuel closed a sermon in the field at Gilgal amid thunder and rain, by which the Lord rebuked the people, and drove them to their knees. Elijah stood on Carmel, and challenged the vacillating nation with the question, 'How long halt ye between two opinions?' Jonah, whose spirit was somewhat similar, lifted up his cry of warning in the streets of Nineveh, and in all her places of concourse gave forth the warning utterance, 'Yet forty days, and Nineveh shall be overthrown!' To hear Ezra and Nehemiah, 'all the people gathered themselves together as one man into the street that was before the water gate.' Indeed, we find examples of open-air preaching everywhere around us in the records of the Old Testament.

Our Lord Himself, who is yet more our Pattern, delivered the larger proportion of His sermons on the mountain's side, or by the sea-shore, or in the streets. He was, to all intents and purposes, an open-air preacher. He did not remain silent in the synagogue, but He was equally at home in the field. We have no discourse of His on record delivered in the Chapel Royal, but we have the sermon on the mount, and the sermon in the plain; so that the very earliest and most Divine kind of preaching was practised out of doors by Him who 'spake as never man spake.' There were gatherings of His disciples, after His decease, within walls, especially that in the upper room; but the preaching was even then most frequently in the court of the temple, or in such other open spaces as were available.— c.h.s., *in Lectures to my Students.*

Mr. Harrald will remember the truly wonderful open-air service at Stowmarket, in Suffolk. It was held in the garden grounds of Mr. Manning Prentice. The trees were full of people; and they looked like big birds roosting on the branches. I think it was in 1868, and I *know* the text was, 'With his stripes we are healed.' It was a marvellous sermon.—william cuff *to Mrs. C. H. Spurgeon, in a letter.*

6

Open-Air Preaching

IF I had my choice of a place for preaching out of doors, I should prefer to front a rising ground, or an open spot bounded at some little distance by a wall. Of course, there must be sufficient space to allow of the congregation assembling between the pulpit and the limiting object in front, but I like to see an end, and not to shout into boundless space. I do not know a prettier site for a sermon than the one which I have many times occupied in the grounds of my friend, Mr. James Duncan, at Benmore.[1] It was a level sweep of lawn, backed by rising terraces covered with fir trees. The people could either occupy the seats below, or drop down upon the grassy banks, as best comported with their comfort; and thus I had part of my congregation in rising galleries above me, and the rest in the area around me. My voice readily ascended, and I conceive that, if the people had been seated up the hill for half-a-mile, they would have been able to hear me with ease. I should suppose that Wesley's favourite spot at Gwennap Pit must be somewhat after the same order. Amphitheatres and hillsides are always favourite spots with preachers in the fields, and their advantages will be at once evident.

Fresh air, and plenty of it, is a grand thing for every mortal man, woman, and child. I have preached twice, on a Sabbath day, at Blairmore not far from Benmore, on a little height by the side of the sea; and, after discoursing with all my might to large congregations, to be counted by thousands, I have not felt one-half so much exhausted as I often am when addressing a few hundreds in some horrible 'black hole of Calcutta,' called a chapel. I trace my freshness and freedom from lassitude at Blairmore to the fact that the windows could not be shut down by persons afraid of draughts, and that the roof was as high as the heavens are above the earth. My conviction is that a man could preach three or four times on a Sabbath out of doors with less fatigue than would be occasioned by one discourse delivered in an impure atmosphere, heated and poisoned by human breath, and carefully preserved from every refreshing infusion of natural air.

[1] See chapter 15.

I am persuaded that, the more of open-air preaching there is in London, the better. If it should become a nuisance to some people, it will be a blessing to others, if properly conducted. If it be the gospel which is spoken, and if the spirit of the preacher be one of love and truth, the results cannot be doubted: the bread cast upon the waters will be found again after many days. The truth must, however, be preached in a manner worth the hearing, for mere noise-making is an evil rather than a benefit. I know a family almost driven out of their senses by the hideous shouting of monotonous exhortations, and the howling of 'Safe in the arms of Jesus,' near their door every Sabbath afternoon by the year together. They are zealous Christians, and would willingly help their tormentors if they saw the slightest probability of usefulness from the violent bawling; but, as they seldom see a hearer, and do not think that what is spoken would do any good if it were heard, they complain that they are compelled to lose their few hours of quiet because two good men think it their duty to perform a noisy but perfectly use-less service. I once saw a man preaching with no hearer but a dog, which sat upon its tail, and looked up very reverently while its master orated. There were no people at the windows, nor passing by, but the brother and his dog were at their post, whether the people would hear or whether they would forbear. Once, also, I passed an earnest declaimer, whose hat was on the ground before him, filled with papers, and there was not even a dog for an audi-ence, nor anyone within hearing, yet did he 'waste his sweetness on the desert air.' I hope it relieved his own mind. Really, it must be viewed as an essential part of a sermon that somebody should hear it; it cannot be a great benefit to the world to have sermons preached *in vacuo*.

Many years ago, I preached to enormous assemblies in King Edward's Road, Hackney[1] which was then open fields. On those occasions, the rush was perilous to life and limb, and there seemed no limit to the throngs. Half the number would have been safer. That open space has vanished, and it is the same with fields at Brixton, where, in years gone by, it was delightful to see the assembled crowds listening to the Word. Burdened with the rare trouble of drawing too many together, I have been compelled to abstain from these exercises in London, but not from any lessened sense of their importance. With the Tabernacle always full, I have

[1] See *The Early Years*, p. 295.

as large a congregation as I desire at home, and therefore do not preach outside except in the country; but for those ministers whose area under cover is but small, and whose congregations are thin, the open air is the remedy, whether in London or in the provinces.

My friend, Mr. Abraham, once produced for me a grand cathedral in Oxfordshire. The remains of it are still called 'Spurgeon's Tabernacle,' and may be seen near Minster Lovell, in the form of a quadrilateral of oaks. Originally, it was the *beau ideal* of a preaching-place, for it was a cleared spot in the thick forest of Wychwood, and was reached by roads cut through the dense underwood. I shall never forget those 'alleys green' and the verdant walls which shut them in. When you reached the inner temple, it consisted of a large square, out of which the underwood and smaller trees had been cut away, while a sufficient number of young oaks had been left to rise to a considerable height, and then overshadow us with their branches. Here was a really magnificent cathedral, with pillars and arches: a temple not made with hands, of which we might truly say—

> *Father, Thy hand*
> *Hath reared these venerable columns, Thou*
> *Didst weave this verdant roof.*

I have never, either at home or on the Continent, seen architecture which could rival my cathedral. 'Lo, we heard of it at Ephratah: we found it in the fields of the wood.' The blue sky was visible through our clerestory, and from the great window at the further end, the sun smiled upon us toward evening. It was grand, indeed, to worship thus beneath the vaulted firmament, beyond the sound of city hum, where everything around us ministered to quiet fellowship with God. That spot is now cleared, and the place of our assembly has been selected at a little distance from it. It is of much the same character, only that my boundary walls of forest growth have disappeared, to give place to an open expanse of ploughed fields. Only the pillars and the roof of my temple remain, but I am still glad, like the Druids, to worship among the oak trees. One year, a dove had built her nest just above my head; and she continued flying to and fro, to feed her young, while the sermon proceeded. Why not? Where should she be more at home than where the Lord of love and Prince of peace was adored? It is true, my arched cathedral is not waterproof, and other showers besides those of grace have sometimes descended upon the congregation, but this has its advantages, for it makes us the more grateful when the day is propitious, and the very precariousness of the weather excites a large amount of earnest prayer.

I once preached a sermon, in the open air, in haying time, during a violent storm of rain. The text was, 'He shall come down like rain upon the mown grass: as showers that water the earth,' and surely we had the blessing as well as the inconvenience. I was sufficiently wet, and my congregation must have been drenched; but they stood it out, and I never heard that anybody was the worse in health, though, I thank God, I have heard of souls brought to Jesus under that discourse. Once in a while, and under strong excitement, such things do no one any harm; but we are not to expect miracles, nor wantonly venture upon a course of procedure which might kill the sickly, and lay the foundations of disease in the strong.

I well remember preaching between the Cheddar Cliffs. What a noble position! What beauty and sublimity! But there was great danger from falling pieces of stone, moved by the people who sat upon the higher portions of the cliff, and hence I would not choose such a spot again. Concluding a discourse in that place, I called upon those mighty rocks to bear witness that I had preached the gospel to the people, and to be a testimony against them at the last great day, if they rejected the message. Many years afterwards, I heard of a person to whom that appeal was made useful by the Holy Spirit.

[Pastor T. B. Field has kindly furnished the following particulars relating to that memorable visit to Cheddar, on September 10, 1862. The spot chosen for the afternoon service was a natural amphitheatre at the entrance to the cliffs, and it was estimated that at least ten thousand persons were present. A temporary platform had been erected for the preacher, and Spurgeon commenced the service by saying, 'Let us make these old rocks resound to the praise of God.' The first hymn was, 'All people that on earth do dwell'; and another that was sung was, 'Rock of ages, cleft for me.'

The text—John 14. 6, 'I am the way, the truth, and the life: no man cometh unto the Father, but by me'—was written on a great scroll, and fastened to the side of a house, so that the whole congregation could see it. About fifteen hundred persons remained to tea in the Baptist Chapel and burial-ground; and, at the evening service, held in a tent on Bridge Hill just above the cliffs, there was again an enormous crowd. The sermon was upon 'The lifting up of the bowed down,' the text being taken from Luke 13. 11–13. One sentence in the discourse has been remembered even to the present day: 'All the devils in hell could not make the woman crooked again after the Lord had made her straight.'

Mr. Field closes his account of the notable day by saying, 'Such crowds have never been seen in Cheddar since; and the good folks of that little town consider that they have been favoured above many, for the prince of preachers has been there. Mr. Spurgeon's visit has had great influence upon the place; and from that time the Baptist community there has been and still is the most influential church for miles round.]

It would be very easy to prove that revivals of religion have usually been accompanied, if not caused, by a considerable amount of preaching out of doors, or in unusual places. The first avowed proclamation of Protestant doctrine was almost necessarily in the open air, or in buildings which were not dedicated to worship, for these were in the hands of the Papacy. True, Wycliffe for a while preached the gospel in the church of Lutterworth; and Huss, and Jerome, and Savonarola for a time delivered semi-gospel addresses in connection with the ecclesiastical arrangements around them; but when they began more fully to know the gospel, and to publish it abroad, they were driven to find other platforms. The Reformation, when yet a babe, was like the newborn Christ, and had not where to lay its head; but a company of men, comparable to the heavenly host, proclaimed it under the open heavens, where shepherds and common people heard them gladly. Throughout England, we have several trees still remaining, which are called 'gospel oaks'. I have myself preached at Addlestone, in Surrey, under the far-spreading boughs of an ancient oak, beneath which John Knox is said to have proclaimed the gospel during his sojourn in England.

I preached at Bristol, many years ago, in the open air; and the service was specially interesting to me from the fact that I had a repetition in my own experience of the scene which Whitefield had there witnessed long before. He said, concerning one of his sermons to the colliers at Kingswood: 'The first discovery of their being affected was, seeing the white gutters made by their tears, which plentifully fell down their black cheeks, for they had come to the service straight from the coal-pits.' I also had a crowd of sailors and colliers—men with black faces—to listen to me, and when I began to talk to them about Christ's redeeming work, I saw the tears streaming down their cheeks; they put up their hands, as if to brush away something from their faces, but really it was in order to hide their tears. It was an affecting sight to behold those rough men broken down under the preaching of the gospel, and I could fully sympathize with what Whitefield wrote concerning similar services: 'The open firmament above me, the prospect of the adjacent fields, with the sight of thousands and thousands of people, some in coaches, some on horseback, and some in the trees, and, often, all melted to tears—to which sometimes was added the solemnity of the approaching evening—this was almost too much for me to bear; and, occasionally, it quite overcame me.'

Supplementing Spurgeon's own records of preaching in the open air, many friends, in various parts of the country, supplied reminiscences of unforgettable services, but only a few of these can be inserted here. One enthusiastic Welsh brother compiled a list of the outdoor gatherings in Wales addressed by the Pastor. Many of them must have been very notable occasions; the congregations were so large that there was great difficulty in reckoning, with exactness, the number of hearers. Of one assembly, it is said that 'Mr. Spurgeon calculated that 28,000 persons were present;' and of another, 'the people estimated the crowd at 30,000 to 35,000; Mr. Spurgeon said 25,000.'

A memorable incident, connected with an open-air service at Rowlands' Castle, near Havant, Hampshire, is thus reported by Rev. D. A. Doudney, for fifty-three years the Editor of *The Gospel Magazine*. On July 12, 1859, Spurgeon preached twice, in a beautiful valley, to large congregations, and, towards the end of the evening sermon, he made a powerful appeal to his hearers in the manner that Mr. Doudney thus described: 'The valley in which we were assembled was a lovely one. It was surrounded by hills clothed with woods and verdure, and on that evening the atmosphere was perfectly calm and still. The sun, which had been shining brightly all day, was sinking in the West; and the large concourse of people, listening with fixed attention to the earnest pleadings of the young preacher, made altogether a scene which one could not easily forget; but although Mr. Spurgeon had spoken with considerable force and energy during the day, and used his noble voice so that every one of his auditors must have heard him distinctly, I, for one, had not noticed that there was a remarkable echo at the spot. The preacher, however, had evidently observed it, and he used the fact in a most effective way. When he came to the close of his last appeal, he exclaimed, with great deliberation and impressiveness, "Yea, even Nature herself confirms and repeats these gracious invitations, for she too says, again and again (here he raised his voice to its highest pitch, and shouted with wonderful power the words) Come —*Come*—Come." And, instantly, amidst the breathless silence of the congregation, the words were echoed from the hills around, again and again, until they softly died away in the distance—Come— Come—Come—Come—Come. A thrill, like an electric shock, passed through the audience, and probably most of those who were present will remember the circumstance as long as they live.'

William Cuff writes as follows of a service in a meadow at Naunton, on the Cotswold Hills:

'The first time I heard Mr. Spurgeon preach in the open air was in the year 1862. The place was at Naunton, eighteen miles from Cheltenham. I was but a lad, just then converted to God. Of course I had heard of the mighty man, and went to hear him full of wonder and expectation. The service was held in a lovely meadow, through which meanders the famous Naunton Brook. It was a faultless day, and crowds gathered from all parts round about. All classes came. Work in the fields was suspended and smock frocks were plentiful in the audience. Horses were tethered everywhere and the roads seemed blocked with all kinds of vehicles, from a four-wheel waggon to a brougham. The pulpit was a waggon. Thousands had gathered long before the time to commence the service. We waited eagerly, and so we prayed fervently for saving power to be upon preacher and people. One old man standing near me scarcely ceased praying all the time we waited. When Mr. Spurgeon stood up to commence, he said a fervent 'Amen' and 'Lord, help him'. It thrilled me.

I shall never forget the ring and tone of that musical though powerful voice as the words fell on our ears, 'Let us pray'. A profound and holy hush fell on the crowd. It was as still as death. The prayer was simple, short, mighty. Every word was heard. Every tone was felt. It lifted the mass nearer God, and transmuted the meadow into a very house of God. Sinners must have trembled, while saints rejoiced in the presence and power of the Lord. But the prayer was calm and measured. So was the pleader. Mr. Spurgeon did not look or seem the least excited. He stood there as ever he did, like a master of assemblies. The reading and exposition were very powerful, yet most simple and unaffected. Another prayer, not long, but a tender intensely earnest plea that souls might then and there be saved. Then came the text and the sermon—Acts 14. 9, 10, 'The same heard Paul speak: who steadfastly beholding him and perceiving that he had faith to be healed, said with a loud voice, Stand upright on thy feet. And he leaped up and walked'.

Oh, how he did preach! His rich melodious voice seemed more mellow and musical than ever as it sounded and swelled over the audience in sweetest cadences, rising and falling in rousing and melting tones. It swayed and moved the mass of people, and rang round the meadow, and echoed back from the little hills above the valley with majesty and power both human and Divine, for the Lord was there. It was heaven on earth to be there. Ah me! it is only a memory now; but it is very vivid and it abides amongst the most precious treasures of my life. It stirred my soul to its very depths and I there and then vowed that I would preach Jesus Christ as he did, if that could be possible to me.'

William Cuff subsequently became a student at the Pastors' College and then minister of Shoreditch Tabernacle. His testimony, written after Spurgeon's death, is representative of the many Christians whose lives were profoundly influenced by hearing the Word of God through Spurgeon: 'I loved our glorified President from the first time I met him, and I have always said that, under God, I owe to him everything I have done in the Lord's work. The Shoreditch Tabernacle is his far more than it is mine, for it would never have been built but for C. H. Spurgeon. What could I have been, or done, but for the Pastors' College? Those who knew me in my early days know best what the College did for me. I can only lovingly and gratefully revere the memory of Mr. Spurgeon, and bless the Lord that I ever knew him.'

It appears to us that the maintenance of a truly spiritual College is probably the readiest way in which to bless the churches. Granting the possibility of planting such an institution, you are no longer in doubt as to the simplest mode of influencing for good the church and the world. We are certainly not singular in this opinion, for to successful workers in all times the same method has occurred. Without citing the abundant incidents of earlier times, let us remember the importance which John Calvin attached to the College at Geneva. Not by any one of the Reformers personally could the Reformation have been achieved, but they multiplied themselves in their students, and so fresh centres of light were created. In modern times, it is significant that the labours of Carey and Marsham necessitated the founding of Serampore College; while the gracious work in Jamaica called for a somewhat similar institution at Calabar. Wherever a great principle is to be advanced, prudence suggests the necessity of training the men who are to become advancers of it. Our Lord and Saviour did just the same when he elected twelve to be always with him, in order that, by superior instructions, they might become leaders of the church.—C.H.S.

7

The Pastors' College, 1861–1878

WHEN the Tabernacle was opened, the students migrated from the house of Mr. George Rogers to the class-rooms in the new sanctuary, and the Pastor took an early opportunity of bringing the work of the College more distinctly before his church and congregation than he had previously done. On Lord's day morning, May 19, 1861, in reminding his hearers of the object for which the collection had been announced, Spurgeon said:

'It has been thought desirable that I should state a few particulars relative to our Institution for training young men for the ministry. Some five or six years ago, one of the young men of our church gave promise of being a successful minister if he could but have a good education. With the assistance of two friends, I resolved to take him under my charge, send him to a suitable tutor, and train him for the ministry. So useful was that brother, that I was induced to take another, and another, and another. Hitherto, I have been myself committee, secretary, treasurer, and subscriber. I have not, except in one or two instances, even mentioned the matter to anyone; but have been content to spare everything that I could out of my own income, beyond that which is necessary for the support of my household, in order to educate any suitable young men who came in my way, that they might become ministers of the cross of Christ. There are now seven settled out, all of whom have been eminently successful. They are probably not men who will become great or brilliant, but they have been good and useful preachers. I think there are not other seven in the whole Baptist denomination who have had so many converts during the years that they have been settled. They have been the means, most of them, in the hands of God, of adding many members every year to the churches of which they are pastors; and most of those churches are not in provincial towns, but in villages. I have therefore been led still further to increase my number of students, and I have now about sixteen young men wholly to support and train. Beside these, there is a very considerable number of brethren who receive their education in the evening, though they still remain in their own callings. With the wider sphere we now occupy as a church, I propose so to enlarge my scheme that all the members of this church and congregation, who happen to be deficient in the plain rudiments of knowledge, can get an education—a common English education—for themselves. Then, if they display any ability for speaking, without giving up their daily avocations, they shall have classes provided for higher branches of instruction. But should they feel that God has called them to the ministry, I am then prepared—after the use of my own judgment, and the judgment of my friends, as to whether they are fit persons—to give them two years' special tutorship, that they may go forth to preach the Word, thoroughly trained so far as we can effect it in so short a time. I know I am called to this work, and I have had some most singular interpositions of Providence in furnishing funds for it hitherto.'

Generous gifts were contributed following this statement of the work of the College and thereafter the church became publicly united with their pastor's call to train men for the ministry. In this connection a resolution of the church on July 1, 1861, noted: 'Hitherto this good work has been rather a private service for the Lord than one in which the members have had a share; but the church hereby adopts it as part of its own system of Evangelical labours, promises its pecuniary aid, and its constant and earnest prayers.'

Spurgeon, the President of the College Institution, often referred to it as 'his first born and best beloved'. In the pages which follow we continue the narrative in his own words.

It is a grand assistance to our College that it is connected with an active and vigorous Christian church. If union to such a church does not quicken the student's spiritual pulse, it is his own fault. It is a serious strain upon a man's spirituality to be dissociated, during his student-life, from actual Christian work, and from fellowship with more experienced believers. At the Pastors' College, our brethren can not only meet, as they do every day, for prayer by themselves, but they can unite daily in the prayer-meetings of the church, and can assist in earnest efforts of all sorts. Through living in the midst of a church which, despite its faults, is a truly living, intensely zealous, working organization, they gain enlarged ideas, and form practical habits. Even to see church-management and church-work upon an extensive scale, and to share in the prayers and sympathies of a large community of Christian people, must be a stimulus to right-minded men. It has often done me good to hear the students say that they had been warned against losing their spirituality during their College course; but they had, on the contrary, proved that their piety had been deepened and increased through association with their brethren and the many godly men and women with whom they were constantly brought into contact. Our circumstances are peculiarly helpful to growth in grace, and we are grateful to have our Institution so happily surrounded by them.

Encouraged by the readiness with which the first students found spheres of labour, and by their singular success in soul-winning, I enlarged the number, but the whole means of sustaining them came from my own purse.[1] The large sale of my sermons in America, together with my dear wife's economy, enabled me to spend from £600 to £800 a year in my own favourite work; but on a sudden, owing to my denunciations of the then existing slavery in the States, my entire resources from that 'brook Cherith' were dried up. I paid as large sums as I could from my own income, and resolved to spend all I had, and then take the cessation of my means as a voice from the Lord to stay the effort, as I am firmly persuaded that we ought under no pretence to go into debt. On one occasion, I proposed the sale of my horse and carriage, although these were almost absolute necessaries to me on account of my continual journeys in preaching the Word. This my friend Mr. Rogers would not hear of, and actually offered to be the loser rather than this should be done. Then it was that I told my difficulties to my people, and the weekly offering commenced, but the incomings from that source were so meagre as to be hardly worth calculating upon. I was brought to the last pound, when a letter came from a banker in the City, informing me that a lady, whose name I have never been able to discover, had deposited a sum of £200, to be used for the education of young men for the ministry. How did my heart leap for joy! I threw myself then and henceforth upon the bounteous care of the Lord, whom I desired with my whole heart to glorify by this effort. Some weeks later, another £100 came in from the same bank, as I was informed, from another hand. Soon afterwards, a beloved deacon of the church at the Tabernacle began to provide

[1] That is, in the period prior to July, 1861. Truthfully he could write: 'At the day of judgment the world shall know that there has never lived a man upon the face of the earth who has less deserved the calumny of "seeking to enrich himself" than I have.'

an annual supper for the friends of the College, at which considerable sums have from year to year been contributed. A dinner was also given by my liberal publishers, Messrs. Passmore and Alabaster, to celebrate the issue of my five-hundredth weekly sermon, at which £500 was raised and presented to the funds. The College grew every month, and the number of students rapidly advanced. Friends known and unknown, from far and near, were moved to give little or much to my work, and so the supplies increased as the need enlarged. Then another earnest deacon of the church espoused as his special work the weekly offering, which has been, for many years, a steady source of income. There have been, during this period, times of great trial of my faith; but, after a season of straitness, never amounting to absolute want, the Lord has always interposed, and sent me large sums (on one occasion, £1,000) from unknown donors.

Pecuniary needs, however, have made up but a small part of my cares. Many have been my personal exercises in selecting the men. Candidates have always been plentiful, and the choice has been wide; but it is a serious responsibility to reject any, and yet more so to accept them for training. When mistakes have been made, a second burden has been laid upon me in the dismissal of those who appeared to be unfit. Even with the most careful management, and all the assistance of tutors and friends, no human foresight can secure that, in every case, a man shall be what we believed and hoped. A brother may be exceedingly useful as an occasional preacher, he may distinguish himself as a diligent student, he may succeed at first in the ministry, and yet, when trials of temper and character occur in the pastorate, he may be found wanting. We have had comparatively few causes for regret of this sort; but there have been some such, and these have pierced us with many sorrows. I devoutly bless God that He has sent to the College some of the holiest, soundest, and most self-denying preachers I know, and I pray that He may continue to do so; but it would be more than a miracle if all should excel.

In dealing with aspirants for the ministry, I have constantly to fulfil the duty which fell to the lot of Cromwell's 'Triers'. I have to form an opinion as to the advisability of aiding certain men in their attempts to become pastors. This is a most responsible duty, and one which requires no ordinary care. Of course, I do not set myself up to judge whether a man shall enter the ministry or not, but my examination merely aims at answering the question whether the

Pastors' College shall help him or leave him to his own resources. Certain of our charitable neighbours accuse me of having 'a parson manufactory,' but the charge is not true at all. I never tried to make a minister, and should fail if I did; I receive none into the College but those who profess to be ministers already. It would be nearer the truth if they called me 'a parson-killer,' for a goodly number of beginners have received their quietus from me; and I have the fullest ease of conscience in reflecting upon what I have so done. It has often been a hard task for me to discourage a hopeful young brother who has applied for admission to the College. My heart has always leaned to the kindest side, but duty to the churches has compelled me to judge with severe discrimination. After hearing what the candidate has had to say, having read his testimonials and seen his replies to questions, when I have felt convinced that the Lord has not called him, I have been obliged to tell him so.

I had a curious experience with one applicant. His pastor had given him an open letter, warmly commending him to me as a man called to the ministry; but, in another communication, sent to me by post, the minister wrote that the young man was not at all likely ever to become a preacher, and that he had only written the recommendation because the candidate's father was his chief deacon, and he feared to offend him by telling him the truth. I felt that it was quite unjust to put upon me the onus of refusing the young man; so, when he arrived, I gave him the epistle I had received, and left him and his father to settle the matter with their pastor in the best way they could.

Physical infirmities raise a question about the call of some excellent men. I would not, like Eurysthenes, judge men by their features, but their general physique is no small criterion, and I feel assured that, when a man has a contracted chest, with no distance between his shoulders, the all-wise Creator did not intend him habitually to preach. If He had meant him to speak, He would have given him, in some measure, breadth of chest sufficient to yield a reasonable amount of lung force. A man who can scarcely get through a sentence without pain, can hardly be called to 'cry aloud, and spare not.' Brethren with defective mouths and imperfect articulation are not usually qualified to preach the gospel. The same rule applies to brethren with no palate, or an imperfect one. I once had an application for admission to the College from a young man who had a sort of rotary action of his jaw, of the most painful sort to the beholder. His pastor commended him as a very holy man, who had been the means of bringing some to Christ, and he expressed the hope that I would receive him, but I could not see the propriety of it. I could not have looked at him, while he was preaching, without laughter, if all the gold of Tarshish had been my reward, and in all probability nine out of ten of his hearers would have been more sensitive than myself. A man with a big tongue which filled up his mouth and caused indistinctness, another without teeth, another who stammered, another who could not pronounce all the alphabet, I have had the pain of declining on the ground that God had not given them those physical appliances which are, as the Prayerbook would put it, 'generally necessary.'

One brother I have encountered—one did I say?—I have met ten, twenty, a hundred brethren, who have pleaded that they were quite sure that they were called to the ministry—because they had failed in everything else! This is a sort of model story: 'Sir, I was put into a lawyer's office, but I never could bear the confinement, and I could not feel at home in studying law. Providence clearly stopped up my road, for I lost my situation.' 'And what did you do then?' 'Why, sir, I was induced to open a grocer's shop.' 'And did you prosper?' 'Well, I do not think, sir, I was ever meant for trade; and the Lord seemed quite to shut up my way there, for I failed, and was in great difficulties. Since then, I have done a little in a life-assurance agency, and tried to get up a school, beside selling tea, but my path is hedged up, and something within me makes me feel that I ought to be a minister.' My answer generally is, 'Yes, I see; you have failed in everything else, and therefore you think the Lord has especially endowed you for His service; but I fear you have forgotten that the ministry needs the very best of men, and not those who cannot do anything else.' A man who would succeed as a preacher would probably do right well either as a grocer, or a lawyer, or anything else. A really valuable minister would have excelled in any occupation. There is scarcely anything impossible to a man who can keep a congregation together for years, and be the means of edifying them for hundreds of consecutive Sabbaths; he must be possessed of some abilities, and be by no means a fool or a ne'er-do-well. Jesus Christ deserves the best men to preach His gospel, and not the empty-headed and the shiftless.

I do believe that some fellows have a depression in their craniums where there ought to be a bump. I know one young man who tried hard to get into the College, but his mind had so strange a twist that he never could see how it was possible to join things together unless he tied them by their tails. He brought out a book; and when I read it, I found at once that it was full of my stories and illustrations; that is to say, every illustration or story in the book was one that I had used, but there was not one of them that was related as it ought to have been. This man had so told the story that it was not there at all; the very point which I had brought out he had carefully omitted, and every bit of it was told correctly except the one thing that was the essence of the whole. Of course, I was glad that I did not have that brother in the College; he might have been an ornament to us by his deficiencies, but we can do without such ornaments; indeed, we have had enough of them already.

One young gentleman, with whose presence I was once honoured, has left on my mind the photograph of his exquisite self. That face of his looked like the title-page to a whole volume of *conceit* and *deceit*. He sent word into my vestry one Sabbath morning that he must see me at once. His audacity admitted him; and when he was before me, he said, 'Sir, I want to enter your College, and should like to enter it at once.' 'Well, sir,' I said, 'I fear we have no room for you at present, but your case shall be considered.' 'But mine is a very remarkable case, sir; you have probably never received such an application as mine before.' 'Very good, we'll see about it; the secretary will give you one of the application papers, and you can see me on Monday.' He came on the Monday, bringing with him the questions, answered in a most extraordinary manner. As to books, he claimed to have read all ancient and modern literature, and after giving an immense list, he added, 'This is merely a selection; I have read most extensively in all departments.' As to his preaching, he could produce the highest testimonials, but hardly thought they would be needed, as a personal interview would convince me of his ability at once. His surprise was great when I said, 'Sir, I am obliged to tell you that I cannot receive you.' 'Why not, sir?' 'I will tell you plainly. You are so dreadfully clever that I could not insult you by receiving you into our College, where we have none but rather ordinary men; the President, tutors, and students, are all men of moderate attainments, and you would have to condescend too much in coming among us.' He looked at me very severely, and said with dignity, 'Do you mean to say that, because I have an unusual genius, and have produced in myself a gigantic mind such as is rarely seen, I am refused admittance into your College?' 'Yes,' I replied, as calmly as I could, considering the overpowering awe which his genius inspired, 'for that very reason.'

'Then, sir, you ought to allow me a trial of my preaching abilities; select me any text you like, or suggest any subject you please, and here, in this very room, I will speak upon it, or preach upon it without deliberation, and you will be surprised.' 'No, thank you, I would rather not have the trouble of listening to you.' 'Trouble, sir! I assure you it would be the greatest possible pleasure you could have.' I said it might be, but I felt myself unworthy of the privilege, and so bade him a long farewell. The gentleman was unknown to me at the time, but he has since figured in the police court as too clever by half.

Beside those brethren who apply to me for admission to the College, I am often consulted by others who wish me to say whether I think they ought or ought not to preach, and I have more than once felt myself in the position of the Delphic oracle—not wishing to give wrong advice, and therefore hardly able to give any. I had an enquiry from a brother whose minister told him he ought not to preach, and yet he felt that he must do so. I thought I would be safe in the reply I gave him, so I simply said to him, 'My brother, if God has opened your mouth, the devil cannot shut it, but if the devil has opened it, I pray the Lord to shut it directly.' Some time afterwards, I was preaching in the country, and, after the service, a young man came up to me, and thanked me for encouraging him to go on preaching. For the moment, I did not recall the circumstances, so he reminded me of the first part of my reply to his enquiry. 'But,' I said, 'I also told you that, if the devil had opened your mouth, I prayed the Lord to shut it.' 'Ah!' he exclaimed, 'but that part of the message did not apply to me.'

From quite the early days of the College, I arranged for a regular course of lectures on physical science; and many of the brethren have thanked me, not only for the knowledge thus imparted, but also for the wide field of illustration which was thereby thrown open to them. The study of astronomy, as illustrative of Scriptural truth, proved specially interesting. The science itself was very helpful to many of the students. I remember one brother who seemed to be a dreadful dolt; we really thought he never would learn anything, and that we should have to give him up in despair. But I introduced to him a little book called *The Young Astronomer*; and he afterwards said that, as he read it, he felt just as if something had cracked inside his head, or as if some string had been snapped. He had laid hold of such enlarged ideas that I believe his cranium did actually experience an expansion which it ought to have undergone in his child-hood, and which it did undergo by the marvellous force of the thoughts suggested by the study of even the elements of astronomical science. Another student, who evidently had not paid very special attention to the lecturer, wondered whether that star, which always hung just over his chapel, was Jupiter! Of course, the result of his foolish question was that 'Jupiter' became his nickname ever afterwards, even though he was not 'a bright particular' star in our College constellations.

I have often noticed one thing in some who have seemed unable to understand even the elements of science; the Holy Spirit has taught them the Word of God, and they are clear enough about that. When we have been reading a chapter out of some old Puritanic book, or when we have been diving into the depths of theology, these brethren have given me the smartest and sharpest answers of the whole class. When we have been dealing with things experimental and controversial, I find that these men have been able to vanquish their opponents at once, because they are deeply read in the Word of God. The Spirit has taught them the things of Christ, if He has not taught them anything else.

One night, Mr. Selway, in the course of the experiments with which he enlivened his lectures, playfully turned a little jet of water on to one of the students, little dreaming what would be the consequences of the harmless pleasantry which had amused successive batches of the men who had listened to him in the room just at the back of the lower platform in the Tabernacle. In an instant, the young man, who was sitting near the table on which stood the glass tubes, jars, and other apparatus used by the lecturer, swept the whole mass to the floor in a terrific crash before anyone could be aware of his intention, much less prevent him from carrying it into effect. It was a sad exhibition of an ungovernable temper which, I greatly fear, in after years, cost the student far more than the price of the destroyed apparatus which he was required to replace. Mr. Selway, who was a singularly calm, self-possessed individual, simply said, 'That young *gentleman* will some day be sorry for what he has done,' and then proceeded with his lecture—of course, without any more experiments that evening!

Bad as this display of passion was, there was one student who did something which, in certain respects, was worse, for there was an element of deliberation about it which was absent on the other occasion. It has long been our rule that each brother should read in the College at least one discourse which he has himself composed, and which his comrades are expected to criticise. Any attempt at plagiarism would, therefore, be manifestly unfair; and, if detected, would meet with well-merited condemnation. One man, when it came to his turn, was actually reckless and foolish enough to take one of my printed sermons—I suppose condensed—and to read it as though it had been his own composition; and he had to thank his brethren that he was not instantly expelled from the Institution. Several of them at once recognized the discourse; and, as soon as the time for criticism arrived, proceeded to pull it to pieces most mercilessly. They found fault with the introduction, the divisions, the sub-divisions, the illustrations, the application—with everything in fact except the doctrine; I think that was all right! I was so pleased with the critical acumen displayed that I forgave the offender, but I let it be distinctly understood that, for the future, any student repeating the offence, whether with my sermon or anyone else's, would be forthwith dismissed in disgrace.

As a rule, the men who have come to the College have been so anxious to make the best use of their time while with us, that they have laboured at their studies most diligently, but occasionally we have had a lazy student who has tried to shirk his class and other work. One who, in his day, was a conspicuous instance of this lack of appreciation of the privileges placed within his reach, had an experience which ought to have made him both a sadder and a wiser man, though I am not sure that it had either effect. When the other brethren, who resided in the same house, were preparing their lessons, he so often interrupted them with questions about the translation of simple words with which he ought to have been perfectly familiar that one of them determined to try to cure him of the practice. On that particular occasion, he came to enquire the meaning of the Latin word '*omnibus.*' 'Oh!' said the young wag, 'that's easy enough; *omni*—twenty-six, and *bus*—to carry; *omnibus,* a vehicle to carry twenty-six persons! You know that you constantly see the notice in the omnibus, "licensed to carry twenty-six persons." '. The next morning, it so happened that Mr. Gracey asked the lazy man to translate the very passage which contained the word '*omnibus*'. In due course, he gave the rendering which had been supplied to him, with a result that can be better imagined than described.

If he was not diligent in one respect, he was certainly industrious in another direction, and he managed to get engaged to three ladies at once! As soon as I knew of it, I sent for him, and told him that he must make his choice, and I hoped the other two would sue him for breach of promise. I never heard that they did so, and probably they were well rid of a man who could trifle with them in such a fashion. He appeared to do well for a time in the ministry, but he afterwards left the Baptist denomination, and therefore is not now numbered in our ranks.

At one of our closing meetings at the College, before the brethren went away for their vacation, I said that I was a poor man, or I would give every student a present, and I told them what I would have selected if I had been rich. I remember one brother to whom I said that I would give him a corkscrew, because he had a good deal in him, but he could not get it out. 'As to you, my brother,' I said to another student, 'I should give you a sausage-stuffer, for you need to have something put into you.' There was one friend to whom I should have liked to present a canister of Chapman and Hall's gunpowder. He was to have two pounds of it, and someone was to set it alight exactly at the second head of his discourse. Of course, the brethren were amused at the idea, but I advised them to read Foxe's *Book of Martyrs*, where the historian records that Bishop Hooper, and others who were burned, had friends who came with bags of gunpowder, to put under their arms when they were going to the stake. I did not want the students to be made to die, but to be made thoroughly alive, and I promised to talk to my wife about supplying dynamite as well as books to poor ministers, so that they might be stirred up, and made a blessing to their hearers.

I have had some amusing experiences with deacons in search of a minister. One wrote to ask if I would send a student who could 'fill the chapel.' I replied that I had not one big enough, and added that I thought it was the business of the people to try to gather the congregation, but that I could send a brother who would do his best to fill the pulpit, and preach the gospel faithfully. In his next letter, the deacon explained that this was just what he and the church wanted, only he had failed to express his meaning clearly.

At one place, where a student—a brother of no little ability—had preached with considerable acceptance, he was informed that, if he had been a bigger man, he would have been invited to the pastorate! I really could not blame him when I heard that, in reply to this very foolish objection, he said to the deacons, 'If Mr. Spurgeon had known that you wanted bulk instead of brains, he would have sent you a bullock!' He might have told them that, in looking for quantity, instead of quality, they might, possibly, find themselves burdened with the support of a donkey!

The officers of a small church in the country applied to me for a minister; but the salary they were prepared to pay was so small that, in reply to their request, I wrote: 'The only individual I know, who could exist on such a stipend, is the angel Gabriel. He would need neither cash nor clothes; and he could come down from heaven every Sunday morning, and go back at night, so I advise you to invite him.' The corresponding deacon of another church, which was needing a pastor, sent me such a long list of the qualifications that must be possessed by the man whom they could look up to as their leader, that I recommended him to take a large sheet of brown paper, and cut out a minister of the size and shape desired, or else to seek to secure the services of the eminent Dr. So-and-so, who had been for a good many years in glory, for I could not think of anyone else who could fulfil the conditions that such an important church and diaconate seemed to regard as indispensable. Like one of the other deacons, he also wrote again; and his second letter being more reasonable than the first, I was able to recommend a brother with whom the church appeared to be perfectly satisfied.

*

One of Spurgeon's students, W. D. McKinney, who later became a pastor at Ansonia, Connecticut, U.S.A., has written the following graphic description of the ever-memorable Friday afternoon classes when the President addressed the students:

'*Friday afternoon* came at last. The old, familiar clock pointed to three: the door opened on the stroke of the hour, the beloved President appeared, and walked up to the desk—Dr. Gill's pulpit—while hands clapped, feet stamped, and voices cheered, till he had to hold up his hand, and say, "Now, gentlemen, do you not think that is enough? The floor is weak, the ceiling is not very high, and, I am sure, you need all the strength you have for your labours."

In those days, the President was in his prime. His step was firm, his eyes bright, his hair dark and abundant, his voice full of sweetest music and sacred merriment. Before him were gathered a hundred men from all parts of the United Kingdom, and not a few from beyond the seas. They were brought together by the magic of his name, and the attraction of his personal influence. His fame had gone out into all lands. His sermons were published in almost all languages. Many sitting before him were his own sons in the faith. Among his students he was at his ease, as a father in the midst of his own family. The brethren loved him, and he loved them.

Soon, the floods of his pent-up wisdom poured forth; the flashes of his inimitable wit lit up every face, and his pathos brought tears to all eyes. It was an epoch in student-life to hear him deliver his *Lectures to my Students*. What weighty and wise discourse he gave us on the subject of preaching! How gently he corrected faults, and encouraged genuine diffidence! What withering sarcasm for all fops and pretenders! Then came those wonderful imitations of the dear brethren's peculiar mannerisms: one with the hot dumpling in his mouth, trying to speak; another, sweeping his hand up and down from nose to knee; a third, with his hands under his coat-tails, making the figure of a water-wagtail. Then the one with his thumbs in the armholes of his waistcoat, showing the "penguin" style of oratory. By this means, he held the mirror before us so that we could see our faults, yet all the while we were almost convulsed with laughter. He administered the medicine in effervescing draughts.

After this, came the wise counsel, so kind, so grave, so gracious, so fatherly; then the prayer that lifted us to the mercy-seat, where we caught glimpses of glory, and talked face to face with the Master Himself. Afterwards, the giving out of the appointments for the next Lord's day took place; the class was dismissed for tea, and then came the men who wanted advice. Some were in trouble, others in joy; and the President listened patiently to all their tales; anon he would laugh, and then he would weep. At last, he is through, "weary in the work, but not weary of it." His cheery voice gradually dies away as he ascends the stairs to his "sanctum." We did not grieve as we parted from him; for we knew that, God willing, on the next Friday afternoon, we should once more see his bright, genial face, and hear his wit and wisdom again.'

*

The list of students in the College at this early period contained the names of men of God who left their mark upon the age, and whose work as preachers and soul-winners, or as teachers of others, is only second to that of Spurgeon himself. Four of those names stand out conspicuously, David Gracey (who was 'called home' one year after Spurgeon), Frank H. White, Archibald G. Brown, and Charles B. Sawday.

Frank White wrote for this volume the following reminiscences of his student-days:

'Early in 1862, Mr. Henry Hull—who was himself a master in the blessed art of soul-winning—wrote to Mr. Spurgeon with a view to my admission to the Pastors' College. An appointment for an interview was soon made, and with some fear and trembling (for the first and last time—for I never afterwards trembled in his presence, except with delight) I stood before the great preacher in his vestry at the Tabernacle. "The very man I want," was his hearty exclamation the instant I entered the room. I do not remember anything else he said, except, "You must go to Paradise Chapel, Chelsea, next Sunday." Accordingly, to Paradise Chapel I went; and that little riverside sanctuary became a very Eden to me, though its surroundings were often quite the reverse of paradisaical. Only eighteen persons were present at the first morning service at Chelsea; but, by the grace and power of the Lord the Spirit, some eight hundred were baptized before my ministry in that part closed.

What happy days were those we spent in College, and with what eagerness did we, after the intense strain of the study and work of the week, look forward to those delightful Friday afternoons with the President! Being fewer in number, the intercourse was closer than was possible in after days. How favoured we were even in the ordinary course of things. But what of those special opportunities, such as a six-days' driving tour, which was once my happy lot? The letter of invitation is before me now.

"Dear Mr. White,

I am expecting you at my house, at 8 a.m. next Monday, to go for a week's drive. I have reserved a seat in the carriage for you, which I could have filled with some other friend, so that you must not feel free to decline under any consideration whatever. Your charges will all be paid, and your company appreciated. Not to have you with me, would grievously afflict—

Your loving friend,
C. H. SPURGEON.

Breakfast at Nightingale Lane at 8; bound to me till Saturday evening; may reach home by 6 on that evening."

Think whether a poor, worn-out, hard-worked student—such as

Archibald Brown, or myself—would be glad to receive such a command, or not. I must leave it to an abler pen than mine to describe those drives from day to day; but to me, they were indescribably joyous. The very trees of the field clapped their hands; and we were closely examined as to their nomenclature, and then most delightfully instructed as to their peculiarities and characteristics. I wish I could recall some of the dear Governor's conversations as we rode along, but I do remember one thing that he said. We were close by the spot where the Bishop of Winchester fell from his horse, and was killed; and Mr. Spurgeon said that he had just received a letter from a clergyman, who informed him that his bodily sufferings were a judgment from God upon him for speaking against the Church of England. In replying to his unfeeling correspondent, he had asked—If a swollen hand or foot was to be regarded as a mark of Divine displeasure, what was to be said concerning a broken neck? Needless to say, that question remained unanswered.'

Archibald Brown has preserved the following letter inviting him to form one of the party on another of those memorable driving tours:

'Nightingale Lane,
Clapham,
May 23

Dear Friend,

    Will you go out with me and others, on June 15, for a week, or two weeks, or three weeks, or a few days, or whatever time you like? We feel that we should like your company, and we think we might do you good. You are very dear to us; to *me* especially. We shall be very quiet, and jog along with the old greys.

    I pray the Lord to bless and comfort you.

Yours so heartily,
C. H. Spurgeon.'

Two other letters show what a true yoke-fellow Brown was to his beloved President, and with what intense affection and esteem Spurgeon regarded his former student:

'Nightingale Lane,
Clapham

Loving Brother,

    I thank you much for preaching for me, praying for me, and

loving me. I am better, but have had a sharp nip. Lucian says, "I thought a cobra had bitten me, and filled my veins with poison; but it was worse—*it was gout.*" *That was written from experience, I know.* Yet I bless God for this suffering also, and believe that your prophetic card will be truer than Dr. Cumming's vaticinations.

Yours ever lovingly,
C. H. S.'

'Nightingale Lane,
Clapham,
January 29th

Three cheers for you, my true-hearted comrade! The story of your East London gathering of the clans fills me with delight. The Lord be with thee, thou mighty man of valour! Whether, in striking the Spiritualists, you are hitting the devil or a donkey, does not matter much; you have evidently hit hard, or they would not be so fierce. I am not able to take much credit for bringing you up, but I am about as proud of you as I dare be.

I hope we shall have a good meeting on Friday week. It is oil to my bones to see you all.

Yours always lovingly,
C. H. SPURGEON.'

The fourth of the notable students of 1862 was Charles Sawday. Spurgeon wrote to his father when the question of a College training for his son was under discussion:

'Clapham,
April 12th, '62

My Dear Sir,

I scarcely wonder at your preference of Regent's Park College for your son, but I think you labour under some mistake, for it so happens that the ground of your choice is just one of the evils which my Institute seeks to remedy.

The residence of a number of young men in one house encourages and necessarily generates levity; their separation from common social life is a serious injury, and tends to unfit them for the wear and tear of future work among ordinary mortals. When a young man resides in a Christian family, not only is he under the most vigilant oversight, but he never ceases to be one of the people. We are far from putting our men into the way of temptation; on the other hand, we think our arrangement is the most effectual method of preservation. I merely write this because your brief acquaintance with our system may allow me to suppose that this view of the case has not suggested itself to you.

Our tutors are sound scholars; but, as we do not aim at any very profound scholarship, we allot but two years to the course. The young men who have left us have been very useful, and the class now in hand will bear comparison with any body of men living.

I could not, while possessing any self-respect, prepare your son for Dr. Angus;[1] but I shall be delighted to be of any other service to him.

Yours most truly,
C. H. SPURGEON.'

The solution of the problem is given by the subject of it in the following words: 'My dear father was prejudiced against Mr. Spurgeon; and, in his anxiety for me to receive an efficient training for the Baptist ministry, had arranged for my admission to Regent's Park College. But I had heard Mr. Spurgeon several times at the Tabernacle, and I pleaded with my father not to insist on my going to Regent's Park, and with Mr. Spurgeon to admit me to the Pastors' College. In those early days, it was no wonder that my father, whose whole religious life was spent among the Wesleyans, should have been unwilling for his son to be associated with so pronounced a Calvinist as Mr. Spurgeon was, and he had conscientious objections against contributing towards my support. The Pastor met us both, one Sunday morning, after the service, and ended the matter by saying, "Well, Mr. Sawday, your son is set on entering my College, and he shall be trained, if necessary, at my own expense." It is not surprising, therefore, that I feel that I have more cause than many of our brethren for holding in grateful love the memory of our now glorified President.'

Spurgeon could scarcely have imagined that, by this generous offer, he was preparing the way into the ministry for a man who would, for a third of a century, be greatly owned of God as a winner of souls, and, then, after his beloved President's departure, become the able and loyal assistant of *his* son and successor in the pastorate at the Metropolitan Tabernacle. Yet so it was directed by the unerring wisdom of Him who—

---

[1] Principal of Regent's Park College at that time.

Moves in a mysterious way,
His wonders to perform.

There is one series of Spurgeon's sayings to his students which must find a place here—namely, the farewell words spoken to them on leaving College, or on removing to another pastorate. The gracious and gifted William Anderson, when he was going from Warkworth to Reading, received the apostolic injunction, with a new meaning attached to it, 'Give attendance to Reading.' Mr. Dobson relates that the parting message to him was: 'Go to Deal, and fight the De'il. Hit him hard; I owe him no love.' To Harry Wood—a devoted brother whose hair was so bright that his fellow-students used playfully to gather round him to warm their hands at the fire—the President wrote from Mentone a loving letter which concluded: 'You are so well known to me that I think I see you—especially your distinguished head of hair—and I look you in the face with a tear of love in separation, and say, *God bless you, Wood! Go, and blaze away for your Lord.*'

Mr. Welton has thus recorded the remarkable message given to him, in 1867, when he accepted his first pastorate at Thetford: 'I want you to go under an operation before you leave. I am going *to put out one of your eyes, to stop up one of your ears,* and *to put a muzzle on your mouth.* Then you had better have a new suit of clothes before you go, and you must tell the tailor to make *in the coat a pocket without a bottom.* You understand my parable?' 'I think so, sir; but should like your interpretation.' 'Well, there will be many things in your people that you must look at with *the blind eye,* and you must listen to much with *the deaf ear,* while you will often be tempted to say things which had better be left unsaid; then, remember *the muzzle.* Then all the gossip you may hear, when doing pastoral work, must be put into *the bottomless pocket.*'

Several students, at different periods in the history of the College, on being sent out as pioneers to start new churches, received this singular charge: 'Cling tightly with both your hands; when they fail, catch hold with your teeth; and if they give way, hang on by your eyelashes!' Mr. Saville went to Carlisle with these words ringing in his ears, and he obeyed them all too literally. With true heroism, he would not let his dear President know the hardships he was enduring for Christ's sake and the gospel's; but someone, who discovered the plight he was in, wrote about his trials and sufferings; and as soon as the tidings reached Mr. Spurgeon, substantial help was sent to him.

This account of the earlier years of the Pastors' College would not be complete without a specimen of Spurgeon's letters to the students while in College. The following, preserved by Pastor C. L. Gordon, exerted a powerful influence upon the men to whom it was written:

'Nightingale Lane,
Clapham,
September 11th, 1865

Beloved Brethren,

I am called away from you this afternoon; and I should much regret this if it were not that it has come into my heart to suggest to you to spend our usual time in prayer, instead of in teaching and earning. My heart is often heavy with trials, arising out of the College work, which is so dear to me that I am perhaps unduly anxious over it. I am bowed to the very dust when I fear that any brother is erring in doctrine, lacking in grace, or loose in behaviour. I have as little to lament as it is possible there should be where we are all such imperfect creatures. But, my brethren, I would fain have you all the best men living; and when you are not, I am distressed exceedingly. Just now, one brother, by his general self-indulgent habits, has lost the respect of his people, and must move. I do not want to inflict a curse on another congregation, and I do not want to cast him off. Between these two courses, I am perplexed. Pray for me, for him, for all the brethren, and for yourselves.

In your society, I always feel so much at home that I must appear to you to be all happiness and mirth. Alas! it is not so; I am happy in the Lord, and blest in Him; but I am often a poor cast-down mortal, groaning under the burden of excessive labour, and sad at heart because of the follies of those whom I hoped to have seen serving the Lord with zeal and success. Do give me your warmest consideration in your supplications. Believe me when I assure you that you are, for Christ's sake, very dear to me. Do not be led away from the faith which you all professed when you entered the College. Cling to the two great collateral truths of Divine sovereignty and human responsibility. Live near to God, and love the souls of men. I make some sacrifices for your sake; but I count them gain, and my work for you is a delight. But do plead for more grace to rest on us all, and upon those settled in the ministry. Levity of conduct in my brethren brings heaviness of heart to me; and what is inconsistent pleasure to them, is terrible agony to me. Oh, how can the ministers of God be smoking and drinking when souls are dying, and talking lightness and wantonness when sinners are perishing? It must not be so among us. May the Lord prevent it! Seeking ever your soul's best interest, and desiring your fervent prayers,

I am, dearly-beloved brethren,
Your affectionate brother,
C. H. SPURGEON.'

In a lecture one has the advantage of more freedom than in a sermon. One is permitted to take a wider range of subjects, and to use an easier style than a theological discourse allows. I will use this freedom, but my aim will be the same as if I were preaching. I trust my lecture may possibly impress some minds to whom a sermon would seem too dull a business . . . I claim the right to mingle the severe with the lively, the grave with the gay. In due proportions the mixture may be taken with good effect.—C.H.S. *in Introduction to 'Sermons in Candles.'*

I suppose a 'lecture' signifies a *reading*; but enough of my brethren use manuscripts, and I will not compete with them. If I cannot speak extemporaneously I will hold my tongue. To read I am ashamed.—C.H.S.

8

Lectures and Addresses

THE first lecture given by Spurgeon, of which a full report has been preserved, was the one delivered at the Surrey Gardens Music Hall, on Tuesday evening, December 29, 1857, under the title, 'A Christian's Pleasures.' It was a bright, lively talk containing much earnest warning and solid instruction. After speaking upon the so-called pleasures which are absolutely forbidden to a believer in the Lord Jesus Christ, and of others which, though innocent, are utterly absurd and insipid, the lecturer thus referred to certain amusements concerning which there is a great dispute whether Christians ought to indulge in them:

'Some persons ask, "What do you think about dancing?" Well, I never hear the subject mentioned without having an uncomfortable feeling in my throat, for I remember that the first Baptist minister had his head danced off! I am sure I should have to be off my head before I should indulge in that pastime. The usual associations of the ball-room and dancing parties are of such a character that it is marvellous to me how Christians can ever be found taking pleasure in them. A safe rule to apply to all occupations is—"Can I take the Lord Jesus Christ with me if I go there? If not, it is no place for me as one of His followers."

Then I may be asked, "What do you think of games of chance?" Well, I always draw a distinction between games that require the exercise of skill and those that largely depend upon chance, as in the shuffling of cards and the throw of the dice. Some games are to be heartily recommended because they tend to sharpen the mental faculties; I do not think the most precise Christian ought to object to draughts or chess—if not played for money—for they help to develop and improve our powers of thought, and calculation, and judgment. Sometimes, when I am weary with my work, I take down my Euclid, and go over a few propositions; or I work out some of Bland's equations,[1] just by way of amusement. That kind of exercise

---

[1] *Algebraical Problems, Producing Simple and Quadratic Equations, with their Solutions*, by Miles Bland, D.D. On the fly-leaf of Spurgeon's copy of this work he had written,

is as much a recreation to me as running out in the fields would be to a boy at school.

In my opinion, games of skill are not objectionable, but every Christian should object to games of chance. Generally, they are played for gain, and hence they excite covetous desires, and so break the tenth commandment. With regard to the great proportion of games of chance, we hardly need discuss the question. The time has now arrived when all England ought to be heartily sick of every form of gaming. It used to be a comparatively harmless thing for ladies and gentlemen to spend all the evening over a pack of cards, or a box of dice, without any money being at stake, but we have had such practical proof that the worst crimes have sprung from this apparently inoffensive practice, that every Christian mind must revolt from it. Besides, I have always felt that the rattle of the dice in the box would remind me of that game which was played by the soldiers at the foot of Christ's cross, when they cast lots for His vesture, and parted His garments among them. He who sees His Saviour's blood splashed on the dice will never wish to meddle with them.

The mere fact that there is any question about a certain course ought to be sufficient to make us avoid it. Have you never noticed that, when people come to ask you whether a thing is right or not, they usually mean to do it themselves? Frequently, a person comes to me with some scruple of conscience, but the questioner has generally made up his mind what he is going to do before he receives my answer. More than one young person has said to me, "Mr. Spurgeon, I want to ask your advice about a very important matter. You are my minister, and I want you to tell me whether you think I ought to marry So-and-so," but, whatever counsel I may give in such cases, I am quite certain they have usually determined what they are going to do, so often I give no advice at all. Possibly you remember the case of the minister who, on one occasion, was asked by a woman whether she should marry a certain man. "Well," said he, "the best thing you can do is to go out, and listen to the bells as you walk home." As she listened to their tuneful melody, they seemed to say to her—

> *Make haste and get married,*
> *Make haste and get married—*

'C. H. Spurgeon 1848.' The volume bears manifest marks of having been well used, page after page being ticked off as 'done.' In one case, 'wrong?' is written against the answer given in the book.

so she did, and her husband horsewhipped her three weeks afterwards! Then she went again to her minister, and told him that he had given her very bad advice. "Why!" said he, "I never told you to get married; I told you to listen to the bells!" "So I did," replied the woman. "But," said the minister, "perhaps you did not hear their message aright; go and listen again." So she went out, and hearkened once more to the bells—remember, this was after the horsewhipping—and this is what they seemed to say then—

> *Never get married,*
> *Never get married.*

It is just the same with people who come to ask you about debatable amusements. Whatever you tell them, you may be sure that they have made up their minds beforehand. I would leave all such questions to a Christian's own judgment, but let him always remember that, although a thing may be right to other people, it may be wrong to him; and it is wrong to him if he has any doubts about it. The apostle Paul said, "Whatsoever is not of faith is sin;" that is, whatever a man cannot do, believing it to be right, is sin to him. If I have any doubt about anything, it is sin to me; though it may not be sinful in itself. Conscience must be the great judge on those points that do not involve morality or immorality; and we thank our God that He has given to each of us who know His Name that inward Monitor, the Holy Spirit, who is infinitely superior to our own conscience, and if we go on our knees, and ask Him for direction, we shall not be misled as to our amusements or anything else. Our Puritanical forefathers may have been a little too strict, but many, nowadays, have become a great deal too loose. If we became more holy by being more Puritanic and precise, both the Church of Christ and the world at large would have good reason to rejoice.'

The remainder of the lecture was devoted to a consideration of the pleasures which true godliness gives, to make up for those it takes away, and an earnest exhortation to all Christians to endeavour to be happy, and so to attract others to the religion which had brought to them so much gladness and joy.

Spurgeon appears to have regarded the address upon 'A Christian's Pleasures' as an informal talk among his own friends rather than a lecture, for when, on January 4, 1859, he took his place at Exeter Hall as one of the lecturers to the Young Men's

Christian Association, to speak upon the subject announced—*De Propaganda Fide*—he began by saying:

'I do not feel in my place here to-night. This is the very first occasion in my life upon which I have ever presented myself before the public as a lecturer—at least, before any audience worthy of being called a multitude. I have long been in the habit of preaching, and one cannot break through a habit that has been acquired by years of constant practice; and I feel positively certain that, do whatever I may, I shall have to preach a sermon to-night. I cannot lecture, I told your secretary so; and I tell *you* also the same, so that, when you retire from the hall, you may say, "Well, I am disappointed, but it is just as he said it would be."

With regard to the title of my lecture, it is a very strange one, and some people have said, "How could Mr. Spurgeon have selected a Latin title for his lecture? What does he know about Latin? He knows a little about Saxon, but he certainly does not understand Latin." I will just tell you the secret of it: I think there is wisdom in that title. Mr. Shipton asked me, a long time ago, what my subject would be. I said, "I am sure I cannot tell you." I very seldom know twenty-four hours beforehand the subject of any sermon I am going to preach. I have never been able to acquire the habit of elaborate preparation. I usually begin my sermonizing for the Sabbath-day on Saturday evening. I cannot think long upon any one subject; and I always feel that if I do not see through it quickly I shall not be likely to see through it at all, so I give it up, and try another. What my theme for this evening was to be, I did not know, so I thought I would have a Latin title; and then, supposing I did not keep to the subject, people would say I did not understand the Latin, and had made a mistake. I felt sure that, with the title I have chosen, I should have a wide field, because I could either translate it literally, and keep close to the exact words, or else I might use a very free translation, and select almost any topic I pleased.'

Dealing with the subject first negatively, Spurgeon showed that, by the propagation of the faith, he did not mean the nominal Christianization of nations, nor the bringing of large numbers to make a profession of love to Christ, nor the conversion of persons from one sect to another. Then, turning to the positive side of the subject, the lecturer continued:

'What, then, is the propagation of the faith? I suggest another question. *What is the faith?* Here a hundred *isms* rise up, and I put them all aside; they may be phases of the faith, but they are not the faith. What, then, is the faith? Strange to say, the faith of Christians is a *Person*. You may ask all other religions wherein their faith lieth, and they cannot answer on this wise. Our faith is a Person; the gospel that we have to preach is a Person, and go wherever we may, we have something solid and tangible to preach. If you had asked the twelve apostles, in their day, "What do you believe in?" they would not have needed to go round about with a long reply, but they would have pointed to their Master, and they would have said, "We believe Him." "But what are your doctrines?" "There they stand incarnate." "But what is your practice?" "There stands our practice. *He* is our example." "What, then, do you believe?" Hear ye the glorious answer of the apostle Paul, "We preach Christ crucified." Our creed, our body of divinity, our whole theology is summed up in the person of Christ Jesus. The apostle preached doctrine, but the doctrine was Christ. He preached practice, but the practice was all in Christ. There is no summary of the faith of a Christian that can compass all he believes, except that word *Christ*; and that is the Alpha and the Omega of our creed, that is the first and the last rule of our practice—Christ, and Him crucified. To spread the faith, then, is to spread the knowledge of Christ crucified. It is, in fact, to bring men, through the agency of God's Spirit, to feel their need of Christ, to seek Christ, to believe in Christ, to love Christ, and then to live for Christ.'

After mentioning some of the encouraging signs of the times, and certain dangers against which he felt it needful to warn his hearers, Spurgeon continued:

'We must confess that, just now, we have not the outpouring of the Holy Spirit that we could wish. Many are being converted; I hope that few of us are labouring unsuccessfully, but we are none of us labouring as our hearts could desire. Oh, that I could have the Spirit of God in me, till I was filled to the brim, that I might always feel as Baxter did when he said—

> *I preached as never sure to preach again,*
> *And as a dying man to dying men.*

I pant for that inward agony of spirit which has made men preach the gospel as though they knew they would be wrapped in their winding-sheets when they descended from the pulpit, and that they should stand at the bar of God as soon as they had finished their sermons. And I feel that, as we want an agonizing spirit in the pulpit, our hearers need it, too. Oh, if the Spirit of God should come upon those assembled to-night, and upon all the assemblies of the saints, what an effect would be produced! We seek not for extraordinary excitements, those spurious attendants of genuine revivals, but we do seek for the pouring out of the Spirit of God. There is a secret operation which we do not understand; it is like the wind, we know not whence it cometh nor whither it goeth; yet, though we understand it not, we can and do perceive its Divine effect. It is this breath of Heaven which we want. The Spirit is blowing upon our churches now with His genial breath, but it is as a soft evening gale. Oh, that there would come a rushing mighty wind, that should carry everything before it, so that even the dry bones of the Valley of Vision might be filled with life, and be made to stand up before the Lord, an exceeding great army! This is the lack of the times, the great want of our country. May this come as a blessing from the Most High!'

Towards the close of the lecture, there was the following striking passage concerning war and its influence upon heathen nations:

'There is one thing I must say—I often hear Christian men blessing God for that which I cannot but reckon as a curse. They will say, if there is war with China, "The bars of iron will be cut in sunder, and the gates of brass shall be opened to the gospel." Whenever England goes to war, many shout, "It will open a way for the gospel." I cannot understand how the devil is to make a way for Christ; and what is war but an incarnate fiend, the impersonation of all that is hellish in fallen humanity? How, then, shall we rouse the devilry of man's nature—

Cry, Havoc, and let slip the dogs of war—

and then declare it is to make straight in the desert a highway for our God—*a highway knee-deep in gore?* Do you believe it? You cannot. God does overrule evil for good, but I have never seen yet—though I look with the cautious eye of one who has no party to serve—I have never seen the rare fruit which is said to grow upon this vine of Gomorrah. Let any other nation go to war, and it is all well and good for the English to send missionaries to the poor inhabitants of the ravaged countries. In such a case, our people did not make the war, they did not create the devastation, so they may go there to preach, but for English cannon to make a way in Canton for an English missionary, is a lie too glaring for me to believe for a moment. I cannot comprehend the Christianity which talks thus of murder and robbery. If other nations thus choose to fight, and if God lets them open the door for the gospel, I will bless Him, but I must still weep for the slain, and exclaim against the murderers. I blush for my country when I see it committing such terrible crimes in China, for what is the opium traffic but an enormous crime? War arises out of it, and then men say that the gospel is furthered by it: can you see how that result is produced? Then your eye must be singularly fashioned. For my part, I am in the habit of looking straight at a thing—I endeavour to judge it by the Word of God—and in this case it requires but little deliberation in order to arrive at a verdict. It seems to me that, if I were a Chinaman, and I saw an Englishman preaching in the street in China, I should say to him, "What have you got there?" "I am sent to preach the gospel to you." "The gospel! what is that? Is it anything like opium? Does it intoxicate, and blast, and curse, and kill?" "Oh, no!" he would say—but I do not know how he would continue his discourse; he would be staggered and confounded, he could say nothing. There is a very good story told of the Chinese that is quite to the point. A missionary lately went to them with some tracts containing the ten commandments; a Mandarin read them, and then sent back a very polite message to the effect that those tracts were very good indeed, he had never read any laws so good as those, but there was not so much need of them in China as among the English and the French; would the missionary have the goodness to distribute them where they were most wanted?'

Spurgeon concluded by earnestly appealing to the unconverted at once to believe in Jesus, and by exhorting Christians to put into practice what they had heard about propagating the faith. His closing words were: 'I wanted to make this lecture practical. If there is but a little practical result from it, I shall rejoice far more in that than in all this great assembly and in your many plaudits. If you will remember the world's dire necessities—if you will ponder the tremendous value of a soul—if you will think about the dread, immeasurable eternity, to which men are hastening—if you will recollect that the Name of Christ is every day blasphemed—if you will bethink you that false gods usurp the place of the God of the whole earth—and if, with these thoughts in your mind, you will go forth into daily life to propagate the faith as it is in Jesus Christ—if, with prayer, with holy living, with a godly example, and with earnest walking, you shall all of you be missionaries for Christ, then I will be well content, and unto God shall be the honour and glory for ever. Amen.'

One of the most notable of Spurgeon's early lectures was delivered at the Camberwell Institute upon 'Seraphic Zeal, as exhibited in the life of George Whitefield.' Numbers 25. 13, 'He was zealous for his God,' was the lecturer's motto; and he spoke, first, upon the nature of Whitefield's zeal; secondly, upon the effects of his zeal; and then gave anecdotes and general particulars of the great evangelist's life. The manuscript notes of the lecture include the following:

'Years on years, Whitefield continued his arduous labours, never resting. In the intervals of preaching, he was riding, or walking, and composing sermons. He wrote letters, conversed with enquirers, visited gaols and sick-beds—attended to the Orphan House, published various works, preached during his voyages—and at all times, even till the hour of death, was earnest and fervent. He was, as he said, tired *in* the work, but not tired *of* it; and he desired to preach once more, and then to die. He had his wish, for he preached from "Examine yourselves, &c.," and then died at six the next morning, of asthma, at fifty-six years of age. It is wrong to say, "Preaching killed him," for fifty-six is as good an age as the average of men may expect to live to;[1] and if he had never preached, he might have died quite as soon.'

On December 26, 1860—three months before the Metropolitan Tabernacle was completed—Spurgeon delivered in the lecture-hall a lecture upon 'Southwark.' The following extracts appear worthy of a place in this volume:

'In 1163, a certain excellent man named Peter of Colechurch erected a bridge of elm across the River Thames, and he, in 1176, commenced that edifice which stood for six-and-a-quarter centuries, and was considered to be the wonder of its time—Old London Bridge—a bridge which some of you have seen, though I did not; the houses were taken away long before our time. Old Peter of Colechurch seems to have dedicated his life to building that bridge; and then, with a sort of poetic inspiration on his mind, he desired

---

[1] Spurgeon was himself 'called home' at the age of fifty-seven.

that he might be buried in the church or chapel in the middle arch of the bridge—the right place for a good man to be buried, in the very centre of his work. I have often said—Let me die while I am labouring for Christ; and I should not desire a better place for my burial than hard by the spot where I have worked for my God, and been the means of doing good to the souls of men.

The tower on the Southwark side of the bridge had most singular garnishings upon the roof. The regular school-book historians will tell you that, on the tower, the heads of traitors were exposed. Now it so happens that men who are traitors one day become heroes by-and-by; and some men, who were execrated, and put to death for attempts which were only blamed because they were not successful, need yet to have their true histories written. Let none of us be desirous of fame while we live. If fame be worth having at all, it is the fame of an Oliver Cromwell, who comes out glorious a hundred years after his death. That thing which is called fame gets all the better for keeping; and, in due time, people respect a man all the more for the calumny through which he has passed.

Southwark is the borough of Baptists. In Walter Wilson's *History of Dissenting Churches*, I find mention of eighteen distinct communities of Baptists, and there is scarcely one of the other churches which was not "infested" by these troublesome persons, as some people considered them. In 1642, there was a famous disputation in Southwark between Dr. Featley and four Baptists. The Doctor published his own version of the case, with the title of "The Dippers Dipt; or, the Anabaptists ducked and plunged over head and ears at a disputation at Southwark." There was a lane called Dipping Alley, Fair Street, Horsleydown, because there was erected there a baptistery, which was used by several congregations. . . . John Bunyan preached in the old chapel in Zoar Street; with a day's notice, he could get 1,200 people early in the morning, or 3,000 with proper intimation to the public. John Wesley preached in a chapel in Snow's Fields, which had been built for a Unitarian Baptist; but there was a great secession, and the cause does not seem to have ever prospered. The members of the church in Snow's Fields excluded Wesley from their Society, and became perfectionists; he was succeeded by Thomas Charlton, who became a Baptist. . . . Near here, tolled the curfew-bell. Here martyrs for baptism were burned. This is the stronghold of religious liberty, and the very centre of our denomination. There are ten Baptist churches within the liberties of our borough, while we now stand upon its margin.'

C. H. Spurgeon: The Full Harvest

The week before the Tabernacle was opened, Spurgeon paid a visit to Aberdeen, in connection with the Young Men's Christian Association. On Tuesday afternoon and evening, March 12, 1861, he preached twice in the Music Hall to crowded congregations, and the following morning he met between 150 and 160 gentlemen at a breakfast, at which the Earl of Kintore presided.

The subject of Spurgeon's address was, 'Success in Life;' and he spoke upon it first as it concerned secular matters, and then as it related to religious affairs. There were several autobiographical passages such as the following:

'We must be careful as to the line of life we select; our pursuit must be in keeping with our constitutional tendencies. A man born to be a mechanic would never succeed as a poet, and the man with the poetical afflatus would not be successful as a financier. Each man has powers that adapt him to certain work, and he ought to look out for that occupation which will be most congenial with his own disposition. I know that, if I had been bred a collier or a ploughman, I would still have been a preacher, for I must speak. I feel something like Elihu, when he said, "I will speak, that I may be refreshed." I do not regard preaching or speaking as a task or a labour; it is more like a cure for dulness. I feel that there is something I want to get rid of, so I unburden myself by telling it to others.

When you have chosen your pursuit in life, stick to it. Having had a great many young men under training, I have met with some who are—

Everything by turns, and nothing long.

Some men in business are just the same, but I would rather be a cobbler, and stick to my last, than change my calling often, and so be noted for nothing in particular. If a tree is transplanted seven times, it will be a miraculous tree if it brings forth fruit. The man who is first this thing and then that is like a dog hunting six hares at one time, he is certain to catch none. David was a man of great influence, and we must trace all his spiritual power to the Spirit of God, but, with respect to what he accomplished, we may learn a lesson from his own words, "One thing have I desired of the Lord, that will I seek after." That concentration was the source of much of his power. Now, if your energies are allowed to run out in many channels, they will be dissipated, and we shall see no result in the stream of your life; but if you have only one channel for all your powers, it will be deep if not broad, and there may go the galley with many oars, and from it shall proudly float the banner of success.

We have in England some cart-rut ministers. They have got into grooves, and there they remain; they think the ruts should never be filled up, and that the wheels of the waggon should always keep in them. I do believe, if the management of our roads had been left to some of these good men, in place of railways, we should not even have got the length of the four-horse coach yet. These brethren are exceedingly wise; and when they see one take an independent course, they say, "This is a very rash and very hazardous thing." Well, I have been very rash in my time, and I mean to be so again. I find that the best method, in such cases, is to act as David did when his brother said to him, "I know thy pride, and the naughtiness of thine heart; for thou art come down that thou mightest see the battle." David went forth to meet Goliath, taking his sling and his five smooth stones from the brook, and when the youthful shepherd came back bearing in his hand the giant's head dripping with gore, that was the best answer to his brother's accusation. If you have work to do, do not stay to vindicate yourself; the work itself will be your vindication. Remember how it was with Peter and John; when they were brought before the high priest and the rulers, and their accusers saw the man who was healed standing with them, "they could say nothing against it;" and I find that our brethren, when they see that God's blessing is resting upon us, and that God is with us, are usually willing to be with us, too.

It was my lot to go through two or three years of the most virulent abuse, and I thank God for it. I felt it very hard to bear, but I fell upon my knees before God, and told Him that, when I gave Him everything else, I gave Him my character, too. If I had known that by faithfully serving Christ I must ruin my reputation, I think I should not have paused for a single moment. I felt quite sure that if my reputation should be lost here among men it would be safe with my Lord; for at the day of judgment there will be a resurrection of reputations as well as of bodies. Yet it is very hard to bear up under constant slanders; only one good thing comes of it, you can find out your weak points, for your enemies will discover your faults if your friends do not. But if I have God with me, I do not care who may be against me. I remember that once, in London, a man took off his hat, bowed to me, and said, "The Rev. Mr. Spurgeon—a great humbug!" I took off my hat, too, and said, "I am much obliged to you, sir, for the compliment; I am glad to hear that I am a great anything." We parted very amicably, and I have not had the pleasure of meeting him since. . . .

Do not think of waiting until you can do some great thing for God; do little things, and then the Master will bid you go up higher. Eleven years ago, I was addressing Sunday-school children, and these alone. Ten,—nine years ago, I was preaching in little insignificant rooms here and there, generally going out and coming back on foot, and occasionally getting a lift in a cart. It has often happened that, when I have been going out to certain villages, the brooks would be so swollen that they could not be crossed in the usual way, so I would pull off my shoes and stockings, wade through up to my knees, then try to make myself tidy again as I best could, and go on to the little chapel to preach, and return home in the same way. Now, I am perfectly sure that, if I had not been willing to preach to those small gatherings of people in obscure country places, I should never have had the privilege of preaching to thousands of men and women in large buildings all over the land. If one wishes to be a steward in God's house, he must first be prepared to serve as a scullion in the kitchen, and be content to wash out the pots and clean the boots. Remember our Lord's rule, "Whosoever exalteth himself shall be abased; and he that humbleth himself shall be exalted." '

An interesting reminiscence of this visit to Aberdeen is preserved in Dr. W. G. Blaikie's Memoir of Dr. David Brown. Dr. Brown found Spurgeon in an anteroom, surrounded by a number of people who were full of high expectation of the treat they were about to enjoy. One of the Pastor's London friends, who had accompanied him, told Dr. Brown that if he could not have a few minutes' quiet meditation his address would be a failure. Accordingly, the room was cleared, but the great preacher seemed in sore distress of mind, as though he could not get along with his subject. Even in the hall he was manifestly out of sorts and groaning in spirit. Dr. Brown told him that he would hold up his hands in prayer. 'Thank you for that,' was the prompt and cordial answer; and twice he repeated the words, 'Thank you for that; thank you for that.' The address proved to be a brilliant one, and when, at the close, friends came to express their admiration and gratitude, Spurgeon, turning to Dr. Brown, remarked, 'You owe it all to him.'

On October 1, 1861, Spurgeon gave, in the Tabernacle, a lecture which was destined to attract more public attention than any which he had previously delivered. It was entitled, 'The Gorilla and the Land he Inhabits,' and was largely concerned with the volume, then recently published, and severely criticised—*Explorations and Adventures in Equatorial Africa*, by Paul B. Du Chaillu. A. H. Layard, M.P., presided, and by his side sat M. Du Chaillu. In introducing his subject, Spurgeon said:

'Mr. Chairman, and my very good friends, I am very glad to see you here, though you have taken me very much by surprise. I was reckoning upon a quiet evening with a moderate audience, but you have crowded this vast house, and I regret to say there have been great multitudes turned away from the doors. We are doomed to disappointments, but such as these one can afford to endure with equanimity. Perhaps the question will be asked, Why do you deliver a secular lecture? I answer that the question itself is rather late, since it is a time-honoured custom for our ministers occasionally to offer instruction to their congregations in this pleasant and friendly form, and the present is very far from my first attempt in this direction. Casting aside all priestly pretences as mere superstition, I meet you as my friends and fellow-labourers every Sabbath-day, and I then endeavour to stir you up to holy labour; and now to-night, on a common week-evening, we meet by way of recreation to talk cheerfully upon an entertaining subject. We want common things treated religiously, and there may be almost as much good achieved by books and lectures on ordinary topics, thoroughly imbued with a religious spirit, as by sermons or theological treatises. All my Heavenly Father's works are my text-books, and, as a preacher, I have a right to select my subject from either of the great books of Creation or Revelation.

But more; it is the growing conviction of my mind that the human animal will have some sort of amusement or other; and that, if we do not give him the right sort, he will certainly seek the wrong. God has made nature not only for our necessities, but for our pleasures. He has not only made fields of corn, but He has created the violet and the cowslip. Air alone would be sufficient for us to breathe, but see how He has loaded it with perfumes; bread alone might sustain life, but mark the sweet fruits with which nature's lap is brimming. The colours of flowers, the beauties of scenery, the music of birds, the sparkling of gems, and the glories of the rainbow and aurora, all show how the great Creator has cared for the lawful gratification of every sense of man. Nor is it a sin to enjoy these gifts of Heaven; but it would be folly to close one's soul to their charms. Now, in matters of truth, there is an analogy with nature. Those glorious doctrines which we daily preach are as the bread of Heaven, the needful and delicious food of our souls; but other truths, great facts of nature, are as the flowers and the birds, they may not *feed* the spirit, but they are not therefore to be neglected, since they gratify and gladden the mind. Certain is it that the masses will have amusement of some sort; everyone can see that. It is of no use for me to stand up in the pulpit constantly, and say to men who have no fear of God before their eyes, "You must not frequent the public-house and the theatre," for their reply will be, "We want something to excite us, some recreation after our hard day's work" —a speech not quite so unreasonable as the censorious may imagine.

For my own part, I have a good conscience towards God in this matter, for my only object in life is to benefit my fellow-men. I feel that the best way to lift up the lost and degraded from the horrible pit and the miry clay, in a spiritual sense, is to preach to them Jesus Christ and Him crucified, but this need not prevent me from using all measures possible to promote social reform; and I firmly believe that lectures upon useful and scientific subjects, in which a lecturer is able to throw out hints about dress, cookery, children, cleanliness, economy, temperance, and the duties of the household, or to ex-claim against the tally system,[1] the pot-house[2] begging, and puffery,[3] may be very useful.'

After carefully examining the volume written by the traveller, and considering the evidence *pro* and *con*, Spurgeon thus announced his decision concerning it: 'I do verily believe, in spite of all that has been said, that M. Du Chaillu's book is matter of fact. It is not written so carefully as a scientific man might write it, nor so orderly and regularly as the author might re-write it, if he had another seven years to do it in; yet I believe that it is true, and that he himself is worthy of our praise as one of the greatest modern discoverers—a man who has done and dared more for science, and, I think I may add, more for the future spread of religion, than most men of his time.'

Coming to the gorilla—a stuffed specimen of which was on the platform—the lecturer said:

[1] Co-habiting without marriage.
[2] Ale-house.
[3] The practice used by certain vendors at auctions of employing a person to run up the price: to puff up the bidding.

'He is an enormous ape, which claims to approach the nearest to man of any other creature. How nearly he approaches, I leave you to judge. True, his claim to be our first cousin is disputed, on behalf of the koolo-kamba, by several very learned men. If we should, therefore, admit you (addressing the gorilla) to be man's first cousin, we fear that the koolo-kamba might institute a suit at law to claim equal rights, and so many cousins would be far from convenient. Besides, I have heard that if we should admit this gentleman to be our cousin, there is Mr. Darwin, who at once is prepared to prove that our great-grandfather's grandfather's father—keep on for about a millennium or two—was a guinea-pig, and that we were ourselves originally descended from oysters, or seaweeds, or starfishes. Now, I demur to that on my own account. Any bearded gentleman here, who chooses to do so, may claim relationship with the oyster; and others may imagine that they are only developed gorillas, but I, for my own part, believe there is a great gulf fixed between us, so that they who would pass from us to you (again turning to the gorilla) cannot; neither can they come to us who would pass from thence. At the same time, I do not wish to hold an argument with the philosopher who thinks himself related to a gorilla; I do not care to claim the honour for myself, but anyone else is perfectly welcome to it.

Seriously, let us see to what depths men will descend in order to cast a slur upon the Book of God. It is too hard a thing to believe that God made man in His own image, but, forsooth, it is philosophical to hold that man is made in the image of a brute, and is the offspring of "laws of development." O infidelity! thou art a hard master, and thy taxes on our faith are far more burdensome than those which Revelation has ever made. When we have more incredulity than superstition can employ, we may leap into infidel speculation, and find a fitting sphere for the largest powers of belief. But who can deny that there is a likeness between this animal and our own race? . . . There is, we must confess, a wonderful resemblance—so near that it is humiliating to us, and therefore, I hope, beneficial. But while there is such a humiliating likeness, what a difference there is! If there should ever be discovered an animal even more like man than this gorilla is; in fact, if there should be found the exact *facsimile* of man, but destitute of the living soul, the immortal spirit, we must still say that the distance between them is immeasurable.'

After giving an account of the country which the gorilla inhabits, and of the manners and customs of the natives of that region, Spurgeon concluded:

'As for sending missionaries among them, they are ripe and ready for them. They received M. Du Chaillu with the greatest kindness and courtesy, and they even prayed the traveller to tell the white men to send missionaries to them; and where they have teachers, they gladly receive them. If missionaries can be sent to Africa in sufficient numbers, there are happy days in store for that land. What will be the effect upon the world when Ethiopia shall stretch out her hands to Christ? . . .'

At the time of the delivery of the 'gorilla' lecture, M. Blondin was performing at the Crystal Palace, and some wag wrote to him a letter purporting to come from Spurgeon. He sent it on to the Pastor, who endorsed it thus—'This was received by M. Blondin, and is a specimen of the genus "hoax" '—and then put it away for future reference. The envelope contained the following epistle:

'Metropolitan Tabernacle,
Newington,
Oct. 5, 1861

M. Blondin,
Sir,

In consequence of the overflowing attendance at my Tabernacle, on Tuesday evening last, when I gave a lecture on the gorilla, it has occurred to myself, and to my brethren the Managers of the Tabernacle, that to engage your services for an evening (say, next Wednesday) for the following programme, would result in mutual benefit. *You must meet me at the Tabernacle, on Tuesday next*, at 12 o'clock, to confirm or to alter the proposed order of entertainment, which I flatter myself will be highly gratifying to all concerned.

Programme.

At 6 o'clock on Wednesday evening, Oct. 9th, M. Blondin to ascend from the platform in the Tabernacle, by an easy spiral ascent, five times round the interior, to one of the upper windows, opposite to "The Elephant and Castle," thence by an easy incline in at the first-floor window of that inn, and return the same way to the platform. The admission to be, as at the "gorilla" lecture, 6d., 1s., and 2s. 6d.

Yours sincerely,
C. H. Spurgeon'

The lecturer could well afford to laugh at this clumsy attempt to hoax M. Blondin; but some of the newspaper attacks upon him, with reference to the 'gorilla' and other lectures, were of such a character that they could not be reproduced here. One friend was sufficiently influenced by them to write an expostulatory letter to Spurgeon, and this evoked the following reply:

'Clapham,
October 22nd, 1861

My Dear Sir,

I have been dumb under the cruel rebukes of my enemies, and the ungenerous reproofs of pretended friends. I have proved hitherto the power of silence, and although most bitterly tempted, I shall not change my custom, or venture a syllable in order to stay these mad ravings. But your brotherly note deserves one or two words of answer.

1 Have I well weighed what I have done in the matter of these lectures? Aye,—and so weighed it that neither earth nor hell can now move me from my course. I have a life-work to perform, and towards its completion, through evil report and good report, I speed my way.

2 You imagine that my aim is merely to amuse, and you then speak very properly of "stooping." Indeed, if it were so, if I had no higher or nobler aim in view, it would be *stooping* with sorrowful emphasis; but, *then*, think you that the devil would care to roar at me? Why, surely, it would be his best policy to encourage me in forsaking my calling, and degrading my ministry!

3 "Is the Master's eye regarding His servant with pleasure?" Yes, I solemnly feel that it is; nor am I conscious of any act, or motive,—the common infirmity of man excepted,—which could cause me to incur Divine displeasure in connection with that which is, to me, *the* work of my life.

4 With regard to *laughter*—you and I may differ upon this matter, and neither of us be quite infallible in our judgment. To me, a smile is no sin, and a laugh no crime. The Saviour, the Man of sorrows, is our example of morality, but not of misery, for He bore our griefs that we might not bear them; and I am not John the Baptist, nor a monk, nor hermit, nor an ascetic, either in theory or practice. Unhallowed mirth I hate, but I can and do enjoy my Father's works, and the wonders of Creation, none the less, but all the more, because I am a Christian. At any rate, I hold my own views

[135]

upon this point; and, during eleven years of ministry, I have seen no ill effect, but very much good from my preaching, although the charge has always been laid at my door that I sometimes provoke the risible faculties.

5 Concerning "sowing to the flesh," I have *not* done so in these lectures, but have rendered honest and hearty service to my Lord, and believe that spiritual fruit has already been reaped.

6 As to the grief of friends, let them, as well as myself, be ready to bear the cross; and let them not attempt to evade reproach by weeping where no tears are needed. I have given no cause to the enemy to blaspheme, or only such blessed cause as shall be renewed with greater vigour than ever.

And now for my explanation; I have, in connection with my Church, a College for young ministers, which is a work of faith as to temporals, and a labour of love on my part in the highest sense of the term. There are about 150 young men, who are getting an education with a view, in most cases, to preaching the Word in the streets, villages, and towns of this land. Their studies are such as their capacities can receive, and the ministering brethren are mainly given to the searching of the Word; while reading it in the original is the ambition of each. In the course of instruction there are lectures, delivered by myself, a regular lecturer, and other gentlemen. We have had about twenty lectures on English History. I have given lectures on Sabbath-school teaching, Preaching, Church Discipline, Ethnology, &c., &c. The Rev. George Rogers has lectured on Books and Reading, Habit and Instinct, on Ministerial Prerequisites, and on other matters. Various brethren have taken up other topics; and, having attended all the lectures, I can testify that the best spirit has pervaded all, and each lecturer has laboured, not merely to instruct, but to do spiritual good.

My present course is upon Natural History. For the lectures already delivered, especially the abused ones, I have had the thanks of the members passed spontaneously and unanimously; and I believe the lectures have been as acceptable to the audience as any which were ever delivered. We who have seen the wonders of wisdom in anatomy, providential adaptation, and creating perfection, have gone home praising and blessing God. We have laughed, doubtless; and we have wept, too; but, with an audience of 150 young men, and a considerable company of men and women of the working-class, what would be the use of dull, drowsy formality? Last Friday week, the "shrews" lecture came in due course, and I thought it might be useful to give a few words as to the value of love and kindness in Christian families, for which words I have had grateful acknowledgment. We went home, and I have not heard of one of the audience who did not feel that it was an evening well and profitably spent. Many Christian people gave me a hearty shake of the hand and glowing thanks.

But, lo! to our utter amazement, one morning we discovered that the lecture was considered vulgar, coarse, and I know not what. The gentlemen of the press had nothing else just then to do, so they said, "Let us abuse Spurgeon, no matter whether he deserves it or not." Since this abuse, I have asked scores who were there if anything had been said for which one might be sorry, and all have answered, "No, nothing was said at all deserving censure, or anything but approval." Think you that my hearers are all so degraded as to tolerate conduct such as a lying press imputes to me? O my brother, you do ill to judge a servant of the Lord from the lips of his foes, and one, too, who has had abuse enough on former occasions without having given cause of offence, which renders it inexcusable that brethren should readily believe reports concerning him!

This work of my Institution is of God; lectures are a part of the necessary plan, they do good, I have a call to this work, so all this opposition is a spur to increased zeal. I would the Lord's people cared more than they do for these young preachers, for I feel sure that God the Holy Spirit will raise up from our midst many who shall do exploits in His Name. To this work am I called, and the Lord is with me in it. Void of offence towards God and man, trusting for acceptance to Him who has washed away my sin, shall I flee because my conduct is misunderstood and my words are misconstrued? Nay, verily, Jehovah-nissi! And now let hell roar, and saints themselves forsake. Time and eternity will clear the character of one who has given up even his good name to his Master, without reserve.

Yours wearily,
C. H. SPURGEON

P.S.—Get the "gorilla" lecture; read it, and see if there be any evil in it; yet *it* is the *least religious* of them all.—C. H. S.'

Those who have read Spurgeon's *Sermons in Candles* will appreciate the delight which hearers in various parts of the country experienced in listening to his lecture upon that subject. It was repeated many times for a quarter of a century and finally published in 1890. The origin of the lecture is thus explained by Spurgeon:

'In addressing my students in the College, long ago, I was urging upon them the duty and necessity of using plenty of illustrations in their preaching that they might be both interesting and instructive. I reminded them that the Saviour had many *likes* in His discourses. He said, over and over again, "The kingdom of heaven is like;" "The kingdom of heaven is like." "Without a parable spake He not unto them." The common people heard Him gladly, because He was full of emblem and simile. A sermon without illustrations is like a room without windows. One student remarked that the difficulty was to get illustrations in any great abundance. "Yes," I said, "if you do not wake up, but go through the world asleep, you cannot see illustrations; but if your minds were thoroughly aroused, and yet you could see nothing else in the world but a single tallow candle, you might find enough illustrations in that luminary to last you for six months." Now, the young brethren in the College are too well behaved to say "Oh!" or give a groan of unbelief, should I perchance say a strong thing, but they *look*, and they draw their breath, and they wait for an explanation. I understand what they mean, and do not make too heavy a draft upon their faith by long delays in explaining myself. The men who were around me at that particular moment thought that I had made rather a sweeping assertion, and their countenances showed it. "Well," I said, "I will prove my words;" and my attempt to prove them produced the rudiments of this lecture.'

If all Spurgeon's notable addresses could be collected they would fill several substantial volumes and would supply a mass of interesting reading on a great variety of subjects. Those unpublished include three very memorable utterances—one delivered in 1862 in connection with the celebration of the Bi-centenary of the ejection of the two thousand ministers in 1662; another, on 'Bells and Bell-ringing,' given at the Tabernacle in 1869, with musical illustrations; and a third, on 'Ignatius Loyola and the Jesuits'.

Many of his individual lectures were published after their delivery: 'Illustrious Lord Mayors' (November, 1861); 'The Two Wesleys' (December, 1861); 'Counterfeits'; 'Miracles of Modern Times'; 'Poland'; and 'George Fox'. The last named was given by request of the Society of Friends, in November, 1866, at the Friends'

Meeting House, Bishopsgate Street. Among his hearers on that
occasion was Matthew Arnold who afterwards wrote to his mother:
'Last night, Lord Houghton went with me and William Forster to
Spurgeon's lecture. . . . It was well worth hearing, though from
William's getting us places of honour on the bench close behind
Spurgeon we did not see or hear him to such advantage as the less
forward public in the body of the hall. It was a study in the way of
speaking and management of the voice; though his voice is not
beautiful as some people call it, nor is his pronunciation quite
pure. Still, it was a most striking performance, and reminded me
very much of Bright's. Occasionally, there were bits in which he
showed unction and real feeling; sometimes, he was the mere
Dissenting Philistine; but he kept up one's interest and attention
for more than an hour and a half, and that is the great thing. I am
very glad I have heard him.'

In 1878 Spurgeon's *Speeches at Home and Abroad* were published
by Passmore and Alabaster, and, although they had not the benefit
of the speaker's revision, they afford a fairly accurate idea of his
utterances at various public gatherings between the years 1861 and
1878. He had begun revising his own copy of the book, and the
accompanying *facsimile* on page 140 will show the extent of his
alterations, and also his loyalty to Baptist principles. One lecture
which Spurgeon did revise and expand into a book was his *Eccentric
Preachers*, being compelled to do so, as he explains in the Preface, by
mutilated versions of the original lecture which had appeared without his leave. The lecture 'Sermons in Stones', given at the Tabernacle in 1870, was published in 1894 by J. L. Keys, under the title,
'What the Stones Say'. The four volumes of *Lectures to my Students*
are so well known and so highly appreciated that no details as to
their contents need be inserted here. Few works in the whole range
of theological literature have been so helpful to aspirants for the
ministry or to those who have already begun evangelistic, pastoral,
or missionary work.

Doubtless Spurgeon's Lectures were much akin to sermons, a
fact for which he humorously apologized on several occasions by
means of the illustration with which we close this chapter:

'I am not an adept at lecturing, and when I take to it under
constraint, I either signally fail in it, or else the successful production
is a sermon in disguise. You cannot drive out nature by command:
the old pulpit hand must preach, even though you bid him do some-

[Set up new page.]

thus

baptized. We simply stand out, ~~the others~~ for reasons best
known to themselves, slink every man to his tent in the rear,
and escape ~~some of~~ the reproach ~~that~~ we have to bear. Baptists
~~that~~ are members of "respectable" churches, I do not respect you,
having left your brethren and deserted your colours for the sake of
being respectable! We are not "respectable" at all because we put
baptism ~~out of the font~~ into the right place. A man says, "I do
not like to be called a Baptist." "Sir, there is no Baptist ~~that~~
wants you to be; he does not feel so proud of you ~~as~~ think it any
honour ~~to have~~ his name coupled with yours." The oldest name of
all ~~is John the~~ Baptist ~~who~~ existed, as our Welsh friend said, a
long time before there was any Wesleyan, or ~~anything of the sort~~;
~~and we speak with no bated breath when we stand right out for the
sake of the vindication of a rite, as it is called, but which rite draws
with it one-third part of the stars of heaven~~, for the view you take
of that rite affects your view of almost every other truth. A
gentleman once told me he did not care twopence for baptism.
~~the~~ reply ~~is~~, "Why don't you give up ~~the~~ twopenny ~~thing~~, and
have a view of ~~a~~ which it would be worth while caring for,
~~which you would maintain?" Brethren, I have heard of some of
your misfortunes since I have been here, as well as some of your
joys, and I thought nobody would be able to say at Plymouth, you
had been better fed than taught. I only hope that to-day you will
be half as well fed as you have been taught.~~

Marginal annotations:

which

for faith and

Also for

so called;

will

My ... was

as to

Episcopalian Names are small matters but the principle we contend for is precious. baptism

Your

our Lord's teaching

for

the denomination now extant is
certainly that of Baptist, wh was
borne by him who heralded our
Master.

maintain the divine
ordinance of believers' baptism: a rite they call
it, but that rite involves a thousand
other matters

Let others do as they will,
but be it ours to be faithful to
our Lord, to obey his commands, for "to
obey is better than sacrifice, & to hearken than the fat of rams."
May the best of blessings attend you!

thing else. It would be no good sign if it were otherwise; for a man must keep to one thing, and be absorbed in it, or he will not do it well. I have preached now for so many years that use is second nature; and a lecture, a speech, an address, and I fear even a conversation, all have a tendency to mould themselves sermon-fashion.

It is just the old story over again of the artist who had been painting red lions all his life. The landlord of a public-house in a certain street desired to have his establishment known as "The Angel" and he commissioned a clever gentleman of the brush to produced one of those flaming spirits. The budding Academician replied, "You had better have a red lion. I can paint red lions against any man, and they seem the right sign for publicans who do a roaring trade". "But", said Boniface, "there are three of your red lions quite handy already and we want a little variety. I have made up my mind to have an angel. Cannot you arrange it?". "Well", said the artist, "I will see what I can do. You shall have your angel, but it will be awfully like a red lion". So, when I am requested to "lecture", I reply, "I cannot manage it; my business is to preach". But if they press their suit, and I am weak enough to yield, I warn them that my lecture will be wonderfully like a sermon.'

Beloved, when you and I have seen or heard anything which God has revealed to us, let us go and write it, or make it known by some other means. God has not put the treasure into the earthen vessel merely for the vessel's own sake, but that the treasure may afterwards be poured out from it, that others may thereby be enriched. You have not been privileged to see, merely to make glad your eyes, and to charm your soul; you have been permitted to see in order that you may make others see, that you may go forth and report what the Lord has allowed you to perceive. John no sooner became the seer of Patmos than he heard a voice that said to him, 'Write'. He could not speak to others, for he was on an island where he was exiled from his fellows, but he could write, and he did; and, often, he who writes addresses a larger audience than the man who merely uses his tongue. It is a happy thing when the tongue is aided by the pen of a ready writer, and so gets a wider sphere, and a more permanent influence than if it merely uttered certain sounds, and the words died away when the ear had heard them.—c.h.s., *in a sermon at the Tabernacle on the words, 'Write the vision'.*

9

Literary Labours

CONTINUING the record of Spurgeon's publications,[1] we mention to begin with, *Spurgeon's Illustrated Almanack*. This little book was first issued in 1857 under the title of *The New Park Street Almanack*, and the Editor thus explained his object and hope in preparing it: 'It may appear, to some persons, degrading and unseemly for a minister to edit a penny Almanack; but I am not burdened with any notions of false dignity, and I think nothing degrading which may be useful. It is quite certain that, by this little Annual, I shall reach many readers who might not have purchased a larger volume; and I hope, by God's grace, some of them will be impressed with thoughts which may result in conversion, or in other cases afford consolation and edification.'

In his Prefatory Note, 'To the Reader,' in the following issue, Spurgeon wrote: 'Last year, this little Almanack gave me an opportunity of speaking to many thousands; and as I believe it to be my duty to avail myself of every means of proclaiming the gospel, I again address myself to you through this humble medium. If one sinner shall be led to Jesus by this little book, or one saint be assisted in his spiritual warfare, my object will be abundantly answered, and unto God shall be the glory. The thousands of this Almanack, which will be scattered over our land, may be compared to a discharge of grapeshot, which is often far more effective than the larger cannon-ball.'

In 1860, the Editor had the joy of being able to report that his desire had been at least in part realized: 'From one of the remote corners of the earth, I have received the good news of a sinner saved through the Almanack of last year. This has been a most sweet and precious reward for the past, and is a most stimulating encouragement for the future. This little David will yet smite another Goliath, and to God shall be the glory.' Happily, this was by no means a solitary instance of blessing; and, year by year, as the booklet became still more widely known, the Lord signified His

---

1 See Chapter 28 of *C. H. Spurgeon: The Early Years.*

approval of it by using its printed messages to the salvation of sinners and the strengthening of saints. Everything that Spurgeon originated had some practical purpose in view; and, therefore, this small book was employed as the advocate of the College, and the other Institutions as they were founded, and became the means of materially increasing the funds needed for their support and development.

The publication of the Book Almanack was continued without intermission from the year of its inception, the texts for daily meditation being chosen for the most part by Mrs. C. H. Spurgeon, who also, during the 'nineties, wrote many of the articles, most of which were illustrated parables from the garden at Westwood. After 1894, quite a new interest was imparted to the passages of Scripture selected for reading and thought from day to day, for the 'Text Union' was then formed, and all who joined it agreed to learn the Almanack motto, so as to be ready to repeat it when challenged by a fellow-member asking for 'the text for to-day, please.' Many thousands of Christians, in our own and other lands, have thus been banded together in a holy fellowship, which great numbers of them have found to be exceedingly helpful; and some very remarkable instances of the appropriateness of the Scriptural quotations to the cases of different individuals have been reported to Mrs. Spurgeon, or her son Charles, who undertook the onerous task of superintending this department of service for the Saviour.

In 1872, the large penny broadsheet entitled, *John Ploughman's Almanack*, was first issued. Instead of a verse from the Bible, the motto for each day was a proverb, or proverbial saying, either composed or selected by 'John Ploughman.' The task of arranging 365 suitable maxims, with the other contents of the Almanack, was by no means a light one; and Spurgeon evidently had, at first, no intention of repeating the process, and so making a permanent addition to his ever-increasing literary labours; but when 1873 arrived without the sheet to correspond with the one for the previous year, so many friends expressed their disappointment at its non-appearance, that the publication of its homely messages was resumed; and, from 1874, *John Ploughman's Almanack* was a welcome visitor in tens of thousands of homes, and exerted a very considerable influence on behalf of religion, temperance, thrift, and charity. The one for the year 1893 was pathetically interesting from the fact that Spurgeon had been preparing the proverbs for it until within a few days of receiving the home-call.

In January, 1865, a notable 'new departure' was inaugurated by the publication of the first number of the monthly magazine, *The Sword and the Trowel*, which was destined to play such an important part in the after-history of its Editor. Its title derives from the memorable and perilous period when Nehemiah was the Tirshatha, or Governor, of God's ancient people. The motto-text, which appeared on all the volumes, was: 'They which builded on the wall, and they that bare burdens, with those that laded, every one with one of his hands wrought in the work, and with the other hand held a weapon. For the builders, every one had his sword girded by his side, and so builded. And he that sounded the trumpet was by me.' (Neh. 4. 17-18.) Although Spurgeon was such a lover of peace, it is significant that he put the battling before the building, not only in the title, but also in the sub-title of the magazine—'A Record of Combat with Sin and Labour for the Lord.' His purpose in issuing it was clearly set forth in his opening article, which was headed, 'Our Aims and Intentions':

'Our magazine is intended to report the efforts of those churches and Associations which are more or less intimately connected with the Lord's work at the Metropolitan Tabernacle, and to advocate those views of doctrine and church-order which are most certainly received among us. It will address itself to those faithful friends, scattered everywhere, who are our well-wishers and supporters in our work of faith and labour of love. We feel the want of some organ of communication, in which our many plans for God's glory may be brought before believers, and commended to their aid. Our friends are so numerous as to be able to maintain a magazine, and so earnest as to require one. Our monthly message will be a supplement to our weekly sermon, and will enable us to say many things which would be out of place in a discourse. It will inform the general Christian public of our movements, and show our sympathy with all that is good throughout the entire Church of God. It will give us an opportunity of urging the claims of Christ's cause, of advocating the revival of godliness, of denouncing error, of bearing witness for truth, and of encouraging the labourers in the Lord's vineyard.

We do not pretend to be unsectarian,—if by this term be meant the absence of all distinctive principles, and a desire to please parties of all shades of opinion. We believe, and therefore speak. We speak in love; but not in soft words and trimming sentences.

We shall not court controversy, but we shall not shun it when the cause of God demands it.

The many ministers who were students in our College will be our helpers in maintaining a variety and freshness of matter; and their flocks, we trust, will receive a blessing through their stirring words. It is our first and last object to do practical service, and to excite others to active exertion.

We shall supply interesting reading upon general topics; but our chief aim will be to arouse believers to action, and to suggest to them plans by which the Kingdom of Jesus may be extended. To widen the bounds of Zion, and gather together the outcasts of Israel, is our heart's desire. We would sound the trumpet, and lead our comrades to the fight. We would ply the trowel with untiring hand for the building up of Jerusalem's dilapidated walls, and wield the sword with vigour and valour against the enemies of the truth.'

The Sword and the Trowel had, from the beginning, a unique constituency, for which Spurgeon always endeavoured to provide suitable literary and spiritual fare. The annual volumes are a storehouse of interesting information on all manner of subjects. Questions concerning Scripture doctrine, church-government, education, the Ritualistic controversy, Dis-establishment, and other matters both of temporary and permanent importance, are discussed in able fashion; and much of the material remains as valuable as when first published. For instance, an early series of illustrated tracts on Ritualism set forth the Protestant position in such a popular style that they have never been excelled, or even equalled, by anything that has since appeared.

Spurgeon had a number of assistants, some paid and others who delighted to aid him voluntarily, from the commencement of the magazine; but, with the exception of very occasional articles, he made himself personally responsible for all that appeared in its pages, and he often declared that most of the manuscripts and all the proofs passed directly under his own hand and eye, so that it was, in a very special sense, 'his own magazine.' It was also, by the generally-expressed desire of its readers, largely autobiographical.

On one occasion, at least, the magazine was mentioned in the House of Lords, and the phrase used concerning it, in that august assembly, furnished its ever-ready Editor with the title of a short article in its next number: 'A Lively Newspaper, called, *The Sword and the Trowel.*' The opening paragraph was as follows: 'The good

Bishop of Rochester has described *The Sword and the Trowel* to the House of Lords as "a lively newspaper." We are afraid our friend is not so well acquainted with his *Sword and Trowel* as we could wish him to be, for it can hardly be called a newspaper; its shape, form, and monthly period of issue most distinctly place it among magazines. Still, that is near enough for recognition; and the adjective appended is so complimentary that we accept it with pleasure, and consider it rather a feather in our cap. What good can a magazine or any other publication effect, if it is not *lively*? Our trying state of health often makes us fear that we shall grow dull, and we accept the Bishop's kindly criticism as a doctor's certificate that the magazine is up to the mark, and is, in fact, "a lively paper." It is all that we can hope if our readers will add, "and so say all of us".'

The early volumes of *The Sword and the Trowel* soon became specially valuable to ministers and students, because in them the Editor gave his expositions of the Psalms, which were afterwards incorporated in his greatest literary work, *The Treasury of David*. Those seven substantial volumes contain, in addition to Spurgeon's own Commentary, the choicest extracts which he and his helpers could find in ancient and modern literature upon the whole Psalter; and, together, they constitute an indispensable portion of the library of any servant of the Lord who would be furnished for his Saviour's service. The Prefaces to the various volumes give just a glimpse of the delight with which this real labour of love proceeded during the twenty years of the busy author's life in which it was in course of preparation; and his final words, written when the great task was accomplished, indicate how deeply the commentator and compiler had been himself profited by his study of this part of the Sacred Scriptures, and how real was his regret when the last Psalm was reached, and he had to turn to other and less congenial forms of toil for his Master:

'At the end of all these years, the last page of this Commentary is printed, and the seventh Preface is requested. The demand sounds strangely in my ears. A Preface when the work is done? It can be only nominally a Preface, for it is really a farewell. I beg to introduce my closing volume, and then to retire with many apologies for having trespassed so much upon my reader's patience.

A tinge of sadness is on my spirit as I quit *The Treasury of David*, never to find on this earth a richer storehouse, though the whole palace of Revelation is open to me. Blessed have been the days spent in meditating, mourning, hoping, believing, and exulting with David! Can I hope to spend hours more joyous on this side of the golden gate? Perhaps not; for the seasons have been very choice in which the harp of the great poet of the sanctuary has charmed my ears. Yet the training which has come of these heavenly contemplations may, haply, go far to create and sustain a peaceful spirit which will never be without its own happy psalmody, and never without aspirations after something higher than it has yet known. The Book of Psalms instructs us in the use of wings as well as words: it sets us both mounting and singing. Often have I ceased my commenting upon the text, that I might rise with the Psalm, and gaze upon visions of God. If I may only hope that these volumes will be as useful to other hearts in the reading as to mine in the writing, I shall be well rewarded by the prospect.

The former volumes have enjoyed a singular popularity. It may be questioned if, in any age, a Commentary so large, upon a single Book of the Bible, has enjoyed a circulation within measurable distance of that which has been obtained by this work.'

Shortly after Volume I of *The Treasury* was issued, Spurgeon met one of the most eminent of the London publishers; and, in the course of their conversation, his new book was mentioned. As the gentleman had such a wide experience of the success or failure of the works of various authors, the Pastor asked him what he would consider a satisfactory sale of *The Treasury*. He replied, 'Well, Mr. Spurgeon, in the first place, you have fixed the price very much lower than I should have done if I had brought out a valuable theological work of that kind. Fifteen or sixteen shillings would not, in my judgment, have been at all too much to charge for it; but, as you have issued it at eight shillings, and, with the prestige of your name, I should say that you have done very well if you have sold as many as two thousand copies by this time.' 'Oh!' said Spurgeon, 'that number was far exceeded directly it was published, and we have already run into several thousands more. I purposely put the price as low as possible, because I wanted to place the volumes within the reach of as large a number of students of the Word as I could.' The publisher was surprised, yet gratified, to hear of the successful commencement of the series, and the author felt that he had great cause for gratitude to God for giving such a gracious token of approval to this important part of his literary labours.

Before Spurgeon was 'called home,' no less than a hundred and

twenty thousand volumes of *The Treasury* had been sold, and it is
still in constant demand. The complete work was republished in the
United States; Spurgeon's own comments have been translated
into German with a view to publication; and his exposition of
Psalm 119 has been issued separately in a handy volume, entitled,
The Golden Alphabet of the Praises of Holy Scripture. It is impossible
to estimate the blessing that has been conferred upon the whole
Christian Church by *The Treasury of David.* If its author had never
written anything else, it would have been a permanent literary
memorial of no small value; and among the hundred and fifty
volumes (or thereabouts), which bear his name on their title-pages,
this series is unquestionably his *magnum opus.*

The most popular of all Spurgeon's publications—*John Ploughman's Talk*—first saw the light in the pages of his magazine, and
probably helped largely to increase the circle of his readers. Even
some of the Editor's most intimate friends did not recognize their
Pastor's voice when he addressed them in the language of such
godly ploughmen as his old Stambourne friend, Will Richardson;
and he has himself left on record this interesting reminiscence of
what one of the Tabernacle deacons thought of the writings of the
(supposed) man in the smock-frock:

'Many years ago, it came into the head of the Editor of *The Sword
and the Trowel* to write a set of plain papers for the people, in pure
Saxon, and in the style of homely proverbs. He produced, one after
another, the chapters which now make up *John Ploughman's Talk.* As
no one knew who wrote them, amusing things occurred. An
attached friend said to their author, "Why do you put those papers
of that ploughman into the magazine?" The answer was, "Well,
they are lively, and they have a good moral; what is the matter
with them?" "Yes," replied the unsuspecting critic, "they are
rather good for a poor uneducated person like the writer, but they
are too coarse for your magazine." "You think so?" said the
Editor, and with a smile on his face, he went his way. When that
good brother found out who the actual writer was, he felt all sorts
of ways; but never a word was said about his criticism.'

One of the ministers trained in the College, Pastor W. D.
McKinney, in writing to Mrs. Spurgeon concerning her husband
after he was 'called home,' proved that a student penetrated the
disguise through which the deacon could not see. Referring to the

President, he wrote: 'The first gift of books I ever received was two volumes of his sermons, which were presented to me at the close of my first public discourse. Afterwards, I entered the College, and was one of those upon whom he tried the effect of *John Ploughman's Talk*; and I think I was the first who found "John" out. Being one of the senior students, who were dubbed "the twelve apostles," I sat on his right hand on Fridays when he read the "Papers from a Ploughman." He evidently wanted to know what we thought of them, yet decided that our verdict should be unbiassed. "Well," said he, with that merry twinkle of his eye which we knew so well, "McKinney, who do you think this ploughman is?" "I think he is not very far away," I replied, "and that he has enjoyed *his own talk*!" "Aha!" said he, "you know too much!" '

As soon as the volume was published, it attained an immense circulation. At first, the book was issued without illustrations; but, after the publication of *John Ploughman's Pictures; or, More of his Plain Talk for Plain People*, the former work was also illustrated. Nearly six hundred thousand copies of the two volumes were sold in the author's lifetime. Several translations into other languages have been made, but the one that specially pleased 'John Ploughman' was the Dutch version, published at Amsterdam under the title, *Praatjes van Jan Ploeger*. Spurgeon wrote, in *The Sword and the Trowel*, a very amusing article upon 'John Ploughman as a Dutchman,' in which he used and applied proverbs specially suitable to Holland and the Hollanders.

While Spurgeon was travelling, either at home or abroad, he always had his note-book close at hand, and jotted down everything that was likely to be of service afterwards, incidents that could be used as illustrations being specially preserved. Many of these were first published in *The Sword and the Trowel*, and then gathered, with other material of a similar kind, into a small volume, entitled, *Feathers for Arrows, or Illustrations for Preachers and Teachers*, which had a very large sale. In one of the *Lectures to my Students*, Spurgeon related the following incident concerning the book: 'I once met with a High Churchman, who told me that he had purchased *Feathers for Arrows*; "and," said he, "some of the illustrations are very telling; but they have to be used with great discretion." His words seemed to imply that my expressions were possibly a little too strong, and perhaps somewhat rough and unpolished here and there. "Well," I replied, "that is how I wrote them." He looked at me, but he said nothing; probably it had never occurred to him that the same kind of discretion was necessary in making the illustrations as in using them.'

At the close of the year in which the magazine was commenced, another valuable literary work was completed. This was Spurgeon's first volume of daily readings, published under the title of *Morning by Morning*, and concerning which he wrote in the Preface:

'In penning these short reflections upon certain passages of Holy Writ, the author has had in view the assistance of the private meditations of believers. A child may sometimes suggest a consolation which might not otherwise have cheered a desolate heart; and even a flower, smiling upward from the sod, may turn the thoughts heavenward: may we not hope that, by the Holy Spirit's grace, as the reader turns "morning by morning" to our simple page, he will hear in it "a still small voice" whose speech shall be the message of God to his soul? The mind wearies of one thing, and we have therefore studied variety, changing our method constantly; sometimes exhorting, then soliloquizing, then conversing; using the first, second, and third persons, and speaking both in the singular and plural, and all with the desire of avoiding sameness and dulness. Our matter also, we venture to hope, is wide in its range, and not altogether without a dash of freshness; readers of our sermons will recognize many thoughts and expressions which they may have met with in our discourses; but much is, to the author at least, new; and, as far as anything can be which treats of the common salvation, it is original. We have written out of our own heart, and most of the portions are remembrances of words which were refreshing in our own experience; and, therefore, we trust the daily meditations will not be without savour to our brethren; in fact, we know they will not, if the Spirit of God shall rest upon them.

Our ambition has led us to hope that our little volume may also aid the worship of families where God's altar is honoured in the morning. We know that it has been the custom in some households to read Mason, Hawker, Bogatsky, Smith, or Jay; and without wishing to usurp the place of any of these, our *Morning by Morning* aspires to a position among them. Our happiness will overflow should we be made a blessing to Christian households. Family worship is beyond measure important, both for the present and succeeding generations; and to be in part a chaplain in the houses of our friends, we shall esteem to be a very great honour.'

The work so admirably answered all the ends designed by Spurgeon that, in a little over two years, he issued the sequel, *Evening by Evening*, and wrote in the Preface:

'Having had the seal of our Master's approval set upon our former volume, entitled, *Morning by Morning*, we have felt encouraged to give our best attention to the present series of brief meditations, and we send them forth with importunate prayer for a blessing to rest upon every reader. Already, more than twenty thousand readers are among our morning fellow-worshippers. Oh, that all may receive grace from the Lord by means of the portion read; and when a similar number shall be gathered to read the evening selection, may the Father's smile be their benison!

We have striven to keep out of the common track; and, hence, we have selected unusual texts, and have brought forward neglected subjects. The vice of many religious works is their dulness. From this fault we have striven to be free; our friends must judge how far we have succeeded. If we may lead upward one heart which otherwise would have drooped, or sow in a single mind a holy purpose which else had never been conceived, we shall be grateful. The Lord send us such results in thousands of instances, and His shall be all the praise! The longer we live, the more deeply are we conscious that the Holy Spirit alone can make truth profitable to the heart; and, therefore, in earnest prayer, we commit this volume and its companion to His care.'

Both the books had a remarkable circulation and their ministry continues. After the author's home-going, the publishers carried out an idea that he had long cherished, and issued the two sets of meditations, printed on India paper, in a dainty little volume that can be carried in the pocket, and used for private meditation, or for the visitation of the sick.

A singular instance of the appropriateness of one of the readings in *Evening by Evening* was often narrated by Spurgeon. Lady Burgoyne (wife of Sir John F. Burgoyne, Constable of the Tower, and mother of the first Mrs. J. A. Spurgeon) was a member of the church at the Tabernacle. The Pastor gave, in his sermon[1] entitled, 'Speak for yourself: A Challenge!' the following testimony concerning her Christian character and witness-bearing for her Lord:

'We had one among us, whose rank entitled her to move in an upper

[1] Sermon No. 1393 (*Metropolitan Tabernacle Pulpit*, 1878).

[152]

sphere of "society"; but her choice enabled her to prefer the humble companionship of the church to which she belonged. Some of you well remember her silvery locks. She has left us now, and gone home to glory. Her lot was cast amongst the aristocracy; yet, with gentle, quiet, bland simplicity, she introduced the gospel wherever she went. Many and many have come to these pews, to listen to your minister, who would never have been here but for her calm, beautiful, unobtrusive, holy life, and the nerve with which, anywhere, and at any time, she could say, "Yes, I am a Christian; what is more, I am a Nonconformist; and what you will consider worse, I am a Baptist; and what you will think worst of all, I am a member of the church at the Tabernacle." She never blushed to own our dear Redeemer's Name, nor yet to acknowledge and be-friend the lowliest of His disciples; and you will do well to imitate her faith, and follow her example.'

On September 7, 1870, Lady Burgoyne took up her copy of *Evening by Evening*, and began to read the text and exposition for that date: 'There is sorrow on the sea; it cannot be quiet. Jeremiah 49. 23. Little know we what sorrow may be upon the sea at this moment. We are safe in our quiet chamber; but, far away on the salt sea, the hurricane may be cruelly seeking for the lives of men. Hear how the death-fiends howl among the cordage; how every timber starts as the waves beat like battering-rams upon the vessel! God help you, poor drenched and wearied ones!'—when she exclaimed, 'Something dreadful has happened to poor Hugh'; and so it proved, for her son, Captain Hugh Burgoyne, commander of H.M.S. *Captain*, an ironclad turret-ship, had, that very morning, been lost off Cape Finisterre with his vessel and over five hundred of his officers and crew, as well as Captain Cowper Coles, the designer of the ship, who was on board as a visitor. The providential arrangement of the message in *Evening by Evening* somewhat prepared the bereaved family for the terrible tidings that soon after reached them.

Another book, prepared by Spurgeon as an aid to family devotion, was duly published under the title of *The Interpreter*, and consisted of selected passages of the Word of God for reading every morning and evening throughout the year, together with brief comments and suitable hymns. It was issued first in monthly parts, and afterwards as a very substantial volume, in various styles of binding. It proved a great help in the private worship of thousands of households; such men of mark as Earl Cairns and Earl Shaftesbury were among the many who have borne testimony to its value. Spurgeon always felt that he might have added largely to its circulation if he had in one respect changed the character of the work; but he explained, in the Preface, the reason for his decision upon that matter: 'I have been earnestly urged to add *prayers*, but my conscience will not allow me to do so, although it would greatly increase the sale of the work. Let every Christian parent try to pray from his heart; and, though at first it may be difficult, it will soon become a delight, by the aid of the Holy Ghost, to pour out the desires of his soul in the midst of his family. To some persons, the use of forms of prayer appears to be lawful; but, as I cannot coincide with that opinion, it would be the height of hypocrisy for me to compose prayers for the use of others.'

In 1866, another formidable yet happy task was accomplished in the compilation of *Our Own Hymn-Book*. The worshippers at the Tabernacle might have continued longer to employ in their service of praise the selections of Dr. Watts and Dr. Rippon, if it had not been for the complicated arrangement of the various books and parts, which proved so puzzling to strangers. So, taking pity upon them, Spurgeon commenced this new undertaking; and when he had completed it, he wrote this explanation of the motive which had actuated him, and the methods he had followed to make the new book as perfect as possible:

'None of the collections already published are exactly what our congregation needs, or we would have cheerfully adopted one of them. They are good in their way, but we need something more. Our congregation has distinctive features which are not suited by every compilation—not, indeed, by any known to us. We thought it best to issue a selection which would contain the cream of the books already in use among us, together with the best of all others extant up to the hour of going to press; and having sought a blessing upon the project, we set about it with all our might, and at last have brought it to a conclusion. Our best diligence has been given to the work, and we have spared no expense. May God's richest benediction rest upon the result of our arduous labours! Unto His glory we dedicate *Our Own Hymn-Book*.

The area of our researches has been as wide as the bounds of existing religious literature—American and British, Protestant and Romish, ancient and modern. Whatever may be thought of our taste, we have exercised it without prejudice; and a good hymn has not been rejected because of the character of its author, or the heresies of the church in whose hymnal it first appeared; so long as the language and the spirit of it commended the hymn to our heart, we included it, and we believe that we have thereby enriched our collection. The range of subjects is very extensive, comprising not only direct praise, but doctrine, experience, and exhortation, thus enabling the saints, according to apostolical command, to edify one another in their spiritual songs.

If any object that some of the hymns are penitential or doctrinal, and therefore unfit to be sung, we reply that we find examples of such in the Book of Psalms, which we have made our model in compiling our work; there we have Maschils as well as Hosannahs, and penitential odes as well as Hallelujahs. We have not been able to fall in with modern scruples, but have rested content with ancient precedents.

We hope that, in some few churches of the land, we may be helpful to their service of sacred song, and aid them in praising the Lord. The Editor has inserted, with great diffidence, a very few of his own compositions—chiefly among the Psalms—and his only apology for so doing is the fact that, of certain difficult Psalms, he could find no version at all fitted for singing, and was therefore driven to turn them into verse himself. As these original hymns are but few, it is hoped that they will not prejudice the ordinary reader against the rest of the collection; and, possibly, one or two of them may gratify the generous judgment of our friends.'

The hope that *Our Own Hymn-Book* might be adopted by other congregations beside that at the Tabernacle, was fully realized; and the Editor's own compositions have been prized as much as any in the whole work. Three of them especially—the one written for an early morning prayer-meeting:

> *Sweetly the holy hymn*
> *Breaks on the morning air;*
> *Before the world with smoke is dim,*
> *We meet to offer prayer.*

another, intended for singing at the communion:

> *Amidst us our Belovèd stands,*
> *And bids us view His piercèd hands,*

> *Points to His wounded feet and side,*
> *Blest emblems of the Crucified.*

and a third, commencing:

> *The Holy Ghost is here*
> *Where saints in prayer agree,*
> *As Jesu's parting gift He's near*
> *Each pleading company.*

have been incorporated into many modern hymnals.

Spurgeon often spoke of the compilation of *Our Own Hymn-Book* as having been a great means of grace to his own soul, especially when he was selecting the hymns in praise of the Lord Jesus; and, once, when preaching at Surrey Chapel, he thus explained why he had omitted one hymn that he found in other collections: 'It really is lamentable to see how common, in certain quarters, misery is among the people of God. In many places they are a feeble folk. Mr. Ready-to-Halt, of whom John Bunyan writes, must have been the father of a very large family. I am afraid that the manufacture of crutches will never die out altogether; and really, in some parts, it must be a most lucrative business, for many of the Lord's people never get beyond, "I hope so," or, "I trust so," and no hymn in the hymn-book is so sweet to them as—

> *'Tis a point I long to know.*

I did not put that hymn in *Our Own Hymn-Book*. I had a debate in my own mind about it. I said to myself, "Ah, well! they will know all about that hymn without my putting it into the book;" and I thought that, if you wanted to sing it, you could sing it alone at home; but it did not seem to me to be a hymn that a whole congregation should use. I have to sing it myself sometimes, I am sorry to say. It is an excellent hymn, as expressing the feelings of some of God's people, but it will not do for all of you to get into that state. It is very well for the good wife to have a little black draught at hand when the child needs it sometimes; but to give the whole family the same medicine might be a great deal more injurious than beneficial. And so it is with regard to that class of hymns; it is suitable to a certain case of diseased spiritual condition, but it would be wrong to suppose or to insinuate that all the people of God, at any one time in a congregation, could be found in exactly the same condition of sad decrepitude of faith.'

After being in use for a third of a century, it was felt that there was need to add to Spurgeon's own compilation; so, in the year 1898, a *Supplement* was issued, containing 300 additional hymns; and, providentially, it was ready for use just when the Tabernacle congregation had need of new hymn-books to replace the many that had been burned in the fire which wrought such terrible destruction in their great house of prayer. The new selection closely follows the lines laid down for the former one, and includes many of the best 'psalms, and hymns, and spiritual songs' that have been composed during the last thirty years.

Perhaps, among all Spurgeon's published works, the one that gives the best idea of his familiarity with the whole range of expository literature, is his unpretentious half-crown volume, issued under the unattractive title, *Commenting and Commentaries*. The book has long since been accepted as a most reliable standard of appeal, and its commendations and valuations are frequently quoted in catalogues of theological works. The purpose of the volume, and the labour necessary for its completion, are thus described by its author:

'Divines who have studied the Scriptures have left us great stores of holy thought which we do well to use. Their expositions can never be a substitute for our own meditations; but, as water poured down a dry pump often starts it working to bring up water of its own, so suggestive reading sets the mind in motion on its own account. Here, however, is the difficulty. Students do not find it easy to choose which works to buy, and their slender stores are often wasted on books of a comparatively worthless kind. If I can save a poor man from spending his money for that which is not bread, or, by directing a brother to a good book, may enable him to dig deeper into the mines of truth, I shall be well repaid. For this purpose I have toiled, and read much, and passed under review some three or four thousand volumes. From these I have compiled my catalogue, rejecting many, yet making a very varied selection. Though I have carefully used such judgment as I possess, I have doubtless made many errors; I shall certainly find very few who will agree with all my criticisms, and some persons may be angry at my remarks. I have, however, done my best, and, with as much impartiality as I can command, I have nothing extenuated nor set down aught in malice. He who finds fault will do well to execute the work in better style; only let him remember that he will have my heifer to plough with, and therefore ought in all reason to excel me. I have used a degree of pleasantry in my remarks on the Commentaries, for a catalogue is a dry affair, and, as much for my own sake as for that of my readers, I have indulged the mirthful vein here and there. For this, I hope I shall escape censure, even if I do not win commendation. Few can conceive the amount of toil which this compilation has involved, both to myself and my industrious amanuensis, Mr. J. L. Keys. In almost every case, the books have been actually examined by myself, and my opinion, whatever it may be worth, is an original one. A complete list of all comments has not been attempted. Numbers of volumes have been left out because they were not easily obtainable, or were judged to be worthless, although some of both these classes have been admitted as specimens, or as warnings. Latin authors are not inserted, because few can procure them, and fewer still can read them with ease. We are not, however, ignorant of their value. The writers on the Prophetical Books have completely mastered us; and, after almost completing a full list, we could not in our conscience believe that a tithe of them would yield to the student anything but bewilderment, and therefore we reduced the number to small dimensions. We reverence the teaching of the prophets, and the Apocalypse; but for many of the professed expounders of those inspired Books, we entertain another feeling.'

Anyone who had the opportunity, for the first time, of examining a complete set of Spurgeon's publications might imagine that he had never done anything but write all the days of his life; yet the present volume shows that his literary labours employed only a part of his ministry. Their aim harmonized completely with his one great object, to serve the Lord he loved, and his writing, as his preaching, drew its fulness from one source. What he said on one occasion of John Bunyan was equally applicable to his own words and writings:

'Oh, that you and I might get into the very heart of the Word of God, and get that Word into ourselves! As I have seen the silkworm eat into the leaf, and consume it, so ought we to do with the Word of the Lord;—not crawl over its surface, but eat right into it till we have taken it into our inmost parts. It is idle merely to let the eye glance over the words, or to recollect the poetical expressions, or the historic facts; but it is blessed to eat into the very soul of the

Bible until, at last, you come to talk in Scriptural language, and your very style is fashioned upon Scripture models, and, what is better still, your spirit is flavoured with the words of the Lord. I would quote John Bunyan as an instance of what I mean. Read anything of his, and you will see that it is almost like reading the Bible itself. He had studied our Authorized Version, which will never be bettered, as I judge, till Christ shall come; he had read it till his whole being was saturated with Scripture; and, though his writings are charmingly full of poetry, yet he cannot give us his *Pilgrim's Progress*— that sweetest of all prose poems—without continually making us feel and say, "Why, this man is a living Bible!" Prick him anywhere; and you will find that his blood is Bibline, the very essence of the Bible flows from him. He cannot speak without quoting a text, for his soul is full of the Word of God.'

Never let it be forgotten that, in the mysterious arrangements of Providence, *The Sword and the Trowel* led to the founding of THE STOCKWELL ORPHANAGE. This would be no mean result, if it were all that the Magazine had accomplished; for in that happy home we hope to house a portion of England's orphanhood for many a year to come, receiving the fatherless by an easier door than that which only opens to clamorous competition and laborious canvassing.—C.H.S., *in Preface to 'Sword and Trowel' volume for* 1867.

10

A Home for the Fatherless

ALTHOUGH it is generally known that the Stockwell Orphanage originated in the gift to Spurgeon of £20,000 by Mrs. Hillyard, the widow of a Church of England clergyman, the various circumstances which preceded that noble act of generosity are not so widely known. The story begins with the inclusion of an article in *The Sword and the Trowel* of August, 1866, entitled 'The Holy War of the Present Hour.' In that paper, after the paragraph advocating the widespread dissemination of religious literature, Spurgeon wrote: 'Further, it is laid very heavily on our heart to stir up our friends to rescue some of the scholastic influence of our adversaries out of their hands. In the common schools of England, Church influence is out of all proportion to the respective numbers of the Episcopal body and the Nonconforming churches. We have too much given up our children to the enemy; and if the clergy had possessed the skill to hold them, the mischief might have been terrible; as it is, our Sabbath-schools have neutralized the evil to a large extent, but it ought not to be suffered to exist any longer. A great effort should be made to multiply our day-schools, and to render them distinctly religious, by teaching the gospel in them, and by labouring to bring the children, *as children*, to the Lord Jesus. The silly cry of "Nonsectarian" is duping many into the establishment of schools in which the most important part of wisdom, namely, "the fear of the Lord," is altogether ignored. We trust this folly will soon be given up, and that we shall see schools in which all that we believe and hold dear shall be taught to the children of our poorer adherents.'

When Mrs. Hillyard read these words, and the further plea for the establishment also of religious schools of a higher order, they indicated to her the method by which she might realize the fulfilment of a purpose that she had long cherished in her heart. She had felt specially drawn out in sympathy towards fatherless boys, so she wrote to Spurgeon telling him of her desire, and asking his assistance in carrying it into effect. The Pastor's own mind had been prepared by the Lord for such a proposal through a remarkable experience at the previous Monday evening prayer-meeting at the Tabernacle.

Pastor C. Welton, who was at that time a student in the College, has preserved this interesting record of what happened on that occasion: 'Mr. Spurgeon said, "Dear friends, we are a huge church, and should be doing more for the Lord in this great city. I want us, tonight, to ask Him to send us *some new work*; and if we need money to carry it on, let us pray that *the means may also be sent*." Several of the students had been called to the platform to join with deacons and elders in leading the assembly to the throne of grace, and to plead with God about the matter. While that mighty man of prayer, Mr. William Olney, was wrestling with the Lord, the beloved President knew that the answer had come. Had the Holy Spirit told him? It seemed so, for, walking lightly across the platform to where I was sitting, he said to me softly, "It's all right, Welton; you pray for the conversion of sinners, will you?" A few days after this Tabernacle prayer-meeting, Mrs. Hillyard wrote to the dear Pastor offering to entrust him with £20,000 for the purpose of founding an Orphanage for fatherless children. Here was *the new work and the money with which to begin it*. It was my conviction thirty years ago, as it is to-day, that the Stockwell Orphanage, as well as the money to found it, came from the Lord in answer to the petitions offered that Monday night. Surely, the Orphanage was born of prayer.'

Spurgeon's name had been introduced to Mrs. Hillyard in an extraordinary way; the incident does not appear ever to have come to his knowledge, and it was not made public until some years after he was 'called home.' Speaking at the Orphanage, in June, 1896, Professor Henderson, of Bristol Baptist College, said: 'Mrs. Hillyard and two friends of mine—a husband and wife—were sitting together here in London; and, in the course of their conversation, Mrs. Hillyard said to my friend, "I have a considerable sum of money that I want to employ for beneficent purposes, but I am not competent to administer it myself; I wish you would take this £20,000, and use it for the glory of God." My friend, who was a very sensible man, replied, "I am quite unfit to administer that large amount." It was pressed upon him, but he resolutely declined to accept the charge of it; whereupon Mrs. Hillyard said to him, "Well, if you are not willing to take it, will you advise me as to the disposal of it?" The recommendation he gave was that the money should be put into the hands of a public man, all of whose acts were known to people generally, one who was responsible to the public,

and whose reputation depended upon the proper use of any funds
entrusted to his keeping. This counsel was approved by Mrs.
Hillyard; and now comes the remarkable part of the story. You
know that she did not hold quite the same views that we do, and
the gentleman to whom she was speaking did not share our intense
admiration for Mr. Spurgeon, though he had a kindly feeling towards him, and a high regard for his integrity and uprightness.
When Mrs. Hillyard said to him, "Will you name somebody who
fulfils the conditions you have mentioned?" he told me that the
name of Spurgeon leaped from his lips almost to his own surprise.
Mrs. Hillyard wrote to Mr. Spurgeon about the matter, and you all
know what followed from their correspondence.'

In reply to the first letter from Mrs. Hillyard, Spurgeon asked
for further particulars of her proposed plan, and offered to go to see
her concerning it; she then wrote again, as follows:

'4, Warwick Villas,
Spencer Street,
Canonbury Square,
Islington,
Sept. 3rd, 1866

My Dear Sir,

I beg to thank you for responding so kindly to my very anxious
and humble desire to be used by the Lord of the vineyard in some
small measure of service. He has said, "Occupy till I come," and He
has graciously given me an unceasing longing to do His will in this
particular matter. My oft-repeated enquiry has been, "What shall I
render unto the Lord for all the inestimable benefits He has conferred upon me?" Truly, we can but offer to Him of His own; yet
has He graciously promised to accept this at our hands. That which
the Lord has laid upon my heart, at present, is the great need there
is of an Orphan House, requiring neither votes nor patronage, and
especially one conducted upon simple gospel principles, just such
an one as might be a kind of stepping-stone to your suggested
higher school, and your College; for I think education, to be
effectual, should begin at a very early age.

I have now about £20,000, which I should like (God willing) to
devote to the training and education of a few orphan boys. Of
course, bringing the little ones to Jesus is my first and chief desire.
I doubt not that many dear Christians would like to help in a work
of this kind, under your direction and control; and should such an

[163]

Institution grow to any large extent, I feel sure there would be no
cause to fear the want of means to meet the needs of the dear
orphans, for have they not a rich Father? I shall esteem it a great
favour if you can call and talk the matter over with me on Thursday
next, between the hours of 12 and 4, as you kindly propose; and—
                    I remain, dear sir,
                         Yours truly obliged,
                              ANNE HILLYARD

P.S.—I would leave this matter entirely in the Lord's hand; not
desiring to go before, but to follow His guidance.'

A stained-glass window in the Board-room of the Orphanage
represents the interview between Mrs. Hillyard, Spurgeon, and
William Higgs, whom the Pastor took with him for consultation
with regard to the details of the suggested-scheme. As they
approached the address given in the lady's letter, the very modest
style of the 'villas' made them ask one another whether they were
being hoaxed, for it did not seem likely that anyone living in such a
humble style would have £20,000 to bestow. They discovered,
afterwards, that it was only by the exercise of the most rigid economy that the good woman had been able to save that large sum.
On being admitted to the plainly-furnished room where Mrs.
Hillyard received them, Spurgeon said to her, 'We have called,
Madam, about the £200 you mentioned in your letter.' '£200! did
I write? I meant to have said £20,000.' 'Oh yes!' replied the Pastor,
'you did put £20,000; but I was not sure whether a nought or two
had slipped in by mistake, and thought I would be on the safe side.'
They then discussed the whole question from various points of
view, Spurgeon being specially anxious to ascertain whether
the money ought to go to any relatives, and even suggesting that it
might be handed over to Mr. Müller for his Orphan Homes. The
lady, however, adhered to her determination to entrust the £20,000
to Spurgeon, and to him alone.

After this interview, the proposed scheme made rapid progress.
A preliminary notice was inserted in *The Sword and the Trowel* for
October, 1866; in the following January, the site at Stockwell was
purchased; funds commenced to come in, one of the first large
contributors being Mr. George Moore, of Bow Churchyard, who
gave £250. The sum of £500 was given by Mrs. Tyson, of Upper
Norwood—a lady who long and generously aided both College and

Orphanage, and who, in her will, left £25,000 to the latter Institution, and so became its greatest helper. As the £500 was a present from Mr. Tyson to his wife on the twenty-fifth anniversary of their marriage, the house built with it was called 'Silver-wedding House;' the next one, given by Mr. James Harvey, was named 'The Merchant's House;' the third, presented by Mr. W. Higgs and his workmen, was entitled 'The Workmen's House;' then came 'Unity House,' the gift of 'Father Olney' and his sons, in memory of Mrs. Unity Olney; 'The Testimonial Houses,' erected with funds contributed by the Baptist churches of the United Kingdom as a proof of the high esteem in which they held the President; 'The Sunday-school House', given by the Tabernacle Sunday-school; and 'The College House,' a token of love from brethren educated in the Pastors' College. The head-master's house, dining-hall, play-hall, and infirmary, completed the boys' side of the Institution; and, at a later period, a corresponding portion was erected for girls.

Very early in the history of the Institution, Spurgeon announced the method he intended to adopt in raising the necessary funds. Preaching in the Tabernacle, in 1867, on 'Believing to See,' he said: 'I hope the day may soon come when the noble example which has been set by our esteemed brother, Mr. Müller, of Bristol, will be more constantly followed in all the Lord's work; for, rest assured that, if we will but "believe to see," we shall see great things. I cannot forbear mentioning to you tonight what God has enabled us to see of late as a church. We met together one Monday night, as you will remember, for prayer concerning the Orphanage; and it was not a little remarkable that on the Saturday of that week the Lord should have moved some friend, who knew nothing of our prayers, to give five hundred pounds to that object. It astonished some of you that, on the following Monday, God should have influenced another to give six hundred pounds! When I told you of that, at the next prayer-meeting, you did not think perhaps that the Lord had something else in store, and that, the following Tuesday, another friend would come with five hundred pounds! It was just the same in the building of this Tabernacle. We were a few and poor people when we commenced, but still we moved on by faith, and never went into debt. We trusted in God, and the house was built, to the eternal honour of Him who hears and answers prayer. And, mark you, it will be so in the erection of this Orphan Home. We shall see greater things than these if only our faith will precede our sight. But if we go upon the old custom of our general Societies,

and first look out for a regular income, and get our subscribers, and
send round our collectors, and pay our percentages—that is, do
not trust God, but trust our subscribers—if we go by that rule, we
shall see very little, and have no room for believing. But if we shall
just trust God, and believe that He never did leave a work that He
put upon us, and never sets us to do a thing without meaning to
help us through with it, we shall soon see that the God of Israel
still lives, and that His arm is not shortened.'

Many notable interpositions of Providence have occurred in connection with the building and maintenance of the Institution. One
of the earliest and most memorable took place on November 20,
1867, concerning which Spurgeon wrote, several years afterwards,
among his other personal recollections of Dr. Brock: 'We remember when, being somewhat indisposed, as is, alas! too often our lot,
we went to spend a quiet day or two at a beloved friend's mansion
in Regent's Park. We were dining, and Dr. Brock was one of our
little company. Mention was made that the Stockwell Orphanage
was being built, and that cash for the builder would be needed in a
day or two, but was not yet in hand. We declared our confidence
in God that the need would be supplied, and that we should never
owe any man a pound for the Lord's work. Our friend agreed that,
in the review of the past, such confidence was natural, and was due
to our ever-faithful Lord. As we closed the meal, a servant entered,
with a telegram from our secretary, to the effect that A. B., an unknown donor, had sent £1,000 for the Orphanage. No sooner had
we read the words than the Doctor rose from the table, and poured
out his utterances of gratitude in the most joyful manner, closing
with the suggestion that the very least thing we could do was to fall
upon our knees at once, and magnify the Lord. The prayer and
praise which he then poured out, we shall never forget; he seemed a
psalmist while, with full heart and grandeur both of words and
sound, singularly suitable to the occasion, he addressed the ever-
faithful One. He knew our feebleness at the time, and while he
looked upon the gift of God as a great tenderness to us in our
infirmity, he also seemed to feel such perfect oneness with us in our
delight that he took the duty of expressing it quite out of our hands,
and spoke in our name as well as his own. If a fortune had been
left him, he could not have been more delighted than he was at the
liberal supply of our needs in the Lord's work. We sat around the
fire, and talked together of the goodness of God, and our heart was
lifted up in the ways of the Lord. Among the very latest things we

spoke of, when we last met on earth, was that evening at our friend's house, and the great goodness of the Lord in response to our faith. While we write the record, our heart wells up with new gratitude for the choice benefit. Surely, if in Heaven the saints shall converse together of the things of earth, this will be one of the subjects upon which two comrades of twenty years may be expected to commune.'

A few weeks later, the same anonymous donor dropped into the President's letter-box two bank-notes for £1,000 each—one for the College, and the other for the Orphanage—with a letter in which the generous giver said, 'The latter led me to contribute to the former.' This intimation was specially cheering to Spurgeon, for he had feared, perhaps naturally, that the new Institution would be likely to impoverish the older one.

In November, 1869, when the President was suddenly laid aside by an attack of small-pox, a friend, who knew nothing of his illness, called and left £500 for the Orphanage; and, a few days later, an anonymous donor, who also was unaware of Spurgeon's affliction, sent £1,000 for the same purpose. At one meeting of the Trustees, the financial report was, 'all bills paid, but only £3 left in hand.' Prayer was offered, and the stream of liberality soon began to flow again. On another occasion, the funds were completely exhausted, and the Managers were driven to special supplication on behalf of the work. That very day, nearly £400 was poured into the treasury, and the hearts of the pleaders were gladdened and encouraged.

The President's usual plan, when supplies ran short, was first to give all he could, and ask his fellow-Trustees to do the same, and then to lay the case before the Lord in the full belief that He would incline His stewards to send in all that was required. As long as he was able to do so, Spurgeon presided at the meetings of the Trustees; and, afterwards, he was kept informed of their proceedings by copies of the Minutes, while the most important items of business were decided 'subject to the approval of the President.' In the earlier days, he used personally to see the applicants—an experience which often proved expensive, for he could not listen to the sad stories of the poor widows without relieving their temporal necessities, whatever might be the decision concerning the admission of their children. Sometimes, there was a humorous side to the situation, and he was quick to notice it. One day, a woman came with quite a little tribe of boys and girls; and, in reply to the enquiries put to her, said that she had been twice left a widow, and her second husband, whom she had recently lost, had been previously married; and then, separating the children into three groups, she said, 'These are his, those are mine, and these are ours.' In relating the story afterwards, Spurgeon used to say that he did not remember any other instance in which possessive pronouns had proved so useful!

In February, 1869, the President wrote in *The Sword and the Trowel*: 'At the Orphanage, we are still set fast for want of a master. The Lord will, we trust, guide us to the right man; but, out of many applicants, not one has seemed to us to be suitable.' Two months later, however, Spurgeon was able to report: 'Mr. Charlesworth, assistant-minister to Mr. Newman Hall, of Surrey Chapel, has accepted the post of master to the Orphanage. He called in—as we are wont to say—by accident, at the very moment when a letter was handed to us from the previously-elected master declining to fulfil his engagement. Our disappointment was considerable at the loss of the man of our choice; but when we found that this dear friend had been thinking of the work, and was ready to undertake it, we were filled with gratitude to the over-ruling hand of God.'

The election of a pædo-baptist to such an important position was another instance of the catholicity of spirit that Spurgeon had manifested in appointing a Congregationalist (George Rogers) to the post of Principal of the Pastor's College, and choosing another member of the same denomination (W. R. Selway) to be the Scientific Lecturer to that Institution. The undenominational character of the Orphanage is apparent from a glance at the table showing the religious views of the parents of the children received. Up to the close of the century, out of the 527 orphans who had found a happy home at Stockwell, no less than 166 had come from Church of England families, while Baptists were only represented by 121, Congregationalists by 64, Wesleyans by 58, and other bodies by still smaller numbers.

Spurgeon never had occasion to regret the choice of Vernon J. Charlesworth as the first master of the Orphanage. He proved himself to be admirably fitted for the position. On one occasion, shortly after there had been an addition to his family, he became the subject of a humorous remark passed by Spurgeon at a meeting of the Trustees. In a tone of apparent seriousness Spurgeon told them that he had to call their attention to the fact that the head-master had introduced a child into the Orphanage without their permission, and he added that this was not the first time such a thing had happened! One of the brethren, not noticing the merry twinkle in the President's eye, proposed that Mr. Charlesworth should be called in, and questioned concerning the matter, and also that he should be very distinctly informed that such a proceeding must not be repeated! The resolution was probably not put to the meeting, and a truthful historian must record that there were several similar occurrences in after years.

Everyone at all acquainted with the inner working of the Orphanage knows with what affection, mingled with reverence, the children at Stockwell always regarded Spurgeon. He was indeed a father to the fatherless; and, while no boy ever presumed upon the tender familiarity which the President permitted, every one of them fully prized the privilege of his friendship. There was no mistaking the ringing cheer which greeted his arrival; everybody on the premises instantly knew what that shout meant, and passed round the cheering message, 'Mr. Spurgeon has come.' In the 'In Memoriam' Stockwell Orphanage Tract, issued in 1892, after Spurgeon was 'called home,' Charlesworth wrote, concerning the 'promoted' President: 'The children loved him; and his visits always called forth the most boisterous demonstrations of delight. His appearance was the signal for a general movement towards the centre of attraction, and he often said, "They compassed me about like bees!" The eagerness with which they sought to grasp his hand, often involved the younger children in the risk of being trampled upon by others; but, with ready tact and condescension, he singled out those who were at a disadvantage, and extended to them his hand. At the Memorial Service, conducted by the head-master, it was ascertained that every boy present had shaken hands with the President—a fact of no small significance! Every visit cost him as many pennies as there were children in the Orphanage. Proud as they were to possess the coin for its spending power, it was regarded as having an augmented value from the fact that it was the gift of Mr. Spurgeon.'

A simple incident related in one of the earlier issues of *The Sword and the Trowel*, showed how even the most friendless of the orphans felt that he might tell his troubles into the sympathetic ear of the great preacher:

'Sitting down upon one of the seats in the Orphanage grounds, we were talking with one of our brother Trustees, when a little fellow, we should think about eight years of age, left the other boys who were playing around us, and came deliberately up to us. He opened fire upon us thus, "Please, Mr. Spurgeon, I want to come and sit down on that seat between you two gentlemen." "Come along, Bob, and tell us what you want." "Please, Mr. Spurgeon, suppose there was a little boy who had no father, who lived in a Orphanage with a lot of other little boys who had no fathers; and suppose those little boys had mothers and aunts who comed once a month, and brought them apples and oranges, and gave them pennies; and suppose this little boy had no mother, and no aunt, and so nobody never came to bring him nice things, don't you think somebody ought to give him a penny? 'Cause, Mr. Spurgeon, that's me." "Somebody" felt something wet in his eye, and Bob got a sixpence, and went off in a great state of delight. Poor little soul, he had seized the opportunity to pour out a bitterness which had rankled in his little heart, and made him miserable when the monthly visiting day came round, and, as he said, "Nobody never came to bring him nice things." '

The narrative, of course, brought 'little Bob' a plentiful supply of pocket-money, and was the means of helping others of the orphans who, like him, were motherless and fatherless; and it also served the President many a time as an illustration of the way in which a personal appeal might be made effectual. One of the best pleas for the Institution that Spurgeon ever issued was dictated to his secretary under the olives at Mentone. It was addressed, 'To those who are happily married, or hope to be;' and after allusion to the bliss of a true marriage union, and the consequent sorrow when one of the twain is removed by death, the writer showed how, often, poverty made the bereavement even more painful, and then pointed out the blessing that a home for the fatherless became to the poor struggling widow suddenly left with a large family. The article contained special references to the Stockwell Orphanage; and it was, in due time, published in *The Sword and the Trowel*. As soon as it appeared, one gentleman sent £100 as a thankoffering from himself and his wife for their many years of happy married life, and other donors sent small amounts. The 'plea' commenced thus: 'We do not write for those people who are married but not mated. When a cat and a dog are tied together, they seldom sorrow much at the prospect of separation. When marriage is *merry-age*, it is natural to desire a long life of it; but when it is *mar-age*, the thought of parting is more endurable. Mr. and Mrs. Naggleton will be sure to put on mourning should one or other of them decease, but the garb of sorrow will be all the sorrow he or she will know; the black will soon turn brown, if not white, and the weeds will probably give place to flowers. We address ourselves to those who have the happiness of being joined together by wedded love as well as by wedlock.' It was a source of much amusement to Spurgeon to receive, among the other contributions for the Orphanage, as the result of his appeal, a donation 'from Mr. and Mrs. Naggleton,' who did not, however, give their real name and address!

In asking for the support of the Christian public in this enterprise, Spurgeon supplied the following information:

'We have heard it objected to Orphanages that the children are dressed uniformly, and in other ways are made to look like paupers. This is earnestly avoided at the Stockwell Orphanage, and if any friend will step in and look at the boys and girls, he will have to put on peculiar spectacles to be able to detect a shade of the pauper look in countenance, garments, speech, limb, or movement.

Another fault that has been found is that the boys and girls by living in one great institution are unfitted for domestic life in small families. There is probably much truth in this allegation, but at Stockwell we have laboured to avoid it by dividing the children into different families, which are located in separate houses. The lads do the domestic work; there is a matron to each house, and no servants are kept; the lads do all, and thus become as handy as young sailors. Those who take them as apprentices shall be our witnesses.

"But", it is said by someone, "there is such a deal of trouble in getting a child into an orphanage, and the practice of canvassing for votes is so laborious to the widow, and in many other ways objectionable". We are of much the same opinion and we heartily wish that everybody else would think in like manner. There is a great deal to be said for the plan of election by votes given to subscribers, and if it is not the best possible way, it has nevertheless served a very useful turn, and many institutions have been founded and successfully carried on under that system. Still, we shall be glad to get rid of it, and supply its place in a more excellent way. We have found it possible to leave the choice of the orphans with the trustees, who are pledged to select the most destitute cases. In the Stockwell Orphanage no canvassing can be of the slightest use, for the trustees personally, or through appointed visitors, examine each application, and endeavour to allot the vacancies where the need is greatest. They do not deviate from their rules under pressure or persuasion, but as much as possible exercise impartiality.

The Orphanage receives fatherless boys and girls between the ages of 6 and 10. It is conducted on the Cottage System, each home being presided over by a godly matron. It is unsectarian, children being received, irrespective of their denominational connection, from all parts of the United Kingdom. The children receive a plain but thorough English education and training. The supreme aim of the managers is always kept in view—to "bring them up in the nurture and admonition of the Lord".'

It is difficult to say where Mr. Spurgeon may be considered most at home; for his time is spent in moving quickly to and from the Tabernacle, the Pastors' College, the schools, alms-houses, and orphanages, of which he is the guiding spirit. Perhaps the most hard-working man on the Surrey side of the Thames, he finds but little leisure for taking his ease in his house in Nightingale Lane—a quiet nook hard by Wandsworth Common. He passes his life, when not actually preaching or working, in a pony chaise, varied by occasional hansom cabs. Wrapped in a rough blue overcoat, with a species of soft deerstalking hat on his head, a loose black necktie round his massive throat, and a cigar burning merrily in his mouth, he is surely the most unclerical of all preachers of the Gospel.— THE WORLD, October 4, 1876.

11

The New Helensburgh House

WHILE Spurgeon was so diligently, and in such self-denying fashion, caring for students and colporteurs, widows and orphans, some of his friends thought it was time for a little more comfort to be provided for himself and his household. Many hallowed associations had endeared the old house at Nightingale Lane[1] to its happy inmates; but they were not blind to the disadvantages of their ancient dwelling, and all rejoiced greatly when, in 1869, it was pulled down, and the new Helensburgh House was erected in its place. The large amount of money expended by the owner in his many departments of service for the Lord would have made it impossible for him to meet the necessary outlay, so a few of his most liberal and devoted helpers determined to defray the principal part of the cost, as a token of their appreciation of his public ministry and private friendship. The work was entrusted to the charge of Mr. William Higgs, and the plans were drawn by his eldest son, William, who was later to become a deacon at the Tabernacle.

Before the new house was ready for occupation, Spurgeon met the generous donors; and Mrs. Spurgeon, who had been for some time staying in Brighton, came up to London in order to be present at that memorable gathering. In a tiny notebook which has been preserved, the Pastor wrote the introduction and outline of the speech in which he expressed his gratitude for the gift he had received. It was a most exceptional thing for him to make, for any occasion, more than a bare skeleton of the address or sermon he was about to deliver, so the high value he set upon the presentation is manifest from the fact that he was moved to compose what may well be called a prose-poem of thanksgiving for it:

'It was a law of Abdul the Merciful that no man should be compelled to speak when overwhelmed by kindness. Doth a man sing when his mouth is full of the sherbet of Shiraz, or a prince dance when he wears on his head the crown of Ali with its hundredweight of jewels? Or, as Job saith, "Doth the wild ass bray when he hath

---

[1] See *The Early Years*, pp. 498-505.

grass? Or loweth the ox over his fodder?" As he that marrieth a virgin is excused from war, so he that receiveth a great gift is exempted from a public speech. My heart is as full of thanks as Paradise was full of peace. As the banks of Lugano ring with the songs of nightingales, so my whole being reverberates with gratitude; and there is another, for whom I may also speak, who echoes all I utter, as the cliffs of Meringen prolong with manifold sweetness the music of the horn.

From you, it comes with double pleasure, like the nuts and the almonds that were carried to Joseph fresh from his father's tents. From my brethren, it is a flower dripping with the dew of Hermon, and perfumed with the fragrance of affection. From my fellow-soldiers, it comes as a cup of generous wine in which we pledge each other for future battles. From my children in the faith, as a love-token such as a tender father treasures. From the church, it is offered as a sacrifice of sweet smell, acceptable unto God.

A house, founded in love, walled with sincerity, roofed in with generosity. Its windows are agates, its gates carbuncles. The beam out of the wall shall talk with me, and the stones shall give me sermons. I shall see your names engraven on every room; and I shall read, in a mystic handwriting, the record that your love was weighed in the balances, and was *not* found wanting.

The time of your love. During my life—not like the poor philosopher, who was starved to death, but who afterwards had a pillar erected in his honour. This house will be a monument of your generosity, and so it will be a double memorial. Your own presents made it needful. I am like the man who received a white elephant as a gift from his prince, and, with it, a sufficient sum of money to enable him to keep it. The damp and decay in the old house rendered a new one necessary; the other was "a pleasant place to live out of."

The difficulty of my position. My dear wife and I have firmly resolved that we will never go into debt for anything, yet you know something of the continual claims upon us in connection with the work of the Lord. You are also aware that, for the sake of my service for the Master here, I have refused to avail myself of many opportunities that I have had of acquiring wealth. You have all heard that I might have gone to America, and, in a few weeks, have obtained more than I am likely to receive in connection with my ministry for many years. Yet I feel that I acted rightly, in the sight of God, in declining all such offers that had been made to me.

The fear of making too much of a minister. There is no intent on my part to rest now that I have a new house. If possible, I shall work harder than before, and preach better than ever.'

There is a very memorable incident which belongs to the history of both husband and wife during this period when the new Helensburgh House was being prepared. In her volume, *Ten Years After!*, Mrs. Spurgeon thus wrote concerning the story of the opal ring and the piping bullfinch:

'This incident got into print somehow, and has been told, with varying incorrectness and sundry brilliant embellishments, in many papers, both in England and America. I think it must have been because my beloved so often spoke of it, and delighted to tell of the tender providence which, in so remarkable a way, gratified his sick wife's lightest wishes. As this book is as much of an autobiography as will ever be written by me, it seems well to give a correct version of the sweet true story in these pages. It was during a time of long and painful suffering that it occurred. Dark days those were, both for husband and wife, for a serious disease had invaded my frame, and little alleviation could be found from the constant, wearying pain it caused. My beloved husband, always so fully engaged about his Master's business, yet managed to secure many precious moments by my side, when he would tell me how the work of the Lord was prospering in his hands, and we would exchange sympathies, he comforting me in my suffering, and I cheering him on in his labour.

One ever-recurring question when he had to leave me was, "What can I bring you, wifey?" I seldom answered him by a *request*, for I had all things richly to enjoy, except *health*. But, one day, when he put the usual query, I said, playfully, "*I should like an opal ring, and a piping bullfinch!*" He looked surprised, and rather amused; but simply replied, "Ah, you know I cannot get those for you!" Two or three days we made merry over my singular choice of desirable articles; but, one Thursday evening, on his return from the Tabernacle, he came into my room with such a beaming face, and such love-lighted eyes, that I knew something had delighted him very much. In his hand he held a tiny box, and I am sure his pleasure exceeded mine as he took from it a beautiful little ring, and placed it on my finger. "There is your opal ring, my darling," he said, and then he told me of the strange way in which it had come. An old lady, whom he had once seen when she was ill, sent a note to the Tabernacle to say she desired to give Mrs. Spurgeon a small present, and could someone be sent to her to receive it? Mr. Spurgeon's private secretary went, accordingly, and brought the little parcel, which, when opened, was found to contain this *opal ring*! How we talked of the Lord's tender love for His stricken child, and of His condescension in thus stooping to supply an unnecessary gratification to His dear servant's sick one, I must leave my readers to imagine; but I can remember feeling that the Lord was very near to us.

Not long after that, I was moved to Brighton, there to pass a crisis in my life, the result of which would be a restoration to better health—or death. One evening, when my dear husband came from London, he brought a large package with him, and, uncovering it, disclosed a cage containing a lovely *piping bullfinch*! My astonishment was great, my joy unbounded, and these emotions were intensified as he related the way in which he became possessed of the coveted treasure. He had been to see a dear friend of ours, whose husband was sick unto death; and, after commending the sufferer to God in prayer, Mrs. T—— said to him, "I want you to take my pet bird to Mrs. Spurgeon, I would give him to none but her; his songs are too much for my poor husband in his weak state, and I know that 'Bully' will interest and amuse Mrs. Spurgeon in her loneliness while you are so much away from her." Dear Mr. Spurgeon then told her of my desire for such a companion, and together they rejoiced over the care of the loving Heavenly Father, who had so wondrously provided the very gift His child had longed for. With that cage beside him, the journey to Brighton was a very short one; and when "Bully" piped his pretty song, and took a hemp seed as a reward from the lips of his new mistress, there were eyes with joyful tears in them, and hearts overflowing with praise to God, in the little room by the sea that night; and the dear Pastor's comment was, "I think you are one of your Heavenly Father's spoiled children, and He just gives you whatever you ask for."

Does anyone doubt that this bird was a direct love-gift from the pitiful Father? Do I hear someone say, "Oh! it was all 'chance' that brought about such coincidences as these"? Ah, dear friends! those of you who have been similarly indulged by Him *know*, of a certainty, that it is not so. He who cares for all the works of His hand, cares with infinite tenderness for the children of His love, and thinks nothing which concerns them too small or too trivial to notice. If

*1   The accepted architect's drawing of the Metropolitan Tabernacle:
the towers were subsequently deleted from the plans*

2 *The laying of the foundation stone of the Metropolitan Tabernacle*

THE LONDON GUIDE

AND

Photographic Album.

Programmes of Concerts, Entertainments, and Theatres; and
Guide to the Public Buildings and Sights of London.

THE METROPOLITAN TABERNACLE.

THE SITE of the Metropolitan Tabernacle was purchased in January, 1859, for five thousand pounds, a sum collected entirely from the voluntary contributions of Mr. Spurgeon's congregation at the Surrey Music Hall. The first stone was laid in August of the same year, and the popularity of this preacher having, if possible, increased, nearly seventeen thousand pounds were then in hand. In April, 1861 the building was completed, and the first of a series of opening services was performed. The Tabernacle is 146 feet long by 81 feet broad, and 62 feet high. There are 5,500 sittings, and standing room for some five hundred persons, without excessive crowding. There are in the basement schoolrooms for 1,000 children, six class rooms, kitchen, lavatory, retiring rooms and a lecture-hall capable of holding about 900. On the ground floor there is a room for ladies' working meetings, a young men's class room, and on the first floor there are three vestries. The accommodation, large at it seems, is felt to be too limited for the work to be carried on.

It would be out of place here to criticise the mission that Mr. Spurgeon has undertaken, it will suffice to say that for the last twenty years he has never ceased to attract large and attentive congregations, not only from the vicinity of the tabernacle, but from the whole of London and the suburbs within a radius of many miles. The panic that occurred in 1856 when Mr. Spurgeon was holding forth to 7,000 people is still fresh in the memory of most of our readers, and it is satisfactory to know that in the present building the means of exit are sufficient to meet any similar emergency.

PUBLISHING OFFICE, 3, BOUVERIE STREET, FLEET STREET, LONDON.

3   *The Metropolitan Tabernacle, from a contemporary paper*

4 & 5   *An artist's impression of the congregation inside the Tabernacle*

6   The Metropolitan Tabernacle – as viewed from the entrance doors

7 '*A gorilla lecturing on Mr Spurgeon*'. *This and the following three illustrations are cartoons from contemporary newspapers*

8   C. H. Spurgeon as 'Gulliver'

9 'A Rome-Antic sketch'

10 'Signposts'

1855.

1860.

1864.

1878.

1869.

1872.

1875.

11   Portraits of C. H. Spurgeon

12   Mrs C. H. Spurgeon

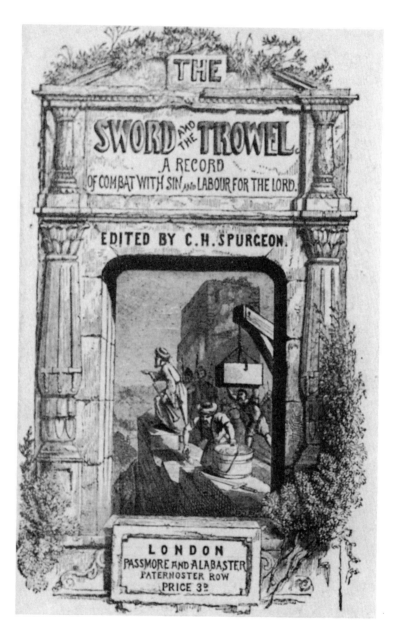

13 *The cover to* The Sword and the Trowel
14 [*Right*] *Life Assurance Proposal, filled in by Spurgeon*

Eagle, Star & British Dominions Insurance Company, Ltd., 1807

STAR LIFE ASSURANCE SOCIETY.

48, MOORGATE STREET, LONDON, E.C.

LIFE PROPOSAL.

If on the Life of another, state the interest the Assurer has in that Life

1. Name, Residence, and Occupation of the Life to be Assured — Charles Haddon Spurgeon, Nightingale Lane, Clapham — Minister of the Gospel

2. Name, Residence, and Occupation of the person by whom the Proposal is made —

3. Place of Birth — Kelvedon Essex. Date of Birth — 19th day of June 1834. Age next Birthday 35 Years.

4. Sum to be Assured, and for what term (State whether the Premium is to be paid Annually, Half Yearly, or Quarterly) — £1000 paid annually

5. Whether the Life proposed has ever been afflicted with Gout, Asthma, Rupture, Palsy, Dropsy, or Rheumatic Fever — Gout or Rheumatic gout only

6. Whether the Life proposed has ever been afflicted with any Fits or Convulsions since Infancy — No, unless convulsions of laughter are meant

7. Whether the Life proposed has ever been afflicted with Insanity, Spitting of Blood, Disease of the Lungs, Habitual or Periodical Cough, Affliction of the Liver, or any other Disease, Ailment, or Infirmity, or addicted to any habit tending to shorten Life — Probable affection of Kidneys causing abundance of infirmities but none yet recognisable by the

8. Whether the Life proposed has had the Small-Pox, or been Vaccinated — Vaccinated at least so I have always believed

9. Whether Single or Married — Married

10. Whether the Life proposed has resided abroad, and if so, where, and for what Period — Travelled but resided in England

11. Whether employed in the Military or Naval Service —

12. Are the Parents living or dead? If living, give their age and state of health. If deceased, at what ages did they die, and of what complaints? — Father John Spurgeon — 58 — Mother Eliza Spurgeon — 56 generally well and not ill. both living at Geneva Road Brixton

13. Have any Brothers or Sisters of the Life proposed died since Infancy? If so, at what ages and of what complaints? — None

14. How many Brothers and Sisters are now living? — Seven

15. Have either of the Parents or any near relatives died of Consumption? — Not that I know of

16. Has a Proposal been made to Assure the Life in this or any other Office? If so, was it declined, or accepted on the usual terms? Or on what terms? — In British Equitable some 14 years ago accepted — First Class.

17. Name and Residence of present Medical Attendant, and how long known to him, for reference as to present and general health and habits — Dr Palfrey Finsbury Place. Physician Twelve years or more

Name any other Medical Gentleman whose advice has been sought, and state for what complaint, and when his services were required — Nobody. One doctor is quite enough for any man to survive

18. Name and Residence of Two Intimate Friends fully acquainted with the Life proposed — Jesse Hobson, 48 Moorgate St, Joseph Passmore, Little Britain, Charles Blackshaw, 78 Penrose Street Walworth

I, the above-named **Charles Haddon Spurgeon** do propose to the Directors of the Star Life Assurance Society to make an Assurance with that Society, in the sum of **One thousand** pounds, on the life of **myself**

And I do hereby declare that the above Particulars and Statements are true, and that I have not withheld any material circumstance or information touching past or present state of health or habits of life; And I agree that the above Particulars and Statements shall be the basis of the Contract between me and the Directors of the same Society for the above Assurance, and shall be referred to in the Policy about to be granted by the said Society; and that if any untrue statement is at any time hereafter found to be contained in this Declaration, all moneys which may then have been paid upon account of the aforesaid Assurance shall be forfeited, and the Contract between me and the Directors of the said Society shall be void. And I further agree that the Assurance hereby proposed shall not be binding upon the Directors of the said Society, until the amount of the premium in respect thereof shall have been paid.

Signed by me, this 3rd day of October one thousand eight hundred and sixty 8

Chas Blackshaw   C. H. Spurgeon

The above Declaration was signed in my presence

Metropolitan Tabernacle
Newington
Decr 26th 1878.

Dear Pastor,
        It is with much earnestness
and love that we your Church Officers wish to
lay before you this our united appeal.
    We consider it to be the path of wisdom for you
to lay on one side for three months your Public
duties in our midst, so as to obtain the complete
rest you so much require. Your many labours in
season and out of season in which we heartily rejoice
have led us to the conclusion that unless you
renew your powers by a long cessation from
active work you will be prevented from a
continuance of it in the future. Our hearts have
sorely grieved over the suffering and weakness which
have seized you so often of late and we therefore
deem it imperative that you should try the
effect of an entire change of scene for three
months. We will make any arrangements you
may desire for the carrying on of your work
while you are away, but most affectionately
yet firmly we press our unanimous judgment
upon you for your consideration. We shall miss
you sadly and shall hail with joy your return
to your loved and prosperous labours; still we
cannot but see that you are wearing yourself away
at your post and must spare yourself for the
future welfare and service not only of our own

beloved Church but of the whole Christian
World.

May our Heavenly Father speedily restore
you and yet more abundantly bless you

pray your loving fellow workers

James A. Spurgeon
William Olney
— McMurell
Thomas Greenwood
Wm Payne
William Higgs
W. Mills
Benj Weldon Carr
T. Passmore
Thomas H. Olney
S. R. Phillips

John T. Dunn
William Perkins
Charles Cornell
M. Bowker
S. R. Pearce
G. Croker
W. H. Hale
M. Llewellyn
J. Nicholson
George Copuit
Edward Binfield
Vernon J. Charlesworth
G. E. Elvin
Geo T. Colston

G. J. Marshall
E. J. Everett

16   The new 'Helensburgh House' (front view)

17   Helensburgh House from the garden, with C.H.S. on the balcony of his study

our faith were stronger, and our love more perfect, we should see far greater marvels than these in our daily lives.

There is not much more to tell. "Bully's" sweet little life and ministry ended at Brighton; but the memory of the Lord's tenderness in giving him to me, is a life-long treasure; and the opal ring glistens on my finger as I write this paragraph.'

The experiences of that trying time need not be described, but mention must be made of the great kindness of Sir James Y. Simpson, who travelled twice from Edinburgh to Brighton to render all the aid that the highest surgical skill could suggest. When the operation was over, Spurgeon asked Sir James about his fee, and he replied, 'Well, I suppose it should be a thousand guineas; and when you are Archbishop of Canterbury, I shall expect you to pay it. Till then, let us consider it settled by love.'

After the meeting of donors, mentioned earlier in this chapter, Mrs. Spurgeon went back to Brighton until the house was ready to receive its long-absent mistress. The thought and care which her husband bestowed upon its furnishing, would have surprised even those who thought they knew him. How lovingly and tenderly he 'reported progress' as the various articles of furniture were being purchased, the following letter will show:

'My Own Dear Sufferer,

I am pained indeed to learn, from T——'s kind note, that you are still in so sad a condition! Oh, may the ever-merciful God be pleased to give you ease!

I have been quite a long round to-day—if a "round" can be "long." First, to Finsbury, to buy the wardrobe—a beauty. I hope you will live long to hang your garments in it, every thread of them precious to me for your dear sake. Next, to Hewlett's, for a chandelier for the dining-room. Found one quite to my taste and yours. Then, to Negretti & Zambra's, to buy a barometer for my very own fancy, for I have long promised to treat myself to one. On the road, I obtained the Presburg biscuits, and within their box I send this note, hoping it may reach you the more quickly. They are sweetened with my love and prayers.

The bedroom will look well with the wardrobe in it; at least, so I hope. It is well made; and, I believe, as nearly as I could tell, precisely all you wished for. Joe [Mr. Passmore gave this handsome present] is very good, and should have a wee note whenever darling feels she could write it without too much fatigue; but not yet. I bought also a table for you in case you should have to keep your bed. It rises or falls by a screw, and also winds sideways, so as to go over the bed, and then it has a flap for a book or paper, so that my dear one may read or write in comfort while lying down. I could not resist the pleasure of making this little gift to my poor suffering wifey, only hoping it might not often be in requisition, but might be a help when there was a needs-be for it. Remember, all I buy, I pay for. I have paid for everything as yet with the earnings of my pen, graciously sent me in time of need. It is my ambition to leave nothing for you to be anxious about. I shall find the money for the curtains, etc., and you will amuse yourself by giving orders for them after your own delightful taste.

I must not write more; and, indeed, matter runs short, except the old, old story of a love which grieves over you, and would fain work a miracle, and raise you up to perfect health. I fear the heat afflicts you. Well did the elder say to John in Patmos, concerning those who are before the throne of God, 'neither shall the sun light on them, nor any heat.'

Yours to love in life, and death, and eternally,

C. H. S.'

There was a very small room, by the side of Spurgeon's study, which was specially fitted up for his wife's use; and nothing had been forgotten which could in any way conduce to the comfort of an invalid almost entirely confined to her couch. Never will the rapture with which he welcomed her home be forgotten, nor the joyful pride with which he pointed out all the arrangements he had made so that her captivity should have every possible compensation and alleviation. There was a cunningly-contrived cupboard in one corner of the room, into which he had gathered all the details of his loving care for her. When the doors were opened, a dainty washing apparatus was disclosed, with hot and cold water laid on, so that no fatigue in ascending and descending the stairways should be neces- sary, and even the towels were embroidered with her name. He had thought of all things that might please; and there were such tender touches of devoted love upon all the surroundings of the little room that no words can describe her emotions when first she gazed upon them, and afterwards when she proved, by practical experi- ence, their great usefulness and value.

Even when the new house was finished, Mrs. Spurgeon was still detained at Brighton, and her husband had, for a while, to occupy it without her. He used often to say, during that time of loneliness, that he and the cat (old 'Dick') went up and down the stairs *mewing for the mistress.*

The new Helensburgh House was dedicated to God with much prayer and praise. Spurgeon always felt that it was a gift from the Lord, through His faithful stewards; and, therefore, all its charms and comforts were accepted as a sacred trust to be employed for his Master's glory. The claims laid to his many forms of Christian service were so numerous, and so constant, that his home could hardly at any period have been called a *private* house; but there were 'high days and holidays' when the students would gather in the garden, at the commencement of the Autumn session, or on some other special occasion when they were invited to meet with their tutors and brethren, and to listen to the wit and wisdom of their President. At such times, there were always many sincere enquiries for 'the Mother of the College,' though, for some years, she had to be content with quietly peeping, from a corner of her bedroom window, at the merry throng down below. On one memorable occasion, she was carried down, in a chair, to the dining-room, and the students sang for her especial benefit some of the sweet songs of Zion.

The garden was rearranged under the direction of Shirley Hibberd, who very ingeniously made the most of a comparatively small area, so that it formed a still more delightful retreat for the oft-weary preacher and toiler when he could steal away for a brief respite from his almost incessant service. Among other alterations, a new lawn was specially prepared, where father and sons, and a few favoured visitors, might play at the old Puritan game of 'bowls.' It was a healthy and not too tiring exercise; but its chief attraction probably was that it had been the favourite amusement of the great uncrowned king of England, Oliver Cromwell, and some of the mightiest masters of theology that the world has ever seen. Spurgeon used frequently to say that the expression 'the bias of the will' must have been connected in their minds with 'the bias of the bowl,' and that he would have greatly prized the privilege of witnessing the game as it was played by the Lord Protector and such notable divines as Thomas Goodwin, John Howe, Thomas Manton, John Owen, and other eminent preachers of the golden age of England's civil and religious history.

Some time after that particular part of the garden was newly turfed, it furnished an interesting instance of the latent power of vegetable life. In digging up the ground ready for the levelling process, the men had evidently disturbed certain roots which had been deeply buried beneath the earth; so it happened before long, that horseradish forced its way up in various places, to the manifest disfigurement of the lawn. It was a very troublesome task to eradicate the old tenant of the soil, but the preacher saw in it a striking simile of the development of long-hidden evil in the human heart, and of the difficulty of getting rid of it.

G. H. Pike who became acquainted with Spurgeon not long after the completion of the new Helensburgh House has given the following description of the home:

'Helensburgh House struck the visitor as being not only an elegant villa, but one which was well planned to suit the requirements of the family. There was a neat garden in front, charming grounds of some extent in the rear. When you entered the house from Nightingale Lane all the domestic arrangements would strike you as being exceedingly comfortable; but there was nothing provided for mere show. At each end the dining-room opened into a conservatory, which was also an aviary, whose feathered inmates maintained a kind of cheerful chorus. There were pictures on the walls of some attraction; but probably the one you would stand still to look at would be the one consisting of photographs of the pastor's twin sons. Once a year, until the two came of age, a new photograph was taken, so that the progress of humanity from babyhood to young manhood was seen at a glance. "Ah," said the great preacher to me when I once showed some interest in this collection, "if one could only grow in grace like that!"

Well, it is past three o'clock on a Saturday afternoon—dinner is over and for one who can claim the privilege this is the time to see the pastor more at ease than on any other day in the week. "Is Mr. Spurgeon at home?" "Yes; and all alone in the study." To reach the study you ascend some stairs. The greeting is thoroughly cordial; but, at the same time, it would appear that this ever-busy man has been interrupted in his work. There may be a number of newly-written letters before him, the ink on the last being not yet dry. In any case there will be a number of printer's proofs on the table, some already corrected, while others are awaiting the process. The room at once struck you as being all and containing all that an ardent student could require. The apartment was large; it was sufficiently lofty, and was, of course, richly furnished with books, new and old, some being of sufficient rarity to cause a bibliophile's mouth to water. These books, collected with great care and judgment, were not only on the shelves and a sight to see—they were well used; and, notwithstanding the very natural astonishment of a class of good folks who never enter a library without expressing the opinion that the possessor can never have read, nor can ever hope to read, so many books, you would have found some difficulty in reaching down a volume with the contents of which the master was not partially or fully acquainted. In addition to the printed books there were also divers unpublished MSS., some being the productions of seventeenth-century Puritan divines. The fact was, a number of second-hand booksellers had the intimation made to them that whenever a MS. of this kind came into their possession the treasure would find a ready purchaser at Clapham. The wonder was how, with such demands on his time, Spurgeon contrived to get through so much reading as he did; but the more you conversed with him in that charming room, the more clearly did you perceive that the mind of your companion was the garner of an omnivorous reader. He could not only read at lightning speed, but when he had gone through a book the contents became permanently his own.

Saturday afternoon was a time of unbending and of free intercourse, if such a term as *unbending* may be applied to a man who never carried about with him any airs of the "great man." Still, at such times, when he was surrounded by friends, he would relate things which he would not have told in public; and such was the interest of his reminiscences and his opinions on men, books, and great public movements, that even his dog Punch seemed to be an interested auditor.

"You know, I am not the reverend gentleman," I once heard him remark; and it was at once realized that he spoke what he felt. He wished all of his visitors to be as much at ease as he was himself. I am not a lukewarm admirer of Boswell's *Life of Johnson*; but I am persuaded that, with all his powers, the literary monarch of the eighteenth century did not surpass Spurgeon as a conversationalist.

At Helensburgh House you found yourself in a charming home, where indoors and out were all things to add pleasure or attraction to life; but so fully is the master occupied with the business which seems to fire him with enthusiasm, that all seem to exist for others rather than for him. The house was supposed to be out of the great highway of city life; and when he went there the young pastor, of course, fervently hoped that the place would afford him a retreat from the crowd of callers, including even begging impostors, who seem naturally to be attracted by the popular minister, and whom they regard as their legitimate prey. As popular preachers know to their cost, however, it is impossible to keep the crowd of intruders altogether at bay.'

Many were the welcome visitors who came to Nightingale Lane. Along with such friends as his publishers, Passmore and Alabaster, the Principal of his College, George Rogers, and his church officers at the Tabernacle, there were missionaries and preachers who called, including sympathizers from America and the Colonies. The circumstances in which some came to the house, however, were not always so happy as the following story, which Spurgeon told to the students of the Pastors' College many years later, indicates:

'There is a Divine discipline always going on in the Church of Christ, of which, sometimes, we are not fully aware. I remember one terrible instance, which occurred many years ago, of a man who often tried to annoy and offend me; but that is not a thing that can be done so easily as some suppose. The individual to whom I refer had long attempted it, and failed. At last, one Sabbath, when he had been peculiarly troublesome, I said to him, "Brother So-and-so, will you come and see me to-morrow morning?" In a very surly tone, he replied, "I have got my living to earn, and I can't see you after five o'clock in the morning." "Oh!" I answered, "that will suit me very well, and I will be at your service, and have a cup of coffee ready for you to-morrow morning at five o'clock." I was at the door at the appointed time, ready to let him in; his temper had led him to walk all those miles out to my house that he might tell me of his latest grievance. It appeared that he had lost £25 for something or other that he had done, he said for the church, but we all felt that it was his own private speculation, and we were not responsible. However, he told me that he could not afford to lose such a large amount, so I counted out five £5 notes, and gave them to him. He looked at me, and asked me this question, "Do you give me this money out of any of the church funds?" "No," I replied, "I feel that you cannot afford such a loss, and though it is no concern of mine, I willingly give you the money." I noticed a strange look come over his face, but he said very little more, and I prayed with him, and he went away.

At five o'clock in the afternoon, the man sent round for my brother to go to see him. When he returned, he said to me, "Brother, you have killed that man by your kindness; he cannot live much longer. He confessed to me that he had broken up two churches before, and that he had come into the Tabernacle church on purpose to act in the same way, and he had specially sought to put you out of temper with him—which he never could do—and he told me that he was a devil, and not a Christian. I said to him, "My brother once proposed to have you as an elder of the church." He seemed very surprised, and asked me, "Did he really think so much of me as that?" I answered, "Yes, but the other elders said that you had such a dreadful temper that there would be no peace in their midst if you were brought in among them."

About the middle of the prayer-meeting, a note was passed to me saying that the poor fellow had cut his throat. I felt his death terribly, and the effect of it upon the people generally was much the same as when Ananias and Sapphira were slain because of their lying unto the Holy Ghost: "Great fear came upon all the church, and upon as many as heard these things." I had often spoken of "killing people by kindness," but I never wished to have another instance of it in my own experience.'

Another visitor arrived at Helensburgh House in dramatic circumstances and his coming might have had very serious consequences if the master of the house had not been graciously guided in his mode of dealing with the madman. Spurgeon happened to be passing the entrance-hall just as someone rapped rather loudly at the door; and, without considering who might be seeking admission in that unceremonious fashion, he opened it. In an instant, a wild-looking man, armed with a huge stick, sprang in, slammed the door, stood with his back against it, and, in a most menacing manner, announced that he had come to kill Mr. Spurgeon! The situation was extremely critical, for there was no way either to escape from the maniac or to summon assistance to get rid of him; so Spurgeon said, 'You must mean my brother, his name is Spurgeon';—knowing, of course, that he could give him timely warning if there was any fear of the man going to Croydon. 'Ah!' said the crazy fellow, 'it is the man that makes jokes that I mean to kill.' 'Oh, then, you must go to my brother, for he makes jokes!' 'No,' he said, 'I believe you are the man,' and then suddenly he exclaimed, 'Do you know the asylum at ———? That's where I live, and it takes ten men to hold me.' Then Spurgeon saw his opportunity, and drawing himself up to his full height, he said, in his most impressive tones, 'Ten men! that is nothing; you don't know how strong I am. Give me that stick.' The poor creature, thoroughly cowed, handed over the formidable weapon. Seizing it, and opening the door, Spurgeon almost shouted, 'If you are not out of the house this very moment, I'll break every bone in your body.' The man quickly fled, some-one was at once sent to give information to the police, and it was a great relief to hear that, before long, the escaped madman was again under restraint.

Spurgeon used often to describe the encounter he had with one of his neighbours at Nightingale Lane. After a long and painful illness from gout, he was starting for a short drive, in the hope of gaining a little strength, when this gentleman came up to the carriage, and pointing to the sufferer's bandaged hand and foot, said, with all the scorn and contempt he could compress into the words, ' "Whom the Lord loveth, he chasteneth." I would not have such a God as that.' In relating the story, Spurgeon always said, 'I felt my blood boil with indignation, and I answered, "I rejoice that I have such a God as that; and if He were to chasten me a thousand times worse than this, I would still love Him; yea, though He slay me, yet will I trust in Him." '

Another time, the same gentleman was in rather a different mood, and he then said to the Pastor, 'I don't believe in shutting myself up with a lot of people in a stuffy building; I like plenty of fresh air, and I worship the God of nature.' 'Yes,' replied Spurgeon, who knew that his neighbour had a skittle-alley, 'your god is made of wood, is he not? and his worship is carried on with a great deal of noise, isn't it? I hear you at your little game before I start for the Tabernacle on a Sunday morning.'

Spurgeon knew how to turn everything to account in his great life-work of preaching the gospel. A simple incident, associated with the new house and garden, furnished him with amost effective illustration for a sermon in the Tabernacle. Long after he had left Nightingale Lane, he recalled the circumstances; and, in urging his hearers who had found the Saviour to seek to bring others to Him, he said:

'In the depth of winter, at a time when I had a balcony to my study, I put some crumbs out upon it, and there came a robin redbreast first, who pecked and ate all he could. I do not know his language, but I fancy I can tell what he said, for he went away, and presently returned with ever so many sparrows and other birds. He had no doubt said to them, "There are crumbs up there; come with me, and get them." So they followed him, and they came in greater numbers every day, and I do not know how it was except that they told one another. One day, whether it was the robin or the sparrows, I cannot say, but some of them told a blackbird, and he was a bigger fellow than any of them; when he came, he stood near, for I should think, a minute, and then he spied me inside, and he flew away, for he thought, "That good man does not like blackbirds." But he did not know me; for I was pleased to see him, and I should have liked to see a lot of such birds. So the robin went up to him, and told him that he had been there for the last three or four days, and I had never even threatened him; and then, after being persuaded a little, the blackbird came back, and the robin seemed to me to be quite pleased to think that he had converted his big companion, and brought him back, for they dropped down together on the crumbs, and they had such a joyful feast that they returned to the balcony again and again as long as the wintry weather lasted.

There are some of you, dear robin redbreasts, who have been here ever so long, eating my Master's crumbs, and you have brought some sparrows to the feast; now try to entice a blackbird, and if there is one blackbird bigger and blacker than the rest, go and bring him, for Jesus says that He will cast out none that come to Him by faith; and you may be sure that it is true, for He is "a Friend of publicans and sinners." '

At another service, Spurgeon thus turned to practical account the wiles of the bird-catchers who carried on their operations not far from his home:

'There is a common hard by the place where I live; and, on Sundays, Londoners come down by scores, and occupy themselves in this way upon it. They bring with them little birds in cages, and use them to lure other birds from the sky, that they may entrap them. Only the other Sabbath, as I was going to the house of God, I saw a little robin sitting on his perch in a wire cage, and he was diligently whistling so as to attract other birds to the fowlers' snare. I assure you that it was a good lesson to me; for I said to myself, "These men know that it is no use for them to frighten the birds; but if they want to catch them, they must put one of their own kind into a cage, and the little captive, by its song, attracts its fellows." Suppose one of those fowlers should be stupid enough to put a cat into the cage, it would not allure any robins; or suppose he was to put in an owl, that sleepy creature would not attract any larks. The arts of the bird-catcher teach us that, when God would save a sinner, He usually takes one of the same sort, first converts Him by His grace, and then sets him to preach, or teach, or sing, or to do something which attracts and allures others.'

That same common also furnished Spurgeon with an illustration which he thus related to his students:

'I shall never forget the manner in which a thirsty individual once begged of me upon Clapham Common. I saw him with a very large truck, in which he was carrying an extremely small parcel, and I wondered why he had not put the parcel into his pocket, and left the machine at home. I said to him, "It looks odd to see so large a truck for such a small load." He stopped, and looking me seriously in the face, he said, "Yes, sir, it is a very odd thing; but, do you know, I have met with an odder thing than that this very day. I've been about, working and sweating all this 'ere blessed day, and till now I haven't met a single gentleman that looked as if he'd give me a pint of beer, till I saw you." I considered that turn of the conversation very neatly managed; and we, with a far better subject upon our minds, ought to be equally able to introduce the theme upon which our heart is set. There was an ease in the man's manner which I envied, for I did not find it quite so simple a matter to introduce my own topic to his notice; yet, if I had been thinking as much about how I could do him good as he had upon how to obtain a drink, I feel sure I should have succeeded in reaching my point.'

There still stands, on Clapham Common, an ancient tree under which Spurgeon preached to ten thousand persons on Lord's-day afternoon, July 10, 1859. A fortnight earlier, a violent storm passed over the South of London. The tree was struck by lightning, and a man who had sought shelter beneath it was killed. Spurgeon, who was greatly impressed by the solemn event, resolved to preach on the fatal spot, and to make a collection for the widow of the man who had been killed. This arrangement was duly carried out, a waggon beneath the tree serving for a pulpit, and the congregation contributing £27 10s. 4d. for the poor bereaved woman.[1] The text

---

[1] The sermon appears in full in *The Sword and the Trowel* for May, 1897.

was taken from Luke 12. 14, 'Be ye therefore ready also;' and in commencing his discourse, the preacher said:

'Happily for us, it is not often that men are struck dead by lightning. Remember all the multitudes of men existing upon the face of the earth, then calculate the number of thunderstorms, and you will see that, after all, many of the fears which disturb our minds in time of tempest and of storm are far more groundless than we are apt to imagine. It is but here and there, and now and then, that the scathing blast smites the earth, and one of our fellow-creatures is launched into eternity. When, however, such a solemn event occurs, we ought to hear in it the voice of God, and listen to what He says to us. I thought, as I passed this tree a short time since, what a sermon it might preach if it could speak! How the rustle of its leaves would forewarn us of the stealthy footsteps of death; and, as it towers upward to the skies, how it might be regarded as a finger directing us to look toward heaven and seek the Lord of grace and mercy!'

Spurgeon's closing words were: 'May the Lord now add His blessing! May He grant, moreover, that a more solemn impression than I can hope to make may be made upon you, as once again you gaze upon this spot! There is, in St. Paul's Cathedral, a little chisel-mark still visible, which you may never have noticed, but which some time may be shown to you. It is the memorial of the death of a man who, being employed at work on the dome, fell down, and was dashed to pieces. What a solemn spot is *that*; and what a solemn spot is *this*! My dear hearers, ere you go away, breathe a prayer for pardon; and, as often as you pass this place, think of your past lives, and of the world to come. It is said that we often walk over our own graves without knowing it, and that we often come to other men's graves and death-places without being aware of it; but *there*, in that tree, stands the monument of the awfully sudden death of a fellow-creature; and let it be so remembered. May God bless the widow; may He bless the orphans; and may He bless all of you! But, my dear friends, ere we go away this afternoon, will not each one of you pray for himself that his sins may be pardoned? Will you all separate, having come together in vain? I do beseech and pray you to lift up your hearts to God, and every one of you to cry, 'God be merciful to me a sinner!' Look this very instant to Christ Jesus, who died upon the cross. We cannot all hope ever to meet again until the last tremendous day; oh, may we, without one exception meet then at the right hand of God! Amen.'

C. H. Spurgeon: The Full Harvest

One of the inmates of the study in the new Helensburgh House, on certain days of the week, was John Lewis Keys, who was for a quarter of a century Spurgeon's secretary and literary assistant, and concerning whom the Pastor wrote in the Preface to Volume I of *The Treasury of David*: 'The research expended on this volume would have occupied far too much of my time, had not my friend and amanuensis, Mr. John L. Keys, most diligently aided me in investigations at the British Museum, Dr. Williams' Library, and other treasuries of theological lore. With his help, I have ransacked books by the hundred; often, without finding a memorable line as a reward; but, at other times, with the most satisfactory result.' In succeeding volumes, Spurgeon repeated his testimony to the value of Mr. Keys' help in the great task happily completed in 1885; and he also mentioned the many courtesies shown to himself, through his secretary, while searching for extracts in Church of England and other libraries.

All Spurgeon's publications, from 1867 to 1891, passed through the hands of J. L. Keys; and he not only read the proofs of the sermons, *Sword and Trowel*, Almanacks, and many books issued during that period, but he also contributed several interesting articles to the Magazine; and he was, for a great part of the time, engaged in evangelistic and pastoral labours at Wimbledon, Whitstable, and Streatham. After Spurgeon's death he struggled on, amid failing health and many difficulties, till, on January 7, 1899, he entered into rest. His suitability for and efficiency in the work he fulfilled are beyond all praise.

One who became a permanent member of the Spurgeon household at Nightingale Lane was George Lovejoy, or 'Old George' as he was familiarly called. Spurgeon's faithful servant for many years, he would certainly have been kindly mentioned if his master had been spared to complete the present record. The two men were first brought together after the death of Mr. Thorne (father of Mrs. Spurgeon's companion). Mr. Thorne's butler said to the Pastor, 'Ah, sir! I closed my old master's eyes, and now Pil-garlic's[1] occupation is gone.' 'Well, George, what do you say to coming to take care of me?' 'Do you really mean it, sir?' 'Yes, of course I do.' 'Oh! then I'll dance for joy, for nothing would please me more, and I'll serve you faithfully as long as you will let me stay with you.'

[1] Pil-garlic: a term used in the Tudor period for a bald-headed man ('peeled garlic'). In later years it was used of a man forsaken by his fellows, and, humorously, or in a self-pitying way, of oneself.

Spurgeon often said that George reminded him of Mr. Pickwick's Sam Weller, and he certainly had many quaint sayings which that worthy might have uttered. If anyone asked him his name, he answered, 'George Lovejoy. Don't you know what the apostle says, "The fruit of the Spirit is love, joy"?' 'You're a rum 'un, George,' his dear master often said to him; and he would reply, 'Yes, sir; there were only two of us came over in three ships, and the other one was drowned.' 'Well, George, how are you this morning?' was often Spurgeon's enquiry; and the invariable answer was, 'First-rate, sir; as fresh as a salt fish.' George's hair was much darker than his beard and moustache, which his master playfully suggested was the result of having used his jaws more than his brains; and, on one occasion at least, Spurgeon said that his name could be properly spelt without using one of the right letters—thus, *Jawj*.

'No man is a hero to his valet,' was never true concerning Spurgeon. Everyone who came under his influence felt the power of his gracious character; and, while there was never in him any affectation of pride or superiority, all felt instinctively that they were in the presence of a truly noble and kingly man. There was no more sincere mourner, among the tens of thousands at Newington and Norwood in February, 1892, than the faithful 'Old George,' who had been superannuated through increasing infirmities which he was unwilling to confess; and, after continuing to the bereaved mistress such service as he was able occasionally to render, he also was 'called home' on January 6, 1898.

No one living knows the toil and care I have to bear. I ask for no sympathy but ask indulgence if I sometimes forget something. I have to look after the Orphanage, have charge of a church with four thousand members, sometimes there are marriages and burials to be undertaken, there is the weekly sermon to be revised, *The Sword and the Trowel* to be edited, and besides all that, a weekly average of five hundred letters to be answered. This, however, is only half my duty, for there are innumerable churches established by friends, with the affairs of which I am closely connected, to say nothing of those cases of difficulty which are constantly being referred to me.— C.H.S.

The greatest—nay, the sole—event of importance which has occurred in Rome during the last few days is the arrival of Mr. Spurgeon, and his intended sojourn here till the 1st instant. Mr. Spurgeon in Rome! How strange do those words sound! The enemy of monks and nuns, the denouncer of idolatry and Mariolatry, the foremost among Dissenters in the greatest Dissenting country on the face of the earth, has arrived in the city of Pius IX and preached a sermon against Popery within a trumpet's call of the Vatican. . . . He described Rome, in one of the most eloquent sermons he ever preached, as an "idolatrous city", and he warned his hearers against idolatry in terms as startling as they were persuasive, with a look and gesture worthy of a really great actor, which he undoubtedly is.—*The Daily Telegraph*, December 13, 1871.

12

In Suffering and Sunshine

FOLLOWING close upon Mrs. Spurgeon's illness there appeared unmistakable signs in the year 1869 that Spurgeon's own constitution was impaired. Without doubt, the main cause was sheer over-work. By the age of thirty he had been used to do much more than is usually expected from a life-time in the ministry and now, at the age of thirty-five, the demands upon him were immense. In terms of financial responsibility alone an annual income of between twenty and thirty thousand pounds was necessary to maintain the various works which he had begun. G. H. Pike, whose personal acquaintance with Spurgeon dates from this period, wrote: 'It might seem the easiest thing in the world for such a man to preach or to write what he did; but that it was quite otherwise was shown by his dread of crowds, and by the signs of wear which each year now became more visible. How he laid upon himself a burden of work which was not easily borne was well known to all who were closely connected with him; but I am not sure that the public ever properly realized the fact.'

Spurgeon himself well understood the cause of his weakened health but, while he counselled other ministers to husband their strength, his sense of spiritual obligation allowed him to take little or no respite. In a sermon 'For the Sick and Afflicted', published in 1876, he said: 'People said to me years ago, "You will break your constitution down with preaching ten times a week," and the like. Well, if I have done so, I am glad of it. I would do the same again. If I had fifty constitutions I would rejoice to break them down in the service of the Lord Jesus Christ. You young men that are strong, overcome the wicked one and fight for the Lord while you can. You will never regret having done all that lies in you for our blessed Lord and Master.'

In 1869, however, rest was temporarily forced upon the Pastor of the Tabernacle and this was to become a recurring pattern in his life. From the age of thirty-five, scarcely a year passed without one

[193]

kind of illness or another laying him low. Approximately one third of the last twenty-two years of his ministry was spent out of the pulpit, either suffering, convalescing, or taking precautions against the return of illness. One of the first of many subsequent notices on his health occurred in *The Sword and the Trowel* for October, 1869: 'The Editor's painful indisposition compels him to forego his usual monthly notes, and also the Exposition of the Psalms. Too great pressure of work has produced a disorder whose root is more mental than physical. Wearisome pain, added to relative affliction and ever-increasing responsibility, make up a burden under the weight of which unaided mortal strength must sink. An all-sufficient God is our joy and rejoicing'.

Later in the same year he suffered from an attack of small-pox, though happily not in its worst form. This was followed, in December, by his first experience of gout, one of the most painful diseases known to man. The name 'gout' seems to be derived from the belief that drops of pain-creating material originating in the blood-stream fall into the joints, crystallize there, and produce those symptoms which sufferers have described as the very distillation of agony. The feet are the members of the body most commonly affected, it may be one foot only or both simultaneously. After an attack is over the patient may feel better in health than for a long time before, for which reason it was long popularly believed that a fit of the gout was capable of curing all other ailments of the body. But the idea will not bear investigation. Also, the disease tends to recur in previously-affected members of the body and to extend gradually to other parts, until, at the worst, the whole system is brought under the tyranny of the disease.

By 1871 it appeared probable that his affliction had taken a per-manent hold on Spurgeon's system. After the Pastors' Conference at the end of March in that year, he wrote: 'On the last day of the Annual Conference we were laid prostrate by an attack of one very painful malady. It will, we fear, be our cross till death. We have been comparatively free from it ever since Christmas, 1869; but on this occasion it came upon us as an armed man, and great has been our bodily anguish beneath its strokes'.

After enforced rest he was back in his pulpit on Sunday, April 23, but weeks of pain followed. Through May and June, 1871, when he should have been on a previously-arranged continental tour, he lay suffering. In a letter to the congregation at the Tabernacle he opened his heart to them:

'Clapham.

Dear Friends,

The furnace still glows around me. Since I last preached to you, I have been brought very low; my flesh has been tortured with pain, and my spirit has been prostrate with depression. Yet, in all this, I see and submit to my Father's hand; yea, more, I bless Him that His paternal love has been more than ever clear to me. With some difficulty, I write these lines in my bed, mingling them with the groans of pain and the songs of hope.

The peace of God be with every one of you, my beloved! My love in Christ Jesus be with you all! I rejoice that my very dear friend, Mr. Hugh Stowell Brown, is with you to-day. May his words be marrow and fatness to your souls!

It must, under the most favourable circumstances, be long before you see me again, for the highest medical authorities are agreed that only long rest can restore me. I wish it were otherwise. My heart is in my work, and with you; but God's will must be done. When I am able to move, I must go away. I try to cast all my cares on God, but sometimes I fear that you may get scattered. O my dear brethren, do not wander, for this would break my heart! I might also feel deep anxiety for my great works, but I am sure my Lord will carry them on. It is, however, my duty to tell you what you can do, and what is needed. The Orphanage funds are lower just now than they have been these two years. God will provide, but you know that you are His stewards.

You do pray for me, I know; but I entreat you not to cease your supplications. I am as a potter's vessel when it is utterly broken, useless, and laid aside. Nights of watching, and days of weeping have been mine, but I hope the cloud is passing. Alas! I can only say this for my own personal and light affliction; there is one who lies nearest my heart whose sorrows are not relieved by such a hope. In this relative trial, a very keen one, I again ask your prayers. The Lord be with you evermore!'

On June 18, the eve of his birthday, he wrote in another letter to the congregation:

'On the closing day of my thirty-seventh year, I find myself the Pastor of a beloved flock, who have borne the test of twelve Sabbaths of their minister's absence, and the severer test of more than seventeen years of the same ministry, and are now exhibiting more love to him than ever. I bless God, but I also thank you, and assure you that I never felt happier in the midst of my people than I do now in the prospect of returning to you. I am still weak, but the improvement in strength this week has been very surprising. I hardly dare speak of the future; but I earnestly hope we shall look each other in the face on the first Sabbath of July.'

This hope was realized when he preached at the Tabernacle on the morning of Sunday July 2, 1871, from Psalm 71. 14, 'But I will hope continually, and will yet praise thee more and more.' A short article entitled, 'Great Mercies', which appeared from his pen in the July issue of *The Sword and the Trowel* revealed something of what he had passed through:

'It is a great mercy to be able to change sides when lying in bed . . . Did you ever lie a week on one side? Did you ever try to turn, and find yourself quite helpless? Did others lift you, and by their kindness only reveal to you the miserable fact that they must lift you back again at once into the old position, for, bad as it was, it was preferable to any other? . . . It is a great mercy to get one hour's sleep at night . . . Some of us know what it is, night after night, to long for slumber and find it not. O how sweet has an hour's sleep been when it has interposed between long stretches of pain, like a span of heaven's blue between the masses of thunder-cloud! We have blessed God more for those dear moments of repose than for whole weeks of prosperity . . . What a mercy have I felt it to have only one knee tortured at a time! What a blessing to be able to put the foot on the ground again, if but for a minute! What a still greater mercy to be able to get from the bed to a chair and back again!

We call those things mercies which please us, ease us, suit our wants, and fall in with our cravings. Truly they are so, but not less gracious are those benefits which cross us, pain us, and lay us low. The tender love which chastises us, the gentle kindness which bruises us, the fond affection which crushes us to the ground—these we do not so readily recount; yet is there as much of divine love in a smart as in a sweet, as great a depth of tenderness in buffet-ing as in consoling. We must count our crosses, diseases and pains if we would number up our blessings. Doubtless it is a mercy to be spared affliction, but he would be a wise man who should tell which of the two was the greater boon—to be for the present without chastisement or to be chastened. We judge that in either case it is well with the righteous, but we will not have a word said to the disparagement of affliction. Granted that the cross is very bitter, we maintain with equal confidence that it is also very sweet.'

Preaching at the Tabernacle, later in 1871, Spurgeon thus described how he wrestled in prayer, and prevailed with the Lord, in what proved to be the crisis of that season of suffering: 'I have found it a blessed thing, in my own experience, to plead before God that I am His child. When, some months ago, I was racked with pain to an extreme degree, so that I could no longer bear it without crying out, I asked all to go from the room, and leave me alone; and then I had nothing I could say to God but this, "Thou art my Father, and I am Thy child; and Thou, as a Father, art tender and full of mercy. I could not bear to see my child suffer as Thou makest me suffer; and if I saw him tormented as I am now, I would do what I could to help him and put my arms under him to sustain him. Wilt Thou hide Thy face from me, my Father? Wilt Thou still lay on me Thy heavy hand, and not give me a smile from Thy countenance?" I talked to the Lord as Luther would have done, and pleaded His Fatherhood in real earnest. "Like as a father pitieth his children, so the Lord pitieth them that fear Him." If He be a Father, let Him show Himself a Father—so I pleaded; and I ventured to say, when they came back who watched me, "I shall never have such agony again from this moment, for God has heard my prayer." I bless God that ease came, and the racking pain never returned. Faith mastered it by laying hold upon God in His own revealed character—that character in which, in our darkest hour, we are best able to appreciate Him. I think this is why that prayer, *Our Father* which art in Heaven," is given to us, because, when we are lowest, we can still say, "Our Father," and when it is very dark, and we are very weak, our childlike appeal can go up, "Father, help me! Father, rescue me!" '

This experience made so deep an impression upon Spurgeon's mind and heart that he never forgot it. Those who are familiar with his writings must have noticed how often he referred to it, and how he urged other tried believers to do as he had done.

Though Spurgeon had quietly resumed work in the summer of 1871, preaching once on each Sunday through August, a real holiday was essential if his health was to be re-established before the chill and damp of winter aggravated his complaint. Thus in November he left home for Italy. As the following pages will show, great was his pleasure in exploring Rome, Naples and Pompeii.

More important for the future course of his life, he learned the practical lesson that if his work in London was to continue then winter visits to the warmth and sunshine of the Mediterranean would need to become a regular event. Yet Mrs. Spurgeon, his delighted companion on earlier visits to the Continent, could no longer be with him, as she explains in this section which follows.

*

In 1868, my travelling days were done. Henceforth, for many years, I was a prisoner in a sick-chamber, and my beloved had to leave me when the strain of his many labours and responsibilities compelled him to seek rest far away from home. These separations were very painful to hearts so tenderly united as were ours, but we each bore our share of the sorrow as heroically as we could, and softened it as far as possible by constant correspondence. 'God bless you,' he wrote once, 'and help you to bear my absence. Better that I should be away well, than at home suffering—better to your loving heart, I know. Do not fancy, even for a moment, that absence could make our hearts colder to each other; our attachment is now a perfect union, indissoluble for ever. My sense of your value, and experience of your goodness, are now united to the deep passion of love which was there at the first alone. Every year casts out another anchor to hold me even more firmly to you, though none was needed even from the first. May my own Lord, whose chastening hand has necessitated this absence, give you a secret inward recompense in soul, and also another recompense in the healing of the body! All my heart remains in your keeping.'

It is marvellous to me, as I survey the yearly packets of letters which are now such precious treasures, how my husband could have managed, amidst the bustle and excitement of foreign travel, to have written so much and so often. I many times begged him to spare himself in this matter, but he constantly assured me that it delighted him to do it; he said, 'Every word I write is a pleasure to me, as much as ever it can be to you; it is only a lot of odds and ends I send you, but I put them down as they come, so that you may see it costs me no labour, but is just a happy scribble. Don't fret because I write you so many letters, it is such a pleasure to tell out my joy.' Every day his dear messages came to me, except, of course, when a long railway journey intervened—and, sometimes, as an unexpected gladness, he would post two in one day, that I might be comforted concerning him. On an important tour the letters would be illustrated by many amusing pen-and-ink sketches, of people, costumes, landscapes, trees, wells, or anything which particularly struck him. Plans of the rooms he occupied in the various hotels were very frequent, and enabled me better to imagine the comfort or otherwise of his surroundings.

The letters themselves are not set forth as examples of elegant style or well-rounded periods, or even of graceful phraseology; they are simply a loving husband's daily notes to his sick wife, a record of his journeyings gladly and faithfully persevered in with the sole object of pleasing her, and relieving her sorrowful loneliness.

*

EXTRACTS FROM SPURGEON'S LETTERS TO HIS WIFE

We are in Rome. Let a man say what he will, there is a thrill passes through his soul, at the thought of being in Rome, that he cannot experience anywhere else, except in the city of our Lord— Jerusalem. There are interests and associations that cluster about 'the eternal city' that a man must feel, if he has any soul at all. You remember that, last year, we started off for our first day's sightseeing without a guide, and wandered about without knowing whither we went; this time, I can act as guide and interpreter, and am able to observe much which, on a former occasion, I had not noticed. Today, we went down the Corso, and up the Capitol. There are new excavations at its foot. We passed down the other side to the Forum, where they are still digging. Rome of the olden time is buried beneath itself, under its own ruins, and the Forum lies some ten, fifteen, and in some places thirty feet of earth below the present level. I soon found myself on what I knew to be the Via Sacra, along which the triumphal processions passed when the great generals returned from war, and climbed the Capitol in state; and it was a memorable thing to stand before the Arch of Titus, and gaze upon its bas-reliefs. There is Titus returning from the siege of Jerusalem, with the seven-branched golden candlestick, and the silver trumpets; and, while these things stand there, it is idle for infidels to say that the Bible is not true. It is good history. Nobody doubts what is written in stone upon the Arch of Titus, but the same story is found in the Book; and the more discoveries that are made of ancient cities, especially in Palestine, the more will the truth of the Book be confirmed, and the record upon stone will be found to tally with what is written on the tablets of God's Word.

Then we came to the Colosseum. What a place it is! Two-thirds of it are gone, and yet enough remains wherewith to build a great city! I climbed to the very top. Under an arch of one of the great corridors we sat down, and sang, 'Am I a soldier of the cross?' 'I'm not ashamed to own my Lord,' and 'Jesu's tremendous name;' and then I preached a little sermon from the text, 'Come, behold the works of the Lord, what desolations He hath made in the earth;' then we prayed, and sang, 'Ashamed of Jesus?' Just then, two persons went by, and said, in broad American, 'Don't let us disturb you.' To which I answered, 'Come and join,' but they replied, 'Our time is too short,' so we sang the Doxology, and went on. Pretty bold this, in such a public place, but very sweet to be remembered. 'Boylston' rolled along the vaulted tunnels like a battle-song.

We went down to the Appian Way, and on to the baths of Titus. By a mistake, I took the party up a lane, and through the wrong gate; but, after all, this was fortunate, for it brought us to the top of the immense structure; and, looking down, we saw the rooms which before I had only seen from below, and this view gave us a better idea of their vastness and mystery. The building is a huge ruin, built upon a ruin. Nero had a golden palace here, but when Titus came into power, he buried it. Its roof was made of great arches, massive and strong, so he bored holes through them, and poured in rubbish till the place was filled up, and then he built his baths on the top of all. *His* work is ruined; but now, part of the palace below has been dug out, and they have found gems of art, enough to fill hundreds of museums. Getting to the right entrance, we came across the custodian, an old wounded soldier, who showed us over the whole place, as far as practicable, telling us all he knew, pointing out every fresco, and putting a delightful zest into it for us all. It is a place of marvels! Its passages and rooms are countless, vast, weird, and most impressive; one could spend a week there, and then begin again. The excavations have brought to light treasures of porphyry, marble, and statues; and the paintings and frescoes of eighteen hundred years ago are as fresh as if they were painted yesterday. Your guide has a long pole, into which he screws another long pole with a lighted candle at the end, this he holds up as high as possible, and you see the paintings on the roof of Nero's palace. There are said to be two hundred rooms still unexcavated, and no one knows what treasures of art they may conceal. Strange to say, there is yet another house beneath this golden palace, for Nero built over the house of Mecænas, the friend of Horace; and, after digging deep down, they have come to the mosaic pavements of the first structure erected on this extraordinary spot. I want a bigger head, to take all these wonders in, and hold my thoughts!

After all this, we went a little further, to the Palace of the Cæsars, which is a mile and a half round, and is being excavated. All is ruined, but it is so far opened up as to show the lower rooms, and the first, or Imperial floor. It consisted of many palaces, and would take a month to explore. In one part, I saw rooms just dug out, as fresh as when originally decorated, and remarkably like the Pompeian house in the Crystal Palace. There was Cæsar's great hall, the place of his throne, the bath of the harem, the library, the academy or residence for philosophers, and the rooms for the Pretorian guard. In fact, the whole Palatine Hill is a palace; and as they dig down, they come to vast chambers and corridors which seem endless. One of these, quite as long as our Nightingale Lane, has its mosaic pavement all complete; we looked down from a great height upon it, and there were opened places far below that. The walls are usually seven to ten feet thick, so the work must be very heavy. I should think all kinds of marble in the world can be picked up here; it is just a vast quarry! What heaps of broken wine-jars— the champagne bottles of the Cæsars! It is a mountain of ruins of porphyry, alabaster, and all precious things! From its top you see other great ruins of temples, basilicas, palaces, and theatres!

Then the guide said, 'Now you must come and see the baths of Caracalla.' I was bewildered, lost, confounded; but I went, and found a building more than a mile in length, which beat all we had seen before, and made me feel as if my senses would give way. These enormous baths could accommodate 1,600 persons at a time; they were in tiers, one for men, another for women, the third for slaves. There were hot baths, cold baths, steam baths, swimming baths; and all these were floored with mosaics which we saw uncovered as we stood there. The roof was destroyed by the Goths; and when it fell in, it smashed the floor; but here and there great portions—as big as our lawn—are left intact, and one could see the lovely patterns of the mosaic,—each room different. The huge brick walls still stand, but the marble facing is almost all gone. I think no living man can conceive what the place must have been in its glory. I needed to go to bed, to sleep off my stupor of wonder! I am foolish to try to write about it. It is like a tadpole describing a sea! The Farnese family have taken the fine statues and other treasures to Naples; but there are acres yet to be dug out, in which, doubtless, many more are buried, but it is too great an expense to dig away very fast. I had one delicious half-hour during the day. I sat down alone opposite to St. Peter's, and felt as if in Elysium. The snow gone, the sun shining, and on the great obelisk I saw words which cheered my soul; they were these, 'Christ conquers, Christ reigns, Christ rules, Christ defends His people from all evil.' The Lord be praised; this is true, and the Pope and all the world shall know it! I love my love amidst all these great thoughts. She is my palace, my throne, my empress, my Rome, my world; yet I have more, my Saviour, my Heaven! Bless you, my own!

Today is the Sabbath, and has been up till now most sweetly calm and happy. We had our little service, with breaking of bread, and the Lord was with us. I read a sermon, and our song and prayer were 'in the spirit.' May it please the Lord of peace to give the like holy rest to my beloved! We then walked on the Pincian, where there are few people during the day, but lovely groves, and beds of roses, with seats in every corner, and all Rome at one's feet. It was truly Sabbatic. All that nature and art can do, is to be seen in these gardens, where the loveliest statues look down upon you, and fountains ripple to tunes of peace, and aromatic trees breathe perfume. A statue of Jochebed laying Moses in his ark of bulrushes among the reeds, struck me as charming to the last degree. It stood as the centre of a fountain, reeds and water-lilies grew at the rocky base, and the ripples of the little hidden jets made wavelets round the ark. Can you imagine it! Nothing in modern art has pleased me more—perhaps nothing so much. This has been a blessed day to me, and I have been feeling so well; I almost tremble lest it should be too good to continue.

Another day of wonders! This morning, we drove to the great amphitheatre of Marcellus, which once held 20,000 persons, and is far older than the Colosseum. It is buried for fourteen feet, and much built over and hidden; around it is a market for the poor, where I saw baskets full of cigar-ends which had no doubt been picked up in the street, and were being sold to be smoked in pipes. What would Marcellus have thought of this? Then we saw the long covered way which led from the theatre to the baths of Agrippa—a great colonnade, of which some pillars are visible, and others are built into the houses of the street which occupies its place. From thence to the Jews' quarter, where the same use of old stones is apparent; capitals, friezes, cornices, and all sorts of marbles are let into the walls of the dwellings. Ah! the cruelties the Jews have suffered in that Ghetto, the barbarities which have there been in-flicted upon God's ancient people! Their district is often flooded by the Tiber; and, on one occasion, when they made an appeal to the papal authorities, because their houses were ten or twelve feet under water, the only answer they received was that the water would do the Jews good! There was a law in Rome, only lately repealed, that a hundred men and fifty women from the Jewish quarter must go to the Church of St. Angelo every Sunday, and they were driven there with whips; and if one of them went to sleep, there was a whip to wake him up, that he might hear himself and his forefathers bitterly abused. On certain days of the Carnival, the Jews were obliged to run races in the Corso, stripped of almost all their cloth-ing, and then the people showered execrations and curses upon them. Time would fail to tell of their sufferings and privations, besides which they were forced to pay large sums of money to their oppressors. Matters have mended somewhat lately, and they are relieved from many of the most cruel persecutions of former days; but they are oppressed still, and I was greatly moved when, in the Church in the Ghetto, I saw this message from the Lord plainly set forth before them, 'All day long I have stretched forth My hands unto a disobedient and gainsaying people.'

To-day we went several miles along the Appian Way. What bliss ever to see it! On both sides, for many miles, it is skirted by tombs, temples, *columbaria*, and ruins of villas in continuous lines. It is a British Museum ten miles long! I felt a strange joy in walking along the same road which Paul trod, when the brethren from Rome came to meet him. From it can be seen Tusculum and Tivoli, and the long line of the Claudian aqueduct, on arches all the way from the moun-tains into Rome, as also the temple of Romulus, and the great circus of Maxentius. What a world of wonders! We went as far as the Casale Rotundo, a round tomb so large that, being full of rubbish, there is a house, and stables, and an olive garden on the top. We wanted to investigate, so climbed up, and were rewarded by the sight of a family of very scantily-clothed children; their mother and an old woman were baking maize bread in a hole in the wall of the tomb. They had *kneaded* it in a wheelbarrow, and the children looked as if they *needed* it, too.

On our way back, when nearly as far as the old walls, we turned down a lane to visit the catacombs of Calixtus. Candles were provided, and we went down to the second tier; there are five of these, one below another. I do not know how far we went, but it seemed miles; passages just wide enough for me to pass through, opening into rooms every now and then, and with many cross-roads where one could soon be lost. Here were countless graves, here and there skeletons, emblems, places for lamps, frescoes of ancient date, and many interesting memorials. It was a new scene to me, but deeply solemn and touching. Think of it—that this was only one set of chambers and passages, and that there was one above, and three deeper down! There are from five to six graves, one above the other, in each passage, and the whole place is full right along. These tombs are open in most cases, for the doors or stones which closed them are taken away to museums. This is the best and most convenient catacomb for tourists to see; but there are, I believe, sixty others. They have no Popery in them, and I would sooner live and die in them than live in this city of Babylon. It is nothing less than what the Bible calls it; it is full of idols, filthy rag, bone, and rubbish worship of the most abominable kind. I have cursed it all, as Paul did those who preach 'another gospel.'

Then we drove to St. John Lateran, 'the mother of all churches,' and I shall here only dare to write of one thing which, to my dying day, I shall never forget. I do not know that I ever felt my blood boil so with indignation or my heart melt so much with pity as when I saw the Santa Scala, down which our blessed Lord is said to have come from Pilate's hall. It was a pitiable sight to see old people, grey-headed men, young women, and little children with their mothers, crawling up and down this staircase on their knees, kissing the bottom step, and touching it with their forehead, and doing likewise to the middle and top steps, because they say our Saviour fainted at those places. As I stood there, I could only pray that another Luther might arise, and thunder forth the fact that men are not justified by works, but by faith alone. It was an awful thought to me that all these poor creatures should believe that they gained a hundred days' indulgence and the pardon of their sins every time they crawled up that staircase, and that every step their knees kneeled on meant so many days less of purgatory for them. The stairs are covered with wood, which has been three times renewed, having been worn away by the knees of the votaries! My heart feels all on a blaze with righteous anger. O miserable world, thus to dishonour the ever-blessed Lamb! O infinite mercy, which permits such insulters to live! I have seen them adoring thigh-bones, skulls, arms, and hands; yes, actually *adoring* these things as if they were Divine! Pagan Rome never went this length.

We went to St. Peter's to finish the day with music, and it was fine indeed; but I was jostled in a crowd of people so highly perfumed with garlic, that I soon made my escape to the outskirts to have another look round the great joss-house. Here I learned some English history, for I saw Canova's tomb to the memory of James III, Charles III, and Henry IX, Kings of England! Ask the boys if they ever read of them. They were the last of the Stuarts—the Pretender—his son, Charles Edward, or 'bonnie Prince Charlie,'—and his son. What hundreds of other things I have seen this day, cannot now, and perhaps never will be told. I have stayed up late to put this down for fear of forgetting it, and also because it may be I shall have less time to-morrow when preparing to preach. God bless thee, dearest, and be thou glad, with me, that no 'strong delusion to believe a lie' has fallen upon us. To-day has taught me a year's learning. The Lord make it useful to His Church!

I send a picture of the Pope's coachman. What a swell he is! I think you will like the portrait of a brigand's wife. It is very well executed, and if you like it too much to part with it, be sure to keep it. The fellow in red is awful; these *confratelli* are in all colours according to the degree of the buried person. They are good fellows, who bury the dead '*pour l'amour de Dieu*,' and they belong to all ranks in Rome. They cover themselves up in this manner to avoid recognition, and escape praise. They are universally respected, but look horribly ugly. I think they will make a sensation in the magic-lantern.

Yesterday morning, when I preached in the Presbyterian Chapel, all was quiet and delightful; but at night, in Rome, while my words were being translated by Mr. Wall, we were stopped by questioners.[1] It was requested that they would reserve their enquiries till the end of the service, but the opponents were impatient. A paper was passed up from a Catholic lady, to say that a secular priest was present, a man of great ability, and a personal friend of the Pope, and that he was sent on purpose to discuss. So, presently, a man of unprepossessing appearance began to assail us with arguments from a sceptical standpoint, upon which he received such an answer that he shifted his ground, and declared that none had any

[1] The date was December 10. The Presbyterian congregation was that of the Free Church of Scotland. Mr. Wall was pastor of the Baptist meeting-house.

right to teach save 'the Church.' Mr. Wall replied to this, and the man changed his tactics again. Then, up rose a Waldensian minister, who spoke so well that the people broke out in cheers and clapping. This was suppressed, and again the enemy thundered forth his threats. He was answered by several, and told that he had shifted his ground, and was a priest; and Mr. Wall challenged him to a public dispute at any place he chose to name. This he declined, and seeing that the people grew warm, he wisely withdrew. One word from us, and he would have been put out of the window. The incident pleased Mr. Wall, for it created excitement, and will bring more to hear; but I was far from happy about it, and would gladly have been spared such a scene. Glory be to God, there is a living church in Rome, and the way in which they have gained converts has been by opposition; the notoriety which it has given them has brought many to hear the gospel. Bravely the work goes on, and the baptized lead the way. The leaders are two good fellows, pronounced Baptists, believing firmly that their church is that of the catacombs, and the only true Church of Christ in Rome; the others, they say, are the churches of Luther, and Knox, and Wesley, and Waldo—theirs is the only old original. I gently combat their restrictiveness, but do not wonder at it.

We have been to another catacomb, one not often visited. It is named after St. Ponziano, and is situated outside Rome, in a vineyard, a good way from the walls, and though truly ancient, it is not very far opened up, but you have to go down very deep. A man, who calls himself 'the dove of the catacombs' (he must mean 'bat'), took us down. We went a long, long way, each of us carrying a taper, and at last we came to a place where some eight roads meet underground. Seven of these were closed, but we found what we had specially come to see. This was a baptistery. It was full of sweet, clear, running water, about four feet deep, and above it was a painting in fresco of our Lord standing up to his waist in the water, and John putting his hand on the sacred head, that it, too, might be immersed—he was not *pouring* the water on him. Here we stood, and prayed to the blessed One into whose Name we had been buried by baptism. It was a solemn moment.

I had two such precious letters from you this morning, worth to me far more than all the gems of ancient or modern art. The material of which they are composed is their main value, though there is also no mean skill revealed in its manipulation. They are pure as alabaster, far more precious than porphyry or verd antique; no mention shall be made of malachite or onyx, for love surpasses them all.

We are off to Naples to-day.

This morning, we drove through Naples for, I should think, six or seven miles or more. It is a crowded city, full of stirs, full of business, and full of pleasure. Horses seem innumerable, they are decorated profusely, and the carriages are very comfortable; but, I am sorry to say, the men drive furiously, and make me very nervous. Old women are numerous and hideous, beggars pestiferous, and dealers intensely persevering. But what a bay! What a sea and climate! No one ought to be ill here.

We have been over the museum—full of frescoes from Pompeii, gleanings from the catacombs, pickings from the Appian Way, stealings from the baths of Caracalla and other places. Naples has taken away from Rome the best of the ancient statuary and treasures, and prepared a vast museum for the spoils. We saw thousands of precious things, enough for a year's inspection; but the Pompeian remains were the most important. There were surgical instruments exactly like those of the present day; cottage-loaves of bread, stewpans, colanders, ladles, and all cookery things just like our own. The safes for money were just like old plate-chests. There were cotton, silk, and thread, in skeins and hanks, and large knitting and netting needles. Indeed, the people then had all we have now; even earthen money-boxes with a slit in the top, such as the children have in our country villages. There were plenty of proofs that the people were sinners, and of a scarlet dye, too. It was curious to see the colours in a painter's shop, the bottles and drugs of a chemist, and the tools of other traders. We saw also a splendid collection of ancient gems and cameos, most costly and lovely. I never saw so many gathered together before.

We drove from the museum to the site of a new field of lava, which flowed down from Vesuvius last April. It is just beyond the houses of suburban Naples, and was very different from what I had expected. It had crossed our road, and passed on through a vineyard—this was one tongue of the stream. Then we crossed a second by a road made near it, and came to a village through which the largest stream had burned its way. It is a huge incandescent sea of the outflow of the volcano; men were blasting and using pickaxes to open up the road which the flood had completely blocked. We were soon upon the lava; it has a surface like a heap of ashes, supposing that every ash should weigh a ton or two. It is still hot, and in some places smoking. I should have investigated it carefully, and with interest, only a horde of children, beggars, and women with babies gave us no rest, but continued crying, and imploring alms, and offering us pieces picked out of the mass. Much of the strange material is far too hot to hold, and our feet felt the heat as we walked across the surface. The stream has partly destroyed several houses, and cut the village in two; people are living in the half of a house which stands, the other half being burned and filled up with the molten substance. Vesuvius, high above us, is only giving out a little smoke, and seems quiet enough. As I could never climb up to the crater, I think we shall be content to have seen this lava torrent.

Our hotel here is vast and empty; we have excellent rooms, and are thoroughly comfortable. There is music continually, and very fair music, too, though not so sweet as silence. Everybody makes all the noise possible, and quiet dwells beyond the sea. Rome is a sepulchre, this city teems with life. You are not out of the door a moment before you are entreated to have a carriage, buy fruit, fish, pictures, papers, or something. The side streets swarm with people, who appear to live in them; there they eat, cook, work, catch fleas, hunt over each other's heads like so many monkeys, etc., etc. It is like living in a museum; but as to the beauty and gracefulness of which we read so much, I cannot detect it, though really looking for it. Persons over forty look worn out, and females at that age are haggard; over that period, they are ghastly and mummified. Macaroni hangs out, in some quarters, before the doors on lines to dry; and the flies, which are numerous upon it, give it anything but an attractive appearance. Tomorrow, we hope to go to Pompeii. I am now thinking about next month's magazine, and devoutly wish I could light upon a subject for an article, but my brain is dull.

We have seen Pompeii. We drove there, and it took us three hours, almost all of it between long lines of houses, like one continuous street. At the town of Resina, we passed Herculaneum, but did not enter it, as Pompeii is more worth seeing. Then we went through a town which has, I think, been seven times destroyed by Vesuvius, and is now crowded with people. There we saw the lava by the side of, and under the houses, hard as a rock; and the roads are generally paved with great flags of the same material. Though driving by the shore of the bay, we seldom saw the water, for even where there was no town, there were high walls, and, worst of all, off the stones the white dust was suffocating, and made us all look like millers. However, we reached Pompeii at last, and I can only say, in a sentence, it exceeds in interest all I have seen before, even in Rome. I walked on, on, on, from twelve to four o'clock, lost in wonder amid the miles of streets of this buried city, now silent and open to the gazer's eye. To convey a worthy idea of it to you, would be impossible, even in a ream of paper.

We entered at the Street of Tombs, which was outside the gate. In it were houses, shops, taverns, a fountain, and several tombs. The house of Diomed greatly interested us. We went upstairs and downstairs, and then into the cellars where were still the amphoræ, or wine-bottles, leaning against the wall in rows, the pointed end being stuck into the ground, and the rows set together in dry dust, in exactly the same way as we place articles in sawdust. In the cellars were found eighteen skeletons of women who had fled there for shelter. The photograph I send shows the garden, with covered walk round it, and tank for live fish. In this street were several places for seats in the shade, made in great semicircles, so that a score of persons could rest at once. Near the gate was the niche where the soldier was found who kept his watch while others fled. We could not think of going up and down all the streets; it would need many days to see all. The city was, I should think, a watering-place for the wealthy. No poor class of houses has yet been discovered. It was paved with great slabs of stone, which are worn deeply with cart or chariot wheels. Across the streets were huge stepping-stones, just wide enough to allow wheels to go on each side; but either they had no horses to the cars in these streets, or else they must have been trained to step over. In some places were horsing-blocks, in others there were holes in the kerbstone to pass a rope through to tie up a horse. The houses are many of them palaces, and contained great treasures of art, which are now in museums, but enough is left in each case to show what they were. Frescoes remain in abundance, and grottoes, and garden fountains, and marble terraces for cascades of water. It is a world of wonders.

In one part of the city, a noble owner had let the corner of his house to a vendor of warm wines, and there is his marble counter, with the holes therein for his warming-pots. Stains of wine were on the counter when it was first uncovered. We saw the back parlour of a drinking-shop, with pictures on the wall of a decidedly non-teetotal character. There were several bakers' shops with hand-mills, the tops of which turned round on a stone, and ground well, no doubt. In one, we saw the oven, with a water-jar near it; in this place were found 183 loaves of bread.

In the doctors' and chemists' shops, when opened, they saw the medicines as they were when entombed, and even pills left in the process of rolling! In the custom-house were standard weights and measures. Soap factories have their evaporating-pans remaining. Oil vessels abound; and in one, made of glass, some of the oil may still be seen. Cookshops had in them all the stewpans, gridirons, and other necessities of the trade. We saw jewellers' shops, artists' studios, and streets of grocers' and drapers' shops, many with signs over their doors.

The baths impressed me much, for they had been newly built when the awful tragedy took place, and look as if they were opened yesterday; a fine cold plunge-bath, with water carried high for a 'shower', a dressing-room with niches for brushes, combs, and pomades—all of which were there, but have been removed to museums; and a great brazier in green bronze, with seats round it for the bathers to dry themselves; a warm bath, and a vapour bath all perfect, and looking ready for use to-morrow.

The Forum was vast, and had in it the façades of several magnificent temples, the remains of which reveal their former glory. The pedestals of the statues of the eminent men of the town remain with their names upon them. We saw the tragic and comic theatres, and the amphitheatre which held 20,000 persons, in which the people were assembled when the eruption came, and from which they escaped, but had to flee to the fields, and leave their houses for ever.

In the Temple of Isis, we saw the places where the priests were concealed when they made the goddess deliver her oracles! We saw the lady herself in the museum, with a pipe at the back of her head, which was fixed in the wall, and served as the secret speaking-tube. The priests of Isis were found dead at her shrine; one of them with an axe had cut through two walls to get out, but had not succeeded. Poor creature!

In a money-changer's house, we saw his skeleton, lying on its face, with outstretched arms and hands; much money was found near him. In the barracks were sixty-three persons, soldiers' and officers' wives. Here were the stocks which had been used for the punishment of refractory soldiers.

In the Street of Mercury is a triumphal arch, on which stood a statue of Nero, found nearly perfect. Here, too, we noted a drinking-fountain, and a house with its exterior richly adorned with red frescoes. In a vast Hall of Justice were cells under the magistrates' bench; and in these, three prisoners were found, inside an iron ring which went round their waists. They were, perhaps, waiting to be brought up before the aldermen for some misdemeanour, and expecting to be fined 'five shillings and costs,' but they perished like their betters, and were summoned before a higher tribunal.

Out of so great a city, I suppose comparatively few were destroyed; so, as the bodies of these are found, they are preserved, especially if anything remarkable is to be seen in connection with them.

We saw the digging still going on, and the mounds of removed rubbish were like high railway embankments. No roofs remain, but spouts for the rain-water are there in great abundance; they are in the form of dogs' and lions' heads and other quaint devices. No stables have yet been uncovered; but the carts, which stood at the inn doors, have left their iron tyres, the skeletons of the horses, and their bits, to bear witness to their former existence. Skeletons of dogs and cats were there, and in a pan was a sucking pig prepared and just ready for roasting! I saw also a pot on a tripod, or trivet, which, when discovered, actually had water in it! I feel ashamed to write so badly on such a theme, but I cannot do better. It is too vast a task for me, and I fail to recollect a tithe of it. I must cease writing tonight, but I continue to breathe loving assurances to my sweet wifey.

We have been in a steamer to the Island of Capri, calling at Sorrento on the way; a glorious excursion, but we failed in our great object, which was, to see the Blue Grotto. The sea was too rough to permit entrance, as the opening is only three feet high, and no one can get in except during smooth water, and when the wind is from a certain quarter. However, we stayed a couple of hours on the island, which is precipitous, so I did not climb, but sat on a balcony, enjoying the marvellous scene. We reached Naples late, for the boat was slow; but first the sunset, and then the moonlight, gave us two charming effects, to which Vesuvius added by smoking almost continuously. This little trip served as a pleasant rest and refreshment after the toil and the dust of Pompeii.

Today, we have had a long and splendid drive to the other side of the bay. First along the quay, then through a tunnel almost half a mile long, and then skirting the bay, by road to Puteoli, where Paul landed; we saw the spot (as is supposed), and the commencement of the Appian Way which he followed till he reached Rome. At Puteoli, we first went into the crater of the Solfatara, a semi-extinct volcano, which has not been in eruption since 1198, when it destroyed ancient Puteoli. It is grown over with shrubs and small trees. Passing by Virgil's Elysian fields, and manifold wonders, we came to Misenum, and the village of Bacoli. Here we left the carriage, and ascended the hill to see what is called the Piscina Mirabilis,—a vast underground reservoir, which once contained water brought by the Julian aqueduct from some fifty miles' distance. It is dry now, and we descended a long flight of steps to the bottom. It has a roof supported by forty-eight huge columns; it is 220 feet long, and 82 feet broad. There are traces of water having filled it up to the spring of the arches, and the place where the water entered is very plainly to be seen. There are great openings in the roof, down which hang festoons of creeping plants. The place was very chilly, and coming up forty steps out of it seemed like leaving a sepulchre. Yet it was a sight to be remembered to one's dying day. We descended through the foul and loathsome village street, where cholera may well rage in summer. We could not explore villas of Julius Cæsar, prisons of Nero, villa of Agrippina, and other places, for we were tired, and I felt afraid of more vaults and their horrible damps. So we went into Baiæ, and entered a queer little *osteria*, or inn, and had some poor would-be oysters, bread and butter, and green lemons, freshly gathered from the tree. The view was glorious indeed, nothing could excel it; great ruined temples and villas were everywhere, and made a picture of exceeding beauty.

The drive home was by the sea, and we could perceive buildings down at the bottom, under the clear blue water. These have been brought down by the depression of the land upon which they stood, owing to earthquakes. We crossed a lava torrent which had come from Monte Nuova, and then we went on by our former road through Puteoli, till we left it to return to Naples without traversing the tunnel. This road took us up on one side of the promontory of Posilippo, whence we saw Ischia, Puteoli, Baiæ, and Misenum; and then we went down the other side, with Capri, Sorrento, Vesuvius, and Naples, all in full view. We were quickly down among the grand equipages which fill the Riviera di Chiaia; and, dashing along as fast as any of them, we were soon at the hotel door; and, since *table d'hôte*, I have been writing this long narration for you. The air here is balmy, the atmosphere dry, the heat great in the sun, but bearable in the shade. Mosquitoes are fewer and less voracious than in Venice. Everything is restorative to the system, and exhilarating. Even the beggars seem to be happy. None are miserable but the old women and the priests. Organs are far too plentiful, and music of all sorts is *ad nauseam*. Of religion, I have only seen one trace, namely, the bowing down of everyone when 'the host' was being carried under an umbrella to some sick person. Beggars swarm, and dealers in little wares assail you at all points, and will not cease their importunities. Tomorrow will be the Sabbath, and in this I rejoice, for rest is sweet, and sweetest when made 'holiness to the Lord.' I send tons of love to you, hot as fresh lava. God bless you with His best blessings!

It is the Sabbath, quiet and restful. We have had a delightful service, and I have written for my note-book and the magazine; so there will be a little less for my dear one, but there is nothing new to tell. I have been so grandly well all this time that I do not know how to be grateful enough, and my heart is light because you are better; my soul is at rest, my spirit leaps. I am indeed a debtor to Him who restoreth my soul. Blessed be His holy Name for ever and ever! We are very quiet, for there are no other visitors in the house; we have the best rooms, nice beds, well-curtained from mosquitoes. There is a house between us and the sea, but we can see the bay on each side of it, and Vesuvius if we go out on the balcony. The climate is like heaven below, and cannot but be a medicine to the sick. To-morrow we hope to be travelling; God be with thee, mine own, and give thee peace and healing! My heart is ever thine.

Again in Rome. Waking somewhat early this morning, I have risen to write to mine own darling wife. The fact is, I am afraid there will be a gap in the correspondence, and I shall be very sorry if it turns out to be so. Just as we left Naples, the rain began to descend, the warmth was gone, and we had a cool, if not a cold journey here. The fall in the temperature seemed to affect me, and I had a very disturbed and uncomfortable night. I am, however, so grateful for my long spell of rest, night by night, that this does not depress me, although I hoped that I was getting beyond the reach of such restless hours.

Yesterday was wet every now and then, but I had to devote the day to the magazine, and therefore it mattered not. I stole out to the Pantheon, and the Lateran, and then in again. Not being in harness, I worked slowly, and the matter came not until the mind

88888

8888888

---

had been much squeezed. How much more pleasant is the outbursting juice of the grape when it yields its streams to the lightest pressure of the vintner's hand! Yet duty had to be done, and I did it; but have more yet to do. Three dear letters awaited me here. 'Not worth sixpence,' did you say? They are worth a mint to me; they are mosaics of which every little bit is a gem. Naples has been a great treat; how I wish you could have been there, but I should not like you to see how horses are treated, it would make you quite unhappy. The Neapolitans load up their carriages most cruelly. I never saw so many horses, mules, and donkeys in my life before in proportion to the people. Everybody drives or rides, and they are all in a great hurry, too.

Mentone.—We came here yesterday from Genoa.

Today, while I was lying on the beach, and Mark Tapley was slyly filling our pockets with stones, and rolling Mr. Passmore over, who should walk up but Mr. McLaren, of Manchester, with whom I had a long and pleasant chat. We are to go to Monaco to-morrow together. He has three months' holiday. I am glad I have not; but I should wish I had, if I had my dear wife with me to enjoy it. Poor little soul! she must suffer while I ramble. Two clergymen have had a long talk with me this evening. It began by one saying aloud to the other, 'I hear Mr. Spurgeon has been here.' This caused a titter round the table, for I was sitting opposite to him. Mentone is charming, but not very warm. It is as I like it, and is calculated to make a sick man leap with health. How I wish you could be here!

The two parsons here are High Church and Low Church, and I have had a talk with both. Just before dinner, who should go by but the Earl of Shaftesbury, with whom I had half-an-hour's converse. He was very low in spirit, and talked as if all things in the world were going wrong; but I reminded him that our God was yet alive, and that dark days were only the signs of better times coming. He is a real nobleman, and man of God. Everybody in the hotel is courteous and kind, and I have quite a circle of acquaintances already. I have enjoyed the rest very much; but young married couples remind me of our early days, and the cloud which covers us now. Still, He who sent both sun and shade is our ever-tender Father, and knows best; and if it be good for us, He can restore all that He has withdrawn, and more; and if not, He designs our yet greater good. There is nothing more to write, except the

ever true and never tiresome message—my perfect love be with
thee, and the Lord's love be over thee for ever! In a few more days
I shall see thee, and it will be a fairer sight than any my eyes have
rested on during my absence.

Yesterday, Mr. and Mrs. Müller went with me to Dr. Bennet's
garden, and I had a most profitable conversation with him, one to
be remembered for many a day with delight. Dr. Bennet came up,
and I was amused to hear Müller teaching him the power of prayer,
and recommending him to pray about one of the terraces which he
wants to buy, but the owner asks a hundred times its value. Dr. B.
thought it too trifling a matter to take to the Lord; he said that Mr.
Müller might very properly pray about the Orphanage, but as to
this terrace, to complete his garden—he thought he could not make
out a good case about it. Mr. M. said it encouraged people in sin
if we yielded to covetous demands, so he thought the Dr. might
pray that the owners should be kept from exorbitant claims; but
Dr. B. said that, as ignorant peasants, they were very excusable for
trying either to keep their land, or to get all they could from an
Englishman whom they imagined to be a living gold mine! The
spirit of both was good; but, of course, the simple, child-like holy
trust of Müller was overpowering. He is not a sanctimonious
person; but full of real joy, and sweet peace, and innocent pleasure.

Nice.—In this place we have been put up four flights of stairs,
and, alas! into very cold rooms. I woke in the night, and felt as if
I were freezing in a vault, and my ankles were in great pain. I was
much cast down; and, on getting out of bed, found the carpet and
floor both very damp. I had a very bad night, and am now in much
pain in the left foot. Yet I believe I shall get over it soon, and I
mean to have no more of these climbings up stairs, and sleeping in
horrid cells. Nice is a very grand place, and I am sorry we left
Mentone to come to it. But I must not write in a grumbling vein.
Here have I had nearly five weeks of good health, and have grown
stronger every day; why should I care for one little relapse? We will
be off to Cannes and Hyères, and see what God has in store for us.
He will deal graciously with me as He has ever done.

Cannes.—I was too ill yesterday to write. After the deadly chill of
Thursday night at Nice, I felt the gout coming on, but resolved to
escape from that inhospitable hotel. An hour brought us here, but
it rained mercilessly, and all around was damp and chill. I got upstairs into beautiful rooms, but had to go to bed, which I have only

left for a moment or two since, while it was being arranged. My left foot is badly swollen, and the knee-joint is following suit. I have had very little sleep, and am very low; but, oh, the kindness of these friends! They sit up with me all night by turns, and cheer me with promises. I hope I shall get home in time for Sunday, but have some fears of it. Do not fret about me, I may be well before this reaches you; and if I am, I will telegraph and say so. I have every comfort here but home, and my dear wifey's sweet words. I am sad that my journey should end so, but the Lord's will be done!

Two days later.—I have had a heavy time of pain, my dearest, but am now better. God has changed the weather; yesterday was warm, to-day is hot, so we think it best to hurry on, and, if possible, have a *coupé-lit* right through to Paris. I feel well in myself, but the knee will not bear me, though I think I should be as strong as a horse after a day or two of this weather. How much I have to thank the Lord for! Such kind friends! They have proved their love beyond all praise. I was never alone. Even the *femme de chambre* pitied '*pauvre monsieur*,' and did her best for me. I hope now to get home in time for Sunday. My soul loves you, and longs to see you.

Paris.—In the hope that one more letter may reach you before I come personally, I give myself the delight of writing it. The telegram will have told you that, at the very prudent advice of the doctor, I left Cannes at 3.15 on Tuesday in a *coupé-lit* to travel direct to Paris. It has proved a very wise step. A lady lent her Bath-chair to take me to the station, and porters lifted me into the carriage. There I had a nice sofa-bed and every convenience. I lay there with great comfort till we reached Marseilles; then came the night, and I had hoped to sleep, but the extreme oscillation of the train quite prevented that. Once only I dozed for a few minutes, yet I was kept restful till six o'clock, when my dear friends got me some warm soup, and I had a refreshing wash. Then, all day long, I was at peace till 6 p.m. From Lyons, the country is flooded all along the road; we seemed to ride through a vast river. I naturally felt the chill of this, and my knees complained. Near Paris it rained hard, and at Paris heavily. After much stress and difficulty, I was put into a cab, and we drove to this hotel. I went to bed immediately, and slept on, on, on, till eight o'clock the next morning, awaking then refreshed, and, happily, none the worse for the long journey. I meant to stay in bed all day, and sent my friends out, so that I might not always be a drag upon them; but, at about noon, I rose and dressed, and when they came in, I had flown—to a sitting-room and a sofa by a cosy fire! I can walk now a little, and hope to be all right for Sunday. Bless the Lord, O my soul; and may He bless thee, too, my dear heart of love! I hope to have a *coupé*, and to-morrow lie down again while travelling, and so home to my tender wifey. Who could hope to escape rheumatic pains when all the world is wet through to the centre? It must not grieve you that I suffer, but you must rejoice that I escaped so long. Why, even rocks might feel this marvellous, long-continued wetting! I am indeed grateful to God for His goodness; still, 'there's no place like home.' This brings great loads of love all flaming. God bless thee ever!

Carriage at Victoria at 5.45, Friday!

I was sitting, one day, in the New Forest, under a beech tree. I like to look at the beech, and study it, as I do many other trees, for every one has its own peculiarities and habits, its special ways of twisting its boughs, and growing its bark, and opening its leaves, and so forth. As I looked up at that beech, and admired the wisdom of God in making it, I saw a squirrel running round and round the trunk, and up the branches, and I thought to myself, 'Ah! this beech tree is a great deal more to you than it is to me, for it is your home, your living, your all.' Its big branches were the main streets of his city, and its little boughs were the lanes; somewhere in that tree he had his house, and the beech-mast was his daily food, he lived on it. Well, now, the way to deal with God's Word is not merely to contemplate it, or to study it, as a student does; but to live on it, as that squirrel lives on his beech tree. Let it be to you, spiritually, your house, your home, your food, your medicine, your clothing, the one essential element of your soul's life and growth.—c.h.s., *in a sermon at the Tabernacle.*

13

A Holiday Drive to the New Forest

ONE of my dear husband's most congenial recreations consisted in spending a long day in the country—driving over hill and dale, and through the lanes and pretty villages of our charming county of Surrey. Many sweet days of rest have thus been snatched from weeks of heavy toil, and a furlough of a few hours has helped to restore and refresh the overworked brain and heart. He would go out in good time, taking with him some choice companion, or, perchance, another weary worker; and, driving slowly, they would jog along till noon, when, at a pleasant wayside inn, they would rest the horse, and have their luncheon, returning in the cool of the evening for high tea at home at six or seven o'clock.

Such rest Mr. Spurgeon found very delightful; but this was surpassed and completed when a fortnight of similar days could be linked together to form a perfect holiday. Then, instead of driving back in the sunset, he would go forward; and the trip would extend itself to many towns, and bring him into pleasant acquaintance with new objects of interest, and novel impressions of places and people. It was amusing, at these times, to note that his ideas of comfort, and his disregard of external appearances, were equally conspicuous. He liked a cosy seat, and easy travelling; but he cared nothing for the style of his equipage; an old horse—most inappropriately named 'Peacock'—and a shabby carriage were matters of perfect indifference to him, so long as they were safe and trustworthy, and carried him out of the noise of the crowded world, into the stillness and beauty of nature's quiet resting-places.

I well remember—aye, and with a present thrill of regret that I ever laughed at it—his purchasing, for these jaunts, a vehicle of so antiquated a pattern, and of such unfashionable proportions, that it was immediately dubbed 'Punch's coach,' and ever after bore that name. Its mirth-provoking aspect was increased when it was packed and prepared for a journey, for there was an arrangement behind, which supported a board for luggage, and added exceedingly to its grotesque and inelegant appearance. However, this convenient provision was, in the dear owner's estimation, one of its chief advantages, if not the very climax of its beauty; and though I laughed afresh at every glimpse of it, I loved him so dearly that I even learned to appreciate 'Punch's coach' for his sweet sake. As I write, and the memories of the old days surge over my mind like the billows from a distant shore, I rejoice to know that his slightest wishes were tenderly indulged, and that his beaming, loving, satisfied face, as he started off on one of these country tours, is far more deeply impressed on my heart than the remembrance of his unsightly holiday caravan! Never was he more happy and exultant than when making excursions of this kind; and those who were privileged to accompany him, saw him at his social best, and with one accord they have testified to the grace and charm of his companionship.

From the pages of his daily letters to me, on one of these notable occasions, I have woven the story of his holiday drive into this single bright chapter; which, in consequence, possesses all the attractiveness of a personal narrative, and I think it well sets forth some traits in his lovely character which could in no other way have been so naturally revealed—his intense delight in the works of God, his fine appreciation of the minute or half-concealed lovelinesses of nature, his care for all living creatures, his calm and contented spirit, his devotion under all circumstances to his Master and His work; all these are brought into distinct relief by the lively touches of his own vigorous pen and pencil.

Perhaps, out of respect for the 'old horse' previously mentioned, and which made so many delightful journeys for my beloved, I ought to explain that the 'noble greys' referred to in the opening sentences of the letters were owned and driven, in this particular instance, by a member of the party; but they had to draw 'Punch's coach' for all that!

*

Alton. June, 1873.—I am having a grand time. The horses are noble greys; the carriage, with my luggage-basket behind, most comfortable. We go along with an ease and dignity seldom equalled, and never surpassed. From Guildford, we drove to the foot of Martha's Chapel, and climbed to the very summit. What a view! Then down, and back to Guildford, and up the Hog's Back. Mistaking the route, we went up an old deserted Roman road, immensely broad, and all green. What a piece of country! The road itself was a sight, and the views on either side were sublime. So on to Farnham, where we dined, and went into the Bishop's park, which you will remember, with its deer, and avenue of elms. From Farnham to Alton is pretty and fruitful, but there were no incidents. I revised part of a sermon last night, and went to bed at 11.30; fell asleep at once, and neither stirred nor dreamed. I awoke at 6, then got up, and finished the sermon. Already, I am so much better that I feel able to go to work again—quite. We go to Selborne this afternoon. How I wish you were with me! But you shall know anything I see which can help you to realize where I am, and what I am doing. By the way, this morning we went into the church here, and saw an old door which was riddled by the Parliamentarians; we were also regaled with a superabundance of organ music which a young gentleman volunteered. The church is restored very beautifully, and in good taste.

Same day, later:—The drive was delicious, and I feel so well. Selborne is a little heaven of delights. It is Switzerland in miniature, where every turn changes the scene. If it were in a foreign land, all the world would crowd to it. We were all charmed; who could be otherwise? Well might White write so prettily upon so choice a subject. Hill, dell, bourne, hanger, down, lane, and wood—one has them all within a very small compass, and with endless variety. We have returned to Alton to send off some of our party; and now, at a council of war, we have decided to visit Selborne again tomorrow, and see more of that gem of a village.

Selborne.—What a grand morning we have had! Up the Hanger above the village we climbed by a zigzag path, and had a very extensive view. It was delicious to ramble among the tall beeches, and peep down upon the village, and then to descend into the place itself by winding paths. We went to White's house, and were received very kindly by Professor Bell and his wife, both very aged persons. We were soon known, and had in honour. The poor complain of the parson's neglect of them, and their lack of anything to hear which they can understand. We rambled about as in a paradise, and then were off to Alresford. What enjoyment I have had, and what health is upon me! I never felt better in my life. We are all so happy with the scenery, that we do not know how to be grateful enough. Oh, that you were here! One of these days, I hope and pray you may be able to come.

From Alresford, we have driven here (Winchester), along the

beautiful valley of the Itchen, and your dear note was all I wanted to make me full of joy. Letters had accumulated here up to Wednesday. I have already answered twenty-five, and Mr. B—— many others; so we are keeping the work under.

Winchester is a rare old place. We went first to the Hospital of St. Cross, and had a piece of bread, and a cup of beer. The cups are of horn, with five silver crosses on them; and my trio of friends bought one for me as a *souvenir*, and present for my coming birthday.

I noticed that *poor* men took a hunch of bread, while gentlemen were satisfied to receive a mere mouthful; and I thought—Ah! none feed on Christ so fully as the poor and hungry. The dole is exhausted about noon, but the mercy of God continues to the eleventh hour.

Having tasted of the hospitality of St. Cross, we passed into its rectangle, under the arch of the Beaufort Tower. It is here that the dole is given, and here we saw some of the old brethren in their gowns with crosses; there are thirteen of these old pensioners, and they get two quarts of beer to drink every day, and on 'gaudy days' gin and beer hot! Indeed, these old Saxon institutions appear to have regarded beer as the grand necessary of life! We walked and talked, and then sat down on the steps leading up into the dining-hall, and quietly looked on the curious scene. In the days when the place was built, chimneys were a new invention, and therefore they are all *external*, and have a grotesque appearance. On one side are the cloisters, and at the further end is a noble church, in which service is performed twice a day.

Our next visit was to St. Catherine's Hill, but as I could not pretend to climb it, we kept along the river-bank till we reached the cathedral. Here, a most intelligent guide made a couple of hours pass away as if they had only been so many minutes. I know more about architecture now than I had ever imagined I could learn, and am able to talk quite fluently about Early English, Decorated, Norman, etc., etc. It was strange to see the chests in which were the bones of Edgar, Ethelwulf, and all those old Saxon kings, and the sarcophagus of William Rufus. There is a kaleidoscopic window, all of the true old material, but no design, order, or arrangement; it reminded me of some men's theological knowledge—their system is of the 'anyhow' character. The thing which pleased us most was a pulpit, into which I ascended. The whole place was full of interest, even down to the crypt, into which we ventured.

After the cathedral, we visited the famous school of William

Wykeham, where the 'tunding' took place. It is like one of the Cambridge Colleges, and very quaint are its ways. The photograph I send you shows the tower of the school-chapel, and the Quakers'-meeting-looking place in front is the French school. We saw the dining-hall, and the great buttery hatches through which the meat and *beer* are passed, of which the boys have as much as they choose—Saxon again! Near the kitchen, is the ancient painting of 'the faithful servant,' which seems to be held in high repute at Winchester, but I think it a very poor thing. I have also been up St. Giles' Hill, above Winchester, and watched the setting sun, and have seen the lamps lit one after another all along the hill. It was very beautiful indeed, and the evening was so cool and calm it did me a world of good.

Salisbury.—To-day has been very dull and wet. Our drive through Hursley to Romsey was all very well; but from Romsey here, there was a constant downpour, and it got to be rather wearisome. It rains still, and I feel very tired; but a sunny day to-morrow will set me up again. I don't like big hotels in towns like dear old 'Hatches' and the blessed trees.

Amesbury. Sabbath.—Last evening, we went into the grounds of the Abbey Park, the property of Sir Edward Antrobus. The river Avon runs through the domain, in many windings, branchings, and twistings. The grounds are thickly wooded, but so little frequented that we heard the hoarse crow of the pheasant, the coo of pigeons, the cry of waterfowl, the song of countless birds, and the plash of leaping fish, but no sound of man's profaning footsteps. We sat on an ornamental bridge, and listened to the eloquence of nature, while the river hastened along beneath us. The family being away, we had leave to wander anywhere, and we enjoyed the liberty very much. I was up this morning at six o'clock, dressing slowly, and meditating; then I came down, and had an hour's work at *The Interpreter*. I do not mean to preach to-day, except with my pen; and it is a great pleasure to me to use that instrument when thought flows freely. May you also have a quiet day, and gather strength! May the Lord God of Israel bless my own best-beloved, and cause His face to shine upon her!

We had a nice little service yesterday morning, and after dinner, we went into the woods again. How I wish you could have been with me! Imagine a series of cathedrals of beech trees; the pillars all of silver, and the roof of emerald lace-work and twinkling stars of sunlight; the walls of dense yew trees, and the floor ankle-deep of red and brown leaves, softer than a velvet carpet. Rain fell; but, under the yews, we only heard it patter; and as we lay still, we could hear the wild ducks on the stream, far down below, making love,—and war. Presently, the sun came out, and we walked through the grand avenues up to a hill, which stood as a cliff above the Avon, with the Abbey House full in view, and Beacon Hill and the Wiltshire range of Downs with plentiful *tumuli*. Here again we saw pheasants in the mead on the other side, one white one among them, and wild ducks and coots on the river, diving, swimming, and flying after one another. Swallows were all around us. Wood-pigeons came every now and then, and some were in the trees cooing constantly. Hawks poised themselves in the air, flocks of starlings flew overhead, like November meteors, thrushes and blackbirds sang; and, last of all, there came, on downy yellow pinions, white-breasted and round-faced, your friend the owl, who sped into the wood, and was soon followed by another, whose soft course, on noiseless broad-sailing wings, would have made you nestle up to me for joy, and whisper, 'Oh, husband, how lovely!' All the while, the fish leaped as if they were quite at home, for we were as high above them and all the other things as if we were on a church spire. We then walked down green alleys, and startled the rabbits in families; and, as we stood still, we saw their gambols, and marked the hares sitting upright, so that, seeing only their backs, they might have been mistaken for stumps of trees, if it had not been for their ears. I send you a sketch of them. A sneeze made them run, or rather, leap away. Then we came on young partridges and hen-coops, which we left at once, for fear of offending; and so came in to tea, walking along the river-bank, and smelling the new-mown hay. It was a sweet Sabbath. To-day and yesterday, I have done twenty-four pages of *The Interpreter*, and have sixteen more to do when I can. Love as deep as the sea and as broad, I send thee, my dear one.

Lyndhurst.—Three dainty notes have I devoured; real delicacies, flavoured with the love I prize above all earthly things. This place is so beautiful that, to linger here for a week or two, will be delightful, and better than going elsewhere. On the way here, we drove to Broadlands, and had a good view of the interior. There is as fine a collection of pictures as I ever saw, distributed over a house replete with comforts and conveniences. The Temples and Palmerstons were set forth in noble portraits, but there were many works of Sir Joshua Reynolds, Sir Peter Lely, Wouverman, and other great masters; many Dutch pictures, and a large number full of interest, and truly instructive works of art. A mile further, we saw Embley Park, where Miss Nightingale was born, and another four or five miles brought us into the forest amid the wildest scenery, and boundless wilderness of shade. Here we came upon the Rufus Stone, of which I send you all three sides. I bought them of a poor boy in a smock-frock, on the spot. 'Mother paints 'em, Sor,' was the answer of this youth to my question, 'Where do you buy them?' What are the Selbornians after to have no photographs of their sweet village? Evidently, this 'Mrs. Hodge' of the New Forest is an advanced woman! How vivid history becomes when such memorials are before one's eyes! The top of the iron pillar is grated, so that we could look in, and see the stone which it encases. Here it began to rain, but we had only about four miles to drive to Lyndhurst, so we went along very gently in alternate shower and shine.

So ends this week's chronicle. I do not think more could well have been seen; certainly, more could not be enjoyed by any living man in the absence of a dear wife to share his pleasure. How I should have loved you to have seen the partridges, and rabbits, and birds of all kinds, and forest trees and cedars, and roses and honeysuckles! It may yet be. The Lord cheer thy heart, thou dearest among women! Accept my most fervent love, hot from my inmost heart!

Sabbath.—I have been to the little Baptist Chapel, and have been much refreshed with a plain sermon from 'Master, carest Thou not that we perish?' We then walked in the wood, and talked and meditated. It is a grand thing to be lost in the forest within five minutes of coming out of a meeting-house!

Monday.—This morning, we have been in the forest again from ten till twelve. There are great masses of beech in one place, then oak, then underwood and small trees. Amid these are green lawns, and verdant valleys, glades, dells, hills, and vales. Sometimes trees disappear, and all is common, with gorse, heather, and low bushes. Cottages surprise you everywhere, in nooks as secret as the haunts of fairies. Cattle with bells create an Alpine tinkling, horses and hogs go in troops. Everything is picturesque, and the space seems boundless. One might soon be lost, for the roads, and tracks, and mere trails, are countless. Birds and insects abound, and wild flowers and mosses. It is a world of beauty, I can say no less. The trunks of the stately trees, all aglow with lichen and moss, are loveliness itself; and the weird oaks are sometimes grotesque, and at other times solemn. Lyndhurst is only a village, but it is in the forest, and that is its charm. You can ramble where you will, and no man can threaten you for trespassing. We hoped to see some of the fallow deer, and the squirrels; but have not succeeded as yet. We tracked a little brawling brook this morning; and if ever perfect beauty has existed on earth since the Fall, we saw it. What with foxgloves on the banks, and rare ferns at the river's brim, and the rippling waters among mossy mole-mounds, and thyme-bearing knolls, and the red floor beneath the temple of beech shade—it was matchless! I am as happy as half a being can be without the other half! It would be bliss indeed if you were here to share my joys.

Tuesday.—An evening drive has been supremely delightful from its coolness, and from the shadows and the gleams of glory from the setting sun, which here and there lit up the tree-tops, blazed among the old roots, and gilded the lofty forest columns. I feel as peaceful as serenity itself. No place upon earth could so fitly minister to a wearied brain by giving such perfect rest. It is better than cities, pictures, or even mountains, for all is peace, and there is not even sublimity to excite the emotions of the mind. One rests, and gazes on a spider's web all silvered o'er, and set with diamonds of dew; a beetle flying heavily; a dragon-fly dashing forward like a cavalier charging the foe, then hesitating and irresolute until another fit of energy seizes him; a foal frisking with delight at its mother's side; a snake rustling hurriedly away among the red leaves, or a partridge scurrying across the heather! Thank God for such peaceful scenes!

We have been through Boldre Wood and Mark Ash, and seen the most wonderful forest scenery I have ever beheld or even dreamed of. The huge beeches and oaks are so fantastic as to seem grotesque and wizard-like. They are beyond measure marvellous, and one could visit them twelve times a day, and yet not see half their beauties. The most singular thing of all is the flying buttress of the beech trees, which I never observed before. A long bough will be supported by another which joins it from lower down, and grows into it, so as to hold it up. This habit in the beech leads to great curiosities of growth, for there are sometimes threefold bracings, and great branches will be thus locked together, while, in other instances, one bough will curl under another in order, apparently, to hold it up. There are shapes most unshapely, and twistings most queer and unexpected, but the one object appears to be to buttress one another, and contribute to each other's strength by this strange interlacing. Just so should believers aid one another; are they not all branches of one tree?

June 19, 1873.—This is my thirty-ninth birthday, and I desire to bless God for sparing and blessing me, and for giving me, as one of His choicest gifts, my own dear, precious wife. May we be spared to one another for many a day, and dwell together for ever hereafter! Thank you for your dear fond letter. Truly, it is sweet to be so dearly loved, and to love in return with an eagerness which could understand limping expressions, much more the tender words which you employ. God bless thee! It has rained all day, so we have all been to be photographed, gratifying our vanity, since we could not indulge our observation. I am promised a copy of the group to-night before this is posted, though it will not have been long enough in water to prevent its fading; but if it pleases you for a moment, it will answer my purpose.

What do you think of your old 'hub' in the forest? Does he not look calm and happy?

I think the old log just suits him, and the shabby old coat, too! I like the photograph better than any portrait ever taken of me; I wonder if you will?

After I wrote to you yesterday, I worked a little while at *The Interpreter*, but soon felt one of my old attacks coming on, so we set off for a long walk, and at some time past ten o'clock at night we lost our way in the thick of the forest, only we knew the direction of Lyndhurst by the chimes. After breaking through the long grass, brambles, bracken, and underwood, we came to the edge of the dense enclosed wood in which we had been wandering, but a ditch and a pond barred our way. However, there were some rails of fencing across, and over this we climbed, and went along it above the water. We landed in a field of high grass, and made tracks for a cottage, got into the garden, down the path, and out at the front gate, nobody challenging us. This adventure did me good, and procured me a fair night's sleep.

To-day, we have been to look at the scene of our night wandering, and to find out where we missed our way. We have roamed in the wood for two hours, and have never seen a soul. Birds, rabbits, flies, ants, and spiders have been our only company, save the ONE with whom we have held sweet converse, and of whose Word we have spoken to each other.

We have been for a drive to Lymington. It was charming to pass through the forest. Each road has its own character, and there is no sameness. I had a fine supply of tracts, and sowed the region well. Lymington is quite a considerable place, but I could not get a good photograph of it for you. We went down to the quay, and took the steamboat to Yarmouth in the Isle of Wight. It was about thirty minutes' steaming, and we saw Hurst Castle and the Needles to the right of us. Yarmouth is a poor little place, but we walked along the beach, and sat down for a while, and enjoyed the lovely view. Fine yachts went sailing by, and porpoises were in great plenty. After being kept in by the wet, the lovely weather of to-day is doubly pleasing. Returning to Lymington at seven o'clock, we then drove back to Lyndhurst, where I found a very specially sweet note from my beloved awaiting me. I am so glad you like the photo. It gives me real delight to afford you pleasure. I feel wonderfully well. My precious one, may the Lord give thee restoration also, and make thee happy with me in journeys yet to be planned! How I should rejoice to show you about this grand forest, the noblest in all England!

Yesterday afternoon was spent most deliciously. We drove along the Christchurch Road, and took the photographer and his apparatus with us, hoping to secure some charming pictures. Our purpose was, however, thwarted by the absence of the sun, for he kept behind a cloud. We then sent back the carriage, and followed on foot the little brook called the Millifont, in all its winding ways. Ah! my darling, what choice bits we came across! Here, the water had worn out the earth from under the trees, and left bare a wattling of roots; there, in another place, clustered the water-lilies, and the green leaves with which they paved the brook. At one moment, we were on a sand island in the middle of the rivulet; at another, the bank was high above the water, like the Rhine hills, in miniature, above that mighty flood. Strange moths and dragon-flies frequented the pools and lakelets, and here and there a fish leaped out, while shoals of minnows flashed away when our shadows fell upon them. We crossed the current upon a single fir tree, rough and unsquared; if we had tumbled into the water, it would not have mattered much, except that we could not quickly have changed our clothes. All this walk was in solitude, among great trees. It was so singular to sit down in the silence, broken only by the warble of the brook's liquid notes, or by the noise of a moving bird, or the scream of a water-fowl, or the surprise of hearing a great crack, such as furniture will give in certain weathers. A dog saluted us with pertinacious bark-ing, and we found his mistress, an artist, sitting down on a sand-bank in the stream, sketching. The dog evidently felt that he was her protector, but I do not think we should have seen the lady if he had not called our attention to her presence. Oh! it was delicious to lie on a bed of moss, beneath a shady beech, with ferns and foxgloves all around, and the water rippling at one's feet! It was balm and cordial to me.

Bishop's Waltham.—We left delightful Lyndhurst at about nine o'clock this morning, and drove along a charming road till we reached Southampton, and crossed by the horse-ferry to go to Netley, and explore the ruins of its Abbey. Certainly, no place could be more congenial for an hour or so of rest. One can clamber up to the top in some places, especially in the South transept, where there is a walk on a sort of narrow ledge under the arches below the window. I was greatly interested, but could only keep on saying to myself, 'How I wish my dear wifey were here!' From there we went to see the Victoria Hospital, driving along by the edge of Southamp-ton Water—such a fine drive! The Hospital is the longest building in England; I should think it is nearly half a mile long. Then we went over the hills to Botley, where the views are boundless, and so on to this queer old town. We have been wandering among the ruins of a castle-palace, where Henry II. and Cœur-de-Lion have feasted in the days gone by. It has been a cool, lovely day, and the way splendid.

Liphook.—We left Waltham this morning, and drove along a ridge which gave us glorious views. We turned off the good roads, and made for Winchester Hill—a great Roman or British earthwork upon an eminence. The tradition is that Winchester once stood here, but I cannot believe it. On the vast Down there are several *tumuli*; indeed, in the region we traversed to-day, *tumuli* are as plentiful as blackberries. What air we breathed! How fresh it blew up from the sea! It was a fair requital for the puffing which it cost me to climb the hill! Then we came down to East Meon, where is an ancient church, and then we traversed a long valley between two great ranges of Downs. Such exquisite views! Nobody need go to Switzerland for the sublime! At Petersfield, I found a sweet note from my darling. May all God's blessings be heaped upon her! As the way had been too short for a day's journey, we came on to Liphook this evening, and saw gems of views, which filled us with admiration. Here is a great inn, of ancient date, stately and roomy. It is mentioned by old Pepys; but since the coaching days, its glories have departed, though it still remains comfortable and vast. I am now looking forward to my work, and hope to keep on for a long time.

Ockley.—We strolled into the park, and sat on a fallen tree. Presently, a squirrel came and peeped at us, and not knowing our faces, he scudded away, and went up a beech. Anon he came down again, waving his tail on high, and passed us to another tree. Then came a doe and fawn, and stood and stared; and others followed, and in Indian file went slowly off. It became cold, so we trotted in to tea; and this done, I pen a line to my darling, almost the last she will get before my return.

A dear little note has just come from you, and rejoiced my heart. What joy to meet my beloved again, and find her better! On Sunday, we went and sat with the Quakers, and created an event. A portly female was moved to speak, and also to admonish us against water-baptism! She was one of the old school, and evidently relieved her soul by her exhortation. In the afternoon, we had a fine storm and refreshing rain, and I revised a sermon, and wrote on a Psalm. Receive a great flood-tide of love from my heart to yours. May God bless us in returning to each other's beloved society, and spare us for many years to one another!

I am sure that, if a minister wants conversions, he must identify himself with his people. There are persons, nowadays, who make a difficulty about Moses praying for Israel, 'If thou wilt forgive their sin——; and if not, blot me, I pray thee, out of thy book which thou hast written;' and they raise questions about Paul being willing to be separated from Christ for his brethren, his kinsmen according to the flesh. Oh, but there is no difficulty in the matter if you once get to feel such an intense love for the souls of men that you would, as it were, pawn your own salvation, and count it little if you might but bring the people to the Saviour's feet! A man who has never felt that willingness does not yet know the true throb of a pastor's heart; he has not been ordained to be a shepherd if he would not lay down his life for the flock, if it were necessary.
—C.H.S., *in a sermon preached at the Tabernacle, August* 23, 1883.

14

Enquirers and Converts

IN one of the sermons preached in connection with his pastoral silver wedding,[1] Spurgeon called attention to the fact that, during his twenty-five years' ministry in London, more than nine thousand persons had joined the church; while, probably, an equal or still larger number had been converted through hearing or reading his sermons, although they had not become members at the Tabernacle. The previous volume of the *Autobiography* contained many references to these converts, and records of the means blessed to their salvation; but it appears necessary to devote a chapter in the present volume to the same subject in order adequately to set forth this most important part of the Pastor's service, and to show how abundantly the favour of God rested upon it from its commencement to its close. It is a cause for devout thankfulness that, in a great measure, a similar blessing still accompanies his published words, both in the English tongue, and in many of the languages into which they have been translated. The following narrative is given in Spurgeon's own words; the latter portion consists of the instances of usefulness which various friends have described; and, to make the chapter as varied and as complete as possible, there are included several specimens of his methods of dealing with anxious enquirers and sinners seeking the Saviour. The cases of blessing here recorded are selected from the whole of his London ministry; and are, therefore, all the more representative of the continued usefulness of his work for the Lord during the long period from 1853 to 1892.

*

There are some passages of Scripture which have been more abundantly blessed to the conversion of souls than others have; they may be called salvation texts. We may not be able to discover how it is, or why it is; but, certainly, it is the fact that some chosen verses have been more used of God than any others in His Word to bring men to the cross of Christ. They are not more inspired than other parts of the Bible, but I suppose they are more noticeable

[1] 1879.

either from their position, or from their peculiar phraseology, by reason of which they are more adapted to catch the eye of the reader, and are more suitable to a widely prevailing spiritual condition. All the stars in the heavens shine very brightly, but only a few catch the eye of the mariner, and direct his course; the reason is this, that those few stars, from their peculiar grouping, are more readily distinguished, and the eye easily fixes upon them. So I suppose it is with those passages of God's Word which especially attract attention, and direct the sinner to the cross of Christ. One of the chief of those texts is Isaiah 43. 25: 'I, even I, am He that blotteth out thy transgressions for mine own sake, and will not remember thy sins.' I have proved it to be a most useful one; for, out of the thousands of persons who have come to me to narrate their conversion and religious experience, I have found a very large proportion who have traced the Divine change which has been wrought in their hearts to the hearing of this precious declaration of sovereign mercy, and the application of it with power to their souls by the Holy Spirit.

Some who come to see me, with the view of joining the church, cannot say much, and they think that I shall be very dissatisfied with them because they make a great muddle of their narrative, but the people with whom I am least satisfied are those who reel off their yarn by the yard; they have it all ready to repeat, and everything is arranged as prettily as possible. As I listen to it, I know that someone has told them what to say, and they have learned it all for me to hear. I like far better the testimony that I have to pick out in little bits, but which I know comes fresh from the heart of the trembling convert. Sometimes, it costs the poor soul a tear or a real good cry, and I have to go round about in all manner of ways to get hold of the story at all; but that shows that it is true, and that the man never borrowed it. I like to hear the experience of a believer, when he comes straight out of the world, and out of the ways of sin, to confess his faith in Christ. He does not know anything about the terms that Christian people use, he has not learned our phrases; and it is a great delight to hear it all fresh and new. Yet it is always the same story in all the essential parts of it. However strangely he may narrate it, it tallies with that of others in the main points. Take the experience of a Christian man who has been brought up in the sanctuary from his childhood, and extract the pith and marrow of it. Now take the experience of a man who has been a horse-racer, a drunkard, a swearer, but who has been truly converted, and extract the essence of that. Talk to a peer of the realm who has become an heir of the kingdom of heaven, and take the substance of his experience. Now speak to a chimney-sweep who has been brought to the Lord, and get the gist of his experience; put them all side by side, and you will not know one from the other. There are always the same essential marks—death, birth, life, food. Christ in the death, the birth, the life, the food—repentance, faith, joy, the work of the Spirit of God. But it is very sweet to hear the story told in the many different ways in which the converts tell it. The true child of grace is ever the same in heart, although the outward appearance may continually vary.

Among the many thousands of souls who have been brought to know the Lord under my instrumentality, I have often noticed that a considerable proportion of these, and of the best members of our church, too, were won to the Saviour, not by legal terrors, but by gentler means. Sitting on one occasion to see enquirers, I should think that there were as many as twelve out of the twenty-three whose convictions of sin were not distinctly marked with the terrors of the law. I asked an excellent young woman, 'What was the first thought that set you really seeking the Saviour?' 'Oh, sir!' she replied, 'it was Christ's lovely character that first made me long to be His disciple. I saw how kind, how good, how disinterested, how self-sacrificing He was, and that made me feel how different I was. I thought, "Oh! I am not like Jesus!" and that sent me to my room, and I began to pray, and so I came to trust in Him.' 'The first religious impression I ever had,' said another, 'that set me seeking the Saviour, was this; a young companion of mine fell into sin, and I knew that I was likely to do the same if I was not kept by someone stronger than myself. I therefore sought the Lord, not so much at first on account of past transgression, but because I was afraid of some great future sin. God visited me, and I then felt conviction of sin, and was brought to Christ.'

Singularly enough, too, I have met with scores of persons who have trusted in Christ, and then have mourned their sins more afterwards than they did before they believed. Their convictions have been more terrible after they have known their interest in Christ than they were at first. They have seen the enormity of the evil after they have escaped from it; they have been plucked out of the miry clay, and their feet set upon the rock; and then, afterwards, they have seen more fully the depth of that horrible pit out of which they have been snatched. It is not true that all who are saved suffer such convictions and terrors as some of us had to endure; there are very many who are drawn with the cords of a man and the bands of love. There are some who, like Lydia, have their hearts opened, not by the crowbar of conviction, but by the picklock of Divine grace. Sweetly drawn, almost silently enchanted by the loveliness of Jesus, they say, 'Draw me, we will run after thee.'

A young woman came to me one day after a service, to ask me whether I really meant what I said when I declared that he that believed in Jesus Christ was saved there and then. 'Yes,' I replied; and I gave her the Scriptural warrant for the statement. 'Why!' she exclaimed, 'my grandfather told me that when he found religion, it took him six months, and they had nearly to put him into a lunatic asylum, he was in such a dreadful state of mind.' 'Well, well,' I answered, 'that sometimes happens; but that distress of his did not save him. That was simply his conscience and Satan together keeping him away from Christ. When he was saved, it was not by his deep feelings; it was by his believing in Jesus Christ.' I then went on to set the Saviour before her as our sole ground of hope in opposition to inward feelings. 'I see it,' she said; and I rejoiced as I noticed the bright light that passed over her face, a flash of heavenly sunshine which I have often seen on the countenances of those who have believed in Jesus Christ, when peace fills the soul even to the brim, and lights up the countenance with a minor transfiguration. Scores of times, when I have been talking with those who have been utterly bowed down beneath sin's burden, they have looked as though they were qualifying for an asylum through inward grief; but as soon as they have caught this thought, 'Christ stood as the Substitute for me; and if I trust in Him, I have the proof that He did so, and I am clear,' their faces have been lit up as with the very glory of heaven.

Some persons have come to me for spiritual guidance because they have been misled by others. One lady who called upon me said that she had not heard me preach, but she had been reading my sermons, and God had been pleased to bless them to her, not only to her conviction, but to her conversion. She went to the clergyman of the parish, full of joy at having found the Saviour, and began to tell him of her gladness, and how she rejoiced that all her sins were blotted out. He stopped her, and said, 'My good woman, that is all a delusion; you have no right to believe that your sins are pardoned, till you have led several years of piety and devotion.' She went away sad, and she came to ask me if what the clergyman said was true; and when I quoted that verse:

The moment a sinner believes,
And trusts in his crucified God,
His pardon at once he receives,
Redemption in full through His blood.

'Oh!' she said, 'I see it clearly now;' and when I went on to tell her that many, who had believed in Christ, had been black sinners one moment, and white as snow the next, and that, by casting themselves simply on Christ, they had instantly found peace, she could not but take to her heart the precious promises of Christ, and, believing in Jesus, being justified by faith, she had the peace of God that passeth all understanding, and she went away rejoicing in Jesus.

I was going to preach in the country on one occasion, and before I went, I received a letter from a young man who wrote: 'Dear Sir,— When you come to this town, do preach a sermon that will fit me; for I have heard it said that we must all think ourselves to be the wickedest people in the world, or else we cannot be saved. I try to think so, but I cannot, because I have not been the wickedest. I want to be saved, but I do not know how to repent enough.' Of course, I told him that God does not require every man to think himself the wickedest in the world, because that would sometimes be to think a falsehood, for there are some men who are not so sinful as others are. What God requires is that a man should say, 'I know more of myself than I do of other people; and from what I see of myself, not merely of my actions, but of my heart, I do think there can be few worse than I am. They may be more wicked openly; but then I have had more light, more privileges, more opportunities, more warnings, and therefore I am, in my own opinion at least, more guilty than they are.'

Some friends have really made an obstacle out of the very thing for which they ought to have been most grateful. An excellent and amiable young woman, when converted to God, said to me, 'You know, sir, I used almost to wish that I was one of those very bad sinners whom you so often invite to come to Jesus, because I thought then I should feel my need more; that was my difficulty, I could not feel my need of Christ.' It is a pity that any should make a hindrance of this matter; yet they do, and others make a difficulty for the opposite reason; they say, 'Oh! we could trust Christ if we had kept from sin.' The fact is, that unbelieving souls will not trust Christ whichever way they have lived; for, from some quarter or other, they will find cause for doubting; but, when the Lord the Spirit gives them faith, big sinners will trust Christ quite as readily as those who have not been great offenders openly; and those who have been preserved from open sin will trust Him as joyfully as the vilest transgressors.

We have had, in the Tabernacle, many very remarkable instances of how God does still bless the outcasts and the very chief of sinners. There was a man, known in the village where he lived by the name of 'Satan', because of his being so thoroughly depraved. He was a sailor, and as another seaman in that place had been the means of the conversion of all the sailors in a vessel belonging to the port, this man desired to sail with him to try to beat his religion out of him. He did his best—or rather, his worst—but he signally failed; and when the ship came to London, the Christian man asked the ungodly one whether he would come to the Tabernacle. He did not mind coming to hear me, for, as it happened, I was brought up near the place where he lived. This 'Satan' came, on the Lord's-day morning when the text was upon soul-murder; and, by the Holy Spirit's gracious application of the Word to his heart, he sat, and sobbed, and cried under the sermon at such a rate that he could only say, 'People are noticing me, I had better go out;' but his companion would not let him go out; and, from that day forth, he became a new creature in Christ Jesus, and he is living and walking in the truth, an earnest believer, singularly clear in his doctrinal knowledge, and doing all that he can for the spread of the Kingdom of Christ.

On another occasion, on a Lord's-day morning, I preached upon the words of the leper, who said to Jesus, 'Lord, if thou wilt, thou canst make me clean.' On the following Thursday morning, I received this letter: 'Dear Sir, I feel so happy to tell you that the Lord has pardoned a poor outcast of society. I got into your place, in a crowd, hoping nobody would see me. I had been out all night, and was miserable. While you were preaching about the leper, my whole life of sin rose up before me. I saw myself worse than the leper, cast away by everybody; there is not a sin I was not guilty of. As you went on, I looked straight away to Jesus. A gracious answer came, "Thy sins, which are many, are forgiven." I never heard any more of your sermon, I felt such joy to think that Jesus died even for a poor harlot. Long ere you get this letter, I trust to be on the way to my dear home I ran away from. Do please pray for me that I may be kept by God's almighty power. I can never thank you enough for bringing me to Jesus.' If it had not been for that sentence about going home, I might have had some doubt concerning her conversion, but when a fallen girl goes home to her father and mother, it is a sure case. This letter gave me great joy; to see souls saved is heaven to me.

Not only has there been a great variety in the converts during my ministry, but the means blessed to their conversion have been very varied.[1] One brother, when he came to join the church, told us that, as an ungodly stranger, he was going into Exeter Hall just as I gave out Charles Wesley's hymn '*Jesu, lover of my soul.*' He said to himself, 'Does Jesus really love me? Then, why should I live in enmity to Him?' There and then, he turned unto the Lord; and, not long after, he came boldly out and confessed his faith in Christ, and sought to do all he could to lead others to the Saviour.

I remember one friend coming to me and saying very earnestly, 'I should like, sir, to take a seat in the Tabernacle.' I answered, 'Well, do so, by all manner of means; I am very glad when people do so.' 'But,' said he, 'I may not come up to what you expect of me, for I have heard that if I take a sitting here, you will expect me to be converted, and I cannot guarantee that.' 'No,' I replied, 'I do not want you to guarantee it; I do not mean the word *expect* in that sense at all, but I do hope that it will be so.' 'Oh!' exclaimed he, 'and so do I; I am going to take a sitting with that very view.' And it was so; of course, it was so. When the man wished it, God accepted the wish, and heard the prayer, and he was brought to Christ, and joined the church.

One brother, when he was giving his testimony before being baptized, said: 'The first time I came to hear Mr. Spurgeon in the Tabernacle, if you had asked me about myself, I should have told you that I was as religious a man as ever lived in Newington, and as good a man, certainly, as ever formed part of any congregation; but all this was reversed when I heard the gospel that day. I came out of the building with every feather plucked out of me. I felt

[1] Among the interesting instances of blessing which Spurgeon did not himself record, was the following, which was reported by a friend: 'Mr. Spurgeon went to preach at a prominent chapel, and, after taking tea at the deacon's house, he walked down to the place of worship under the guidance of the son of the household. "Do you love my Master?" was the question which, in his clear, manly way, the Pastor put to his young companion. Before replying, he stopped in the street, and looking his questioner straight in the face, said, "Mr. Spurgeon, I have walked down to this chapel with the ministers for several years, and not one of them ever asked me such a question before." That faithful word was the beginning of a new life; and, seeking God, he found pardon and peace through Christ.'

myself the most wretched sinner who could be on the face of the earth, and I said, "I will never go to hear that man again, for he has altogether spoiled me." But that was the best thing which could have happened to me; I was made to look away from myself, and all that I could do, to God, and to His omnipotent grace, and to understand that I must pass under my Creator's hand again, or I could never see His face with joy. I learned to loathe my own righteousness as filthy rags, fit only for the fire, and then I sought to be robed in the perfect righteousness of Christ.'

Another man, who came to join with us in church-fellowship, owed his conversion, indirectly, to a Jew. He was on an omnibus going by the Tabernacle, one Sunday, and a crowd was standing outside as usual, waiting for the doors to be opened. The person sitting next to him was a well-known Jew. 'Ah!' said the man, 'that humbug always attracts the people.' The Jew turned round to him, and enquired, 'Would not you like to see such a crowd as that round your shop? I should welcome them at my place of business. I have ridden past here these twenty-eight years, and have always seen just such a crowd as that waiting to get in. Now, if your shop had been crowded thus for twenty-eight years, and anybody said that you did not sell a good article, what would you reply? You would probably answer that those people were good judges, and that, if you had not supplied goods that were satisfactory, they would not have kept on coming. Now, I am a Jew, yet I am inclined to go in, and listen to what Mr. Spurgeon has to say, because I see these crowds of people going to hear him.' The man who had at first made the offensive remark was greatly impressed by his companion's observation, and in telling us how it affected him, he said, 'I discovered that I had been buying the wrong article, and I thought the Jew had spoken very sensibly, so I resolved to go, and see and hear for myself.' He came, examined the article that was offered for sale, and bought it on the gospel terms, 'without money and without price.'

One Sabbath evening, while preaching in the Tabernacle, I felt moved to say: 'Dear mother, if you have never talked with your daughter about her soul, do it this very night. "But," you reply, "when I get home, she will be in bed." If so, then wake her up, but do talk and pray with her to-night; and then let her fall asleep again; begin at once this holy service if you have neglected it until now.' One good woman, who was present, went straight home, and did exactly what I had said; she woke her daughter up, and began speaking to her about the Saviour. The dear girl said, 'Oh, mother! I am glad you have spoken to me about Jesus; for months, I have been wishing you would do so.' It was not long before the mother brought her daughter to see me about joining the church, and then told me how the blessing had come to her.

On various occasions, the Lord has set His seal upon a very simple request that I made to my congregation. I asked those who were present, after they reached their homes, to spend a little time quietly and alone, and then, when they had honestly considered their condition in the sight of God, to take a pencil and paper, and to write one of two words. If they felt that they were not believers in the Lord Jesus Christ, I asked them to write the word *Condemned*, but if they were trusting to Him alone for salvation, to put on the paper the word *Forgiven*. Several friends were brought to decision for Christ in that way; amongst them was one young man who at first wrote the word *Condemned*, but, as he looked at it, his tears began to flow, and his heart began to break; and, before long, he fled to Christ, put the paper in the fire, took another piece, wrote on it the word *Forgiven*, and soon came to tell me the good news, and to ask that he might be admitted to church-fellowship. In another case, a man went home, and told his wife that he was going to write the word *Condemned*; she pleaded with him in vain, for he took the pencil, and was just about to make the letter C; but his little daughter, a Christian girl, caught hold of his hand, and said, 'No, father, you shall not write it;' and by the united entreaties of his wife and child, the man was brought to the Saviour, and afterwards became a member with them at the Tabernacle.

My experience goes to show that there have been persons converted to God by doctrines that some might have thought altogether unlikely to produce that result. I have known the doctrine of the resurrection to bring sinners to Christ; I have heard of scores brought to the Saviour by a discourse upon election—the very sort of people who, as far as I can see, would never have been reached if that truth had not happened to be an angular doctrine that just struck their heart in the right place, and fitted into the crevices of their nature. I have often preached a terrible sermon upon the law, and afterwards found that sinners had been comforted by it. God frequently blesses the Word in the very opposite manner to that in which I thought it would be blessed, and He brings very, very many, to know their state by nature by doctrines which I should have thought would rather have comforted believers than awakened the unconverted. I am constantly driven back to the great foundation truth of Divine Sovereignty, and am made to realize that, in grace as well as in providence,

God moves in a mysterious way,
His wonders to perform.

I was talking one day with an aged minister; and I noticed that he put his hand into his waistcoat pocket, and brought out a letter that was well-nigh worn to pieces. As he unfolded it, he exclaimed, 'God Almighty bless you, sir! God Almighty bless you, sir!' I said, 'Thank you, my dear sir, for that blessing, but what makes you give it to me?' The good man replied, 'I had a son, who I thought would be the stay of my old age, but he disgraced himself, and ran away from home, and I could not tell where he had gone, only that he said he was going to America.' When the minister had told me so much of his story, he bade me read the letter, which ran thus: 'Dear Father,—I am here in America; I have found a situation, and God has prospered me. I write to ask your forgiveness for the many wrongs that I have done you, and the grief I have caused you; and to tell you that, blessed be God, I have found the Saviour. I have joined the church here, and hope to spend my life in the Redeemer's service. This great change happened thus. I did not sail for America on the day I expected to start; and, having a leisure hour, I went down to the Tabernacle to see what it was like, and there God met with me. In his sermon, Mr. Spurgeon said, "Perhaps there is a runaway son here. The Lord call him by His grace!" And He did call me.' 'Now,' said the minister, as he folded up the letter, and put it into his pocket again, 'this son of mine is dead, and he has gone to heaven; and I love you, and shall continue to do so as long as I live, because you were the means of bringing him to Christ.' It is very difficult to say which of us was the more happy as we rejoiced together over the wanderer who had thus been brought to the Lord.

On another occasion, a lad, who was just going to sea, came to the Tabernacle, and was converted; and a few hours after was in heaven. He wrote to tell his parents that he had found the Saviour; and, just as they were reading his letter, they received news that the vessel in which he sailed had been in collision, and that he was drowned.

Two enquiring ones came to me in my vestry. They had been

hearing the gospel from me for only a short season, but they had been deeply impressed by it. They expressed their regret that they were about to remove far away, but they added their gratitude that they had heard me at all. I was cheered by their kind thanks, but felt anxious that a more effectual work should be wrought in them, and therefore I asked them, 'Have you in very deed believed in the Lord Jesus Christ? Are you saved?' One of them replied, 'I have been trying hard to believe.' I have often heard this statement, but I will never let it go by me unchallenged. 'No,' I said, 'that will not do. Did you ever tell your father that you tried to believe him?' After I had dwelt awhile upon the matter, they admitted that such language would have been an insult to their father. I then set the gospel very plainly before them in as simple language as I could, and I begged them to believe Jesus, who is more worthy of faith than the best of fathers. One of them replied, 'I cannot realize it; I cannot realize that I am saved.' Then I went on to say, 'God bears testimony to His Son, that whosoever trusts in the Lord Jesus Christ is saved. Will you make Him a liar now, or will you believe His Word?' While I thus spoke, one of them started as if astonished, and she startled us all as she cried, 'Oh, sir, I see it all; I am saved! Do bless Jesus for me; He has shown me the way, and He has saved me. I see it all.' The esteemed sister who had brought these friends to me knelt down with them while, with all our hearts, we blessed and magnified the Lord for a soul brought into the light. The other young woman, however, could not see the gospel as her companion had done, though I feel sure she will do so; but it seemed strange that, both hearing the same words, one should come out into clear light, and the other should remain in the gloom.

When talking with anxious enquirers, I am often amazed at the ingenuity with which they resist the entrance of the truth into their hearts. I do not think I have ever been so much astonished at the invention of locomotive engines, electric telegraphs, or any other feats of human mechanism, as I have been at the marvellous aptitude of simple people in finding out reasons why they should not believe in the Lord Jesus Christ. After I have proved to them to a demonstration that it is the most reasonable and fitting thing in the world for them to trust themselves with Christ, they ask, 'How is this to be done?' or, 'How is that to be accomplished?' and they argue, first one way, and then another, all against their own best interests. Often, I go patiently through the whole process again and again;

and even when that has been done, there comes another objection. I have tracked these people to their holes as diligently as if I had been a fox-hunter, and I have tried to unearth them from their hiding-places, but I find that they can often burrow faster than I can follow them. Oh, the 'ifs' and 'buts' they put; the 'perhaps,' and 'peradventure,' and 'I don't feel this,' and 'I don't feel that'! Oh, that wicked questioning of Christ! While talking with them, endeavouring to comfort them, and I hope not unsuccessfully, I am often led to realize more deeply than before, in my own mind, what an awful crime it is to doubt God, to doubt Him who speaks from above, to doubt Him who hung bleeding on the tree.

Sitting, one day, to see enquirers, a young Dutchman came into the room. He had crossed from Flushing, and desired to tell me his difficulties of soul. He began, 'Sir, I cannot trust in Christ.' My answer was, 'Why not? What has He done that you should speak so ill of Him? I have trusted everything in His hands, and I believe Him to be quite trustworthy. What do you know against His character?'

'Indeed, sir, I know nothing against Him, and I am ashamed that I have so spoken, for I believe the Lord Jesus to be worthy of all confidence. That was not what I meant. May I trust Him to save me?'

'Of course you may, for you are commanded to do so by the gospel, which says, "Believe on the Lord Jesus Christ, and thou shalt be saved." You are warned against not believing by the words, "He that believeth not shall be damned." '

'I may, then, trust Christ; but does He promise to save all who trust Him?'

'Certainly. I have already quoted to you the promise of the gospel. It is also written, "Whosoever shall call upon the Name of the Lord shall be saved." If Jesus does not save you upon your trusting Him, you will be the first He ever cast out.'

'Ah, sir, I see it! Why did I not see it before? I trust, and Jesus saves me. I am well repaid for coming from Flushing.'

I prayed with him, and he went his way trembling for joy.

A lady came to me, after a service in the Tabernacle, and asked me to pray for her. She had been before to speak to me about her soul, so I said to her, on the second occasion, 'I told you very plainly the way of salvation, namely, that you are to trust yourself in Christ's hands, relying on His atoning sacrifice. Have you done that?' She answered, 'No,' and then asked me whether I would pray for her. I said, 'No, certainly I will not.' She looked at me with astonishment, and again asked, 'Will you not pray for me?' 'No,' I replied, 'I have nothing for which to pray for you. I have set the way of salvation before you so simply that, if you will not walk in it, you will be lost; but if you trust Christ now, you will be saved. I have nothing further to say to you; but, in God's Name, to set before you life or death.' Still she pleaded, 'Do pray for me!' 'No,' I answered, 'would you have me ask God to shape His gospel so as to let you in as an exception? I do not see why He should. His plan of salvation is the only one that ever has been or ever will be of any avail; and if you will not trust to it, I am not going to ask God anything, for I do not see what else is wanted from Him. I put this question plainly to you, "Will you believe in the Lord Jesus Christ?" ' I certainly was somewhat surprised when the sister said, very deliberately, 'If it be so, then, that salvation will come to me by believing, I do believe what the Scripture says concerning Christ; and, moreover, I feel that I can trust myself with Him, because He is God, and He has offered a sufficient sacrifice for my sins; and I do trust myself to Him just now; and I feel such a strange peace stealing over me at this very moment. I have trusted Him, and I am certain that I am saved;' and, in an instant, she said to me, 'Good evening, sir; there are other people waiting to see you,' and away she went, like a common-sense woman as she was; and she has often told me since how glad she was that I refused to pray for her, and so brought her to the decision to trust Christ for herself, and thus to receive the assurance of her salvation.

There is a great contrast between the ways in which different converts begin their new life. I have sometimes thought that if a man does not become a high-class Christian during the first three months after his conversion, he probably never will. I have noticed some people who have commenced their Christian career in a very feeble fashion. I hope they so began that they were really saved; but, still, they started doubting and fearing, and they kept on in the same style till they went to heaven. 'Ah, sir!' said one to me once, 'either all the world has altered, or else I have, for people I once delighted in I am now afraid of. The things that once made me glad now make me unhappy, and those that I thought melancholy are now the very things in which I find my highest joy.' I am always thankful when our friends get a very decided conversion, because, though I am not going to say a word against those who come to

Christ very gradually, yet their experience is rather cloudy. No doubt they are just as safe as others, but they lack a good deal of comfort afterwards; and, sometimes, persons who are very readily converted, and who have no very deep sense of sin, are more apt to play with evil than others are who have had a clearer sight of its enormity. Some begin by serving the Lord stingily, not giving Him their whole hearts; or they commence coldly, and so they never get hot with zeal all their lives. I am glad when a young convert is red-hot, or even white-hot; I like to see him too full of zeal, if that is possible, because, when he cools down, he will come just to the right temperature if he is too hot at first but, if he is cool at the beginning, what will he come to by-and-by? There are no labourers for the Master who are so useful as those who begin to serve Him while they are young. Sometimes, God converts men in middle life, or even in old age, and uses them in His service; but, still, I venture to assert that Church history will show that the most useful servants of Christ were those who were caught early, and who from their youth up bore testimony to the gospel of Jesus. In the case of some old people, who have been professors of religion for years, but who have done next to nothing for Christ, I find it very difficult ever to stir them up at all. When I do get a saddle on them, they are very restive creatures, like a horse that has never been broken in; but if I break them in while they are colts, they get used to their work, it becomes a delight to them, and they would not be happy unless they had something to do for the Lord Jesus. I remember having a considerable share of sneers, and rebukes not a few, from some who thought themselves very wise men, because I began preaching at the age of sixteen. I was recommended to tarry at Jericho till my beard had grown, and a great many other pieces of advice were given to me; but I have never regretted that I was a 'boy-preacher' of the Word; and if I could have my time over again, I would like to do just the same as I did then.

I have been delighted as I have noticed the earnest efforts of many of my church-members in seeking to bring sinners to the Tabernacle to hear the gospel. Two of our brethren, both working-men, one of whom has been a famous runner, and who has won prizes in many running-matches, are accustomed, as they say, to hunt in couples for souls. Their usual method is for one to go on one side of the street, and his friend on the other, on the Lord's-day morning, in those parts of London where Sabbath trading is carried on to the greatest extent. One morning, one of them was giving a tract to a person as the other was crossing over to join him, to communicate with him on some subject. As the second friend met the man who had received the tract, he heard him say, with an oath, 'What is the use of giving me this tract? I shall be in hell in an hour!' He said to his fellow-labourer, on reaching him, 'Did you hear what that man said?' 'No,' he answered, 'I did not notice; what was it?' 'He appeared very wild, and talked of being in hell in an hour; he is either insane, or he is intending to commit suicide.' 'Do you think so? Then we will be after him.' They followed him, and the second one, on coming up to the man, said to him, 'What did you say when you took that tract?' 'That's no concern of yours,' he answered, 'mind your own business.' 'Oh!' was the reply, 'but it is my business, for, if I heard aright, you said that you would be in hell in an hour.' 'Yes, I did say so; this world is worse than hell, and I'll be out of it in an hour.' 'No, you won't,' said our friend, 'for I mean to stick by you; and I won't leave you for an hour, go where you may.'

The poor creature then succumbed, and the godly men took him into a coffee-shop, and gave him a good breakfast. The man felt less like committing suicide after that meal. Our friends knew that the best gospel sermon would not be likely to benefit a man who was starving; he had tasted nothing for three days, and had walked the streets all the night. Hence, our brethren wisely felt that they must first feed his hungry body; and after that, they brought him to the Tabernacle. When the service was over, their poor patient looked a little more hopeful, and the soul-doctors thought it best to repeat the dose of solid nutriment. They took him to a house where they were accustomed to dine, in a humble way, and he shared their meal. He went to one of the Bible-classes in the afternoon; and, in the evening, they brought him again to the Tabernacle, and it pleased God to touch the poor man's heart, and bring him to a knowledge of himself and his Saviour. Then he became communicative, and it appeared that he had left his wife for four or five months, and had been living a life of dissipation, sin, and poverty. He gave the name and address of his wife, in the North of England; she was written to, and his fare was paid home; and, after he had gone back, a letter came from the good woman, saying that she had been a member with the Wesleyan Methodists, and had been long praying for her husband, who had been an awful reprobate, and had at last run away from home. Then she thought it was all over with him; but

God had designs of love towards him, and now he had sat down at the Lord's table with her. She did not know what to say, her heart was so full of gratitude to God, and to the dear friends who had been the means of bringing her husband to the Saviour.

At another time, a man came to join the church; and, according to our usual custom, he was asked how he had become converted, when he told us the following story. He said: 'I was employed in driving a horse and van; I never thought of going to any place of worship, and I do not think anybody ever said a word to me about God or Christ until one day when I was crossing over London Bridge when, suddenly, a man jumped up, and climbed into the back of my cart. I took my whip to lash him off, but he said, "Hold hard, mate, I've got a message for you." This was a very curious thing to me, and I asked, "What is it?" "I will tell you, but I may as well sit in front." So he sat down beside me. Then I asked him, "What is your message?" "It is a message from God to your soul." I cursed and swore at him; but that made no difference to him. He said, "You are the very man I was after. I knew you were a swearing man, for it was that first attracted my attention to you, and I am sure my message is for you." I said to him then, "What have you to say? Come, cut it short." He did cut it short, and he put it pretty straight, too. He told me what would become of my soul if I died a swearer, and he talked to me about the world to come. Then he told me that there was a Saviour for sinners, and that, if I trusted Him, I should be saved. Before he left me, he made me promise that I would go to hear you, sir. So I promised, and as I always boasted that I kept my word, I came to hear you, though I was precious sorry that I had promised to do so. I never got up so early on a Sunday morning before; and when the man saw me at the gate, he took me in, and gave me his seat, and stood himself all the service, which I thought was very kind on his part. After the sermon, he asked me, "Did you like it?" I replied, "No, I did not; that is not the sort of thing that I care about; I don't believe in religion." "Ah! but you will," the man said; and he and I parted company at the gate, and I hoped I should never meet him again.

I did not see him for some weeks; but, one day, as I was walking down the Blackfriars Road, I saw him coming along, so I slipped round the first corner, and began to run to avoid him; but, soon, I heard somebody running after me, and he came up to me, and said, "Well, mate, how are you?" "All right." "Are you going on any better?" he asked. I did not give him any answer, and then he told me that he had made up his mind that I should be a Christian one day, and that he never meant to let me alone till that came to pass. I believe he would have gone into my house with me; but, as my wife and I were fond of drink, there was only a little furniture in it, and I did not wish him to come in, and see the miserable place, so, to get rid of him, I proposed to go and hear Mr. Spurgeon on the next Sunday. I kept my promise; and, now, I am happy to say that I do not need anybody to induce me to go to the Tabernacle. I have been here six months, I have found the Saviour for myself, and I have got four of our men to come down to hear the gospel with me.'

Perhaps, next to the joy of actual conversions, the rescue of those who have long been in dense spiritual darkness has given me the greatest delight. Many of God's people are perplexed with questions concerning their interest in Christ, or they are afflicted with deep depression of spirit out of which only the Lord Himself can lift them up. I have tried, upon some of the sorely-troubled ones, all the promises of the Bible which I could remember. I have reminded them of the Person of Christ, and of His consequent power; of the sufferings of Christ, and of His consequent ability to cleanse from sin; but I have many times had this answer given to me, "When God shutteth up, who can deliver?' and I have been very often made to feel that, as Pastor, *I* could not quench the fiery darts of the wicked one for other people, and that I could not break in pieces the sword of the enemy, for others, or even for myself. Yet I have been very happy when the Lord has enabled me to be the means of cheering any desponding or even despairing soul. One day, as I came out of the pulpit, there met me a brother-minister, and he said, 'Sir, I cannot tell you all the particulars now, but I will write to-morrow; my wife is set at liberty.' Afterwards, he wrote to tell me how she had been in despair, and what sorrow she had suffered, and what a grief it had been to him, but while I preached upon the words, 'Cast not away therefore your confidence, which hath great recompence of reward,' she was brought out of bondage. Oh, how I praised and blessed God, and thought that I would like to preach day and night if I might but be the channel of such blessing again and again!

Another case which I remember was that of a man of excellent character, well beloved by his family, and esteemed by his neighbours, who was for twenty years enveloped in unutterable gloom. He ceased to attend the house of God, because he said it was of no use; and although always ready to help in every good work, yet he had an abiding conviction upon him that, personally, he had neither part nor lot in the matter, and never could have. The more anyone talked to him about the things of God, the worse he became; even prayer seemed but to excite him to more fearful despondency. In the providence of God, I was called to preach the Word in his neighbourhood; he was induced to attend, and, by the Holy Spirit's blessing on the sermon, he obtained a joyful liberty. After twenty years of anguish and unrest, he ended his weary roamings at the foot of the cross, to the amazement of his neighbours, the joy of his household, and the glory of God. Nor did his peace of mind subside; for, until the Lord gave him a happy admission into eternal rest, he remained a vigorous believer, trusting and not being afraid.

'Sydney Smith called Scotland "the knuckle-end of England;" but, as to gospel preaching, we have always regarded it as the choicest part of the three kingdoms, and so it is, and so it shall be by the grace of God.'— C. H. SPURGEON *in a review of 'Modern Scottish Pulpit'* in *'The Sword and The Trowel'*, 1881.

15

In Scotland

As recorded in the previous volume, Spurgeon had first preached in Scotland in 1855 at the age of twenty-one. At that time one of his first impressions of a Scottish congregation was hardly encouraging. He wrote of a service at Aberfeldy: 'After prayer and singing I began to preach; but there were no eyes of fire, and no beaming countenances, to cheer me while proclaiming the gospel message. The greater part of the congregation sat in apparent indifference; they seemed made of lumps of ice. I tried all means to move them, but in vain . . . I felt like the Welshman who could make Welshmen jump, but could not move the English. I thought within myself, "Surely your blood is very cold here, for everywhere else I should have seen signs of emotion while preaching Christ and Him crucified." ' Yet this first impression was soon corrected as he goes on to say: 'Feeling rather sad at our singular service, I went into the street, and was delighted to find that, although cold as marble in the building, they were now hearty and full of feeling.' Beneath the sombre countenance of the Highlander Spurgeon found men whose life-long attachment to his gospel-preaching was exceeded by no other part of the British Isles. It was also a benefit to him to gain the acquaintance and friendship of such Scottish evangelicals as Brownlow North, John G. Paton of the New Hebrides and David Livingstone. The last mentioned was present at a service in the Surrey Music Hall in 1857 and after his death, in the heart of Africa in 1873, one of Spurgeon's sermons—turned yellow—was found embedded in one of his journals and inscribed in his neat hand, 'Very good.—D. L.'

Spurgeon's second visit to Scotland was in the early part of March 1861, and included services at Edinburgh, Glasgow, Perth, Dundee, Montrose, and Aberdeen. According to *The Morning Journal* of Glasgow, more than half the clergy of the city were present at the services at the City Hall and at the Queen's Rooms, while in Aberdeen, 5,000 tickets of admission to the service were sold long before the preacher's arrival. On March 10th he preached for his friend John Anderson, Free Church minister of Helensburgh, twice in his church and a third time from a table in the manse garden.

The sum of £391 which he brought back went to the completion of the Metropolitan Tabernacle. On returning to Scotland in 1863 another such Sabbath was spent at Helensburgh. 'Helensburgh', writes G. H. Pike, 'was probably at this time the place which Mr. Spurgeon loved best to visit in Scotland.'

In May, 1866, Spurgeon was in Edinburgh to address the General Assemblies of both the Free Church and the United Presbyterian Church. His speech in the Free Church Assembly on 'Home Missions', delivered on May 29th, was one of the finest of all his addresses. On the previous Sunday he had also preached to packed congregations for his friend Robert Candlish, minister of Free St. George's, and for Andrew Thomson, minister of the United Presbyterian Church.

It was in the 1870's, however, that Spurgeon was to be found most frequently in the North. In May, 1870, after speaking in Edinburgh and Dundee (at the latter for the opening of the M'Cheyne Memorial Church) he proceeded for the first time to Ross-shire. The previous winter he had formed a friendship with Dr. John Kennedy, minister of the Free Church, Dingwall, who had been convalescing in the South after an illness. At that time a new Free Church was being built for Kennedy in the county town of Ross-shire and the Scots leader secured a promise from Spurgeon that he would come to open the new building. The event is well described in Alexander Auld's *Life of John Kennedy*:

Great was the joy of the Highland people, not only in the prospect of hearing Mr. Spurgeon, but also in the realization. His printed sermons and books had prepared the way before him. When he alighted at the railway station a ringing cheer welcomed him. The new church could not hold the multitude of people who came to hear, so Mr. Spurgeon kindly said that he would preach in the open air, and the 17th of May proved to be the first lovely summer day of the season. The old and the delicate could listen without fear of consequences, and even the deaf could hear the splendid clear voice as it poured forth the living, loving message from John 7.37, 38.

As Mr. Spurgeon and his host drove from the tent to the Free Church Manse, the people who lined the streets involuntarily stood and uncovered their heads, anxious to show more than regal honour. An old saint turned round and said, "Are you not thankful that Spurgeon is still so young?" Clergymen from all quarters appeared on that day, and many of them dearly prized the right hand of fellowship extended to them by the metropolitan preacher.

Mr. Spurgeon proved quite as attractive in private as in public; his sparkling wit, his joyous spirit, his ready rejoinder, made time fly all too quickly. His host and other friends remarked a strong similarity between him and John Macdonald, the apostle of the North, even in his movements as well as in his social qualities.

Very soon after Mr. Spurgeon's return to London the following letter was received by Mr. Kennedy:

"MY VERY DEAR BROTHER, You are very kind to express the pleasure my visit gave you, but rest assured mine was quite equal to yours. It was a sunny spot in a very sunny life when I saw you and your dear wife and family, and your beloved people. I shall always look back on it with unfeigned joy, and we will even talk of it in heaven, for 'the Lord was there.' I trust and pray that you may have fully recovered the elasticity of your spirit, which is oil to the bones.

I have had small strokes of the gout, but otherwise was never better—I wish I could add, never nearer to God. Still, I walk in the light, and have fellowship with Him and the blood—ah, there's the joy of it, the blood cleanses me from all sin. I should delight to see a more solemn and deep religious work going on in and around all Churches. We must unite in prayer for this. God has not left us, but we long to sing, 'The right hand of the Lord doeth valiantly.' I am a scant letter-writer; you know how to excuse me; but an epistle from you will always be precious, and, time being given, would find a reply. Present my love in the Lord to Mrs. Kennedy and yours, all of them. My wife is marvellously better. Pray for my two boys when you have the Master's ear. One word more for you. Glory in infirmities, because the power of Christ doth rest upon you. You see the infirmities most, but others see the power and feel it, and glorify God for it.—Your own brother in the Lord's house,

C. H. SPURGEON." '

For three successive years, 1876-1878, Spurgeon spent summer holidays with James Duncan, of Benmore, an estate at the head of Holy Loch on the river Clyde, opposite Gourock and Greenock. Here, amidst scenes of great beauty, there was rest, and in the Duncan's yacht opportunity to be left alone with sky and ocean. Without revealing the precise whereabouts of his retreat, Spurgeon apologized for the absence of the customary editorial notes in

The Sword and the Trowel for September, 1876, with these words:
'The Editor has been out of the way of taking notes of anything
except Highland cattle, sea gulls, herrings, and heather. Hence this
department of the magazine must go bare this month. Perhaps, also,
the rest of this issue may show that the ruling hand is absent; and
if so, gentle reader, forgive the fault. We must rest now and then,
and breathe the ocean air, or else we shall become as flat, stale and
unprofitable as a stagnant pool. What salt could be expected in a
magazine if the editor never went to the sea-side?'

Even at Benmore, however, it was not all rest and Spurgeon
could have reported the service on the hill-side at the Duncans'
home on August 20th when over 3,000 heard him preach. The
following year, 1877, still larger numbers assembled along the
Clyde to hear him. On Sunday, July 22nd, 1877, he preached at
Dunoon skating-rink to some 7,000 persons. An hour before two
o'clock, the time of commencing, the place was so thronged that
there was some danger of the platform being forced down. 'Presumably,' reported one paper, 'all the church-going folk in Dunoon
were present, for all the churches were closed in the afternoon, and
from the surrounding villages and the other side of the water there
were great streams of people. Some of the congregation came as far
as from Garelochhead, a journey involving a walk of about
twenty-two miles, and crossing and re-crossing of two lochs.'

The scene at the time of the service was thus described by one
eye-witness writing in *The Greenock Daily Telegraph*:

'If the weather were to prove unpropitious the new United
Presbyterian church in the town had been agreed upon as the
meeting-place. Several boats containing occupants were lying in
the bay. When Mr. Spurgeon ascended the platform, he advanced
to the front of it, and in a clear, ringing voice remarked that, as
most of his audience were standing, he would not make the service
very long, to which he added that he should have to stand also.
This seemed to tickle his listeners, and though the day was Sunday,
and the scene the shores of a Scotch river, a general laugh could be
heard. Then in a most solemn manner the reverend gentleman
opened the proceedings with prayer. When finished he announced
the 89th Psalm. This he read out, and having asked the crowd to
watch the time in singing, the precentor led to the tune of Martyrdom. The effect was very grand, for the vast concourse of people
seemed to be impressed by the Christian associations which the

meeting recalled, and they sung the psalm with great earnestness, Mr. Spurgeon beating time with his psalm-book.

Another prayer followed, and in it the Deity was addressed as the "God of the Covenanters", and a special appeal was made on behalf of those in the congregation who were unconverted. So well did Mr. Spurgeon speak that at some distance from the shore his voice was distinctly heard, and one remarkable feature was that the echo was so perfect that the words could be understood almost as well as when the speaker uttered them. During the sermon a large number of ladies fainted owing to the great heat and crush; but in spite of the fears which at an earlier stage of the proceedings were entertained as to the stability of the front wall of the rink, the meeting was unattended by any mishap.'

On the evening of the same day a service was held in the grounds of Benmore. The following Saturday he preached at Fort William and on Sunday, July 29th, to 3,000 at Oban. The *Glasgow Herald* reported the striking scene:

'Long before the hour appointed for the commencement of the service the hill-side was well-nigh filled with people, many of whom came a long distance—some twenty and thirty miles—to hear the distinguished preacher . . . From the platform, which was temporarily erected, and covered with tarpaulin to protect the speaker from the weather should it prove unfavourable, Mr. Spurgeon had a full view of the congregation. Speaking of the depravity of man's heart and its antagonism to the will of God, he said that the stars in the firmament were only restrained by Omnipotence from darting baleful fires against those who were obnoxious to God. The Christian, he said, depended upon his God for his spiritual prosperity as much as the vegetable world depended upon the heat of the sun for its growth. He concluded with a most earnest appeal to his hearers to accept of God's salvation through Christ, reminding them all, young and old, that they and he would meet again when heaven and earth would be in a blaze, and on that day none of their blood would be on his head.'

The press though decidedly friendly was not entirely uncritical. The *Greenock Daily Telegraph* wrote:

'Mr. Spurgeon made one mistake in the Highlands. At Dunoon he delivered in his prayer an apostrophe to the "God of the Covenanters;" and at Oban he improved upon this by speaking of the

times of old when the mountains and valleys of the surrounding
country had resounded with the psalms sung by the Covenanters.
The worthy pastor of the Metropolitan Tabernacle, whom we all
hope to see often in this part of the world, must revise his study of
Scottish history against his next visit. He will learn, on further
inquiry, that the parts about Oban, instead of contributing subscribers to the Covenant, provided a pretty large proportion of that
sanguinary "Highland host" which sprinkled some of our Lowland
counties with martyr graves. Happily, a great change has come over
the Land of Lorne, and this was indicated at the close of Mr.
Spurgeon's Oban sermon, when crowds of venerable Highland
peasants, some of the women especially very far advanced in life,
crowded round the great preacher to shake hands with him and
invoke the blessing of God upon himself and his work. Not a few of
the old dames told him how greatly they enjoyed reading his sermons at home, and Mr. Spurgeon was much affected by these
tokens of friendly feeling, so fervently expressed by the sons and
daughters of the Gael, no longer the instruments of despotism and
superstition, but the most ardently Evangelical and Protestant
section of the Scottish nation.'

THE BRONZE STAG AT BENMORE

Among the many lighter moments enjoyed by Spurgeon at 'Benmore' one is reported by William Williams, pastor of Upton Chapel, London, who shared a holiday with 'the President' beside the Clyde. His narrative needs to be read in connection with the picture of Benmore reproduced opposite:

'In the foreground of the picture is a stag lying majestically, with head erect, in the meadow (as though 'Benmore' belonged to him). There is a little incident connected with this stag which I think is worth relating. It may tell a "wee" bit against the writer, but it illustrates Mr. Spurgeon's love of fun. Soon after we were settled down at Benmore, Mr. Duncan said to me, "Can you shoot, Mr. Williams?" "Yes," I replied, "I was almost born with a gun in my hand." "Well then," said he, "I will send to Glasgow for a gun licence for you to-morrow." I had not specially noticed the stag in the meadow, for there were plenty of deer close, too. The next evening, just as it was getting a little dusk, as Mr. Spurgeon, Mr. Duncan, and I were sitting outside the house, Mr. Spurgeon said, "Oh, Mr. Williams, I have asked and obtained permission from Mr. Duncan for you to shoot that fine stage in the meadow; see, he is lying there now. But you are to shoot him as he lies; for, if you get him to move, you won't hit him; and Mr. Duncan says, if you kill him, you can have a haunch of venison to take home with you. Now, there is a chance for you." I expostulated, and said, it was not fair to shoot at the animal sitting; if I were allowed first to make him rise, I would fire. "No, no," said Mr. Spurgeon; "if you don't shoot him sitting, Mr. Duncan is sure you won't shoot him at all. He is a very unusual sort of stag." I yielded and crept quietly behind the trees in front of him until I got within forty yards of the animal, when, dusk as it was, I began to be suspicious, and soon discovered that the stag was bronze. I did not fire, or the reader might be now looking at the singular phenomenon of a lively-looking stag's body without a head. I turned round to find Mr. Spurgeon laughing with all his might. A tougher piece of venison than I should have liked to bring to London, was that stately monarch of the meadow.'

On several accounts his stay on the Clyde in 1878 was one of the most memorable of all. Travelling by carriage he was reported to have experienced a deliverance from what might have been a serious accident if not sudden death. The coachman was allowing his horses to run at considerable speed down a steep hill; on being asked to rein in the horses he responded, 'Oh, we always go like that here,' and continued down a further descent 'at a rate the English preacher had never travelled at before, except in an express train.' At that point the harness broke and the driver lost all control. As the vehicle approached the bottom—a precipice protected by a fence— the passengers anticipated disaster, but the horses of their own accord swung into another road in which an incline brought them to a standstill.

During the same holiday the party proceeded by yacht far out towards the Western Isles. Having touched at Oban, Tobermory, and other places, Spurgeon arrived at Rothesay Bay on Saturday, July 27th. The next day he worshipped at the Baptist Chapel and in the evening he preached from the top of the porch of Provost Orkney's house, his text being Luke 13. 10–17. This weekend was remembered many years later by one of the students of the Pastors' College who happened to be there at the time:

'I was at Rothesay, spending a brief holiday, when our ever-beloved President preached there in 1878. The mere fact that Mr. Spurgeon was announced to preach, created great interest all along the Clyde; and in Rothesay, as the day fixed on (Sunday, July 28,) drew near, every scrap of information concerning the proposed service was greedily devoured. On the Saturday, Bute's bright little capital received a large temporary addition to its summer population. Many yachts, too, came and anchored in the bay. Mr. Duncan's yacht, with Mr. Spurgeon on board, arrived about 3 p.m.; and in a few minutes the word had gone all over Rothesay, "Mr. Spurgeon is in the bay." Directly on his arrival, our dear Brother Crabb (who is still the respected Pastor of the Rothesay Baptist Church) and I went off in a boat to greet our President, and to tell him what preparations had been made for the morrow.

The next evening, Mr. Spurgeon preached, with marvellous power, to a congregation supposed to number from fifteen to twenty thousand persons. I need hardly say that the service was greatly enjoyed by the great company of worshippers. When it was over, the dear preacher rested for a while in the Provost's garden, to allow the crowds to disperse; but they evidently did not intend to leave him quite in that fashion. As they knew that he would have to go in a boat to reach the yacht, they gathered in thousands along the sea-wall. When Mr. Spurgeon stepped into the boat, and the sailors began to ply their oars, as one looked along the crescent-shaped front, it seemed as if every person in that vast gathering had brought a white handkerchief for the special purpose of waving it in his honour. I have witnessed many touching scenes in my day, but I do not think I ever saw anything more impressive than the sight of those thousands of true-hearted Scotch people saying, by their silent action, better than they could have said it in words—"Accept our heartiest thanks for your sermon, and may God bless you at all times!" That was Scotland's way of bidding a Sabbath adieu to the great and good man she loved so well; and not until he was on board the yacht did the farewell signals cease to flutter in the evening breeze.'

In a real sense Rothesay was saying farewell to Spurgeon. The following year, 1879, saw one of the longest of Spurgeon's breakdowns in health, necessitating more than five months on the Continent and thus his succession of summers in the North came to an end. He returned to Scotland in the 1880's and as late as 1885 some four thousand heard him preach again on James Duncan's lawn at Benmore but the more widespread great open-air gatherings of the 1870's were never to be repeated.

In these later years when his declining health was apparent it was viewed with much concern by his friends on the Clyde and a letter on this subject from Mr. Duncan's sister, Mrs. Moubray of Strone House, drew from him a characteristic reply. After mentioning various places she had recently visited which were known to Spurgeon, his Highland correspondent had advised him to desist from overworking himself and to remember that the sixth commandment required 'all lawful endeavours to preserve our own life'. From London, Spurgeon replied:

'Westwood,
Aug. 26, 1885

Dear Mrs. Moubray,
  I heartily thank you for the proverbs, some of which I have used. I think I am well acquainted with the book you have culled from; indeed, I would go far to see a proverb-book which I do not know.

Happy woman to be sailing over the fair seas, and gazing upon those glorious hills! I find abundance to do all day, and every day; but, as the Lord blesses the work, I am not able to weary of it.

I saw Mr. Duncan on Sunday, much to my joy. He is, indeed, a kind and tender friend, and his sister is like unto him. God bless both!

I trust Mr. McKercher will get better, and be restored to you. Truly good men are scarcer than they used to be. The world has gone after the idols of modern thought, and those of us who do not thus wander are esteemed to be "old fogies."

A woman rose in the Tabernacle, last Sunday, just as I entered, and began to talk about *the sixth commandment*! Of course, I pricked up my ears, and wondered whether it was a lady from Strone House! She did not get far before the attendants carried her off. I have not asked her name, but it looks very suspicious. Were *you* up in London last Sunday?

I am studying that commandment, and I begin to think that I must work much harder, for fear somebody should be killed, spiritually, by my failure to preach in season and out of season.

My very kindest regard and heartiest thanks to you.

Yours ever gratefully,

C. H. SPURGEON.'

Spurgeon's sermons were read all over the North and in many a glen and Highland croft there was no gospel preacher more highly esteemed. A colourful example of this was given by Pastor W. Brock in an article 'A Guide to Killiecrankie', published in *The Sword and the Trowel* in 1873. Visiting this beautiful Perthshire glen he had accompanied an agent of the Scottish Tract Society who was accustomed to visit among the homes of the people. Brock thus recalls how they met an elderly member of the Baptist Chapel of Tullymet:

'The good colporteur, finding that I was a Baptist, had hinted to me that it was scarcely less than a duty to call on a certain Annie Sims, living with her brother James, in the heart of a wood not far from the meeting of the rivers. Annie, he said, had been "in the way" for seventy-three years, having been baptized in the river Tay at Dunkeld when sixteen years of age, and it was not every day that you could meet with such a case of faithful pilgrimage as that. So, through rain and mire, I found my way up a cart-track to the cottage, and making known my errand, gained a speedy admission.

Three chairs stood beside the hearth, on which the wood crackled cheerfully. On one of the chairs sat an aged woman, her body bent with the injuries caused by a fall, but with a face smooth and bright like a girl's, and a happy voice that charmed you at once. The brother, a man of eight-four, took his seat opposite, and we were soon in for a "crack." Yes, she had been a church member all those years, and was now hoping for the blessed end. She remembered her baptism well—Mr. Macleod preached from a boat in the river to the people on the bank, and someone else baptized the candidates. It was nearly twenty years since she had been in the church; she could not move from the house, and should never leave it now. But she had her Gaelic Bible, and could read it easily, with her glasses, and Mr. B. (the colporteur) often paid her a visit, and brought her books. Then the talk took another turn. Where was the visitor from? From Perth or Edinburgh? What! from London? Ah, the brother had been there, thirty years ago, and a wonderful big place it was; but they kent of naebody there now but Mr. Spurgeon, and they had his sermons every month, and sent them on to friends in Ireland. And did I know Mr. Spurgeon; and how old was he; and how many bairns had he; and how many would his Tabernacle hold; and could they all hear him and see him when he preached? Now the communion question came up. Mr. Spurgeon admitted persons to the communion who were not baptized, did he? The answer was "Yes;" hereupon a difference of opinion ensued, the brother, a Presbyterian, highly approving; the sister questioning, "There were sae mony deceivers about now; the church at Tullymet had great need to take care whom they admitted." "Ay, but they mak it no longer the Lord's table, but their ain," objects the brother. And then we went to higher thoughts and future times, when all shall be one, sitting down together at Christ's table, in his kingdom. Prayer followed; and as we said good-bye, the aged believer repeated once and again her favourite text, "In the world ye shall have tribulation; but be of good cheer; I have overcome the world."

I had reached the door, when a hospitable thought struck Annie, and she called after me, "We have *nae bottle* here, but we can gie you a cup o' tea, gin ye will tak it." Then we parted, and the cottage was soon lost to sight among the trees. But in how many such corners of our land, hidden from the eye even of the church, the jewels of our Lord lie, waiting his hour to be set in their own place upon his crown.

I promised Annie that I would tell Mr. Spurgeon, when I saw him, of his readers and friends on the top of that distant Highland brae.'

In some memories of his father Charles Spurgeon wrote of a good lady of Loch Etive who had a glimpse of the preacher in unexpected circumstances:

'It has been my privilege to accompany dear father, on many occasions, to "the land o' cakes" and the county of lakes; and never had any tourist a more excellent guide. He was a veritable walking Encyclopædia; so full of information, and so gracious in imparting it, that a holiday spent with him was as instructive as a term at school, and to me, far preferable. It sometimes became amusing to see how eager folks were to show any little kindness to him. On one occasion, we were passengers on Mr. Duncan's yacht, *Varina*, and had made the passage of the Caledonian Canal, as far as Loch Etive, where, in one of the sheltered and picturesque bays, we had anchored for the night. Next morning, when breakfast was being prepared, the steward discovered that the supply of milk had run short, and that he must needs visit the shore to replenish the store. Standing on deck, I watched the progress of our caterer as he climbed the hillside, and made application at a small cottage on the border of the wood which covered the slope. Presently, a woman made her appearance, and then it soon became evident that she and the steward were having a somewhat lively conversation. In a few minutes, the man returned; but, alas! minus the milk.

He told us, when he came back, that the lady of the house would only supply it on condition that he would let her see Mr. Spurgeon, whose name he had used as his last argument. Upon my dear father learning that his appearance was required for this purpose, with his usual readiness to supply "the milk of human kindness," he came up on deck, and waved his hand in the direction of the cottage. The woman at once recognized him, and commenced a "Scotch reel" of delight. The steward had, meanwhile, again pulled to the shore; he soon disappeared within the house, and, in a few seconds, he came out, bearing a huge jug, brimful of pure milk, for which the worthy dame would not accept even twopence a quart!'

After Spurgeon's death another striking instance of God's blessing on his sermons in Scotland came to light with this report from T. G. Owens:

'On July 6th, 1893, I was on board a steamer going to Islay, the most Westerly of the Southern Hebrides, and, as is my custom when travelling, I distributed some of the sermons to my fellow-passengers and to the ship's crew. Among the rest I gave one to the chief engineer who then made the following statement, which I noted down: "Ten years ago I was converted by reading one of Spurgeon's sermons. My wife was converted two years before me; but I then hated religion and strongly opposed her attending the Sabbath and week-night services. She tried hard to persuade me to accompany her to the house of God, but her entreaties only excited my evil passions, and I angrily refused, and threatened her saying, 'If you go to the prayer meeting, I will go to the public house'. She, however, persisted in her efforts; but on the very Sabbath before my conversion I said to her, 'It is of no use for me to go with you to church; my day of grace is past'. I was at that time so terrified at the remembrance of my sins that I was afraid to fall asleep at night, lest I should open my eyes in hell before morning. I despaired of my salvation and was sure that my sins were so aggravated that God *could not* forgive me. I have been a seaman for forty years. On Monday, January 15th, 1883, I was starting out on a voyage and my wife (who has since died) put into my portmanteau six of Mr. Spurgeon's Sermons, bound together. That very night I read one of the sermons. The text of it was 2 Cor. 5. 14: 'For the love of Christ constraineth us, because we thus judge, that if one died for all, then were all dead' (No. 1411). That sermon was the means God used for my conversion.'

We conclude this chapter with a letter written to Spurgeon while he was on holiday one year at 'Benmore'. It is a reminder that the preacher's sermons were sometimes *heard* in the North even when he did not deliver them! Spurgeon gladly gave his consent to the unusual proposal which the writer made:

'19, Ardbeg Road,
Rothesay,
30th July, 1885

My Dear Rev. Sir,

For many years, I have perused your weekly sermons with great benefit to body and soul. I now trouble you to say that I purpose delivering your admirable discourse on "Coming Judgment of the Secrets of Men," with your permission, in the oldest Episcopal Church of Scotland. If you veto this, I will hold fire. I mean to give it *verbatim*; the only lack will be the voice of the living author.

Were it in my power, you should have the first vacant mitre in honour and appreciation of your singular gifts. Pardon this obtrusion on the rest which you so much need for your unwearied tax of strength, and believe me to be,

Yours most truly in Christ,
J. F. S. Gordon, D.D.,
St. Andrew's Episcopal Church, Glasgow.'

Charlie and Tommy are good little boys;
When they're asleep, they don't make any noise.

C.H.S.

That is a very precious Name which Christ puts into our mouths when He bids us say to God, 'Our Father, which art in Heaven;' and there is a wonderful sweetness when we come to know that we may call Him our Husband. I do not like to compare the two, and say which title is to be preferred—whether Husband or Father— they are both unutterably sweet when they are enjoyed to the full.—C.H.S., *in sermon preached at the Tabernacle, March* 1, 1883.

16

A Son's Memories

CHARLES SPURGEON JR

THE earliest recollections of my father which I have retained are naturally those associated with my childhood and my heart is filled anew with joyful pleasures as I think again and again of the doings of the days gone by. I must have been a very small boy when I capered about, with great delight, because my father had provided, for the entertainment of the natives of Walton-on-the-Naze, a firework display on the sands; and, among the visitors at the then slightly-known and out-of-the-way watering-place, little Charlie was made glad by looking at sky-rockets, and listening to the bang of squibs. This may seem a small matter to report, but it is indicative of a prominent feature in my father's character, inasmuch as he constantly rejoiced in giving pleasant surprises wherever he could; nor was this the only time when, to give his children some fun, he made the fifth of November an excuse for indulging in works of fire.

I well remember, too, how an improvised swing had been hung between two trees for the amusement of the boys; but an untimely fall of one of the twins precluded all further use of this out-door gymnasium. Father felt, however, that athletic exercises were conducive to the health of growing lads, so he arranged for the erection of a substantial horizontal bar and swing for their use, thus giving evidence of his thoughtful love and sympathetic consideration for their well-being.

I seem to see, as if it were but yesterday, his bright face beaming with smiles, as he gave his would-be carpenter sons a present, in the form of a basket of tools and a box of nails. All the implements needed for the full equipment of a master in the trade were to be found within that workman's basket; and I shall never forget how father watched and waited for us to discover, among the tools, a neat roll of rag! While we were puzzling our brains to find out why this was included, he laughingly explained that, in all probability, when we had cut our fingers, we should find out the use of it. The providing of the bandage for wounded amateurs, exemplified his power of forethought, and also his profound common sense.

I prize immensely the first letter I ever received from my father. It was written while he was staying in Heligoland and at the head of his note-paper was a coloured view of the populated end of the island, with some houses on the cliffs and others on the sands far below. It runs thus:

'My Dear Charlie,
    I am very glad that you wrote a nice little note to your dear mother, and I hope it is a sign that you are always going to be diligent and thoughtful, and this will be a glad thing indeed. . . . I am delighted to hear that you are doing so well at College. Give my love to all the students, and tell Mr. Rogers that it always cheers me to know that the brethren bear me up in their prayers.

On this little island, there is a lighthouse. It is much needed, for many vessels are wrecked here. We live down below, on the beach, near the square tower with a flag on it; that is a bathhouse. Steamers come every two days, and then we can send letters; at other times, we are far off from everybody, alone in the wide, wide sea. We have sheep's milk, for there is no room for cows. Fish is very plentiful, and very good.

My dear boy, I trust that you will prove, by the whole of your future life, that you are truly converted to God. Your actions must be the chief proof. Remember, trees are known by their fruit, and Christians by their deeds. God bless you for ever and ever! Mother sends her kindest love, and so does—
Your loving father,
C. H. SPURGEON.'

The reference to 'doing so well at College,' needs an explanation for I was at that time only a little boy. One of the students was then our tutor and, naturally, father took a deep interest in our educational progress. Pastor Harry Rylands Brown, now of Darjeeling, was the good brother who had us in training, and, from that day to this, teacher and pupil have been close friends.

When I was about twelve years of age I was riding home with my father in the brougham after an evening service at the Tabernacle. It was 'blowing great guns,' there was a heavy downpour of rain, and a keen East wind, with a cutting edge, was driving it upon the pavement. It was a dark, dreary night; and, as we came to a point where cross-roads met, father's quick eye discerned a person, whom he judged to be a poor woman, hurriedly rushing across the stones through the storm. With her skirt gathered over her head, she looked a weird spectacle; and in a moment, his heart was moved with compassion toward her. He cried out, 'Charlie, stop the coachman; jump out, and see if there is anything wrong with that poor creature, and find out whether you can help her.' Of course, I sprang out of the carriage at once; but I wondered what I was going to say to the woman. I overtook her, and said, 'Excuse me, but is there anything the matter? Are you in trouble?' She replied, 'Oh, dear, no! I have been to see a friend, and have been caught in the storm. I came out without an umbrella, so I am running home as fast as I can.' As I repeated to father what she had said, he exclaimed, 'That is a relief to me!' But what would he have done if she had been in distress? He was glad that she was all right; but I remember thinking, as I sat there by his side, 'Dear me! That woman is nothing to him, yet his heart went out towards her in pity and sympathy.' It went out after everyone who was in need and distress; and if his hand could help, its bounty speedily followed the leadings of his great heart of love.

While my brother and I were at Mr. Olding's school at Brighton, I wrote to tell my father that we had started a little prayer-meeting in the master's drawing-room, among our school-fellows. In reply, he wrote: 'Dear boy,—One of my sweetest joys is to hear that a spirit of prayer is in your school, and that you participate in it. To know that you love the Lord, and are mighty in prayer, would be my crowning joy; the hope that you do so already is a happy one to me. I should like you to *preach*, but it is best that you pray; many a preacher has proved a castaway, but never one who has truly learned to pray.'

I remember the great enjoyment father gave his two sons, in August, 1871, when he took us to Antwerp. As we went through the different churches there, he seemed to know all about every picture, each pulpit, and even the tombs; and he could tell us about the famous artists, sculptors, and carvers, upon whose works we were gazing in boyish wonderment.

I well remember, too, how father's righteous indignation was kindled as we stood in the famous cathedral, and witnessed the absurdities connected with the funeral obsequies of some great personage. No sooner had the gloomy *cortège* quitted the building, to a slow and solemn dirge rendered by the chorister monks, than a gorgeous wedding procession, with all the joyous accompaniments of marriage festivities, took its place; and thus the whole scene was quickly changed, and the mournful '*miserere*' was succeeded by the nuptial *'jubilate.'* The experienced preacher extemporized a brief discourse upon the ever-varying vicissitudes of human life, as set forth by the two events; and the truths he thus inculcated still abide, as we remember that our joys and sorrows are not so far apart as we are apt to think, for sunbeams and shadows are closely allied, after all. *Sic est vita.*

At another time, I was staying with my father in a much-loved, and oft-frequented spot in Surrey, where his presence was always looked upon as a high honour. The villagers had been successful in securing a fine large carp from the pond which skirted the green, and they thought that such a good catch should at once be sent to their notable visitor; so, with great ceremony, a deputation of rustics was appointed to wait upon him. The best that they could give to him was not reckoned too good for the man they loved; and though the gift was small, it was sufficient to prove the affectionate regard in which he was held by these simple rustics.

One of the most notable events of which I still have vivid recollections was the occasion of my baptism. An entry in the Tabernacle church-book, dated September 14, 1874, reads as follows: 'Charles and Thomas Spurgeon, of Nightingale Lane, Clapham, were proposed for church-membership, and Brother Payne was appointed messenger.

Charles and Thomas Spurgeon came before the church, and gave a satisfactory statement of the work of grace in their souls, and the messenger reporting favourably, it was agreed that, after baptism, they should be received into communion with the church.'

On the following Lord's-day morning, father preached at the Tabernacle, from Isaiah 8. 18, a sermon to which he gave the title, 'I and the Children.' The next evening, September 21, he baptized his twin sons, who had, on the previous day, celebrated their eighteenth birthday. As the beloved Pastor had not, for a long time, been able to baptize, and also, perhaps, because the candidates were his own sons, the great edifice was crowded with an interested concourse of people who had come to witness the solemn ceremony. Dr. Brock, of Bloomsbury Chapel, was present, according to promise, and delivered a forcible address, which was emphasized by some of father's telling utterances.

When it was put into my heart to serve the Lord, and to begin to speak for Him, I of course sought my father's counsel. He was then laid aside with a painful illness at Brighton, but he wrote to me thus:

'My own dear son,

I think it very kind and thoughtful of you to write to your father, and the more so because the time you have to yourself is not very long. I am glad you desire to do something for the Lord, and shall be still more pleased when you actually set about it. Time flies; and the opportunity for doing good flies with it. However diligent you may be in the future, you can only do the work of 1875 in 1875; and if you leave it undone now, it will be undone to all eternity. The diligent attention which you give to business, the careful purity of your daily life, and your concern to do common things in a right spirit, are all real service for the Lord. The hours in which your earthly calling is industriously followed for Christ's sake, are really hours of work for Jesus; but, still, this cannot satisfy you, or, at least, I hope it cannot. As redeemed by the precious blood of Jesus, you feel that you belong to Him, and you long to show your love to Him by actions *directly* meant to extend His Kingdom, and gather in sinners whom He loves to bless. When once such efforts are commenced, they become easier, and a kind of hunger to do more seizes upon the heart. It is not toil, but pleasure; and if God blesses what we do, it rises from being a common pleasure to become a sacred delight. "Whatsoever thy hand findeth to do, do it with thy might." It is not for me to suggest what form your service shall take, that must be left to yourself; and half the pleasure of it will lie in the exercise of a sacred ingenuity in discovering the work for which you are best adapted.

I was very thankful to read that you rejoiced in prayer; may it always be so, and yet more and more; for nothing gives us such strength, or affords us such guidance. The Lord bless you *there*, and all must be well. I have always hoped to see you a leader in the host of God. How it will be, I know not; but that so it may be, is one of my increasing prayers. Dear son, may all blessings abound towards you; you know I love you very dearly. It is a very dull Sabbath here, as to weather; I hope you are having a bright and happy day at home.

Your loving father,
C. H. Spurgeon.'

During the period I spent as a student in the Pastors' College, my father was always interested, not only in my own welfare, but in that of all the brethren. Perhaps at no time in the history of the

Institution was he better acquainted than he was then with the whole of the men, and the internal work and hidden life of our 'Alma Mater.' It was not looked upon as 'telling tales out of school' when the son answered the enquiries of the sire. On two occasions, I was privileged to receive from him letters containing notes which he desired me to read to all the brethren. No less than eleven outlines of discourses were given in the following letter, and from them I have chosen one specimen:

'Mentone.

Beloved Brethren,

Always make hay while the sun shines, and store up notes of sermons when your mind is fertile, for there are seasons of famine as well as of plenty, and every Joseph should lay up a store against the time of need. I fear I am not just now in the right order for sermonizing; but, if "silver and gold have I none," "such as I have give I you." By the way, that would not be a bad subject—*What we would give if we could, not half so valuable as what we can bestow if we will.* Or, (1) Talents we do not possess are not to be the source of repining, of sloth, or of indifference to men's wants; (2) Talents we do possess are to be used for the good of men, in faith, in the Name of Jesus, to the glory of God.

Turn to Acts 19, which is rich in texts. Verse 8. (1) The characteristic of a useful ministry: "he spake boldly." (2) The subject of such a ministry: "persuading the things concerning the Kingdom of God."

(i) The consistency of it with the Old Testament.
(ii) The binding character of its claims.
(iii) Its blessedness.
(iv) Its immediate requirements.'

At the end of the eleven skeletons of sermons, father wrote:

'This is all I can do to-day. I am much better, and send my love to you all, and thanks for capital letters, all of which are beyond criticism.

Yours ever heartily,
C. H. SPURGEON.'

Those ever-memorable Friday afternoons produced many rich seasons for storing up homiletic hints and outlines. This exercise seemed to be a recreation to the President, for if ever there was a brief interval that needed filling in between a bracing talk and a brilliant exposition, he would quietly make some such remark as this: 'Here's a good text: "HE restoreth my soul"—

(1) To life, by regeneration.
(2) To hope, by the revelation of His Son.
(3) To strength, by being my food.
(4) To wealth, by being my Father.
(5) To a Kingdom in Christ.
(6) To Paradise with Christ.'

As my College course was drawing to a close, my father wrote to me: 'Your time will soon be up, and I should like you to begin in some sphere, not too large, nor too small, from which you may step into a life-long position. I think you will maintain a good congregation; and, by God's blessing, will be useful. We must not push or strive to get you a position, but wait on the Lord, and He will do better for you than I can. When Bishops look out for livings for their sons or nephews, we condemn their nepotism, so we must not fall into the same evil ourselves. You will be patient and believing, and the right door will open.'

When the time came for me to settle in the ministry, my father's counsel was a great factor in helping me to decide to accept the 'call' from the members of South Street Baptist Church, Greenwich, and if afforded me no little joy to have him as the preacher on the occasion of my recognition as Pastor. A striking injunction, from the discourse he then delivered, stands out vividly in my memory, and has been a constant inspiration to me. Leaning over the pulpit rail, and looking down upon me, as I sat on the lower platform, he said, in tender, yet thrilling tones, 'Preach up Christ, my boy! Preach HIM up!!'

Among my father's letters that I treasure beyond the price of gold, are those which relate to the help rendered to him in times of sickness. Some of them look almost like hieroglyphics, because they were hurriedly scribbled, when his poor hands were swollen with gout, on a Sunday morning, and sent to Greenwich by a special messenger, asking me to take his service. Here is one: 'I am too full of pain to preach this morning; will you go to Tabernacle? I telegraphed Dunn to go to you, but if you have anyone else available, let him be ready. Your poor father—C. H. S.'

The first time that ever it was my honour to stand in his place, and thus occupy the pulpit in the Metropolitan Tabernacle on the Lord's day, called forth from him the following letter:

'Nightingale Lane,
Balham,
Surrey,
December 14, '78

My Dear Son,

I pray earnestly for you under the solemn responsibility of to-morrow. May your father's God lift you out of yourself, giving you lowly dependence on His Spirit, and pleading earnestness that men may come to Christ! I am very ill, or I would be in my pulpit. I am ready to weep on being still away; but, dear son, the Lord is so good in giving me you, that I dare not think of repining. Only lean thou wholly on Him, and be nothing before Him. He has been my stay these many years.

Tell the people that, night and day, I am full of pain; and as these three times I have promised to be with them, and have failed, I fear to hope any more. Only they will be all sure that it will be my highest joy to be back among them, to see their loving faces, and to speak to them the good Word of God. I am an exiled prisoner, and the iron enters into my soul; but the Lord is good, and in His Name do I hope.

With best love from your dear mother, and—

Your poor father,
C. H. Spurgeon.'

The deep interest he ever took in my work at Greenwich, and his ardent affection for my beloved mother, are set forth in many of his letters, as the following extract from a letter written at Mentone shows:

'May you, some quarter of a century hence, enjoy the pleasure of having your son Charles to preach for you! It is a great delight to me to receive such loving letters from the "Bishop" of Greenwich, who is also my son and heir; and it is even more joy to see that God is prospering you, and making your work successful. I think you have made specially good progress in the time. Stick to your studies. Read *Matthew Henry* right through, if you can, before you are married; for, after that event, I fear that Jacob may supplant him. Remember me to Mr. Huntley, and all the good people.'

At my marriage, on April 11, 1881, both my parents were present; the happy ceremony was performed by my father, and I can even now recall some of his words after the legal portion of the service had been completed: 'As this ring is round, so may your love be endless! As it is made of pure gold, so may your affection be pure.' Continuing to say all manner of nice, kind things, he added: 'It is exceedingly necessary that a minister, especially a young minister, should have a wife. The duties a minister's wife has to fulfil are very important, for she is expected to be a combination of all impossible virtues; in fact, altogether a wonder.' Glancing lovingly at dear mother, he said: 'I know one minister's wife who has greatly strengthened her husband in the Lord.' Never shall I forget the beautiful prayer in which he commended 'the happy couple' to God; the answers to those petitions we continue to receive even to this day.

I must relate an incident which, at the time, afforded my father a large amount of pleasure; and which is, I should think, unique in ministerial life. He had been announced to preach on behalf of a small Baptist church in the East End of London, and the Congregationalists had kindly lent their large place of worship for the occasion. Long before the appointed hour of service, a great crowd had gathered both within and around the building, so that, when the preacher entered the pulpit, many hundreds were still seeking admission. Turning to me, as I sat just behind him, he asked me whether I would take an overflow meeting in the sanctuary opposite. I readily assented; whereupon he rose, and told the people to pass word on to those outside, 'that his son Charles would preach just over the way, in the Baptist Chapel.' He continued his own service, and I retired to fulfil my promise, and had a crowded audience in the smaller building. It had been arranged that I should preach, in the evening, in the Baptist Chapel; and it turned out that the experience of the father was to be repeated with the son, for the place was filled in every part, and a large number in vain sought admission, so I despatched a pencilled note to the great preacher of the afternoon, asking him if he would kindly come and take *my* overflow in the schoolroom opposite! As we journeyed home together, he said, 'Well, Charlie, I do not suppose it has ever happened before, that father and son should be preaching opposite to one another at the same time; but, thank God, dear boy, not in opposition.'

I remember, too, in connection with this visit, that, as we passed through the great meat-market at Smithfield, he called my attention to the immense quantities of provisions, remarking, as he did so, 'Whatever will become of it all?' But we had not gone far down the Mile End Road, before the ever-moving mass of humanity caused another enquiry to rise to mind and lip, which was expressed in the Scriptural question, 'From whence can a man satisfy these?' The conversation, which might very naturally have taken the form of a discussion upon the law of supply and demand, and such kindred themes as social and political economy, was, however, diverted into the higher channel of talk about the gospel amply meeting the spiritual needs of the masses—a truth which was shortly after to receive its exemplification through the ministry of father and son.

On another occasion, it was my high privilege to preach to some three or four thousand people, who were the *residue* of a congregation numbering one thousand, gathered to hear my father in a church at Pollockshaws, Scotland. The intense joy, which seemed to ripple over his face and sparkle in his eyes, when he learned that his son had the larger audience, increased the already large measure of happiness which delighted my heart. The crowds surged round him, blocking the thoroughfare, and rendering it impassable, until 'the gude man' had shaken hands with his Scotch friends; and joyous cheers rang out again and again as the carriage conveyed the two preachers away from the place of their joint ministry.

A large book could be written concerning the experiences of persons who had the honour and delight of meeting with my father during his visits to different parts of the country. I often wish that I had had it in my power to preserve, more securely than in mere mental jottings, many of the wise sayings reported to me by those who remember their interviews with him.

To a friend, who had called upon him, he said, 'I was looking at myself in the glass, this morning, when the words of the psalmist came to my mind: "Who is the health of my countenance, and my God." I saw no signs of health upon my countenance, and thought that they were far away; but my heart was comforted by the latter portion of the text, for none can rob me of "my God." '

To the same friend, he said, 'I am going to preach, one day, upon "bad lodgers." You get them here, for they come into your house to eat the food that you provide, and spoil the furniture in your home, and then leave without paying. I am not going to talk about this class of lodgers; but shall try to answer the question, "How long shall thy vain thoughts lodge within thee?" ' He was as good as his word, for he preached in the Tabernacle from Jeremiah 4. 14, and the sermon is published under the title, 'Bad Lodgers, and How to Treat them.'

On one occasion, it was my lot to have to go some distance from a countryside station to the village where I was to conduct some special services. A horse and cart were in waiting to convey me to my destination, the driver being a local farmer. We had not gone very far upon the road before his rustic voice broke the silence. 'So you be Mr. Spurgeon, be you, the son of the great man in Lunnon? I bin once in Lunnon, and 'eard him. I was up at the cattle show, and went over to his big chapel, and he preached about sheep. Bless you, he knew more about sheep than I do; and yet I've bin a farmer all my life!' The conversation did not lack in vivacity for the rest of the journey, as my newly-found acquaintance gave his town friend some agricultural education, second-hand, his tutor having been the worthy Pastor of the Metropolitan Tabernacle! My father was a living 'Enquire Within upon Everything.' All who ever heard him can well understand how his almost universal knowledge furnished him with striking simile, matchless metaphor, forceful figure, and instructive illustration.

Entering, only the other day, an establishment which, in years long gone by, was frequented by both father and son—as the former sought after some old Puritan, to add to his library, and the latter interested himself in conning picture-books, which were lying all around—I fancied I could see the form of my father, sitting, as was his wont, in a particular corner of the shop, (and he would sit in no other place) and I could hear him say, 'Well, friend Smith, have you any new old books—something rich and rare?' And the proprietor of the store would speedily bring forth from his treasures 'things new and old.'

Following in my father's footsteps, I had betaken myself to this market of material for the mind; and, naturally, memories of former visits made me desirous to have a little talk with the worthy proprietor, who is now well on in years. With thoughtful mien, and moist eye, he recounted to an attentive listener several personal reminiscences of his friend. He told me that he once journeyed to London, to see the great preacher, and upon entering the precincts of the Tabernacle, my father turned to the caretaker of what is now the Jubilee House, and gave the following instructions, 'Please get dinner for two at one.' In due course, the bookseller and the book-reader returned to partake of the ordered meal, when, to their dismay, they found the table bare. Summoning the good woman into his presence, the following explanation was forthcoming, 'Why, sir!' said she, 'you ordered dinner for one at two.' The mistake caused great merriment to the would-be host and his guest; and, while waiting for the repast to be prepared, the dear Pastor discovered others whose expectations had not been realized. A number of old women had gathered in one of the rooms at the Tabernacle, in the hope of receiving gifts from the Benevolent Society; but the ladies in charge of that agency were not present, as some mistake had been made in the day and hour. The 'fellow-feeling' that always made him 'wondrous kind,' moved him to thrust his hand into his pocket, to bring forth a number of shillings, and to bestow one upon each of the erstwhile disappointed applicants, saying as he did so, 'There's a trifle for you, so you haven't had quite a lost journey.' His benevolence was one of the best and brightest traits in his character. There are secrets concerning his generous gifts, and the self-sacrifice they often entailed, which will never be revealed on earth; I do not know whether they will be unveiled even in Heaven.

If ever a man was sent of God, my father was—a true apostle and a faithful ambassador of Jesus Christ. Although my judgment may be deemed very partial, I venture to express the opinion that, since the days of Paul, there has not lived a greater or more powerful exponent of the doctrines of grace, or a more able and successful preacher of the 'saying' which is 'worthy of all acceptation, that Christ Jesus came into the world to save sinners.' There was no one who could preach like my father. In inexhaustible variety, witty wisdom, vigorous proclamation, loving entreaty, and lucid teaching, with a multitude of other qualities, he must, at least in my opinion, ever be regarded as the prince of preachers. From the days when, as a little boy, I sat behind the platform, in the high-backed and well-cushioned seat in the dear old Tabernacle, with silver pencil-case and neat pocket-book, to take notes of my beloved father's sermons, until this present time, I have looked upon him as 'the prime minister of England.'

There was one trait in his noble and godly character, which, among many others, always shone with a lustre peculiarly its own. His humility was of a Christlike character. Words of eulogy concerning himself were ever painful to him, his motto in this, as in all other matters, being, 'not I, but Christ;' yet, from his own child some meed of praise may surely come, and the son would fain render all due honour to the best of fathers. His blameless example, his holy consistency, his genial love, his generous liberality, his wise counsel, and his fearless fidelity to God and His truth, are all on a par with his fatherliness; and in my heart, as in all those with whom he came into contact, these qualities have been enshrined. The matchless grace and goodness, manifested in the home, found their counterpart in his public career, and proved how completely the spirit of the Master permeated the whole life of His servant. What my father was to me, to the Church of Christ, and to the world at large, none can ever fully estimate, but those who knew him best understood the secret of his magic power, for they felt that he 'had been with Jesus,' and that Jesus lived in him.

Let me describe certain Baptists in this hotel. (1) A father and son;—the father, rather lame; the son, very attentive to the father; in fact, a model; father improving as to health, but nothing to boast of. (2) An old man-servant with a grey beard,—an odd customer, commonly called 'Old George.' (3) Mrs. Godwin, daughter of Dr. Acworth, of Rawdon, and wife to the son of Dr. Godwin, of the same place. With her are two daughters, once pupils of Miss Dransfield, excellent ladies. (4) An old round-faced Dutchman, a Mennonite, with his daughter, another Mennonite;—haters of baby-baptism, and very glad to see Mynheer Spuūrjeoon!—c.h.s., *in letter written home during the furlough*, 1879.

17

The Furlough and Semi-Jubilee of 1879

WHEN the year which was to mark the completion of Spurgeon's twenty-five years in London commenced, the preacher was once more laid aside from his work. His regular ministry had been broken off after Sunday, November 3, 1878 and, with the exception of Sunday, December 22, he was not heard again in the Tabernacle until Easter Sunday, April 13, 1879. In *The Sword and the Trowel* for January, 1879, he wrote: 'Should there be error in the notes . . . the editor's ill-health will be sufficient apology. We have done our best; but with a pained and wearied brain, which is the root of our malady, we cannot but fail in many ways.' The same month he left for Mentone (*Fr.* Menton) on the Riviera Mediterranean coast. Since his visit to Italy in 1871, regular—frequently annual—breaks in the sunny South, away from the chill and damp of English winters, had become a necessity, and Mentone, about fifteen miles east of Nice, was now firmly established as his favourite second home. The resort enjoys what has been described as 'a delicious climate', and even in the winter the temperature is usually about 72°F in the sun and 55°F in the shade. Frost is a rarity. Its Bay faces south-east and is sheltered on the north and west by mountains the slopes of which are covered by lemon, olive and pine. In 1860 it was purchased by Napoleon III's France from the Prince of Monaco, and when, in the same year, Nice was ceded to France by Piedmont-Sardinia, it was added to the Department of the Alpes Maritimes which was then formed.

The visit in 1879 was memorable on account of the presence with him of his twin-son, Thomas, then in his twenty-second year. On account of a lung weakness, it had been advised in 1877 that Thomas should take a sea voyage and accordingly that year he had terminated his apprenticeship in the engraving business (to which his considerable artistic gifts had inclined him) and sailed for Australia. As he himself notes at the commencement of his narrative which continues below, the illness of his mother summoned him back from Australia in September, 1878. It was during this stay overseas that Thomas first became recognized as a preacher and his

[281]

home-coming was marked by a call to stand for the first time in his father's pulpit on November 10, following the latter's breakdown.

*

'MOTHER WORSE, RETURN', was the sad, brief message that hurried me home from Australia in 1878. How joyful was the discovery, on arriving at Plymouth, that the crisis of her illness was past! But, alas! alas! dear father soon fell sick; and what with helping to nurse him at home, and attempting to take his place at the Tabernacle, it really looked as if it was on *his* account, rather than on mother's, that Providence had led me back. This surmise was further strengthened when, much to my surprise, it was proposed that I should accompany the convalescent to Mentone.

It might be thought that I should have jumped at such a privilege; but, if the truth is told, I must admit that I was by no means keen on going. Perhaps I was a little weary of travelling; may be, I wanted to get at some permanent employment; perchance, I was loth to leave my mother, still so sorely sick. I fancy, too, that I had pardonable fears that I could not provide for my father such companionship as he deserved and desired. I had yet to learn how easy it was to please him. As it happened, I had not been a week with him ere I could write, 'What a good father he is, to be sure! I loved him much although away from him and now my affection will increase by being with him.' So, indeed, it did. Three months at Mentone, under the varying experiences of earnest work and happy recreation, of growing health and sad relapse, of fair and stormy weather, gave me an insight into his character such as I could not have gained in any other way. Many a time since then have the memories of that sojourn in the South been an inspiration to me.

Of our journey to the land of sunshine, little need be said. The invalid began to improve directly we started. He seemed better at Folkestone, and better still at Paris. Even the long night-journey to Marseilles did not unduly tire him. Ere we left the gay capital, we had knelt in prayer, asking for peace and pleasure on our way; and, at the very start, we had an answer in the shape of a pleasing interview with a converted Jew who was acting as Cook's agent. He spoke very earnestly about the blessed Book, and his dear Saviour Jesus Christ. On the journey, father amused us for some time with arithmetical puzzles, in which, of course, he had the best of it. The night was bitterly cold, our breath froze on the carriage windows, yet the sick preacher took no harm. Our prayers were answered most graciously; we had journeying mercies rich and rare. I should have said that our party consisted of father and son, Mr. Joseph Passmore—that kindest and most genial of travelling companions and old George Lovejoy.

A brief halt at Marseilles was helpful, but the rest of the journey proved slow and wearisome. How shall I speak of the joy with which the Pastor hailed his chosen resting-place? What though the weather was so unfavourable for a while, that he had constantly to say, 'This is not Mentone,' the very sight of the hills, and the olives, and the sea, revived his spirit. He knew that, when the sun did shine on them, they would be surpassingly lovely. The closing days of January were 'as fine as fine could be', so, though the limbs were not yet strong, it was possible to get to Dr. Bennet's garden,[1] or to watch the fishermen draw in their nets, and even to saunter up one or other of the charming valleys. But progress was all too slow, and an alarming relapse supervened. It was a black Thursday when I had to send word home, 'Dear father's right foot is wrong, and he is fearful that it will get worse.' On the first of March, the most that could be said was, that where the path was pretty level, he managed well enough alone, but every now and then he had to lean upon my shoulder. Gladder tidings were sent to England a week later, 'All is full of mercy with us. Dear father still continues to improve, though his knees are certainly not hurrying to fulness of strength.' However, he gradually rallied. Great was my grief that the closing week was stormy and dismal. I had so hoped that he could be in the healing sunshine just to receive the finishing touches. On the fourth of April, I had the joy of recording, 'Father pronounces himself better than ever this morning.' That was the last bulletin.

I was particularly struck with the welcome accorded by all to the great preacher. It was hardly the sort of welcome usual in such cases. There was no undue familiarity in it, but it was hearty, spontaneous, and, I might even say, affectionate. Everybody was delighted to see him. The foreigners, who called him 'Meester Sparegen,' vied with Englishmen in assuring him of their joy at his return. He had a genial smile and a cheery word for all. The Hôtel de la Paix was still more peaceful when he became its guest. Old acquaintances and ministers of the gospel had a specially hearty reception from him. Even the clergyman, who claimed to be 'a

---

[1] Henry Bennet was a Christian resident in Mentone, who, as recorded earlier in this volume, appreciated the company of men such as Spurgeon and George Müller. Spurgeon had leave to come and go in his garden as he pleased.

friend of more than twenty years' standing, because,' said he, 'I have been cribbing from you all that time,' was favoured with quite a large slice of attention. Most to his mind, however, were the King's three mighty men, George Müller, John Bost, and Hudson Taylor. In the company of these kindred spirits he literally revelled. Was I not honoured to be an onlooker?

Family worship was a delightful item of each day's doings. It was, of course, usually conducted by C.H.S., but he sometimes asked others to take part. His unstudied comments, and his marvellous prayers, were an inspiration indeed. I did not wonder that requests were received for a share in this privilege. My journal contains the following interesting entry for March 3: 'We had two fresh arrivals to morning prayers. Strangers to father, they had requested, through the waiter, admission to our worship, so a stately mother and a tall daughter from Belgrave Square were made right welcome.'

It was often directly after breakfast that the work had to be seen to; for it must be known that C. H. Spurgeon's holidays were by no means altogether devoted to so-called pleasure-taking. He found his truest delight in active service. Sometimes, if the truth must be told, it appeared to all of us that he rested insufficiently. There were those ceaseless letters; how they worried me, for he *would* answer them himself, when I wanted him to be by the sea, or under the olives! How he loved the olive trees, chiefly because they told him of his Lord and of Gethsemane!

I confess that I begrudged him the time he spent in corresponding with all save mother and the Tabernacle Church. This is how I wrote at the time concerning this matter: 'As to his other letters, I wish folk would not bother him with nonsensical epistles. I must admit that it does not seem any great labour to him to answer them; still, the time would be far better spent in the sunshine; but what can't be cured must be endured.' I think I understand better, by this time, why he answered almost everyone. He knew so well the power of letter-writing. He knew also how glad the recipients would be, and what life-long friends he would secure. Quite recently, a venerable saint, in his eighty-ninth year, sent me, 'just to look at,' a letter he had received from my father at Mentone. It was in answer to a message of gratitude for a sermon in *The Christian Herald*, and ran like this:

'My Dear Brother,

I thank you for your word of good cheer. It is a great joy to be the means of comfort to an aged believer. You will very likely get home before I shall, but tell them I am coming as fast as the gout will let me. The Lord will not leave you now that hoary hairs have come, but will now carry you in His bosom. Peace be unto you!

Yours heartily,

C. H. SPURGEON.'

Who can tell the joy that brief, bright, brotherly note brought the octogenarian, who, after all, was not the first to 'get home'?

But there was other work to be done. The weekly sermon had to be revised, and the magazine edited. Here is a striking *holiday* item: 'He is very busy with the magazine, and fears he cannot write to you to-day.' Moreover, there was generally some book on the stocks, and since he who would write books must read them—a maxim which obtained even with so original a thinker as he was— it is written in my diary—'We have beguiled many of our hours by reading, and father has been culling flowers of thought to be arranged in fragrant nosegays by-and-by.' The only mishap on our journey to Mentone was the temporary loss of a bag full of books; but a more serious loss than that seemed scarcely possible to the author and devourer of books. He was as a workman bereft of his tools. He was in terrible distress, and refused to be comforted till the satchel was forthcoming. Great was his joy on finding his peculiar treasure.

With very special delight I recall the fact that I, too, was set to work, and that I had the President of the Pastors' College as my private tutor. Let me give a few quotations which will sufficiently indicate the curriculum of the Mentone branch of that Institution: 'I read Chapter 1 of a French history from which father questioned me afterwards. I then stuck to Hodge[1] till dinner-time, and by to-morrow I hope to get into real working order. It is very good of father to interest himself so in my welfare. I shall do my very best to prevent him ever regretting it.' 'Father and son worked at history and Hodge. *The driest matter bursts into a blaze when C.H.S. puts some of his fire to it.*' 'Father is now on a sofa, at an open window, inspecting a primer of political economy, prior to my study of it. I wonder if this College course extraordinary will admit me to the Conference; I greatly hope so.' 'I have just completed an examination in history, and am, as usual, top of the class. A still more interesting way of studying French history was introduced yesterday. Father borrowed Carlyle's *French Revolution*, and read it to us!' It was glorious to hear C. H. Spurgeon read Carlyle!

[1] Presumably this means Charles Hodge's *Systematic Theology*.

Every day, when the weather favoured, and health permitted, we had an outing of some sort. It often consisted only of a drive up one of the valleys, and a stroll back; but we generally took our lunch, and 'Old George' was sorely tried because there was no spot sufficiently level for his cloth, and no centre-piece more elegant than an orange; but these were trifles which our sharpened appetites scorned. How the Pastor gloried in the freedom of these rambles! The spring flowers and the trap-door spiders, no less than the towering hills and dashing rills, filled his soul with prayer, and praise, and poetry. The prayer and praise constantly found expression, and once at least the poetry overflowed. 'We lunched beneath the fir trees. Meanwhile, the birds were singing to us. No wonder, then, that the poetic fire burst forth, and C.H.S. gave vent to his delight in extempore rhyme. It should be perhaps explained that we had been reading Cowper together before the meal.'

But Dr. Bennet's garden was our chief resort—a veritable paradise on the side of a rocky steep. How many times it was visited, I cannot tell. It was near at hand, and no special invitation was necessary. Father loved to look on the town from this viewpoint, and desired me to sketch the scene. It was not the first time my pencil had been at his service; and great was my joy to transfer to my sketch-book the scenes which particularly interested him, such as some queer specimens of architecture in the old town, the tunnel-pierced cliff with the Italian guard-house on its brow, the ruined castle and running fountain at Roquebrune or a specially gnarled and twisted olive tree. Never had aspiring artist a more indulgent patron.

After dinner, there was generally an adjournment to the smoking-room, where father chatted freely with the other visitors at the hotel, who were by no means loth to exchange sentiments with the distinguished preacher. And he could discourse on almost any theme. How pleased he was to meet an aged Mennonite Baptist there! An Alsatian baron, who had translated some of the sermons, and had come all the way from Cannes to see him, was received, one evening, with due ceremony, in his private sitting-room.

Will anyone be surprised to hear that, on one occasion, Mr. Spurgeon witnessed a conjuring performance? 'We were entertained at a '*brillante séance de magie*,' given by '*Le Professeur Presti-digitateur*, B. Marchelli.' The performance was very good for that of a strolling conjuror. Father seemed to enjoy it mightily, especially when the Professor produced a turtle-dove from 'Old George's' pocket in first-rate style.' Almost every evening, we had some reading of a light description—*The Ingoldsby Legends* being a favourite work. It was my privilege, also, to add to the paternal merriment by reading certain humorous sketches of my Australian experiences, sometimes amid a shower of newspapers and other missiles.

We enjoyed our Sundays thoroughly. The Presbyterian Church was not then built, so we worshipped in a room of Mrs. Dudgeon's villa. Dr. Hanna and others preached, and *our* Pastor was often an interested listener. He always had unstinted praise for a sermon which exalted Jesus, and proclaimed His dying love. 'That was a very sweet sermon,' he used to say when such a discourse had been delivered. How delighted he was to hear George Müller on 'Patient waiting upon God.' Especially did he rejoice in the man behind the message. The preacher came to our communion service, and closed it with prayer. I remember that, after asking great things for my beloved parents, he prayed very earnestly for 'the dear son in Australia.' I had great pleasure in informing him that I was the son in Australia; and oh! how warmly did he grasp my hand! Little did we dream then that, nine years after, he would help to marry me in New Zealand.

Perhaps I may venture to add, concerning our Sundays, that it was my joyful privilege to conduct several services. On one occasion, the Pastor of the Metropolitan Tabernacle occupied a seat under the verandah. I told him, afterwards, how fortunate it was that I did not happen to address 'outsiders.' I cannot forget the loving encouragement he gave me. Not less did I prize the lenient criticisms and valuable hints as to style and delivery. I may be pardoned, too, for treasuring the memory of how, during this happy holiday, he conceived the idea of having me ever with him, and of instituting a Sunday afternoon service that I might conduct. But the Master willed it otherwise.

We had a whole day with George Müller in Dr. Bennet's garden, and I am able to copy from my letter of the following date this striking testimony to the advantage of such fellowship—'Father declares himself far better able to "trust and not be afraid" through intercourse with Mr. Müller.' The stimulus to faith was greatly needed then. How well God times His aid! In the same epistle, after recording our sorrow at mother's continued illness, these words occur: 'Another source of anxiety is the lack of funds for the Colportage Association. This matter also we have believingly commended to the God of all grace, who will surely not let His servants want. Father has been in many straits before, and has always been delivered. In this trouble also the Lord will befriend him—for what is £700 to Him?'

As soon as a measure of health returned, the eager worker looked longingly towards home. His head nurse declared that he was not fit to go back, but the patient was impatient to be in harness again. Here is the official bulletin for March 17: 'He seems, to my mind, hardly strong enough to undertake the thousand duties of his gigantic work; but he will not hear of staying longer, and has already engaged a sleeping-car.' Urgent representations from the Tabernacle, that he should remain away till thoroughly restored, came to hand; but an extra week was all that the combined efforts could secure. He was as a greyhound in the leash till he was back at his post.

And what a home-coming it was! Nightingale Lane then heard sweeter music than ever Philomel produced—the music of loving welcome to dear ones mingled with fervent gratitude to God. And when the blessed ministry at the Tabernacle was resumed, there rose to heaven a doxology, loud as the voice of many waters, from a church and congregation that loved their Pastor almost as well as he loved them.

*

The first great event after Spurgeon's return to the Tabernacle in April, 1879, was the celebration of his pastoral silver wedding—the conclusion of his twenty-five years in London. It was felt that so notable a period of Christian service should not be allowed to pass without due recognition, and many desired to avail themselves of the opportunity to present to their Pastor a testimonial of their loving esteem. The commemoration was spread over three days, commencing Sunday, May 18th. On Monday evening the meeting was mainly devoted to praising God for His goodness to both Pastor and people. On Tuesday a tea preceded the assembling of a great congregation in the Tabernacle. After prayer and praise, B. W. Carr summarized the church's progress during Spurgeon's ministry; Dr. Charles Stanford followed with an address on 'The Baptist Churches, twenty-five years ago and now'. After a few more brief addresses the Pastor said:

'We will sing our Tabernacle National Anthem, that glorious hymn,

Grace, 'tis a charming sound

to the tune "Cranbrook", which a critic has called "execrable". I am such a heretic as to like "Cranbrook"; and if you will only sing it as we generally do, we will make some of these heathen here to-night like it. The way of singing now (continued Spurgeon, in affected tones to imitate the parties to whom he alluded) is, "Let us sing to the praise and glory of God, and rattle through it as fast as possible, with never a fugue or a repeat, and get it over and done, for we are sick to death of it."'

The hymn was sung to the tune 'Cranbrook' as only a Tabernacle audience of six thousand people could sing it. Then followed the presentation of the testimonial. Spurgeon had previously agreed to accept such a gift on condition that it could be devoted to the Church's work of supporting the poor members and especially for maintaining the women's Almshouses. Once the deacons agreed to this stipulation Spurgeon characteristically urged the raising of £5,000. The actual amount in the testimonial was £6,233, and the Pastor was urged to receive the £1,200 surplus. On no account would he do so and he alluded to his reasons as he brought the meeting to a close:

'When I gave myself up to Him at first to be His minister I never reckoned that He would give anything except raiment to put on and bread to eat. I recollect when my income was forty-five pounds a year. Well, I do not know, but I think I had more money to spare than I have got now. I had not many things to drag at me then; I never wanted anything. When I came to London I desired to keep up the feeling that I was to serve God altogether, and give myself and all that I should ever get entirely to Him, and just be a gentle-man-commoner upon the bounty of God, whose livery would always be found him, whose bread would be given him, and whose water would be sure. So I have lived. I get sometimes requests for loans of hundreds of pounds, under the supposition that I am a very rich man. I never was a rich man, and never shall be; and yet I am the richest man in England, if you can make that out, because there is nothing that I want on earth but I have it. I have not any wishes which are not gratified and satisfied, except that I always want to be doing more for Jesus Christ, if possible.'

A sermon entitled 'Crowning Blessings ascribed to God' was preached by Spurgeon on the Sunday evening preceding the presentation. He spoke as follows:

'This very house of prayer has been to some of you a quiet resting-place. You have been more at home here than when you have been at home. I will be bound to say that you recollect more happy times that you have had here than anywhere else, and these have put out of your memory the sad records of your hard battling in the world, even for a livelihood. I know that many of you live by your Sabbaths. You step over the intervening space from Lord's-day to Lord's-day, as if the Lord had made a ladder of Sabbaths for you to climb to heaven by; and you have been fed, as well as rested, in God's house. I know you have, for he who deals out the meat has had his own portion; and when he is fed, he knows that others have like appetites, and need like food, and know when they get it. You have clapped your hands for very joy when redeeming grace and dying love have been the theme, and infinite, sovereign, changeless mercy has been the subject of discourse.

Well now, by every happy Sabbath you have had, my brethren; by every holy Monday evening prayer-meeting; by every occasion on which God has met with you in any of the rooms of this building, when a few of you, at early morning, or late in the evening, have gathered together for prayer; by everytime in which the realization of Jesu's love has charmed your soul up to heaven's gate, bless and magnify His Name, who has crowned the years with His goodness. There had been no food for us if the Lord had not given us manna from heaven. There had been no comfortable rest for us if He had not breathed peace upon us. There had been no coming in of new converts, nor going out with rapturous joy of the perfected ones up to the seats above, if the Lord had not been with us, and, therefore, to Him be all the praise.

I do not suppose that any strangers here will understand this matter. It may even be that they will judge that we are indulging in self-gratulation under a thin disguise; but this evil we must endure for once. You, my brothers and sisters, who have been together these many years, comprehend what is meant; and you know that it is not within the compass of an angel's tongue to express the gratitude which many of us feel who, for these five-and-twenty years, have been banded together in closest and heartiest Christian brotherhood in the service of our Lord and Master. Strangers cannot guess how happy has been our fellowship, or how true our love. Eternity alone shall reveal the multitude of mercies with which God has visited us by means of our association in this church; it is to some of us friend, nurse, mother, home, all in one. During all these years, the Lord has been pleased, in infinite mercy, to prepare men's hearts to listen to the Word. It was not possible, they said, that great places could be filled with crowds to hear the old-fashioned gospel. The pulpit had lost its power—so unbelievers told us; and yet, no sooner did we begin to preach in simple strains the gospel of Christ, than the people flew as a cloud, and as doves to their windows. And what listening there was at New Park Street, where we scarcely had enough air to breathe! And when we got into the larger place, what attention was manifest! What power seemed to go with every word that was spoken; I say it, though I was the preacher; for it was not I, but the grace of God which was with me. There were, stricken down among us, some of the most unlikely ones. There were brought into the church, and added to God's people, some of those who had wandered far away from the path of truth and righteousness; and these, by their penitent love, quickened our life, and increased our zeal. The Lord gave the people more and more a willingness to hear, and there was no pause either in the flowing stream of hearers, or in the incoming of converts. The Holy Spirit came down like showers which saturate the soil till the clods are ready for the breaking; and then it was not long before, on the right and on the left, we heard the cry, "What must we do to be saved?" We were busy enough, in those days, in seeing converts; and, thank God, we have been so ever since. We had some among us who gave themselves up to watch for the souls of men, and we have a goodly number of such helpers now, perhaps more than ever we had; and, thank God, these found and still find many souls to watch over. Still the arrows fly, and still the smitten cry out for help, and ask that they may be guided to the great healing Lord. Blessed be God's Name for this! He went with us all those early days, and gave us sheaves even at the first sowing, so that we began with mercy; and He has been with us even until now, till our life has become one long harvest-home.

I am bound to acknowledge, with deep thankfulness, that, during these twenty-five years, the Word has been given me to speak when the time has come for preaching. It may look to you a small thing that I should be able to come before you in due time; but it will not seem so to my brethren in the ministry who recollect that, for twenty-five years, my sermons have been printed as they have been delivered. It must be an easy thing to go and buy discourses at sixpence or a shilling each, ready lithographed, and read them off, as hirelings do; but to speak your heart out every time, and yet to have something fresh to say for twenty-five years, is no child's play. Who shall do it unless he cries unto God for help? I read, but the other day, a newspaper criticism upon myself, in which the writer expressed his wonder that a man should keep on year after year with so few themes, and such a narrow groove to travel in; but, my brethren, it is not so, our themes are infinite for number and fulness. Every text of Scripture is boundless in its meaning; we could preach from the Bible throughout eternity, and not exhaust it. The groove narrow? The thoughts of God narrow? The Word of the Lord narrow? They who say so do not know it, for His commandment is exceeding broad. Had we to speak of politics or philosophy, we should have run dry long ago; but when we have to preach the Saviour's everlasting love, the theme is always fresh, always new. The incarnate God, the atoning blood, the risen Lord, the coming glory, these are subjects which defy exhaustion. When I recollect how, as a boy, I stood among you, and feebly began to preach Jesus Christ, and how these twenty-five years, without dissension, ay, without the dream of dissension, in perfect love compacted as one man, you have gone on from one work of God to another, and have never halted, hesitated, or drawn back, I must and will bless and magnify Him who hath crowned these years with His goodness.

Now I come to my closing point. It is this—the crowning blessing is confessed to be of God. Some churches have one crown, and some another; our crown, under God, has been this—the poor have the gospel preached unto them, souls are saved, and Christ is glorified. O my beloved church, hold fast that thou hast, that no man take this crown away from thee! As for me, by God's help, the first and last thing that I long for is to bring men to Christ. I care nothing about fine language, or about the pretty speculations of prophecy, or a hundred dainty things; but to break the heart and bind it up, to lay hold on a sheep of Christ and bring it back into the fold, is the one thing I would live for. You also are of the same mind, are you not? Well, we have had this crowning blessing that, as nearly as I can estimate, since I came amongst you, more than nine thousand persons have joined this church.[1] If they were all alive now, or all with us now, what a company they would be! I find that, during these twenty-five years, there have gone from us, to the upper realms, about eight hundred who had named the Name of

[1] At the beginning of 1879 the membership of the Tabernacle was 5,066, even though over 250 had recently been encouraged to leave in order to form a church at Peckham. 'The pastor,' says G. H. Pike, 'was always pleased when such a battalion left the main army to carry on operations elsewhere'.

Jesus. Professing their faith in Christ, living in His fear, dying in the faith, they gave us no cause to doubt their sincerity; and, therefore, we may not question their eternal safety. Many of them gave us, in life and in death, all the tokens we could ask for of their being in Christ; and, therefore, we sorrow not as those that are without hope. Why, when I think of them—many of them my sons and daughters in the faith—now before the throne, they fill me with solemn exultation! Do you not see them in their white robes? Eight hundred souls redeemed by blood! These are only those whom we knew of, and had enrolled on our church books. How many more there may have been converted, who never joined our earthly fellowship, but, nevertheless, have gone home, I cannot tell. There probably have been more than those whose names we know, if we consider the wide area over which the printed sermons circulate. They are gathering home one by one, but they make a goodly company. Our name is Gad, for "a troop cometh." Happy shall we be to overtake those who have outmarched us, and entered into the Promised Land before us. Let us remember them, and by faith join our hands with theirs. Flash a thought to unite the broken family, for we are not far from them, nor are they far from us, since we are one in Christ.'

A sequel to the commemoration meetings was thus noted at the time by Spurgeon: 'The testimonial which celebrated our twenty-five years of pastoral work was presented on Tuesday, May 20, and there and then dedicated to the Lord. On the following Thursday evening, we commenced a new period in our church history; and it is a singularly pleasing coincidence that, at the church-meeting held on that evening, no less than thirty-seven candidates came before the church, and confessed their faith in Christ—the largest number that we have ever received at one church-meeting. This was the more remarkable as it happened entirely without arrangement on the part of the Pastor or anyone else. We regard it as "a token for good," and look for "greater things than these."'

We have often been advised to rise from Nightingale Lane to higher ground, to escape a portion of the fogs and damps which hang almost always over our smoky city. In the good providence of God, we have been led to do so, and we are now upon the Southern heights. We did not seek out the place, but it came into our hands in a very remarkable manner, and we were bound to accept it. We have left the room which has been so long our study, and the delightful garden where we were wont to walk and meditate. Not without many a regret have we transferred our nest from our dear old home to the Hill of Beulah.

What a type of our departure out of this world is a removal from an abode in which we have lived for years! Many thoughts have thronged our mind while we have been on the wing from the spot where we have dwelt for more than twenty years.—C.H.S., *in 'Spurgeon's Illustrated Almanack' for* 1881.

18

Westwood

THE Spurgeon household occupied Helensburgh House, Nightingale Lane, Clapham, for 1857 to 1880, the rebuilding taking place in 1869, as already mentioned. Concerning the removal to Westwood, situated on the rising ground known as Beulah Hill, Upper Norwood, Spurgeon often said, 'I did not arrange it myself; the Lord just put a spade underneath me, and transplanted me to Norwood.'[1] The change came to pass in the following way. In the year 1880, a great trouble arose through what was intended to be only a joy and a help. Mrs. Tyson, who had long been a generous donor to all the Tabernacle Institutions, made a will by which she meant to leave to the College and Orphanage the greater part of her estate, subject to the payment of certain annuities to a number of aged pensioners upon her bounty. The kind testatrix appointed Spurgeon and a clerical friend, as her executors, explaining that she did so on purpose to ensure that there should be no question about the carrying out of her intentions; but unhappily, the bequests included her real as well as personal property, and therefore came within the scope of the Law of Mortmain. The whole affair was complicated in so many ways that the executors were obliged to arrange with the Trustees of the College and Orphanage to institute a friendly suit in the Court of Chancery in order to have an authoritative decision upon the points about which there was uncertainty. This involved a heavy addition to the Pastor's work, and necessitated many journeys to White Lodge, Biggin Hill, Upper Norwood, where Mrs. Tyson had lived.

After the executors had paid one of their periodical visits, Spurgeon suggested that, before returning home, they should drive as far as the front of the Crystal Palace. Proceeding along Beulah Hill, the notice of a house and estate for sale caught his eye as he passed a gateway which was afterwards to become very familiar to

---

[1] According to G. H. Pike the new residence was about the same size as Helensburgh House but the grounds were considerably larger. In 1972 the second Helensburgh House still stands—enlarged since Spurgeon's day—while no trace of Westwood remains, the site having been levelled and a girls' school built upon it.

him. He had long felt the need to remove to higher ground, and to a more secluded spot than the once rural Nightingale Lane had become, and he had been making enquiries in various directions; but, so far, he had not heard of any place which was sufficiently near the Tabernacle, and, at the same time, fairly clear of the smoke and fog of London. On reaching the Palace, the return journey was commenced; and, soon, the carriage was back in Beulah Hill, and nearing the gate where the board had been seen. Bidding the coachman stop, the Pastor asked his secretary to find out what the notice said. It appeared that cards to view the property were required; but, on asking at the house, permission was at once given for Spurgeon to see all he wished, and then, for the first time, he passed down the drive, and beheld his future home.

As soon as he caught sight of Westwood, he exclaimed, 'Oh, that place is far too grand for me!' and, after a very brief inspection, he left without having any anticipation of becoming its owner. So completely did he give up all thought of living there, that he did not even send anyone to the sale; but, a few days afterwards, he received a note telling him that the reserve price had not been reached, and asking if he would make an offer for the estate. Then came what Spurgeon always regarded as the providential interposition of God in the matter. That very day, the builder, whom he always employed for all work needed at Helensburgh House, called to enquire if he wanted to sell his home; because, if so, one of his neighbours wished to buy it as a residence for his son-in-law who was returning from abroad. The Pastor then mentioned the house he had seen at Norwood, and added, 'If I could get for this place anything like what is needed to purchase the other, I should be glad to make the exchange.' A consultation was held as to the price to be asked, a sum was stated, and duly reported to the neighbour, who at once said, 'I should not think of offering Mr. Spurgeon any less, for I am sure he would only fix a fair value; I will give you a deposit to seal the bargain.' The builder soon returned with the message and cheque; but Mr. Spurgeon said, 'I must wait to see if I can buy Westwood, or I shall be out of house and home.' He drove again to Beulah Hill, found that he could, without difficulty, meet the difference in the price of the two places, and, within a few hours, the old home was sold, and the new one secured, as he always believed, by Divine arrangement.

The incoming residents at Helensburgh House desired to have some permanent memorial of their predecessor's occupancy of the house, so Spurgeon wrote the following inscription, and had it engraved, and fixed underneath the large painted window at the end of the study:

> *Farewell, fair room, I leave thee to a friend:*
> *Peace dwell with him and all his kin!*
> *May angels evermore the house defend!*
> *Their Lord hath often been within.*

'What a type of our departure out of this world' wrote Spurgeon, 'is a removal from any abode in which we have lived for years! Many thoughts have thronged our mind while we have been on the wing from the spot where we have dwelt for more than twenty years'. In August, the removal took place, and in the next number of *The Sword and the Trowel*, the Editor wrote: 'Simple as the matter of change of residence may be, it has sufficed to create all sorts of stories, among which is the statement that *"Mr. Spurgeon's people have given him a house."* My ever-generous friends would give me whatever was needful; but, as I had only to sell one house and buy another, there was no necessity for their doing so. Having once accepted a noble presentation from them, and having there and then handed it over to the Almshouses, it would by no means be according to my mind to receive a second public testimonial. One friend who heard of my change of residence right generously sent help towards the expense of removal; but, beyond this, it is entirely my own concern, and a matter about which I should have said nothing if it had not been for this gossip.'

Though Spurgeon had described Westwood as being far too grand for him, he was very much vexed when an American visitor published a grossly-exaggerated account of 'its park, and meadows, and lakes, and streams, and statuary, and stables,' which were supposed to rival those of the Queen at Windsor Castle! It would be difficult to find the 'park' for the whole estate comprised less than nine acres—three of which were leasehold; and the numerous 'lakes and streams' which the imaginative D.D. fancied that he saw, were all contained in the modest piece of water across which the prettiest view of the house can be obtained.

Spurgeon hoped that one effect of his removal to Westwood would be that he might enjoy better health than he had at Clapham; he even cherished the notion that the change would be so beneficial that he would not need to go to Mentone in the winter. But over-work exacted the same penalties in the new home as in the old one.

For a time, the hydropathic appliances at the near-by Beulah Spa seemed to afford relief; but, by-and-by, they also failed, and the Pastor, in his own expressive way, said that he had resolved to go to heaven as the Israelites crossed the Jordan, dryshod. The friendly connection with the hydropathic establishment was, however, still maintained, for its proprietor was permitted to have a pipe running from his house to the well in Spurgeon's garden, so that any of the guests who desired to drink the Beulah Spa water might have a supply of it. The prospectus, issued at the time that Westwood was offered for sale, contained a very elaborate description of the virtues of the water, and its medicinal value as compared with that of other springs in England and on the Continent; but Spurgeon never concerned himself much about it, though he occasionally drank it himself, and gave others the opportunity of following his example.

Apart from its private uses, perhaps Westwood was never more thoroughly utilized than on the occasions when tutors and students gathered there, to spend a long and delightful day with their President. The rose-garden was the usual place of meeting; and here, after partaking of refreshments, a brief devotional service was held, followed by the introduction of the new students. The name of nearly every one of them, or something about his previous calling, or the place from which he had come, furnished material for that ready wit with which Spurgeon brightened all parts of his service; and the freshmen were always warned that the festive proceedings of the opening day were not to be regarded as representative of the rest of their College career, which must be one of real hard work, so that they might derive all possible benefit from the season of preparation for the ministry.

As the brethren dispersed to their various forms of recreation, a number of them always chose the Puritan game of bowls; and in the summerhouse overlooking the lawn, the President and tutors watched them, and, at the same time, talked over any matters on which they might need to consult. Thus, on one occasion, a brother was called from his play to receive a commission to go to the Falkland Islands; another was summoned to go to the mission-field; while to others was entrusted the honour of reviving some decaying church in an English village, or starting a new one amidst the dense population of London or some provincial town.

The top of the round tower, visible from the lawn, is the place from which a wide extent of country can be seen; and many of the students, in days past, sought and secured permission to 'view the landscape o'er.' The grand stand at Epsom was plainly discernible from the grounds; but, from the greater height, the tower on Leith Hill, and, in a peculiarly favourable state of the atmosphere, Windsor Castle also, could be descried.

The steps leading down to the lawn often formed a convenient rallying-point for the evening meeting, though sometimes the brethren were grouped around the upper summerhouse. Far away across Thornton Heath rolled the great volume of sound as the male choir of eighty to a hundred voices sang the songs of Zion, of which the College anthem—'Hallelujah for the Cross!'—was certain to be one. The words spoken by the President at those gatherings were gratefully remembered by brethren as they laboured for the Lord in various parts of the world.

During the day, informal meetings were held under 'The Question Oak,' which gained that name because, beneath its widely-spreading branches, Mr. Spurgeon allowed the students to put to him any enquiry that they pleased, and he answered them all without a moment's hesitation, and often interspersed his replies with the narration of striking incidents in his own experience.

The lake is not likely to be forgotten by some of the Pastors' College brethren who are now in the ministry. In the first visit of the students to Westwood, the President told them to go wherever they pleased, and to explore the whole place. It was not very long before some of them discovered that there was a boat on the lake, and not many minutes more before the boat and all its crew had gone down into the mud!

Happily, the coachman's cottage was close by, so it became a place of refuge for the shipwrecked collegians, who received the sympathetic attentions of their brethren while their garments were being restored to a wearable condition; and they were themselves temporarily clothed from the wardrobe of Spurgeon and the coachman. As the students were not so stout as the former, nor so tall as the latter, they were not very comfortable in their borrowed raiment; but, later in the day, they appeared in their proper garb, and the President then turned the adventure to practical account by warning them to keep clear of the muddy waters of doubt, and not to trust themselves off *terra firma* unless they were sure of the trustworthiness of their boat and the skill of the oarsman.

In addition to the students of the Pastors' College, many other visitors were from time to time welcomed at Westwood. On one occasion, a party of American friends, who had been worshipping at the Tabernacle on the Sabbath, sought permission to see the preacher at his home. This was readily accorded; and one of their number wrote, after Spurgeon's home-going, a long and interesting account of their reception. The following extract will convey a good idea of the impressions made upon the Transatlantic visitors that day, and also on many others who, at different times, saw the Pastor in his own house and garden:

'Turning into the open gateway, a short drive along the thickly-shaded carriage-way brings us to the house itself, now and ever to be known by the familiar name of "Westwood." Mr. Spurgeon is at the carriage before we alight, and gives us such a cordial greeting that we immediately feel at home ourselves. We spend a few moments, in the rose-garden, in further social intercourse. Then, with cheerful, though somewhat laboured, steps, our genial host leads us along the grass-bordered walks around the house, down a winding pathway sheltered by overhanging trees, over a little rustic bridge, and along the edge of a miniature lake; then out upon a sloping stretch of open ground, from the summit of which the "Westwood" dwelling sends down its sunny glances, and beyond which the widening expanse of a picturesque English landscape suggests to heart and voice alike the familiar melody "Sweet Beulah Land."

At every step, we find ourselves drawn closer and closer to the man himself, as, with unaffected simplicity, and with easy, brilliant, entertaining conversation, he makes the moments pass too quickly by. Recalling these glimpses of the social and domestic life of the great preacher, leads me to indicate a few of the impressions that are most tenderly cherished. I was especially struck with his love of nature. He lived in loving acquaintance with his beautiful surroundings. He seemed to be on terms of closest intimacy with every leaf, and plant, and flower; and, without question, this may very largely account for his own marked naturalness in speech and movement, both in the pulpit and out of it. Like the leaves, and plants, and flowers, he loved to be just what God made him.

"Come into my picture gallery," said he, "and let me show you some pictures painted by God Himself." Again we found ourselves at the entrance to the rose-garden, where our attention was directed to certain openings which had been made in the dense foliage.

Placing us in the proper positions before these open spaces, he invited us to look through them; and, as we did so, we found ourselves gazing upon natural pictures that were all the more beautiful because they enabled us, as well as the owner of the gallery, to "look through nature up to nature's God." In all these methods of expression, there was not the least show of affectation, or any assumption of sanctimoniousness. The entire conduct and conversation of the man, both in his private walks and public ways, breathed out the fervour and the frankness of a soul who knows and loves God, and who lives and communes with his Saviour.'

A visitor at Westwood, who professed to have come from the United States, was received by Mr. Spurgeon with considerable cordiality because he announced himself as 'Captain Beecher, the son of Henry Ward Beecher.' He was conducted through the grounds, and had the special attractions of the place pointed out to him; and he, on his part, managed very well to sustain the *rôle* he had assumed until, just before leaving, he said, 'Oh, Mr. Spurgeon! excuse me for making such a request, but could you change a cheque for me? Unfortunately, I waited until after the bank was closed, and I want some money very particularly to-night.' The Pastor's suspicions were at once aroused, and he said, with pardonable severity, 'I do not think you ought to make such a request to me. If you are really Mr. Beecher's son, you must be able, through the American consul, or some friend, to get your cheque cashed, without coming to a complete stranger;' and, foiled in his attempt, the young man departed. A few days afterwards, a gentleman was murdered in a carriage on the Brighton railway; and when the portrait of the criminal, Lefroy, was published in the papers, Spurgeon immediately recognized the features of his recent visitor, though he never understood the reason for the man's strange call at Westwood.

One place to which Westwood visitors were sure to be taken was the fernery; and among the many treasures to which their attention was directed, the mother-fern was never forgotten, and most of them received from the Pastor, as living mementoes of their visit, some of the baby-ferns growing on the parent-plant. At one of the Tabernacle prayer-meetings, Spurgeon gave an address upon the mother-fern, in which he urged his hearers to seek to be spiritually what it was naturally, and, by the grace of God, to be the means of reproducing themselves in their converts, in whom the same blessed process might be repeated by the effectual working of the Holy Spirit.

At one time, bees were kept at Westwood, and Spurgeon was intensely interested in watching them whenever he had a few minutes to spare, or any visitors who could explain their various movements. The scientific lecturer at the Pastors' College at that period was Professor Frank Cheshire—a great authority on bees and bee-culture; and he was delighted to place his wide knowledge of the subject at the President's disposal. One day, he brought with him a Ligurian queen, which he had procured on purpose to add to the value of Spurgeon's own bees, and he was delighted to see how quickly her majesty made herself at home among her English subjects.

After a while, Spurgeon noticed that the little creatures appeared to have to fly so far afield, to 'gather honey all the day,' that they seemed quite tired out when they reached the hives, or fell exhausted before they could get back to their homes. There was also much difficulty in keeping them alive through the winter; so he reluctantly parted with them. Before he did so, however, he had one experience, connected with them, which he never forgot. On a calm summer's evening, he was standing to watch them, when, without giving him any warning, hundreds of them settled on his clothes, and began crawling all over him. He rushed upstairs, stripped off all his garments, threw them quickly out of the bedroom window, and, marvellous to relate, he escaped without a single sting.

One Monday morning, not long after removing to Westwood, the whole household was in a state of consternation because there had been a burglary during the night. On the Sabbath evening, a service had been held in the study, and a small window had been opened for ventilation. It was not noticed at the time for locking up, so it remained open, and made it a comparatively easy matter for a thief to enter. He did not get much for his pains, and his principal plunder almost led to his arrest. Mr. John B. Gough had given to Mr. Spurgeon a valuable stick as a token of his affection; this was amongst the burglar's booty, and, after hammering out of shape the gold with which it was adorned, he offered it for sale at a pawnbroker's in the Borough. It was possible still to read the name, C. H. Spurgeon, in the precious metal, so an assistant was despatched for the police; but, before they arrived, the man decamped, and was not seen again.

Annoying as the incident was, the Pastor always said that he was decidedly a gainer by the transaction. With the amount he received for the battered gold, he bought some books which were of more use to him than the handsome stick would ever have been. Then the Trustees of the Orphanage felt that, as he was the Treasurer of the various Institutions, and often had money, and documents of value, belonging to them, in his possession, he ought to have a safe in which to keep them, so they presented one to him. The burglar had thrown down, in the study, a number of lighted matches, and the loose papers in various parts of the room were set on fire, so that a great conflagration might easily have resulted, if the Lord had not graciously prevented such a calamity. Thankfulness for this providential escape was followed by the recollection that, since the transfer of the property from the former owner, the premises had not been insured, so that the loss, in case of fire, would have been serious. That neglect was speedily remedied; and, by means of electric bells, and other arrangements, special protection was provided for the future.

News of the burglary was published, in various papers, with considerable exaggeration; and, perhaps as the result of the publicity thus given, Spurgeon received a letter, purporting to have been written by the thief; and it bore so many marks of being a genuine epistle that it was really believed that it came from the man himself. Among other things, he said that he didn't know it was 'the horflings' Spurgin' who lived there, for he would not have robbed *him*, and he put the very pertinent question, 'Why don't you shut your windows and keep a dog?' From that time, dates the entry to Westwood of 'Punch'—the pug concerning whom his master testified that he knew more than any dog ever ought to know!

One Thursday evening, when preaching at the Tabernacle, Spurgeon introduced his canine friend into the sermon, and turned to good account his pugnacious propensities: 'I think that I have heard preachers who have seemed to me to bring out a doctrine on purpose to fight over it. I have a dog, that has a rug in which he sleeps; and when I go home to-night, he will bring it out, and shake it before me, not that he particularly cares for his rug, but because he knows that I shall say, "I'll have it," and then he will bark at me, and in his language say, "No, you won't." There are some people who fetch out the doctrines of grace just in that way. I can see them trotting along with the doctrine of election just in order that some Arminian brother may dispute with them about it, and that then they may bark at him. Do not act so, beloved.'

In many of his letters from Mentone, Spurgeon mentioned his dog; a few extracts will show how fond he was of the intelligent creature: 'I wonder whether Punchie thinks of his master. When we drove from the station here, a certain doggie barked at the horses in true Punchistic style, and reminded me of my old friend. . . . Punchie sending me his love pleased me very much. Poor doggie, pat him for me, and give him a tit-bit for my sake. . . . I dreamed of old Punch; I hope the poor dog is better. . . . Kind memories to all, including Punch. How is he getting on? I rejoice that his life is prolonged, and hope he will live till my return. May his afflictions be a blessing to him in the sweetening of his temper! . . . Tell Punchie, "Master is coming!" '

It was at Westwood that the celebration of Spurgeon's silver wedding took place. There was some intention of holding a special meeting at the Tabernacle, to congratulate the Pastor and his wife, on Monday, January 10, 1881—two days after the actual date; but, unhappily, Spurgeon was laid aside at the time, so that idea had to be abandoned, although both were very sympathetically remembered in the supplications of those who were assembled that evening in the house of prayer. Ultimately, the commemoration took the form of a private gathering of friends, at Westwood, on Wednesday, February 2.

It was characteristic of my beloved's devotion to his Lord's service, [wrote Mrs. Spurgeon] and of the intimate union existing between himself and his church-officers, that such an event in our family history should have been celebrated in connection with a meeting of the deacons at our home. I might not have remembered that circumstance had I not been favoured with the loan of one of the invitations issued by the dear Pastor, a *facsimile* of which is here reproduced. I am not aware that he ever signed another letter with our united initials, and the date on which this one was written gives it now a specially tender interest. I have no very vivid recollections of the evening's proceedings; but I know that Mr. William Olney and Mr. Carr, as the spokesmen on behalf of their brother-deacons, made most sympathetic references to both the parents and their twin-sons, and that, after the interchange of many cheering reminiscences, and a time of holy fellowship, the whole household joined us for family worship, which was conducted by Mr. Spurgeon with his usual fervour and impressiveness.

[304]

Westwood
Beulah Hill
Upper Norwood
Jan. 31, 1881.

Dear Friend,

Lest you should forget it, I beg to remind you that the Deacons' Meeting will commence here at 5 on Wednesday next.

At 6.30, we will meet for tea, & after tea, we hope to celebrate with you our silver wedding with great thankfulness to God.

Please come as early as you can that we may get through business before tea.

Yours heartily
C.H. & S. Spurgeon

[305]

Among my dear husband's papers, I find a letter, relating to this happy season, from his old Cambridge friend, Mr. J. S. Watts. This epistle so sweetly links the beginning of our wedded life with the twenty-fifth anniversary of our marriage, that it appears to me to deserve a place in this chapter.

'Regent Street,
Cambridge,
January 8, 1881

My Dear Friend,

My mind reverts to the month of January, twenty-five years ago, when a certain newly-married juvenile Pastor and his wife came to me for a few days, and solaced themselves in their mutual love for each other at my house.

Many things have happened since that time; but their faithfulness and their affection for each other have not been impaired; and now that they are about to celebrate their silver wedding, I ask permission to remind them of those early days, and to add my hearty congratulations at this auspicious period.

May the 8th of January, 1881, ring in a strain of joyful music over the strings of the past, assuring them that "golden days" are yet to come, even before they "walk the golden streets." So prays,
Their old friend and well-wisher,

J. S. WATTS.'

Another letter, written at that period by Dr. W. Morley Punshon, is also worthy of preservation here:

'Tranby,
Brixton Rise, S.W.,
Jan., 1881

My Dear Sir and Brother,

The papers tell us that the 8th inst. will be a memorable day to you; and, amid hosts of greeting friends, my wife and I (than whom you have none truer, though our love can rarely exhibit itself but in wishful thought and prayer,) would fain express our good wishes in a line.

We trust there is good foundation for the rumour, which has lately reached us, of great and permanent improvement in Mrs. Spurgeon's health; and we pray that, if it be the Lord's will, you may be continued to each other in happy fellowship until the "silvern" shall have become "golden" by the lapse of years.

18   Charles and Thomas Spurgeon with their mother

19   Charles and Thomas at the age of twenty-one

20   *Family portraits*

Rev James Spurgeon of Stambourne
Mrs C. H. Spurgeon   *Mrs John Spurgeon*
Rev John Spurgeon   *Rev J. A. Spurgeon*

21 *The Old Town, Mentone, from the breakwater, a favourite view of Spurgeon's. Although this photograph was taken in 1972, the scene has changed remarkably little in an hundred years*

22 *A contemporary view of the bay at Mentone taken from the hillside above Hotel Beau Rivage on a damp but warm February afternoon*

23 Harrald and Spurgeon in the garden of Villa les Grottes, Mentone

24   *The Mentone Group, 1880*

25   Westwood

26   The library at Westwood

27   *The study at Westwood*

28   *A corner of 'the den'*

29   *Hotel Beau Rivage, Mentone*

30   *Hotel Beau Rivage (close view). The first floor balcony-window at right hand corner was customarily Spurgeon's sitting room, and the window around the same corner was his bedroom*

PARSONS IN THE PULPIT.
MR. SPURGEON.

31   Cartoons in a London periodical

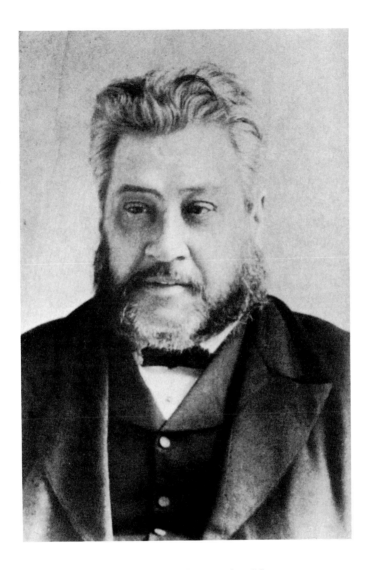

32 One of the last photographs of Spurgeon

33   The funeral cortège at Mentone

34 *The announcement. This and
the following three pictures are
artists' drawings at the time of
Spurgeon's death*

35 *The lift under
construction at
the Tabernacle*

36   Funeral procession

37   Funeral procession entering West Norwood Cemetery

THIS MONUMENT WAS ERECTED IN LOVING MEMORY OF

C. H. SPURGEON,

WHO WAS BORN AT KELVEDON, ESSEX, JUNE 19TH 1834,
AND FELL ASLEEP IN JESUS AT MENTONE, FRANCE JANY 31ST 1892.

"E'ER SINCE BY FAITH I SAW THE STREAM,
THY FLOWING WOUNDS SUPPLY,
REDEEMING LOVE HAS BEEN MY THEME,
AND SHALL BE TILL I DIE.

THEN IN A NOBLER SWEETER SONG,
I'LL SING THY POWER TO SAVE,
WHEN THIS POOR LISPING STAMMERING TONGUE,
LIES SILENT IN THE GRAVE."

38   The monument above the grave at West Norwood

Like most of God's anointed, it seems as if you are to be "made meet by consecrated pain." May the Refiner sit always by the furnace! *You know* that the fire will never be kindled a whit too fiercely, nor burn a moment too long.

There are many, whom you know not, who thank God, in these times of rebuke, for your fidelity to the old gospel, and who watch you with solicitude and prayer.

Wishing, for Mrs. Spurgeon and yourself, happiness, and the blessedness which is better—the Lord's unutterable peace, long and useful lives, and the "abundant entrance" at last, I am, in my wife's name and my own,

Yours very affectionately,

W. Morley Punshon.'

Three months later, when Dr. Punshon was 'called home,' Spurgeon gratefully referred to this letter, and sought to comfort the bereaved family in their season of sorrow.

The man who finds the ministry an easy life will also find that it will bring a hard death. If we are not labourers, we are not true stewards; for we are to be examples of diligence to the King's household. I like Adam Clarke's precept: 'Kill yourselves with work, and then pray yourselves alive again'.—C.H.S.

'If I have any message to give from my own bed of sickness it would be this—if you do not wish to be full of regrets when you are obliged to lie still, work while you can. If you desire to make a sick bed as soft as it can be, do not stuff it with the mournful reflection that you wasted time while you were in health and strength. People said to me years ago, 'You will break your constitution down with preaching ten times a week,' and the like. Well, if I have done so, I am glad of it. I would do the same again. If I had fifty constitutions I would rejoice to break them down in the service of the Lord Jesus Christ. You young men that are strong, overcome the wicked one and fight for the Lord while you can. You will never regret having done all that lies in you for our blessed Lord and Master. Crowd as much as you can into every day, and postpone no work till to-morrow. 'Whatsoever thy hand findeth to do, do it with thy might'—C.H.S., 1876.

19

A Typical Week's Work

MANY people have wondered how it was possible for Spurgeon to do all the work that he was able to perform, for so many years, with such happy results. He had efficient helpers in various departments of his service, and he was always ready to render to them their full meed of praise. Yet, with all the assistance upon which he could rely, there still remained for the chief worker a vast amount of toil which he could not delegate to anyone. He was a splendid organizer, and he could find employment suited to the capacity of many individuals with greatly varied qualifications; and while he could keep them all busily occupied, he was himself so quick in all his labour that he would probably do single-handed as much as all of them combined could accomplish.

The following description of a typical week's work will afford at least a glimpse of the way in which my husband spent a considerable portion of his time, and it will also indicate some of the methods adopted by him in discharging the heavy responsibilities which devolved upon him. In such an active and far-reaching life as his was, no one week in the year could be quite like the rest, nor indeed did the occupations of any two days exactly resemble one another; but the particulars here given will supply all that needs to be known about a fairly representative week's work.

The week must consist of seven days, for the Day of Rest was, in many respects, the beloved preacher's busiest time; and, although he often tried hard to get a Sabbath for himself on the Wednesday, the ever-increasing and not always reasonable requests for 'services,' all over the kingdom, frequently encroached upon the brief period of relaxation to which he was rightfully entitled, and which the claims of health imperatively demanded. He was, perhaps, all the more willing to take a long holiday in the winter because he had toiled so strenuously and almost continuously through all the other months of the year; though it must also be recorded that, during his seasons of rest, he probably did as much as most men do when in full work. The sermon had to be issued every week, and the magazine every month, material for the Almanacks had to be arranged, there were always some new books in course of preparation, many letters followed the absent minister wherever he might go, and the care of his own church and many others, and the many forms of holy service in which he was interested, left all too little leisure for the weary brain and the oft-suffering body. But if his holiday was a time of toil, what must have been the pressure when, for weeks and months at a stretch, it was almost literally 'all work and no play'?

In describing a typical week's work, a beginning can most appropriately be made with an account of the preparation for the hallowed engagements of the Sabbath. Up to six o'clock, every Saturday evening, visitors were welcomed at Westwood, the dear master doing the honours of the garden in such a way that many, with whom he thus walked and talked, treasure the memory of their visit as a very precious thing. At the tea-table, the conversation was bright, witty, and always interesting. After the meal was over, an adjournment was made to the study for family worship, and it was at these seasons that my beloved's prayers were remarkable for their tender childlikeness, their spiritual pathos, and their intense devotion. He seemed to come as near to God as a little child to a loving father, and we were often moved to tears as he talked thus face to face with his Lord. At six o'clock, every visitor left, for Mr. Spurgeon would often playfully say, 'Now, dear friends, I must bid you "Good-bye," and turn you out of this study; you know what a number of chickens I have to scratch for, and I want to give them a good meal to-morrow.' So, with a hearty 'God bless you!' he shook hands with them, and shut himself in to companionship with his God. The inmates of the house went quietly about their several duties, and a holy silence seemed to brood over the place. What familiar intercourse with the Saviour he so greatly loved, was then vouchsafed to him, we can never know, for, even while I write, I hear a whisper, 'The place whereon thou standest is holy ground.' No human ear ever heard the mighty pleadings with God, for himself, and his people, which rose from his study on those solemn evenings; no mortal eyes ever beheld him as he wrestled with the Angel of the covenant until he prevailed, and came back from his brook Jabbok with the message he was to deliver in his Master's Name. His grandest and most fruitful sermons were those which cost him most soul-travail and spiritual anguish; not in their preparation or arrangement, but in his own overwhelming sense of accountability to God for the souls to whom he had to preach the gospel of salvation by faith in Jesus Christ. Though he had the gift of utterance above many, preaching was to him no light or trifling task; his whole heart was absorbed in it; all his spiritual force was engaged in it; all the intellectual power, with which God had so richly endowed him, was pressed into this glorious service, and then laid humbly and thankfully at the feet of his Lord and Saviour, to be used and blessed by Him according to His gracious will and purpose.

Sometimes, but not often, he would leave the study for a few moments, to seek me, and say, with a troubled tone in his voice, 'Wifey, what shall I do? God has not given me my text yet.' I would comfort him as well as I could; and, after a little talk, he would return to his work, and wait and watch for the Word to be given. It was, to me, a cause for peculiar thankfulness when I was able to suggest to him a passage from which he could preach; and, afterwards, in referring to the sermon, he seemed so pleased to say, 'You gave me that text.'

Many years ago, on a Friday evening in the week of the Annual College Conference, a number of the ministers met at Westwood, as was usual with them, to talk over the doings of the past days, and to enjoy a chat with the President in his own home. During the evening, it was suggested that each one should explain his method of procedure in the most important matter of sermon-making; and the idea found great favour with the little company. Many of the brethren responded, and told, more or less interestingly, their manner of preparation; but it was evident that all awaited with impatience the moment when 'the Governor' should speak, and reveal to them the secrets of his Saturday nights' work. Very eager were the faces turned to him as he sat, blissfully happy in his easy chair, the strain of the week over, and in full enjoyment of the free and holy fellowship which obtained on such occasions. I cannot recall his very words, but the purport of them was something like this: 'Brethren, it is not easy for me to tell you precisely how I make my sermons. All through the week I am on the look-out for material that I can use on the Sabbath; but the actual work of arranging it is necessarily left until Saturday evening, for every other moment is fully occupied in the Lord's service. I have often said that my greatest difficulty is to fix my mind upon the particular texts which are to be the subjects of discourse on the following day; or, to speak more correctly, to know what topics the Holy Spirit would have me bring before the congregation. As soon as any passage of Scripture really grips my heart and soul, I concentrate my whole attention upon it, look at the precise meaning of the original, closely examine the context so as to see the special aspect of the text in its surroundings, and roughly jot down all the thoughts that occur to me concerning the subject, leaving to a later period the orderly marshalling of them for presentation to my hearers.

When I have reached this point, I am often stopped by an obstacle which is only a trouble to those of us whose sermons are regularly printed. I turn to my own Bible, which contains a complete record

of all my published discourses; and, looking at those I have preached upon the text, I find perhaps that the general run of thought is so similar to that which I have marked out, that I have to abandon the subject, and seek another. Happily, a text of Scripture is like a diamond with many facets, which sparkles and flashes whichever way it is held, so that, although I may have, already printed, several sermons upon a particular passage, there is still a fresh setting possible for the priceless gem, and I can go forward with my work. I like next to see what others have to say about my text; and, as a rule, my experience is that, if its teaching is perfectly plain, the commentators, to a man, explain it at great length whereas, with equal unanimity, they studiously avoid or evade the verses which Peter might have described as 'things hard to be understood.' I am very much obliged to them for leaving me so many nuts to crack;

but I should have been just as grateful if they had made more use of their own theological teeth or nut-crackers. However, among the many who have written upon the Word, I generally find some who can at least help to throw a side-light upon it; and when I have arrived at that part of my preparation, I am glad to call my dear wife to my assistance. She reads to me until I get a clear idea of the whole subject; and, gradually, I am guided to the best form of outline, which I copy out, on a half-sheet of notepaper, for use in the pulpit. This relates only to the morning sermon; for the evening, I am usually content if I can decide upon the text, and have a general notion of the lessons to be drawn from it, leaving to the Lord's-day afternoon the final arrangement of divisions, sub-divisions, and illustrations.'

This is, as nearly as I can recollect, the preacher's own explanation of his mode of preparing his discourses. 'Will you come and help me to-night, wifey?' he would say on those memorable Saturday evenings, as if I were doing him a favour, though the service was one which an angel might have coveted. I always found, when I went into the study, an easy chair drawn up to the table, by his side, and a big heap of books piled one upon the other, and opened at the place where he desired me to read. With those old volumes around him, he was like a honey-bee amid the flowers; he seemed to know how to extract and carry off the sweet spoils from the most unpromising-looking tome among them. His acquaintance with them was so familiar and complete, that he could at once place his hand on any author who had written upon the portion of Scripture which was engaging his attention; and I was, in this pleasant fashion, introduced to many of the Puritan and other divines whom, otherwise, I might not have known.

Never was occupation more delightful, instructive, and spiritually helpful; my heart has burned within me, as the meaning of some passage of God's Word has been opened up, and the hidden stores of wisdom and knowledge have been revealed; or when the marrow and fatness of a precious promise or doctrine have been spread like a dainty banquet before my longing eyes. Shall I ever forget those solemn evenings when the sufferings of the Lord Jesus were the theme of tearful meditation; when, with 'love and grief our hearts dividing,' we followed Him throughout the night on which He was betrayed, weeping, like the daughters of Jerusalem, and saying, 'There was never sorrow like unto His sorrow'; or the more rapturous time when the topic for the morrow was to be, 'the exceeding riches of His grace,' and we were fairly bewildered by the inexhaustible treasures of love and mercy to be found in that fair 'land of Havilah, where there is gold'? Gracious hours are those thus spent, and unspeakably precious to my soul; for, while the servant of the Lord is reaping the corn of the Kingdom for the longing multitude who expect to be fed by his hand, I can glean between the sheaves, and gather the 'handfuls of purpose' which are let fall so lovingly.

There come delightful pauses in my reading, when the book is laid down, and I listen to the dear voice of my beloved as he explains what I cannot understand, or unfolds meanings which I fail to see, often condensing into a few clear, choice sentences whole pages of those discursive old divines in whom he delights, and pressing from the gathered thoughts all the richest nectar of their hidden sweetness. Thus, a *poor prisoner* has the first sip of the 'wines on the lees, well-refined,'—the first morsel from the loaves with which the thousands are to be fed and refreshed on the morrow. How shall I sufficiently thank God for this drink of the brook by the way, this 'holy place' within my home where the Lord deigns to meet with me, and draw out my heart in adoration and worship?

On Lord's-day morning Spurgeon always set a good example to his people by being early at the sanctuary. He usually reached the Tabernacle at least half an hour before the time for commencing the service. During that interval, he attended to any matters that were of special urgency, selected the hymns that were to be sung, and arranged with the precentor the tunes best adapted to them; the remaining minutes were spent in prayer with all the deacons and elders who were not already on duty elsewhere. The preacher himself greatly valued this season of devotion, and his sermons contain many references to the petitions presented by the brethren in his vestry before joining in the public worship of the great congregation. During the thirty years that he preached in the beautiful building he had so largely helped to erect, there was practically no difference in the size of his audience, for the Tabernacle was always crowded, though sometimes the number of friends unable to gain admission, when the outer gates were closed, was larger than on other occasions. Punctually at eleven o'clock, Mr. Spurgeon was seen descending the steps leading to the platform, followed by the long train of office-bearers, and, after a brief pause for silent supplication, the service began.

Spurgeon himself often said that the pulpit was his throne, and that, when preaching, he envied no monarch in all the world, nor felt the slightest desire to exchange places with any man upon the face of the earth. Yet was there, even to him, an inner shrine—the very holy of holies—which was more sacred still. Many times he has testified that, when leading the great congregation in prayer, he has been so rapt in adoration, and so completely absorbed in the supplication or thanksgiving he has been presenting, that he has quite forgotten all his surroundings, and has felt even a measure of regret, upon closing his petition, and opening his eyes, to find that he was still in the flesh, in the company of men of like passions with himself, instead of being in the immediate presence of the Most High, sharing in the higher worship of the holy angels and the spirits of just men made perfect. D. L. Moody must have been very deeply in sympathy with Spurgeon upon this matter, for he declared that, greatly as he had been blessed every time he heard the pastor preach, he had been even more impressed as he had heard him pray. Other notable servants of Christ have borne a similar testimony.

The service being ended, if it was the second Sabbath in the month the Pastor joined the large company of communicants who usually filled the spacious lecture-hall; and there, around the table of their Lord, another half-hour of hallowed Christian fellowship was enjoyed, completing and consummating the blessing received in the public assembly. To many of the most earnest workers of the Tabernacle Church, the morning was the only time when they could meet with their brethren and sisters in Christ in their own house of prayer; for the afternoon and evening were devoted to Sunday-school and mission work, open-air preaching, or the many forms of Christian service in which they were engaged. The Pastor constantly referred to this happy arrangement; and urged others of the members to adopt the same method of both getting good and doing good, as it would help to develop their own gifts and graces, and it would also make the more room for the unconverted who desired to come to hear the Word at night.

Each Sabbath, except the second, the ordinance of the Lord's supper was observed at the close of the evening service, the first Lord's-day evening in each month being the time for the great communion in the Tabernacle, when the area and the larger part of the first gallery were reserved for communicants, and many hundreds of spectators were able to remain in other parts of the building.

It was a most impressive scene—sublime in its simplicity—and those who have ever taken part in it can never forget it. Spurgeon had long held and taught that the apostolic precedents all appeared to indicate that the celebration of the sacred supper should take place each Lord's day, and, therefore, whether at home or abroad, he always attended the communion every Sabbath if it was possible and he often bore his willing witness that the frequent participation in the holy feast increased rather than diminished its value as a constant reminder of Him who said to His disciples, 'This do in remembrance of me.'

On every Sabbath morning in the month, except the second, there was usually a long procession of friends from the country, or from foreign lands, waiting for just a shake of the hand and a greeting from the Pastor; and it was interesting to notice how quickly he recognized those whom he had seen before, even if years had elapsed since they last met. All through the summer season, some hundreds of visitors from the United States helped, at each service, to swell the contingents from other parts; and most of them afterwards sought to secure a personal interview with him. Among them were usually some of the most noted of the American ministers of various denominations, to whom a hearty invitation was given to take part in the evening service, or the prayer-meeting the next night. Spurgeon loved to quote what one of these brethren said to him: 'Well, Brother Spurgeon, I was here ten years ago, and heard you preach , and I find that you have not altered your doctrine in the least. You stand to-day exactly where you stood then.' 'Yes,' replied the Pastor, 'and if you come again in another ten years, you will, by the grace of God, find me still preaching the very same gospel, unless the Lord has, in the meantime, called me home.' Among the special friends from across the Atlantic were such divines as Dr. John Hall, Dr. W. M. Taylor, Dr. Cuyler, Dr. Armitage, Dr. MacArthur, Dr. Lorimer, and Dr. H. L. Wayland; and they were sure to be invited to call during the week at the Pastor's home, and some of them had the still greater delight of spending a quiet day with him in the country, when that rare privilege was possible. Others, at mutually-convenient times, visited the Orphanage, and the rest of the Institutions, under his guidance, and thus they heard from his own lips the charming story of how the Lord had led him and blessed him in connection with all the different branches of his service.

The informal reception being over at last, the Pastor was able to leave, unless, as not seldom happened, some poor trembling soul was waiting in the hope of having a word or two of cheer and direction from him, or one of the earnest workers, always on the watch for anxious enquirers, came forward, with radiant face, bringing one or another who had sought and found the Saviour either during or since the service. While Mr. Spurgeon was residing at Helensburgh House, he was able to return home to dinner on the Lord's-day; but, after removing to Westwood, he soon found that the distance was too great, so he remained for the afternoon within easy reach of the Tabernacle, with friends who were only too glad to minister in any way to his comfort and refreshing. Sometimes there was a sick member whom the Pastor felt that he must visit after dinner; otherwise, he had an hour or so of rest and Christian conversation before retiring, at about four o'clock, for the preparation of his evening discourse. Some, who were very little children then, can probably remember the injunction given to them on such occasions, 'You must be very quiet, for Mr. Spurgeon is getting his sermon.' Ere he was summoned to tea, the brief notes which he was going to use in the pulpit were duly arranged. The evening sermon was usually shorter than the one delivered in the morning, and somewhat more evangelistic, in order to be specially adapted to the larger number of casual worshippers who might then be present. Yet, often, that order was changed; and the morning discourse more nearly resembled an earnest evangelist's address, while the sermon in the evening was a closely-reasoned exposition of the doctrines of grace, which again and again led to the conversion of more sinners than did some of the appeals directly addressed to them.

For some years, once a quarter, the Tabernacle was thrown open, on the Lord's-day evening, to anybody who liked to come, the members of the church and congregation being asked to stay away for that night. The experiment was crowned with abundant success from the first. The preacher said, afterwards, that his regular hearers had so loyally complied with his request that they should worship elsewhere for that one occasion, that, in addition to the seat-stewards and other workers who were present, he could not recognize half-a-dozen persons in the whole assembly of five or six thousand people. The discourses delivered to such a promiscuous audience were, naturally, evangelistic, and many were brought to the Lord through these special services.

Before the evening worship, on ordinary Sabbaths, the Pastor often saw an enquirer, or a candidate for church-fellowship, who found it difficult to get to the Tabernacle during the week; and, after preaching, except on communion nights, however weary he might be, he was never too tired to point a poor sinner to the Saviour, and to act the part of the true shepherd of souls to those who were seeking entrance into the fold. Even when he reached his home his day's labour was not always finished; for, if he was going to preach in a distant area on the morrow, he was obliged to start at once revising the report of the discourse which he had delivered in the morning. That, however, was quite an exceptional arrangement; and, as a general rule, his first work, every Monday, was the revision of the Lord's-day morning's sermon.

This was always a labour of love, yet it was a labour; and it is not surprising that, during a very severe illness, when his friends induced him to see an eminent physician, the doctor urged and almost ordered him to abandon this heavy task so soon after the great strain of the Sabbath services. But the Pastor knew that, to delay the publication even for a week, would materially affect the circulation. He also said that, if he was to continue his gifts to the Lord's cause on the scale to which he had been accustomed, he must keep all his literary work up to the highest mark, and he could not bear the thought of lessening the help that he saw to be required in so many different directions. He used also playfully to say that the earth itself would cease to revolve if the sermon was not published every Thursday morning; and, in advising the students occasionally to follow his early example, and to write out their discourses in full— but not to read or recite them—he told them that the revision of his sermons for the press gave him all the benefits that other preachers might derive from writing theirs.

As soon as the messenger brought the reporter's manuscript, Mr. Spurgeon glanced at the number of sheets to see whether the discourse was longer or shorter than usual, so that he might judge whether he had to lengthen or to reduce it in order that it might, when printed, fill the requisite space,—twelve octavo pages; and at once began revising it. The *facsimile*, on the opposite page, will show how carefully and thoroughly this part of his work was done.

After Mr. Spurgeon had made the alterations which he deemed advisable, his literary secretary Mr. Keys, who sat on his left-hand in the study, was entrusted with the duty of verifying quotations, and seeing that the punctuation and other minor matters were all in order. Then, when about a third of the manuscript was ready, the

When you & I reach the shores of heaven, the glory. When we come forth out of our graves it will not be with loss, but with enrichment.

We shall leave corruption & I warm behind us he will bring us forth also with silver & gold. What golden songs, what silver notes, what piths of communion with our Lord will adorn our raiment! If we too, acquainted with grief, how much more fully shall we enter into joy of our Lord because we entered into his sorrow! He also has suffered for them, he has done battle for God against the enemy, he also has borne reproach, he comes aliens to our mother's children, he has been bruised in heel, & yet in death conquered death, even as He did; only by grace. Hence the fellowship with him through eternity. What we else shall tell angels, principalities, powers, & I gems o our grateful history of our trials & deliverances. Coming up from death to eternal life, we shall see that it is sure of it, feeling He brought us forth also with silver & gold."

messenger started off with it to the printers, returning for a second supply, and sometimes even for a third if the word of revision was at all delayed.

There was a little breathing-space for the busy toiler after the boy was sent away with the first portion of the sermon manuscript, but, usually, other work at once claimed the Pastor's attention. During the time that Mr. Spurgeon was revising the sermon, his private secretary, J. W. Harrald, would be busy opening the morning's letters, and arranging those that required immediate answers. If there were any that he knew would be specially cheering, they were always placed where they would at once catch the eye of 'the Governor.' This was always the case with large and unexpected donations for the Lord's work under his care, such as a cheque for £500, which came as a substantial token of a father's gratitude for Mr. Spurgeon's efforts to be the means of blessing to the gentleman's son at Mentone. Sometimes, there were anonymous letters— complaining, or abusive, or even blasphemous—and it was with peculiar satisfaction that they were prevented from ever wounding the servant of the Lord for whom they were intended by those who wrote them. The Pastor occasionally dictated replies to a few of the letters before continuing his sermon-revising; but, more often, with his own hand, he wrote the answers in full, for he never spared himself if he could give greater pleasure to others. In later years the number of donors to the various Institutions so increased that he was obliged to have a set of receipts lithographed in *facsimile*, but, even when using these, he added a few words which greatly enhanced their value in the opinion of those who received them. He found it necessary also to have a considerable variety of lithographed letters prepared, ready to send to applicants for admission to the College and Orphanage, or persons seeking situations, asking him to read manuscripts, or to write the Prefaces for new books, or to do any of the thousand and one things by which so many people sought to steal away his precious moments, and at the same time to augment the revenue of the Post Office.

It was usually far into Monday afternoon before the last sheet of the sermon was reached, and the messenger was able to start with it to the printing-office. Then there were more letters to be answered, possibly books to be reviewed, magazine proofs to be read, or other literary work to be advanced to the next stage; and it was with the utmost difficulty that even a few minutes could be secured for a quiet walk in the lovely garden that, all day long, seemed to be inviting the ceaseless worker to come and admire its many charms. He could also hear the voice of duty calling him in another direction, and soon it was time to get ready to start for the Tabernacle.

Frequently he reached the Tabernacle by half-past five, either to meet the elders, and consider with them the very important matters relating to the church's spiritual state which specially came under their notice, or to preside at the first part of a church-meeting, which often lasted throughout the whole evening, and was mainly occupied with the delightful business of receiving new members. As seven o'clock approached, he left the meeting in the charge of his brother, or one of the deacons or elders, that he might be at liberty to begin the prayer-meeting at the appointed hour. Sometimes, if he had engagements which would prevent him from being at the Tabernacle on Tuesday or Wednesday, he would get his sermon-revision completed by mid-day and directly after dinner go up to see enquirers and candidates—a congenial but exhausting form of service which often continued right up to the hour of prayer.

On certain special Mondays in the year, the annual meetings of some of the smaller Societies were held, and on those occasions Mr. Spurgeon was at the lecture-hall in time to give out the 'grace before tea.' His presence was greatly prized by the earnest and energetic sisters who carried on the various works of charity and beneficence; and they were much encouraged by his hearty words of cheer, and by the financial help which always accompanied them. It was really surprising to notice, year after year, how much he varied his addresses at these gatherings, for the audience mainly consisted of the same persons each time.

A little before seven o'clock, the happy season of talk was brought to a close, a brief prayer for a blessing on the work and workers followed, and then the whole company ascended to the Tabernacle for the prayer-meeting. All who are familiar with Spurgeon's writings, know that he regarded the prayer-meeting as the thermometer of the church; and, judging by that test, the spiritual temperature of the large community under his charge stood very high. Not that he could ever induce all the members to be regularly present on the Monday night; but, for many years, the numbers attending filled a large portion of the area and first gallery, and the world-wide testimony was that the meeting was altogether unique, the only one that at all approached it being Archibald G. Brown's Saturday night prayer-meeting at the East London Tabernacle. Nor was it remarkable simply for its size, but the whole spirit of the gathering made it a source of peculiar helpfulness to all who were in constant attendance, while occasional visitors carried away with them even to distant lands influences and impulses which they never wished to lose or to forget. In Spurgeon's eyes the prayer-meeting was the most important meeting of the week. He often said that it was not surprising if churches did not prosper, when they regarded it as of so little value that one evening in the week was made to suffice for a feeble combination of service and prayer-meeting.

The gatherings at the Tabernacle on Monday nights were constantly varied. Usually, some of 'our own men' labouring in the country or abroad were present, and took part, while missionaries going out to China, or North Africa, or other parts of the foreign field, or returning home on furlough, helped to add to the spiritual profit of the proceedings. The Pastor always gave one or more brief addresses, and never allowed the interest to flag. All too soon, half-past eight arrived, and the meeting had to be concluded, for many of the workers had other prayer-meetings or services following closely upon that one.

Spurgeon's day's work was not yet complete, for various visitors were waiting for an interview; and, with them, some candidates or enquirers needed and secured a few precious minutes—the conversation and prayer at such times being something to be remembered with gratitude as long as they lived. On some Monday nights, an extra service was squeezed in; and, leaving the Tabernacle a little before eight o'clock, the Pastor preached at Christ Church, Upton Chapel, Walworth Road Chapel, or some other neighbouring place of worship; or spoke at some special local gathering, such as a meeting at the Newington Vestry Hall on behalf of the Hospital Sunday Fund. When, at last, he was really *en route* for home, his first question was—'Has the sermon come?' and the second—'What is the length of it?' If the reply was, 'Just right,' it was joyfully received, for the labour of adding to or cutting out any part made the task of revising the proof still more arduous; and, if a distant preaching engagement had to be fulfilled the next day, it was essential for the revision to be completed that night, or very early in the morning. On one occasion, when the London Baptist Association Committee met at Westwood for breakfast and business, it transpired that their host had taken time by the forelock, and begun his day's work at four o'clock.

Ordinarily, the correction of the proof of the sermon was completed by about eleven o'clock on Tuesday morning, leaving a couple of hours for replying to letters, and attending to the most pressing literary work. When there were only four Thursdays in the month, an extra sermon was required to make the usual number for the monthly part, and that entailed heavy labour. The discourses available for this purpose were the shorter ones delivered on the Sabbath and Thursday evenings; and, as a rule, two or three pages had to be added to them. The *facsimile* on page 324 is a good example of the method adopted in lengthening the sermon which had been set up from the reporter's transcript, unrevised, and it is specially suitable to the present volume as it contains a striking passage in the preacher's autobiography.

Tuesday afternoon, with rare exceptions, was devoted to the truly pastoral and important work of seeing candidates and enquirers at the Tabernacle; and in no part of his service was Spurgeon more happy and more completely at home. On reaching his vestry at three o'clock, he always found some of his elders already at their post; and usually they had, by that time, conversed with the first arrivals, and given them the cards which were to introduce them to the Pastor. If he was satisfied with the person's own testimony, he put the name of the friend upon the list of those to be proposed for church-fellowship, and indicated the elder or deacon to be appointed as visitor, to make the necessary enquiries before the applicant could be admitted to baptism and membership. In the course of three or four hours, twenty, thirty, or even forty individuals were thus seen; and anyone who has had much experience in such service knows how exhausting it is. Sometimes, the number was smaller, or it was made up with those who came about other matters. These were seen by Mr. Harrald, or by the elders, and interviews with the Pastor were arranged if they were deemed advisable. At five o'clock, a brief interval was secured for tea; and, during that half-hour, the Pastor compared notes with his helpers concerning those with whom he had conversed, and related specially interesting incidents which some of the candidates had described to him. Then he returned to the happy task, and kept on as long as any were waiting; and, often, as the crowning of his day's labour, he went down to the lecture-hall, to preside at the annual meeting of one or other of the Tabernacle Societies, such as the Sunday-school, the Almshouses Day-schools, the Evangelists' Association, the Country Mission, the Loan Tract Society, or the Spurgeon's Sermons' Tract Society. He frequently said that the number of Institutions, Societies,

"The burden of the word of the Lord."—Malachi i. 1.

THE prophets of old were no triflers. They carried a burden. Those who still speak in God's name, if the Lord has sent them, dare not play with their work. They have a burden to carry—"The burden of the word of the Lord." I am often astounded at the way in which some who profess to be the servants of God make light of their work. I read of one who said, "I got on very well for a year or two in my pulpit, for my great uncle had left me a large store of manuscripts, so I read them." The Lord have mercy on his guilty soul! Another is able to get on well with his preaching because he pays so much a quarter to the bookseller, and is supplied with regular manuscript sermons. I have seen the things. What must God think of such people as these? But in the old times, those whom God sent did not borrow their messages. They had their message directly from God, and that message was weighty—so weighty that they called it "the burden of the Lord." He that does not find his ministry a burden now will find it a burden hereafter which will sink him lower than the lowest hell. A ministry that never burdens the heart and the conscience in this life will be like a millstone about a man's neck in the world to come. The servants of God mean business. They do not talk for talking's sake. They are not sent into the world to tickle men's ears, nor to make a display of elocution. They have a something to say that presses upon them, and they must say it. They have an inward weight, they have will, have an inward fire, and they must give vent to them; for the Word of the Lord is as fire in their bones, consuming them, if, indeed, they be the servants of God. The servants of God are not triflers, for they have the burden of the Lord.

And in their message, the true servants of God have something to carry. There is something in their message. It is not froth and foam, words and verbiage, and stories and pretty things, and oratory, and all that. There is weight in it, and if ever there were men in this world who ought to speak in earnest, they are the men they speak for God, and, if there is nothing in what they have to say, then God never commissioned them. If there is no importance—yea, if their message be not of the first and of the last importance—why in the name of God do they profess to speak in the name of God? It must be so, that the true servant of God has no light weight. He does not run merrily as one that has nothing to carry, but he bears that he bears, the burden of the word of the Lord.

Yet, do not let me be misunderstood at the beginning. God's true servants, who are burdened with his word, cheerfully carry that burden. I would not be without it for all the world. Sometimes, do you know, we get tempted, when things do not go right, to run away from it. When some of you do not behave yourselves, and things get a little out of order, I say to myself, "I wish I could give this up," but then I think of Jonah, and whales are scarcer now than they were then, and I do not seem inclined to run that risk. So I stick to my business, and keep to the message of God; for one might not be brought to land quite so safely as the runaway prophet was. God's servants would do nothing else but bear this burden, even if they could make a change. Remember how William Carey, speaking of one of his sons says, "Poor Felix has drivelled into an ambassador." He was a missionary once, and he was employed by the British Government as an ambassador, "That is what his father thought of that promotion." "Poor Felix has drivelled into an ambassador." It would be a drivelling down, indeed, from bearing the burden of the Lord, if one were to wear a crown, or be first in a senate of philosophers.

The burden which the true preacher of God bears is for God, and on Christ's behalf, and for the souls of others. He has a natural instinct which makes him care for the souls of others, and his anxiety is that none should perish. Like the Christ who longed to save, so does the true Malachi, or messenger of God, go forth with this as his happy, joyful, cheerfully-borne burden, but yet, as a burden, for all that, and of that I am going to speak to-night. There is the practical truth arising out of this. "The burden of the word of the Lord."

I. And why is it a burden? Well, first, BECAUSE IT IS THE WORD of the Lord. If what we preach is only of man, we may preach as we like, but there is no burden in it; but if this Book be inspired—if Jehovah be the only God, if Jesus Christ be God incarnate, if there be no salvation save, through his precious blood—then there is a great solemnity about that, which a minister of Christ is called upon to preach. It hence becomes a burden to him.

And, first, it becomes a burden in the reception of it. I do not think that any man could ever preach the gospel aright until he has had it borne into his own soul. You cannot preach conviction of sin

[324]

Missions, and Sunday-schools connected with the Tabernacle was so large that it would have been possible to arrange for an anniversary of one of them every week in the year! The secretaries or leaders of many of these works always secured his presence and help at their meetings, if possible; and he used to describe the lecture-hall as his happy hunting-ground where he found recruits for the College. Some who later became successful ministers and missionaries spoke tremblingly before him, for the first time, at these week-night gatherings. They might scarcely recognize themselves by the description the President gave of some of them then, as he pictured the 'fledglings, with their callow wings, trying to soar away to the empyrean, but falling down flop into the arena!'

Sometimes, instead of meeting with a few hundreds of friends in the lecture-hall, the Pastor presided over many thousands in the Tabernacle. One such gathering took place on the night when the Jubilee Singers sang, and, by that one effort, the sum of £220 was added to the funds of the Fisk University; another notable meeting was held when our own black brethren, Johnson and Richardson, and their wives, had their farewell before proceeding to Africa, 'the land of their fathers'—and an equally memorable occasion was the evening when Mr. John B. Gough gave one of his marvellous oratorical displays on behalf of the Pastors' College, and, in recognition of his kindness, the Pastor presented to him a complete set of his sermons. At other times Spurgeon was not the chairman of the meeting, but he helped to contribute to the success of the proceedings by delivering an earnest address in aid of the Primitive Methodist Missionary Society, the Liberation Society, or some other great public movement for which the Tabernacle had been lent, and for which his personal advocacy was also desired.

Wednesday was the only possible time available as a mid-week 'Sabbath'; and whenever it could be secured for rest, its benefits were immediately manifest. Each year, on his return from Mentone, Spurgeon told his secretary to keep his diary clear of all engagements on that day; but, alas! soon one, and then another, and yet others, had to be given up in response to the importunate appeals to which the self-sacrificing preacher had not the heart to say, 'No,' although he knew that the inevitable result would be a breakdown in health, and the cancelling for a time of all arrangements for extra services. Then, when he appeared to have recovered, the same process would be repeated, with an exactly similar sequel; but the requests for sermons, speeches, and lectures poured in upon him even during his worst illnesses, and it always pained him when he felt that he must refuse them.

But there were some outstanding days when, with one or more congenial companions, he would go off for a long drive into the country. Yet, even then, before he started in the morning, or after he returned at night, he often accomplished what many other people would have considered enough for a hard day's work. When there were only two or three hours available for a drive, a favourite route was over the Shirley Hills, and through Addington Park. The Archbishop of Canterbury kindly sent, each year, a card giving the right of free passage through his spacious grounds, and he, on several occasions, expressed his wish to have the pleasure of entertaining Spurgeon at Addington. On the acceptance of one invitation to lunch, Dr. Benson greeted his guest very heartily, and, pointing to his butler and footman, said, 'There are two members of your congregation, Mr. Spurgeon. When I am in residence at Lambeth, they always go to the Tabernacle. I don't blame them, for I would do the same myself if I had the chance. When your coachman gets round to the stables, he will recognize another Tabernacle attendant; and I can truly say that they are all a credit to the instruction they receive from you.' This testimony was very pleasing to the Pastor, and he was further cheered by hearing of others on the estate who were readers of his sermons. The two preachers spent a very enjoyable time together; and, later on, during Spurgeon's long illness, one of the letters which gave him great comfort was written by the Primate. In his friendly intercourse with the Tabernacle Pastor, Dr. Benson followed in the footsteps of one of his own predecessors, for, during the time that the bill for the abolition of church rates was before Parliament, Archbishop Tait frequently consulted Spurgeon upon several of the details of the measure.

Sometimes, instead of going through Addington Park, Spurgeon paid a visit to the Bishop of Rochester at Selsdon Park. A very intimate friendship existed between Bishop Thorold and the Pastor, and they enjoyed many happy hours together in the Selsdon home and under the elms of the garden. Usually, each year, as the time approached for the preparation of the addresses to be delivered in connection with his episcopal visitation, the Bishop invited Spurgeon to spend a long quiet day with him in prayer and conversation upon such matters as would help to put him in a right state of heart for the responsible task before him. On several occasions he also visited his friend at Westwood, and the season of spiritual fellow-ship in the study must have been mutually profitable, for, when it was over, and the visitor was gone, Spurgeon always remarked, 'Oh, we have had such a delightful time of talk and prayer together!'

Thursday morning was principally devoted to letter-writing and literary work in general. Spurgeon's position naturally brought him into correspondence with vast numbers of people all over the world. Yet he often felt that he could have employed his time to far better purpose. Again and again, he sorrowfully said, 'I am only a poor clerk, driving the pen hour after hour; here is another whole morning gone, and nothing done but letters, letters, letters!' When reminded of the joy and comfort he was ministering to many troubled hearts by that very drudgery, he agreed that it was work for the Lord as truly as the preaching in which he so much more delighted. Still, we often felt that quite an unnecessary addition to his already too-heavy load was made by the thoughtless and often frivolous communications to which he was expected personally to reply.

If Spurgeon's correspondence was not quite as burdensome as usual, or if he had literary work that had to be done—when the weather permitted, he liked to retire to his favourite retreat, a summer-house in the garden, where the hours fled all too swiftly as he wrote his comments on the Psalms, or some of the other books that now remain as permanent memorials of his studious and in-dustrious life.

After dinner, definite preparation for the Thursday evening ser-vice began, though the subject had probably been, as he often said, 'simmering' in his mind all the morning. The Saturday evening procedure was to a great extent repeated, but one of his secretaries had the privilege of looking up anything that might help him to get the true meaning of his text. His private study, commonly called 'the den,' became, on such occasions, his place for secret retirement and prayer; and very joyously he generally came forth, carrying in his hand his brief pulpit-notes; though, at other times, the message he was to deliver only came to him just in time.

For many years, Spurgeon had on Thursday evening in the Taber-nacle lecture-hall, from six o'clock till nearly seven, what he termed 'The Pastor's prayer-meeting.' This was an extra gathering, specially convened for the purpose of pleading for a blessing upon the Word he was about to preach; and most refreshing and helpful it always proved both to himself and the people. From the New Park Street days, he had made little or no difference between the services on the Lord's-day and on week-nights; and, throughout the whole course of his ministry, the Thursday evening worship afforded an opportunity for the attendance of many Christian workers of all denominations who were not able to be present on the Sabbath; and, among them, were numerous Church of England clergymen and Nonconformist ministers. At the close, some of these hearers usually desired a few minutes' conversation with the preacher, so that it was late before he could get away; and then, though not weary of his work, he was certainly weary in it.

On Friday morning, the usual routine of answering correspondence had, to some extent, to give way to the more urgent work of preparation for his talk to the students of the College. He regarded this part of his service as so important that he devoted all his powers of heart and mind to it, and it was indeed a rich store of mental and spiritual instruction that he carrried up, each week, to his 'school of the prophets.' Hundreds of 'our own men' have testified that, greatly as they profited by the rest of their College curriculum, Spurgeon's Friday afternoon class was far beyond everything else in its abiding influence upon their life and ministry. With such a responsive and appreciative audience, he was at his very best; and both students and ministers often declared that, not even in his most brilliant pulpit utterances, did he excel, or even equal, what it was their delight to hear from his lips in those never-to-be-forgotten days. From three till about five o'clock, there was a continuous stream of wit and wisdom, counsel and warning, exhortation and doctrine, all converging to the one end of helping the men before him to become good ministers of Jesus Christ. Then, when the class was dismissed, another hour, or more, was ungrudgingly devoted to interviews with any of the brethren who desired personally to consult the President; and that this privilege was highly prized was very evident from the way in which it was exercised.

Now and then, the Friday afternoon was made even more memorable by a special sermon to the students, at the close of which the Lord's supper was observed, the whole service being peculiarly helpful to the spiritual life of the brethren. On other occasions, students from Harley House, or Regent's Park, or Cheshunt College paid a fraternal visit to Newington; and, in due course, the Pastors'

College men returned the visit. At such times, Presidents, tutors, and students vied with one another in making their guests feel at home, and in conveying to them all possible pleasure and profit.

Perhaps, between six and seven o'clock, Mr. Spurgeon was free to start for home; but, more likely, there was another anniversary meeting—possibly, of the Evening Classes connected with the College, at which he had promised to preside; or there was some mission-hall, at which he had engaged to preach or speak; or there was a sick or dying member of the church to whom he had sent word that he would call on his way back from the College. It was utterly impossible for him to make any systematic pastoral visitation of his great flock—that work was undertaken by the elders—but he found many opportunities of visiting individual members; and his sermons contain frequent references to the triumphant deathbed scenes that he had witnessed. He could not often conduct funeral services, yet there were some cases in which he felt bound to make an exception to his usual rule, as he did also in the matter of weddings. *The Sword and the Trowel*[1] has recorded typical instances of how thoroughly, on such occasions, he sorrowed with those who wept, and rejoiced with those who were full of happiness. Add to all this, the constant interruptions from callers, and the many minor worries to which every public man is subject, and readers may well wonder when Spurgeon could find time for reading, and study, and all the work he constantly accomplished! If they had known how much he was continually doing, they might have marvelled even more than they did. Surely, there never was a busier life than his; not an atom more of sacred service could have been crowded into it.

Saturday morning was the time for the Pastor and his private secretary to clear off, as far as possible, any arrears of work that had accumulated during the week. The huge pile of letters was again attacked; various financial matters were settled, and cheques despatched to chapel-building ministers or those engaged in pioneer and mission work, or needing some special assistance in their labour for the Lord. The secretary also then reported the result of interviews with students, and various officials and workers in connection with the different Institutions, and received instructions as to the replies to be given to their requests, or with regard to various

[1] See for example, the volume for 1894, page 109, 'Mr. Spurgeon at a Funeral;' and page 157, 'Mr. Spurgeon at a Wedding.'

matters tending to the general efficiency of the whole work. It was usual, often, on that morning, for the President to see some of the applicants for admission to the College, or to examine the papers of others, and to dictate the letters conveying his decision, or making further enquiries if there was a doubt either with regard to acceptance or rejection. Brethren just leaving for the foreign mission field, or some other distant sphere of service, were glad of the opportunity of a personal farewell, and of the tender, touching prayer, and tokens of practical sympathy, with which they were speeded on their way. Then there were magazine articles to be written or revised, Almanacks to be prepared, books to be read and reviewed, or sent to some of the brethren who helped in that department of *The Sword and the Trowel*; and, by the time the gong sounded for dinner, the Pastor was often heard to say, 'Well, we have got through a good morning's work, even if there is not much to show for it.'

The greater part of the afternoon was spent in the garden, if the weather was favourable. One of the few luxuries the master of Westwood enjoyed was to stroll down to the most secluded portion of the grounds of Westwood and to rest awhile in the summer-house, to which he gave the singularly appropriate title, 'Out of the world.' Here, with his wife, or some choice friend, the precious minutes quickly passed; and by-and-by, other visitors arrived for a cheery chat and a peep at the numerous interesting things that were to be seen. It is needless to give the names of the many who shared in the delights of those happy afternoons; most of Mr. Spurgeon's special ministerial and other friends and acquaintances were included amongst them. One visitor who was always welcome was the Earl of Shaftesbury. His life also was a very busy one, so that his visits were infrequent; but, every now and then, when he was more than usually depressed and troubled by the aspect of affairs, religiously and socially, he found it a relief to have a talk with his Baptist friend, who largely shared his views concerning the state of the Church in general, but who also saw some signs of better and brighter days which the venerable nobleman had not perceived.

God gave Elijah forty days' meat at one meal: do you, dear friends, ever get such meals as that? I do when I read certain books—not modern-thought books. Give me no such fare as that—a grain of meal to a gallon of water; but let me have one of the good solid Puritan volumes that are so little prized nowadays, and my soul can feed upon such blessed food as that, and be satisfied with it.—C.H.S., *in sermon preached at the Tabernacle, June* 24, 1883.

If you can read a tainted book that denies the inspiration of the Scriptures, and attacks the truth of God, and if you derive any profit from it, you must be a very different being from myself. I have to read such books, I must read them sometimes to know what is said by the enemies of the gospel, that I may defend the faith, and help the weaklings of the flock; but it is a sorry business. When those who are qualified to do so are reading these heretical works, if they are doing it really in the fear of God for the good of their fellow-men, they remind me of Sir James Simpson and the two other doctors when they discovered the medical and surgical value of chloroform. They sat at the table, and scarcely knew what was going to happen; but they took a dose each, risking their lives by so doing; and when they came back to consciousness, they had certainly made a great discovery.—C.H.S., *in sermon preached at the Tabernacle, October* 29, 1885.

20

In the Study at Westwood

No life of Spurgeon would be complete unless it contained information concerning the books he read and owned. All who have been
intimately acquainted with him, from his childhood, or in later
years, have testified to the omnivorous character of his reading.
While he was but a little lad, the boy and the books were insep-
arable. When he advanced from the position of scholar to that of
teacher, he gladly availed himself of the increased opportunities of
reading and learning everything that might be turned to good
account in his future career; and when he had become a follower of
Christ, and an earnest worker for his Lord, he spent all that he could
honestly afford in the purchase of the classical and theological books
which were likely to be of the greatest service to him.

At the time of his death he possessed at least 12,000 volumes.
The number would have been far larger if he had not given so
generously to the libraries of the Pastors' College and of many of
the ministers trained within its walls, and if he had not also, from
his abundant stores, so freely enriched other friends. His books
almost filled the shelves of two large rooms—the study and the
library, one smaller room—'the den', and the vestibule adjoining
the study. He knew the proper place and at least the principal contents of nearly every book in his possession; he could have fetched
almost any one of them in the dark, and if any had been taken away
by a dishonest visitor, he would speedily have missed them.
Probably, a great many of his precious treasures did become permanently lost to him through being lent, for all who borrowed from
him were not as particular in returning other people's property as
he himself was. Addressing his students, on one occasion, he said:

'I lately met with a statement by a clergyman which has very
much raised my opinion of human nature, for he declares that he
has a personal acquaintance with three gentlemen who have actually
returned borrowed umbrellas! I am sorry to say that he moves in a
more favoured circle than I do, for I have personal acquaintance
with several young men who have borrowed books, and never
returned them. The other day, a certain minister, who had lent me

five volumes, which I have used for two years or more, wrote to me a note to request the return of *three* of them. To his surprise, he had them back by the next parcels' delivery, and with them two others which he had forgotten. I had carefully kept a list of books borrowed, and, therefore, could make a complete return to the owner. I am sure he did not expect their prompt arrival, for he wrote me a letter of mingled astonishment and gratitude; and when I visit his study again, I feel sure I shall be welcome to another loan. You know the rhyme which has been written in many a man's book—

> *If thou art borrowed by a friend,*
> *Right welcome shall he be*
> *To read, to study, not to lend,*
> *But to return to me.*
> *Not that imparted knowledge doth*
> *Diminish learning's store;*
> *But books, I find, when once they're lent,*
> *Return to me no more.*

Sir Walter Scott used to say that his friends might be indifferent accountants, but he was sure they were good "book-keepers".'

If Spurgeon could return to his study, he would have no difficulty in finding his books, for they are still arranged according to the method he long ago adopted.[1] Beginning at the right-hand side of the cupboard in the centre of illustration no. 27 the volumes commence with Commentaries on Genesis, and continue in consecutive order, through the whole of the long side of the room, to the end of Revelation. Then follow Cyclopædias of anecdotes, illustrations, and emblems, with dictionaries and other works of reference indispensable to a literary man. These books fill up half the other end of the study. Then, on the further side of the doorway leading into 'the den' (see illustration no. 28), is a choicely-bound set of the Pastor's sermons. These formed part of the background of one of the latest and best of his photographs that was ever taken.

On the shelves above and below Spurgeon's volumes of sermons, is a large assortment of theological works, sufficiently numerous to overflow to the revolving bookcase, which also contains

---

[1] This volume was, of course, originally compiled before the sale of Westwood in 1905, at which time the library was purchased by William Jewell College, Missouri, where it remains today.

biographies and miscellaneous literature for general reading. At the opposite end of the room, on the left-hand side of the cupboard shown in illustration no. 27, are more theological works, somewhat less modern than those mentioned on the previous page.

Several thousands of the books that belonged to Spurgeon occupied the spacious shelves in the library, a view of which is shown in illustration no. 26. The volumes here preserved, like those in the study, are also arranged in sections. Beginning at the side nearest the windows, one whole bay is filled with works on natural history and the sciences; the next is devoted to records of missions, travels, and adventures; then follow biographies, which require almost the whole of the space in the two wide sets of shelves, the remainder being allotted to books on Bible lands. The shelves visible on the left-hand side of the picture (illustration no. 26) are filled with poetry and the hymnals used in the compilation of *Our Own Hymn Book*, with later additions, and some sermonic and other literature not usually needed in the study. Beyond the doorway, bound volumes of periodicals, both for juveniles and adults, and more general literature, with a large store of books of proverbs and anecdotes, need several sets of shelves; next follow historical and denominational works, a collection of topographical books; a great number of old folios, mostly the writings of Latin authors; and last, but certainly not least, more than a whole bay is required for the American and other reprints of Spurgeon's sermons and other works, and the translations of them into various foreign languages. He was never able to procure anything like a complete set of his writings as reproduced in other tongues, and the number of translations has been greatly increased since his home-going; they include Arabic, Armenian, Bengali, Bulgarian, Castilian (for the Argentine Republic), Chinese, Congo, Czech, Danish, Dutch, Esthonian, French, Gaelic, German, Hindi, Hungarian, Italian, Japanese, Kaffir, Karen, Lettish, Maori, Norwegian, Polish, Russian, Servian, Spanish, Swedish, Syriac, Tamil, Telugu, Urdu, Welsh, with sermons in Moon and Braille type for the blind, making, with the preacher's mother-tongue, nearly forty languages in which he continues, from the printed page, to proclaim the unsearchable riches of Christ. The text most commonly used concerning him is, 'He being dead yet speaketh.' Dr. Newman Hall, referring to Spurgeon, gave a new rendering to that passage: 'Then, as he yet speaketh, he is not dead.'

The foregoing account of the arrangement of Spurgeon's books is necessarily incomplete, and many hundreds of his highly-valued volumes may thus have escaped classification; but it gives a general idea of the books he owned, and loved, and used, and with which he was so well acquainted that he was prepared to discuss their contents with any visitor who called to see him.

On removing to Westwood, and fitting up with oak bookshelves two sides of the room used by the former occupants of the house as a drawing-room, Spurgeon found that the space at his disposal proved too large even for the thousands of books which had over-taxed the accommodation at Helensburgh House. He therefore purchased many works which he had long desired to possess, and added them to his previous store; and, as he had still to say, 'Yet there is room,' he hit upon an ingenious expedient for temporarily filling the empty shelves at the top of the library and study. He had a number of dummy volumes made by his bookbinder, and had some of them lettered to correspond with the sets of books already in his possession, such as *Carlyle's Works, Macaulay's Works, Alison's History of Europe, Hume's History of England, The Homilist,* etc. In other cases, the titles were reversed; as, for instance, *Job on Caryl,* made to stand not far from *Caryl on Job.* The lettering of some of the large sets of dummies was amusing. Anyone who handled the volumes entitled *Wretched Scandals, by the Talkers' Sisters,* would find that there was nothing in them! Similar sets bore the titles, *Mischief by Boys, Windows Ventilated by Stone, Gunpowder Magazine by Plumstead,* and *Padlock on the Understanding.* But it was upon the names of the single volumes that the Pastor exercised the greatest ingenuity. He often referred to the meaning of Mrs. Spurgeon's Christian name, Susannah, a lily, and associated it with Shushan, so it was not surprising that one of the titles he used was *Lilies of Shushan,* while the name of Mrs. Spurgeon's companion suggested *Thorn on Roses.* The Pastor's two secretaries were represented by the volumes entitled *Mysteries Opened by J. L. Keys,* and *The Character of William the Conqueror, by Harrald.* The tutors and students of the Pastors' College were represented by the following and other titles: *Joseph, Samuel, and Abraham, corrected by G. Rogers; Sublime and Beautiful, by D. Gracey; Goodly Pearls, by Marchant; Eastward Ho! by A. G. Brown; Cuff on the Head; Knell on Death; Carter on the Road; Cricket on the Green, by Batts; Over the Stream, by Bridge; Hook and I; Tydeman on Cleanliness; Hammer and Tongs, by Smith; Aches and Pains, by Feltham* (felt 'em); *Country Retreats, by Greenwood*; *Grindery in all its Branches, by Miller*; *Do it Again, by Dunnett* (done it); *Starling, Swift, Finch, and another Bird*; and *Flight on the Wings of a Dove*.

Among the amusing descriptions there might also be found *Hints on Honey Pots, by A.B.*; *Weaver's Meditations among the Looms*; *Gilpin on Riding Horses*; *Tick on Sheep*; *Skid on the Wheel*; *Cat on Hot Bricks*; *Pancakes on Shrove Tuesday*; *Lectures to my Servants, by a Shrew*; and *Sticking up for One's Self, by a Pole*.

Before very long, the number of books increased at such a rapid rate that, instead of dummies being required to fill vacant shelves, real and substantial volumes were standing or lying about, in various directions, because there was no proper place available for them. It was then decided that Spurgeon must have the use of the bookshelves in the vestibule between the hall and the study, which up to that time had been employed as the depôt and packing-room for the works distributed in connection with Mrs. Spurgeon's Book Fund. The nearness of this set of shelves to the study made it a very valuable annexe, and a room in another part of the house was adapted and fitted up for the use of the Manager of the Book Fund and her helpers.

Still later, a greater alteration was made, by which additional accommodation was provided for the ever-multiplying books. During Spurgeon's absence at Mentone, one winter, a new room was built, connecting the study with the small conservatory, where he liked to sit for a few minutes admiring the choice flowers, watching the fishes and grasses in the miniature aquarium, and reading or meditating upon the theme of some anticipated address or sermon. One result of the altered arrangements was that, in wet weather, the Pastor could have a continuous walk, under shelter, from the fernery at one side of the house to the greenhouses at the other end. By steadily tramping the whole distance, backwards and forwards, several times, a very fair amount of exercise could be obtained when it was not possible to be out of doors. It had also long been felt that Spurgeon needed another and more private study, into which he could retire for devotion and pulpit preparation, or for interviews with special visitors. This room was always called 'the den,' though it was a very different kind of place from Bunyan's apartment in the Bedford prison to which the immortal dreamer gave that name. In this favoured spot, the works of the Puritan divines were lovingly arranged by the one who always repudiated the title many times accorded to him—*Ultimus Puri-*

tanorum, the last of the Puritans—for he believed that he had helped to train hundreds of men who would continue the Puritanical succession after he was gone from their midst, and he also knew that there were, in other denominations and other lands, multitudes of believers in the truths which the Puritans taught, and for which many of them suffered even unto death.

In addition to the Puritans, 'the den' contained a large quantity of homiletical, exegetical, and proverbial literature, with a number of miscellaneous volumes for general reading. The new room was a great boon to the busy Pastor, and many a powerful sermon for the congregation at the Tabernacle, or weighty address for the students of the Pastors' College, or bright article for *The Sword and the Trowel*, first saw the light in the quiet seclusion of 'the den.'

Spurgeon never cared to buy a book simply because it was rare, unless it was one of the Puritans that he needed for his collection. He valued literary works for their usefulness, not simply for their market price; yet he possessed a great many volumes, bearing their authors' autograph inscriptions, which he highly prized; and, among them, some of Ruskin's were always accorded a prominent position as reminders of the early and cordial friendship which existed between him and the Pastor. Sir A. H. Layard, Dr. Livingstone, M. Paul B. Du Chaillu, Mr. C. W. M. van de Velde, Dr. W. M. Thomson, Dr. William Wright, Dr. Lansdell, Mr. John MacGregor ('Rob Roy'), and many other travellers were represented at Westwood by their works duly inscribed, or by letters from them fastened in their books. It was one of Spurgeon's few 'hobbies' to have the photographs and autographs of all authors, as far as he could, with portions of the manuscripts of their works, or other specimens of their handwriting, inserted in one or more of their volumes, thus materially increasing their value, at least in his estimation. Perhaps it was this fancy which made him so freely give his own signature to other collectors of autographs, even if they did not always enclose stamps with their applications; and the same reason may also have prompted him to write in the many hundreds of books that he gave to his friends, who now prize them all the more because of the tender and loving inscriptions with which he enhanced the intrinsic worth of his gifts.

One of his letters shows that, in his anxiety to secure the signature of a friend whose writings he valued, he unintentionally wrote a second time to the same individual:

'Nightingale Lane,
Clapham,
May 11.

Dear Sir,

I have to apologize for having troubled you twice about so small a matter as your autograph; but the fact is, I did not recognize Dr. David Brown, of *Duncan's Memoir* as the David Brown of the *Commentary*. Pray excuse me.

I am getting to fear and tremble about the Browns. You must know that the President and Vice-President of our Baptist Union are both Browns, and that the chairman of our London Association is also a Brown. Browns to the right of us, Browns to the left of us, etc. God bless them all!

Yours heartily,
C. H. SPURGEON.'

In reply to a letter from Spurgeon to Dr. Andrew A. Bonar, asking for his portrait and autograph to insert in his *Commentary on the Book of Leviticus*, the beloved author sent his photograph, and the following characteristic note:

'Dear Brother,

I cannot refuse what you are so kind as to ask. But if you had only waited a little while, it would have been really worth having—for "we shall be *like Him*" (1 John 3. 2). Meantime, the enclosed may hint to you that sometimes you should pray for me.

Yours, with all brotherly love,
ANDREW A. BONAR.'

The same writer's volume, *Christ and His Church in the Book of Psalms,* contains the inscription: 'This book was given to me by my dear friend, Mr. Bonar, and the corrections are made by his own hand.—C. H. SPURGEON.' Dr. Horatius Bonar's volume, *Earth's Morning; or, Thoughts on Genesis,* is thus commended: 'A deeply thoughtful and thought-creating book.'

In *The Book of Psalms, a New Translation, with Introductions and Notes, Explanatory and Critical,* by J. J. Stewart Perowne, Spurgeon wrote: 'For a modern book, this has become very rare. It is most accurate and valuable.' The volume also contains a letter from the author in which he said: 'I thank you heartily for your kind words about my book on the Psalms. I am the more sensible of your approbation, because you have yourself conferred so inestimable a

boon upon the Church by the publication of your *Treasury of David.*
There is no book like it as an aid to devout meditation on one of the
most precious portions of God's Word. I hope some day you will
visit Peterborough. It would be a pleasure to me to show you our
beautiful cathedral.'

The volume of *Expository Thoughts on the Gospels,* by the Bishop
of Liverpool (Dr. J. C. Ryle), contains his portrait, and a letter
which he wrote to Spurgeon, in 1875, when he was vicar of Strad-
broke, in which he said: 'You want no praise of man, and you know
its worthlessness. But I must tell you how much I like your *Lectures
to my Students.* I have rarely seen so many nails hit right on the head.
I should like to give a copy to every young clergyman in the Church
of England! I hope you are pretty well. I have had much illness in
the last four years, and feel nearer home than I ever felt before.'

Yet he has been spared to continue his faithful testimony for
nearly another quarter of a century; and only towards the close of
1899 has he felt compelled to intimate his approaching resignation
of his bishopric, while his younger friend, to whom he wrote so
heartily, has been 'at home' for nearly eight years!

Spurgeon desired to possess a specimen of the manuscript of Dr.
Charles Hodge, Professor in the Theological Seminary, Princeton,
New Jersey, U.S.A.; and, in reply to a note to that effect, addressed
to his son, Dr. A. A. Hodge, the latter wrote as follows:

'Princeton,
New Jersey,
July 1st, 1879

Rev. Charles H. Spurgeon,
    Dear Sir,
        I thank you very much for your kind note, relating to the
Outlines, received yesterday. Your many friends, on this side of the
ocean, have been anxious about your health, as we have received
irregular, and imperfect, and perhaps irresponsible reports of it
from time to time. I sincerely trust that it is re-established funda-
mentally and permanently. Yet I am sure that God has warned you, as
the trusted steward of His gifts, not to work so hard and continuously.

I send you, herewith, two of my father's papers, prepared for the
Conferences held by the Professors and students, every Sabbath
afternoon, in our Oratory. Nelson, of Edinburgh, has just published
a volume containing 249 of them. These I send you are originals in
my father's handwriting.

May the Father, and the Son, and the Spirit, bless you with *all* blessings in Christ Jesus *our* Lord!

Give my best respects to Mrs. Spurgeon.

Yours sincerely,
A. A. HODGE.'

Spurgeon's copy of Dr. A. A. Hodge's *Outlines of Theology* contains his autograph, and this entry in Mr. Spurgeon's handwriting: 'Autograph written in my study, Aug. 8, 1877.—C.H.S.'

In addition to the letters, manuscripts, photographs, and autographs of the authors, which Spurgeon preserved in his copies of their works, whenever he could obtain them, he also wrote his own name in many of the volumes, with an expression of his opinion of their contents. There are, perhaps, among his books, some hundreds of these inscriptions; many of them are autobiographical, and for that reason deserve a place in the present work. It is worthy of note that, while this chapter has been in course of preparation, the compilers have met with an interesting article by Mr. Andrew Lang, entitled 'Scrawls on Books,' which shows that he approved of the custom which the Pastor so extensively observed. Among other things, he wrote: 'The practice of scribbling on fly-leaves and margins has many enemies. I confess that I am not among these purists. I like to see these footprints on the sands of literature, left by dead generations, and to learn from them something about previous owners of books, if it be but their names. . . . We should all write our names, at least; no more of us may ever reach posterity. . . . As a rule, tidy and self-respecting people do not even write their names on their fly-leaves, still less do they scribble marginalia. Collectors love a clean book, but a book scrawled on may have other merits. Thackeray's countless caricatures add a delight to his old school-books; the comments of Scott are always to the purpose; but how few books once owned by great authors come into the general market! Where is Dr. Johnson's library, which must bear traces of his buttered toast? Sir Mark Sykes used to record the date and place of purchase, with the price—an excellent habit. These things are more personal than book-plates, which may be and are detached by collectors, and pasted into volumes. The selling value of a book may be lowered even by a written owner's name; but many a book, otherwise worthless, is redeemed by an interesting note. Even the uninteresting notes gradually acquire an antiquarian value, if contemporary with the author. They represent the mind of a dead age, and perhaps the common scribbler is not unaware of this; otherwise, he is indeed without excuse. For the great owners of the past, certainly, we regret that they were so sparing in marginalia.'

Spurgeon commenced the practice which Mr. Lang commends quite early in his ministry for the inscriptions in Dr. Gill's *Commentary* date back to 1852. In Martin Luther's *Commentary on the Epistle to the Galatians,* is written: 'This volume is one of my earliest friends; needs no letter of commendation.—C. H. SPURGEON, 1852.'

The following remarkable commendation is inserted on the fly-leaf of the first volume of *A Compleat History and Mystery of the Old and New Testament, logically discussed and theologically improved,* by Christopher Ness: 'Reader, Here is something worth all thy time, though thou read it all day long. Give eyes and heart a feast here. Here is goodly word-painting and rich heart-breathing.—C. H. SPURGEON.' The third volume is marked 'much valued'; and the fourth has this inscription:—'I reckon these four volumes to be worth their weight in gold. They may contain some eccentric conceits, but these are as the dust upon a palace. I doubt not that Matthew Henry borrowed very extensively from Ness, and certainly showed his wisdom in so doing. If these volumes shall become the property of another, I charge him either to read them carefully and prayerfully, or else to give or lend them to some godly person who can appreciate them. Such a treasure should be out at interest.— C. H. SPURGEON. Nov., '58.'

In 1857, Spurgeon wrote in Matthew Poole's *Annotations*: 'Poole is a most excellent expositor.' Dr. John Mayer's *Commentarie upon the New Testament* bears the inscription: 'Mayer is one of my greatest favourites.—C. H. SPURGEON, 1859.' The same author's volume on the Historical Books is described as 'excellent, full of research, and rare learning.'

Two volumes of Dr. Adam Clarke's *Commentary* contain lengthy but not commendatory notes. In volume 1, Spurgeon wrote, just below the portrait of the commentator: 'who discovered that an *ape,* and not a serpent, deceived Adam.' At the top of the title-page is this warning: 'Take heed, reader! This is dangerous ground for those who are not grounded and settled.' Volume 6 has this inscription: 'Adam Clarke is as immortal as his monkey, and other errors; see notes on Genesis. He is always to be read with caution, for his sentiments are, in my judgment, most unscriptural.—C. H. SPURGEON.' On the title-page, after the words, 'A Commentary and

Critical Notes,' there is added: 'Adapted to blind the eye, and prevent the truth in Jesus from shining upon the soul, by Adam Clarke—Arminian twister of the Word.'

By way of contrast, it may be mentioned that Dr. Gill's *Exposition of Solomon's Song* contains Spurgeon's autograph, and the following note: 'This priceless work of my learned predecessor has always been helpful to me.' In different volumes of John Trapp's *Annotations upon the Old and New Testaments*, Spurgeon wrote: 'Prized for its quaintness'; 'A great favourite'; 'Trapp is ever my favourite, 1873.' A large folio edition of Ralph Erskine's Works has two inscriptions: 'The Rev. Joseph Irons, the gift of his father'; and underneath, 'Valued all the more by me as having been the property of Joseph Irons.—C. H. SPURGEON.' Blomfield's *Greek Testament, with English Notes,* is inscribed: 'I value Blomfield exceedingly: I can always make more out of him than out of Alford.— C. H. SPURGEON, Sep., 1872.'

The copy of Cruden's *Concordance*, which Spurgeon always used, contains upon its fly-leaf the following testimony:

'For these ten years this has been the book at my left hand when the Word of God has been at my right. What a precious assistant! Notes I had written have been destroyed by the binder to whom I had to send this volume because it was worn all asunder. Blessed be the Lord who has spared me to search His Word with some apprehension of its sweetness these twenty years. C.H.S. Jan. 1869. (This half-crazy Cruden did better service to the Church than half the D.D.s and L.L.D.s of all time. Mar. 1872).'

Taking, almost at random, the works of various authors who wrote on separate Books of the Bible, the following inscriptions will serve as specimens of the comments, favourable and otherwise, inserted in them:

In Dr. James Morison's *Practical Commentary on the Gospel according to Matthew*, Spurgeon wrote: 'Volume greatly valued for its scholarship. Difficult to find much Morisonianism here.' *The Genius of the Gospel*, by Dr. David Thomas, contains this note: 'A suggestive volume, but rather bombastic.' On the title-page of the same writer's work, *The Book of Psalms Exegetically and Practically Considered,* opposite the author's name—David Thomas—Spurgeon added: 'Not David, nor Thomas. David scrabbling, Thomas doubting.' The same writer's *Homiletic Commentary on the Acts of the Apostles* contains his photograph, autograph, and the following remarks: 'Many of the homiletic outlines strike me as "much ado about nothing"; still, if a man should read this work, and get no help from it, it would be his own fault.—C. H. SPURGEON, 1874.'

Three books on the Epistle to the Romans naturally have references to the writers' doctrinal views. Of Dr. F. A. Philippi, Spurgeon wrote: 'Frequently goes out of his way to have a fling at what he thinks to be Calvinism.' Rev. William Tyson's *Expository Lectures* are said to be 'Excellent for an Arminian. I find him sweetly Evangelical in many places.' Dr. David Ritchie's *Lectures, Explanatory and Practical*, are described as 'Unsound in many respects. Of the *Moderate* School, I should judge.'

James Fergusson's *Brief Exposition of the Epistles of Paul* contains the autograph and date, C. H. SPURGEON, 1878; and this note: 'A volume of great worth. Few books have been more frequently consulted by me.—C.H.S.' John Barlow on II *Timothy* 1 *and* 2 is thus commended: 'Though apparently unattractive, this book will richly repay a careful reader.—C. H. SPURGEON.' Nicholas Byfield, on I *Peter* 1–3, is wittily criticised: 'Byfield is discursive, and takes in every by-field which he had better have passed by. Yet, in his Preface, he calls this an abridgment! I am glad it was not my lot to hear him.—C. H. SPURGEON.' Nathanael Hardy on *The First Epistle of John*, is said to be 'a rare divine, this Hardy; an Episcopalian Puritan.'

In Frederick Denison Maurice's *Prophets and Kings of the Old Testament*, Spurgeon wrote: 'Herein we find a great deal of wild doctrine, but yet there is thought of no mean order. We can wash out the gold.' The work of a writer of quite another stamp—*Notes on the Book of Genesis,* by C.H.M.,—is thus described: 'Good in its line, but too cramped. There is also error concealed here and there.' Lange's *Genesis* is said to be 'one of the best of the series'; but his *Isaiah* is characterized as 'very poor.' Dr. Pusey on *The Minor Prophets* bears the unique distinction of being highly commended in a single word: 'Invaluable.—C. H. SPURGEON, 1878.' *Sermons on Judges,* by Richard Rogers, contains this note: 'C. H. Spurgeon much prizes this book.—1882.'

Among other brief but notable notes are the following:

Durham's *Christ Crucified*: 'Much prized.'

Practical Reflections on Every Verse of the Holy Gospels, by a clergyman: 'Good, simple, marred.'

Poetical Works of George Herbert: 'Much valued by C. H. Spurgeon.'

Darling's *Cyclopædia Bibliographica*: 'An invaluable tool.'

Joseph Taylor's volume, *Naturales Curiosæ: Curiosities in Natural*

History, contains the warning, 'Believe not too readily.—C. H. SPURGEON.'

In *Whitefield's Sermons* is the autograph, with the inscription following:—'C. H. Spurgeon, who admires Whitefield as chief of preachers.'

Spurgeon was a very quick reader, but the rapidity of his glance at the page did not interfere with the completeness of his acquaintance with its contents. He could read from cover to cover of a large octavo or folio volume in the course of a very short space of time, and he would thus become perfectly familiar with all that it contained. Dr. William Wright, the late Editorial Superintendent of the British and Foreign Bible Society, gave a remarkable instance of this combination of speed and accuracy, as well as a notable testimony to Spurgeon's literary ability, in the reminiscences which he wrote for *The British Weekly* in February, 1892. The following paragraphs from that article provide a fitting conclusion to one view of Spurgeon in his study:

'Mr. Spurgeon visited Belfast in 1858. I was then preparing to enter College, with a hankering after the Indian Civil Service. Mr. Spurgeon preached in Dr. Cooke's church. He singled me out,—as I thought,—and spoke to me as if no one else was present. There was no thrumming of theology, and no pious posing; but a clear, direct, hot, living, personal appeal that dare not be resisted. . . . Fifteen years later, I went to the Tabernacle, on my way home from Damascus. The same straightforward Englishman was preaching the same straightforward gospel in all its fulness, and without any apology for its severity. After the service, I walked into the vestry without being announced. He had not seen me for ten years, but he recognized me in the crowd without a moment's hesitation. He ran over a list of the books on Syria and Palestine, stating the merits of each, and ended by saying, "I suppose Thomson's *The Land and the Book* is still the best on the manners and customs." He had the whole literature of the Holy Land at his finger-ends.

When I came to be Mr. Spurgeon's near neighbour, I found that his knowledge of all literature was wonderful. His power of reading was perhaps never equalled. He would sit down to five or six large books, and master them at one sitting. He sat with his left hand flat on the page at the left side of the book, and pushing his right hand up the page on the right side until the page projected a little, he turned it over with his finger, and proceeded to the next page. He took in the contents almost at a glance, reading by sentences as others read by words, and his memory never failed him as to what he read. He made a point of reading half-a-dozen of the hardest books every week, as he wished to rub his mind up against the strongest minds; and there was no skipping. I several times had an opportunity of testing the thoroughness of his reading, and I never found him at fault.

Drummond's *Natural Law in the Spiritual World* reached him and me about the same time. I called on Mr. Spurgeon when he was fresh from a perusal of the book. It was then unknown to fame, and he had read it with five or six other books. At tea, we were speaking of the freshness of the illustrations, and the peculiarity of the doctrines taught, when a third party challenged Mr. Spurgeon's recollection of certain points. Mr. Spurgeon thereupon quoted a whole page to show that Drummond spoke of the natural and spiritual laws being identical, and another important page to show how the book erred by defect. On my return home, I looked over the passages quoted, and I believe he scarcely missed a word in the repetition. His power of swift and effective reading was one of the greatest of his many talents. . . .

I was at first surprised to find Mr. Spurgeon consulting both the Hebrew and Greek texts. "They say," said he, "that I am ignorant and unlearned. Well, let them say it; and in everything, by my ignorance, and by my knowledge, let God be glorified."

His exegesis was seldom wrong. He spared no pains to be sure of the exact meaning of his text. On one occasion, he was going to preach on the subject of the olive tree; and he sent his secretary to the keeper of the Natural History Department of the British Museum, with a series of questions regarding the peculiarities of the tree. Mr. Carruthers, the keeper, was so much interested in the enquiry that he wrote out several pages for Mr. Spurgeon; but when the sermon came to be preached, the information had been passed through the crucible of Mr. Spurgeon's mind, and came forth in a few Bunyanesque sentences. . . . Sometimes, when I left him on Saturday evening, he did not know either of his texts for Sunday. But he had a well-stored mind; and when he saw his lines of thought, a few catchwords on a half-sheet of notepaper sufficed. Before we parted, he used to offer up a short prayer which was an inspiration to both of us.

Mr. Spurgeon had a marvellous combination of gifts which contributed to his greatness. A voice that you heard with pleasure,

and could not help hearing. A mind that absorbed all knowledge—
whether from books or nature—that came within its range. An eye
that took in a wide angle, and saw everything within view. A
memory that he treated with confidence, and that never disappointed him. A great heart, on fire with the love of God and the
love of souls. And then he showed a practical common sense in
doing things, both sacred and secular, and a singleness of aim, joined
with transparent honesty, that ensured the confidence of all who
knew him. You could not help loving him if you came within his
spell.'

On several occasions, Spurgeon found himself in the company of
a number of High Church clergymen, and they were always greatly
surprised to find that the Baptist minister was far more familiar
with the works on their side of the controversy than they themselves were. They also discovered that, while he spoke heartily in
commendation of all that appeared to him to be Scriptural in the
writings of Dr. Pusey, Dr. Neale, Dr. Littledale, Isaac Williams,
and other divines of their school of thought, he was able to give
good reasons for not accepting their sacramentarian and sacerdotal
theories. The same characteristic is very manifest in his remarks
upon the Ritualistic works referred to in his *Commenting and Commentaries*.

Other people beside theologians often noticed the extensive and
varied knowledge that Spurgeon possessed. On one of his visits to
Mentone, he was in company with an eminent medical man, and,
after a while, the conversation drifted round to anatomy, physio-
logy, various diseases to which flesh is heir, and the different modes
of treatment adopted for their removal. The doctor was quite
astonished at the completeness of his companion's acquaintance
with every part of the subject, and he afterwards said: 'Mr. Spurgeon is one of the most remarkable men I ever met. He seems to
know as much about the human body as any medical man might
have done; he would have made a splendid physician.'

Among the Pastor's hearers at the Tabernacle, or in various
seaport towns, many sailors have often been found, listening with
intense eagerness; and the men of the sea have often testified that
they have never known him make a mistake in his nautical allusions; and James Neil, who spent twenty years in Palestine, has
borne similar witness to the accuracy of Spurgeon's descriptions of
Biblical manners and customs, thereby confirming the verdict by
Dr. Wright already mentioned.

C. H. Spurgeon: The Full Harvest

Many of 'John Ploughman's' readers have wondered that he could tell them so much about how 'to plough and sow, and reap and mow.' Part of that familiarity with farming affairs, no doubt, dated back to his early visits to Stambourne, and his walks among the furrows by the side of the godly ploughman, Will Richardson; and part must be attributed to his constant preaching in different parts of the kingdom, and to the opportunities thus afforded of obtaining further information concerning agricultural pursuits; but extensive reading also added to the effectiveness of his references to such matters. Among the books of his library were two which bore traces of having been carefully examined and used by him: *A System of Sheep-grazing and Management, as Practised in Romney Marsh*, By Daniel Price, and *Sheep, their Breeds, Management, and Diseases*, by William Youatt.[1] With Spurgeon everything was made subservient to the one great object he had before him, the glory of God in the salvation of sinners and the extension of the Redeemer's Kingdom.

[1] Further information on the breadth of Spurgeon's reading will be found in *Personal Reminiscences of Charles Haddon Spurgeon*, William Williams, 1895.

The influence of Spurgeon was not of those that have passed or can pass away like a dream. Even yet, people will explain his popularity by his voice, his humour, by his oratory, and the like. But the continued life and power of his printed sermons show that his oratory, noble as it was, was not the first thing. Our firm belief is that these sermons will continue to be studied with growing interest and wonder; that they will ultimately be accepted as incomparably the greatest contribution to the literature of experimental Christianity that has been made in this century, and that their message will go on transforming and quickening lives after all other sermons of the period are forgotten.—W. ROBERTSON NICOLL, *printed on back of Sermon* 2572 (1898).

The actual number of copies of the sermons issued from the beginning is not known. So vast is it that all count has been lost, but it is estimated that about a hundred and fifty millions have been disposed of in this form. Add to these the immense number issued abroad in various languages, and those that have been printed in newspapers, and probably more than three hundred millions of Spurgeon's sermons have gone out on their evangelistic mission. The human mind quite fails to grasp what these numbers mean. Take the regular weekly sermons only. If all that have been issued were to be placed side by side they would stretch a distance of 13,889 miles, or more than half-way round the globe. If the pages were torn out and placed end to end they would reach nearly from the earth to the moon. And figures of this kind might be multiplied without limit. There has never been anything like it in the history of printing. The Scriptures have circulated enormously, but nothing to compare with Spurgeon's sermons, and it is pretty safe to say there never will be another publication that can be called a rival.—CHARLES RAY.

21

The Published Sermons and World-Wide Blessing

For twenty years Messrs. Passmore and Alabaster have issued one of my sermons weekly without cessation, indeed, they have done more, for the number published has been five for every month of the twenty years, and has now reached 1,200.[1] In the *Baptist Messenger* a sermon has been inserted every month during the same time, making 240 more; 34 in addition have appeared in three volumes of the *Pulpit Library*, and 16 in *Types and Emblems*. I do not feel that I may allow the twenty years to close without a few words of thanksgiving. The fear of being thought egotistical does not so much affect me as the graver danger of being ungratefully silent. I am inexpressibly thankful to the God of infinite love, and if I did not give my thanks expression the boards of my pulpit might well cry out against me. Life has been spared, strength has been continued, and power to interest the people has been afforded, together with higher and more spiritual blessings, whose preciousness and number must of necessity move the heart of any man who is the recipient of them, if he be not utterly graceless. 'The Lord has done great things for us, whereof we are glad.'

The first seven volumes of *The New Park Street Pulpit* were printed in small type, and the sermons formed only eight pages, but the abolition of the paper duty enabled the publishers to give a more readable type and twelve pages of matter. This has been better in every way, and marks an epoch in the history of the sermons, for their name was at about the same period changed from *The New Park Street* to *The Metropolitan Tabernacle Pulpit*, and their sale was largely increased.

Several sermons in the series have attained a remarkable circulation, but probably the principal one is that upon Baptismal Regeneration. It was delivered with the full expectation that the sale

[1] These words were originally written by Spurgeon in an editorial for the January 1875 issue of *The Sword and the Trowel*. Some of his paragraphs have already been printed in *The Early Years*, chapter 28, but they are repeated here where chronologically they belong.

of the sermons would receive very serious injury; in fact, I mentioned to one of the publishers that I was about to destroy it at a single blow, but that the blow must be struck, cost what it might, for the burden of the Lord lay heavy upon me, and I must deliver my soul. I deliberately counted the cost, and reckoned upon the loss of many an ardent friend and helper, and I expected the assaults of clever and angry foes. I was not mistaken in other respects, but in the matter of the sermons I was altogether out of my reckoning, for they increased greatly in sale at once. That fact was not in any degree to me a test of the right or wrong of my action; I should have felt as well content in heart as I am now as to the rightness of my course had the publication ceased in consequence; but still it was satisfactory to find that though speaking out might lose a man some friends it secured him many others, and if it overturned his influence in one direction it would be compensated elsewhere. No truth is more sure than this, that the path of duty is to be followed thoroughly if peace of mind is to be enjoyed. Results are not to be looked at, we are to keep our conscience clear, come what may, and all considerations of influence and public estimation are to be light as feathers in the scale. In minor matters as well as more important concerns I have spoken my mind fearlessly, and brought down objurgations and anathemas innumerable, but I in nowise regret it, and shall not swerve from the use of outspoken speech in the future any more than in the past. I would scorn to retain a single adherent by such silence as would leave him under misapprehension. After all, men love plain speech.

It would not be seemly for me to tell of the scores of persons who have informed me of their being led to faith in Jesus by single sermons which appear in the twenty volumes, but there are discourses among them of which I may say, without exaggeration, that the Holy Spirit blessed them to the conversion of hundreds; and long after their delivery fresh instances of their usefulness come to light, and are still being brought under our notice. Seldom does a day pass, and certainly never a week, for some years past, without letters from all sorts of places, even at the utmost ends of the earth, declaring the salvation of souls by the means of one or other of the sermons. The price is so small that the sermons are readily procured, and in wonderful condescension the Lord sends the Holy Spirit to work through them. To God be all the glory.

Many singular things have happened in connection with their publication, but the most of them have escaped my memory; the following, however, I may mention. One brother, whose name I must not mention, purchased and gave away no less than 250,000 copies. He had volumes bound in the best style, and presented to every crowned head in Europe. He gave copies containing twelve sermons to all the students of the universities, and to all the members of the two houses of parliament, and he even commenced the work of distributing volumes to the principal householders in the towns of Ireland. May the good results of his laborious seed-sowing be seen many days hence; the self-denial with which this brother saved the expense from a very limited income, and worked personally in the distribution, was beyond all praise; but praise was evaded and observation dreaded by him; the work was done without his left hand knowing what his right hand did.

In the first days of our publishing a city merchant advertised them in all sorts of papers, offering to supply them from his own office. He thus sold large quantities to persons who might otherwise never have heard of them. He was not a Baptist, but held the views of the Society of Friends. It was very long before I knew who he was, and I trust he will pardon me for here mentioning a deed for which I shall ever feel grateful to him.

By my permission, the sermons were printed *as advertisements* in several of the Australian papers: one gentleman spending week by week a sum which we scarcely dare to mention, lest it should not be believed. By this means they were read far away in the bush, and never were results more manifest, for numbers of letters were received in answer to the enquiry as to whether the advertisements should be continued, all bearing testimony to the good accomplished by their being inserted in the newspapers. A selection of these letters was sent to me, and made my heart leap for joy, for they detailed conversions marvellous indeed. Besides these, many epistles come to us of like character, showing that the rough dwellers in the wilds were glad to find in their secular paper the best of all news, the story of pardon bought with blood.

In America, the sale of the edition published there was extremely large, and I believe that it still continues, but dozens of religious papers appropriate the sermons bodily, and therefore it is quite impossible to tell where they go, or rather where they do not go. Of translations the Dutch have been most plentiful, making large volumes. An edition of two volumes of selected sermons has been circulated in the colony of the Cape of Good Hope among the Dutch settlers of that region. In German there are three noble volumes, besides many smaller ones. German publishers, with the exception of Mr. Oncken, of Hamburg, seldom have the courtesy to send the author a copy, and I have picked up in divers places sermons bearing date from Baden, Basel, Carlsruhe, Ludwigsburg, and so on. How many, therefore, may have been sold in Germany I am unable to compute. In French several neat volumes have appeared. In Welsh and Italian one volume each. In Sweden a handsome edition in four volumes has been largely circulated, and the translator informed me of the conversion of some of noble and even royal birth through their perusal. Besides these there are single sermons in Spanish, Gaelic, Danish, Russ, Maori, Telugu, and some other tongues, and permission has been sought and gladly given for the production of a volume in the language of Hungary.[1] For all these opportunities of speaking to the different races of mankind, I cannot but be thankful to God, neither can I refrain from asking the prayers of God's people that the gospel thus widely scattered may not be in vain.

Brethren in the ministry will best be able to judge the mental wear and tear involved in printing one sermon a week, and they will best sympathise in the overflowing gratitude which reviews twenty years of sermons, and magnifies the God of grace for help so long continued. The quarry of Holy Scripture is inexhaustible, I seem hardly to have begun to work in it; but the selection of the next block, and the consideration as to how to work it into form, are matters not so easy as some think. Those who count preaching and its needful preparations to be slight matters have never occupied a pulpit continuously month after month, or they would know better. Chief of all is the responsibility which the preaching of the Word involves; I do not wish to feel this less heavily, rather would I fain feel it more, but it enters largely into the account of a minister's life-work, and tells upon him more than any other part of his mission. Let those preach lightly who dare do so, to me it is the burden of the Lord—joyfully carried as grace is given, but still a burden which at times crushes my whole manhood into the dust of humiliation, and occasionally, when ill-health unites with the mental strain, into depression and anguish of heart.

[1] At a later date there was an increase in the number of his sermons translated into these and other foreign languages. For example, a wealthy Russian, who had read some of the sermons obtained the permission of the censor to publish Russian translations and a million copies were at once prepared. They were approved and licensed by the heads of the Orthodox Church and having been marked on the front cover with the official stamp, to certify that they might be read and circulated by faithful members of the Church, were distributed very widely over the Czar's dominions.

However, let no man mistake me. I would sooner have my work to do than any other under the sun. Preaching Jesus Christ is sweet work, joyful work, heavenly work. Whitefield used to call his pulpit his throne, and those who know the bliss of forgetting everything besides the glorious, all-absorbing topic of Christ crucified, will bear witness that the term was aptly used. It is a bath in the waters of Paradise to preach with the Holy Ghost sent down from heaven. Scarcely is it possible for a man, this side the grave, to be nearer heaven than is a preacher when his Master's presence bears him right away from every care and thought, save the one business in hand, and that the greatest that ever occupied a creature's mind and heart. No tongue can tell the amount of happiness which I have enjoyed in delivering these twenty years of sermons, and so, gentle reader, forgive me if I have wearied you with this grateful record, for I could not refrain from inviting others to aid me in praising my gracious Master. 'Bless the Lord, O my soul, and all that is within me bless his holy name.'

*

Five and a half years after the preceding words were written Spurgeon made the following interesting comment on the extent of the circulation of the sermons. The occasion of this address was the laying of the memorial-stones of four houses for an Orphanage for girls in June, 1880. The day was also his forty-sixth birthday and from gifts received, Spurgeon, with the aid of his publishers, met the building cost of one house which was named after the Sermons:

'It is Sermon House, and is intended specially to commemorate the goodness of God in connection with the sermons; and right it is that there should be a house for that, because the College, the Orphanage, and all our works owe a great deal to the sermons. I have a little church of some 5,500 members over at Newington Butts; but I have a larger church of, I dare say, 56,000 members all over England, Scotland and Ireland, who are always up to the mark if any good work has to be done. . . . Among my birthday gifts of this land there are some coming from distant lands. The people who send them say I am their pastor. They are far away from sermon-makers, and so they read one of mine every Sunday, and think of me as their minister, though I hope that those who read them will never think them to be half so good as listening to those from the lips of a living preacher. . . . This house is to be a record to all time of our thankfulness to God that the sermons have continued to be printed week by week for twenty-five and a half years, and we have now reached the number in regular order of 1,542. That is a considerable number of sermons to be printed week by week, and there seems to be as much good in them for the souls of God's servants now as twenty-five years ago, for which I devoutly bless God. For many a time, when I go forth to look for food for the souls of my people, it is with an earnest cry to heaven, and a consciousness that if I am not helped I have nothing laid up in store, I use up the manna every day, and have none to breed worms. I keep on emptying the barrel, but it fills again.'

*

A great deal could be written on the results arising from the circulation of Spurgeon's Sermons; in the remainder of this chapter an account of the world-wide good that was done will be confined to some representative instances. Occasionally Spurgeon himself related from the pulpit examples of God's blessing coming to men through this means. Referring to one such case, which illustrated the power of faithful prayer, he said:

'At the close of one of our services, a poor woman, accompanied by two of her neighbours, came to my vestry in deep distress. Her husband had fled the country; and, in her sorrow, she had gone to the house of God and something I said in the sermon made her think that I was personally familiar with her case. Of course, I had really known nothing about her; I had made use of a general illustration which just fitted her particular case. She told me her story, and a very sad one it was. I said, "There is nothing that we can do but kneel down, and cry to the Lord for the immediate conversion of your husband." We knelt down, and I prayed that the Lord would touch the heart of the deserter, convert his soul, and bring him back to his home. When we rose from our knees, I said to the poor woman, "Do not fret about the matter. I feel sure your husband will come home; and that he will yet become connected with our church."

She went away, and I forgot all about her. Some months afterwards, she re-appeared, with her neighbours, and a man, whom she introduced to me as her husband. He had indeed come back, and he had returned a converted man. On making enquiry, and comparing notes, we found that, the very day on which we had prayed for his conversion, he, being at that time on board a ship far away on the sea, stumbled most unexpectedly upon a stray copy of one of my sermons. He read it; the truth went to his heart; he repented, and sought the Lord; and, as soon as possible, he came back to his wife and to his daily calling. He was admitted as a member at the Tabernacle, and his wife, who up to that time had not joined the church, was also received into fellowship with us.

That woman does not doubt the power of prayer. All the infidels in the world could not shake her conviction that there is a God that hears and answers the supplications of His people. I should be the most irrational creature in the world if, with a life every day of which is full of experiences so remarkable, I entertained the slightest doubt on the subject. I do not regard it as miraculous; it is part and parcel of the established order of the universe that the shadow of a coming event should fall in advance upon some believing soul in the shape of prayer for its realization. The prayer of faith is a Divine decree commencing its operation.'

Among the many clergy and ministers of religion whose lives were changed by the Sermons was one ritualistic 'priest' whose story Spurgeon thus narrates:

'He told me that he owed everything to me, because I had been the means of leading him to Jesus. He said he was "only a humble vicar of the Church of England," so I asked what his line of teaching had formerly been. "Very high," he replied. "But," I asked, "did you pretend to forgive people's sins?" "Yes," he answered. "Then," I enquired, "how did you get rid of the idea that you were a priest?" "Well," he said, "I sincerely believed myself to be a priest until I read one of your sermons. That convinced me of my own state as a sinner, and the priesthood oozed out of me directly. Now I am trusting the Lord Jesus Christ for salvation, and I point my congregation to Him alone." '

More often news of good done by the Sermons came through letters. The gentleman in Australia referred to earlier who at one period had the sermons printed as advertisements in papers received no less than some four hundred letters from people to whom they had been an immense benefit. One man, from an outlying district in Victoria, wrote:

'Sir,
    Having seen an advertisement lately, at the head of one of the sermons published weekly in *The Australasian*, asking for an expres-

sion of opinion as to their usefulness, I venture respectfully to offer the following plain and brief statement in reply.

I have been, for some five years or more, one of those unfortunates who are commonly called "swagmen." Travelling about, a few months since, looking for employment, I came to a public-house, by the roadside, into which I went for a drink, and an hour's rest, as I was very tired. A newspaper was lying on the counter, containing Mr. Spurgeon's sermon on the text, "Turn O backsliding children, saith the Lord; for I am married unto you." I read it through, with increasing interest as I went along; and it exactly met my case. It aroused me to a sense of my utterly lost condition as a sinner of the deepest dye, and, at the same time, so encouraged me to seek for mercy and peace at the foot of the cross that I could not resist doing so; and I humbly hope and believe that I did not seek in vain.

I left that public-house resolved never to enter one again unless absolutely compelled by circumstances to do so. Since then, I have enjoyed a peace to which I had been long a stranger. I now make God's Word my daily study, and attend Divine service whenever I can. Although nominally a Church of England man, previous to reading the sermon alluded to, I had only been once to church since my arrival in the Colony, now nearly seven years ago.

To my personal knowledge, these sermons are extensively read in the country districts; and, for my own part, I look to the arrival of the weekly paper—which my employer always lends me,—as the messenger of joy and comfort to myself; and I pray that it may prove to be the same to hundreds of others also. I would just, in conclusion, ask you to offer the expression of my humble and heartfelt thanks to the friend who pays for the advertisements of Mr. Spurgeon's sermons.

I am, sir,
Your obedient servant,

————.,

An Australian minister relates another striking case of conversion through the Sermons:

'I was preaching in the Baptist Chapel, Aberdeen Street, Geelong, a few years ago, when, at the close of an evening service, an elderly man came to the platform to bid me "good-night." As he was a stranger, I asked him where he came from, and how long he had known the Lord; he then told me the story of his conversion, and the strange way by which he was led to the Saviour. About five years before, while keeping sheep some miles beyond Ballarat, he *picked up a sheet of a weekly newspaper, which the wind had blown over the plains.* He glanced at a few sentences, and these drew him on to read more, and then he found he was eagerly perusing a sermon by Mr. C. H. Spurgeon. "If I had known it was a sermon," he said, "before I had begun to read it, I should have tossed it away;" but having commenced the discourse, he wanted to see how it finished. It set him thinking; he carefully preserved it, reading it over and over again in deep concern, until finally it became the means of leading him to the cross. For many years he had not entered a place of worship, and he was utterly careless about his soul till this paper was blown to his feet. Now, when he has the opportunity, he always attends some Baptist service; but this is a rare pleasure, owing to his lonely life and employment in the bush. He does, however, get the weekly sermons, which cheer and comfort him with spiritual nourishment.'

A no less remarkable instance of blessing upon one of the sermons published in the papers was once reported to Spurgeon. A parcel, sent from Australia, to the wife of a publican in England, was wrapped up in a newspaper containing one of the discourses delivered in the Metropolitan Tabernacle. The woman read it, and so was led to trust in the Lord Jesus Christ as her Saviour. Surely, that was another proof of the truth of Cowper's lines:

> *God moves in a mysterious way,*
> *His wonders to perform.*

Greatly as the Sermons were thus used in leading sinners to the Saviour it appears they were almost equally blessed in reclaiming backsliders, and in comforting and cheering those who have been in mental or spiritual distress. From Victoria, a lady wrote to Spurgeon the following grateful letter:

'My Dear Sir,
    I have often felt inclined to write to you. Twelve years ago, I lost a darling boy; everything seemed dark, and nothing brought me any comfort. The Word of God, which had been my stay through many previous trials, was all darkness to me. A friend brought me one of your sermons, and asked me to allow her to read it. At first, I refused; but, at last, I consented. I forget the title,

but it was to the effect that everything is ordered by God, and that there is no such thing as chance. I felt, all the time my friend was reading, almost afraid even to breathe; I could only say, "Go on, go on." When she had finished it, I leapt from my couch, and said, "All is right; thank God, my dark mind is all light again!" I have had similar sorrows since, and many other trials; but I could, from my heart, say to the Lord, "Thy will be done; it is all right." At that time, my husband ordered your sermons monthly, and we still continue to have them. Every Sunday evening, we read one of them aloud, for all to hear, and afterwards I send them into the bush.

'My dear sir, go on and preach what you feel; it has often been a great comfort to us that you seemed to feel just as we felt.'

Spurgeon's sermons were also read in New Zealand at an early date. In November, 1861, the church-book of the Metropolitan Tabernacle, recorded that the Sermons were being read regularly by a small group in Auckland, New Zealand, and that God had been pleased to own this instrumentality in the conversion of eleven persons—four natives and seven Europeans. Five thousand copies of one sermon, 'None but Jesus', had been distributed amongst the natives in their own language and an effort was being made to build a Baptist Chapel in the town. The effort succeeded and twenty years later, in 1881, Spurgeon's twin son, Thomas, became the pastor of this growing congregation!

Outside the British Isles the largest circulation of Spurgeon's Sermons was undoubtedly in North America. This was underlined in an article by Dr. Stanford Holme in the American edition of *The Christian Herald*, in January, 1879, along with some comment on the sources of the preacher's literary and spiritual power. Dr. Holme wrote:

'It is a fact worthy of especial notice that the sermons of Mr. Spurgeon have had a circulation in this country entirely without precedent. Of the American edition of his sermons, there have been sold not less than 500,000 volumes. And when, to this vast number, we add the almost innumerable republications of single sermons in the transient periodicals of the day, it is safe to say that no other preacher has had so extensive a hearing in America as Charles H. Spurgeon.

Many of the causes of the wonderful popularity of this distinguished preacher are not difficult to discover. In freshness and vigour of thought, in simplicity and purity of language, in grasp of gospel truth, and in tact and force in its presentation, he is perhaps without a peer in the pulpit.

When, in early life, Mr. Spurgeon commenced his ministrations in the New Park Street Chapel, in London, he quickly filled the old house to overflowing. Soon, he attracted the attention of all England. But he was regarded by many as a brilliant meteor that would soon fade away. Yet Mr. Spurgeon is, to-day, a vastly more efficient and even a more brilliant preacher than he was twenty years ago. He continues to grow in brilliancy as well as in efficiency year by year. No one can yet point to the slightest indication of exhaustion in either his faculties or his resources.

This, doubtless, is attributable, in a measure, to his industry and well-directed application, as well as to natural ability and great personal piety. But Mr. Spurgeon's peculiar views of the Word of God, and his manner of preparation for the pulpit, also tend in no small degree to secure *the inexhaustible variety* which so strikingly characterizes his sermons. It is not his manner to spin his web out of himself. The resources from which he draws are not measured by the strength and the store of his own faculties, but rather by the infinite fulness of the Divine Word. He never preaches from a topic. He always has a text. His text is not a mere motto, but *in it* he finds his sermon. He uses his text with as much apparent reverence and appreciation as if those few words were the only words that God had ever spoken. The text is the germ which furnishes the life, the spirit, and the substance of the discourse. Every sermon has the peculiar flavour, and fragrance, and colour of the Divine seed-truth of which it is the growth. Thus, as the Bible is a store-house of seed-truths, inexhaustible and of infinite variety, so Mr. Spurgeon's sermons are never alike. Every seed yields its fruit after its kind. If he brings you up again and again to the same old truths, it is always on a different side, or in a new light, or with new surroundings.

A very strong confirmation of this view has been afforded to the author in the preparation of an edition of Mr. Spurgeon's works. In making up the index of subjects, it was necessary to go carefully through the entire fourteen volumes, page by page, and to note the different topics discussed, and then to arrange them in alphabetical order. When this work was finished, such was the wonderful variety of subject, of thought, and of illustration, that, in many thousands of references, no two subjects, or thoughts, or illustrations, were found exactly to correspond. The preacher is discussing essentially the same familiar truths over and over again. And yet his setting forth of truth, his shades of thought, and his modes of illustration, always arrange themselves in new forms and colours with well-nigh the endless variety of the combinations and tints of the clouds at the setting of the sun. It is not surprising, therefore, that sermons so varied, fresh, and Evangelical, should have so large a circulation in this country.'

So great, indeed was the American interest in Spurgeon's ministry that, in 1883, a syndicate in the United States, without asking his opinion or consent, arranged for the transmission by telegraph of his Lord's-day morning sermons, and their publication on the following day, in a number of papers in Boston, Chicago, Cincinnati, Philadelphia, and St. Louis, having an aggregate circulation of a million copies. The experiment was doomed to be a failure, for the instructions to the English agents were: 'Cable Spurgeon's Sunday morning sermons, *omitting the little words.*' The attempt to insert those words in the report received on the other side of the Atlantic produced such a strange result that Spurgeon wrote on the first copy he received: 'Sermon a hash, but pretty well, considering the hurry and double transmission to New York, and then to Cincinnati.' Not long after, when the experiment ceased, the preacher noted: 'We much prefer to revise and publish for ourselves; and as these forms of publication are permanent, their usefulness becomes in the long run greater than would come of a wide scattering of faulty reports'.

As in the case of Australia considerable information exists on the good done by the sermons in America. The following interesting case was given in a report appearing in a Baptist paper, published in the United States:

'At our prayer-meeting, the other Sunday evening, a brother, to show the different ways there are of doing good, mentioned an incident that occurred on board a steamer in which, some time before, he was a passenger up the Pacific Coast to Oregon. It was Sunday; and a passenger, who had with him a volume of Spurgeon's sermons, went round asking one and another to read one of them aloud. The passengers declined, till he came to our brother, who consented to act as reader. Quite a company gathered round him, which gradually increased, as he went on with the discourse, until, looking up, after a little time, he saw that, not only the passengers, but all the crew who could possibly be at liberty, were among his audience, and that all were very attentive.

The informal service was soon over. But not so the effect of the sermon; for, some months after, being in San Francisco, he was abruptly saluted in the street, one day, by a stranger—a sailor—who seemed overjoyed at meeting him. "How do you do?" said he. "Don't you know me? Why, I heard you preach!" "I am not a preacher, my friend; so you must have made a mistake." "Oh, no! I have not; I heard you preach. Don't you remember the steamer that was going to Oregon?" "Oh, yes!" replied the gentleman; "I recollect, and I read one of Mr. Spurgeon's sermons." "Well," said the sailor, "I never forgot that sermon; it made me feel that I was a sinner, and I have found Christ, and I am so glad to see you again." '

A Christian, writing to Spurgeon from Florida, spoke for many in this letter:

'My Dear Brother in Christ,
    Once upon a time, a wealthy man, who owned many gardens, sent one of his gardeners to water the plants. The gardener went and adjusted the hose, turned the tap, and watered them far and near. Many of them were near him; but, away in a corner of the garden farthest from the gardener, was a frail flower that had long been pining for the refreshing showers. The gardener, not knowing its need, nevertheless turned the hose in that direction, and the drooping plant revived, and bloomed afresh, to delight all who happened to come near it; and it loved the master, *and the instrument*, though the latter was unknown.
    Several weeks ago, I lay ill, far away from England, in the wilds of Florida. Weak and faint-hearted, I lay pondering on the strange providence of the Master, when one of your sermons was placed in my hands. The refreshing shower revived me, and gave me fresh hope and courage; and I rose from my sick couch to strive still more earnestly to gain access to the hearts of those by whom I am surrounded; and, to-day, in a small class that I have formed out here in the wilderness, the Lord made His presence felt, and blessed us with an awakening that I have never seen here before, and tears of repentance were shed by many. I was so full of joy and gratitude to God that I longed to let you know that your influence, as an instrument, had reached even this far-away spot.'

Two specimens of the usefulness of the Sermons in foreign languages must also be included. India felt their impact. Robert Spurgeon, a cousin of C. H. Spurgeon, as a missionary in India superintended the translation of certain of the Sermons into Bengali and circulated them by post among principal men.

One of the recipients, a Zemindar (landlord), an old man, had a son at school who read the sermons to his father and afterwards wrote the following letter to Robert Spurgeon:

'Dear Sir,

I am coming to you as an unknown youth. I hope that your kind heart will not fail to recognize me as a dear friend. The three pamphlets—The Faithful Saying, Jesus—Name all blessing, and Jesus the Judge—which you have sent to my father, was given to me to read it to him because he is now an old man of 70 years and his eyesight is not better.

First, I read your Faithful Saying only to perform my father's word. But when I met the sentence, "When a sinner comes to Jesus, he need not look back again, he receives salvation as a gift", my mind and heart gathering themselves gave me a fresh mind, and I heartily met with the sentence, "Jesus longs to save the sinner and penitent". "There is life for a look at the Crucified One".

> *But let our debts be what they may,*
> *However great or small,*
> *As soon as we have nought to pay,*
> *Our Lord forgives us all.*

Nearly all the sentences I met with my heart: and so I read all your pamphlets. The word "salvation" which I read in The Faithful Saying often strikes my soul.

Sir, I often wish to read some religious book, but unfortunately I have no religious treatise. Even I have no Bible. I hope that your kind heart will not fail to send me some religious book.

Yours truly,

_____,'

Robert Spurgeon, who translated this letter from Bengali, adds: 'This will give an indication of how the Sermons are working upon the hearts of intelligent Bengalis. Probably hundreds have thus been already awakened. Evangelists especially are helped in presenting the truth by reading them'.

The following record of the Sermons' usefulness came from Syria:

'Many of the Sermons were translated into Arabic and published in Beirut (Syria). A missionary labouring at Zahleh in that country, reported to Mrs. Spurgeon who had donated £5 from her Sermon Fund for the Arabic work, that about 1,500 copies of Sermons had been distributed by school children in the homes of the town, after they had been exhorted by their teachers to read them to their parents. The result was scarcely what had been expected. The missionary wrote to Mrs. Spurgeon in the following words:

The bishop and priests have pronounced a great curse upon all who received and read the sermons. The town is in a *furore*. After pronouncing the curse and reading it in all the eight Catholic churches, the *priests had a public burning of the sermons in their possession*. They then visited the Greek priests and persuaded one of them, formerly a Catholic priest, to pronounce against the sermons in the Greek Church, which he did, though he did not pronounce any curse.

Now the matter turned out the very opposite of what the enraged priests planned for and expected; instead of listening to them the people laughed at them and our schools lost only a very few boys. Of the people, those who could read and had not received the sermons came running to secure copies and so the curse made many more people anxious to study them. Then the priests received rebukes in public and in private from the principal men of the town.

"Holy work for Christmas" and "The sages, the star and the Saviour" (are the sermons) to which they (chiefly) objected. Next time we distribute I think it will be, "Salvation by Works a Criminal Doctrine" (No. 1534) followed by "Faith—What is it? How can it be obtained?" (No. 1609). This experience has taught us all the need of a little more of this active tearing down of old systems of error'.

It was but fitting that, as Spurgeon's sermons had been the means of blessing to so many readers, he should, himself, receive a special message through one of his own discourses. He thus describes how the 'waiter' became, on at least one occasion, 'a guest at the gospel feast':

'I once learnt something in a way one does not often get a lesson. I felt at that time very weary, and very sad, and very heavy at heart; and I began to doubt in my own mind whether I really enjoyed the things which I preached to others. It seemed to be a dreadful thing for me to be only a waiter, and not a guest, at the gospel feast. I went to a certain country town, and on the Sabbath day entered a

Methodist Chapel. The man who conducted the service was an engineer; he read the Scriptures, and prayed, and preached. The tears flowed freely from my eyes; I was moved to the deepest emotion by every sentence of the sermon, and I felt all my difficulty removed, for the gospel, I saw, was very dear to me, and had a wonderful effect upon my own heart. I went to the preacher, and said, "I thank you very much for that sermon." He asked me who I was, and when I told him, he looked as red as possible, and he said, "Why, it was one of your sermons that I preached this morning!" "Yes," I said, "I know it was; but that was the very message that I wanted to hear, because I then saw that I did enjoy the very Word I myself preached." It was happily so arranged in the good providence of God. Had it been his own sermon, it would not have answered the purpose nearly so well as when it turned out to be one of mine.'

I do not think any human being upon earth ever felt so much repose of soul and body as I do. Many years of toil are all rewarded by this blessed rest, which only seems too good to be true. I have no task work, and do more voluntarily, as a recreation,than I have often done of obligation.No idle tongues disturb me, or cares molest me. The burden is taken from the shoulder, and the bit from between the jaws. If anything can make me young and strong again, this will. It is rest of a sort which I never knew before in all its forms; for, at other times, pain, or dulness, or too much company, has made it less enjoyable. I rest on the wing, as the swallow is said to do.— c.h.s., *in letter from Mentone, written in* 1882.

Up in Dr. Bennet's garden, when Harrald read me the following lines, I adopted them as my own:

> *O days of heaven, and nights of equal praise,*
> *Serene and peaceful as those heavenly days,*
> *When souls drawn upward in communion sweet*
> *Enjoy the stillness of some close retreat,*
> *Discourse as if released, and safe at home,*
> *Of dangers past, and wonders yet to come,*
> *And spread the sacred treasures of the breast*
> *Upon the lap of covenanted rest.*   C.H.S.

22

At Mentone

It would have been easy to fill a volume with the account of Spurgeon's experiences in the sunny South, but the many other interesting records of his wondrously full life make it needful greatly to condense the story of about twenty annual visits to the Riviera. He was fairly familiar with most of the favourite resorts on that part of the Mediterranean shore, and he occasionally made a short stay at one or other of them; but Mentone was the place he loved beyond all the rest. Sometimes, after going elsewhere for a change of scene, a few days sufficed for the enjoyment of the beauties and charms of the new region, and then he would say, 'I think we will hasten on to Mentone.' On settling down in his old quarters, he generally exclaimed, with a sigh of relief, 'Ah! now I feel at home.'

Spurgeon's first visit to the Riviera was made before the railway had been completed along the coast; and he used often to describe to his travelling companions in later days the delights of driving from Marseilles to Genoa, and so being able to see, under the most favourable conditions, some of the loveliest views on the face of the earth. On that journey, one incident occurred which was quite unique in the Pastor's experience. While staying for a few days at Nice, he received a letter from the captain of the *Alabama*, an American man-of-war lying in the harbour of Villefranche, inviting him to pay a visit to that vessel. On accepting the invitation, a very pleasant time was spent on board, and then the captain asked Spurgeon to come another day, and preach to his officers and men, and to those of a second man-of-war which was stationed not far off. Though the preacher was seeking rest, he gladly availed himself of the opportunity of conducting the service desired; and after it was over, he chatted for some time with a number of his sailor hearers. Amongst them, he found one who, when a boy, had been in Newington Sunday-school, and whose uncle was a member at the Tabernacle, and another who, as a lad, ran away from his home at Dulwich. Several different nationalities were represented, and a good many Roman Catholics were there; but all seemed exceedingly pleased to listen to the gospel message, and Spurgeon said that he did not know that he had ever enjoyed preaching more than he did on that occasion, and that he should, ever afterwards, reckon himself an honorary chaplain of the United States Navy.

Tidings of the service at Villefranche probably reached other American vessels, for, several years later, when the U.S.S. *Trenton*, the flagship of the European squadron, was at Gravesend, the chaplain wrote to Spurgeon: 'Could it be possible for you, amid your abundant labours, to come down some day, and address our officers and men, it would be esteemed a great favour, and I know it would be the means of doing incalculable good. All through the cruise, it has been my desire that the ship might go to some port in your vicinity, hoping thereby that you might oblige us with a visit.' The Pastor was unable to accede to the request so kindly conveyed, but he fully appreciated the honour, and perhaps all the more because he was never invited to preach on board a British man-of-war.

One of the travelling companions on the first visit to the Riviera was the Pastor's friend, deacon, and publisher, Joseph Passmore; and he was usually a member of the little company which gathered at Mentone year by year; though, latterly, his partner, James Alabaster, had the joy of taking his turn at holiday-making with the author whose works he had so long published. In 1879, Joseph Harrald, Spurgeon's personal secretary and 'armour-bearer', went for the first time; and, from that year, until the never-to-be-forgotten last visit of 1891-2, he was only absent twice, when his services seemed more urgently required at home.

Extracts from his letters of the same period will furnish details of the manner in which some of his days of holiday were pleasantly and profitably spent:

'I went up to Dr. Bennet's garden at 11 o'clock, and remained there alone with Harrald till 3.30. He read to me, and then I dictated to him, changing to a talk, a walk, a pun, some fun, and then reading and speechifying again, the electric shorthand bottling all up for future use. I did enjoy it, though the mistral blew savagely. We were in a corner of the kiosque, out of all the wind, and yet in the open air, with mountains, and sea, and garden all around. No one disturbed us; it was the *beau ideal* of an artistic author's studio.'

'Harrald read to me, yesterday, *The Life of Cromwell*—grand, soul-inspiring. How the man trusted in the Lord! How sweet is the life of faith, and how splendid are its triumphs! I would live equally above joys and sorrows, and find my all in the Lord Himself.'

'It came on to blow, so Harrald and I resorted to Dr. Bennet's garden from 10 to 3, having a grand read all alone till about 2 o'clock, and then admitting the other friends to be silent disciples among us. I gathered sheaves of texts for sermons, and a few subjects for articles, and had a very happy day. The wind blew in hurricanes, but we sat with a wall at our backs, and the sun shining upon our faces. Trees were bending in the gale, and the swift ships were flying across the main; but we had a hiding-place from the wind, and sat therein with comfort.'

Spurgeon never saw cyclamen growing anywhere without recalling an amusing incident which happened in Dr. Bennet's garden at the time when visitors were freely welcomed there in the morning. The Pastor and his secretary had found a sheltered spot where they were completely hidden from view, and during one of the pauses in the reading or dictating, they were greatly interested in hearing a young lady, quite near them, exclaim, in unmistakable Transatlantic tones, 'O mother, du come here! There are some lovely sickly men (cyclamen) just here. I du love sickly men!' Perhaps the speaker would not have been quite so enthusiastic if she had been aware of the proximity of the English listeners who mischievously gave to her words a meaning she never intended them to convey.

Within the garden was an ancient ruined tower which Dr. Bennet restored to usefulness. This done, he placed it at the disposal of Mr. Spurgeon, who at once availed himself of such a delightful retreat. Perched high above the sea, it afforded a view indescribably lovely, while, by turning the key in the lock, absolute immunity from intruders was secured; and, as a result, some of the brightest of the articles in *The Sword and the Trowel* were here written or dictated, and some of the choicest sermons in *The Metropolitan Tabernacle Pulpit* were here composed, at least in outline. Only a short distance away from this tower, and perched on the very edge of the cliff overhanging the sea, stands the Italian guard-house which Spurgeon had to pass every time he went to see his friend, Mr. Thomas Hanbury, at the Palazzo Orengo, La Mortola. The Pastor often told the story of an incident that happened within this building. In the days when the phylloxera was committing such deadly havoc among the vines of France and Italy, the two countries tried to prevent its further spread by forbidding the transport of fruit, flowers, and shrubs from one land to the other. It was a foolish and useless regulation, for the phylloxera was already in possession of both sides of the frontier; and it led to many amusing scenes. One day, Spurgeon was going with a party of friends for a picnic; and, amongst the articles under his charge, were a couple of oranges. He understood sufficient Italian to comprehend that the fruit could not be allowed to pass; but his ready wit suggested the best way out of the difficulty, so he walked into the soldiers' room, peeled the oranges, carefully putting all the peel into the fire, and ate them, to the great amusement of the defenders of the crown rights of the King of Italy! As the story has been published in various papers and books, Spurgeon is represented as having 'stepped back, five or six paces, into France,' in order to defy the Italian guards; whereas, at the time, he was probably one or two hundred yards beyond the boundaries of the Republic.

Dr. Bennet's garden was not the only open-air study that Spurgeon had at Mentone. A cypress walk up the hillside led to numerous quiet nooks where the Pastor and his secretary spent many a delightful day. They started from the hotel soon after the little company of friends who had gathered for morning prayer had dispersed, and if the weather was favourable for a long stay out of doors, they carried the materials for a light lunch with them, a waterproof rug to spread on the ground to ward off rheumatism—and some books, of course, generally including a volume of Brooks, or Manton, or some other Puritan divine, with a biography or other work to give variety to the reading. The reader had to pause, every now and then, to jot down texts that struck the attentive listener as being suggestive, or to preserve, by means of shorthand, any happy and helpful thoughts that might be of service in after days. Sometimes, the dictation would only be sufficient for a paragraph or two, and then the reading would be resumed; on other occasions, a whole article for the magazine would be ready for transcription before the return journey to the hotel. A large part of *The Clue of the Maze*, and several of the *Illustrations and Meditations, or, Flowers from a Puritan's Garden*, were thus recorded.

Occasionally, the time devoted to reading in the open air was spent in one of the many lovely valleys by which Mentone is surrounded. Spurgeon never forgot one experience which he had in a portion of the Gorbio valley:

'In this valley I have spent many a happy day, just climbing to any terrace I preferred, and sitting down to read. I once left *Manton on Psalm* 119 by the roadside, and before the next morning it was returned to me. Here, too, on Christmas-day, 1879, I learned what it is to "Walk in the Light." I had been ill with gout; and, on recovering, we arranged to drive up this valley as far as the road would serve, and then send away the carriage, walk further on, have our lunch, and, in the afternoon, walk gently back to the spot where we left the conveyance, the man having orders to be there again by three. Alas! I had forgotten that, as far as the upper portion of the valley is concerned, the sun was gone soon after twelve! I found myself in the shade before lunch was over, and shade meant sharp frost; for, wherever the sun had not shone, the earth was frozen hard as a rock. To be caught in this cold, would mean a long illness for me; so, leaning on the shoulder of my faithful secretary, I set forth to hobble down the valley. The sun shone on me, and I could just move fast enough to keep his bright disc above the top of the hill. He seemed to be rolling downward along the gradually descending ridge, like a great wheel of fire; and I, painfully and laboriously stumbling along, still remained in his light. Of course, it was not the time for our Jehu to be at the appointed

THE GORBIO VALLEY, NEAR MENTONE

spot; so, with many a groan, I had to stagger on until a stray conveyance came in our direction. Out of the sunshine, all is winter: in in the sunlight alone is summer. Oh, that spiritually I could always walk in the light of God's countenance as that day I managed to keep in the sun's rays!

> *Like Enoch, let me walk with God,*
> *And thus walk out my day;*
> *Attended still with heavenly light,*
> *Upon the King's highway.*

The Gorbio valley was one of the special haunts of the trap-door spiders until visitors so ruthlessly destroyed their wonderful underground homes. Concerning these and other curious creatures, the Pastor wrote to Mrs. Spurgeon: 'How I wish you could be here to see the spiders' trap-doors! There are thousands of them here, and the harvesting ants also, though the wise men declared that Solomon was mistaken when he said, "They prepare their meat in the summer." I shall send you a book about them all.' When the volume arrived, it proved to be *Harvesting Ants and Trap-door Spiders*, by J. Traherne Moggridge. On its fly-leaf was the choice inscription:

I cannot bring you to this land,
Nor bring this land to you,
But here the artist's skilful hand
Has set before your view
Two tribes of creatures dwelling here
Most wonderful to see:
Gaze on the insects without fear,
And, gazing, think on me. *C.H.S.*

One of the charms of Mentone to Spurgeon was that he could constantly see there illustrations of Biblical scenes and manners and customs. He frequently said he had no desire to visit Palestine in its forlorn condition, for he had before his eyes, in the Riviera, an almost exact representation of the Holy Land as it was in the days of our Lord. He was greatly interested in an article written by Hugh Macmillan upon this subject, in which that devoted student of nature traced many minute resemblances between the climate, the conformation of the country, the fauna and flora, and the habits of the people in the South of France of to-day, and those of the East in the time when the Lord trod 'those holy fields.' In several of his Sabbath afternoon communion addresses, the Pastor alluded to the many things that continually reminded him of 'Immanuel's land,' while the olive trees were a never-failing source of interest and illustration. One of the works, with which he had made very considerable progress, was intended to be, if possible, an explanation of all the Scriptural references to the olive.[1]

Spurgeon often remarked that there were many Biblical allusions which could not be understood apart from their Oriental associations; and, as an instance, he said that some people had failed altogether to catch the meaning of Isaiah 57. 20, 'The wicked are like the troubled sea, when it cannot rest, whose waters cast up mire and dirt.' Those who have affirmed that the sea never can rest have not seen the Mediterranean in its most placid mood, when for days or even weeks at a time there is scarcely a ripple upon its surface. During that calm period, all sorts of refuse accumulate along the shore; and then, when the time of tempest comes, anyone who walks by the side of the agitated waters can see that they do 'cast up mire and dirt.' Usually, during the Pastor's stay at Mentone, there was at least one great storm, either far out at sea, or near at hand. In 1882, in one of his letters home, he wrote the following graphic description of the scene he had just witnessed:

'This afternoon, I have been out to watch the sea. There was a storm last night, and the sea cannot forgive the rude winds, so it is avenging its wrongs upon the shore. The sun shone at 3 o'clock, and there was no wind here; but away over the waters hung an awful cloud, and to our left a rainbow adorned another frowning mass of blackness. Though much mud was under foot, all the world turned out to watch the hungry billows rush upon the beach. In one place, they rolled against the esplanade, and then rose, like the waterworks at Versailles, high into the air, over the walk, and across the road, making people run and dodge, and leaving thousands of pebbles on the pavement. In another place, the sea removed all the foreshore, undermined the walls, carried them away, and then assailed the broad path, which it destroyed in mouthfuls, much as a rustic eats bread-and-butter! Here and there, it took away the curb; I saw some twelve feet of it go, and then it attacked the road. It was

---

[1] See for example, *Metropolitan Tabernacle Pulpit*, sermon preached on 17/4/1879 and published on 16/12/1909, with the title ,'The Beauty of the Olive Tree'.

amusing to see the people move as a specially big wave dashed up. The lamp-posts were going when I came in, and an erection of solid stone, used as the site of a pump, was on the move. Numbers of people were around this as I came in at sundown; it was under-mined, and a chasm was opening between it and the road. Men were getting up the gas pipes, or digging into the road to cut the gas off. I should not wonder if the road is partly gone by the morning. Though splashed with mud, I could not resist the delight of seeing the huge waves, and the sea birds flashing among them like soft lightnings. The deep sigh, the stern howl, the solemn hush, the booming roar, and the hollow mutter of the ocean were terrible and grand to me. Then the rosy haze of the far-ascending spray, and the imperial purple and azure of the more-distant part of the waters, together with the snow-white manes of certain breakers on a line of rock, made up a spectacle never to be forgotten. Far away, in the East, I saw just a few yards of rainbow standing on the sea. It seemed like a lighthouse glimmering there, or a ship in gala array, dressed out with the flags of all nations. O my God, how glorious art Thou! I love Thee the better for being so great, so terrible, so good, so true. "This God is *our* God, for ever and ever." '

Another phenomenon was thus described in a letter of the same period:

'About six in the evening, we were all called out into the road to see a superb Aurora Borealis—a sight that is very rarely seen here. Natives say that it is twelve years since the last appearance, and that it means a cold winter which will drive people to Mentone. Our mountains are to the North, and yet, above their tops, we saw the red glare of this wonderful visitant. *"Castella is on fire,"* said an old lady, as if the conflagration of a million such hamlets could cause the faintest approximation to the Aurora, which looked like the first sight of a world on fire, or the blaze of the day of doom.'

Spurgeon had been at Mentone on so many occasions that he had watched its growth from little more than a village to a town of considerable size. He had so thoroughly explored it that he knew every nook and cranny, and there was not a walk or drive in the neighbourhood with which he was not perfectly familiar. His articles, in *The Sword and the Trowel*, on the journey from 'Westwood' to Mentone, and the drives around his winter resort, have been most useful to later travellers, and far more interesting than ordinary guide-books. Many of the villas and hotels were associated with visits to invalids or other friends, and some were the scenes of notable incidents which could not easily be forgotten.

At the Hôtel d'Italie, the Pastor called to see John Bright, who was just then in anything but a bright frame of mind. He was in a very uncomfortable room, and was full of complaints of the variations in temperature in the sunshine and in the shade. His visitor tried to give him a description of Mentone as he had known it for many years, but the great tribune of the people seemed only anxious to get away to more congenial quarters. The Earl of Shaftesbury was another of the notable Mentone visitors whom the Pastor tried to cheer when he was depressed about religious and social affairs in England and on the Continent.

The genial Sir Wilfrid Lawson, Member of Parliament and temperance advocate, scarcely needed anyone to raise his spirits, for he was in one of his merriest moods when he met Mr. Spurgeon at the hotel door, and the half-hour they spent together was indeed a lively time. The Right Hon. G. J. Shaw-Lefevre was another politician[1] whom the Pastor met at Mentone. The subject of Home Rule for Ireland was just then coming to the front, and the Liberal statesman heard that day what Mr. Spurgeon thought of Mr. Gladstone's plans; the time came when the opinions then expressed privately were published widely throughout the United Kingdom, and materially contributed to the great leader's defeat in 1886.

In the earlier visits to Mentone, the Pastor stayed at the Hôtel des Anglais. In later years he used often to say that he never passed that spot without looking at a certain room, and thanking God for the merciful deliverance which he there experienced. One day he was lying in that room, very ill, but he had insisted upon the friends who were with him going out for a little exercise. Scarcely had they left, when a madman who had eluded the vigilance of his keepers rushed in, and said, 'I want you to save my soul.' With great presence of mind, the dear sufferer bade the poor fellow kneel down by the side of the bed, and prayed for him as best he could under the circumstances. Spurgeon then told him to go away, and return in half an hour. Providentially, he obeyed. As soon as he was gone, the doctor and servants were summoned, but they were not able to overtake the madman before he had stabbed someone in the street. Only a very few days later, he met with a terribly tragic end.

[1] Shaw-Lefevre became Postmaster General during Gladstone's Second Ministry; his introduction of sixpenny telegrams brought him additional fame.

In the garden of the same hotel, the Pastor once had an unusual and amusing experience. A poor organ-grinder was working away at his instrument; but, evidently, was evoking more sound than sympathy. Spurgeon, moved with pity at his want of success, took his place, and ground out the tunes while the man busily occupied himself in picking up the coins thrown by the numerous company that soon gathered at the windows and on the balconies to see and hear the English preacher play the organ! When he left off, other guests also had a turn at the machine; and, although they were not so successful as the first amateur player had been, when the organ-man departed he carried away a heavier purse and a happier heart than he usually took home.

It was while staying at the Hôtel des Anglais that the Pastor adopted a very original method of vindicating one of the two Christian ordinances which were always very dear to him. At a social gathering, at which Spurgeon and a large number of friends were present, John Edward Jenkins, M.P., the author of *Ginx's Baby*,[1] persistently ridiculed believers' baptism. It was a matter of surprise to many that he did not at once get the answer that he might have been sure he would receive sooner or later. The party broke up, however, without anything having been said by the Pastor upon the question, but it was arranged that, the next day, all of them should visit Ventimiglia, about six miles to the East. On reaching the cathedral, Spurgeon led the way to the baptistery in the crypt; and when all the company had gathered round the old man who was explaining the objects of interest, the Pastor said to his anti-immersionist friend, 'Mr. Jenkins, you understand Italian better than we do, will you kindly interpret for us what the guide is saying?' Thus fairly trapped, the assailant of the previous evening began, 'This is an ancient baptistery. He says that, in the early Christian Church, baptism was always administered by immersion.' The crypt at once rang with laughter, in which the interpreter joined as heartily as anyone, admitting that he had been as neatly 'sold' as a man well could be. He was not the only one who learnt that the combatant who crossed swords with our Mr. Great-heart might not find the conflict to his permanent advantage.

For several years, Mr. Spurgeon stayed at the Hôtel Beau Rivage. As he generally had several companions, or friends who wished to be near him, his party usually occupied a considerable portion of the small building, and the general arrangements were as homelike as

---

[1] A satirical novel published anonymously in London in 1871.

possible, even to the ringing of a bell when it was time for family prayer. Not only were there guests in the house who desired to be present, but many came from other hotels and villas in the neighbourhood, and felt well rewarded by the brief exposition of the Scriptures and the prayer which followed it. Those of the company who were members of any Christian church asked permission to attend the Lord's-day afternoon communion service, and it frequently happened that the large sitting-room was quite full, and the folding doors had to be thrown back, so that some communicants might be in the room adjoining. On the Sabbath morning, the Pastor usually worshipped with the Presbyterian friends at the Villa les Grottes; occasionally giving an address before the observance of the Lord's supper, and sometimes taking the whole service. Although away for rest, an opportunity was generally made for him to preach, at least once during the season, at the French Protestant Church, when a very substantial sum was collected for the poor of Mentone. He also took part in the united prayer-meetings in the first week of the year, and sometimes spoke upon the topic selected for the occasion.

It is scarcely possible to tell how many people were blessed under the semi-private ministry which Spurgeon was able to exercise during his holiday. He used, at times, to feel that the burden became almost too great to be borne, for it seemed as if all who were suffering from depression of spirit, whether living in Mentone, Nice, Cannes, Bordighera, or San Remo, found him out, and sought the relief which his sympathetic heart was ever ready to bestow. In one case, a poor soul, greatly in need of comfort, was marvellously helped by a brief conversation with him. The Pastor himself thus related the story, when preaching in the Tabernacle, in June, 1883:

'Some years ago, I was away in the South of France; I had been very ill there, and was sitting in my room alone, for my friends had all gone down to the mid-day meal. All at once it struck me that I had something to do out of doors; I did not know what it was, but I walked out, and sat down on a seat. There came and sat next to me on the seat a poor, pale, emaciated woman in the last stage of consumption; and looking at me, she said, "O Mr. Spurgeon, I have read your sermons for years, and I have learned to trust the Saviour! I know I cannot live long, but I am very sad as I think of it, for I am so afraid to die." Then I knew why I had gone out there, and I began to try to cheer her. I found that it was very hard work. After a little conversation, I said to her, "Then you would like to go to heaven, but not to die?" "Yes, just so," she answered. "Well, how do you wish to go there? Would you like to ascend in a chariot of fire?" That method had not occurred to her, but she answered, "Yes, oh, yes!" "Well," I said, "suppose there should be, just round this corner, horses all on fire, and a blazing chariot waiting there to take you up to heaven; do you feel ready to step into such a chariot?" She looked up at me, and she said, "No, I should be afraid to do that." "Ah!" I said, "and so should I; I should tremble a great deal more at getting into a chariot of fire than I should at dying. I am not fond of being behind fiery horses, I would rather be excused from taking such a ride as that." Then I said to her, "Let me tell you what will probably happen to you; you will most likely go to bed some night, and you will wake up in heaven." That is just what did occur not long after; her husband wrote to tell me that, after our conversation, she had never had any more trouble about dying; she felt that it was the easiest way into heaven, after all, and far better than going there in a whirlwind with horses of fire and chariots of fire, and she gave herself up for her heavenly Father to take her home in His own way; and so she passed away, as I expected, in her sleep.'

The testimony of one American minister is probably typical of that of many others who came under Spurgeon's influence at Mentone. In one of his letters to *The Chicago Standard*, Rev. W. H. Geistweit wrote: 'It has been said that, to know a man, you must live with him. For two months, every morning, I found myself in Mr. Spurgeon's sitting-room, facing the sea, with the friends who had gathered there for the reading of the Word and prayer. To me, it is far sweeter to recall those little meetings than to think of him merely as the great preacher of the Tabernacle. Multitudes heard him there while but few had the peculiar privilege accorded to me. His solicitude for others constantly shone out. An incident in illustration of this fact will never be forgotten by me. He had been very ill for a week, during which time, although I went daily to his hotel, he did not leave his bed, and could not be seen. His suffering was excruciating. A little later, I was walking in the street, one morning, when he spied me from his carriage. He hailed me, and when I approached him, he held out his left hand, and said cheerily, "Oh, you are worth five shillings a pound more than when I saw

you last!" And letting his voice fall to a tone of deep earnestness, he
added, "*Spend it all for the Lord.*" '

A gentleman, who was staying in the hotel at Mentone, where
the Pastor spent the winter of 1883, wrote: 'As an instance of the
rapidity of Mr. Spurgeon's preparation, the following incident may
be given. There came to him, from London, a large parcel of
Christmas and New Year's cards. These were shown to some of the
residents at the hotel, and a lady of our party was requested to
choose one from them. The card she selected was a Scriptural one;
it was headed, "The New Year's Guest," and in harmony with the
idea of hospitality, two texts were linked together: "I was a stranger, and ye took me in;" and "As many as received him, to them
gave he power to become the sons of God, even to them that believe
on his name." The card was taken away by the lady; but, on the
following Lord's-day, after lunch, Spurgeon requested that it might
be lent to him for a short time. The same afternoon, a service was
held in his private room, and he then gave a most beautiful and
impressive address upon the texts on the card. The sermonette[1] was
printed in *The Metropolitan Tabernacle Pulpit* shortly after that date,
and has always seemed to me a wonderful illustration of Spurgeon's
great power. Later in the day, he showed me the notes he had made
in the half-hour which elapsed between the time the card came into
his possession and the service at which the address was delivered;
and these, written on a half-sheet of notepaper, consisted of the
two main divisions, each one with several sub-divisions, exactly as
they appear in the printed address.'

Occasionally, Spurgeon sent home the outline which he had used
at the Sabbath afternoon communion, with some account of the
service. The address upon the words, 'Thou hast visited me in the
night,' which was published in December, 1886, under the title,
'Mysterious Visits,'[2] contained quite a number of autobiographical
allusions, such as the following: 'I hope that you and I have had
many visits from our Lord. Some of us have had them, especially in
the night, when we have been compelled to count the sleepless
hours. "Heaven's gate opens when this world's is shut." The night
is still; everybody is away; work is done; care is forgotten; and then
the Lord Himself draws near. Possibly there may be pain to be
endured, the head may be aching, and the heart may be throbbing;
but if Jesus comes to visit us, our bed of languishing becomes a
throne of glory. Though it is true that "He giveth His beloved

[1] Sermon No. 1757 (1884).   [2] In *The Sword and the Trowel* (December 1886).

sleep," yet, at such times, He gives them something better than sleep, namely, His own presence, and the fulness of joy which comes with it. By night, upon our bed, we have seen the unseen. I have tried sometimes not to sleep under an excess of joy, when the company of Christ has been sweetly mine.'

The closing paragraph is a good illustration of the way in which Spurgeon made use of the scenes around him to impress his message upon his hearers:

'Go forth, beloved, and talk with Jesus on the beach, for He oft resorted to the sea-shore. Commune with Him amid the olive groves so dear to Him in many a night of wrestling prayer. If ever there was a country in which men should see traces of Jesus, next to the Holy Land, this Riviera is the favoured spot. It is a land of vines, and figs, and olives, and palms; I have called it "Thy land, O Immanuel." While in this Mentone, I often fancy that I am looking out upon the Lake of Gennesaret, or walking at the foot of the Mount of Olives, or peering into the mysterious gloom of the Garden of Gethsemane. The narrow streets of the old town are such as Jesus traversed, these villages are such as He inhabited. Have your hearts right with Him, and He will visit you often, until every day you shall walk with God, as Enoch did, and so turn weekdays into Sabbaths, meals into sacraments, homes into temples, and earth into heaven. So be it with us! Amen.'

The river of our peace at certain seasons overflows its banks; and, at times, the believer's joy is exceeding great. Even princes, who fare sumptuously every day, have their special banquets; and this Jubilee of my life is a true Jubilee of joy, not only to myself, but to every member of my family.—c.h.s., *in sermon preached at the Tabernacle in celebration of the completion of his fiftieth year.*

'The most surprising thing to most people will be the discovery that Mr. Spurgeon is only fifty years old. He has been so constantly before the public for so many years that the first impression on most minds on hearing of his jubilee is that it is the celebration of the fiftieth year of his ministry, not the fiftieth year of his life. But Mr. Spurgeon is in reality only fifty years old, although for thirty years he has been one of the best-known men of the time. At first he was a curiosity, then a notoriety; but he has long since been recognized as one of the first celebrities of his day. His position is absolutely unique. —*The Pall Mall Gazette,* June 18th, 1884

23

The Jubilee of 1884

JUNE 19, 1884, was one of the red-letter days in Spurgeon's history for he then completed the fiftieth year of his life. The year which was to witness this joyful celebration, however, opened for him under trying circumstances. Having gone to Mentone for rest the previous November, January, 1884, found him very ill despite the advantages of his winter retreat. With the pre-arranged duration of his 'holiday' almost completed he had reluctantly to accept a delay in his return as the following letter to the Tabernacle explains:

'Mentone,
Jan. 10th, 1884.

Dear Friends,

I am altogether stranded. I am not able to leave my bed, or to find much rest upon it. The pains of rheumatism, lumbago, and sciatica, mingled together, are exceedingly sharp. If I happen to turn a little to the right hand or to the left, I am soon aware that I am dwelling in a body capable of the most acute suffering.

However, I am as happy and cheerful as a man can be. I feel it such a great relief that I am not yet robbing the Lord of my work, for my holiday has not quite run out. A man has a right to have the rheumatism if he likes when his time is his own. The worst of it is, that I am afraid I shall have to intrude into my Master's domains, and draw again upon your patience. Unless I get better very soon, I cannot get home in due time; and I am very much afraid that, if I did return at the date arranged, I should be of no use to you, for I should be sure to be laid aside.

The deacons have written me a letter, in which they unanimously recommend me to take two more Sundays, so that I may get well, and not return to you an invalid. I wrote to them saying that I thought I must take a week; but as I do not get a bit better, but am rather worse, I am afraid I shall have to make it a fortnight, as they proposed.'

He was able to recommence preaching at the Tabernacle in February but was too unwell to take the services on Sunday, the

24th of the month. Being still disabled a week later, he wrote again to the people:

'Westwood,

March 2nd, 1884.

Dear Friends,

It is to my intense sorrow that I find myself "shut up" for another week. I hoped that I had escaped my enemy among the olives, but he threw me down at my own door. The Lord's will must be done, and we are bound to bear it without a repining thought . . . I shall not fall lower, but the difficulty is to rise up again. Literally my trouble is to get on my feet again. I am a poor creature. Evidently I am in the extreme of physical weakness. Nevertheless the Lord can cause His spiritual power to be shown in me, and I believe He will. Your great love will bear with me, and I shall be in the front again, bearing witness to the faithfulness of the Lord.'

During the enforced rest Spurgeon prepared a leading article for the March issue of *The Sword and the Trowel*, entitled 'In my Fiftieth Year, and getting Old.' Its reflections are well worthy of inclusion in this Autobiography:

*

This fiftieth year of mine has not been without its peculiar heart-searchings. When feeling weary with an unbroken stretch of work, I began to fear that it was the age of the man, as well as the work of the office, which was causing sluggishness of mind. We all remember how Bunyan says of his '*Pilgrim's Progress*,' 'as I pulled, it came.' So did my sermons; but they wanted more pulling, and yet more. This is not a good sign for the quality of the discourses. If I judge rightly, the best juice of the mind's vintage is that which leaps from the cluster at the first gentle pressure of the feet; that which is squeezed out by heavy machinery is poor stuff: and therefore I have feared that, with increasing labour, I might only manage to force forth a viscid liquid acceptable to none. I hope it has not been so; I cannot judge my own productions, but I think, if I had greatly flagged, some of those delicious people, called "candid friends," would have been so kind as to drop the acid information into my wounds at a time when they perceived that the vinegar would cause the most smart. Still, the critics may have formed very humiliating judgments on the subject, and may have been so fearful of the consequences to my feeble mind that they have in great tenderness repressed their verdict. An American brother says that 'People's tastes are such that preachers on the wrong side of fifty may consider that they are about done with the gospel trumpet.' Judicious friends may have reached that stage of feeling with regard to me, but may not care to express it.

Such were my lucubrations: they were humbling, and so far healthy; but one can drink so much of the waters of self-depreciation as to grow faint of heart; and this is not healthy, but the reverse.

Over all this, in the worn-out hours, came the dark suspicion that the morning time was over, and the dew was gone, and that the beams of the sun were falling more aslant, and had less light and warmth in them; and the dread that the gloom of eventide would soon darken thought and expression, and show that the prime of the work-day was past. Faith saw the God-ward side of the matter, and sang, 'At evening time it shall be light'; but prudence also whispered that the human side must be considered too, and that dulness would injure force, and weaken interest, and diminish usefulness.

In my rest-time I have been able to survey the situation with some fair measure of deliberate impartiality, and also to call in the aid of a considerable observation of the result of years upon other men. No one can deny that there is such a thing as 'the tameness at forty, and the going-to-seed at fifty.' The lively evangelist of former years has sobered down into the prosy sermon-reader, a man much respected by all who know him, but rather endured than enjoyed by his regular congregation. The brother who flashed and flamed has, by reason of age, become a strangely quiet fire: a live coal, no doubt, but by no means dangerous to the driest fuel. A brother of our own profession, by no means censorious, has said, 'A very little examination will convince the most sceptical that an appalling percentage of preachers are dull, dry, and tiresome.' Surely these men did not begin at this pitch, or why were they allowed to begin at all? They must have grown into a routine of sermonizing, and have settled down into a flat, unprofitable style through the lapse of time. They were green and juicy once, but they have dried in the suns of many years, till the vulgar speak of them as 'sticks'. Shall we all go that way? Must my next volumes of sermons, if the sermons ever see the light in that form, become mere faggots, which none but the old man in the moon would care to be burdened with? A heart-rending question to me. I fear my personal observation of the bulk of preachers does not help me to a consolatory answer. Perhaps the remark may offend my brethren. Courage, my heart, it will not offend those of whom it is not true; and those of whom it is true will be sure not to take it to themselves, and so I may escape.

But this writer whom I have quoted, whose somewhat lengthy and Latinized words persist in ringing in my ears, has done much to cheer me. He says, 'The dismal decadence of a multitude of well-intentioned men is quite preventable.' Brave news! I will bestir myself to prevent it in my own case, if it be preventable. He adds, 'No doubt any of us can number a score of men, in the range of our personal knowledge, who at sixty are fresher in thought, more attractive in manner, and in higher demand in the churches, than they were twenty years ago.' I am not sure about 'a score' whom I know at this present; but I certainly know, or have known, more than that number who answer to the description. There rises before me now a brother, whose age I will not even guess at, but he is certainly over sixty, who is as vigorous as he was twenty years ago, and more prominently useful than ever before throughout a singularly useful life. I knew another who, towards his later days, largely increased the number of his always numerous hard words, and did not therefore increase the pleasure of his auditors; but with this exception he hardly showed a sign of flagging, and went off the field because his wisdom urged him to make room for a younger man, and not because he could not still have held his post with honour. A third conspicuous instance is before me of a preacher, who, however he may have declined in faith, and erred in doctrine, to the inexpressible grief of thousands, is still mentally as vigorous and fresh as aforetime. Our statesmen are many of them ancients; our greatest political leader is 'the Grand Old Man.' Observation therefore gives a second deliverance, which, if it does not reverse, at least qualifies the former verdict.

'Soon ripe, soon rotten,' is a proverb which warns the precocious of what they may expect. He who is a shepherd at sixteen may be a mere sheep at sixty. One can hardly eat his cake and have it too. When a third of a century of work has already been done, the labourer may hardly expect the day to last much longer. In my own case, the early strain has been followed by a continuous draft upon the strength through the perpetual printing of all that I have spoken. Twenty-nine years of sermons on those shelves; yet one must go plodding on, issuing more, and yet more, which must all be in some measure bright and fresh, or the public will speedily intimate their weariness. The outlook to those eyes which are only in the head is not cheering. Happily there are other optics, and they shall be used.

It is the Rev. Martyn L. Williston that I have quoted, and I will borrow from him again.[1] 'It is not the first instrusion of gray hairs in the pulpit which is a signal of alarm to the pews. No man, in average health, should be less of a man at fifty, or seem so, than at twenty-five; but many are so in appearance and in fact; and to them, not to the people, is chargeable the slackening demand for their services. The most of our professional feebleness is traceable to our own want of mental virility. If we will, we can remove a great deal of uneasiness from our congregations. Preachers who grow duller as they count their years, this side of sixty at least, do so from simple mental shiftlessness, very much as the Virginian planters have let their lands run waste from mere depletion. We must perpetually replenish heart and brain, or the fields of thought will turn meagre and barren.'

This is sound sense, and stirs the aging man to an increase of diligence in reading and study. But it should also be clear to him that he must have more time than ever for these purposes. He must conscientiously use his hours, and his people must as conscientiously yield them to him. The Israelites made bricks without straw, but they could not have made them without time. Increased space will be needed for collecting useful materials, and preparing them for the upbuilding of the church.

The peculiar danger of advancing years is *length of discourse*. Two honoured brethren have lately fallen asleep, whose later years were an infliction upon their friends. To describe one is to depict the other. He is so good and great, and has done such service that you must ask him to speak. He expects you to do so. You make bold to propose that he will occupy only a few minutes. He will occupy those few minutes, and a great many more minutes, and your meeting will die out under his protracted periods. Your audience moves, all interest is gone, your meeting is a failure, and all through a dear old man whose very name is an inspiration. The difficulty is not to start these grand old men, but to stop them when started: they appear to be wound up like clocks, and they must run down. This is a seductive habit to be guarded against when years increase: it may be wise to resolve upon being shorter as age inclines us to be longer. It would be a pity to shorten our congregation by lengthening our discourse.

It is also frequently true that elderly speakers become somewhat

[1] *Lobb's Theological Quarterly* No. 1 Vol. I. A paper upon 'The Imaginative Element in Preaching.'

negligent in their oratory. It has been said that a young man is mainly taken up with the question—'How shall I say it?' and hence he attains a good and pleasing style; while the older man thinks only of—'What shall I say?' and thus, while he improves as to the matter of his discourse, his manner is all too apt to become slovenly and drowsy. If it be so, it ought not to be so. We ought to improve in all respects, so far as our powers have not declined. We cannot be blamed if memory does not serve us quite so nimbly as aforetime, or if imagination is not quite so luxuriant; but we deserve to be censured if in any point within our power we decline even a hair's breadth. We must not make a mistake as to what really is improvement. It is possible to preach better according to the canons of taste, and to preach worse as to real usefulness: God grant that we may not improve in this fatal way! It is easy to become more weighty, and at the same time more dull, so that though more is taught less is learned; may we have grace to avoid this form of unenviable progress! The art of growing old wisely will need to be taught us from above. May we be willing scholars of the Great Teacher!

When all is said and done, the jubilation of our Jubilee does not call for any great blowing of trumpets, but rather for uplifting of hand and heart in prayer to God for further help. It may be that we are only in mid-voyage. May that voyage end in landing our freight in port, and not as some life-passages have terminated, namely, in an utter wreck of every hope! Our friends and fellow-helpers will, we trust, supplicate on our behalf that we may receive a fresh anointing from on high, and we will begin life again without fear. The Scripture remains as our inexhaustible textbook, the Lord Jesus as our boundless subject, and the Holy Ghost as our infinite Helper—what therefore have we to fear? What is lost in sparkle may be gained in value; the departure of vivacity may be made up by the incoming of experience; and thus the old man may be as useful as the young. 'Such an one as Paul the aged' is an honour to the church: we are not such as yet, but grace can cause the middle-aged to mellow into fathers of that order.

*

Spurgeon was able to resume his ministry on Sunday, March 16, 1884, and preparations were in hand for the celebration of his Jubilee. This had been decided at a church meeting in February when the following resolution was unanimously and enthusiastically passed:

'That the church gratefully recognizes the goodness of Almighty God in sparing to it, and to the Christian Church at large, the invaluable life of our beloved Pastor, C. H. Spurgeon; and that, in order worthily to celebrate his Jubilee, a suitable memorial be raised, and presented to him; and that it be an instruction to the deacons to take this matter vigorously in hand, and to carry it forward as they may deem best.'

The deacons were faced with a difficulty in knowing how to make any presentation of money to Spurgeon which he would not employ entirely for the Lord's work. They remembered how the testimonial of £6,500 presented to him in 1879 had all gone to the various Institutions under his charge and they were also aware that the people wanted to raise a gift which would go to the Pastor himself. A decision was made to use part of the money to pay for the Jubilee House which was then being erected at the back of the Tabernacle as a permanent memorial of the Pastor's fiftieth birthday; yet this did not answer the main intention of the congregation. In the outcome the problem was only solved when Spurgeon was persuaded to promise he would use at least some part of the money people donated for himself.

As the date of the celebration of the Jubilee approached, many references to it appeared in the religious and secular newspapers, the most noteworthy being the articles in the *Pall Mall Gazette* of June 18 and 19, 1884. They were the result of Mr. Spurgeon's compliance with the request contained in the following letter from W. T. Stead, the Editor:

'Dear Sir,

You are, I am aware, one of the busiest men in London. But I venture to ask you to spare me a morsel of your leisure to have a talk over things in view of your approaching Jubilee—your long and successful labours in London, and the general result at which you have arrived after going through it all. That, of course, for the paper and the public. Besides this, I should be very glad to have an opportunity personally of placing myself in immediate communication with one who has been such a power for good in London and throughout the world. I also am very busy, but any day after 12 I am at your service if you can spare me time for an interview. I have the honour to be,

Your obedient servant,

W. T. Stead.'

Stead's report of the interview contained allusions to many subjects either of passing or permanent interest:

'Mr. Spurgeon is one of the most genial of hosts, and in the course of a couple of hours spent in strolling about his well-wooded grounds, or in gossiping in his library, his visitor was able to gather his views concerning a great number of the questions of the day. He found Mr. Spurgeon, as is not to be wondered at, a strong believer in the one-man power. "Wherever anything is to be done," said he, "either in the Church or the world, you may depend upon it, it is done by one man. The whole history of the Church, from the earliest ages, teaches the same lesson. A Moses, a Gideon, an Isaiah, and a Paul are from time to time raised up to do an appointed work; and when they pass away, their work appears to cease. Nor is it given to everyone, as it was to Moses, to see the Joshua who is destined to carry on his work to completion. God can raise up a successor to each man, but the man himself is not to worry about that matter, or he may do harm. Hence I am against all endowments for religion; it is better to spend the money for immediate needs. I am not even in favour of endowing my own College. Someone made me an offer, the other day, to found a scholarship in connection with it, but I declined it. Why should I gather money, which would remain after I am gone, to uphold teaching of which I might entirely disapprove? No! let each generation provide for its own wants. Let my successor, if I have one in the College, do as I have done, and secure the funds which he needs for his own teaching. I wish there were no religious endowments of any shape or kind among Dissenters or Churchmen, for I never yet knew a chapel, possessing an endowment, which did not find that, instead of its being a blessing; it was a curse. One great object of every religious teacher should be to prevent the creation of external appliances to make his teaching appear to live when it is dead. If there were no endowments, an error would soon burst up, whereas an artificial vitality is imparted to it by bolstering it up with endowments."

"Then you have faith for yourself, Mr. Spurgeon, but none for your successor?" queried the visitor.

"A man does very well," was the reply, "who has faith for himself; but how can he undertake to have faith for another? I am no believer in sponsorship. Who knows where my successor may be? He may be in America, or in Australia, or I know not where. As for the Tabernacle, the man who occupies my place, when I pass away, will have to depend upon his own resources, upon the support of his people, and the grace of God, as I have done; and if he cannot do that, let him come to the ground, for he will not be the fitting man for the post." '

One other paragraph may be quoted, partly because of the reference made to it by Dr. Peter Bayne:

' "In theology," said Spurgeon, "I stand where I did when I began preaching, and I stand almost alone. If I ever did such a thing, I could preach my earliest sermons now without change so far as the essential doctrines are concerned. I stand almost exactly where Calvin stood in his maturer years; not where he stood in his *Institutes*, which he wrote when quite a young man, but in his later works; that position is taken by few. Even those who occupy Baptist pulpits do not preach exactly the same truths that I preach. They see things differently; and, of course, they preach in their own way. Although few will deny the wonderful power of the truth as it has been preached at the Tabernacle, it is not according to their method; yet it is the Calvinistic way of looking at things which causes my sermons to have such acceptance in Scotland, in Holland, and even in the Transvaal, where a recent traveller expressed his astonishment at finding translations of them lying beside the family Bible in a great many of the farmsteads of the country. I am aware that my preaching repels many; that I cannot help. If, for instance, a man does not believe in the inspiration of the Bible, he may come, and hear me once; and if he comes no more, that is his responsibility, and not mine. My doctrine has no attraction for that man; but I cannot change my doctrine to suit him." '

The actual celebration of the Jubilee commenced on Wednesday, June 18, 1884. when the Pastor sat in his vestry, from twelve to five o'clock, to receive the congratulations of friends, and contributions to be passed on to the treasurers of the testimonial fund. Then several hundreds of the church-members were entertained at tea in the rooms under the Tabernacle, and afterwards the great sanctuary was crowded with an enthusiastic audience. Such vast numbers of people were anxious to be present that two evenings had to be set apart for the meetings; and, even then, hundreds of applicants for tickets had to be refused, for so many applied that, if the building had been twice as large, there would have been no difficulty in filling it on both nights.

Little did the cheering thousands know of the intense anxiety that was felt by a few of the Tabernacle officials, and other friends who shared with them a terrible secret. Just at that time, in various quarters of London, there had been threats of desperate deeds by Fenians, or those in sympathy with them; and an intimation, which the police authorities dared not disregard, had been given that the Tabernacle was to be blown up on the night of Spurgeon's Jubilee. It seemed scarcely possible that such a diabolical scheme of wholesale destruction of human life could have been devised; but every precaution was taken to prevent it becoming an awful reality. There probably had never been so many detectives and policemen in the building before; and when the proceedings on the second night were over, and the delighted audience had dispersed, there were private but grateful thanksgivings that all had gone off without even a note of alarm; yet, for a considerable period afterwards, it was deemed advisable to have a special watch kept in case any attempt of the kind indicated might be made. With thoughtful and tender solicitude, all knowledge of the threatened explosion was kept from the Pastor; and it was only when he was in the carriage, on his way home, that Mrs. Spurgeon told him the alarming news which had occupied her thoughts during the evening, and together they gave thanks that the evil had been averted.

The Wednesday evening meeting was specially intended for the members of the church and congregation, and representatives of the many missions, schools, and agencies connected with the Tabernacle. The number of these various forms of work for the Lord may be judged from the fact that the list of them occupied more than half a page in *The Sword and the Trowel*, while nearly as large a space was required for the names of the various religious societies, at home and abroad, from which addresses of congratulation had been received.

The Pastor presided, and it was to him a source of intense thankfulness that Mrs. Spurgeon was able to be present on both the evenings, to share with him the joys of the Jubilee, after so many years' enforced absence from the Tabernacle through severe illness. The keynote of the whole of the gatherings was struck, at the commencement of the meeting, by the Pastor's opening sentences:

'I do not think anybody imagines that I ought to speak at any great length tonight, but I should like to say very much in very little. I feel overwhelmed with gratitude to you, dear friends, and because of you, to God. After the kind words which many of you have spoken to me, I have much to do not to cry; indeed, I have had a little distillation of the eyes quietly, and I feel very much like weeping now, at the remembrance of all the good and gracious things that have been said to me this day. But let me say this for my speech: the blessing which I have had here, for many years, must be entirely attributed to the grace of God, and to the working of God's Holy Spirit among us. Let that stand as a matter, not only taken for granted, but as a fact distinctly recognized among us. I hope, brethren, that none of you will say that I have kept back the glorious work of the Holy Spirit. I have tried to remind you of it, whenever I have read a chapter, by praying that God the Holy Spirit would open that chapter to our minds. I hope I have never preached without an entire dependence on the Holy Ghost. Our reliance upon prayer has been very conspicuous; at least, I think so. We have not begun, we have not continued, we have not ended anything without prayer. We have been plunged into it up to the hilt. We have not prayed as we should; but, still, we have so prayed as to prevail; and we wish it to be on record that we owe our success, as a church, to the work of the Holy Spirit, principally through its leading us to pray. Neither, as a church, have we been without a full conviction that, if we are honest in our asking, we must be earnest in acting. It is no use asking God to give us a blessing if we do not mean it; and if we mean it, we shall use all the means appointed for the gaining of that boon; and that we have done.

'Next it behoves me to say that I owe the prosperity I have had in preaching the gospel to the gospel which I have preached. I wish everybody thought as much, but there are some who will have it that there is something very particular and special about the preacher. Well, I believe that there may be something peculiar about the man, something odd, perhaps. He cannot help that, but he begs to say there is nothing about him that can possibly account for the great and long-continued success attending his labours. Our American friends are generally very 'cute judges, and I have a good many times read their opinion of me, and they say over and over again, "Well, he is no orator. We have scores of better preachers in America than Mr. Spurgeon, but it is evident that he preaches the gospel as certain of our celebrated men do not preach it." I so preach the gospel that people coming to hear it are impressed by it, and rejoice to rally to the standard. I have tried, and I think successfully, to saturate our dear friends with the doctrines of grace. I defy the devil himself ever to get that truth out of you if God the Holy Spirit once puts it into you. That grand doctrine of substitution, which is at the root of every other—you have heard it over and over and over and over again, and you have taken a sure grip of it. Never let it go. And I say to all preachers who fail in this matter, that I wish they would preach more of Christ, and try to preach more plainly. Death to fine preaching! There is no good in it. All the glory of words and the wisdom of men will certainly come to nought; but the simple testimony of the goodwill of God to men, and of His sovereign choice of His own people, will stand the test, not only of the few years during which I have preached it, but of all the ages of this world till Christ shall come. I thank you, dear friends, for all your love and your kindness to me, but I do attribute even that, in great measure, to the fact that you have been fed with the pure gospel of the grace of God. I do not believe that the dry, dead doctrine of some men could ever have evoked such sympathy in people's hearts as my gospel has aroused in yours. I cannot see any reason in myself why you should love me. I confess that I would not go across the street to hear myself preach; but I dare not say more upon that matter, because my wife is here. It is the only point upon which we decidedly differ; I differ *in toto* from her estimate of me, and from your estimate of me, too; but yet I do not wish you to alter it.'

B. W. Carr read the congratulatory address which was published at the time in *The Sword and the Trowel*; the Pastor's father, brother, and son Charles briefly spoke; Archibald G. Brown and H. H. Driver represented the past and present students of the College; S. R. Pearce was the speaker on behalf of the Sunday-school; W. J. Orsman and W. Olney were the representatives of the missions which had grown out of the church's work; and Pastor W. L. Lang presented an address from the Baptist ministers of France; but, remembering the world-wide influence of the American evangelist, D. L. Moody, probably the most important utterance that night was the testimony he gave to the blessing he had derived from the Pastor's printed and spoken messages:

'Mr. Spurgeon has said, to-night, that he has felt like weeping. I have tried to keep back the tears, but I have not succeeded very well. I remember, seventeen years ago, coming into this building a perfect stranger. Twenty-five years ago, after I was converted, I began to read of a young man preaching in London with great power, and a desire seized me to hear him, never expecting that, some day, I should myself be a preacher. Everything I could get hold of in print that he ever said, I read. I knew very little about religious things when I was converted. I did not have what he has had—a praying father. My father died before I was four years old. I was thinking of that, tonight, as I saw Mr. Spurgeon's venerable father here by his side. He has the advantage of me in that respect, and he perhaps got an earlier start than he would have got if he had not had that praying father. His mother I have not met; but most good men have praying mothers—God bless them!

In 1867, I made my way across the sea; and if ever there was a sea-sick man for fourteen days, I was that one. The first place to which I came was this building. I was told that I could not get in without a ticket, but I made up my mind to get in somehow, and I succeeded. I well remember seating myself in this gallery. I recollect the very seat, and I should like to take it back to America with me. As your dear Pastor walked down to the platform, my eyes just feasted upon him, and my heart's desire for years was at last accomplished. It happened to be the year he preached in the Agricultural Hall. I followed him up there, and he sent me back to America a better man. Then I began to try and preach myself, though at the time I little thought I should ever be able to do so. While I was here, I followed Mr. Spurgeon everywhere; and when, at home, people asked if I had gone to this and that cathedral, I had to say "No," and confess I was ignorant of them; but I could tell them something about the meetings addressed by Mr. Spurgeon. In 1872, I thought I would come over again to learn a little more, and I found my way back to this gallery. I have been here a great many times since, and I never come into the building without getting a blessing to my soul. I think I have had as great a one here tonight as at any other time I have been in this Tabernacle. When I look down on these orphan boys, when I think of the 600 servants of God who have gone out from the College to preach the gospel, of the 1,500 or 2,000 sermons from this pulpit that are in print, and of the multitude of books that have come from the Pastor's pen, (Scripture says, "Of making many books there is no end," and in his case it is indeed true,) I would fain enlarge upon all these good works, but the clock shows me that, if I do, I shall not get to my other meeting in time.

But let me just say this, if God can use Mr. Spurgeon, why should

He not use the rest of us, and why should we not all just lay our-selves at the Master's feet, and say to Him, "Send me, use me"? It is not Mr. Spurgeon who does the work, after all; it is God. He is as weak as any other man apart from his Lord. Moses was nothing, but Moses' God was almighty. Samson was nothing when he lost his strength; but when it came back to him, then he was a mighty man; and so, dear friends, bear in mind that, if we can just link our weakness to God's strength, we can go forth, and be a blessing in the world. Now, there are others to speak, and I have also to hasten away to another meeting, but I want to say to you, Mr. Spurgeon, "God bless you! I know that you love me, but I assure you that I love you a thousand times more than you can ever love me, because you have been such a blessing to me, while I have been a very little blessing to you. I have read your sermons for twenty-five years. You are never going to die. John Wesley lives more to-day than when he was in the flesh; Whitefield lives more to-day than when he was on this earth; John Knox lives more to-day than at any other period of his life; and Martin Luther, who has been gone over three hundred years, still lives." Bear in mind, friends, that our dear brother is to live for ever. We may never meet together again in the flesh; but, by the blessing of God, I will meet you up yonder.'

It was a fitting accompaniment to Moody's address that among the many resolutions of congratulation received at the Jubilee celebration was one from the Philadelphia Conference of Baptist ministers. To this Spurgeon subsequently sent the following reply:

'Dear Sir,

I beg you to thank all the brethren on my behalf. I am deeply affected by your brotherly love. One touch of grace has, in a truer sense than a touch of nature, made us all akin. I rejoice every day in the prosperity of the Church of God in the United States. Your nation is but in its youth, and you are educating it for a high career; ours is old, and slow to learn, and we are with much difficulty lighting its candle, lending it spectacles, and opening the Bible before it. We cannot expect to teach Mr. Bull quite so readily as you teach Master Jonathan. We will, however, do our best; and you will pray for us, and God will bless us.

I feel as if I was even now squeezing the hand of each minister, and receiving a return grip. Take it as done. Thank you! God bless you!

Yours heartily,

C. H. SPURGEON.'

On Thursday evening, June 19, the Tabernacle was packed to its utmost capacity,[1] while crowds in vain sought admission. The Earl of Shaftesbury presided and delivered a notable testimony to the Pastor's faithfulness from the first days of his ministry until that hour; addresses were also given by the Revs. Canon Wilberforce, J. P. Chown, O. P. Gifford (Boston, U.S.A.), Newman Hall, W. Williams (Upton Chapel), Dr. Joseph Parker, and Sir William McArthur, M.P.; the Jubilee address was again read by Mr. Carr, and the treasurers of the testimonial fund presented to Spurgeon a cheque for £4,500, 'free from any condition, and to remain absolutely at his disposal.' In reply, the Pastor said:

'The affectionate words to which I have listened have sunk into my heart. I can take a very great deal of encouragement without being lifted up even to the ordinary level, and all I have received will operate upon me more afterwards than just now. But I am sure that the kindly pressure of the hand, and the way in which friends, one after another, have told me that I led them to the Saviour, or that I comforted them in the time of trouble, have been a very great joy to me. To God be all the praise; to me it is an overwhelming honour to be His servant. Had there been no money whatever accompanying this celebration, I should have been as well pleased as I am now; for I never proposed a gift, and I never thought of it.

I have coveted no man's silver or gold. I have desired nothing at your hands, but that you love the Lord Jesus Christ, and serve Him with all your might. But I have coveted, and I do still covet to have a generous people about me, because I am sure that it is to God's glory and to your own advantage to be liberal to His cause. Poor men should give that they may not be always poor. Rich men should give that they may not become poor. These are selfish motives; but, still, they are worthy to be mentioned. "There is that scattereth, and yet increaseth; and there is that withholdeth more than is meet, but it tendeth to poverty." As a general rule, he that keeps his substance will not find it multiply under his hands; but he that gives shall find that it is given back to him, "good measure, pressed down, and shaken together, and running over." Besides, I do not think much of giving when I have plenty to give with; I like it better when I can pinch myself. If you pinch yourself, there is a sweetness about giving to the Lord. What you do not want, you can dispense with, and exhibit small love; but when you come to

---

[1] G. H. Pike estimated the number to be 7,000.

what you do want, and give that to the Lord, then there comes to your own heart the comfortable assurance that you are really doing it unto the Lord, because of the needs of His cause.

Now I thank everybody who has given a hundred pounds, and everybody who has given a penny. God bless you, and return it to you in every way! One of our brethren told you, the other night, what once happened to me. I had been preaching in a country place, and a good woman gave me five shillings. I said to her, "Well, my dear friend, I do not want your money." She said, "But you must take it; I give it to you because I got good from you." I said, "Shall I give it to the College?" She answered, "I don't care about the College; I care about you." "Then I will give it to the Orphanage." "No," she said, "you take it yourself." I said, "You need it more than I do." She replied, "Now, do you think that your Lord and Master would have talked like that to the woman who came and broke the alabaster box over Him? I do not think He would." She added, "I know you do not mean to be unkind; I worked extra to earn it, and I give it to you." I told her that she owed me nothing, and that woman owed the Lord everything, and asked, "What am I to do with it?" She said, "Buy anything you like with it; I do not care what. Only, mind, you must have it for yourself." I mention the incident because it is much in that spirit that the friends have given this noble testimonial.

The Lord bless you! The Lord bless you! The Lord bless you, yet more and more, you and your children!'

Two days later the series of celebrations was concluded with a meeting at the Orphanage when the greetings of children and staff were conveyed to Spurgeon by Mr. Charlesworth and 'the little ones seemed overjoyed to give their President a rug for his carriage.'

'I have chosen thee in the furnace of affliction'—This has long been the motto fixed before our eye upon the wall of our bed-chamber, and in many ways it has also been written on our heart. It is no mean thing to be chosen of God. God's choice makes chosen men choice men. . . . We are chosen, not in the palace, but in the furnace. In the furnace, beauty is marred, fashion is destroyed, strength is melted, glory is consumed; yet here eternal love reveals its secrets, and declares its choice. So has it been in our case . . . Therefore, if to-day the furnace be heated seven times hotter, we will not dread it, for the glorious Son of God will walk with us amid the glowing coals.—C.H.S., *in 'The Cheque Book of the Bank of Faith'*.

24

The Furnace of Affliction

IN the months following the Jubilee celebration Spurgeon's work continued with the vigour which always marked his periods of comparative health. But the duration of these periods was now growing shorter and by October, 1884, the customary effects of the burden of his labours had re-appeared. *The Sword and the Trowel* for that month contained the editorial note:

'Solicited on all sides to preach abroad, and abundantly willing to do so, we made another trial of labouring in the provinces, with the same result as on former occasions, an utter breakdown, a sharp agony, and a long weakness. . . . We must again cancel all promises, and for a while do home work and nothing more. Crowded chapels, windows necessarily opened, and consequent cold draughts, foul air from below, and cold air from above, make up an arrangement which must arouse rheumatism when it slumbers in the constitution.'

Nevertheless, despite some days when suffering was severe, Spurgeon remained at his post. On December 9th, at the annual College meeting, he mentioned his extreme weakness. Two days later his brother had to take the Thursday evening service at the Tabernacle, though Spurgeon was hoping, as he wrote to his brother, to be able to preach at the week-end: 'Tell the good people to look for me. I think I can get away on January 5th. I must try to hold out till then on Sundays.' His Winter ministry at the Tabernacle did continue until Sunday, January 4th, 1885 but the following day he was too ill to leave for Mentone as intended. It was not until January 27th that he was fit enough to travel. During the intervening weeks, he received the following letter from a special church meeting:

'January 12

Dear Pastor,
    We have heard, with profound grief, that you have been unable to go out on your proposed visit to Mentone in consequence of severe and painful illness during the past week. Our poignant

sympathy is rather increased than lessened by the reflection that this season of affliction has not been borrowed from your time of service for the church, but from the period of recreation to which you have a perfect right as well as a hearty welcome.

While devoutly recognizing the hand of the Lord in this and in all other dispensations of His providence, we feel that it cannot be irreverent to seek some clear interpretation of the will of our Heavenly Father. Can we be mistaken in supposing that the lesson to us and to yourself is transparent? Your arduous labours, and your incessant anxieties, so far exceed the average strength of your constitution, that there is an imperative demand for you to take longer and more frequent occasions of retirement, and to take them, not when you have used up 'the last ounce of your strength', but when you are in unimpaired vigour.

Under present circumstances, we earnestly entreat you to consecrate at least three months to entire relaxation from the duties of your sacred office; and if it seem good to you, let the appointment of supplies for your pulpit be left to the Co-pastor and the deacons, subject always to their accepting any suggestion of yours, and their communicating to you every arrangement of theirs, as is their habitual wont.

And accept herewith our assurance, as a church, that we will all unite in a strong determination to support the good work of the Tabernacle by constant attendance, both on Sundays and week-evenings, and by offering our full contributions to the support of the various institutions of the church.

With sincere affection, and unceasing prayers for your recovery,
We are, dear Pastor,
Yours ever lovingly,
(Signed by the church-officers)'

After his departure the annual church-meeting was held as usual in February and in writing to this meeting from Mentone the Pastor referred to the subject of the previous letter:

'Mentone,
February 9, 1885.

To the Church in the Tabernacle,
Beloved in the Lord,

I salute you all right heartily. I regret that an annual church-meeting should be held without me; but I know that all things will be done rightly, for the Spirit of God is among you.

I write only to send my love, and to assure you that I am greatly profiting by the rest which has been given me. I am weak indeed, but I feel much more myself again. I have learned, by experience, that I must go away in November each year, or else I shall be at home ill. If the Lord will help me through the other months of the year, I might rest in November and December with a clear economy of time. I want to do the most possible; and, on looking over the past, this appears to be the wisest way.

The other matter is,—the elders propose special services, and my whole heart says "Yes." If the church takes it up, the result will be, with the Divine blessing, a great ingathering. Members canvassing from door to door, and leaving a sermon, might do much good. I will subscribe £5 towards a fund for sermons, suitably selected, to be given away. The chief point is, to get the people in, not by bribing them with tea, etc., but by fair persuasion. Oh, for a great blessing!

I feel grieved to be out of the running, but I cannot help it. I can pray, and I do. Rally round your leaders. Pray with double earnestness. Be instant in season and out of season. Attempt great things, and expect great things.

May the Lord bless, guide, comfort, strengthen and uphold the Co-pastor, deacons, elders, and every one of you, for Jesus' sake!

Yours in hearty affection,

C. H. SPURGEON.'

The March, 1885, issue of *The Sword and the Trowel* reported: 'Resting at Mentone, bathing in the sunlight, the invalid finds his pain gone, and his strength returning'. On Sunday, April 12, Spurgeon was once more back in the Tabernacle pulpit. At the College Conference in May he mentioned that he was trying a vegetarian diet and that he had enjoyed life during the preceding ten days more than during the last ten years. The same point is referred to in the October issue of the magazine: 'The editor begs to report himself as for the present enjoying vigorous health, and working at express speed. . . . So far, abstinence from flesh has been a more effectual preservative from rheumatism and gout than any of the many systems hitherto tried. . . . It is a great joy to be bright of heart and vigorous in frame.'

Clearly Spurgeon did not mean to stop preaching when he felt in this condition and the intention expressed to the church-meeting in his February letter was thus not executed. Before long, however, his hopes were dashed as illness returned to lay him low. The December, 1885, magazine gave the news: 'After doing our utmost to remain at our post through the Winter, we are compelled to succumb. Neuralgia has marked us for her own for some time past. The brain is weary and refuses to perform its office with its usual ease. A whole day is needed to produce the thought-fabric which, in better times, was woven in half-an-hour. . . . The net will break if it be not mended. Day after day of wretched pain, and golden hours lost in miserable incompetence, warn us that true economy requires the most willing worker to have his due proportion of Sabbath.'

From his room at Westwood he wrote to the Church on Sunday, December 6: 'I should have been greatly disappointed if I had not learned that the Lord's appointments are those which must serve His children. I can form no idea as to how long I may be shut up in this room. My Lord is not bound to give me any account of His matters. Beloved, seek the prosperity of our Zion with all your hearts.'

On December 11, 1885, Spurgeon was able to leave England for two months. Thereafter, apart from a handful of Sundays, he was not to be in his own pulpit again during the Novembers, Decembers and Januarys of the few years which remained. By this time there was also more frequent illness in the months which earlier had usually left him comparatively free of suffering. In May, 1886, he could not be present at the Annual Conference on the day when his address was expected. The next morning, however, he arrived and a member of the Conference later wrote: 'Those who were present at the Conference on the following morning are not likely ever to forget the sudden appearance in the room of the suffering President, "his arm in a sling, his face looking like a battle-field of contending pains." The address which followed was such as might have come from a strong man in buoyant health.'

The June, 1886, issue of *The Sword and the Trowel* gave further news of his health: 'Once more the editor has been called to pass through the fiery furnace of pain. This sad state of affairs has largely resulted from the extra services which he has been induced to undertake lately. Nearly every day requests have come in, begging for sermons, addresses, etc., on behalf of all sorts of objects at home and abroad. Many of these have been refused with regret but there are some to which a denial could not be given, and this is the consequence. . . . The question continually comes up—is not this too heavy a price to pay for the privilege of rendering occasional service to deserving objects outside our own immediate circle?'

Spurgeon wrote nothing on his health for his Autobiography, and, in general he made scant reference to the subject. The reader of his sermons is not often given any indication of the suffering which, in later years, frequently preceded, or even accompanied, their delivery. It is this fact which gives additional importance to the occasional autobiographical notes on his recurring illness in *The Sword and the Trowel*. Though these notes were originally written to explain his absence from the Tabernacle pulpit, they are now essential to a proper understanding of his life. We therefore give the following extracts from his closing years and these tell their own story:

'November, 1886: Within five weeks of his time of vacation the editor has had a wretched break-down which makes him feel that the sooner he goes the better. The strain of his work is incessant. . . . It is a joyous thing to work on for the Lord Jesus and His people, but poor flesh and blood at last give way, and pain and sickness render service impossible.

July, 1888: The editor is so completely prostrate that his brain will not think, and his right hand cannot hold a pen . . . There is always some circumstance of grace about the heaviest trial. The thorn-bush bears its rose. The Lord lets us see a bright light in the clouds even when they gather in grimmest fashion.

November, 1888: When the time arrived for making up the Notes for the magazine, the editor was quite prostrate, and suffering so severely that he was unable to write even a sentence. . . . With both feet and one hand a mass of pain he was obliged to postpone everything. . . . If well enough to travel, he will leave home early in November for a season of sorely-needed rest.

December, 1888: Long has our motto been, 'I have chosen thee in the furnace of affliction' and it proves itself to be true. . . . The furnace has been fiercely hot; and besides the dross which we hope we have parted with, we have certainly lost a great deal of strength, which it will take us long to recover. . . . Writing on November 4, we are in this dilemma—we cannot get better until we are in another climate, and we cannot reach that other climate till we get better. . . . The Lord whom we serve will not allow our unavoidable lack of service to be a serious injury to the church which is His joy and care. . . . We leave amid a sound of abundance of rain.

C. H. Spurgeon: The Full Harvest

January, 1889: On the last Sabbath of the year . . . friends at the Presbyterian Meeting-room (i.e. at Mentone) held their Communion Service, and according to our custom our own service was absorbed thereby, that we might in no way divide, but ever unite the family of our Lord. Having given a word from the heart to the hearts of those around the table, our work was done. This left the Sabbath afternoon quite free; and in order to enjoy as complete a rest as possible, four of us walked a short distance from the hotel to an empty villa where we could sit, and sing, and read, and pray, and no one could visit us, because no one knew where we were. During that afternoon, sitting upon the covered balcony, we had the rolling sea below us, and the smiling hills around us, and enjoyed hearty Christian fellowship. The rising of a cold and blustering wind rendered it expedient to retire within . . . I quietly led the way downstairs . . . I trusted to my walking stick; it slipped, as it was most natural that it should do, upon the smooth marble and down went the massive form which was so little prepared for the consequent descent. The more those who were present reflect upon the incident of that one ill step, the more are they amazed that it led to nothing worse. With bowed head the sufferer from that fall adores the Lord, who has said, "Underneath are the everlasting arms". [After speaking of lost teeth and trembling limbs, Spurgeon continues] Our friends were in sad concern, and we rallied them with a cheery word about painless dentistry, sat down upon a chair, and joined with them in singing praise to God for so special an escape. The Sabbath evening closed in with no great evil to deplore; a bruised knee seemed to be the only evil token. But soon the Scripture, which assures us that, if one member suffers, all the other members suffer with it, had a very emphatic illustration in our flesh, and bones, and tendons and nerves. And in a day or two we also learned how intimate is the connection between flesh and spirit. To anguish of body followed shattering of mind, so that thought was confused. We now tell the story with a running pen, but a week ago we could not have written a line without blundering, or even forgetting what we had intended to have said. . . I felt called on to telegraph to the beloved congregation at the Tabernacle . . . and the writing which was delivered to the clerk was in terms of clearest accuracy . . . I gave for a text, Matthew 6.34, "Take therefore no thought for the morrow. Sufficient unto the day is the evil thereof". Alas! it pleased the movers of the wires to resort to the fifth instead of the sixth chapter, and consequently my brethren received the admonition, "Swear not at all"—a superfluity, to say no more! . .

The good hand of the Lord is with us, and let His Name be praised. Tribulation worketh patience, and patience experience, and the experience of one is for the profit of many, and the glory of God. I hope to be back as soon as I can walk, and to preach as soon as I can think out a sermon and stand long enough to preach it.

March, 1889: I can walk a moderate distance. How great is the goodness of God in granting me this happy restoration. . . . Will those members of the Christian public who are making up their minds to ask for a sermon, a lecture, a speech, a bazaar-opening, or something or other, be so very gracious to me as to note the following letter which I have received from the deacons of the Tabernacle [the letter urges him to desist from overmuch work]. I think I must obey their thoughtful admonition, for what will become of all order and discipline if a minister does not pay heed to his deacons! I have frequently gone a little beyond my tether, and have suffered a month's pain in consequence; and as soon as I have been half-well, somebody else has pleaded with me almost to tears to do the same thing again. I must this year be a little hard-hearted and let the pleaders plead in vain. If I do my home-work, it is more than enough for one mortal man. I would indeed be grateful if friends would and could believe that I have not the strength of earlier years, and would excuse me when I cannot grant their requests. It is constantly the case that I have to write several letters before they will accept my answer in the negative; and this is one of the inflictions which I think I ought to be spared. It is painful to me to say 'No' once; but it adds to the burden when another and another letter or deputation come with the same plea.

October, 1889: Some years ago my death was reported, and a kind friend improved the occasion with a funeral address, which turned out to be rather premature. Now the papers announce that I am about to retire from my post, and one of them even proceeds to arrange for my early death and distribution of my worldly goods. . . . Now all this is utterly untrue. I hope to work on for many years, if my life be spared, and if the present age be continued. . . . I have had nearly eight months' continuous preaching, and it is long since I have been favoured with so great a privilege. The fall of the year has come, and with it symptoms that the old enemy is lurking about. . . . I have had a better year than usual.'

[409]

Extracts of a similar nature may also be found in earlier issues of *The Sword and the Trowel*, for Spurgeon's fear in 1871 that his malady would be 'our cross till death' had proved correct. 'My disease is like original sin in the regenerate: it is there even when it does not manifest itself.' During the last twenty-two years of his life illness was never far from him and when attacks came they frequently brought with them a bout of depression. 'During the time that I have been preaching the gospel in this place,' he said in 1879, 'I have suffered many times from severe sickness and frightful mental depression, sinking almost to despair. Almost every year I have been laid aside for a season; for flesh and blood cannot bear the strain, at least such flesh and blood as mine. I believe the affliction was necessary to me and has answered salutary ends; but I would, if it were God's will, escape from such frequent illness: that must be according to His will and not mine.'

While the physical tendency to depression was the accompaniment of his disease there can be no doubt that it was aggravated by the unique circumstances of his ministry. His presence was so much needed, and the necessity of being out of his pulpit so repeatedly troubled him deeply. In 1871 he wrote to his people: 'The highest medical authorities are agreed that only long rest can restore me. I wish it were otherwise. My heart is in my work, and with you; but God's will must be done . . . I try to cast all my cares on God; but, sometimes, I fear that you may get scattered. O my dear brethren, do not wander, for this would break my heart!' Again, in 1879, 'If I should grow worse and worse, and be even more frequently unwell, have patience with me. . . . I always will be at my post when I can.' In 1885, 'It would be well if I could write without mentioning myself, and for your edification only. Forgive the need which there is of alluding to my health; it would best please me if I could work right on, and never have the least item of self to mention. . . . Our frequent illnesses are very trying to the Church and its progress; but if all at home will pray and watch and work, as they have often done before, there will be less falling off than there might otherwise have been.'

Notwithstanding the affectionate letters which came to the Pastor from his church-officers during the periods of absence, and their reassurances that the pulpit was being well supplied, he knew the difficulty of providing the great congregation with such preaching as had previously drawn them together. Furthermore, a sudden return of illness would not infrequently leave him with no time to announce his absence beforehand and scarce time to call upon his brother, or someone else, to undertake a service for him. Among the letters which James Spurgeon received from his elder brother there were a number like the following:

'Dear Brother, I am attacked with such violent neuralgia in my head that I cannot keep up, and must beg you to preach for me tonight. I will come if I get better, but fear there is no hope. I took cold in a dreadful crowd and draught last night.—Yours lovingly'

'Dear Brother, I feel a great nausea this afternoon, and my legs are heavy with the gout feeling. I shall not be up to the meeting at six; please go down to it. Perhaps I may come at seven. If not, take up all the works separately, and pray hard.—Yours lovingly.'

'Westwood

Dear Brother, I am feeling better, but Barrett told me that if I stood upon the foot on Thursday I might make a bad case of it and be laid up on Sunday.

I believe it will pass away, and that I shall preach on Thursday; but I cannot, unless the red swelling somewhat abates.

I am anxious to preach, and will never lay on you what I can do myself, but at this moment I cannot be sure.

Blue pill and black draft have had a fair trial, and I think will carry me through; but it is a huge foot and full of fire, and I cannot be sure of a swift deliverance.

Be ready, and I will be there if I can do so safely.—Your loving brother.'

With so much uncertainty over who would occupy the Tabernacle pulpit there was justification for Spurgeon's concern in case the attendance began to fail. Even in 1879 he had said at the semi-jubilee of his ministry that if the time came when he was 'too often ill' he would wish 'to leave the position to an abler occupant'. This thought was preying upon his mind when he lay bed-ridden at Benmore, Scotland, in July, 1883. The following letter to his brother is not characteristic of Spurgeon but it reveals the anxiety with which he had to struggle when the disease brought him low:

'Benmore, *Friday.*

DEAR BROTHER, I am very distrustful of my mental powers; indeed, I should not like to give a decision upon anything, for I am so entirely broken down and crushed; but I cannot, by the use of my strongest imagination, conceive of an argument for the postponement of the time of cleaning the Tabernacle. That seems to me to have been settled upon by us all with great judgment and deliberation; and I have been looking forward to preaching at Exeter Hall, and praying to be re-established in time for that event. There will now be a fortnight to be spent by me in a sort of shuttle-cocking, preaching to a people who will not know where to go to hear me, as I shall be reported to be both at Exeter Hall and the Tabernacle. I think that last fortnight will be the ounce which will settle the camel's back for ever. I should have been so glad to have got at the work, and to have got it over. Is it supposed that its horrors will diminish by being dangled before my eyes for another fortnight. But I leave it. I would think the course of action wise if I knew of any way in which to place it in which it reflected a scintilla of common sense. I am, however, so utterly ill that I do not want my judgment to weigh with you at all. Do what seems good in your eyes.

'As to the cost of cleaning the Tabernacle, I am thunderstruck. I thought it was done on one occasion for £600, and on another for £800. My judgment upon that can be of no value to you whatever. All I can do is to say, 'Get it done, omit anything that can be omitted, but let it be done thoroughly.'

'Dear brother, my hand and arm do not seem to improve, and the incessant pain is wearing me down. What is to be the end of this perpetually recurring affliction? Cleaning the Tabernacle seems almost a trifling matter. If only *this* poor tabernacle could be cleaned and repaired, there would be some sense in it. I am evidently occupying a position for which I am not qualified, and serious thought must be given to the imperative need of alterations which will be suggested from without by enemies, if they are not first of all perceived by friends.

'I wish I had been well enough to rejoice in the joy of your household. I did up to the measure of my poor capacity, but how shall mountains of misery break forth into singing in harmony with the high hills of gladness? With hearty love to you all,—I am, your loving brother,

C. H. Spurgeon'

The mood passed and a month later from Westwood he could write to James, 'Ranges of the mountains of gloom are now dis solving though some lesser hills remain.' None the less there could be no relief from the profound sense of responsibility which weighed Spurgeon down. His anxiety for the spiritual prosperity of the Tabernacle was far removed from any regard to the maintenance of his own reputation. What did need to be maintained were the many evangelical agencies and Institutions which depended upon the help of the Church which stood at the centre. His own estimate of himself was brief, 'How unimportant we are! God's cause goes on without us', but in the view of the Christian public he was the leader to whom they would gladly entrust their money for the Lord's work. This being so, the question was a very real one, how the orphans, the students, and the old people in the almshouses were to be provided for if he were not seen to be at the seat of operations. The following words, written at different periods in *The Sword and the Trowel*, indicate how impossible it was for him when incapacitated by illness to lay down this burden of care for others which he had gladly received from God:

'We have received many prescriptions for the gout, both for inward and outward application, and should have been dead long ago if we had tried half of them. We are grateful for the kindness although we cannot utilize it. Those who would really aid in the restoration of our health can best do so by preventing our having any anxiety about either College, Orphanage, or Colportage while we are away.'

'For some reason or other subscriptions slacken and almost stop as soon as we leave home, nor do they rally till we return. If this continues we must come back at all hazards, for otherwise we shall have our ships aground. . . . We are sure that the Lord will provide, but when one is ill and weary, it is pleasant not to have faith much tried. At such a time it is a double comfort to be remembered by friends, and to see that they will not allow the holy cause to suffer because the chief worker is laid aside. Satan loses one of his fiery darts when he can no longer whisper, "God forsakes you, and your friends forget you". This weapon is forged out of lies, but he is none the less ready to use it in the dark and dreary hour.

'Oh, for power to pursue our work! Troops of orphans, students, colporteurs and evangelists seem to march through our poor brain both sleeping and waking. All must be left with the Lord. Where could they be better?'

C. H. Spurgeon: The Full Harvest

It is not undeserving of mention that the large measure of humour which belonged to Spurgeon's character did not forsake him even in times of pain. His words to his distressed companions, following his fall in Mentone in 1889, recorded earlier in this chapter, are a case in point. Likewise his descriptions of himself to friends at times of illness are altogether characteristic: 'No dealer would buy me except for cat's meat, and I'm not worth so much for that as I was, for I am many pounds lighter.' 'I am doing nothing—can do nothing. I am only a pin cushion of pain-pins.' 'I am creeping on like a snail; but I am going upward with my horns out in hope'. 'How much he suffered,' writes G. H. Pike, 'no mortal knew save himself; yet neither pain nor weakness seemed to be able to repress the flow of his spirits or check his wit. He once remarked to one who had been writing about some phases of London life: 'You might have added the advertisement of the undertaker who said, in large letters, "Why endure the ills of life when you can be comfortably buried for three pound ten?"'

Undergirding all Spurgeon's experience in suffering was his conviction that his ill-health was God's gift. He gained from illness a wealth of knowledge and sympathy which he could not have gained elsewhere. In the realms of sorrow he was blessed. With his own experience in view he warned his students near the end of his life against making a mistake over what is a blessing: 'In the matter of faith-healing, health is set before us as if it were the great thing to be desired above all other things. Is it so? I venture to say that the greatest earthly blessing that God can give to any of us is health, *with the exception of sickness.* Sickness has frequently been of more use to the saints of God than health has. . . . A sick wife, a newly-made grave, poverty, slander, sinking of spirit, might teach us lessons nowhere else to be learned so well. Trials drive us to the realities of religion.'

The benefits which Spurgeon gained, became, under God's providential hand, the possession of many others. In this connection Charles Spurgeon, Junior, wrote: 'I know of no one who could, more sweetly than my dear father, impart comfort to bleeding hearts and sad spirits. As the crushing of the flower causes it to yield its aroma, so he, having endured in the long-continued illness of my beloved mother, and also constant pains in himself, was able to sympathize most tenderly with all sufferers.'

Spurgeon himself once gave a striking instance of how his own experience had prepared him to help another. In the course of speaking at a Monday evening prayer-meeting at the Tabernacle on the personal preparation which a soul-winner may have to go through in order to his greater usefulness, he said:

'Some years ago, I was the subject of fearful depression of spirit. Various troublous events had happened to me; I was also unwell, and my heart sank within me. Out of the depths I was forced to cry unto the Lord. Just before I went away to Mentone for rest, I suffered greatly in body, but far more in soul, for my spirit was overwhelmed. Under this pressure, I preached a sermon from the words, "My God, my God, why hast thou forsaken me?" I was as much qualified to preach from that text as ever I expect to be; indeed, I hope that few of my brethren could have entered so deeply into those heart-breaking words. I felt to the full of my measure the horror of a soul forsaken of God. Now that was not a desirable experience. I tremble at the bare idea of passing again through that eclipse of soul; I pray that I may never suffer in that fashion again unless the same result should hang upon it.

That night, after the service, there came into my vestry a man who was as nearly insane as he could be to be out of an asylum. His eyes seemed ready to start from his head, and he said that he should utterly have despaired if he had not heard that discourse, which had made him feel that there was one man alive who understood his feelings, and could describe his experience. I talked with him, and tried to encourage him, and asked him to come again on the Monday night, when I should have a little more time to speak with him. I saw the brother again, and I told him that I thought he was a hopeful patient, and I was glad that the word had been so suited to his case. Apparently, he put aside the comfort which I presented for his acceptance, and yet I had the consciousness upon me that the precious truth which he had heard was at work upon his mind, and that the storm of his soul would soon subside into a deep calm.

Now hear the sequel. Last night, of all the times in the year, when, strange to say, I was preaching from the words, "The Almighty hath vexed my soul," after the service, in walked this self-same brother who had called on me five years before. This time, he looked as different as noonday from midnight, or as life from death. I said to him, "I am glad to see you, for I have often thought about you, and wondered whether you were brought into perfect peace." I told you that I went to Mentone, and my patient also went into the country, so that we had not met for five years. To my enquiries, this brother replied, "Yes, you said I was a hopeful patient, and I am sure you will be glad to know that I have walked in the sunlight from that day till now. Everything is changed and altered with me." Dear friends, as soon as I saw my poor despairing patient the first time, I blessed God that my fearful experience had prepared me to sympathize with him and guide him; but last night, when I saw him perfectly restored, my heart overflowed with gratitude to God for my former sorrowful feelings. I would go into the deeps a hundred times to cheer a downcast spirit: it is good for me to have been afflicted that I might know how to speak a word in season to one that is weary.'

If Spurgeon's sickness brought new wealth to his preaching it is equally true that those silent Sabbaths, when there was disappointment at the Tabernacle at his absence, worked together for the good of that great number in different countries and generations who were to be his readers. As one of the Pastor's favourite Puritans declared, 'Books may speak when the author cannot, and what is more, when he is not.' Spurgeon's literary labours would never have become what they were had it not been for the many periods of enforced absence from the pulpit. In days of illness or convalescence, when in the eyes of the public he was doing nothing, he was, in reality, producing his most enduring work. To the very end of his life he continued to write, and each winter at Mentone brought a new project. In the winter of 1887–8, when Spurgeon had come through many months of heart-ache and trial over the 'Down-Grade' controversy, he solaced himself in writing *The Cheque Book of the Bank of Faith*, his testimony to the gain which the 'furnace of affliction' had brought to him:

'To the cheering Scriptures, I have added testimonies of my own, the fruit of trial and experience. I believe all the promises of God, but many of them I have personally tried and proved. . . . I commenced these daily portions when I was wading in the surf of controversy. Since then, I have been cast into 'waters to swim in,' which, but for God's upholding hand, would have proved waters to drown in. . . . I do not mention this to exact sympathy, but simply to let the reader see that I am no dry-land sailor. I have traversed those oceans which are not Pacific full many a time: I know the roll of the billows, and the rush of the winds. Never were the promises of Jehovah so precious to me as at this hour. Some of them I never understood till now; I had not reached the date at which they matured, for I was not myself mature enough to perceive their meaning. How much more wonderful is the Bible to me now than it was a few months ago! In obeying the Lord, and bearing His reproach outside the camp, I have not received new promises; but the result to me is much the same as if I had done so, for the old ones have opened up to me with richer stores.'

What a storehouse the Bible is, since a man may continue to preach from it for years, and still find that there is more to preach from than when he began to discourse upon it! What pyramids of books have been written upon the Bible, and yet we who are students find no portion over-expounded, but large parts which are scarcely touched! If you take Darling's *Cyclopaedia* and look at a text which one divine has preached upon, you will see that dozens have done the same; but there are hundreds of texts which remain like virgin summits, whereon the foot of the preacher has never stood. I might almost say that the major part of the Word of God is in that condition; it is still an Eldorado unexplored, a land whose dust is gold.—C.H.S., *in speech at a Bible Society Meeting,* 1882.

Perhaps you will allow me to say a word or two about his power as a writer—his power to express himself in writing. In this democratic age, when sympathy with the masses is on everyone's lips, it often seems to me wonderful that the power of communicating with the multitude is so rare. We have scores of ministers who are ambitious of writing for the world of the cultivated; but a book frankly and successfully addressing the average man, in language which he can understand, is one of the rarest products of the press. It really requires very exceptional power. It requires knowledge of human nature, and knowledge of life. It requires common sense; it requires wit and humour; and it requires command of simple and powerful Saxon. Whatever the requirements may be, Mr. Spurgeon had them in an unexampled degree.—DR. JAMES STALKER, *in an address at the unveiling of the C. H. Spurgeon Memorial, at the Stockwell Orphanage,* June 20, 1894.

25

Later Literary Works

NOT only did Spurgeon, to the end of his life, continue to read vast numbers of the works written by ancient and modern authors, but he also kept on writing books for other people to read, and when he was 'called home' he had so many in course of preparation that his posthumous works form quite a numerous company. Many people appear to have thought that it was hardly possible for Spurgeon, with the almost incessant demands upon his time and strength, to devote much personal attention to certain portions of his literary labours, so they attributed to his helpers a good deal of the toil that devolved upon him. One person was credited with the compilation of the *Book Almanack*, although its Editor never entrusted it to anyone but himself until the year of his long illness; and on one occasion, at least, he felt it needful to remind his readers that his connection with *The Sword and the Trowel* was not by any means a merely nominal one, but was very real and practical. In his 'Notes' for April, 1885, anticipating his return from Mentone, he wrote:

'A kindly reviewer speaks of our March number as vivacious and good, "notwithstanding the absence of the Editor." The fact is, that the Editor is never absent from the magazine; but personally reads every line of each number. Friends now and then write, blaming some supposed subordinate, if their tastes are not pleased; but the Editor hides behind nobody, friends must please blame *him*, for he is personally responsible. Our writers are able men, and are quite able to fight their own battles, should battles occur; but the Editor never wishes it to be imagined that he merely puts his name on the cover of the magazine, and leaves it to be produced by other people. No; it is our continual endeavour to make this serial as good as we can make it, and we would do better if we could. Notwithstanding illness, or absence from home, we have never been obliged to delegate our duties to anyone else; on the contrary, we have given all the more time to this work when we have been debarred from other labours.'

C. H. Spurgeon: The Full Harvest

The twenty-eight volumes of *The Sword and the Trowel*, from 1865 to 1892, contain notices of many thousands of books that the beloved Editor either read through, or examined sufficiently to be able to write reviews of them. He also read many that he did not review, for he was well aware that an unfavourable notice in his magazine would help to advertise erroneous teaching, and he thought the wiser course was to ignore such works altogether. His usual method of dealing with a thoroughly bad book—either morally or doctrinally—was to tear it into little pieces too small to do harm to anyone, or to commit it bodily to the flames. This was the sentence executed upon many volumes that cast doubt upon the Divinity of our Lord, the efficacy of His atoning sacrifice, or the inspiration of the Scriptures, though some works of that kind were allowed to remain as evidences of the character of the writings of some of the religious leaders of the day.

Taking the books published by Spurgeon during the last fourteen years of his life in chronological order, the first to be noted is *The Clue of the Maze, a Voice Lifted up on behalf of Honest Faith*. The Preface describes its autobiographical character: 'How I have personally threaded the labyrinth of life, thus far, may be of helpful interest to some other soul which just now is in a maze.' The subtitle is thus explained: 'A great poet let fall the expression, "honest doubt."[1] How greedily it was clutched at! Modern unbelief is so short of the quality that it seized the label, and, in season and out of season, it has advertised itself as HONEST doubt. It was in dire need of a character. Feeble as our voice may be, we lift it on behalf of HONEST FAITH.' The author was greatly gratified as he heard, from time to time, that his purpose in writing it had been happily fulfilled; and he was specially cheered by the testimony of a notable literary man who had been, through reading it, lifted up from blank atheism to saving faith in the Lord Jesus Christ. The little book has been translated into several foreign languages.

About the same time as *The Clue of the Maze* was published, the Pastor was busily occupied with the first of his four volumes, entitled *My Sermon Notes*. They were issued in response to an oft-repeated request for outlines of discourses which might be helpful to 'lay' or local preachers who have but little time for their pulpit preparation, or who find a difficulty in selecting suitable subjects for sermons and addresses. In order that the notes might be of still greater service to such brethren, they were made rather more ample

[1] Tennyson, in *In Memoriam* (section 95).

and detailed than when Spurgeon himself preached from them; and, for the same reason, appropriate extracts and illustrations were added to them. That the work met an urgent need was speedily apparent; and it was not long before a 'Note' to the following effect appeared in *The Sword and the Trowel*:

'Our first half-crown volume of outline sermons has met with a very cordial reception, the first edition of 5,000 being very nearly cleared out, though only so lately presented to the public. Taking this as a token for good, we shall soon issue the second portion, which contains our notes of sermons from Ecclesiastes to Malachi. Brethren whose time is much occupied with business cares, who nevertheless delight to preach the Word of God, will find these *Sermon Notes* to be a great assistance. With that view we have prepared them, and to that end we trust that God will bless them. They are not sufficiently *in extenso* to suit the idler, and yet we trust there is enough of them to aid the embarrassed worker. The preparation of this volume has enabled us to while away the evenings and the occasional wet and cloudy days of our rustication at Mentone. As its fragmentary nature allowed us to take it up and lay it down at will, it was just the sort of occupation to afford us happy recreation. To have nothing to do, is bondage; but such congenial employment as this has aided us in being perfectly at ease.'

In due time, the whole set was completed, and it had a very large sale. Two years after the Pastor's home-going, another volume of a somewhat similar character was published—*C. H. Spurgeon's Facsimile Pulpit-Notes, with the Sermons Preached from them in the Metropolitan Tabernacle*. The book originated in rather a singular way. A paragraph appeared in various newspapers, announcing that some of the notes used by Spurgeon, while preaching at the Tabernacle, were about to be reproduced in *facsimile*, and the writer intimated that the work would be certain to have a favourable reception. As a matter of fact, up to that time, no such arrangement had been made; but the idea seemed so good, and the publicity given to it was so helpful, that a dozen suitable outlines were selected, and, with the discourses delivered from them, were made into a volume which at once became an interesting memento of the preacher, and a striking illustration of his method of sermon construction.

The book which has the double distinction of having been translated into more foreign languages and of having been blessed to the salvation of more souls than any other of Spurgeon's works, as

[421]

far as is known, is the small volume entitled *All of Grace: an Earnest Word with those who are Seeking Salvation by the Lord Jesus Christ.* Its opening sentences are: 'The object of this book is the salvation of the reader. He who spoke and wrote it will be greatly disappointed if it does not lead many to the Lord Jesus. It is sent forth in childlike dependence upon the power of God the Holy Ghost, to use it in the conversion of millions, if so He pleases.'

One of the many instances of the usefulness of the little volume, of which the Pastor knew before he was 'called home,' was reported to him in the following letter from a doctor who was a member of the Tabernacle church:

'My Dear Sir,

I have a message to give you, and will do it as briefly as I can. For many years, I have had the friendship of a well-known medical man in ———. For some two or three years, he has suffered from diabetes; but he has lived just the same, entirely without Christ. Last Christmas, I sent him a copy of *All of Grace.* A short time ago, when I was at the seaside, I received a letter from a friend in which he said, "I believe Dr. —— is saved, . . . the teaching has been all Mr. Spurgeon's." This I was delighted to hear.

Yesterday, I stood by his side. I found him very ill, suffering from inflammation of the lungs, consequent on the diabetes. He took my hands, and, as well as he could between his tears, and the shortness of breath, told me that he was saved, that he was a child of God, that his sins were all forgiven, that he was washed in the blood of his Saviour, and clothed in the robe of His perfect righteousness; and recovering his breath, he said, very solemnly, "Will you tell Mr. Spurgeon that this has all come, in God's mercy to me a poor sinner, by that book,"—pointing to *All of Grace*, which was lying open on his bed—"Will you let him know what a blessing that book has been to me?"

Dear sir, I have delivered the message. I know you will be pleased to receive it, and will you remember my dear friend in prayer?

Believe me to be,

Yours deeply-indebted,

———.'

The book having been so manifestly owned of God, Spurgeon prepared a companion volume, *According to Promise; or, the Lord's Method of Dealing with His Chosen People*; and, some time later, he issued *Around the Wicket Gate; or, a Friendly Talk with Seekers con-*

cerning Faith in the Lord Jesus Christ, both of which have had a wide circulation, and have been greatly blessed.

The volume which, more than any other of Spurgeon's writings, illustrates his power of rapid composition, is *The Cheque Book of the Bank of Faith*. It consists of 366 Scripture promises, arranged for daily use, with brief experimental comments suitable for reading at family worship or as a help to private devotion. During the Pastor's stay at Mentone, in the winter of 1887–8, there was one Monday when the rain poured down incessantly in such tropical fashion that he was compelled to remain indoors all day. His companions were not aware that he was contemplating the commencement of another new book, but they noticed how rapidly he was covering sheet after sheet of foreign notepaper. After a while, he explained that he had begun a volume of daily meditations; and, before he went to bed, that night, he had finished the portions for the month of January, and handed them to Mr. Passmore to send off to London for the printers. They were so carefully written that they needed but little correction; and anyone who has the book, and examines the first thirty-one pages in it, will be able to estimate both the quantity and the quality of one wet day's work while the Pastor was supposed to be on his holiday in the sunny South.

Spurgeon had many proofs of the usefulness of *The Cheque Book* volume; one that interested and amused him was thus related by Pastor W. Williams, of Upton Chapel:

'Opposite my study-window are several gardens, affording during summertime a pleasant outlook; but, in the first of them, there *was* tied up, until recently, a large retriever dog. His incessant barking made study and thought quite out of the question. I let his owner know this in a quiet way; but still the dog was there. I wondered if I should pray about the matter: it seemed rather comical to pray about the barking of a dog; besides, I could not bring to mind a promise about such a thing which I could mention in prayer, until one day I opened Mr. Spurgeon's *Cheque Book of the Bank of Faith*, at page 157, where the text is, "But against any of the children of Israel shall not a dog move his tongue," the comment on which begins, "What! has God power over the tongues of dogs? Can He keep curs from barking? Yes, it is even so." I was startled, for no dog ever laid hold with greater tenacity than this text did on me. There and then I knelt down, and asked that the dog might be removed.

The dog has gone, and the owner, too; but mark, the arrangements to go were made by the owner just about the time that the prayer was offered! How true it is that—

> *More things are wrought by prayer*
> *Than this world dreams of!'*

Following *The Cheque Book*, Spurgeon published two volumes of quite a different character—*The Salt-cellars, being a Collection of Proverbs, together with Homely Notes thereon.* For nearly twenty years, he had issued *John Ploughman's Almanack*, and the labour involved in collecting or composing so many thousands of proverbs, maxims, and mottoes, seemed to justify their preservation in a more permanent form than the annual broadsheet ensured. Accordingly, they were arranged alphabetically, in two sections, 'Proverbs and Quaint Sayings,' and 'Sayings of a more Spiritual Sort;' and, in nearly every instance, 'Homely Notes' were added.

Each of the volumes, as it was published, received a most hearty welcome both from the press and the public, and their contents have ever since been frequently quoted in the pulpit and on the platform. Spurgeon sent the two books to George Augustus Sala, with a request that he would review them in *The Daily Telegraph* if he judged them worthy of such a notice. In reply, Sala wrote a long and cordial letter, in the course of which he said: 'Your two volumes were such pleasant reading that I thought the best way to meet your views would be to make *The Salt Cellars* the text for a leading article, which I now have much pleasure in sending you. Naturally, I was struck (and amused) by the maxim, "Newspapers are the Bibles of worldings." *That is exactly so*; and it is eminently fitting that it *should* be so; because, to a journalist who is aware of the usefulness and respects the dignity of his calling, the press is a pulpit whence, on week-days, he preaches lay sermons, leaving Sunday to you and your brethren.'

The opening and closing paragraphs of the 'leading article' ran as follows:

'A really busy man has usually the largest amount of leisure at his disposal, and Mr. C. H. Spurgeon, amidst the multifarious labours and responsibilities which devolve on him as Pastor of an immense congregation, has found time to dig and delve very deeply indeed in that richest of colloquial mines—the treasury of English proverbs. Under the title of *The Salt Cellars*, Mr. Spurgeon has just issued two comely and handy volumes, which will derive much value, not only from the fact that the work is one presenting evidence of indefatigable industry of research and considerable acumen in selection, but also from the circumstance that the compiler has graced his chosen proverbs with a running commentary of what he modestly calls "homely notes." In reality, they are often humorous as well as homely, and are always replete with that spirit of cheerful piety, quite devoid of cant or bigotry, which renders Mr. Spurgeon's utterances always acceptable even to those who differ from him most widely in dogma. . . .

Mr. Spurgeon has chosen to select, as a proverb, that which appears to us to be more of the nature of a pulpit platitude, "Newspapers are the Bibles of worldlings"; and to this we have the homely note, "How diligently they read them! Here they find their law and profits, their judges and chronicles, their epistles and revelations." The newspapers, however, must take their chance of being abused, even by those who most diligently read them. Journalists are a long-suffering race, and it curiously happens that, among old Howell's proverbs, collected more than two centuries since, we find this one, "A diurnal-maker is the sub-amner to a historian."[1] We have no quarrel, therefore, with Mr. Spurgeon on this account. What he says about newspapers has long since been said at the Antipodes, where the vast weekly budgets of the Sydney and Melbourne journals are habitually called "The Bushman's Bible," constituting, as they do, the almost exclusive reading of the shepherds and stockriders far away in the bush. Altogether, *The Salt Cellars* may be welcomed as an equally entertaining and edifying compilation; and the scheme, as well as the actual accomplishment of the work, is alike creditable to the heart and the head of an estimable minister of religion who has long since won the rank of an English worthy.'

If there had been sufficient space available, an interesting chapter might have been compiled concerning 'Mr. Spurgeon as a Poet and Hymn-writer.' As that is not possible, one specimen of his poetry must be included here, partly because of its autobiographical character, but also because it was the last that he ever wrote. He put at the top of it, as the motto-text, 'I will make the dry land springs of

---

[1] The meaning is: 'A journal-maker (i.e. a journalist) is sub-almoner to a historian': in other words, 'Journalists supply source-material for 'historians' (the first known occurrence of the proverb is dated 1654).

water'; and as the title, 'The Drop which Grew into a Torrent. A Personal Experience.'

All my soul was dry and dead
Till I learned that Jesus bled;
Bled and suffer'd in my place,
Bearing sin in matchless grace.

Then a drop of Heavenly love
Fell upon me from above,
And by secret, mystic art
Reached the centre of my heart.

Glad the story I recount,
How that drop became a fount,
Bubbled up a living well,
Made my heart begin to swell.

All within my soul was praise,
Praise increasing all my days;
Praise which could not silent be:
Floods were struggling to be free.

More and more the waters grew,
Open wide the flood-gates flew,
Leaping forth in streams of song
Flowed my happy life along.

Lo! a river clear and sweet
Laved my glad, obedient feet!
Soon it rose up to my knees,
And I praised and prayed with ease.

Now my soul in praises swims,
Bathes in songs, and psalms, and hymns;
Plunges down into the deeps,
All her powers in worship steeps.

Hallelujah! O my Lord,
Torrents from my soul are poured!
I am carried clean away,
Praising, praising all the day.

In an ocean of delight,
Praising God with all my might,

Self is drowned. So let it be:
Only Christ remains to me.

The hymn was written in the early part of the year 1890, and was inserted in the programme used at the next College Conference. Those who were present, on that occasion, are not likely to forget the thrilling effect produced when the five hundred ministers and students joined in singing it to the tune 'Nottingham'. At the commencement, all sat and sang; but as they came to the later verses, they spontaneously rose, the time was quickened, and Mr. Manton Smith's cornet helped to swell the volume of praise expressed by the writer.

The next literary work was one of the smallest of Spurgeon's many volumes, yet its history and associations place it among the most notable of his publications. At the College Conference, in 1891, the Presidential Address struck all who heard it as being a peculiarly timely and weighty utterance; and some who listened to it, and to the sermon which followed it, three days later, afterwards said that they had a kind of premonitory conviction that their beloved President would never again meet the members and associates of the Pastors' College Evangelical Association in conference on earth; and so it proved to be.

On the Monday evening of that memorable week, at the public meeting in Upton Chapel, Spurgeon took, as the subject of his address, Ephesians 6. 16: 'Above all, taking the shield of faith, wherewith ye shall be able to quench all the fiery darts of the wicked.' This proved to be the prelude and preparation for the martial topic on which he intended to speak the next morning, and which he summarized under three heads, (1) *our armoury*, the Word of God; (2) *our army*, the Church of God; and (3) *our strength*, the Holy Spirit. It was a fitting climax to the long series of Inaugural Addresses, which were always reckoned, by those who were privileged to hear them, as the most solemn and forceful of all Spurgeon's utterances. It was rapturously received by the crowded and enthusiastic assembly; and, at its close, such urgent requests were presented for its publication in pamphlet form, that consent was at once given, on condition that the brethren would help to make it known when it was issued.

During the week following the Conference, the reporter's transcript was revised, considerable additions being made to the manuscript, and it was promptly published under the title, *The Greatest Fight in the World*. It immediately attained a very wide circulation; it was reprinted in the United States, translated into French and German, and passed through several large editions. Then, after Spurgeon's home-going, a generous gentleman, who had been with him on the platform during its delivery, felt that one of the best ways of honouring his memory was to perpetuate his testimony, and therefore arranged that a copy of it, bearing the additional title, 'C. H. Spurgeon's Final Manifesto,' should be sent, through Mrs. Spurgeon's Book Fund, to every clergyman and minister of every denomination in England. In this way, 34,500 more copies were circulated, with abundant evidence that the Lord had owned and blessed the effort.

Another small volume, which has very tender associations connected with it, is *Memories of Stambourne*. It was commenced before Spurgeon's long illness in 1891, and it was completed during the time of partial restoration which was graciously granted to him later in that year. The little book was really the first portion of *C. H. Spurgeon's Autobiography*, telling the story of his childhood as he wished it to go forth to the public, and for that reason it was largely used in the compilation of the early chapters of this Standard Life. For several years, the Pastor visited Stambourne and its neighbourhood, partly because of his early recollections of his grandfather's country, and partly that he might gather up all available material concerning some of the memorable scenes of his boyhood. On the last occasion, he took with him Mr. T. H. Nash, who kindly photographed a number of views for reproduction in the volume then being written. It was during the last such visit that the 'overpowering headache' came on, of which Spurgeon afterwards wrote, adding, 'I had to hurry home, to go up to that chamber wherein, for three months, I suffered beyond measure, and was often between the jaws of death.' In answer to the almost universal prayer of believers in all lands, he was raised up for a time, and had the satisfaction of seeing his little book of reminiscences not only finished and published, but also widely welcomed and greatly enjoyed.

But there was another volume, in progress at the same time, which was destined to have a still more pathetic interest attaching to it. That was *The Gospel of the Kingdom; a Popular Exposition of the Gospel according to Matthew*, concerning which Mrs. Spurgeon wrote, after her husband's promotion to glory: 'It stands alone in its sacred and sorrowful significance. It is the tired worker's final labour of

love for his Lord. It is the last sweet song from lips that were ever
sounding forth the praises of his King. It is the dying shout of
victory from the standard-bearer, who bore his Captain's colours
unflinchingly through the thickest of the fight. . . . Much of the
later portion of the work was written on the very borderland of
heaven, amid the nearing glories of the unseen world, and almost
within sight of the Golden Gates.'

Spurgeon's intention, in preparing the volume, was to produce a
devotional Commentary, specially calling attention to the Kingship
of the Lord Jesus Christ, which is the prominent feature of the
Gospel according to Matthew. He proceeded with the work very
leisurely, and a great part of it was written during his winter
sojourns on the sunny shores of the Mediterranean. Towards the
latter part of 1891, when Spurgeon was sufficiently restored to be
able to travel to Mentone, he eagerly resumed his delightful service
of expounding the first Gospel, and he wrote some portion of it,
day by day, until he was finally laid aside. To the last, his handwriting was as clear, and distinct, and firm as ever, and there was no
sign of the rapidly approaching collapse which was to send such a
thrill of sorrow through the whole of Christendom. Mentally and
spiritually, the work was equal to the best efforts of his brightest
years; but he was not permitted to finish it, for he was called up to
see the King of whom he had been writing, and to share in the
glories of the Kingdom of which he had so long been preaching to
others.

After due consideration, it was resolved that, instead of leaving
his last literary work to stand like a broken column, it should be
completed as nearly as possible in the way he would himself have
ended it, had he been spared long enough. He had so often expounded the closing chapters of Matthew's Gospel that there was
abundant material for the latter portion of his Commentary to be
compiled *entirely from his own spoken and written words*. This delicate
duty was entrusted to his private secretary. The Editor of *The
British Weekly* indirectly paid a high compliment to the compiler of
the later chapters when he said that there should have been some
indication as to where Spurgeon's manuscript ended. Evidently,
'the worker in mosaics' had so skilfully joined together the precious
treasures committed to his charge that even this keen critic could
not discover any break in the connection.

Another literary work, upon which Spurgeon was busily occupied when the home-call came to him at Mentone, was *Messages to the*

Multitude, the eighth volume in 'The Preachers of the Age' series, issued by Messrs. Sampson Low, Marston, and Co. It was intended to set forth the style of the Pastor's preaching at various periods of his long ministry; and, to that end, the sermons selected ranged from one delivered in the Surrey Gardens Music Hall, in 1859, to another, which was almost the last preached in the Tabernacle, in 1891.

Many other volumes had been either commenced or planned by Spurgeon; and several of them have been completed since his death. The first of these was *The Art of Illustration*, forming the third series of *Lectures to my Students*, and containing exceedingly valuable information concerning the use of illustrations in preaching, and the books in which anecdotes, illustrations, fables, emblems, and parables are to be found. The following extract shows how Spurgeon turned an illustration used by Henry Ward Beecher to quite a different purpose from the one intended by the eminent American preacher:

'When a critical adversary attacks our metaphors, he generally makes short work of them. To friendly minds, images are arguments; but to opponents, they are opportunities for attack; the enemy climbs up by the window. Comparisons are swords with two edges, which cut both ways; and, frequently, what seems a sharp and telling illustration may be wittily turned against you, so as to cause a laugh at your expense: therefore, do not rely upon your metaphors and parables. Even a second-rate man may defend himself from a superior mind if he can dexterously turn his assailant's gun upon himself. Here is an instance which concerns myself, and I give it for that reason, since these lectures have all along been autobiographical. I give a cutting from one of our religious papers: "Mr. Beecher has been neatly tripped up in *The Sword and the Trowel*. In his *Lectures on Preaching*, he asserts that Mr. Spurgeon has succeeded 'in spite of his Calvinism'; adding the remark that 'the camel does not travel any better, nor is it any more useful, because of the hump on its back.' The illustration is not a felicitous one, for Mr. Spurgeon thus retorts: 'Naturalists assure us that the camel's hump is of great importance in the eyes of the Arabs, who judge of the condition of their beasts by the size, shape, and firmness of their humps. The camel feeds upon his hump when he traverses the wilderness, so that in proportion as the animal travels over the sandy wastes, and suffers from privation and fatigue, the mass diminishes; and he is not fit for a long journey till the hump has regained its usual proportions. Calvinism, then, is the spiritual meat which enables a man to labour on in the ways of Christian service; and, though ridiculed as a hump by those who are only lookers-on, those who traverse the weary paths of a wilderness experience know too well its value to be willing to part with it, even if a Beecher's splendid talents could be given in exchange." '

Next followed one of the choicest volumes in the whole of Spurgeon's works, *'Till He Come': Communion Meditations and Addresses.* It consists very largely of the quiet, homely talks of the Pastor to the little companies of Christians who gathered with him around the table of the Lord in his sitting-room at Mentone; but it also includes some of his more public utterances when thousands of believers met for communion in the Tabernacle. The value of the ordinance, and the spiritual benefit to be derived from its frequent observance, are clearly set forth; and it seems impossible for any lover of the Lord to read the book without being brought into still closer fellowship with the Saviour, and a deeper appreciation of the great atoning sacrifice symbolized by the broken bread and the filled cup. The volume has proved invaluable as an aid to private devotion, and as a guide to those who are called to preside at the celebration of the sacred feast of love.

Another book, which Christian workers have found to be of great service to them, is *The Soul-winner; or, How to Lead Sinners to the Saviour.* Containing several lectures to the students of the Pastors' College, addresses to Sunday-school teachers and open-air preachers, and sermons upon what Spurgeon termed 'that most royal employment—soul-winning,' it has been compiled for the help of those who desire to become wise in winning souls, while it explains some of the secrets of the author's own power as one of the greatest of all soul-winners.

Beside the new works published since Spurgeon's death, there have been already issued no less than eight different sets of his sermons: *The Parables of our Lord*; *The Miracles* (two volumes); *The Most Holy Place* (fifty-two discourses on the Song of Solomon); *The Messiah, our Lord's Names, Titles, and Attributes*; *Christ in the Old Testament*; *The Everlasting Gospel*; and *The Gospel for the People.* Ten smaller volumes contain shorter passages from his writings, suitable for various classes of readers: *Teachings of Nature in the Kingdom of Grace, Words of Wisdom, Words of Warning,* and *Words of*

C. H. Spurgeon: The Full Harvest

Cheer for Daily Life, Words of Counsel for Christian Workers, Words of Advice for Seekers, We Endeavour, Come, ye Children, Gospel Extracts from C. H. Spurgeon, and *Glorious Themes for Saints and Sinners.* The last-named book has been printed in very large type so as to adapt it to the needs of old people and little children.

It is impossible to estimate the total number of volumes of Spurgeon's works that have been issued in this country, in the United States, and in many other lands in which they have been translated into foreign languages. Many millions of copies must already have been sold; and, although it is now eight years since he was 'called home,' there is, apparently, no diminution in the demand for them. Indeed, the many new works from his lips and pen published since his promotion to higher service, the still larger number of reprints or extracts from his writings, and the ever-increasing circulation of his sermons, make it almost certain that his publications are distributed even more widely now than they were during his lifetime on earth, while testimony to their usefulness is constantly being received from all quarters of the globe. It may, therefore, be concluded that, great as was his influence in the pulpit, his power through the press is not a whit less; and there seems to be no valid reason why his testimony to the truth should not be continued, by means of the printed page, until the Lord Himself returns.

It is a sort of tradition of the fathers that it is wrong to laugh on Sundays. The eleventh commandment is, that we are to love one another; and then, according to some people, the twelfth is, 'Thou shalt pull a long face on Sunday.' I must confess that I would rather hear people laugh than I would see them asleep in the house of God; and I would rather get the truth into them through the medium of ridicule than I would have it neglected, or leave the people to perish through lack of reception of the message. I do believe, in my heart, that there may be as much holiness in a laugh as in a cry; and that, sometimes, to laugh is the better thing of the two, for I may weep, and be murmuring, and repining, and thinking all sorts of bitter thoughts against God; while, at another time, I may laugh the laugh of sarcasm against sin, and so evince a holy earnestness in the defence of the truth. I do not know why ridicule is to be given up to Satan as a weapon to be used against us, and not to be employed by us as a weapon against him. I will venture to affirm that the Reformation owed almost as much to the sense of the ridiculous in human nature as to anything else, and that those humorous squibs and caricatures, that were issued by the friends of Luther, did more to open the eyes of Germany to the abominations of the priesthood than the more solid and ponderous arguments against Romanism. I know no reason why we should not, on suitable occasions, try the same style of reasoning. 'It is a dangerous weapon,' it will be said, 'and many men will cut their fingers with it.' Well, that is their own lookout; but I do not know why we should be so particular about their cutting their fingers if they can, at the same time, cut the throat of sin, and do serious damage to the great adversary of souls.—C.H.S., *in 'Lectures to my Students.'*

26

Pure Fun

GLEAMS of Spurgeon's ready humour have been visible at intervals throughout preceding chapters and will remain visible to the end of the volume, but it was felt that the record of his happy life would not be complete unless at least one chapter was filled with specimens of that pure fun which was as characteristic of him as was his 'precious faith.' All who were brought into the closest contact with him know that his wit was as abundant as his wisdom; indeed, full often, the wisdom found its most effective utterance by means of the witty words which gained an entrance for the message which might otherwise have been rejected. His fun was always pure, with an emphasis; and he showed how it was possible for the highest spirituality to find a fitting exemplification in the brightest and cheeriest character. Some of his most intimate friends have often said that there was not the slightest incongruity, after one of his brilliant witticisms which had set the whole company laughing, in hearing him say, 'Let us pray,' for both the merriment and the devotion were sanctified. He had no sympathy with the hymn-tinkerer who altered even the glorious hundredth Psalm by putting 'fear' instead of 'mirth' in the third line of the first verse; and he always sang it according to the authorized version, as it appears in *Our Own Hymn-Book*—

> *All people that on earth do dwell,*
> *Sing to the Lord with cheerful voice;*
> *Him serve with* mirth, *His praise forth tell;*
> *Come ye before Him, and rejoice.*

In making a rather rough classification of Spurgeon's pure fun, as manifested under various aspects throughout his long public career, first may be placed a few incidents associated with a matter which he always regarded as of great importance—punctuality.

Everyone who was acquainted with him knows how scrupulously punctual he was at all services and meetings, and that, unless something very unusual had detained him, he was ready to commence either the worship or the business proceedings at the exact

[435]

minute fixed. In the New Park Street days, he was unavoidably late on one occasion when he was to meet the deacons. One of them, the most pompous of the whole company, who was himself noted for his punctuality, pulled out his watch, and held it up reproachfully before the young minister. Looking at it in a critical fashion, Spurgeon said, 'Yes; it's a very good watch, I have no doubt, but it is rather old-fashioned, isn't it?'

He had often to suffer inconvenience and loss of time because those who had asked for interviews with him were not at the place arranged at the appointed hour. Frequently, after allowing a few minutes' grace, he would go away to attend to other service, leaving word that, as those he expected had not come according to the arrangement made, they must wait until he could find some other convenient opportunity of meeting them. This was to him a method of giving a lesson which many greatly needed. 'Punctuality is the politeness of kings'; yet some who are 'kings and priests unto God' are sadly deficient in that particular virtue. Sometimes, the Pastor would laughingly say that perhaps those who came so late were qualifying to act as lawyers, whose motto would be, 'Procrastination is the hinge of business; punctuality is the thief of time.'

'General' Booth once sent an *'aide-de-camp'* to Spurgeon to ask for an interview for himself. The hour for him to come was named but it was several minutes past the time when he arrived. Spurgeon, though sympathizing with the efforts of the Salvation Army, never approved of what he called their 'playing at soldiers,' so he said, in a tone of gentle irony, 'Oh, General! military men should be punctual!' It appeared that the object of 'General' Booth was to ascertain if the Tabernacle could be lent to the Army for some great gathering; but he would not ask for the loan of the building until the Pastor gave him some sign that, if he did make such a request, it would be granted. There the matter rested.

The Pastor once had occasion to see Gladstone, the Prime Minister, at Downing Street. Having asked for an interview of ten minutes, he arrived punctually, and, having transacted the business about which he had called, rose to leave directly the allotted time had expired. 'The grand old man' was not willing to allow his visitor to go away so quickly—though he said he wished others who called upon him would be as prompt both in arriving and departing—and 'the two prime ministers,' as they were often designated, continued chatting for a good while longer. It was during the conversation which ensued that Spurgeon suggested to the great Liberal leader a grander measure of reform than any he had ever introduced. His proposal was, that all the servants of the State, whether in the Church, the Army, the Navy, or the Civil Service, should be excluded from Parliament, just as the servants in a private family are not allowed to make the rules and regulations under which the household is governed. Possibly, archbishops, bishops, generals, admirals, noble lords, and right honourable gentlemen might imagine that this suggestion was a sample of Mr. Spurgeon's pure fun, but he introduced it to Mr. Gladstone with the utmost seriousness, and he often referred to it as a plan which would greatly and permanently benefit the whole nation, and which he believed his fellow-countrymen would adopt if it were laid before them by the great statesman to whom he submitted it.

*

During a General Election, it was discovered, one Monday morning, that the front gates and walls of 'Helensburgh House' had been, in the course of the night, very plentifully daubed over with paint to correspond with the colours of the Conservative candidates for that division of Surrey. In speaking, at the Tabernacle, the same evening, concerning the disfigurement of his premises, Spurgeon said, 'It is *notorious* that I am *no Tory*, so I shall not trouble to remove the paint; perhaps those who put it on will take it off when it has been there long enough to please them'; and, in due time, they did so.

The mention of a General Election recalls a characteristic anecdote which Spurgeon delighted to tell. He had gone to preach for his friend, John Offord, and quite unavoidably was a little late in arriving. He explained that there had been a block on the road, which had delayed him; and, in addition, he had stopped on the way to vote. 'To vote!' exclaimed the good man; 'but my dear brother, I thought you were a citizen of the New Jerusalem!' 'So I am,' replied Spurgeon, 'but my "old man" is a citizen of this world.' 'Ah! but you should mortify your "old man." ' 'That is exactly what I did; for my "old man" is a Tory, and I made him vote for the Liberals!'

When the Tabernacle was about to be opened, tickets of admission to the various gatherings were printed. The one intended as a pass to the first service seemed to Mr. Spurgeon so unsuitable to the occasion that he turned it into a sweep's advertisement by annotating the front of it in this humorous style:

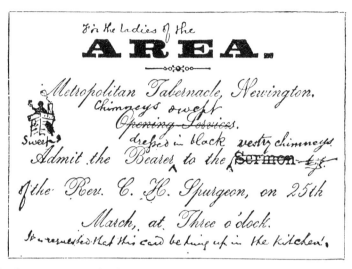

He also wrote on the back the comments and queries here reproduced in *facsimile*—

and sent the card to Mr. Passmore.

One matter that always afforded Spurgeon the opportunity of poking a little good-natured fun at his esteemed publishers (Messrs. Passmore and Alabaster) was the non-arrival of proofs for which he was looking. Frequently, at Mentone, or at some other place where the author was combining rest and work, Mr. Passmore or Mr.

Alabaster would be asked about the 'Cock Robin shop' that he had left for a while. (A 'Cock Robin shop' is the trade designation of a small printing-office where cheap booklets, such as *The Death of Cock Robin*, are issued.) It was a theme for perennial merriment, and no protestations of the publishers availed to put an end to it. If sermon or magazine proofs were delayed, the invariable explanation was, 'Perhaps they have had another order for *Cock Robins*, so my work has had to wait.'

On one occasion, Spurgeon and his secretary had gone to Bournemouth for a week; and, not knowing beforehand where they would be staying, the printers were instructed to send proofs to the Post Office, to be left till called for. On enquiry, the officials declared that they had nothing for Spurgeon, so the following telegram was despatched to London:—'When you have finished *Cock Robins*, please forward proofs of sermon and magazine.' It turned out that the fault was with the postal authorities, for they had only looked for letters, whereas the printed matter was in the office all the while in the compartment allotted to bookpost packets.

At one of the meetings when contributions for the new Tabernacle were brought in, the names of Knight and Duke were read out from the list of subscribers, whereupon Spurgeon said, 'Really, we are in grand company with a knight and a duke!' Presently, 'Mr. King, five shillings,' was reported, when the Pastor exclaimed, 'Why, the king has actually given his crown! What a liberal monarch!' Directly afterwards, it was announced that Mr. Pig had contributed a guinea. 'That,' said Mr. Spurgeon, 'is a guinea-pig.'

The propensity of punning upon people's names was often indulged by the Pastor. Spurgeon could remember, in a very remarkable fashion, the faces and names of those whom he had once met; and if he made any mistake in addressing them, he would speedily and felicitously rectify it. A gentlemen, who had been at one of the annual College suppers, was again present the following year. The President saluted him with the hearty greeting, 'Glad to see you, Mr. Partridge.' The visitor was surprised to find himself recognized, but he replied, 'My name is Patridge, sir, not Partridge.' 'Ah, yes!' was the instant rejoinder, 'I won't make *game* of you any more.'

A lady in Worcestershire, writing to Mrs. Spurgeon concerning a service at Dunnington, near Evesham, says:—'Mr. Spurgeon shook hands with *seventy* members of one family, named Bomford, who had gone to hear him. One of our deacons, a Mr. Alway, was at the same time introduced to him; and, in his own inimitable and ready way, he exclaimed, "Rejoice in the Lord, Alway!"' '

Dr. John Campbell was once in a second-hand bookseller's shop with Spurgeon, and, pointing to *Thorn on Infant Baptism*, he said, 'There is "a thorn in the flesh" for you.' Mr. Spurgeon at once replied, 'Finish the quotation, my brother—"the messenger of Satan to buffet me."' '

During the Baptismal Regeneration Controversy, a friend said to Spurgeon, 'I hear that you are in hot water.' 'Oh, dear no!' he replied; 'it is the other fellows who are in the hot water; I am the stoker, the man who makes the water boil!'

*

Spurgeon made a very sparing use of his wit in the pulpit, though all his wits were always utilized there to the utmost. To one who objected to some humorous expression to which he had given utterance while preaching, he replied, 'If you had known how many others I kept back, you would not have found fault with that one, but you would have commended me for the restraint I had exercised.' He often said that he never went out of his way to make a joke—or to avoid one; and only the last great day will reveal how many were first attracted by some playful reference or amusing anecdote, which was like the bait to the fish, and concealed the hook on which they were soon happily caught.

At the last service in New Park Street Chapel, the Pastor reminded his hearers that the new Tabernacle, which they were about to enter, was close to 'The Elephant and Castle,' and then, urging them all to take their own share of the enlarged responsibilities resting upon them as a church and people, he said, 'Let every elephant bear his castle when we get there.' This was simply translating, into the dialect of Newington, Paul's words, 'Every man shall bear his own burden,' and, doubtless, the form of the injunction helped to impress it upon the memory of all who heard it.

No student of the Pastors' College, who listened to the notable sermon delivered in the desk-room by the beloved President, would be likely ever to forget the text of the discourse after it had been thus emphasized:—'Brethren, take care that this is always one of the Newington Butts—"*But* we preach Christ crucified." Let others hold up Jesus simply as an Example, if they will; "but *we* preach Christ *crucified*." Let any, who like to do so, proclaim "another gospel, which is not another"; "but *we* preach *Christ crucified*."' '

On one occasion, when Mr. Spurgeon was to preach in a Non-conformist 'church' where the service was of a very elaborate character, someone else had been asked to conduct 'the preliminaries.' The preacher remained in the vestry until the voluntary, the lessons, the prayers, and the anthem were finished, then entering the pulpit, he said, 'Now, brethren, let us *pray*'; and the tone in which the last word was uttered indicated plainly enough what he thought of all that had gone before.

When William Cuff was minister at Providence Chapel, Hackney, one of the College Conference meetings was held there. The President presided, and in the course of his speech, he pointed to the organ, and said, 'I look upon that as an innovation; and if I were here, I should want it to be an outovation, and then we would have an ovation over its departure. I was once asked to open an organ—I suppose the people wanted me to preach in connection with the introduction of the new instrument. I said that I was quite willing to open it as Simple Simon opened his mother's bellows, to see where the wind came from, but I could not take any other part in the ceremony.'

Preaching at a chapel in the country, Mr. Spurgeon gave out Isaac Watts' version of the 91st Psalm—

> *He that hath made his refuge God,*
> *Shall find a most secure abode;—*

and then added, 'We'll sing it to the tune "Refuge" '. The organist leaned over from the gallery, and whispered to the preacher, 'It is not in our tune-book, sir.' 'Then it ought to be,' answered Spurgeon; 'no tune-book is complete unless "Refuge" is in it;' and, turning to the congregation, he said, 'The last time I was here, you people praised God for yourselves, but now you have a machine to do the praising for you. If it can't play "Refuge", we'll have it all the same, and I'll start it myself.'

Relating to his students some of his experiences in his early ministerial days, the President said:—'I remember going to a little village to preach; the forms had no back to them, and on the front bench were seated some ancient dames, each wearing a cloak and hood, like Little Red Riding Hood's, which made me feel that Solomon in all his glory was not arrayed like one of these. After the service had commenced, the front seat gave way with a crash, and down came all its occupants. This was too much for my gravity, and it was no use to go on with the sermon from the selected text, so I made the enquiry, "Where did that form come from? Was it borrowed from the Established Church!" "No, sir," replied someone; "it came from the Wesleyan Chapel." "Well then, you see, dear friends," I said, "Dissenting forms are no safer than those used by the Church of England, so I would advise you not to trust to any forms or ceremonies, but to the Lord Jesus Christ, for He alone can save you." That accident gave me a subject on which I was able to speak with freedom, and I hope with profit also, to my rustic hearers, who would probably long recollect my warning against borrowing any mere formal religion from either the Church or Dissent.'

*

Spurgeon was, even on ordinary occasions, so happy and joyous, and the means of communicating so much pleasure to others, that it is not surprising that his services were in great demand when his friends were about to be married. Some of the sweetest reminiscences of the loving couples who survived him are associated with the brightness that his presence and counsel imparted to their wedding-day. Naturally, the addresses given on such occasions bore considerable resemblance to one another, although there was always something special in each case. The earliest marriage service conducted by Spurgeon, of which the record has been preserved, was that of Pastor T. W. Medhurst and his first wife, Miss M. A. Cranfield. The wedding took place on May 26, 1859, at Kingston-on-Thames, where the first student of the Pastors' College had been ministering for more than two years. Mr. Spurgeon announced, at the commencement of the proceedings, that he was not going to perform the ceremony as if he were reading the burial service, nor as if he were about to thrust his two young friends into prison, and make their feet fast in the stocks. He also said that he hoped their wedded life would not be like the Church of England marriage service, which begins with 'Dearly beloved' and ends with 'amazement.' He trusted that they would both be 'dearly beloved' not only at the beginning of their united career, but all through to the end, and then for ever and ever; and that, while their sorrows would be mutually shared, their joys would all be multiplied. In expounding Ephesians 5. 23, the Pastor, addressing the bride, said, 'According to the teaching of the apostle, "The husband is the head of the wife." Don't you try to be the head; but you be the neck, then you can turn the head whichever way you like.'

At another marriage service, many years afterwards, Spurgeon, commenting on the same passage, said to the bridegroom, another of 'our own men,' 'My dear friend, don't you begin to feel proud because Paul says that the husband is the head of the wife. Solomon says that "a virtuous woman is a crown to her husband", and the crown is the top of the head. Still, the governing faculty should rest with the head; and the family will never be ordered aright unless we each keep our proper place.' On the same occasion, he thus humorously described the difficulties and privileges of a pastor's wife:—'If I was a young woman, and was thinking of being married, I would not marry a minister, because the position of minister's wife is a very difficult one for anyone to fill. Churches do not give a married minister two salaries, one for the husband and the other for the wife; but, in many cases, they look for the services of the wife, whether they pay for them or not. The Pastor's wife is expected to know everything about the church, and in another sense she is to know nothing of it; and she is equally blamed by some people whether she knows everything or nothing. Her duties consist in being *always at home* to attend to her husband and her family, and being *always out*, visiting other people, and doing all sorts of things for the whole church! Well, of course, that is impossible; she cannot be at everybody's beck and call, and she cannot expect to please everybody. Her husband cannot do *that*, and I think he is very foolish if he tries to do it; and I am certain that, as the husband cannot please everybody, neither can the wife. There will be sure to be somebody or other who will be displeased, especially if that somebody had herself half hoped to be the minister's wife! Difficulties arise continually in the best-regulated churches; and the position of the minister's wife is always a very trying one. Still, I think, that if I was a Christian young woman, I would marry a Christian minister if I could, because there is an opportunity of doing so much good in helping him in his service for Christ. It is a great assistance to the cause of God to keep the minister himself in good order for his work. It is his wife's duty to see that he is not uncomfortable at home; for, if everything there is happy, and free from care, he can give all his thoughts to his preparation for the pulpit; and the godly woman, who thus helps her husband to preach better, is herself a preacher though she never speaks in public, and she becomes to the highest degree useful to that portion of the Church of Christ which is committed to her husband's charge.'

Wedding breakfasts naturally afforded Spurgeon the opportunity of making many kind and witty remarks. He was very fond of saying to the bridegroom, 'I really cannot compliment you upon your great discrimination in choosing your bride;' and then, when the poor fellow was blushing to the roots of his hair, and the guests all round the table (if they had not previously heard the joke) were saying to one another, 'What can Mr. Spurgeon mean?' he quietly added, 'Any stupid, with half an eye, could see that she would make a man a good wife, so no discrimination was needed in your case, and I very heartily congratulate you upon your choice.' The neat turn of the speech not only set the whole company at their ease, but proved a notable addition to the harmless merriment that always prevailed on such occasions until the time came for the closing devotional service before the happy couple started for their honeymoon.

At one wedding breakfast, Spurgeon made an amusing allusion to the fact that the bridegroom, a missionary from Japan, had been previously married. Speaking to the bride, he said, 'You must not be too proud of your husband, Mrs. ———, for he is only second-hand; yet he is as good as new, for he has been Japanned!'[1]

Even when he had not been present at the marriage of his friends, Spurgeon often managed to make merriment for them out of something which he heard or knew concerning the happy event. A notable instance of this occurred when 'one of our own men' and his bride went to Mentone for their honeymoon, Spurgeon himself being there at the time, and someone sent to the beloved President a newspaper containing a full report of the service, and the details generally published on such occasions. In the course of conversation with the happy couple, Mr. Spurgeon said to the bride, 'Mrs. ———, if I was a young lady, going to be married, I should wear so-and-so and so-and-so.' Turning to her husband, she exclaimed, 'Oh, ———! Isn't it funny? That's just how I was dressed.' 'Then,' said Mr. Spurgeon, 'I should have so many bridesmaids, and they should wear such-and-such dresses and such-and-such hats.' 'Oh, ———! Why, that is just how many bridesmaids I had, and they were dressed exactly like that.' 'Then, for presents,' said the Pastor, 'I should like so-and-so and so-and-so.' 'Oh, ———! Isn't it funny? That is just what we had.' It is not certain that the good lady ever knew how it came to pass that the great preacher's wishes and her own coincided so singularly! Certainly, he extracted a considerable quantity of pure fun out of her amazement as he proceeded with his recital of things to be desired at a wedding.

[1] 'Japanned'. Made like new by the use of lacquer.

On one of his visits to Mentone, a friend asked him, 'In what coloured ink should a promise of marriage be written?' He guessed all the colours he could think of, and then was informed that the right answer was, 'in violet' (inviolate). He was so delighted with the conundrum,—both for its wit, and for its confirmation of the solemnity of an engagement with a view to marriage,—that he often propounded it to his friends, and seldom found one who was more successful in seeing through it than he himself had been, though all thought the answer to it was admirable.

*

Spurgeon once spent an evening with a few of Her Majesty's judges at the house of Mr. Justice Lush, who was his highly esteemed personal friend. After dinner, with an air of apparent seriousness, the Pastor said that he had a point of law that he should like to submit to the eminent authorities present. There was a man who had been lying in Camberwell for the last fortnight, and yet nobody would bury him; his friends would not arrange for his funeral, and neither the police nor the parish officials had been able to get him interred. The learned judges began consulting with one another, and quoting various Acts of Parliament that applied to such a case, and said that, if the relatives persistently refused to bury the man, the requisite power remained with certain local authorities whom they named. They were, however, considerably nonplussed when Spurgeon very quietly said, 'There was one little item in the case that I omitted to mention, *the man is not dead yet*!' 'Are you not afraid of the consequences of taking in Her Majesty's judges like that?' enquired Mr. Justice Lush, adding, 'You really ought to be committed for contempt of court; but as you seem to be well up in legal matters, tell me—Ought a man to be allowed to marry his widow's sister?' 'Oh, yes!' exclaimed the Pastor, not suspecting the trap that had been laid for him, and in the excitement of the moment thinking that the question had been, 'Ought a man to be allowed to marry his deceased wife's sister?' 'Then,' said the judge, 'we will cry quits, for even your friend in Camberwell could not marry his *widow's* sister!'

Later in the evening, Spurgeon told a story that invariably elicited the wrong reply, and that occasion was no exception to the rule. 'A lady and gentleman were engaged to be married; they were walking along the sea-shore, when some dispute arose, and the lady, in a fit of temper, snatched the engagement ring from her finger, and threw it into the water. After a while, she found another lover, to whom she was married, and they went down to Scarborough to spend the honeymoon. On the first morning, they had fish for breakfast; and, as the bridegroom was dividing it, he felt something hard; what do you suppose the knife had cut against?' Of course, the judges, like everybody else, exclaimed, 'The ring.' 'No,' said Spurgeon, 'it was only a bone!'

Charles Spurgeon, the Pastor's son, mentions a service conducted by his father at Pollockshaws. During that visit to Scotland, Mr. Spurgeon was introduced to the Dean of Guild. 'The Dean of Guild: Oh, you are the gentleman who can go through every tollgate in England without paying!' 'I was not aware that any such privilege was attached to my office.' 'It is quite true, sir,' replied the Pastor; '*you* can go through every tollgate without paying, but the gatekeeper will charge for your horse and carriage!'

All the students of the Pastors' College, who have recorded their reminiscences of the time spent in connection with that Institution, have testified to the bright and joyous atmosphere which pervaded all the classes, and which has made that period in their history ever memorable to them. From the very beginning of Spurgeon's work of training young men for the Christian ministry, hard study and a happy spirit were delightfully combined. Even before there was any College, when a solitary student was under the charge of George Rogers, coming events cast their *sunshine* before, as the two following paragraphs, supplied by Thomas William Medhurst, Spurgeon's first student, clearly prove:

'Soon after I went to live with Mr. Rogers,[1] one Saturday morning Mr. Spurgeon called to see what progress we were making, when the following conversation took place:—"Well, friend Rogers," enquired the Governor, "how are you getting on with this zealous young Baptist?" "Oh!" replied the tutor, "we get along very nicely; but we don't say much about baptism. You know, Mr. Spurgeon, that when the Samaritan woman found the Saviour, she left her waterpot." "Yes, friend Rogers," was the prompt answer, "she left her sprinkling machine, for the Lord Jesus had shown her the 'much water' that there was in the deep well."

On another occasion, there had been a snowstorm during the night; so, in the morning, I joined Mr. Rogers' sons in a game of snowballing in front of the house. This, precise Mrs. Rogers con-

[1] Rogers, as a Congregationalist, held with infant sprinkling.

sidered very unbecoming on the part of a ministerial student! Mr. Spurgeon called shortly afterwards, on the same day, and the good old lady (she was a dear kind soul) asked him what he thought of me for so far forgetting what was due to my position as a candidate for the Christian ministry. Mr. Spurgeon replied, "Well, Mrs. Rogers, I greatly admire the prevenient grace of God that did not allow me to come earlier this morning; for had I been here, I fear I should have been tempted to join in the snowballing." Then, turning to me, he said, in a tone of assumed solemnity, "Young man, you are forgiven this time; but see that you transgress no more—until the next fall of snow!" '

Spurgeon evidently had great confidence, both in George Rogers and in those who were trained by him, or he would not have committed to his care the hundreds of students who passed through the College during the long period of his principalship. It is to the credit of both tutor and taught that, although some few of the men became Pædo-Baptists, no one of them was ever known to attribute his change of sentiments to the influence of the Congregational Principal. Yet the subject of believers' baptism *versus* infant sprinkling was very often under discussion; and probably all the students, at some time or other, sought to lead George Rogers into what they regarded as the light upon this important matter. The President used to say that the brethren treated their tutor as a kind of hone on which they tried to sharpen their Baptistic arguments, and he himself had many an encounter with the sturdy old Independent. A favourite simile with him was that the Pædo-Baptist tutor of Baptist students resembled a hen sitting on ducks' eggs, and he humorously described the agitation of the poor bird as she stood trembling on the edge of the pond while the ducklings took to the water according to their nature! This comparison was greatly enjoyed by the merry audience, and they were not less pleased with George Rogers' ready reply, 'If I am as silly as an old hen, I have always managed up to the present to keep my head above water!'

Pastor Harry Abraham has supplied the following description of a lively scene which may be regarded as fairly representative of many similar occurrences in the history of the College:

'The summer holidays had ended. The opening day of a new session was ever a time of glad greetings, and of pleasant preparations for the tasks which lay before us. Old friends were speaking mutual welcomes, and new students were regarded with kindly curiosity. The tutors were heartily received, as being at once our fathers and our brothers; for so was it ever in the days of George Rogers, David Gracey, and Archibald Fergusson; while the dear President, C. H. Spurgeon, was still the best-loved—most paternal and most fraternal of all.

On the morning to which I now refer, the three tutors were in their places on the platform in the College lecture-hall, and nearly a hundred of us occupied the benches. The venerable and venerated George Rogers was telling, in characteristic fashion, how he had spent the vacation: attending recognition services, delivering charges, preaching sermons, and speaking at various meetings in places where "our own men" were doing the Great Master's work. The dear old man could never resist an opportunity of making some playful allusion to his own Pædo-Baptist views, in contrast with those which his hearers held—always to the advantage of his own position, of course. An observation of this kind, which had just fallen from his lips, led Professor Gracey to interject the sentence, "But *you won't be baptized.*" "Yes, I will," replied the nimble-witted sage, "if you'll let me *stand up to be done!*" But the Irish wit of the classical tutor was equally quick, and he answered, "We're quite willing to let you stand up *if only the water is deep enough!*"—a retort which the students emphasized with a merry peal of laughter and ringing cheers. "Ah!" said the old man, in the familiar tone which always seemed gravest when his spirit was gayest, "you can't find anything *deep enough for Mr. Gracey!*"

In the very midst of the applause which followed this smart rejoinder, in came the President! Only those who knew how much he was beloved, and what a gladsome spirit of freedom was always associated with his coming upon such a scene, could have understood, or perhaps excused, the boisterous burst of welcome—laughter, cheers, and a general din of delight—which sent the echoes flying about the lecture-room for a while. Ere the noise subsided, Mr. Spurgeon had reached the platform steps, where he paused, lifted his right hand, and exclaimed, "Brethren! brethren! I feel like Moses coming down from the mount; true, there isn't much music, you are not exactly dancing, but you are making a great row; and, lo! I see that you are *worshipping—an Essex calf!*"[1] In an instant, Mr. Rogers had seized the sharp shaft of good-tempered humour, and, with exquisite grace and skill, had sent it flying back, by simply and swiftly *dropping into his chair*, with a profound

[1] Essex has long been famous for its calves, often facetiously called lions.

and courtly bow, *leaving the President standing alone upon the platform, himself the Essex calf to whom the homage was being rendered!* A more perfect *tu quoque* in action could not be conceived, and no words can indicate the wonderful way in which it was done. It was the wittiest thing I ever saw, even from the most witty of octogenarians whom I have ever met. But the merry scene was not quite at an end even then. "Well, friend Rogers, what does all the noise mean?" asked the genial "Governor." "Oh, sir! Mr. Gracey has been trying to put me down." Like a flash came the Roland for the Oliver. "Why, that's what I have been trying to do for the last twenty years, you old sinner, and *you won't go down!*"

All the sparkling fun lingers in the memory,—pure as the holy joy of angels—for there strangely mingles with it the recollection of the hallowed moments spent at the throne of grace before that meeting ended; and between the playfulness and the prayer there seemed to be no abrupt transition, no discord, no incongruity— but all was perfect harmony and happiness.'

Many other amusing reminiscences of College days have been preserved, but space can be spared for only one more, which relates to a certain period when the College library had been closed for a while, mainly because some of its choice volumes were reported missing. It seemed a long time to the students before they were able again to avail themselves of the privilege of consulting the many valuable books collected in that spacious room at the top of the building. One Friday afternoon, when the President took his place on the platform of the desk-room, he looked up at the clock, and seeing that it had stopped, said, 'I cannot understand what is wrong with that clock; we have had it repaired several times, yet it won't go.' One of the students thought he saw an opportunity of calling attention to another matter in which he and all the brethren were interested, so he said, 'It's like the library, sir, it is shut up.' 'Yes,' replied Spurgeon, 'and very probably for the same reason, because some of the "works" have been taken away!'

At the close of the annual Conferences, it was the President's custom to invite from a dozen to a score of the ministers to spend the Friday afternoon and evening at his house; not only for their own enjoyment, but also in order that they might repeat for Mrs. Spurgeon's benefit as many as possible of the notable sayings during the week, or recall any incident in which she would be specially interested. It was a very delightful winding-up of the meetings; and with prayer, and speech, and song, the time swiftly passed. On one of those occasions, the whole company started to march round the garden, singing, 'Hold the fort.' Spurgeon was walking in front of his little band of picked soldiers of the cross; but, as soon as the first verse of the hymn was finished, he cried, 'Halt! Right about face! Quick march! *Now* you may sing—

> *See the mighty host advancing,*
> Satan leading on.'

*

This chapter cannot be better concluded than by inserting a selection of autobiographical anecdotes related in Spurgeon's own words.

Soon after I came to London, an eccentric individual called to see me, with the view of setting me right on various points in which he did not agree with the doctrine I preached. When he failed to convince me that my teaching was unscriptural, he rose and said, 'Then I will shake off the dust of my feet against you.' 'Please don't do that,' I answered, 'you might make the carpet dirty; you will find a scraper and a mat at the front door, they will answer the purpose quite as well!'

A man who had made a special study of 'the number of the beast' mentioned in the Book of Revelation, wrote to me and said that he could make the names of W. E. Gladstone and the Emperor Napoleon III. agree with the mystic number, 666; but he could not make the numerical value of the letters in my name fit in with it, and he wanted me to explain how I accounted for that fact. 'Why,' I replied, 'I suppose it must be because I am not the beast, and that, therefore, 666 is not the number of my name!'

Dean Stanley once invited me to dine with him; and when I arrived, I found Mr. Rogers, of Bishopsgate ('Hang Theology' Rogers), was also a guest. We had a merry time, especially when the question of Disestablishment was under discussion. The Dean jocularly said to me, 'When that time comes, would you like to have the Abbey?' 'No, thank you,' I replied, 'I have not horses enough to fill it.' 'Well,' said the genial ecclesiastic, 'I did not think you would have made that objection, but really the place is more adapted for stables than for preaching the gospel to such crowds as gather around you. But, seriously, Mr. Spurgeon, if the Church is disestablished, what will become of friend Rogers and myself?' 'Why,'

I answered, 'you will have to do as I do, live upon what your people give you.' 'Oh dear! Oh dear!' cried both gentlemen at once, 'if we only had what our people gave us, it would be a poor living.' I encouraged them to do all they could to educate their congregations in the Scriptural system of giving before the day of their emancipation arrived.

A young man, who had been 'in fellowship with the brethren,' wished to join the church at the Tabernacle. I knew that they would not grant him a transfer to us, so I wrote to ask if there was anything in his moral character which should prevent us from receiving him. The reply they sent was laconic, but not particularly lucid:— 'The man —— has too much of the flesh.' When he called to hear the result of his application, I sent for a yard or two of string, and asked one of our friends to take my measure, and then to take his. As I found that I had much more 'flesh' than he had, and as his former associates had nothing else to allege against him, I proposed him for church-membership, and he was in due course accepted.

Once when I was going through a gentleman's garden, in company with the owner, we suddenly came to a rosemary bush, and I playfully said to him,—not dreaming that my words could have any personal application—'Oh! rosemary! you know what people say about it, I suppose? "Where the rosemary grows, the missus is the master." ' The next time I went there, I saw that the bush had been cut down! Then I knew who was the master!

A gentleman said to me, one day, 'Ah! Mr. Spurgeon, I don't agree with you about religion; I am an agnostic.' 'Yes!' I replied, 'that is a Greek word, and the exact equivalent is ignoramus; if you like to claim that title, you are quite welcome to it.' I do not think he cared to accept that designation, for he thought himself anything but an ignoramus!

*

The compilers are regretfully aware that the chapter on 'Pure Fun' does not adequately set forth the vivacity of his wit, or the geniality of his humour. They cannot reproduce the soft rich tones of his voice, the merry twinkle in his eye, or the grace of gesture which accompanied all his utterances. His fun was so natural, so spontaneous, and so hearty, that any description of it fails to do justice to the effect it produced at the time. The *esprit* of his jests and repartee cannot be written down; it was as fugitive as the colours of those iridescent fish of which we read that, the moment they are drawn up in the nets, the rainbow hues vanish, and their singular beauty has faded away.

Perhaps it is better so. We prefer to recall Mr. Spurgeon's solidity of thought, steadfastness of purpose, and unfaltering faith in God as the chief characteristics of his life—the firmament across which the flashes of his wit would sometimes play, like the harmless lightning of a summer's eve.

College, Orphanage, Colportage Association, and Society of Evangelists, might any one of them be regarded as works of Christian inventiveness, but it would be by far the smaller half of the truth to look at them from that point of view. These enterprises have succeeded each other, by a natural rule and order of Providence, as inevitably as the links of a chain follow one another. We have heard kind friends speak of 'genius for organization' and 'great practical common sense' as abiding in the leader of these various works for the Lord; but, indeed, it would be far nearer the truth to say that he followed with implicit, and almost blind confidence what he took to be the intimations of the Divine will, and hitherto these intimations have proved to be what he thought them. At the close of twenty-five years, we see a vast machinery in vigorous operation, in better working condition than ever it was; and, as to means and funds, perfectly equipped, although it has no other resources than the promise, 'My God shall supply all your need, according to His riches in glory by Christ Jesus.' Gratitude bows her head, and sings her own song to her Well-beloved, to whom it belongs.—C.H.S., *in Preface to 'The Sword and the Trowel' volume for* 1878.

27

The Growth of the Institutions

THE last decade of Spurgeon's life proved to be a prolific period both for the Tabernacle Church and the various Institutions connected with it. These Institutions and agencies were now manifold and the Pastor gave attention to them all, although it was the College which remained his first concern. Writing at the time of the Down-Grade controversy he said: 'It costs me one solid day each week to prepare for my men, to spend the afternoon in the class-room in lecture and exposition, and then to see one by one such men as need special direction. Friday is to me a heavy but happy day. . . . I would cheerfully die a hundred times over to see in this our land a sure succession of sound and able ministers of the New Covenant. On all sides there is a falling away from the truth of the gospel and a tendency to seek out some new thing. . . . This is my great longing: to see men go forth who will preach *the gospel*, and commit it in their turn to faithful men who will teach others also.'

For some fourteen years after the opening of the Tabernacle the College classes were held in various rooms below the sanctuary but growing numbers made the accommodation inadequate and in the 1870's ground close by was purchased from the Ecclesiastical Commissioners; in his own characteristic fashion Spurgeon told the brethren at one of the Annual Conferences that he had secured the parson's garden, behind the Tabernacle, as the site for the new College, and he was going to cultivate it for him by growing Dissenters on it! The new College buildings became a vital part of the Tabernacle's facilities. Shortly after their erection an incident occurred which was soon talked of in South London. A deputation from the local council authority visited the new premises to decide the amount at which they should be rated. While conducting these gentlemen through the different rooms, the President briefly narrated the history of the Institution, and recounted various instances in which the money necessary for carrying on the work had come directly in answer to prayer. The chairman of the deputation, who evidently did not believe that the funds came in any such way, said, 'That is your idea, Mr. Spurgeon, but the fact is, certain good people have confidence in you, and therefore they send you contributions for your College and Orphanage.' 'Yes,' replied the Pastor, 'there may be some truth in that remark, but if the good people did not think of me, God would send the devil with the money rather than let His cause suffer.' No further reference was made to the matter until the men had finished their investigations and consulted as to the value to be fixed for rating purposes, when the chairman, speaking for his colleagues, said to Spurgeon, 'We have been greatly interested in all that we have seen and heard, and we look upon this College as a valuable addition to the educational advantages of the parish. We should be very glad if we could let it go without being rated at all, but we have a duty to perform to the public, so that is not possible. We have agreed to fix the amount at ——, which we think you will consider satisfactory; and, personally, I think it is such a capital Institution that I shall be glad if you will accept ten pounds towards its maintenance.' The President thanked him very heartily, and then added, 'You said that it was the *good* people who gave me the money; I hope that adjective applies to you?' 'Oh, dear no!' replied the gentleman, 'certainly not;' and his companions appeared very surprised at the whole transaction. Afterwards, whenever anyone in the local council wanted to raise the question of the rating of the College, he always said, 'Well, if you like to go to see Spurgeon about it, you may; my last visit cost me ten pounds, and I am not going again, and I should advise you to leave the good man alone. He is a benefactor to the whole district, and ought to be encouraged, and not hindered.'

The total cost of the new building and furnishing was £15,000, largely raised by Spurgeon's own endeavours. In later years the President expressed an objection to providing an endowment to secure the future of his College, on the grounds that such a provision would be no safeguard to preserving a succession in soundness of doctrine. None the less he was, in a very singular way, and quite unintentionally, the means of providing a large portion of the funds for its maintenance for several years after he had been 'called home.' The story greatly amused him when he heard it related; it was to this effect. The conductor of an omnibus, while waiting on the City side of London Bridge, endeavoured to attract passengers by shouting out, 'Over the water to Charlie!' A gentleman enquired what he meant by this unusual cry, and he explained that the 'bus was going over the Thames, and past the Tabernacle, where

C. H. Spurgeon was announced to preach. It happened that the stranger had never heard the Pastor; indeed, as the tale is told, it appears that he was not in the habit of attending any place of worship; but he went on that occasion, and for the rest of his life he was a diligent reader of the printed sermons. When he made his will, he bequeathed a large sum to Spurgeon for the Pastors' College.

At the end of 1878, over five hundred students had been trained in the Institution, of whom twenty-five had been 'called home.' Of the four hundred and fifty then engaged as Baptist pastors, evangelists, and missionaries, less than three hundred filled up the statistical forms, which showed that, during the year, they had baptized 3,600 persons; and during the previous fourteen years there had been a net increase to the churches of 33,319 members. The sons of the College had also found their way into all four quarters of the globe and the President's prayer that the missionary spirit should be increased among the brethren was being graciously answered, for some of them had gone forth to India, China, Japan, Africa, Spain, Italy, the West Indies and South America, beside a considerable contingent in the Australasian and Canadian colonies and the United States.

The Pastors' College Missionary Association was formed to support the men overseas but due to an insufficiency of funds this did not go beyond maintaining two missionaries in North Africa and giving assistance to another two in Spain. Spurgeon was glad that so many of his students were enabled to go to various lands under the auspices of the Baptist Missionary Society, the American Baptist Missionary Union, or the China Inland Mission. 'The day shall declare' what these men did.

Also working in conjunction with the College was the Pastors' College Society of Evangelists, an association of men who were entirely set apart for evangelistic work. It should also be mentioned that long before the College Society of Evangelists was organized there had existed two large and useful companies of so-called 'lay' brethren—the Tabernacle Evangelists' Association and Country Mission—under the leadership of devoted elders of the Tabernacle Church. Many of the students first began to speak for the Lord in connection with one or other of these useful agencies, and, during their College career, they continued, by this means, to help in the evangelization of the metropolis and its suburbs, and the towns and villages in the adjacent counties.

There were both changes and great advances in the College in the last fourteen years of Spurgeon's life, from 1878 to 1892. George Rogers—'Father Rogers'—who was spared to see his first student succeeded by more then eight hundred others, continued to hold the office of Principal until 1881, and he afterwards rendered occasional help at the College until 1884, when he finally retired. Then, after spending seven restful years in his peaceful home at South Norwood, at the ripe age of ninety-two he entered the glory-land only about four months before the Pastor and President with whom he had been so long and so happily associated in the important work of training men for the Christian ministry. Professor Gracey was appointed Principal in 1881, and he faithfully discharged the duties of that responsible position until he also was 'called home' just a year after Spurgeon.

One of the most important events in the later years of the College was the formation, in 1888, of the Pastors' College Evangelical Association. This was one of the direct results of the 'Downgrade' Controversy. When Spurgeon found that many of his own former students had accepted various forms of modern-thought teaching, he felt compelled to withdraw from further fellowship with them in the annual Conferences, at which they were practically his guests for the week. The only method of attaining that end, so far as he could see, was to reorganize the Association, and to define more clearly the doctrinal basis, which had been in existence from its commencement, although there had been no need to call attention to it while all had been heartily united in the 'one faith' as well as the 'one Lord' and the 'one baptism.' It was a great grief to the President that some brethren, who were firmly attached to Evangelical doctrine, remained outside the new fraternal band; but the gap in the ranks which was caused by their absence was quickly filled by an equal number of ministers, who, though not trained in the Pastors' College, were in heart and soul one with Spurgeon, especially in his great protest against error and worldliness in the Church. A special clause was inserted in the constitution of the reorganized fraternity by which they were admitted, as associates, to share the privileges enjoyed by the members.

Up to the time of the President's death nearly nine hundred brethren had been educated in the Institution, of whom a large number had gone to the foreign mission field or to other distant spheres of service. The statistical account for the year 1891–2 showed that, in the churches under the charge of the ministers who furnished the figures for that Annual Report—and it was never possible to get returns from anything like all of them—nearly 100,000 persons had been baptized since the year 1865, when the statistics were first collected; and, after making all deductions, there had been a clear increase of 80,000 members. Truly, if Spurgeon had done nothing beyond founding and carrying on the Pastors' College, it would have been a noble life-work. His own estimate of the importance of such work gives the final explanation why it was so prominent in his ministry. Writing in *The Sword and the Trowel* in 1882 he said:

'When we think of the value of a well-instructed minister of the Gospel, we sometimes think the work of training ministers to be superior to all other services done to the Lord and His church. We wonder not that Colleges should be liberally supported, but the rather we marvel that more lovers of the Lord do not devote their substance to this superior purpose . . . Those who helped the poor boy Luther to pay for his learning made a grand investment of their monies. The possibilities which lie around one single preaching man of God are such as may make the College lecture-hall one of the most solemn spots beneath God's heaven.'

Of the several agencies linked to the Pastors' College the most important was the Colportage Association which had its base on the College premises. This work had resulted from an article written by Spurgeon in 1866. 'The Holy War of the Present Hour'. Reflecting upon the growth of Catholic influence, particularly through the teaching of the Anglicans of the Tractarian school (such as E. B. Pusey), he called for this remedy:

'We would urge the propriety of a very large distribution of religious literature bearing upon the Puseyite controversy. Very little has been done in this respect. Tractarianism owed its origin to tracts, as its name implies; why may not its downfall come from the same means, if well used? If several millions of copies of forcible, Scriptural testimonies could be scattered over the land, the results might far exceed all expectation. Of course, controversy would arise out of such a distribution; but this is most desirable, since it is only error which could suffer by the question being everywhere discussed. We should like to see the country flooded, and even the walls placarded, with bold exposures of error and plain expositions of truth. We will take our own share in the effort if any friends should be moved to work with us; at the same time, we shall be equally glad if they will do the work alone; only let it be done, and done well, and at once. If the expense of the tracts should involve a sacrifice, it will be sweet to the true heart to serve the Lord with his substance, and none will desire to offer to Him that which costs them nothing. . . .'

The plea did not fall upon deaf ears, a member of the Tabernacle came forward to support the proposal liberally and accordingly a committee was formed in September, 1866, having as its object, 'to extend the circulation of the Scriptures, and to increase the diffusion of sound religious literature, in order to counteract the evils arising from the perusal of works of a decided Romish tendency.' Once the work began it was speedily discovered that the undertaking was too heavy to be carried out properly by gentlemen who were occupied in their various callings during the day and thus a paid officer of the Association was soon arranged. Ultimately, in 1872, W. Corden Jones was elected secretary, a post which he continued in until 1894.

By the year 1878 there were 94 colporteurs engaged in the work and their sales for the twelve months of that year amounted to £8,276, these sales resulting from 926,290 visits in many parts of the country. The work continued with great steadiness, and from year to year a Report of considerable length was inserted in *The Sword and the Trowel*. The Report of the last year of Spurgeon's life showed that 95 colporteurs were at work, that 689,284 'visits to families' had been made, that 10,147 'services and addresses' had been engaged in, that the sales of Christian literature totalled £11,255, and that donations and subscriptions almost reached £4,000. The Report recorded 'an immense amount of devoted labour, considering that each man (colporteur) had to travel nearly 2,000 miles during the year to dispose of the goods, which range in price mainly from one penny to one shilling. The salutary influence of so large a quantity of literature scattered over the land must be immense.'

Closely associated with colportage was a work which was equally dear to the hearts of the Metropolitan Tabernacle pastor and his wife. It was known as 'Mrs. Spurgeon's Book Fund' and dated from 1875. By that year Mrs. Spurgeon was a chronic invalid, unable to take any part in public Christian work or to attend a service at the Tabernacle. At times life itself had been in the balance. Many were the prayers that restoration might be granted. This, however, was not the will of the Lord. But in the long-drawn-out weariness of illness He directed her into an activity suited to her state, which gave her great joy and brought her into touch by gift and by letter with a considerable number of Christian workers at home and abroad.

The Book Fund originated at Helensburgh House, Clapham. 'How do you like *Lectures to My Students*?' Spurgeon said one day to his wife. 'I wish I could place it in the hands of every minister in England' was the reply. 'Then why not do so? How much will you give?' The question caused the wife to ponder, 'How much can I spare from housekeeping or personal expenditure to start such a scheme?' 'Then,' says Mrs. Spurgeon,' came the wonderful part. I found the money ready and waiting. Upstairs in a little drawer were some carefully hoarded crown pieces which, owing to some foolish fancy, I had been gathering for years whenever chance threw one in my way. These I now counted out and found that they made a sum *exactly* sufficient to pay for one hundred copies of the work'.

Never was a wife more pleased with her assignment, and in the years which followed tens of thousands of volumes (preferably those written by her husband himself) were dispersed from the home. It was not long after the commencement of the work that she wrote:

'I have been doing a brave business in Wales through the magnificent generosity of a stranger whom now we count as a friend. He sent £100 to Mr. Spurgeon, £50 of which was for my Book Fund. I was greatly gratified at receiving so large a sum at one time and set about spending it as quickly as possible. . . . John Ploughman says that "Spend, and God will send" is the motto of a *spend*-thrift. Now I must not dispute this, for dear John is always right, and moreover, knows all about everything, but I should like this motto to be handed over to me at once and for ever for my Book Fund, for again and again has it been proved most blessedly true in my experience. I have spent ungrudgingly, feeling sure that the Lord would send after the same fashion, and indeed He has done so, even "exceeding abundantly above all I could ask or even think . . ."

The friend who gave the £50 wished to give a copy of *Lectures to my Students* to *every* Calvinistic Methodist minister, preacher and student in North Wales (of whom there are 500) if I would undertake the "trouble" of sending them. Trouble!! The word was inadmissible! With intense joy and gratitude to God I received the charge, and *another* £50 to meet expenses! And as soon as 400 copies had been given in the northern part I received authority from the same noble donor to continue at his expense the distribution throughout South Wales also . . . Nor does the matter rest here; other ministers besides Calvinistic Methodists coveted the precious volume and wrote to me asking why they should be left out. I have supplied all who have written and at this present moment I have promised copies to all the Wesleyan ministers of South Wales, and when they are satisfied, I doubt not their northern brethren will request the same favour . . . These copies of course are provided by my Book Fund, our friend's gift being confined to his own denomination; but you see, dear friends, I never can be the least troubled at a large expenditure because I have the firmest possible faith in my motto, "Spend and God will send".'

After the commencement of this work, which Mrs. Spurgeon carried on personally from their home, she composed a report annually for *The Sword and the Trowel* on its progress. In the 1878 report she wrote: 'I recall with glad satisfaction the very first donation which reached me "for sending books to ministers". It came anonymously and was but five shillings worth of stamps, yet it was very precious, and proved like a revelation to me, for it opened up a vista of possible usefulness and exceeding brightness. The mustard seed of my faith grew forthwith into "a great tree", and sweet birds of hope and expectation sat singing in its branches. "You'll see", I said to my boys, "the Lord will send me *hundreds of pounds* for this work". For many a day afterwards mother's "hundreds of pounds" became "a household word"!'

A special article in *The Sword and the Trowel* for May, 1882, commended the Book Fund's Annual Report to readers. Spurgeon wrote: 'It is one of the delights of our life that our beloved wife has made ministers' libraries her great concern. The dear soul gives herself wholly to it. You should see her stores, her book-room, her busy helpers on the parcel-day, and the waggon-load of books each fortnight. The Book Fund at certain hours is the ruling idea of our house. Every day it occupies the head and heart of its manager. The reader has scant idea of the book-keeping involved in the book-giving; but this may be said—the loving manager has more than 6000 names on her lists, and yet she knows every volume that each man has received from the first day until now. The work is not muddled, but done as if by clockwork, yet it is performed with a hearty desire to give pleasure to all receivers, and to trouble no applicant with needless inquiries.'

Thus the work continued, year in, year out. Up to 1890, when the Book Fund had been in existence fifteen years, no fewer than 122,129 volumes had been distributed. In that year the recipients numbered 484, including Baptists, Independents, Methodists, Anglicans (the largest group helped), Presbyterians, Lutherans, Moravians, and 'missionaries'. Of the *Treasury of David*, 1305 volumes were donated, of the *Sermons* 510 volumes. *Lectures to my Students* accounted for 668 volumes, *My Sermon Notes* for 488. 76 copies of Watson's *Body of Divinity* were included in the gifts; *Selected Sermons* numbered 498; smaller works by Spurgeon, 898. 1,134 Books given by friends were also included in the distribution, besides 'smaller quantities of other valuable works'.

Spurgeon commended the 1890 Report to readers in parabolic fashion:

'I saw in my dream a man worn and weary with working the handle of a pump from which no water came. Hard by was his garden, and all the plants and flowers were pining for water; but he had none to give them. Then I saw a woman coming towards him, bearing a pitcher of water. She stopped and spoke cheeringly to the weary one; and anon she smilingly poured the contents of her pitcher down the pump, and immediately it began to work, and pour forth waters of its own. How the husbandman blessed her!

'I think I know that woman; and sure I am that often the reading of a new book, sent from the Book Fund, enables a mind to work with success, which previously had been exhausted by labour in vain in the Lord'.

There is, finally, another agency which must be included in this record of growth, the work of the Orphanage. As a child, Spurgeon had himself benefited largely from the help of older Christians and, in turn, he always acted on the principle that the best way to influence the future was to guide the young. The commencement of the Stockwell Orphanage for boys in 1867 has already been described and the girls' Orphanage, which followed in 1880 has also been referred to. The Pastor had indeed some hesitation before committing himself to the proposal of a girls' work.

He reported his feelings at a meeting in the Tabernacle in 1879:

C. H. *Spurgeon: The Full Harvest*

'A day or two ago, the lady who founded the Boys' Orphanage sent me £50 for the Girls' Orphanage. I wrote to her somewhat to this effect: "I am very grateful for the proposal; but I am not very well, and the times are not very hopeful, so I had rather not begin any new work just yet." I proposed to keep the £50 in case we did build an Orphanage for girls; and if not, to hand it over to the boys. "No" said our friend, "you are right in your judgment, but take the £50 as the first brick, for I am fully assured that many more bricks will shortly be added."'

Probably his hesitation was far less than his words suggest for at the same meeting he proposed that £50 of the surplus of the testimonial, collected for his semi-jubilee, be added to the first £50, and that the inauguration of a Girls' Orphanage would be a good note upon which to start a 'second twenty-five years of pastorate'. Anticipating the probable feelings of some present, he concluded: ' "What next?" says somebody. I cannot tell you what I may suggest to you next; but, you see, I am driven to this Girls' Orphanage. I have this £50 forced upon me, and I cannot get rid of it; would you have me refuse to use this money for poor fatherless girls? No, your hearts would not so counsel me. Thus, of my own free will, compelled by constraining grace, I accept a further charge, and look to see prayer and faith open a new chapter of marvels.'

Thus a girls' home shortly took its place beside that of the boys in Clapham Road, and these together sheltered the helpless children of hundreds of bereaved families. Up to the time of Spurgeon's death, nearly sixteen hundred boys and girls were provided for in the Orphanage and not infrequently there was evidence that the homes had brought not only happiness but spiritual blessing. The following letters from each sex are instances which gave great joy to the President:

'Dear Mr. Spurgeon,
    In closing the list, to-day, for March *Sword and Trowel*, you will, I am sure, be pleased to know that it contains donations from "some of the old boys" (about forty), to the amount of £17 . 17 . 0. *Every one*, in forwarding his subscription, wishes it were ten times or a hundred times as much; and it is accompanied with every expression of gratitude for the benefits received at the Stockwell Orphanage, and of warmest love to yourself—the earthly father to this large orphan family; and they all pray that our Heavenly Father

may spare you, for many, many years, to lead and direct this blessed work of caring for the widow and the fatherless.

I am,

Dear Mr. Spurgeon,

Ever yours sincerely,

F. G. Ladds.'

'Dear Mr. Spurgeon,

You must excuse the liberty I am taking in writing to you; but you will not mind when you know the reason. I must, first of all, tell you that I am one of your old orphan girls; but the Lord having found me, and made me His child, before I left the Orphanage, I knew it would cheer your heart if I wrote and told you. I thought, when my father died, I could never have another to equal him; but when I came to your Orphanage, I discovered my mistake, for I found a better and truer Father, who will never leave me nor forsake me, and to whom I can take my every trouble, however small it may be. It seems almost too good to be true that Jesus was really crucified to save me. When I think of all the years I grieved and pained Him, it only makes me want to try and please Him ever so much more for the future.

I must tell you that I was in the Orphanage seven-and-a-half years, and was very happy indeed, and wish myself back again. Now I think I must close, thanking you for your kindness in giving us such a beautiful home to live in. It will always be something to look back on with pleasure for the rest of our lives, and for which we can never thank you enough. I myself hope shortly to come forward, and, by baptism, publicly let the world know that I have accepted Jesus as my Saviour; or, rather, I should say, that He has accepted me as His child.

I remain,

One of your old orphan girls,

————.'

One of Spurgeon's last visits to the Orphanage occurred in the autumn of 1890 under circumstances which are not likely to be forgotten by any who were then present. His own account of the afternoon, illustrating as it does so well the motive which had led him to take up so many endeavours, will be a fitting conclusion to this chapter of his Standard Life:

'I went to the Stockwell Orphanage, on Tuesday, September 23, to walk round with an artist, and select bits for his pencil, to be

[465]

inserted in a Christmas book for the Institution. We had not gone many yards before it began to rain. Umbrellas were forthcoming, and we tried to continue our perambulation of the whole square of the boys' and girls' houses; but the rain persisted in descending, and speedily increased into a downpour. Nothing short of being amphibious would have enabled us to face the torrent. There was no other course but to turn into the play-hall, where the boys gave tremendous cheers at our advent—cheers almost as deafening as the thunder which responded to them. Go out we could not, for the shower was swollen into a deluge, so I resolved to turn the season to account. A chair was forthcoming, and there I sat, the centre of a dense throng of juvenile humanity, which could scarcely be kept off from a nearness which showed the warmth of their reception of their friend. Our artist, who, standing in the throng, made a hurried sketch, could not be afforded space enough to put in the hundreds of boys.

It was certainly a melting moment as to heat, and fresh air was not abundant; but anything was better than the storm outside. Flash after flash made everybody feel sober, and prompted me to talk with the boys about that freedom from fear which comes through faith in the Lord Jesus. The story was told of a very young believer,[1] who was in his uncle's house, one night, during a tremendous tempest. The older folk were all afraid; but he had really trusted himself with the Lord Jesus, and he did not dare to fear. The baby was upstairs, and nobody was brave enough to fetch it down because of a big window on the stairs. This lad went up to the bedroom, brought the baby to its mother, and then read a Psalm, and prayed with his relatives, who were trembling with fear. There was real danger, for a stack was set on fire a short distance away; but the youth was as calm as on a summer's day of sunshine, not because he was naturally brave, but because he truly trusted in the Lord.

While I was thus speaking, the darkness increased, and the storm overhead seemed brooding over us with black wings. It was growing dark before its hour. Most appropriately, one of the boys suggested a verse, which all sang sweetly and reverently,

> *Abide with me! fast falls the eventide;*
> *The darkness deepens; Lord, with me abide!*
> *When other helpers fail, and comforts flee,*
> *Help of the helpless, O abide with me!*

---

[1] This was, of course, himself.

This ended, there followed a word about the ground of the believer's trust: he was forgiven, and therefore dreaded no condemnation; he was in his Heavenly Father's hand, and therefore, feared no evil. If we were at enmity against God, and had all our sins resting upon our guilty heads, we might be afraid to die; yes, and even afraid to live; but, when reconciled to Him by the death of His Son, we said farewell to fear. With God against us, we are in a state of war; but with God for us, we dwell in perfect peace. Here came flashes of lightning and peals of thunder which might well make us start; but no one was afraid. It is true we all felt awed, but we were restful, and somehow there was a quiet but general cry for "*perfect peace.*" On enquiring what this meant, I was answered by all the boys singing right joyfully,

> *Like a river glorious is God's perfect peace,*
> *Over all victorious in its bright increase,*
> *Perfect, yet it floweth fuller every day;*
> *Perfect, yet it groweth deeper all the way.*
> *Stayed upon Jehovah, hearts are fully blest,*
> *Finding, as He promised, perfect peace and rest.*

This sung, we covered our faces reverently, and the boys were very silent, while I lifted up my voice in prayer. Then we opened our eyes again, and it was very dark, as if night had come before its time. While the flames of fire leaped in through the windows and skylights, the noise of the rain upon the roof and the tremendous thunder scarcely permitted me to say much upon Jesus as being our peace, through His bearing our sins in His own body on the tree. Yet, as well as I could, I set forth the cross of Christ as the place of peace-making, peace-speaking, and peace-finding, both for boys and men; and then we all sang, to the accompaniment of the storm-music,

> *How sweet the Name of Jesus sounds*
> *In a believer's ear!*
> *It soothes his sorrows, heals his wounds,*
> *And drives away his fear.*

I need not write more. The storm abated. I hurried off to see inquirers at the Tabernacle, but not till one and another had said to me, "The boys will never forget this. It will abide with them throughout eternity". So be it, for Christ's sake! Amen'.

Controversy is never a very happy element for the child of God: he would far rather be in communion with his Lord than be engaged in defending the faith, or in attacking error. But the soldier of Christ knows no choice in his Master's commands. He may feel it to be better for him to lie upon the bed of rest than to stand covered with the sweat and dust of battle; but, as a soldier, he has learned to obey, and the rule of his obedience is not his personal comfort, but his Lord's absolute command. The servant of God must endeavour to maintain all the truth which his Master has revealed to him, because as a Christian soldier, this is part of his duty. But while he does so, he accords to others the liberty which he himself enjoys.—c.h.s., *in address at the Tabernacle,* 1861.

I am a disciple of the old-fashioned doctrine as much when it is covered with obloquy and rebuke as when it shall again display its power, as it surely shall. Sceptics may seem to take the truth, and bind it, and scourge it, and crucify it, and say that it is dead; and they may endeavour to bury it in scorn, but the Lord has many a Joseph and a Nicodemus who will see that all due honour is done even to the body of truth, and will wrap the despised creed in sweet spices, and hide it away in their hearts. They may, perhaps, be half afraid that it is really dead, as the wise men assert; yet it is precious to their souls, and they will come forth right gladly to espouse its cause, and to confess that they are its disciples. We will sit down in sorrow, but not in despair; and watch until the stone is rolled away, and Christ in His truth shall live again, and be openly triumphant.—c.h.s., *in sermon at the Tabernacle,* 1878.

I might not have had such an intense loathing of the new theology if I had not seen so much of its evil effects. I could tell you of a preacher of unbelief, whom I have seen, in my own vestry, utterly broken down, driven almost to despair, and having no rest for the sole of his foot until he came back to simple trust in the atoning sacrifice. If he were speaking to you, he would say, 'Cling to your faith, brethren; if you once throw away your shield, you will lay yourself open to imminent dangers and countless wounds; for nothing can protect you but the shield of faith.—c.h.s., *in address at College Conference,* 1891.

28

The 'Down-grade' Controversy,
from Spurgeon's Standpoint

THIS Standard Life could not be complete without a reference to that most sorrowful but important episode, The 'Down-grade' Controversy; yet how shall I dare to touch the strings of that rifted lute? The lightest and most skilful fingers could scarcely draw harmony from it now, and I would fain not be expected to awaken any of its discords. Oh, for the guiding Hand to be laid on heart and brain and pen, that gently and tenderly, albeit truthfully, the outlines of the sad story may be given!

There are many dear and able friends who could write the full history of the Controversy;[1] but, after much thought and prayer, I have been led to allow the shadow of the past to rest upon it in a measure, and to conceal, under a generous silence, most of the documentary and other evidence which could be produced to prove the perfect uprightness, veracity, and fidelity of my dear husband throughout the whole of the solemn protest which culminated in the 'vote of censure' by the Council of the Baptist Union! Therefore, in accordance with the autobiographical character of this record, the Controversy is sketched from Mr. Spurgeon's own point of view; he tells the story in his own way, so that only as much as he chose to make known of the deepest grief of his life is chronicled in these pages.

From August, 1887, to February, 1892, scarcely any number of

---

[1] The Down-grade Controversy was occasioned by articles in *The Sword and the Trowel*, in 1887, which gave warning of the general defection from Biblical truth which was proceeding in the Nonconformist churches; the charge was vigorously repelled in many quarters and ignored by the autumn meetings of the Baptist Union. Privately Spurgeon placed evidence of the unbelief of ministers in the Baptist Union before the secretary of the Union, S. H. Booth, and when it became evident to him that no action would be taken he withdrew from the Union on October 28, 1887.

No 'full history' of the controversy has ever been published and some of the materials necessary for such a record appear to have been lost. This chapter gives important side-lights on the private thoughts of Spurgeon and his wife; his public utterances will be found, at length, in the volumes of *The Metropolitan Tabernacle Pulpit* for these years (now reprinted) and in *The Sword and The Trowel*. The reader will find an account of the Down-grade Controversy in several more recent books including *The Forgotten Spurgeon*, Iain Murray, 1966 and reprinted 1973.

The Sword and the Trowel appeared without some reference to the Controversy and its various issues. The most pathetic 'Note' of all was written within a few days of my dear husband's home-going, for in it he revealed the fact, already known to all who were nearest and dearest to him, that his fight for the faith had cost him his life. Yet he never regretted the step he had taken; for, throughout the whole affair, he felt such a Divine compulsion as Luther realized when he said, 'I can do no other.'

So far as the Baptist Union was concerned, little was accomplished by Mr. Spurgeon's witness-bearing and withdrawal. The compromise at the City Temple, in April, 1888, confirmed the position of the modern-thought men in the Union, and made 'the vote of censure' the act of the whole assembly with the exception of the noble seven who voted against it. But, in other respects, I have had abundant proofs that the protest was not in vain. Many, who were far gone on 'the Down-grade,' were stopped in their perilous descent, and, by God's grace, were brought back to the Up-line; others, who were unconsciously slipping, were made to stand firmly upon the Rock; while, at least for a time, in all the churches, Evangelical doctrines were preached with a clearness and emphasis which had long been lacking.

The ultimate results of the whole matter must be left in the hands of Him who never makes a mistake, and who will, in His own right way, vindicate His obedient and faithful servant from the 'censure' so unjustly passed upon him.

Not long after Mr. Spurgeon's withdrawal from the Baptist Union, he went to the South of France for much-needed rest; and the letters he there wrote, during that time of suffering and reproach, contained many allusions to the painful subject. Naturally, those written to me referred to the more personal and private aspects of the Controversy, as the following extracts will show:

'I was greatly surprised at the note from —— (one of "our own men"), but when we are in a battle, we must expect calamities. It is a serious matter to know *how* to act; but one thing is plain enough, I must go on clearing myself of union with those who belong to the broad school. I felt so well, this afternoon, when sitting under the palms, and as happy as a birdie beneath the blue sky. Then came the letter, just to sober me, and drive me from the sunshine to my Lord, who is the Sun itself. I can bear anything for Jesus while His everlasting arms are underneath me. The hills around Hyères are called "the mountains of paradise," but the serpent comes even here. Ah, well! the Serpent-Killer is with us, and He will subdue all things unto Himself. I am sorry that the evil flood should carry away one of my men; but the wonder is, that more have not gone. It shows how much more evil was abroad than I dreamed of. I have done my duty, even if all men forsake me. Those who write in *The Freeman* and *The Christian World* show how everything I do can be misconstrued. Nevertheless, I know what I have done, and why I did it; and the Lord will bear me through. In Him I rest, and I am in no haste to answer opponents, nor even to think about them in a depressing way. What a providence that I am here, out of call! Luther was best at the Wartburg, was he not? I did not plan this, nor plan anything.

What a farce about my seeing these brethren, privately, according to Matt. 18. 15! Why, I saw the Secretary and the President again and again; and then I printed my plaint, and only left the Union when nothing could be done. Now, something will be done. Not until I took the decided step could I effect anything. Luther was very wrong to nail up his theses on the church door; he should have seen the Pope, and prayed with him! Do not let these things distress you, for my sake. The Lord will give both of us the heroic spirit and we shall neither fear men, nor become ungenerous toward them.'

'Canon Sidebotham called yesterday to assure me of the sympathy of all Christian Churchmen, and his belief that my stand for truth will help all believers. He told me that he meets with amazing scepticism among young men whom he has been called to visit in sickness, and he believes there is an epidemic of it everywhere. He says the antidote was needed, and came just at the right time. So may God grant!

How I do delight in the Lord! I am now consciously nearer to Him than ever before, and I revel in a sense of blessedness. I am delivered from all fear of failing in this battle; and the Lord, whom I sought to honour, bows me low at His feet in gratitude for His tender mercies. We are safe in His hands. This is where I love to feel that I am, and that you are, and the dear boys, and the Church, and the College, and "the Down-grade," and all!'

I trust I may be made stronger for the stern task which awaits me; but I try not even to think of *that*, but just to abandon myself to a bath of rest. This, I trust, is the wisest course; and yet I keep on longing to be doing some good, or bearing some fruit unto the Lord. Little occasions for this do occur, and I am eager to use them aright.

Yesterday was eventful. First came a telegram, saying that there had been a hot discussion, and that my brother had left the Council meeting in indignation because my veracity had been impugned. Just as I was going to rest came another telegram: "Council has appointed Culross, McLaren, Clifford, and myself to confer with you at Mentone, without delay, to deliberate with you how the unity of our denomination in truth, and love, and good works may be maintained. When can we see you? Letter sent. Booth." Think of four doctors of divinity coming all this way to see me! I was in great perplexity, and knew not what to reply. I don't quite see what it all means. I lay awake till one o'clock, and then got a pencil, and wrote out a telegram:—"Cannot reply without further information. Respectfully request deputation to await my return. Tone of discussion suggests caution. Will write." Afterwards, I wrote a letter. Briefly, I urge them not to come so far:—it would be four to one, and I should be at the disadvantage of having been the cause of great expense. If they really mean brotherly conference, I will see them when I return, right gladly; that is to say, if I find there is any use in it. Now I shall need wisdom. I do not fear four doctors, but I think it a very wise move on their part. If it means that they will surrender, it is well; but if it is meant to fix on me the odium of being implacable, it is another matter. In any case, the Lord will prepare me for all that is to happen. It is of His mercy that I am here, or I should not be able to bear it all; but being quiet, and rested, and not worried by personal assaults, I can look round the question calmly.

The four doctors are not coming. Very likely my brother will call to tell you about the affray. He was justly wroth, and describes the Council meeting as "horrible." For Dr. Booth to say I never complained, is amazing. God knows all about it, and He will see me righted. I have just received a letter from England in the words of Jer. 15. 19, 20.'

That passage was so peculiarly appropriate to the circumstances of the case, that many friends afterwards sent it to my beloved, who was greatly comforted by the reassuring message which was thus conveyed to him.

During that visit to Mentone, an incident occurred, to which my husband often gratefully referred as a remarkable token of the Lord's approval of his protest against false doctrine and worldliness. Before I give extracts from his letters concerning it, a brief explanation is necessary. For many years before this eventful period of my husband's life, he had been most generously aided in all his beneficent plans and purposes by a friend to whom God had given abundance of this world's wealth. These supplies came with loving freeness, and invariable regularity; and more than a mere hint was given that they might be depended on while the donor had it in his power to be thus royally open-handed. However, Mr. Spurgeon's attitude in the 'Down-grade' Controversy alienated the heart of this friend, and caused him to withdraw altogether the splendid help which had, for so long a period, exempted my beloved from much financial anxiety.

The letter, announcing this failure of friendship and sympathy, arrived during Mr. Spurgeon's absence at Mentone, and it therefore became my duty to open and read it. Then followed one of those hallowed enlargements of heart which leave their mark for ever on the life of the person experiencing them. At once, I took the letter, and spread it before the Lord, pleading, as Hezekiah did, that He would 'hear and see' the words written therein; and He gave me so strong a confidence in His overruling and delivering power that, as I knelt in His presence, and told Him how completely I trusted Him on my husband's behalf, the words of petition ceased from my lips, and I absolutely *laughed aloud*, so little did I fear what man could do, and so blessedly reliant did He make me on His own love and omnipotence!

In this exultant frame of mind, I wrote to Mentone, making light of the trouble, and endeavouring to parry the blow which I knew must sorely wound the sensitive heart of my beloved. I told him, too, how the Lord had 'made me to laugh' as I was laying the matter before Him, and had filled me with righteous scorn and indignation at the means used to dishearten him in his sublime stand for the truths of the old gospel. So, as far as I was able, being absent from him, I comforted and upheld my much-tried spouse. In less time than I had thought possible, I received this telegram: 'I laugh with you. The Lord will not fail us, nor forsake us;' and, by the next post, there came a letter recording the dear writer's un-swerving faith in the God whose he was, and whom he served, and to whom he left all the issues of that painful trial. The following extract will indicate the spirit in which he wrote:

'Mentone,
Nov. 18, 1887

You are as an angel of God unto me. When I began to read your letter, I trembled, for I could not tell what was coming; but when I finished it, I could laugh with you. Bravest of women, strong in faith, you have ministered unto me indeed and of a truth. God bless thee out of the seventh heavens!

I do not know that I have ever before really suffered any loss for Christ's sake; I feel decorated and elevated by this honour. His yoke is easy, and His burden is light. But our friend uses a queer sort of argument! I am to be set right; therefore, stop the supplies to God's work! The fire must be put out; whip the child! I do not see the connection between the end desired and the means used. Your loving sympathy has fully repaid me already. I rejoice in the Lord who has dealt bountifully with me hitherto. All that I possess belongs to Him.

> *There, take an inventory of all I have,*
> *To the last penny; 'tis the King's.'*

While this correspondence was passing to and fro, the Lord was working on behalf of His servant in a wonderful way. Writing to one of his deacons, Mr. Spurgeon said: 'I have had a very remarkable deliverance out of a pecuniary difficulty inflicted upon me in consequence of the "Down-grade" Controversy. It is as nearly a miracle as anything I ever heard of. The living God guards me on every side, and covers my head. To Him be praise!'

A lady from the Antipodes, who was staying in London, afterwards related that, during the time under consideration, she felt an overpowering impression that she must go to Mr. Spurgeon, in the South of France, and carry him some financial help to meet a special emergency. She said that, on other occasions, when similar intimations had come to her, she had obeyed her Lord's commands, and in each instance had found that she had been infallibly guided by Him, so she at once made arrangements for the thousand miles' journey. The amount she was to give was not at first revealed to her, nor did she know exactly where she was to go, as it had been announced that Mr. Spurgeon would be moving from place to place. However, the Lord, who had entrusted her with the commission, directed her to Mentone; and, on her arrival there, she was further guided to the Hôtel Beau Rivage. What happened there, my beloved thus records:

'An awe is upon me as I write to you, for I feel the Lord to be so near. On Tuesday evening, there came to this hotel three ladies who asked if Mr. Spurgeon were here, and left cards. The next morning, they were at our family worship; and, to-day, Mrs. R——gave me the enclosed letter, and cheque for £100! I told her of my trouble afterwards, I had not mentioned it before, and I read to her a few sentences of your letter. "There," she said, "that is the Lord's reason for moving me to give it to you; *let it go to make up the lack for the next six months.*" I worshipped the Lord with a thrilling joy. She added, "I do not doubt but that the Lord will see you right through the difficulty." I believe so, too, and that all the help will come from someone who does *not* know of my special need, so that it will be the more conspicuously "of the Lord." The money will be surer from Him than from Mr. ——, although he promised it for life. It may be very childish of me, but I could not help sending you the very cheque and letter, that you may see with your eyes what the Lord sent me. How this lady came to know my hotel, I cannot imagine, but Mr. Harrald says that HE who sent her knew where I was.

'Our College men have met, with grand result; the only dissentient being one who is, practically, out of the ministry. Yesterday, I went to see an afflicted gentleman,[1] whose deceased wife was Miss Havergal's sister. His doctor met me, just now, and told me that I had done his patient great good. I was, however, the greater gainer, for he read me three letters from his son, a clergyman in Islington, in which he told his father to be sure to meet me, and wrote very many kind things, which I am not egotistical enough to repeat; but he said that all who loved the Lord, whom he knew, were bearing me up on their hearts. Truly, I am delivered from all fear of failing in this battle, which is the Lord's, not mine. I feel as if I must not write about anything else upon these two sheets. "Holiness unto the Lord," is written on them; and the domestic matters must go on another sheet of paper. Oh, how I praise the Lord for *you*! You are dear to me, as a woman and a wife, beyond all expression; but now, more fully than ever, we wear the yoke of Christ together, and mutually bear the double burden of service and suffering for Him.'

---

[1] After Spurgeon's return from Mentone, he wrote to this friend, concerning the Controversy:— 'I have had to lean on the bare arm of God. It is a grand sensation. An arm of flesh loses all charms after we have once leaned on the greater power. What a Lord we serve! True indeed is His Word, and it is profitable to be made to prove its truth in storm and wreck. What folly it seems to try to explain it away! Its keenest edge wounds nothing but that which is false and foul. I would sooner be slain by the Word of the Lord than live by the lie of the devil.'

Less than a week after the above letter was received, my husband wrote as follows:

'Prepare for further rejoicing. We had been out driving all day, and when I came in, I found your letter, and saw you sitting "in Expectation Corner," *with the door open.* Please receive the fresh token which the Lord has sent in the form of a second £100! Letter and cheque enclosed. What hath God wrought! I never gave Mrs. R—— a shadow of a hint. I never thought she would do more. Why should she? But, as you say, "the living God does deliver His children." How I praise Him! Or, rather, how I do wish I could praise Him, but I feel as if my gratitude was cold and superficial when contrasted with His great goodness! Blessed be His Name for ever!

What a dear soul you are! How I love you! Our inward and spiritual union has come out in this trial and deliverance. We will record all this to the glory of the Lord our God. The weather here is rather of heaven than of earth; warm, clear, bright, and yet life-giving and refreshing. The toothache touches me every now and then; but, moderated by interludes of ease, I hardly ought to mention it, my mercies are so great. What are pains when God is so near? This one theme is so predominant in my soul, that I cannot write about anything else. The Lord liveth, and blessed be my Rock!

Send cheque to Bank. Sing the Doxology. Keep all my love, and rest under the blessing of the Lord our God.'

After the letters to myself, probably those written to the friends at the Tabernacle expressed most fully what was in the Pastor's heart. Shortly after he reached the South of France, he wrote thus to them:

'I wish to thank you all most heartily for your constancy of love during four-and-thirty years of fellowship. We have been many in number, but only one in heart, all through these years. Specially is this true in the present hour of controversy, for my heartiest sympathizers are in my own church. Several enthusiastic ones proposed a general meeting of church-members, to express their fervent agreement with their Pastor; but the ever-faithful deacons and elders had taken time by the forelock, and presented to me a letter signed by them all as representing their brethren and sisters. Such unity comes from the grace of God, proves that His blessing is now with us, and prophesies future happiness. What can I do but thank you all, love you in return, labour for you as long as strength remains, and pray for you till I die? The infinite blessing of the Eternal God be with you for ever!'

In reply to the letter from the church-officers, and to a further communication sent by them, the Pastor wrote:

'Mentone,
Nov. 27, 1887.

To the Co-Pastor and the Deacons,
My Own Dear Brethren,

I am touched by your loving letter. It is just like you; but it is so tenderly, so considerately done, that it has a peculiar sweetness about it. May the Lord deal with each one of you as you have dealt towards me, even in tender love and true faithfulness!

The more you know of this Controversy, the more will your judgments, as well as your hearts, go with me. It is not possible for me to communicate to anyone all that has passed under my knowledge; but I have had abundant reason for every step I have taken, as the day of days will reveal. All over the various churches there is the same evil, in all denominations in measure; and from believers, in all quarters, comes the same thankful expression of delight that the schemes of errorists have been defeated by pouring light upon them.

I cannot, at this present, tell you what spite has been used against me, or you would wonder indeed; but the love of God first, and your love next, are my comfort and stay. We may, perhaps, be made to feel some of the brunt of the battle in our various funds; but the Lord liveth. My eminent predecessor, Dr. Gill, was told, by a certain member of his congregation who ought to have know better, that, if he published his book, *The Cause of God and Truth*, he would lose some of his best friends, and that his income would fall off. The doctor said, "I can afford to be poor, but I cannot afford to injure my conscience;" and he has left his mantle as well as his chair in our vestry.

I should like to see you all walk in here, and to hear your loving voices in prayer, for I feel knit to you all more and more.

Yours for ever,
C. H. SPURGEON.'

Among the letters written by Mr. Spurgeon, at that period, is one that is of special and permanent importance, first, because it was

[477]

the reply to a kind communication from Dr. Culross, the President of the Baptist Union; and, next, because it sets forth so clearly the reason for Mr. Spurgeon's protest and action:

'Mentone,

Nov. 26, 1887

My Dear Dr. Culross,

I think it most kind of you to write me. Your brethren have usually fired at me through the newspapers their loving appeals and advices. Of this I do not complain; but, assuredly, yours is a way which commands an answer. Letters to the papers are literature, and may or may not be worth one's notice; yours is a letter sent to me, and I will at least heartily thank you for it.

Do I need to say that, with you, and such brethren as Dr. McLaren, Mr. Aldis, and Dr. Angus, I have no sort of disagreement, except that you stay in the Union and I am out of it? We shall, according to our light, labour for the same cause. We are all Christians and Baptists, and can find many ways of co-operation.

The "Metropolitan men" in London request the Union to devise some way by which I, with others, can return to it. This is very right from their point of view, but I wish you to understand, as President of the Union, that *the request is not mine*. I do not ask you to do what I am sure you cannot do. If I had thought that you could have done anything which would enable me to return if I retired, I should have asked you to do it before retiring.

So long as an Association without a creed has no aliens in it, nobody can wish for a creed *formally*, for the spirit is there; but at a time when "strange children" have entered, what is to be done? Whatever may theoretically be in your power, you *practically* have no power whatever. You will go on as you are; and, unless God's grace calls back the wanderers, their numbers will increase, and their courage will cause them to speak out more plainly, to the sorrow of the faithful ones who shielded them in patient hope of better things.

I have followed out our Lord's mind as to private remonstrance by seeing Presidents and Secretary on former occasions, and I have written my remonstrances again and again without avail. I had no course but to withdraw. Surely, no sane person thinks that I should have made a tour to deal with the individual errorists. I have no jurisdiction over them, and should have been regarded as offensively intrusive if I had gone to them; and justly so. My question is

[478]

with the Union, and with that alone. I have dealt with it all along.

Your very clear declaration, that the Union could not have a creed, or, as I read it, could not declare its doctrinal views otherwise than by practising baptism and the Lord's supper, closes the door finally against me. Neither do I knock at that door, nor wish for another door to be made. The good men who formed the Union, I fancy, had no idea that it would become what it now is, or they would have fashioned it otherwise. It has, by its centralization and absorption of various Societies, become far other than at the first. This is a good thing, but it involves a strain on the frail fabric which it is ill adapted to bear. So I think; but time will be the best proof of *that*.

I wish I could have worked with you in this particular way; but, as I cannot, we are not therefore deprived of a thousand other ways of fellowship. You feel union of heart with men who publicly preach Universal Restitution: *I do not*. I mean, you feel enough fellowship to remain in the Union with them: *I do not*. It is the same with other errors. Still, I am in fellowship with *you*—Union or no Union. If I think you wrong in your course—as I surely do—I will tell you so in the same spirit as that in which you have written to me.

From the Council of the Union I cannot look for anything which I should care to consider as the voice of the Union. It is too largely committed to a latitudinarian policy beforehand, and I have no question to refer to it.

I am happily free from all responsibility for its actions, and all allegiance to its sovereignty.

Very heartily yours,

C. H. Spurgeon.'

I have received, from many friends, copies of my dear husband's letters written during this trying period; but I do not think any good purpose can be served by the publication of more than I have here given. Those who sympathized with him in his protest need nothing to convince them of the need and the wisdom of his action; while those who were opposed to him would probably remain in the same mind, whatever might be said, so there the matter must rest as far as I am concerned.

Dec 28. 85

From the sunny shore of the central sea
There cometh thee cooing note unto thee; -
My turtle-dove it is well with me:
Thou wilt need no more of minstrelsy
And I go to bask in the sun.

Menton. Jan. 5. 86

From sunny lands my spirit flies to thee,
And doth salute thee in the chilly day;
Long hast thou been a summer's sun to me,
Fain would I chase thine every cloud away
Though I dark thy skies, I would thy light increase,
By one short message of my pen can tell:
It brings thy love some little light of peace
To know that with thy husband all is well

C. H. S.

FACSIMILES OF POST CARDS FROM MENTONE.

29

Last Letters from Mentone

Mrs. C. H. Spurgeon

THE love-letters of twenty blessed years have been reluctantly lifted from their hiding-place, and re-read with unspeakable love and sorrow. They are full of brightness, and the fragrance of a deep and abiding affection; and filled with every detail concerning my beloved and his doings which could be precious to the heart of a loving wife. But, alas! each year, some part of the holiday time at Mentone was overshadowed by what appeared to be an inevitable illness, when the dear preacher was laid aside, and days and nights of wearisome pain were appointed to him. He had always worked up to the latest moment, and to the utmost point of endurance, so it was not surprising that, when the tension was relaxed, nature revenged herself upon the weary body by setting every nerve on fire, and loading every vein with gout-poison, to act as fuel to the consuming flame. 'I feel as if I were emerging from a volcano,' he wrote, at the beginning of a convalescent period; but even at such a time his sense of humour asserted itself, for his pen had sketched the outlines of a conical hill, out of the crater of which his head and shoulders were slowly rising, while the still-imprisoned lower limbs set forth the sad truth that all was not yet well with them.

These chronicles would scarcely be complete without some further particulars concerning his life on the Riviera—how he enjoyed his pleasures, how he bore his pains, how he worked when God gave him relief from sickness, and how, always and ever, his loving heart was 'at home' with me. He kept up a daily correspondence with unflagging regularity; and when unable to use his pen, through severe suffering or weakness, the letter came as usual, either dictated by him, or altogether written by his devoted secretary.

I have selected, as the material for this chapter, the *last* letters which were written to me from Mentone, and which cover a period of nearly three months, for he left London on November 11, 1890, and returned February 5, 1891.

Passing over the days of travel, which had no special interest, the arrival at Mentone is thus recorded on a post card:—'What heavenly sunshine! This is like another world. I cannot quite believe myself to be on the same planet. God grant that this may set me all right! Only three other visitors in the hotel—three American ladies—*room for you.* So far, we have had royal weather, all but the Tuesday. Now the sea shines like a mirror before us. The palms in front of the windows are as still as in the Jubilee above. The air is warm, soft, balmy. We are idle—writing, reading, dawdling. Mentone is the same as ever, but it has abolished its own time, and goes by Paris.'

This bright opening of the holiday was quickly overclouded, for the next day came the sad news that gout had fastened upon the patient's right hand and arm, and caused him weary pain. Yet he wrote: 'The day is like one in Eden before our first parents fell. When my head is better, I shall enjoy it. I have *eau de Cologne* dripped on to my hot brain-box; and, as I have nothing to do but to look out on the perfect scene before me, my case is not a bad one.' But, alas! the 'case' proved to be very serious, and a painful time followed. These sudden attacks of the virulent enemy were greatly distressing and discouraging; one day, Mr. Spurgeon would be in apparent health and good spirits; and the next, his hand, or foot, or knee, would be swollen and inflamed, gout would have developed, and all the attendant evils of fever, unrest, sleeplessness, and acute suffering, would manifest themselves with more or less severity.

In the present instance, the battle raged for eight days with much fury, and then God gave victory to the anxious combatants, and partial deliverance to the prisoner. Daily letters, written by Mr. Harrald during this period, were very tender records of the sickroom experiences—every detail told, and every possible consolation offered—but it was a weary season of suspense for the loving heart a thousand miles distant, and the trial of absence was multiplied tenfold by the distress of anxiety.

In the first letter Mr. Harrald wrote, he said: 'The one continual cry from Mr. Spurgeon is, "I wish I were at home! I must get home!" Just to pacify him, I have promised to enquire about the through trains to London; but, of course, it would be impossible for him to travel in his present condition. Everyone is very kind, sympathetic, attentive, and ready to do anything that can be done to relieve or cheer the dear sufferer. I have just asked what message he wishes to send to you. He says, "Give her my love, and say I am very bad, and I wish I were at home for her to nurse me; but, as I am not, I shall be helped through somehow." '

Curiously enough, *The Times* of the following day had a paragraph to the effect that 'Mr. Spurgeon will stay at Mentone till February;' and when Mr. Harrald read this aloud, the dear patient remarked, 'I have not said so, but I am afraid I shall have to do it;' and the prophecy was fulfilled.

After eight days and nights of alternate progress and drawback, there came to me a half-sheet of paper, covered with extraordinary hieroglyphic characters, at first sight almost unreadable. But love deciphered them, and this is what they said: 'Beloved, to lose right hand, is to be dumb. I am better, except at night. Could not love his darling more. Wished myself at home when pains came; but when worst, this soft, clear air helps me. It is as heaven's gate. All is well. Thus have I stammered a line or two. Not quite dumb, bless the Lord! What a good Lord He is! I shall yet praise Him. Sleeplessness cannot so embitter the night as to make me fear when He is near.' This pathetic little note is signed, 'Your own beloved *Benjamite*,' for it was the work of his left hand.

I think the effort was too much for him, for two more letters were written by Mr. Harrald; but a tender pleasantry, recorded in one of them, showed me that my beloved was on the road to recovery. 'Our dear Tirshatha,' says Mr. Harrald, 'has been greatly pleased with your letter received to-day; your exhilaration appears to have favourably affected him. He says that he hopes the time will speedily arrive when *he will be able to offer you his hand*!'

After this, the daily correspondence from his own pen is resumed, and in the first letter he strikes his usual key-note of praise to God: 'Bless the Lord! I feel lighter and better; but oh, how weak! Happily, having nothing to do, it does not matter. I have nearly lost a whole month of life since I first broke down, but the Lord will restore this breach.'

The next day—date of letter, Dec. 1, 1890,—he writes to his 'poor lamb in the snow' to tell her that 'this poor sheep cannot get its forefoot right yet, but it is far better than it was'—followed by the quaint petition, 'May the Good Shepherd dig you out of the snow, and many may the mangolds and the swedes be which He shall lay in the fold for His half-frozen sheep!'

Our Arctic experiences in England were balanced by wintry weather on the Riviera. 'We have had two gloriously terrific storms,' he says; 'the sea wrought, and was tempestuous; it flew before the wind like glass dust, or powdered snow. The tempest howled, yelled, screamed, and shrieked. The heavens seemed on fire, and the skies reverberated like the boom of gigantic kettle-drums. Hail rattled down, and then rain poured. It was a time of clamours and confusions. I went to bed at ten, and left the storm to itself; and I woke at seven, much refreshed. I ought to be well, but I am not, and don't know why.'

Dec. 3, 1890.—'We had two drives yesterday, and saw some of the mischief wrought by the storm. The woodman, Wind, took down his keenest axe, and went straight on his way, hewing out a clean path through the olives and the pines. Here he rent off an arm, there he cut off a head, and yonder he tore a trunk asunder, like some fierce Assyrian in the days ere pity was born. The poor cottagers were gathering the olives from the road, trying to clear off the broken boughs before they bore down other trees, and putting up fences which the storm had levelled with the ground. They looked so sad as they saw that we commiserated them. To-day, so fair, so calm, so bright, so warm, is as a leaf from the evergreen trees of Heaven. Oh, that you were here!'

For the next four days, I received post cards only. There was a loving arrangement between us that these missives should be used when we were busy, or had not much to tell; but my beloved could always say a great many things on these little messengers. He knew how to condense and crystallize his thoughts, so that a few brief choice sentences conveyed volumes of tender meaning. I have commenced this chapter with *facsimiles* of two of his poetical post cards of earlier date; here are two specimens belonging to the period of which I am writing:

'Mentone,
Sunday, Dec. 7, '90

Mia Carissima,

Your praise of my letters prompts me to write more; but your royal commands restrict me to a card; and they are wise. Much love. Parcel has arrived—all that I want. If specially good books come, you might get Mr. Keys to take two or three to Cook's office, for Haskoll to bring to me. He travels every week to and fro.

It was wet yesterday; but I went out a very little walk. Mean to walk every day, but find my feet painful, as if I could count all my bones, yet I am each day better. Today is dull, and by no means tropical; but, oh, so quiet! I am praying that the "Report" may flow as streams in the desert. In our port, some vessels have all sails spread, but it is only to dry them; better have ever so little a bit of canvas filled with the breath of heaven. I feel as if I were drying; may you have the breeze!'

'Mentone,
Monday, 8/12/90.

Out of that obedience which has so long been habitual to me, I did not write this morning; but, finding that there is an evening post, my rebellious nature seized the occasion to indulge itself. TO-DAY I DRESSED MYSELF! A childish glee is on me as I record the fact. To have the use of one's hands again is a big mercy. We have had a heavenly day, and spent the morning in a long drive. Afternoon, I went for a walk. I was entreated to attend laying of first stone in Scotch Church, but I would not yield. H. went, and it was cold and draughty—enough to lay me up again. Wisdom did me a good turn when she bade me walk in the sun. Mr. A. has sent home some flowers; he despatched some rosebuds to you from me. They will be perfumed *à parfait amour*. You write so sweetly. Yours is a hand which sets to music all it writes to me. God bless you! But you don't say how you are. If you do not, I will write every day. We have fifteen in the hotel now. I have not commenced morning prayer with them yet, but think of doing so soon. Remember me to T. and old George.'

Such post cards were as good as letters, and I could have been well content had my husband sent me only these; but he was lavish in his love, and insisted that the letters should outnumber the smaller missives. I had long protested, and sincerely, too, against what I feared was a tax upon his precious holiday time; but, to the end, (for these are his *very* last letters to me,) he persevered in his tender, self-imposed task; and, now, the memory of his goodness is inexpressibly precious.

In the succeeding communication, there is a reference to the burning question of the hour—Home Rule—which may interest readers who indulge a *penchant* for politics:

'We have had two of the loveliest of days; and, after a morning drive, I have had an afternoon's walk, each day walking just a little more. It is not much now, but it was and is much to me. The Dr. says that, in the heart-cure, they have a zigzag up a mountain, and the patient tries a turn each day; and when he can walk to the top and down, he goes home. My little perambulations are somewhat after this fashion. This place is delicious. It is just 8 a.m., and I have both windows open, and I am writing to the low soft cadence of a rippling sea. Oh, that you were here!

That Irish stew! The last dose was well peppered, and served up hot! Perhaps now that they are separated they will get together; they seem to have been greatly divided while they were united! Poor G.O.M.! How he must feel the insults of those for whom he has forfeited everything! Yet he seems to hold on to their scheme though he knows that it is not only dangerous, but unattainable. I am glad I am neither of Gladstone nor of Parnell. He that wades not up to the ankles, will not go in up to the loins.'

Midwinter in England brought also to Mentone some cold, wet days, and these acted on the Pastor's sensitive frame as the atmosphere operates on a barometer. Dull and dreary days depressed him; but when they came, they were welcomed, for he would then turn to his literary work with redoubled energy, and get through an amazing quantity of it in an incredibly short space of time; but he revelled in the sunshine, and enjoyed basking in its warm beams; and his pity for those who had to endure the severities of fog, frost, and snow, was very real and sincere.

'Poor darling,' he wrote, 'to be so cold. The Lord will soon hear prayer, and send the soft South wind upon you, and then I also shall get well, and go out for walks, and praise His Name. I wish I could think of something to cast a gleam of sunlight over "Westwood." If my love were light, you would live in the sun. I shall send some roses to-morrow, and they will prophesy of better days.' Alas! the 'better days' moved very tardily towards him on this occasion; and, though of course we did not know it at the time, the deadly mischief, which afterwards proved fatal, had already begun to work in his poor body. 'I cannot say that I am as I should like to be,' he writes; 'two cold, windy afternoons have kept me in, and so I have missed my walk; and my hand, inside, is white and chalky, and outside, on its back, it is still somewhat swollen, and you see I cannot write so well. To-day, I have been for a drive, but it was rather cold. I sleep well, take physic often, and try to be right, and am really much better, but the mischief hangs about me.' Undoubtedly it did, and this was 'the beginning of the end,' though our eyes were holden, so that we could not see it.

The loving ministries of his Mentone life began again, however. He 'went to see a sick Baroness, and prayed with her, and helped her to feel at rest through submission to our Lord's will;' and the morning meetings for worship were recommenced, the conduct of which gave him much joy and encouragement.

Next morning, the aneroid marked a higher figure, but only for a few hours: 'This has been so far a lovely, sunny, warm day, and we have been out for a long drive, and enjoyed it much. Seen the mountains of Italy covered with their white millers' hats; and fields of roses, red, white, and yellow! We had a drink of very cold water from the fountain which gushes, apparently, from the heart of an olive. Now the day is darkening down with clouds, and probably a cold blast will come. Yes, the angels are letting loose the winds from their fists, and the palm trees are waving their fronds in token of victory over the sun which has retreated behind the clouds. These palms in front of the windows constantly remind me of the words in the Revelation, "with palms in their hands," for we are on a level with their grand fronds. I should think they measure ten or twelve feet from where they start. They are magnificent emblems of victory. We shall wave better than these when we are with the Lord, and celebrate His triumph!'

Day after day, these barometric fluctuations agitated the dear patient, and seemed to retard his recovery; but they were only the outward indications of the deep-seated internal trouble. It is wonderful how blind we were; so used, I expect, to the alternations of my beloved's condition, and so happily accustomed to see his 'rare power of recuperation,' as the Dr. called it, manifesting itself at the end of an illness, that we had learned to anticipate complete recovery from all his sicknesses. God be praised for the merciful veil which hides the future from our eyes!

'Mentone,
Dec. 18, '90.

Yesterday morning was wet and cold, and we rejoiced in the fire of olive logs. After lunch, the clouds were gone, the winds fell asleep, the sun in beneficent splendour gave us two hours of summer, during which your Prince Charlie went forth in his chariot, and was so pleased with the light, colour, warmth, and tone of everything, that he felt no spot or time could ever be more enjoyable unless his dear consort could be with him. I want someone to show these things to—and there is only one "someone" who would fulfil my ideal.

After morning prayer, we went down town to get the parcel from

Cook's man. All right. Books well selected. Hearty thanks. The tracts from Drummond's we can give away. We sent sermons and other periodicals to a Shields collier which has been in this port with coals. After getting our parcel, we returned, for the clouds came up in black armies, and the wind rushed forth. It may alter again, and then "out we go"; but nothing seems to be settled, and I suppose the weather here cannot be quiet, while it is so terrible with you. If the Lord will, I trust the worst of the winter will soon be gone. I have plenty to do, so that a day indoors is not dull, but I wish I could get my walk. This, too, may come. I have one finger purple and swollen, but I feel so greatly better that I could clap my hands if it were not for hurting that poor weak member.'

Till Christmas day, the letters tell of cold and rain, tornadoes of wind, and other evils, with occasional glimpses of the lovely spring weather so much desired. My husband greatly sympathized with us in our endurance of the very severe winter of 1890; it was quite touching to note how constantly he referred to it, and seemed almost to suffer with us in our long period of frost, fog, bitter cold, and darkness.'I keep on praying for change of weather for you, and the poor and sick,' he writes; 'I wish I could send you a brazier of the coals of my heart, which have a most vehement flame.'

Oh, how true this was! God had made him a real philanthropist, and the woes of others were felt, and commiserated, and brought before the Lord, with as much earnestness and sincerity as though they had been his own. His heart was so big, it had room for others' griefs; and it was so full of love and pity, that he had always some to spare for those who needed it.

A carriage drive to Ventimiglia gave him great pleasure just at this time. From a certain part of the road, the Col di Tenda and a considerable portion of the Maritime Alps are visible, in their winter dress of snow; and visitors from Mentone are fond of driving there to see a picture quite unique in its grouping—a foreground of roses, and palms, and tropical vegetation luxuriating in the sunshine—on the one side, the blue waters of the Mediterranean rivalling the brightness of the sky; on the other, the valley of the Roya, with picturesque hamlets on both banks of the river, and, for a distant background, those solemn white Alps proclaiming, in a language which cannot be misunderstood, the greatness and majesty of their Maker.

Christmas day was grey and cold, and was spent in work 'digging away at books and letters.' Friends had lavished upon him a wealth of lovely flowers—roses, carnations, hyacinths, tuberoses, cyclamen—in vases; and a pot of that sweetest of sweet blossoms, lily of the valley; but he could scarcely enjoy them. All night, his bones had 'cried and groaned' with rheumatism; and he must, I think, for the first time, have had some premonition of danger, for he says, 'There is some deep-seated gout in me.'

But even this passes, and the five following days each bring a bright, cheerful little post card to reassure and comfort me. One, written on Monday, December 29, 1890, tells of 'a delightful meeting, last night, in the room above ours. Piano, with hymns *ad lib.*, and I preached from Deut. 32. 10, glad to review the goodness of Him who found, led, taught, and kept me;' and the last of the five—on December 31, 1890—testifies thus graciously to the goodness and faithfulness of God:—'The old year is nearly out—a good old year, a year of loving kindnesses and of tender mercies. I cannot dismiss it with a complaint, but with thankfulness. Oh, for more holiness for myself in the new year, and more health for my beloved spouse! I think I shall get home for February 1, or first Sunday in February, for I now feel as if life had come back to me with enjoyment, and a measure of sprightly thought, for which I would praise the Lord practically by employing it in His service. We had twenty-three to morning prayer to-day—nearly as many as the room can hold. How they do come! Wet and cold do not hinder, and they are so grateful.'

'New Year's Day, Jan. 1, 1891.

'A happy new year to you, my sweetest and best! I would write it in the biggest of capitals if that would show how happy I wish the year to be. I had a praiseful evening yesterday, blessing God for the old year; and now, this morning, we have had a good meeting. We sang No. 1,042 in *Our Own Hymn Book*. Then I read and expounded Psalm 103 and prayed. There were flowers, and cards, and contributions; and, this afternoon, we are going to give our landlord and his wife a present, for the house is not full, and the keeping of the hotel is not profitable. So there will be joy among many as we meet for tea. God is indeed gracious to me, for I feel well, and I turn my face homeward in desire. I have been for a drive in the delicious summer sunshine. Oh, that you had been at my side! I have just read your sweet, sweet letter. You best-beloved of my heart, how I wish I could change your weather! I can only pray;

but prayer moves the hand which moves winds and clouds. The Lord Himself comfort you, and bear you up under all troubles, and make up to you, by His own presence, the absence of health, warmth, and husband!'

When my beloved felt fairly well, his Sundays at Mentone were a great joy and rest to him. He made the day full of sweet, devout service, and still sweeter communion with the Lord! In the morning, after having family prayer, he would, perhaps, go to the Presbyterian place of worship in Mrs. Dudgeon's garden; and afterwards write to me:—'Capital sermon from Mr. Somerville on Rev. 2. 12, 17, splendidly witnessing against the "Down-grade."' In the afternoon, there would be breaking of bread, and one of those choice little addresses, on the love and grace of the Lord Jesus, which melted all hearts, and rekindled the latent fires of devotion in some inconstant breast; and the evening would be spent in singing God's praises, and listening to a brief sermon by Mr. Harrald, or someone else who might have a message to deliver. 'Quite a full day,' he remarks, after one of these occasions, 'but it seemed very short, and as sweet as short. Oh, that you were here!'

The holy, happy influence of these Sabbaths overflowed into the days of the week, which to my beloved were as much 'Lord's days' as those set apart by law and gospel. The company at morning worship grew larger every week, the adjoining room had to be thrown open, and one very cold day he wrote: 'I wondered to see my visitors assemble to the great number of forty-one, and they do not want to go away from what some of them call "this dear room." Truly, the Lord is here, and His Word is sweet both to them and to me, as we read it morning by morning. What a text is Isaiah 62. 7, in the Revised Version: "Ye that are the Lord's remembrancers, take ye no rest, and give Him no rest." Oh, for such importunate prayers for His Church now that evil times have come!'

A tender, loving birthday letter, which set all the joy-bells in my heart ringing, comes next in order, and I quote a few extracts from it: 'I trust this will reach you on your own dear birthday. Ten thousand benedictions be upon you! . . . What an immeasurable blessing you have been to me, and are still! Your patience in suffering, and diligence in service, are works of the Holy Spirit in you, for which I adore His Name. Your love to me is not only a product of nature, but it has been so sanctified by grace that it has become a spiritual blessing to me. May you still be upheld; and if you may not be kept from suffering, may you be preserved from sinking! . . . My love to you grows, and yet I do not know how at any time it could have been greater. I am thinking which I shall do—drive out, and send you flowers, or walk, and get Mr. A. to send them. I know which way your vote would go, and I shall act accordingly, if our friend will undertake the commission. If flowers do not come, please know that it was in my heart to send them.'

A few days after, a reference is made to my reply in these words: 'I had your letter, last night, which was written on your birthday. I am so glad the flowers reached you, and made you glad. There is a happy tone about "the old woman's" letter which does the old man good. God bless you, darling, and delight your heart with trucks and sacks of good things for others!' This latter sentence refers to the generous action of one of our near neighbours, on Beulah Hill, who, knowing that I was interesting myself for the poor in Thornton Heath, had placed a truckload of coals at my disposal for them. The long and dreary winter had severely tried them, and we opened a soup-kitchen at 'Westwood,' which ministered daily to their necessities. My beloved felt sorely troubled for the distress which came so close to our doors, and did not fail to take his share in the pitying help rendered to those you could not help themselves during the time of that awful frost. 'I am so glad you feed the poor,' he wrote; 'spend £10 for me, please; don't stint anything. As I look at the pictures in *The Graphic*, my spirits sink, but my prayer rises.' And a few days later he returns to the same subject:—'I pray day and night for a thaw to come and end this great distress by allowing the people to work. Do spend my £10, which I will send by next post.'

The grey, cold days, which prevailed at Mentone during the early part of the year 1891, gave the dear preacher an opportunity for working hard, of which he willingly availed himself. He heartily enjoyed the pleasurable leisure of driving, which seemed to soothe his brain, and refresh both body and spirit; but he was never idle; and, after returning from his excursions, he would apply himself immediately to the work in hand, and his busy pen would fly over the sheets of paper with untiring energy. The secret of the amazing wealth of literary labour, which he left as a legacy to the world, lay in the fact that he was constantly gathering up the seed-pearls of small opportunities while never neglecting the greater occasions of enrichment. Receiving and imparting, gaining that he might give, labouring not for himself but for others, the redeemed minutes soon multiplied into hours, and the hours grew into days, and so his life, like a field well-dressed and tended, bore hundred-fold crops to the praise and glory of the Great Husbandman.

Sabbath, Jan. 18, 1891, he wrote: 'I have not gone to service this morning, as I had sermons to revise, and one to get for this afternoon. I have chosen Psalm 32. 9, and want to show the joy of having a good understanding with the Lord, so as to need no bit, but to be left free to go on in His way with liberty. Two things are to be dreaded,—*Irreverent familiarity*: "lest they come near unto thee;" (A.V.)—*Disobedient departure*: "else they will not come near unto thee." (R.V.) Are not the two renderings curious? To me, they set forth the same thing in different lights. Note, in R.V., "whose trappings must be bit and bridle," as if even these were made ornamental, and our inflictions and afflictions became our decorative equipment,—yet even then not desirable. Oh, to be guided by the Lord's eye!'

Further on, I am told that he had 'a good service from the text mentioned,' and then that he had been able to revise six sermons ready for printing when double numbers were wanted, or 'to be used if I should be ill.' Was this another premonition? If it were, the shadow soon passed, for the next letter describes a visit to Beaulieu—'a lovely drive, in the warm sunshine, to a place which I should like to stop at for a time another year, if it please God.' This little outing must have benefited the dear patient, for, the next morning, he writes: 'I am working with windows wide open; and when I have done, I hope to take my long walk round the red rocks. I forgot to tell you that, on Thursday, Mr. Cheyne Brady came over from Cannes, and we walked out a mile or more, and talked, and prayed, and then came back. He returned alone because he had to hurry to catch a train, but I walked both ways with great pleasure; indeed, it was the best time I have spent since I came here. The sun, the air, the sea, all ministered to me; and I ministered to the Lord in grateful praise.'

The Pastor had consented to open the new Scotch Church on Thursday, January 29, 1891; but, on the Wednesday, while out walking, a sudden seizure of gout in both hands and one foot threatened to lay him aside once more. It is most touching to read how he fought the disease both with physic and by dieting. 'The enemy is going,' he writes; 'driven out by medicine, starved out by oatmeal and nothing else for lunches and dinners.' He took the service at the Scotch Church, though so utterly unfit for it, and 'got through the sermon with trembling knees, and the bell gone out of my voice.'

Extremely sensitive as my beloved was to any degree of pain, it was simply marvellous how he overcame this weakness of body, and served while suffering, when work for the Master called forth his spiritual energies. Many a time, at the Tabernacle, has he painfully limped into his pulpit, leaning heavily on his stick, and, unable to stand, has preached, kneeling with one knee on a chair; but even then, the astonished congregation has seen him, warming to his work, and inspired by his all-consuming zeal, push the chair aside, and, grasping the rail of the platform with both hands, stand there for the rest of the service, apparently forgetful of his bodily distress, because absorbed by his passionate desire to persuade poor sinners to come to Christ.

But this is a digression. We must return to Mentone for the few days yet remaining.

One of the dear preacher's last ministrations, on this occasion, was to hold a funeral service over the body of the Baroness von H., whom he had so often visited and comforted in her last sickness. He writes:—'There was a great blaze of candles on both sides of the coffin, and palm branches and white flowers upon it. She is now to be carried to Russia, and I should think the journey will occupy a fortnight. Why can't they let a body be? I would prefer to be buried wherever I might die; yet, as she wished to lie in the same tomb with her husband, there is an argument on that side also.'

Now the record draws quickly to a close. It had been a time of strangely mingled experiences of rest and rack, of cold and heat, of storm and sunshine, of pain and pleasure—but, over all, the peace of God brooded like a dove, and the home-coming was safe and happy; not even a shadow of the dark dispensation, which fell upon us in June, then rested on our spirits. The *last* communication from Mentone was a post card, which, from the extracts I give, will be seen to have been written in quite good spirits, and suitably closes this chapter:

'Mentone,

Monday, February 2, '91.

Mine Own,

I telegraphed you to-day, and I hope your anxiety has ceased. There! at this moment, a mosquito popped on my nose, and Harrald has killed him! So may all your fears end! I am very much better; indeed, well. Archibald Brown has been with me for an

[493]

hour; and the sight of him, and a little prayer with him, have set me up. I rested well yesterday. We are all in a muddle packing; H., in his shirt-sleeves, almost wants to pack *me* up! I am writing notes of "Good-bye" to friends. I hope soon to follow where this card is going; how delighted I am with the prospect! I am already with you in spirit. My heart has never left you. Blessed be God that we are spared to each other!'

Blessed is that man to whom the Lord has said, 'The blood shall be to you for a token.' Death's terrors are gone to him who has the blood for a token. Lay me down on my bed! There let me endure the allotted pain and weakness, till the clammy sweat stands on my brow, and needs to be constantly wiped away: lay me down, I say, and I will calmly fall asleep like a child tired with a day's play.

'A token,' say you, 'what is it? Is it some line extracted from the golden book of God's election? Is it a gem taken from the diadem which is prepared for him in heaven?' No, no, it is not this. 'Has he in his sleep beheld a vision and seen the shining ones walking the golden streets, or has he heard an audible celestial voice saying to him, "Thou art mine"?' No, he has none of these, he has neither dream nor vision nor anything that men call superhuman, but he is resting in the precious blood, and this blood is the token of friendship between God and his soul; by this he knows the love of God, and by this God communes with him. They meet at the blood. God delights in the sacrifice of Christ, and the believing soul delights in it too; they have thus a common love and a common joy, and this has bound the two together by a bond which never can be broken. This it is which makes some of us sing—

And when I'm to die,
Receive me, I'll cry,
For Jesus has loved me,
I cannot tell why;
But this thing I find,
We two are so joined,
He won't be in heaven
And leave me behind.

C.H.S.

30

The Last Year

THE first Sabbath after his return from the sunny South—February 8, 1891—the Pastor preached at the Tabernacle from Isaiah 62. 6, 7, using both the Authorized and Revised Versions, as he had done when speaking upon that passage at Mentone. On that occasion, he said to his secretary, 'You need not transcribe your report, for I expect to have this subject again when I get home.' He had been specially struck with the Revisers' rendering of the text: 'Ye that are the Lord's remembrancers, take ye no rest, and give Him no rest, till He establish, and till He make Jerusalem a praise in the earth.' The sermon was intended to be the key-note of the year's service for God; it was a powerful call to prayer and testimony, yet probably even the preacher himself did not then fully realize how appropriate was his message in preparing the people for that long season of almost ceaseless intercession while he was enduring the heaviest affliction of his life, and from which he was never really to recover.

Although there were ominous indications that his health was by no means all that could be desired, he did not spare himself, but laboured with the utmost earnestness and zeal to extend his Master's Kingdom. A brief 'Note' in *The Sword and the Trowel* of that period gives just a glimpse of the great spiritual prosperity which was being enjoyed only a little while before the startling breakdown which proved to be 'the beginning of the end': 'The month of March has been a memorable one for the church in the Tabernacle. Pastor C. H. S. continued to see persons who wished to join the church, and out of these he had eighty-four to propose for fellowship. How much of joyous labour all these involved, is best known to the Pastor and the sympathizing reapers who shared his delightful toil. To God alone be glory.'

The last College Conference at which Spurgeon was present was held from Monday, April 20, to Friday, April 24. In the June number of *The Sword and the Trowel*, the Editor inserted the following 'Note' concerning the Sabbath night after the meetings: 'To the President, the week of Conference was one of exhausting delight.

Every day, everything went well. . . . Of course, there was a reaction for the one who was the centre of all this; and, for the first time in a ministry of forty years, we entered the pulpit on the Sunday evening, and were obliged to hurry out of it; for a low, nervous condition shut us up. Happily, Mr. Stott[1] could take up the story there and then; and he did so.' It was very remarkable that, in his letter, written to Mr. Stott, four months previously, concerning his appointment as assistant-minister for the year 1891, Spurgeon said: 'It would be a great relief to me if I knew that someone was on the spot to take the pulpit should I su-ddenly fail.' That expression almost implies a premonition of what took place on that Sabbath night, April 26, 1891.

This unprecedented experience was an indication of a very serious state of affairs; yet the following Lord's-day morning, May 3, the Pastor was in his pulpit again; and he delivered the discourse which he had prepared for the previous week, prefacing it with a reference to the 'overpowering nervousness' which had then oppressed him, and pointing out the lessons which that strange occurrence was probably intended to teach to himself and his hearers. He preached again at night; on the following afternoon, he was at the Tabernacle, seeing enquirers and candidates for church-fellowship; and in the evening, he presided at the prayer-meeting. In the course of the proceedings, he asked for earnest supplication on behalf of the special services in which he was to be occupied during the week. These comprised the annual sermon to Sunday-school teachers, at Bloomsbury Chapel on the Tuesday evening; a sermon at the Tabernacle, on the Thursday night, in aid of the British and Foreign Sailors' Society, preceded by a prayer-meeting in the lecture-hall; and two meetings at Hendon, on the Friday, in connection with the "Fraternal" of which Spurgeon was a member. In the June number of *The Sword and the Trowel*, the Editor gave a brief account of all these gatherings, and some others that followed shortly afterwards; and his 'Notes' indicate that the long illness had commenced, although he was not then aware of its serious nature or its probable duration. The concluding paragraphs were as follows:

'Friends will note that *all the above meetings were held in one week*, which also included two Sabbath services and the great communion at the Tabernacle, beside all the regular home-work, correspondence

---

[1] William Stott of Abbey Road Chapel, St. John's Wood. Though not a Pastors' College man, he had been acquainted with Spurgeon for many years and was held in high esteem.

etc. In addition, the Lord's-day morning sermon had to be revised, and published the following Thursday; and the sermons to Sunday-school teachers and sailors were received for revision, and duly attended to. Is it any wonder that the worker gets weary, and has to beg friends not to impose further burdens on one who is already terribly overladen?

On Friday evening, May 15, Mr. Spurgeon spoke at the Presbyterian missionary meeting at Exeter Hall. It was a time of peculiar bodily weakness, and of special spiritual strength. God bless our friends who so kindly received the message and the messenger!

On Sunday evening, May 17, Mr. Spurgeon could not preach; and on the Monday, the doctor found him laid aside with congestion of the lungs and other matters, which forbid his quitting his chamber for some little time to come. "My times are in Thy hand." We would always be preaching: howbeit, the Lord thinketh not so.'

The text quoted by the Pastor was the subject of his Sabbath morning sermon on May 17, which many have supposed to be his last discourse in the Tabernacle. It was not, however, for there was one more message which he was to be permitted to speak to the great congregation before that 'long silence' which was only temporarily broken at Mentone on the following New Year's Eve. On Lord's-day morning, June 7, 1891, Spurgeon stood for the last time on that platform which, for thirty years, had been his pulpit throne, and from which he had proclaimed the gospel to at least twenty millions of hearers, while, by means of the printed page, he had been brought into communication with a far greater number of readers in all quarters of the globe. His text, on that ever-memorable morning, was 1 Samuel 30. 21–25; and the sermon was published, as No. 2,208 in the regular weekly issue, under the title, 'The Statute of David for the Sharing of the Spoil.' The whole discourse was a noble conclusion to the Pastor's ministry in the beautiful sanctuary which was ever to him what Zion was to the Jews; but the final sentences were specially noteworthy:

'If you wear the livery of Christ, you will find Him so meek and lowly of heart that you will find rest unto your souls. He is the most magnanimous of captains. There never was His like among the choicest of princes. He is always to be found in the thickest part of the battle. When the wind blows cold He always takes the bleak side of the hill. The heaviest end of the cross lies ever on His shoulders. If He bids us carry a burden, He carries it also. If there is anything that is gracious, generous, kind, and tender, yea, lavish and superabundant in love, you always find it in Him. His service is life, peace, joy. Oh, that you would enter on it at once! God help you to enlist under the banner of JESUS CHRIST!'

On the following morning, Spurgeon went into the country, to be the guest of Mr. Gurteen, of Haverhill (Suffolk), in order that he might again visit Stambourne and its neighbourhood, that his photographer friend might take the views which he wished to have reproduced for his little volume, *Memories of Stambourne*. In the course of the week, however, a renewal of his malady set in and on the Friday he was compelled to hurry home; then, for three months, he was completely laid aside.

For a while, all that medical skill, patient watching, and careful nursing could do, appeared to be of no avail; and, with the use of all means that seemed wise and right, prayer was being offered, unceasingly, by believers all over the world. The Tabernacle Church, beginning with a whole day of intercession for the suffering Pastor, continued to meet, morning, noon, and night, to plead for his recovery. In hundreds and perhaps thousands of Nonconformist places of worship, sympathetic petitions were presented on his behalf. The Chief Rabbi of the Jews, although holding very different views from Spurgeon's, remembered him in the Synagogue service during his season of suffering. Many of the clergy of the Established Church, with their congregations, were equally earnest in praying for him, the ecclesiastical dignitaries officiating at St. Paul's Cathedral and Westminster Abbey joining with the Archbishops and many of the Bishops in interceding on his behalf.

The secular and religious press of our own and other lands devoted much space to accounts of his illness, and particulars of his work—not always accurate, though, on the whole, exceedingly kind and appreciative. Telegrams, letters, and resolutions of sympathy poured into 'Westwood' in a continuous stream, while those who called or sent to enquire after the sufferer were of all ranks, from the Prince of Wales and a great proportion of the nobility of the country to the poorest of the poor.

The progress towards a measure of recovery may be briefly traced. On August 9, the following letter, the first written by the Pastor's own hand after his long illness, was read to the congregation at the Tabernacle, and was received both as an answer to prayer, and an encouragement to continued intercession:—

'Dear Brethren,

The Lord's Name be praised for first *giving* and then hearing the loving prayers of His people! Through these prayers my life is prolonged. I feel greatly humbled, and very grateful, at being the object of so great a love and so wonderful an outburst of prayer.

I have not strength to say more. Let the Name of the Lord be glorified.

Yours most heartily,

C. H. SPURGEON.'

Even after the first signs of improvement were manifest, a long and wearisome time followed, hopeful advances alternating with disappointing relapses. At last, the patient was able to be carried downstairs, and to be wheeled round his garden, where the fresh air seemed to work wonders for him. On entering his study, for the first time, and catching sight of the final proofs of *John Ploughman's Almanack* and *Spurgeon's Illustrated Almanack*, and then asking for copies of the recently-issued sermons and magazine, he exclaimed, 'Why! you have carried on everything just as if I had been here.' Those who were responsible for the work felt that, if possible, nothing must be allowed to suffer during his absence; and it was a great joy to them to find how highly their services were appreciated by the Pastor.

As the autumn advanced, and the patient's weakness remained, it became certain that he must go to Mentone for the winter if he could journey so far. The renewed offer of Dr. Pierson, to cross the Atlantic if he could be of any service to the Pastor, appeared to everyone another providential arrangement; and, ultimately, it was settled that he should commence his service at the Tabernacle on Lord's-day, October 25.[1] In order to test the invalid's power to travel, an experimental visit was paid to Eastbourne from October 3 to 16. This proved most satisfactory, and it also further indicated the absolute necessity of a prolonged rest in the sunny South. Accordingly, on Monday, October 26, Pastor and Mrs. C. H. Spurgeon, Pastor and Mrs. J. A. Spurgeon, and Joseph Harrald started on their thousand miles' journey, arriving at their destination on Thursday, October 29.

It was a tender token of the Lord's loving kindness that husband

[1] Arthur T. Pierson, 1837–1911, of the Presbyterian Church in America, had preached at the Tabernacle and made a deep impression on a number of the members in December, 1889. In prayer with Pierson at 'Westwood', before he left for Mentone, Spurgeon said, 'Lord, we do not tell Thee how to work or what to do, only work like Thyself'. Pierson maintained a consecutive ministry at the Tabernacle until June, 1892.

and wife were, for once, permitted to travel together to Mentone, and to spend there three months of perfect happiness before the sorrowful separation which had been so long dreaded, but which came at last almost without warning. Spurgeon's oft-expressed longing—'Oh, that my dear wifey could see all the beauties and glories of this land of sunshine and flowers!'—was at length realized; and he had the joy of pointing out to her the many scenes with which he had been familiar for years, but which became doubly precious to him under such delightful circumstances. The rooms in the Hôtel Beau Rivage, which he and his friends had occupied year by year, soon began to give evidence of a lady's presence in them. A special improvement was made in the large sitting-room which had become a peculiarly hallowed spot to all the members of the Pastor's Mentone circle because of the morning gatherings there for the reading of the Word and prayer, and the still more sacred Sabbath afternoon meetings around the table of the Lord.

Mr. Spurgeon's weakness prevented him from resuming those much-prized hotel services, during his last sojourn 'on the sunny shore,' except on the memorable occasions hereafter mentioned; but he lost no time in beginning such literary work as he felt able to accomplish, and would never admit that he was doing too much for an invalid. His chief employment was the continuation of his Exposition of the Gospel according to Matthew. Articles for *The Sword and the Trowel*, with 'Notes' and reviews of books, also came from his busy pen; but he expressly said that he only occupied the editorial chair while he wrote the Preface to the magazine volume for 1891. The important work of sermon-revision was also left almost entirely in the hands of those upon whom it had devolved during his long illness, the only exceptions being the two notable discourses, 'Gratitude for Deliverance from the Grave,' and 'A Stanza of Deliverance,' intended for reading on the first and last Lord's-days in January, 1892.

The December number of *The Sword and the Trowel* opened with an article by Spurgeon under the suggestive title, '? ? ?'. In his usual graphic fashion he described his own physical condition, and made use of it in suggesting enquiries concerning his readers' spiritual state. In that paper, he referred to the two things which were characteristic of a great part of his time of partial convalescence —the deceptive appearance of a return to health, and the fact that the deadly disease was still firmly entrenched within his system, and ready at any moment to end his earthly existence.

One great help to him was the bright sunshine in which he was able to spend so much of his time. He almost lived in the open air, usually going for a drive in the morning, and in the afternoon having a ride in a Bath chair, along the Promenade St. Louis. This was the scene of the walking exercise in which the engaged so perseveringly in the winter of 1890-1.

A favourite route for a short drive was, around the Boulevard Victoria, and along the breakwater, as Spurgeon always admired the view of the old town across the harbour. One of the longest and latest drives that the Pastor and Mrs. Spurgeon took together is mentioned on a post card, written to Mr. Passmore, which reads as follows:

'I have only good news to send you. I have not gone backward, but doctor says I am a shade better as to my disease. In other respects I feel up to the mark, Mrs. S. is well. Beautiful ride this morning. Weather has been bad, but today is heavenly. Snow on the mountains just makes us the more grateful. . . . I sent telegram of sympathy to Sandringham.[1] I could not help it, as the Prince had so kindly thought of me. May the Lord save all you love from this fell disease'.

On the New Year's Eve and the following morning, Mr. Spurgeon gave to a privileged circle of friends the two addresses, which he afterwards revised for publication in the magazine, under the title, 'Breaking the Long Silence.' He also conducted two short services in his sitting-room, on January 10 and 17, when he was persuaded not to attempt to give a new address, and rather reluctantly consented to read portions of his early sermon on Psalm 73. 28, and his Exposition of Matthew 15. 21-28. On the second Sabbath evening—January 17, 1892—before offering the closing prayer at the final service in which he took part on earth, he gave out the last hymn he was ever to announce to a company of worshippers here below. If he could have foreseen what was to happen only a fortnight later, he could hardly have chosen a more appropriate farewell than the poem founded on some words of Samuel Rutherford—

The sands of time are sinking,
The dawn of heaven breaks,
The summer morn I've sighed for,
The fair, sweet morn awakes,

[1] The telegram related to the death of the Duke of Clarence, eldest son of the Prince of Wales and grandson of Queen Victoria.

C. H. Spurgeon: The Full Harvest

Dark, dark hath been the midnight,
But dayspring is at hand,
And glory, glory dwelleth
In Immanuel's land.'

On the two following days, the wind was very rough, so Mr. Spurgeon went only for short drives; but on Wednesday morning, he was able to go as far as the little village of Monti. In the afternoon, signs of gout appeared in his right hand; later in the day other serious symptoms were manifest and he had to retire to the bed from which he never again rose. It soon became evident that a crisis was approaching, though there were intervals of improvement which gave ground for slight hope. Towards the end of the week, the Pastor said to his secretary, 'My work is done,' and spoke of some matters in a way that indicated his own conviction that he was not going to recover.

Tuesday, January 26, was the day on which thankofferings were brought to the Tabernacle, in grateful acknowledgment of the Pastor's partial restoration. By that time, he had become so much worse that he was for a long while only partly conscious; but he had not forgotten the special character of the day, and he sent a telegram which, under the circumstances, was peculiarly significant:—'*Self and wife, £100, hearty thankoffering towards Tabernacle General Expenses. Love to all friends.*' That was his last act and his last message; for, shortly afterwards he became totally unconscious, and remained so until five minutes past eleven on the Sabbath night—January 31, 1892—when, like his namesake, Mr. Valiant-for-truth, 'he passed over, and all the trumpets sounded for him on the other side.'

Shortly the news was being flashed all over the world, and in every quarter of the globe many felt a sense of personal loss as they read or heard it. The telegraph wires at Mentone were speedily blocked with the multitudes of messages to Mrs. Spurgeon, the Prince and Princess of Wales being among the first to 'desire to express their deep sympathy with her in her great sorrow.'

Flowers in abundance were sent by friends, but Mrs. Spurgeon intimated her preference for palm branches as the most suitable emblems of her husband's victorious entrance into 'the presence of the King.' At the head and foot of the olive casket, were plates bearing the following inscription:

The Last Year

In ever-loving memory of
CHARLES HADDON SPURGEON,
Born at Kelvedon, June 19, 1834;
Fell asleep in Jesus at Mentone, January 31, 1892.
'I have fought a good fight, I have finished my course, I have kept
the faith.'

In the early years of his visits to Wotton, in Surrey, the Pastor had always said that he would like to be buried in the churchyard of that village. Later, he expressed the wish to lie in the centre of the Stockwell Orphanage grounds, for he thought that many would come to look at his grave, and then help the orphans in whom he took so deep an interest; but when the Electric Railway caused such a disturbance to the Institution, he abandoned that idea. At one time, he said he would like to be buried at Mentone, but after he had attended the funeral of a friend there he gave up that notion. Last of all, it was mentioned that he had pointed to a site in Norwood cemetery—in a far less conspicuous position than the one ultimately chosen—and asked that it might be reserved for him; so that, in death as in life, he might be surrounded by his church-officers and members, many hundreds of whom are buried there. The Tabernacle deacons sent an urgent request to Mrs. Spurgeon, asking that this might be the arrangement, and the matter was so settled.

The memorial and funeral services at the Tabernacle from Sunday, the 7th February to the Thursday following, when the interment took place, were attended as it was estimated by not less than 100,000 people. The Bible on the top of the olivewood casket was that which Spurgeon had so long used at the Tabernacle. It was opened at Isaiah 45. 22: 'Look unto me, and be ye saved, all the ends of the earth', the text which on January 6, 1850 had been blessed to his conversion.

Now, when his own preaching of that Word was ended, the number of members on the church roll was 5,311, and during his long pastorate no less than 14,691 had been received into fellow-ship. At the end of 1891, there were 22 mission stations, and 27 Sunday and Ragged Schools, with 612 teachers, 8,034 scholars, and accommodation for 3,840 worshippers in the various halls used for public services. Comparing this great host with the little company of anxious but praying people to whom 'the boy-preacher' delivered his first discourse, in New Park Street Chapel, on that historic morning, in December, 1853, one can only say, as he said, times without number, when speaking of the blessing which the Lord had graciously vouchsafed to his ministry, 'What hath God wrought!'

Never had the South of London witnessed such a procession as that day, Thursday, February 11, 1892, slowly moved from the Tabernacle to the cemetery; and never had such crowds assembled along that five-mile route to Norwood. More than eighteen years before, the Pastor had given a description of the scene; but probably even he had no conception of the throng that would gather to do honour to his memory. At the close of his sermon, on Lord's-day evening, December 27, 1874, he said: 'In a little while there will be a concourse of persons in the streets. Methinks I hear someone enquiring, "What are all these people waiting for?" "Do you not know? He is to be buried to-day." "And who is that?" "It is Spurgeon." "What! the man that preached at the Tabernacle?" "Yes; he is to be buried to-day." That will happen very soon; and when you see my coffin carried to the silent grave, I should like every one of you, whether converted or not, to be constrained to say, "He did earnestly urge us, in plain and simple language, not to put off the consideration of eternal things. He did entreat us to look to Christ. Now he is gone, our blood is not at his door if we perish." God grant that you may not have to bear the bitter reproach of your own conscience! But, as I feel "the time is short," I will stir you up so long as I am in this Tabernacle.'

Though the scene along the route was striking, that presented at the cemetery was, in some respects, even more so. The long line of ministers, and students, and other friends, all in mourning garb, reaching from the entrance to the grave itself, was a sight that could never be forgotten by those who saw it. At length, the vast throng clustered in a dense mass around and upon the slope outside the cemetery chapel, where the last service was to be conducted. The principal part in the closing ceremony fell to the share of Pastor Archibald G. Brown, and nothing could have been more suitable than his solemn and touching words. They came straight from his heart: they entered thousands of other hearts. With great pathos and many pauses, he said—

'Beloved President, Faithful Pastor, Prince of Preachers, Brother Beloved, Dear Spurgeon—We bid thee not "farewell," but only for a little while "good-night." Thou shalt rise soon, at the first dawn of the resurrection day of the redeemed. Yet is not the "good-night" ours to bid, but thine. It is we who linger in the darkness; thou art in God's own light. Our night, too, shall soon be past, and with it all our weeping. Then, with thine, our songs shall greet the morning of a day that knows no cloud nor close, for there is no night there.

Hard Worker in the field, thy toil is ended! Straight has been the furrow thou hast ploughed. No looking back has marred thy course. Harvests have followed thy patient sowing, and heaven is already rich with thine ingathered sheaves, and shall be still enriched through years yet lying in eternity.

Champion of God, thy battle long and nobly fought is over! The sword, which clave to thine hand, has dropped at last; the palm branch takes its place. No longer does the helmet press thy brow, oft weary with its surging thoughts of battle; the victor's wreath from the Great Commander's hand has already proved thy full reward.

Here, for a little while, shall rest thy precious dust. Then shall thy Well-Beloved come, and at His voice thou shalt spring from thy couch of earth, fashioned like unto His glorious body. Then spirit, soul, and body shall magnify thy Lord's redemption. Until then, beloved, sleep! We praise God *for* thee; and by the blood of the everlasting covenant, we hope and expect to praise God *with* thee. Amen.'

The memorial number of *The Sword and the Trowel* contained the following paragraphs, which will fitly close the account of that memorable season:

'While we gathered around the grave, a little patch of blue sky appeared, just over our heads, as if to remind us of the glory-land above; and while Mr. Brown was speaking, a dove flew from the direction of the Tabernacle towards the tomb, and, wheeling in its flight over the crowd, almost seemed to pause. In ancient days, it would have been an augury: to us, it spoke only peace. As the service proceeded, a little robin poured forth its liquid note all the while from a neighbouring tombstone; the redbreast made appropriate music, fabled as it was to have had its crimson coat ever since it picked a thorn from the Saviour's bleeding brow. Well, we do not believe that; but we believe what we sang at the grave, the truth that Spurgeon lived to preach, and died to defend,

C. H. Spurgeon: The Full Harvest

Dear dying Lamb, Thy precious blood
Shall never lose its power,
Till all the ransomed Church of God
Be saved to sin no more.

Many remarked that the whole of the memorial services, unique as
they were, were characterized by a simplicity and heartiness completely in harmony with the entire life of the beloved Pastor; and it
was most significant that, when the olive casket was lowered into
the vault, not even the glorified preacher's name was visible—it
was just as *he* would have wished it—there was nothing to be seen
but the text at the foot of the coffin, and the open Bible. Of course,
the Bible was not buried; it is not dead, it 'liveth and abideth for
ever;' and who knows whether it may not prove, more than ever,
the means of quickening the dead, now that he, who loved it dearer
than his life, can no longer proclaim its blessed truths with the
living voice? God grant it!'

INDEX

Nightingale, Florence 225
Nightingale Lane (Wandsworth):
see Helensburgh House
Noel, Baptist W. 57
Nero, Emperor 200
New Zealand 360
North, Brownlow 53, 253
Norwood 295, 506
Nottingham (hymn-tune) 427

O

Oak, Question 299
Oaks, Gospel 91
Oban 257–8, 260
Ockley 230
Offord, John 437
Olive (trees) 284, 346, 375, 505, 507
Olney, Thomas 10, 69
Olney, William P. 10, 71, 78, 162, 165, 304, 396
Opal Ring 177–8
Opium War (China) 124–5
Organ-grinder 378
Orphanage: see Stockwell Orphanage
Orsman, W. J. 396
Orthodox Church (Russia) 354
(Syria) 365
Our Own Hymn-Book 154–7, 335, 435, 489
Outlines of Theology (A. A. Hodge) 341
Owen, John 181
Owens, T. G. 264

P

Pall Mall Gazette 391
Paris 216–17
Parker, Joseph 399
Parnell, C. S. 487
Passmore, Joseph 179, 214, 283, 370, 423, 438
Passmore & Alabaster 100, 139, 184, 351, 438
Pastors' College 96–115, 136, 165, 168, 184, 271, 325, 328–9, 330, 333, 440, 446–9, 454
its origins 97–8
its costs 98–100, 456–7

applicants and their qualifications 100–4
its teaching of physical science 104–5
its methods 106
Spurgeon's lectures 108
notable students 109–13
Spurgeon's farewell words to students 114
its students visit Westwood 298–9
its library 449
its development 455–8
its statistics 457, 459
the Down-grade 458
its Evangelical Association 58, 427
its Missionary Association 457
its Society of Evangelists 457
its Annual Conference 194, 311, 405–6, 427, 441, 449–50, 455, 458, 497–8
Paton, John G. 253
Peacock (horse) 218
Pearce, S. R. 396
Pepys, Samuel 230
Perowne, J. J. Stewart 340
Perth 253
Peter of Colechurch 126
Peto, Sir Samuel Morton 3, 8, 10, 14
Philadelphia Baptist Conference 398
Philippi, F. A. 344
Pierson, Dr. A. T. 501
Pike, G. H. xi, xii, 182, 193, 254, 292, 295, 399n, 414
Pil-garlic 190
Piping Bullfinch 177–9
Pius IX (Pope) 192
Pleasures, A Christian's 119–21
Pocock, W. W. 7
Poland 138
Pollockshaws 276, 446
Pompeii 207–11
Poole, Matthew 342
Prayer, forms of, 154
Prayer-meetings: see Metropolitan Tabernacle

Index